# ALLONS-Y!
## LE FRANÇAIS PAR ÉTAPES

INSTRUCTOR'S ANNOTATED ÉDITION VOLUME 1

**JEANNETTE D. BRAGGER**
The Pennsylvania State University

**DONALD B. RICE**
Hamline University

**PREMIÈRE PARTIE:** Étape préliminaire, Chapitre 1 à Chapitre 4
**DEUXIÈME PARTIE:** Chapitre 5 à Chapitre 8

**HH** Heinle & Heinle Publishers
I⊤P An International Thomson Publishing Company
Boston, Massachusetts 02116 USA

ISBN: 0-8384-6471-8

10  9  8  7  6  5  4  3  2  1

# CONTENTS
## of the
## INSTRUCTOR'S GUIDE

Canada

Québec

Nouveau-Brunswick

Québec
Montréal

St-Pierre-et-Miquelon

*Amérique du Nord*
États-Unis

Maine

Nouvelle-Écosse

Nouvelle-Angleterre

Louisiane

*Océan Atlantique*

La Nouvelle-Orléans

Haïti

Les Antilles
Guadeloupe
Martinique

Port-au-Prince

*Océan Pacifique*

Cayenne

Guyane française

*Amérique du Sud*

Wallis et Futuna

Polynésie française

Vanuatu

Tahiti

*Australie*

Nouvelle-Calédonie

# *Le monde francophone*

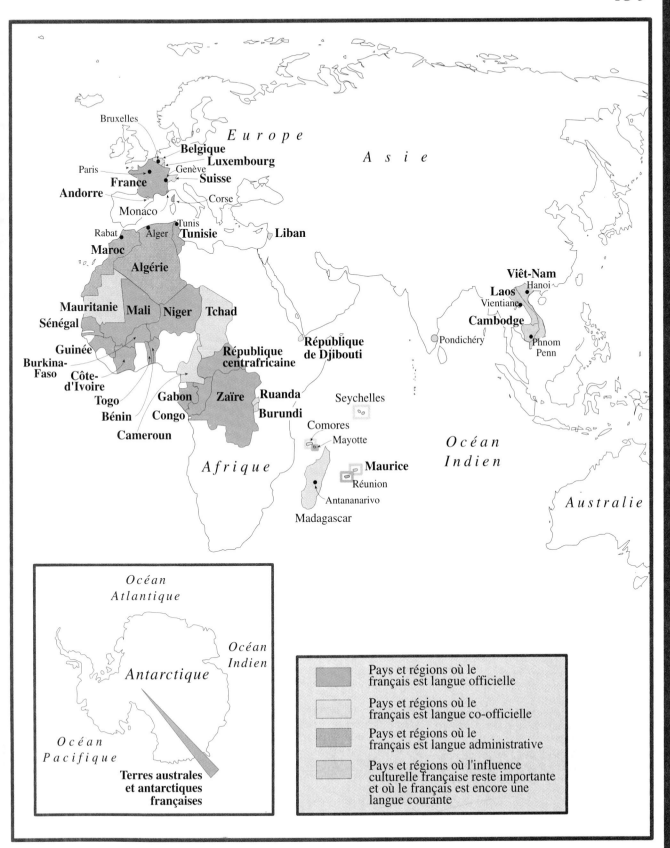

# France

MER DU NORD

Pays-Bas

Angleterre

Allemagne

Dunkerque

Calais

Belgique

NORD-PAS-DE-CALAIS

Lille

Valenciennes

Luxembourg

LA MANCHE

Cherbourg

HAUTE-NORMANDIE

Amiens

PICARDIE

Le Havre

Rouen

Seine

Reims

Metz

LORRAINE

ALSACE

Meuse

Rhin

Caen

BASSE-NORMANDIE

☆Paris

Versailles

ÎLE-DE-FRANCE

CHAMPAGNE-ARDENNE

Nancy

Strasbourg

Saint-Malo

VOSGES

Brest

Fougères

Troyes

Moselle

BRETAGNE

Rennes

Le Mans

Orléans

Seine

Mulhouse

PAYS DE LA LOIRE

Blois

Chambord

BOURGOGNE

Saône

Besançon

JURA

St-Nazaire

Angers

Tours

Dijon

FRANCHE-COMTÉ

Suisse

Nantes

Chinon

Loire

Chenonceaux

Azay-le-Rideau

Bourges

Chalon-sur-Saône

Nevers

CENTRE

Loire

Poitiers

OCÉAN

LIMOUSIN

Vichy

Annecy

Rhône

ATLANTIQUE

POITOU-CHARENTES

Limoges

Clermont-Ferrand

Lyon

La Rochelle

Saint Étienne

RHÔNE-ALPES

Italie

Périgueux

AUVERGNE

Grenoble

ALPES

Bordeaux

MASSIF CENTRAL

Rhône

PROVENCE-ALPES-CÔTE-D'AZUR

AQUITAINE

Garonne

Rodez

Monte-Carlo

MIDI-PYRÉNÉES

Avignon

Grasse

Monaco

Biarritz

Nîmes

Tarascon

Nice

Bayonne

Toulouse

Montpellier

Aix-en-Provence

Pau

Béziers

Marseille

Toulon

Cannes

PYRÉNÉES

Carcassonne

Narbonne

LANGUEDOC-ROUSSILLON

Espagne

Perpignan

Andorre

MER MÉDITERRANÉE

0    75 km

CORSE

Ajaccio

©1993 Magellan Geographix^SM Santa Barbara CA

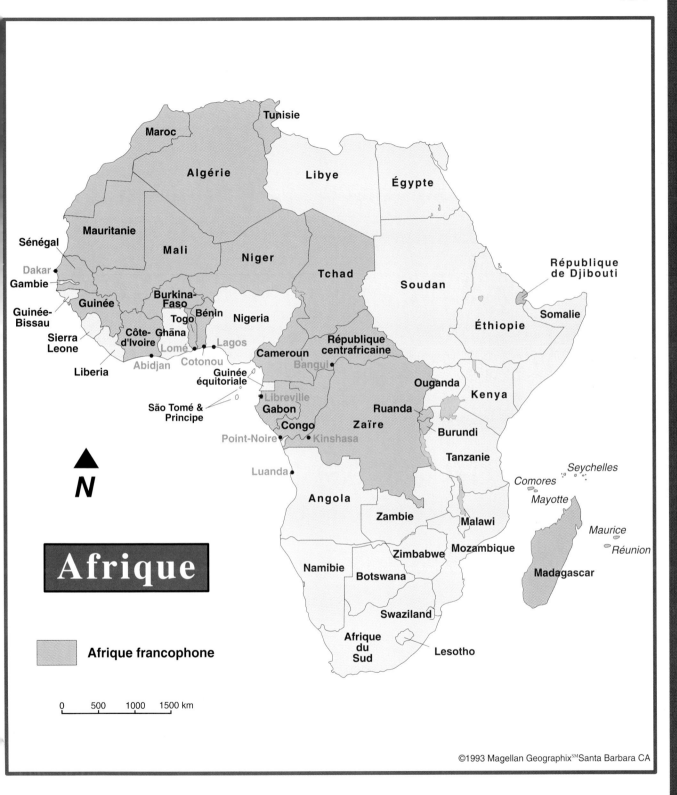

Tunisie
Maroc
Algérie
Libye
Égypte
Sénégal
Dakar
Mauritanie
Mali
Niger
Tchad
Soudan
République de Djibouti
Gambie
Burkina-Faso
Guinée
Bénin
Togo
Nigeria
Somalie
Guinée-Bissau
Côte-d'Ivoire
Ghana
Lagos
Éthiopie
Sierra Leone
Lomé
République centrafricaine
Cameroun
Abidjan
Cotonou
Liberia
Bangui
Guinée équitoriale
Ouganda
São Tomé & Principe
Libreville
Kenya
Gabon
Ruanda
Congo
Zaïre
Burundi
Point-Noire
Kinshasa
Tanzanie
Luanda
Seychelles
Comores
Angola
Mayotte
Zambie
Malawi
Maurice
Zimbabwe
Réunion
Mozambique
Madagascar
Namibie
Botswana
Swaziland
Afrique du Sud
Lesotho

**N**

# Afrique

Afrique francophone

0    500    1000    1500 km

©1993 Magellan Geographix℠Santa Barbara CA

# INSTRUCTOR'S GUIDE to accompany *Allons-y!*, Fourth Edition

## PREFACE

*Allons-y! Le français par étapes,* Fourth Edition, is an integrated learning system that provides beginning-level students with immediately useful and usable language skills in French. *Allons-y!,* Fourth Edition, is a mutually supporting network of learning components:

- a textbook (with student edition annotations)
- a workbook
- student audio tapes and CDs (4)
- a special Instructor's Annotated Edition (conveniently divided into two paperback booklets)
- instructor's audio tapes (2)
- a new culture-based video program
- a testing program in two formats: printed and computerized
- computer software: *Système-D 2.1: Writing Assistant for French*
- multimedia computer software: *Nouvelles dimensions*
- a resource manual for instructors
- an Instructor's Resource Kit

Together, these components provide students with unprecedented opportunities for listening to, speaking, reading, and writing French. They also open up the classroom and language lab to the sights and sounds of the French-speaking world.

Because we are convinced that creative use of language is possible from the outset, we have developed a program that allows for maximum interaction among students and between students and instructors, beginning with the preliminary lessons. Interaction is based on tasks to be accomplished and on effective linguistic functioning in the types of situations likely to be encountered in real life. We have tried to put into practice the principles set forth in the ACTFL Proficiency Guidelines so that we may help students function as accurately as possible in a variety of contexts.

### THE BASIC ORGANIZATION

As suggested above, the basic philosophy of *Allons-y!* has not changed. Nor have we changed the fundamental structure of the book: thematically unified chapters, organized into **étapes,** progress from a **Point de départ** through a series of vocabulary and structure exercises to a concluding set of activities **(Point d'arrivée).** Moreover, we have maintained our emphasis on systematic and continuous review—within the **étape (Débrouillons-nous!),** between **étapes (Reprise),** and throughout the book (via a steady recycling of contexts and structures).

### WHAT IS NEW ABOUT THE FOURTH EDITION?

Based on the comments and suggestions of numerous satisfied users, we have not made major revisions in the fourth edition. This focused revision includes changes to the textbook, the workbook, and the ancillaries.

### TEXTBOOK

Reflecting our continuing effort to make the program as user-friendly as possible, much of the revision of the textbook involves the margin annotations and the Instructor's Annotated Edition. Other changes involve fine-tuning: the design has been revised for improved readability; cultural information and realia pieces have been updated; and some photos have been replaced.

#### ● Margin annotations

We have tried to improve the margin annotations in both the Student Edition and the Instructor's Annotated Edition. The graphics accompanying the annotations have been made more immediately recognizable. At the beginning of each chapter, instructors and students are both provided with a list of materials they will need. Students also receive information on when to use the Student Tapes and what their assignments are in the Workbook. In addition, student annotations key the book-specific video to the content of each chapter. Vocabulary from the video is provided in the *Lexique* of each chapter.

#### ● Instructor's Annotated Edition

The Instructor's Annotated Edition is now divided into two paperback booklets—(Volume 1) Étape préliminaire, Chapters 1 through 8; and (Volume 2) Chapters 9 through 14. Each booklet contains the complete Table of Contents, Verb Appendices, Lexiques, and Index. Each booklet also contains an Instructor's Guide that includes Chapter Notes as well as tapescripts for both the Student Tapes and the Instructor's Tapes.

## WORKBOOK

The changes introduced in the Workbook, involving the addition of self-correcting grammar quizzes and a change in the Student Tapes, reflect our continuing desire both to focus on communicative skills (especially reading, listening, and writing) and to reduce the correction time for instructors. The following paragraphs describe the revised format of the Workbook and explain how it addresses the various skills.

### ● Workbook Organization

Paralleling the first three **étapes** in each textbook chapter are three Workbook **étapes** that include the following sections:

- **Lisons!**—reading strategy, text, comprehension activities
- **Écrivons!**—a self-correcting test on the grammar of the **étape** (students who do not score 80% or above on this test are referred to the computer disk, which contains highly structured review exercises on the topic of the text); semi-controlled and open-ended, authentic writing activities that reinforce the vocabulary and grammar of the **étape.** (Note: For many of these activities, especially in the early chapters, answers are provided in an Answer Key at the back of the Workbook.)

The fourth **étape** of each Workbook chapter parallels the fourth **étape** of the textbook and includes the following sections:

- **Écoutons!**—listening activities correlated with the Student Tape (answers are provided at the back of the Workbook
- **Rédigeons!**—open-ended writing activities that combine the functions, vocabulary, grammar, and theme of the chapter.
- **Travail de fin de chapitre**—an additional activity from the Student Tape and, in most chapters, a word game (crossword puzzle, rebus, anagram, etc.) that reviews some of the vocabulary of the chapter.

### ● Development of Skills

The separation of communicative functions (in the Workbook) and structured grammar practice (in the computer program) places the responsibility on the student and makes the development of communicative skills more interesting and challenging. In turn, this organization relieves the tedium of mechanical exercise correction and allows instructors to give time to the development of the reading, writing, and listening skills.

**Reading** (*Lisons!*) The Workbook contains many authentic texts that include literary excerpts, the popular press, realia, and so forth. In each text, students are directed to apply a specific reading strategy (skimming, scanning, use of cognates, guessing from context, word families, reading for gist, reading for supporting detail). All of these strategies are applied to a variety of text types to assure sufficient practice through regular re-entry.

**Writing** (*Écrivons! / Rédigeons!*) The exercises in these sections are communicative, often personalized, writing assignments that range from lists to sentences to paragraphs to multiple paragraphs. Each chapter ends with an extended writing activity that asks students to use the vocabulary, grammar, and functions learned in the particular chapter as well as in previous ones. The writing tasks are keyed to *Système-D* for students who have access to this writing program.

**L'art d'écrire** Beginning in Chapter 11, this section is included in the first three **étapes** of each chapter. In all, these twelve writing sections constitute a systematic writing development course similar to the typical freshman English writing course. Students are given explanations with examples of a particular writing strategy and are asked to apply the strategy in a series of activities. Among the strategies presented are the expansion of the sentence, punctuation, personal and business letters, the development of an idea, the organization of a paragraph, the linking of sentences (temporal and logical), how to identify key words in a text, how to use the dictionary, how to imitate French syntax.

**Listening** (*Écoutons!*) The Student Tapes that accompany the fourth edition focus on listening comprehension rather than speaking. The material for each chapter (found on the Student Tape for that chapter) usually consists of three segments. The first segment deals with pronunciation and corresponds to the **Prononciation** section of each **étape** in the textbook. (Since these sections only appear in Chapters 1 through 11, the Student Tapes for Chapters 12 through 14 have only two segments each.) The second segment provides a variety of activities: dictation, sound and word discrimination, specific task listening. The final segment offers a conversation or monologue that provides practice in listening for gist and for detail.

## ANCILLARY MATERIALS

The ancillary program of the fourth edition text has also undergone major revisions. The various components are support materials that are fully integrated with the textbook themes and that allow instructors to introduce variety to their classroom activities.

● **Instructor's Annotated Edition**

For your convenience, the Instructor's Annotated Edition is available as two separate booklets — (Volume 1) Étape préliminaire, Chapters 1 through 8, and (Volume 2) Chapters 9 through 14. The Instructor's Guide, found at the beginning of each Instructor's Annotated Edition, includes chapter notes (suggestions for classroom management, supplementary exercises, cultural information), as well as the tapescripts for both the instructor and student audio tapes.

● **Resource Manual: Initiation à la langue et à la culture**

This book (provided in the Instructor's Resource Kit) is divided into four parts. The first part contains five additional **étapes préliminaires** from which the instructor may select one or several (depending on the time frame of the course) as an introduction at the beginning of the term. Some of these **étapes** may also be reserved for an introduction to the second term or as a change of pace at any point in the book.

The second part of the book contains the materials that support the three **Intégrations culturelles** (Paris, France, the Francophone world). For each segment, the instructor is provided with color transparencies (maps, places, monuments), explanations, and activities that can be done in class. This support material is designed to give instructors maximum flexibility in terms of the selection and the time allowed for presentation of these cultural topics.

The third part of the book contains the supplementary readings. They are thematically tied to each chapter. For each chapter there are five readings, including texts from literature, from the press, and from a variety of other sources. In accordance with the linguistic ability of students, these texts range in degree of difficulty from very simple (marked by a single *) to moderately difficult (marked by a double **) to challenging (marked by a triple ***). Each text is followed by at least one comprehension exercise (understanding of the text) and one expansion exercise (work to be done on an aspect of the topic or on a related field).

The fourth part of the book contains activity card masters on perforated pages that can be photocopied and distributed as needed in the classroom. The cards are correlated to specific exercises in the chapters; a correlation sheet is included to use as a guide.

● **Student Tapes**

The purpose of the Student Tapes (sold with the textbook) is to provide students with practice in both pronunciation and listening. The Student Tape program for the fourth edition of *Allons-y!* usually consists of three segments. For the **Étape préliminaire** and Chapters 1–11, Segment 1 deals with pronunciation and corresponds to the **Prononciation** section of each **étape** in the textbook. Segment 2 offers a variety of activities (dictation, sound and word discrimination, or specific task listening) and corresponds to the **Quatrième étape** of the Workbook. Segment 3 offers a conversation or monologue that provides practice in listening for gist and for detail. This segment corresponds to the **Travail de fin de chapitre,** also found in the Workbook.

● **Instructor's Tapes**

In addition to providing supplementary listening comprehension material on each chapter theme, the Instructor's Tapes contains recordings of the conversations from the **Point de départ** (Chapters 1–8), the **Portrait** (Chapters 1–14), the **Relais** (Chapters 9–14), and the conversations from the **Expansions grammaticales** (Chapters 12–14).

● **Video Program**

Video represents real-life listening more closely than audio tapes. In addition, it provides interesting and informative cultural information in an engrossing way. The *Allons-y!* video program combines these two elements to give students a window into the language and culture of the contemporary Francophone world.

The video is divided into 14 **actes,** each of which corresponds thematically to each text chapter. Marginal student annotations in the text suggest when to use the video and provide questions designed to focus attention on the spoken text. Difficult vocabulary is provided at the end of each chapter in the **Lexique** section in a separate video vocabulary box.

A separate video guide contains the video script and a variety of activities designed to enhance the viewers' appreciation of the video's cultural content while practicing both active and passive skills.

● **Transparencies**

A full set of color transparencies accompany the fourth edition of *Allons-y!* Rather than providing primarily duplicates of what is presented in the textbook, these transparencies include alternate examples of realia in support of the chapter theme. They also include the maps for easy use in the classroom.

● **Integrated Testing Program featuring "Testing the Way We Teach"**

Testing components include: proficiency-based speaking tests; achievement-based listening and speaking tests with efficient evaluation instruments; printed tests that check control of structures and vocabulary and check proficiency in reading and writing using culturally relevant contexts.

*Computerized Test Bank.* Printed tests appear in an expanded computerized test bank allowing instructors to tailor quizzes to their own courses.

### ● Software: *Système-D*

Users of the fourth edition of *Allons-y!* will be pleased to learn that the capabilities of version 2.1 of the noted software program *Système-D: Writing Assistant for French* are reflected in the open-ended composition exercises in the Workbook. *Système-D*'s array of on-line tools include:

* a bilingual dictionary of more than 8,000 entries complete with examples of usage
* a verb conjugator that can call up over 500,000 conjugated verb forms
* an on-line reference grammar
* an index to functional phrases
* sets of thematically related vocabulary items

Extensive cross linking between dictionary, grammar, and functions ensures easy access for the student to the very different ways in which English and French sometimes express the same ideas.

An on-line word processor enables students to capture the fruits of their labors in an electronic file that, when printed out, provides both student and teacher with a legible product.

The tracking program, which records every student action within the program, can provide teachers with insights into how individual students approach the writing process (e.g., linearly or recursively) and thus with the means to provide direction to students on an individual basis.

*Système-D* is available to institutions in DOS, Windows, or Macintosh formats via site license agreement. It can be installed either in a stand-alone mode or on a network. A non-networkable stand-alone version is also available for individual purchase by students.

### ● Software: *Nouvelles dimensions*

*Nouvelles dimensions* is designed to develop the cognitive aspects of listening comprehension in French. Available in either CD-ROM or laser disk format, *Nouvelles dimensions* can be used in both a classroom environment and independently in the language lab. By combining video and software, the student's attention is focused on listening for key words and phrases in authentic cultural contexts. Students view scenes from daily life and interact with the program as they practice and test their listening comprehension skills.

### ● Instructor's Resource Kit

The Instructor's Resource Kit contains all the instructor materials in one handy box for easy transport. Included are the following items:

* both Instructor's Annotated Edition booklets
* transparencies
* resource manual
* teacher tapes (2)
* student tapes (4)
* printed tests

### HOW DOES *ALLONS-Y!* FIT INTO THE SCHOOL YEAR?

In order to answer this question fully, it is necessary to address three questions:

**1. How long does it usually take to do a chapter?** In general, we recommend spending six days per chapter. However, these six days can be organized in two basic ways, depending on how you wish to treat the notion of an **étape**—as a day's lesson plan or as a sequence of activities.

If you deal with the **étape** as a built-in lesson plan for a class session, you can devote one day to each of the first three **étapes** in a chapter. You will find that some **étapes** fit perfectly in a class hour while others do not. If you finish early, the program contains ample ancillary material for expansion. If you find that there is too much material for one hour, you can temporarily omit some exercises. These exercises can then be done as part of the **Reprise** the following day or, more likely, during the final three days over which you can spread the **Lecture** (including perhaps a supplementary reading from the Resource Manual), the activities of the **Point d'arrivée,** and the video.

Some instructors may prefer to follow the sequence in the book, i.e., not to save exercises for review at the end of the chapter. In this case, if you cannot finish an **étape** in one day, you simply carry it over to the next. By the end of the sixth day, you will have "caught up" and completed the chapter. If you are carrying material over to the following day, we would suggest, however, that you try to give each day some kind of closure—i.e., a communicative exercise (**Débrouillons-nous!** or the final exercise in an **Application** section).

**2. Can the book be finished in a year by devoting six days to a chapter?** If you proceed at the rate of one chapter every six days, the fourteen chapters can be completed in 84 days. The **Étape préliminaire** requires at least one day. The **Intégrations culturelles** are flexible and can be used for as few as one or two days or as many as four days. Consequently, a minimum of 88 days is needed to get through the text.

The number of classes in courses meeting four times a week for a semester ranges from 104 to 120 class sessions during a school year. Courses meeting four times a week for a quarter also have approximately 120 class sessions per year. You can do seven chapters per semester or five chapters per quarter and have ample time for testing, review sessions, ancillary materials, and even spending an extra day on a few chapters.

Courses that meet five times a week offer even more flexibility. Instructors will thus be able to do extra reading, work more thoroughly with the video tape and the **Intégrations culturelles,** and include more of the **Étapes préliminaires.**

**3. What do I do if my class only meets three times per week?** Classes meeting three times per week can still get the benefit of *Allons-y!*'s emphasis on interactive communication by devoting five days per chapter instead of six. Here are some suggestions for the implementation of the five-day schedule:

- Have students read the **étape** before class.
- Reserve as much class time as possible for communicative practice. Anything the book can do (i.e., explain grammar) should be done outside of class as much as possible (the **Pratique de la grammaire** exercises allow students to work independently).
- Work more frequently in class with the students' books open; this will speed up the time needed to do exercises.
- Limit the **Point d'arrivée** activities to one in class and one for homework.
- Make the video tape available in the lab.
- Reserve supplementary readings for extra credit or for gifted students.

### HOW DO I DEAL IN CLASS WITH EACH SECTION OF AN *ÉTAPE?*

Each chapter contains a sequence of four **étapes,** with the chapter theme amplified from one **étape** to the next. The **Première, Deuxième, and Troisième étapes** have the same basic format: **Point de départ, Reprise** (except in the **Première étape**), **Structure, Prononciation** (Chapters 1–11), **Structure** (variable according to **étape**),

and **Débrouillons-nous!** The **Quatrième étape** contains a **Lecture,** the **Point d'arrivée** activities, the **Portrait,** and the **Profil.** In this Instructor's Guide, you will find detailed suggestions for presenting vocabulary and structures and for implementing unusual exercises. The remainder of this Preface will offer some general suggestions for working with the various parts of the chapters and the **étapes.**

### POINT DE DÉPART

The **Point de départ** section introduces semantic and cultural information associated with the chapter theme. In Chapters 1–8, it usually takes the form of a vocabulary presentation (often by means of photos or drawings) and/or a dialogue (often illustrated). Following are some suggestions for presenting this new material.

● **Vocabulary**

a) The Instructor's Resource Kit contains transparencies that reproduce the drawings and the words (with overlay). Start with the drawings and the overlay, having students repeat the new words. Remove the overlay; have students repeat, then identify the vocabulary items. Be sure to vary the order.

b) Introduce the new vocabulary by personalizing it for the students. If you are dealing with topics such as school supplies, clothing, food, etc., bring in real objects or photos or work with objects in the classroom. If you are dealing with more abstract notions, give a monologue about yourself or ask students questions about themselves, moving from known material to the new vocabulary. Follow up with the transparencies or the visuals from the book as reinforcement.

● **Dialogues**

a) The **Point de départ** dialogues are recorded on the Instructor's Tapes. Begin with a mini-planning strategy to establish a context. Have students listen with books closed, ask general comprehension questions, and then have students read and repeat from the book. Ask questions again, if necessary.

b) Dramatize the dialogue while students listen (and watch) with books closed. You can play both roles or you can ask a good student to read one of them. Ask general comprehension questions. Follow up by having students read and repeat, taking parts.

● **Realia**

In Chapters 9–14, the **Point de départ** consists of authentic realia pieces to introduce the chapter theme through reading comprehension.

a) Do an advance organizer by asking students some personalized questions related to the material in the reading. Then have them look over the material silently. Follow up with the comprehension exercises.

b) Present key vocabulary of the reading as an advance organizer. Then have students look at the comprehension exercise items as they read the realia pieces.

### À VOUS! (Exercices de vocabulaire)

The **À vous** exercises that follow each **Point de départ** are designed to practice the new vocabulary and further develop the chapter theme. They are presented in a variety of formats: visuals for solidifying vocabulary acquisition, dialogues to be imitated for practicing conversational strategies, or practically-oriented reading comprehension activities.

### REPRISE

The **Reprise** exercises (found in **étapes** 2, 3, and 4) provide consistent review of material from the **Point de départ** and the **Structures** of the previous **étapes**. They can be done as a warm-up at the start of the class hour or as a break in the middle of the session.

### STRUCTURE

Each **Structure** section presents a limited grammatical topic with model sentences and a short explanation in English. The topics can be presented to the students "cold" or students can read the grammatical explanations before coming to class. If you present them for the first time in class, we would urge you to follow an inductive method—i.e., to give models and examples (a short monologue about yourself, some statements about students, a question/answer exchange, etc.) before explaining the rule(s) briefly (preferably in French). However, in situations where the topic is particularly complex or where you are pressed for time, it is certainly possible to make a deductive presentation—a short explanation (preferably in French) followed by a few examples.

The format used for presenting grammatical structure in Part 4 (Chapters 12–14) is designed to give students practice in thinking inductively—i.e., in making generalizations from particular examples. Consequently, students first encounter the new structure in a short dialogue, followed immediately by some controlled questions and answers (**À vous de le dire!**) that get them to use the structure contextually (i.e., in reference to the dialogue). The dialogues used in the **Expansion**

**grammaticale** for each chapter deal with the character(s) featured in that chapter. These dialogues are all recorded on the Instructor's Tape; therefore, you can, if you wish, play them all consecutively as a separate listening comprehension activity. There is only one grammatical topic per **étape**; however, in several cases, the topic is divided into subtopics—i.e., two, three, or four short dialogues are used to present all aspects of the topic. The Chapter Notes in this Instructor's Guide provide specific suggestions for the presentation of this material.

### APPLICATION

Following each **Structure** section is a series of exercises that move from structured drills to open-ended activities. The usual progression is:

**1. Mechanical exercises.** These exercises provide both structure and meaning. Since their object is to familiarize students with the structure itself, these exercises are often not contextualized. To maximize student practice, do a couple of items with the entire class, then have students work in pairs, then do some rapid spot-checking for verification.

**2. Meaningful exercises.** These exercises provide the structure, but the students often provide a personalized meaning (e.g., when directed to answer questions about themselves and their families). Start by having students work in pairs or small groups. Then go over the exercises with the entire class in order to verify accuracy.

**3. Communicative exercises.** With these exercises, the students provide both structure and meaning (e.g., when asked to state their feelings about something). Traditionally neglected by many textbooks, these exercises can be done by having one pair or group of students model the exercise in front of the class. Students can then work in groups and report back in a variety of ways. It is very important that these activities be done in class, as they give students the opportunity to show their linguistic independence.

### PRONONCIATION

In Chapters 1–11, students learn the most common French graphemes (letters or letter combinations) along with their phonemes (the sounds that the letters represent). The presentations always move from symbol to sound. Before doing the exercises with the class, you may wish to write a couple of examples on the board as a way of quickly and efficiently underlining the main point or problem. The pronunciation sections are recorded on the Student Tapes for out-of-class reinforcement.

### RELAIS (Chapters 9–14)

The **Relais** sections are model dialogues that incorporate the chapter theme and vocabulary. They also represent one segment of a coherent story line (with the **Point de départ** and the **Expansion grammaticale** dialogues) that incorporates the chapter character(s) and theme. These dialogues are recorded on the Instructor's Tape and can be presented in a similar fashion to the **Point de départ** conversations.

### DÉBROUILLONS-NOUS! (Petite révision de l'étape)

The **Débrouillons-nous!** section usually consists of two exercises: an **Échange** (personalized questions that two students ask each other) and a mini-situation. Both exercises integrate the functions, vocabulary, and structures of the **étape** while the mini-situation prepares students for the type of activities found in the **Point d'arrivée.** In the case of the mini-situation, you may wish to model the exercise with one group of students, then have small groups work individually before you ask one or two groups to redo their conversations for the entire class.

### LECTURE / COMPRÉHENSION

The **Quatrième étape** always begins with a reading selection that is to be used for general comprehension and for the development of reading skills. Each text usually begins with a reading hint, an indication of a strategy (looking for cognates, reading for main ideas, guessing from context, etc.) that may be particularly useful with the passage in question. We urge instructors to follow the basic pattern set up in the margin notes: prereading, reading, comprehension check, postreading. The prereading exercises are designed to give students an advance organizer before they begin to read. They consist of personalized questions, brainstorming of words, visuals, etc. We suggest that the reading itself be timed so that students are given a reasonable but limited amount of time to complete the passage. In this way, they are not allowed to linger over individual words but have to work on reading in larger chunks. Depending on the exercises in the **Compréhension** section, students are sometimes allowed to consult the glosses during the first reading. The postreading exercises aim at linking the reading to the theme of the chapter and to other skills, such as speaking or writing. They can be done in class or for homework.

### POINT D'ARRIVÉE (Activités orales)

Each chapter culminates in this set of purposeful, communicative activities that draw together the vocabulary, functions, structures, and cultural information learned in the first three **étapes.** For the most part, these activities involve pairs or groups of students. The instructions are always in English in order to be precise about the "real" situations in which students might find themselves. Before letting students start to work, it is a good idea to make clear the *mechanics* of the exercise (Who speaks first? Do they change roles? How does it end?); establish a *time limit;* and model and/or brainstorm the activity for the whole class.

In order to help students perform these activities, we have included an **Exprimons-nous!** section that presents expressions for effective communication (e.g., hesitation words, agreeing/disagreeing, asking for and giving an opinion, giving information, recounting a sequence of activities, etc.). Students are asked to incorporate these phrases and expressions into the **Point d'arrivée** conversations.

### PORTRAIT

Each chapter ends with a photo and short portrait of the character(s) in the chapters. The character talks about where he/she is from and gives a personal statement related to the chapter theme. The **Portrait** is recorded on the Instructor's Tape and can be used for additional listening practice.

### PROFIL

The **Profil** at the end of each chapter highlights the city, region, or country of origin for the chapter character. In addition to a small map focusing on that region, it includes pertinent factual information about the area with some discussion questions (**À discuter).**

### LEXIQUE

At the end of each chapter, students can find a vocabulary list (without English translations) to (1) use as a reference during class activities and (2) as a study guide to verify their comprehension of the vocabulary.

### ENDING THE CHAPTER

Before you begin a subsequent chapter, we suggest that you wrap up the chapter you have been working on with one or more of the following activities:

**1. The Instructor's Tapes.** Have students listen to the supplementary conversations. They can be asked either to listen for gist or for specific details.

**2. The Video Program.** Have students watch the scene(s) of the video tape pertaining to the chapter. Basic comprehension questions can be asked in French followed by a more in-depth analysis in English.

**3. Supplementary Readings.** Have students work on one or more of the additional readings both literary and non-literary, found in the Resource Manual.

**4. *Nouvelles dimensions*.** See the Resource Manual for suggestions for using *Nouvelles dimensions* either in class or in the language lab.

We hope that this Preface has answered some of your general questions about the fourth edition *of Allons-y!* For more specific help in preparing daily lessons, consult the notes in the margins as well as the more detailed discussions in the Chapter Notes section of this Instructor's Guide.

# CHAPTER NOTES

## ÉTAPE PRÉLIMINAIRE

Many students arrive in class the first day without their books. The entire **Étape préliminaire** can be done by using the transparencies provided in the Instructor's Resource Kit.

In addition to the **Apprenons une langue étrangère!** section (in the text), the Resource Manual offers five other activities that can be used in the place of, or along with, the principles of learning French. These activities are of varying length and can be photocopied for distribution to students. They include: (1) **Names**— Students learn basic principles of French pronunciation through exposure to French **prénoms.** They also practice some basic greeting and leave-taking. This activity can be used to provide each student with a French name. (2) **Cultural Information Quiz**—Students are introduced to France and the Francophone world. This activity can be used to make students aware of cultural stereotypes. (3) **Total Physical Response**—This option uses Asher's TPR approach to familiarize students with the code of the language and to begin work on listening comprehension. (4) **Bonjour... Comment vas-tu?** Students learn basic social amenities and how to ask some appropriate questions. (5) **La France et la Franco-phonie**—Students learn the basic sounds of French through map work as they study geographical aspects of France and the French-speaking world.

Whatever choice(s) you make, you need to end the preliminary activities by doing the **Point de départ: Allons au café** on p. 7 of the text.

● **Apprenons une langue étrangère!**
Ex. A and D can be done from oral cues. Ex. B, C, E, F, G, and H require that students look at material on the transparency or in photocopied form.

● **Point de départ:** *Allons au café!*
The **Point de départ** sections often present a considerable amount of vocabulary. You may wish to stress (now and as the course progresses) that students are not expected to have active command of every item, particularly in lists such as the drinks in this preliminary **étape,** (to which you may well wish to add a few of your own favorites). Rather, students are given a large choice of vocabulary so that they can express their own interests and preferences. While they should be able to recognize words (e.g., know that **une menthe à l'eau** is something

cold to drink), what is more important is having a selection of seven or eight drinks they like and can therefore order.

## CHAPITRE 1

### PREMIÈRE ÉTAPE

● **Point de départ:** *Commandons!*
The **Point de départ** of each **étape** serves to introduce some aspect of the chapter context and to present new vocabulary. In the first eight chapters, the **Point de départ** consists of a list of vocabulary, presented visually, and/or a short dialogue.

In most instances, the vocabulary images are reproduced on a transparency with an overlay containing the French words. You can thus begin by showing the pictures and having students repeat the French words. Then you can do some simple exercises (with the overlay at first, and then with just the images). Some vocabulary also lends itself to presentation using a TPR approach, i.e., working in class with the actual objects.

The dialogues are all recorded on the Instructor's Tapes, so you can present them in class as a listening comprehension activity.

● **Application:** *Ex. D*
This type of mechanical exercise can easily be done in pairs. If you wish to fix the proper pronunciation, do the first few items with the class (choral or individual responses), then have students continue in groups of two. You can circulate to verify accuracy and pronunciation. Those groups that finish first can continue with the controlled but meaningful exercise that normally follows the first mechanical exercise for each grammatical structure.

● **Structure: Le présent des verbes réguliers en** *-er* **($1^{\text{ère}}$ et $2^{\text{e}}$ personnes)**
You can also present this structure inductively through a series of statements, questions, and answers. However, be careful to avoid getting into situations where students will need to use third-person pronouns and forms. (We have split the presentation of regular **-er** verbs into two parts in order to allow students to practice talking to each other before referring to other people).

Some useful verbs and expressions for an inductive presentation of this topic include: **parler (espagnol), fumer, travailler, chanter (bien, faux), danser.** Begin by stating that you do something (**Je parle espagnol**), then do it. Ask a student: **Vous parlez espagnol? Oui? Allez-y. Parlez.** When you find someone who does, say: **Alors, (Marc) et moi, nous parlons espagnol.** (Write on board: **je, vous, nous.**) Get a student to begin (**Je parle espagnol**), then gesture for him/her to ask someone else. (**Vous parlez espagnol?**) Correct to: **Tu parles espagnol?** Using this technique, you can combine the presentations of the subject pronouns, verb conjugations, yes-no questions, and the negative **ne... pas.**

## DEUXIÈME ÉTAPE

● **Structure: Le présent des verbes réguliers en -er (3e personne)**
An alternative approach is to question three or four students using verbs from the previous **étape: Vous habitez à... ? Vous fumez? Vous étudiez beaucoup?** Then sum up what you have learned using third-person forms: (**Marie) habite à... Elle ne fume pas.**, etc.

● **Application:** *Ex. H*
This exercise type can be a bit complicated the first time it is done. However, once learned it provides an excellent means of working with any new verb or verbal expression, particularly early in the course when students are still getting used to the notion of conjugation. For this reason, you may want to take extra time now to help students see how the exercise works. Basically, it asks students to use all the subject pronouns by identifying them with various people in the group. To ensure that each series involves the three grammatical persons (both singular and plural), a basic pattern is set up: student A asks student B about himself (herself); student A asks student C about himself (herself) and student D; student C asks D in order to answer; then student A asks student C about student B (C can answer on the basis of B's earlier answer); finally, student A asks student B about students C and D (B can answer on the basis of C's earlier answer). With each item, students rotate from position A to B to C, etc.

Suggestion: practice with one group of four students in front of the class before having everyone break into groups. When the exercise works properly, students are manipulating all forms of the verb in a meaningful and personalized fashion.

## TROISIÈME ÉTAPE

● **Structure: Le verbe irrégulier *être***
To present **être** inductively, begin by engaging in a conversation with students about where you and they live and are from. For example, **Moi, j'habite ici, à** Lakewood. **Mais je ne suis pas de Lakewood. Je suis de Jefferson City dans l'état de Missouri. Et vous, Jim? Où est-ce que vous habitez? Est-ce que vous êtes de...?**

## QUATRIÈME ÉTAPE

● **Lecture:** *La Dauphine vous propose*
Emphasize to students that it is unusual for a non-native speaker (and even for a native speaker) to recognize every single item on a menu. Encourage them to make intelligent guesses based on: cognates (e.g., **tomates, aromatisés**), context (e.g., the general category **plats chauds**), word association (e.g., the relationship between **jus pressés** and **citron pressé**). On the other hand, warn them to beware of false cognates (e.g., **crudités**).

## CHAPITRE 2

## PREMIÈRE ÉTAPE

● **Structure: Le verbe irrégulier *avoir***
To present **avoir** inductively, begin by identifying a group of people in the class who all possess the same object: e.g., **Qui a une voiture?** Have several of these people stand in front of the class; question them about the kind of car each has: **Moi, j'ai une Toyota. Et vous, Jane? Ah, vous avez une Ford. Qu'est-ce qu'elle a comme voiture? Elle a une Ford. Et Bill?**

● **Structure: L'adjectif possessif (1ère et 2e personnes)**
Since students already understand the notion of possession, the main problem here is with agreement. We have tried to simplify the situation, at least initially, by eliminating the third-person *his / her* confusion from this **étape.** Whenever possible, work with actual objects in the classroom. When third-person situations occur, deal with them by using the definite article and **de.**

By limiting the initial presentation to first and second persons, we also give students the chance to learn the expressions **c'est** and **ce sont** while avoiding aural confusion with **ses** and **son.** We would recommend that you *not* make a major point of the use of **ce** (as opposed to **il, elle,** etc.) in these expressions. Our experience suggests that students can learn them as fixed expressions, especially when dealing with possession.

## DEUXIÈME ÉTAPE

● **Point de départ: Moi, j'aime beaucoup...**
If you wish to use the **Point de départ** as a listening comprehension activity, prepare students by telling them:

You *are about to hear a conversation between a female student (Christine) and her boyfriend (Robert). Even though they like each other a lot, they have very different interests.* After playing the tape once or twice, ask: **Qui aime la nature? Qui n'aime pas les animaux? Qui aime le football? Qui aime Beethoven et Mozart? Qui n'aime pas beaucoup la politique? Qui a un cours de mathématiques?,** etc. After verifying comprehension, have students read and repeat the dialogue. Ask again those questions with which they had difficulty the first time.

● **Structure: Le présent du verbe irrégulier *faire***
To present the verb **faire** inductively, use the expression **faire du sport.** Begin by saying: **Moi, je fais du sport. Je fais du tennis. Qui d'autre fait du tennis? (Je fais du tennis.) Bon. Jan et moi, nous faisons du tennis. Est-ce que Jan fait du sport?**

## TROISIÈME ÉTAPE

● **Structure: Les adjectifs possessifs (3ᵉ personne)**
In order to underline the fact that possessive adjectives agree with the object (not the possessor), begin by asking: **À qui est ce livre? C'est votre livre? (Oui, c'est mon livre.)** Point to owner. **C'est son livre? (Oui, c'est son livre.)** Point to a student of the opposite sex. **C'est son livre? (Non, ce n'est pas son livre. C'est son livre.)** Continue the presentation with: **calculatrice, clés** (one possessor), **cahiers** (multiple possessors), **chaise** (have two people sit on it).

## CHAPITRE 3

## PREMIÈRE ÉTAPE

● **Structure: Le verbe irrégulier *aller***
If you prefer to present the verb **aller** inductively, you can do so by combining the presentation of the verb with that of the adverbs frequently used with the idea of "going" (see the **Note grammaticale**). Write on the board: **souvent, quelquefois, de temps en temps, toujours, rarement.** Illustrate the meanings with verbs students know already: **étudier, fumer, chanter.** Do this just long enough so that the differences in meaning are clear. Choose a city (one that is nearby or a famous one). Start by telling about yourself: **Moi, je vais rarement à Chicago. Mais je vais très souvent à New York.** Then ask: **Vous allez à Chicago? Souvent? De temps en temps? Ah, (Susan) va à Chicago de temps en temps.**

● **Structure: La préposition *à* + l'article défini**
You may prefer simply to write on the board the names of several places. It is a good idea to group them by gender, in the following order:

| *feminine* | *masc. or fem. beginning with a vowel* | *masculine* |
|---|---|---|
| **pharmacie** | **église** | **cinéma** |
| **gare** | **université** | **musée** |
| **librairie** | **hôpital** | **parc** |

Begin by asking students: **Où allez-vous?** Have them respond: **Nous allons...** beginning with **à la pharmacie... à la gare...** Continue through each list. Then have individual students pick out three places to go: **Où allez-vous? / Je vais à la gare, à l'hôpital, et au parc.**

If you wish, this is a good spot for teaching the expressions **d'abord, ensuite,** and **enfin.** Once the pattern is established, encourage students to substitute other places to go.

## DEUXIÈME ÉTAPE

● **Structure: Le futur immédiat**
To present this structure inductively, begin by asking: **Qu'est-ce que vous allez faire ce soir? Vous allez rester à la maison? Vous allez étudier? Vous allez travailler? Vous allez sortir avec des amis?** (You can introduce the infinitive form of **sortir;** the conjugated form is presented in Chapter 9.) **Moi, je vais rester à la maison. Heidi? (Je vais étudier.) Ah, elle va étudier. Karen aussi? Ah, Karen et Heidi vont étudier.**

● **Structure: La préposition *de* + l'article défini; les prépositions de lieu**
You can combine the presentation of contractions with **de** and contractions with prepositions of place by using the transparency of Tarascon or by drawing part of a city on the board. For best results, figure out ahead of time the order in which you plan to ask questions.

● **Structure: L'impératif**
You may wish to make a more extensive presentation of imperative forms. If so, after having established the basic pattern (see the suggestion in the margin note), invite the class and yourself to look at something: for example, **Regardons la carte de la France!** Gesture to students to start to move; tell some students *not* to look: **Paul! Janice! Ne regardez pas la carte de la France! Regardez le plan de Paris!** Then have someone tell another person what to do: **Jessica, dites à Carl de regarder...** (Carl, regarde...)

## TROISIÈME ÉTAPE

● **Structure: Le verbe irrégulier** *prendre*

To present this verb inductively, begin: **Avec mon dîner, je prends d'habitude comme boisson du café. Et vous, Anne? (Je prends un Coca.) Et vous, Doug, qu'est-ce que vous prenez? (Je prends un Coca aussi.) Anne et Doug prennent un Coca. Qui d'autre prend du café? Jane?**

## CHAPITRE 4

### PREMIÈRE ÉTAPE

● **Point de départ: Vous allez en ville?**

The vocabulary in this **Point de départ** is set up to show that a particular idea can usually be expressed in more than one way. Thus, there are two expressions for each activity in town. It is not necessary that every student learn to produce all the expressions. For weaker students, it is enough to understand them receptively and to be able to use *one* of the expressions for each activity.

● **Structure: Le verbe irrégulier** *vouloir*

To present the verb **vouloir** inductively, choose a context in which the students can indicate something they want to have or do. For example, if you choose a café, talk *about* ordering instead of having students actually order. Begin: **Moi, je veux un thé au lait. Et vous, Scott, qu'est-ce que vous voulez? (Un Perrier.) Ah, il veut un Perrier. Vous aussi, Becky?**

### DEUXIÈME ÉTAPE

● **Structure: Les expressions** *espérer* **et** *avoir l'intention de*

As with **manger** and **voyager,** we do not deal with orthographic changes in verb forms as a major grammatical topic. Since students tend to make the changes orally almost automatically, we treat the spelling changes as a writing problem and treat them in the Workbook, where they get immediate reinforcement by means of a writing exercise. If you feel more comfortable pointing out in class the changes in some forms of **espérer,** by all means do so.

### TROISIÈME ÉTAPE

● **Structure: Le présent des verbes pronominaux**

In the fourth edition of *Allons-y!* pronominal verbs (both reflexive and reciprocal) are introduced in Chapter 4. (They did not appear until Chapter 9 in the first and second editions.) We have elected to present them earlier, using a small number of fairly common verbs, for three reasons:

(1) since students already know the verb endings (all of our examples are regular **-er** verbs), they need only learn the pronoun com-binations (**je me, tu te, il/elle se,** etc.); (2) students will have that much more opportunity to practice their use; and (3) we can provide more natural language in the contexts that follow since we are no longer obliged to avoid (artificially) pronominal verbs until the middle of the text.

## CHAPITRE 5

### PREMIÈRE ÉTAPE

● **Note culturelle**

In most situations, we don't have the time to make accurate mathematical conversions of temperatures. It is therefore important that students have a rough idea of what Celsius temperatures represent (i.e., is it cold or hot outside, what am I going to wear, etc.). To get students used to making these decisions quickly, state various Celsius temperatures and have them respond with one of the following statements: **Il fait très froid, il fait assez froid, il fait frais, il fait assez chaud, il fait très chaud.** For example: **La température est de 32 degrés. (Il fait très chaud.)**

● **Structure: Le passé composé avec** *avoir*

To present the **passé composé** more inductively, you can use the following technique. Write a short paragraph in the present tense on the board and illustrate it with a stick-figure drawing. For example, **D'habitude, Janine quitte la maison, elle tourne à gauche dans la rue Maubert, elle achète un journal au bureau de tabac, elle continue tout droit jusqu'à la place de la République, elle traverse la place et elle passe la matinée au parc.** Then write **hier** on the board along with yesterday's date. Redo the paragraph orally, using the **passé composé.** Question students about Janine's activities, then ask a student to play the role of Janine (**Hier j'ai quitté...**). Finally, have other students say what **Janine / Janine et son mari / Janine et moi** did.

Then quickly show on the board how the **passé composé** is formed. Write out some sentences from the paragraph above, keeping the explanation very simple (i.e., show the conjugation with **avoir** and the past participle with **-é.**) If you feel it is necessary, do a quick review of the present of the verb **avoir.**

### DEUXIÈME ÉTAPE

● **Note culturelle**

The French love the movies. It is their main cultural

activity. For example, almost 50% of the French go to the movies at least once a year (90% of young people between the ages of 15 and 24), and 60% of the people living in Paris see at least 10 films a year. In addition, there are more than 11,000 **ciné-clubs** with over a million members.

Moving pictures were invented in the late nineteenth century by the Lumière brothers (Auguste and Louis). Since then, the French have had a great interest in films—those produced around the world as well as in France, the newest releases as well as the great classics. In addition to the great number of commercial houses in France (over 5,000), there are also, at the **Palais de Chaillot** in Paris, a film museum and theater **(la Cinémathèque)** that show a wide variety of movies from film history every day.

Americans encounter some noteworthy cultural differences when going to the movies in France. For example, you are shown to your place by an usher **(une ouvreuse),** who will expect a small tip. In addition, there is a short break, usually about 20 or 30 minutes after the showing **(la séance)** begins. Between the short subjects and publicity films, the lights go on and the **ouvreuses** move through the theater **(la salle),** selling candy and ice cream before the main feature **(le film)** begins.

*L'Officiel des spectacles* and a similar publication, called *Pariscope,* appear weekly and offer detailed information, not only on movie offerings, but also on plays, concerts, sports events, and other entertainment possibilities. They use a similar style and format. The abbreviations **v.o. (version originale)** and **v.f. (version française)** indicate whether a foreign film is shown with subtitles **(v.o.)** or is dubbed **(v.f.).** The following paragraphs explain the format and abbreviations for the listings of the **Gaumont Les Halles** movie theater and for the film *La Double Vie de Véronique.*

---

**GAUMONT LES HALLES.** Location: rue du Forum, Porte Rambuteau, third level. Métro stop: Châtelet-Les-Halles. Telephone: 40 26 12 12. Handicap access provided. Price of a ticket **(place):** 40 francs. Credit cards accepted: **Carte Bleue Visa.** Special price: 31 francs for students, holders of a **Carte Vermeil** (special entertainment card), large families (between Sunday 8:00 P.M. and Friday 6:00 P.M.) and also children under 18 (between Sunday 8:00 P.M. and Tuesday 6:00 P.M.). Reduced price (26 francs) for the early show every day (11:00 A.M. to 12:45 P.M.).

*La Double Vie de Véronique* (with subtitles). Shows at 11:10, 1:45, 3:50, 5:55, 8:00, 10:05. Film starts 20 minutes after the show time.

---

● **Structure: Le passé composé avec** *être*
Although there are a variety of techniques and mnemonic devices for learning the verbs conjugated with **être,** the most important first step is for students to become accustomed to *using* the verbs conjugated with **être.** Ideally, they should get so much practice that **être** simply "sounds right" with certain verbs. They usually achieve this with **aller** because it is the most frequently used **être** verb. The goal is to do the same with the other verbs, such as **rentrer, entrer, monter, descendre,** and **sortir,** for example. Of particular importance is the verb **rester** since it is the most error-prone of the **être** verbs Even when students have reached higher levels of proficiency, they still tend to use **avoir** with **rester.**

Simple, quick drills done regularly may be a partial answer to having students develop the *habit* of using **être.** The more often students hear and say the forms, the more likely they are to use them correctly. This is one instance where grammar rules may not be as useful as spontaneous practice. For example, you might decide that each time a student uses the wrong helping verb, you will stop and give a rapid drill for correction: **J'ai sorti avec des amis. / Non, il faut dire: Je suis sorti avec des amis. (nous / elles / il / tu / je / vous).**

● **Débrouillons-nous!**
An additional activity, which can be used here or along with the **Reprise** in the next **étape,** involves getting students to survey their classmates. Select a certain number of students to be the questioners. Each one receives a pair of expressions, for example:

- **regarder la télé**
- **aller au cinéma**
- **faire du shopping**
- **rester à la maison**
- **manger un bon dîner**
- **écouter de la musique**
- **écouter des disques**
- **sortir avec des amis**
- **organiser une soirée**
- **faire un voyage**
- **aller à un match de...**
- **faire une promenade (à vélo)**

The questioners can ask about a specific time **(hier, le week-end dernier, récemment)** or use a more general framework **(Quelle est la dernière fois que tu... ?)** (You can take advantage of this activity to show how to say **Je n'ai jamais...** or **Je ne suis jamais...).** You can then ask the questioners to report back to the class.

## TROISIÈME ÉTAPE

● **Structure: Le passé composé des verbes pronominaux**
Perhaps you will have noticed that when introducing the present tense of pronominal verbs in Chapter 4, we did not use many of the verbs traditionally favored for teaching reflexive verbs: for example, **se réveiller, se brosser les dents, s'habiller, se laver la tête et les mains,** etc. These expressions will appear in various contexts of succeeding chapters. However, if you feel the need to introduce these verbs at this point, you can do so as part of an alternative presentation of this topic.

For example, tell students what you did this morning, acting out the activities as you speak. Stress pronominal verbs, but do not hesitate to mix in nonpronominal verbs that fit your narrative. For example, **Ce matin je me suis réveillé(e) assez tard. Par conséquent, je ne suis pas resté(e) au lit. Je me suis levé(e) tout de suite. J'ai pris une douche, je me suis lavé la tête, et je me suis habillé(e) en toute vitesse. Pour le petit déjeuner, j'ai pris seulement une tasse de café et une tartine. Je me suis brossé les dents et j'ai quitté la maison.** Ask students if they noticed how you formed the **passé composé** of verbs such as se **réveiller, se lever, s'habiller, se brosser.** Then question students about their mornings, leading them to generate and use all the other forms. For example, **À quelle heure est-ce que tu t'es réveillé(e) ce matin? Tu t'es levé(e) tout de suite? Et Graham, il s'est réveillé à 6h aussi? Ah, bon. Graham et Lucy se sont réveillés à 6h.** Include yes-no questions in order to introduce the position of **ne... pas** with the **passé composé** of pronominal verbs.

● **Débrouillons-nous!**
Here are some role-playing situations that can be used to practice the **passé composé** with **avoir.**

(1) Have students survey their classmates as to how they spent last evening. In large classes, only about a third of the students should be conducting the survey; the others are to be their respondents. In small classes, each student can both ask and respond. Assign some of the following activities to each questioner:

- **regarder la télévision**
- **étudier (faire les devoirs)**
- **regarder une vidéo**
- **faire une promenade**
- **étudier pour un examen**
- **organiser une soirée**
- **travailler**
- **téléphoner à des amis**
- **écouter de la musique**

- **manger du chocolat**
- **faire du shopping**
- **danser**
- **faire du jogging**
- **aider (quelqu'un)**
- **manger un bon dîner**

Have students record the number of students who say yes and the number who say no to each of the activities. You can then ask them to report to the class. (2) Have students question each other in pairs. Insist that they give precise answers, i.e., that they use one of the time expressions that situate events in the past (**hier matin, l'année dernière,** etc.). Put on the board the model: **Je n'ai jamais** + past participle. When students have finished, have some summarize what they have learned for the class. Example: **Hier soir Susan a téléphoné à son amie Alice. Elle a fait une promenade le week-end dernier. Elle n'a jamais organisée une soirée. Elle a fait du jogging samedi dernier. Elle a fait un voyage il y a un mois. Elle a visité Chicago il y a trois mois. Elle n'a pas mangé de chocolat hier soir. (Elle n'aime pas le chocolat.) Elle a fait du shopping dimanche après-midi.**

● **Additional Cultural Information**
Weather conditions and climate provide excellent springboards for presenting geographical information about France. This can be done partly in French and partly in English. First, you may have students characterize different parts of the United States in terms of climate. Follow up by asking if students think that climate affects the way people think and behave (attitudes, values, etc.). Then do the same thing for France. You may offer some of the following information:

- Geographically, France occupies a privileged position in Western Europe. It is at the center of the main routes connecting all the Western European countries.
- Many different climates can be found in France, which makes its agriculture rich and varied and provides a vast array of tourist attractions. Climates range from semi-tropical in the south (grapes, olives, fruit trees, flowers for perfume, beaches) to alpine in the southeast and east (mushrooms, herbs, winter sports), and mild in the southwest and west (grapes, vegetables, grain).
- France is a country well-irrigated by **fleuves** (which flow into the ocean) and **rivières** (tributaries). Every part of the country has a major river: **le Rhin, la Seine, la Loire, la Garonne, le Rhône.**
- Although one should try to avoid stereotypes, some people feel that the different climates in France have an influence on character traits. For example, in the south,

people seem to be more open, more easy-going, more relaxed, happier, and friendlier. In the colder climates, people are said to be more serious and harder to get to know. In the Atlantic regions, the abundance of rain is said to make people more gloomy. Ask students whether they think there is any validity to this type of characterization and if they have noticed the same things about Americans who live in different parts of the country. At the same time, point out the dangers of cultural stereotyping.

## CHAPITRE 6

### PREMIÈRE ÉTAPE

● **Point de départ: Chez les petits commerçants**
The presentation of the narrative may be accompanied by the transparency of the food items sold in a **boulangerie,** a **pâtisserie,** and a **charcuterie.** Students have the book closed; you point at the items as you present them (orally or using the recording on the Instructor's Tape). This visual presentation will facilitate comprehension and cut down on translation or explanation. An alternative method is to present the vocabulary before having students hear or read the narrative. You might recount a shopping trip you took: **D'abord je suis allé(e) à la boulangerie où j'ai acheté...** (point to items on transparency). **Ensuite je suis allé(e) à la pâtisserie pour acheter un gâteau au chocolat pour l'anniversaire de... J'ai aussi acheté quelques pâtisseries... Moi, j'adore aussi les tartelettes, mais j'ai résisté à la tentation... Enfin, je suis allé(e) à la charcuterie...**

● **Note culturelle**
Point out to students that one usually greets people in a small store upon entering by saying **Bonjour, Monsieur (Madame, Mademoiselle)** and also remind them of the expressions for leave-taking, such as **Au revoir (À demain), Monsieur (Madame, Mademoiselle).** Greetings and leave-takings can be integrated into Ex. A, B, and C. Additional cultural information:

• Although specialized food stores are still very important in France, many people shop at supermarkets.
• Small shopkeepers (**les petits commerçants**) make up an increasingly smaller portion of the work force. In 1960, they numbered over one million; in 1989, there were only 770,000.
• There are **boulangeries** and **pâtisseries** in each **quartier** of Paris and other big cities. During the

summer vacation months (July and August), many may be closed.
• Sample prices of some common items:

  **baguette** (4F)
  **croissant** (4F50)
  **pain au chocolat** (5F)
  **éclair** (8F)
  **gâteau** (60F à 110F)
  **tarte** (40F à 100F)
  **tartelette** (10F à 15F)
  **pâté** (70F le kilo)
  **saucisses** (59F à 82F le kilo)
  **saucisson** (62F le kilo)
  **jambon** (74F le kilo)
  **salade de tomates** (40F le kilo)

● **Structure: Les expressions de quantité**
An alternative way of presenting specific quantities is to bring to class a scale and different amounts of apples (oranges or some other fruit) in plastic bags. (If you don't have a scale, label each bag: **1 livre, 1/2 kilo, 2 kilos**). Also bring different size pieces of cheese (or other food). Show students what you have: **J'ai un kilo de pommes. Et voici un gros morceau (une belle tranche) de fromage.** When you have finished with the food you brought, have them talk about foods they know: **Dans mon frigo, j'ai un litre de lait, une livre de concombres, une bouteille de Coca,** etc. **Qu'est-ce qu'il y a dans votre frigo?**

To give further practice with the expressions of general quality, you can do a **Demandez à... si...** type of exercise: **Demandez à Susan si elle a beaucoup de disques. Demandez à Mike s'il mange beaucoup de viande. Demandez à Peter s'il a beaucoup ou peu de cassettes.** etc.

### DEUXIÈME ÉTAPE

● **Note culturelle**
Some additional cultural information about food and dining habits in France:

• The French often eat fruit for dessert instead of something sweet. A bowl of fruit is on the table, and each person makes a selection. The dessert course follows the cheese course.
• The French often peel fruit that Americans tend to eat with the skin on (apples, peaches, and pears, in particular).
• A French **salade** often uses just Boston lettuce and a vinaigrette dressing (oil, vinegar, mustard, salt, and pepper). They do not add lots of vegetables nor do they

use creamy dressings. This is probably because the salad is eaten after the meal, before the cheese. The vinaigrette dressing is intended to clear the palate for the cheese course.

- Now that students have learned many of the names for foods, you can point out to them the various courses and have them design a meal: hors-d'œuvre, main course(s), salad, cheese, dessert, coffee.
- Until recently, the main meal in France was lunch. Now that more women work and fewer people return home at noon, the trend is slowly shifting to having the main meal at night.
- Dinner is usually eaten later in France than in the United States (starting between 7:30 and 8:00 P.M.).

### ● Structure: Le partitif
The most important thing to remember about a presentation of the partitive is that it should be done as simply as possible; students should not be led to believe that it is a complicated concept. You should probably not expect your students to use it with 100% accuracy in spontaneous situations: they may learn it quite well in highly structured situations, but when involved in a simple conversation, they are likely to revert back to the definite or indefinite articles.

You may wish to isolate for the students those verbs that are likely to take the definite article and those that usually are followed by the partitive:

- definite article:

| | |
|---|---|
| **aimer (bien, assez)** | **adorer** |
| **détester** | **préférer** |

- partitive:

| | |
|---|---|
| **prendre** | **manger** |
| **acheter** | **avoir** |

- and the expressions **il y a** and **je voudrais**

### ● Structure: Les nombres de 100 à 1.000.000
In order to develop the skill of understanding spoken numbers, introduce a sequence of listening comprehension exercises, such as the following:

- You call out the cost of different food items; students write down the price.
- You give a series of dates (year only); students write them down.
- You give the price of something; students write down (or say) the next highest denomination (by tens). For example: **Les croissants, 23F. Voilà 30F.**
- You give students a written list of names of cities (or countries); you then call out the population of each place, and students write down the figure.

## TROISIÈME ÉTAPE

### ● Point de départ: Au centre commercial
You will probably wish to introduce the **centre commercial** by working with one small conversation (i.e., one store) at a time. You can also intersperse your presentations of the dialogues with personalized questions about what students own or prefer, as a way of reinforcing the new vocabulary items for each store.

In France one is beginning to find more and more shopping malls or complexes (**centres commerciaux**). With the exception of a few very large ones (such as **Le Forum des Halles** in Paris or **Le Centre Leclerc** in Toulouse), they tend to be smaller than their American counterparts. Unlike American malls, they often are not attached to major department stores and, in many cases, they are located in the center of cities so that people can travel there via public transportation.

A French **centre commercial** will usually include a large number of specialty stores, for example:

- **un magasin de matériel** (electronics store)
- **une parfumerie**
- **une bijouterie**
- **un magasin de meubles**
- **des boutiques de vêtements (femme, homme, enfant, sport)**
- **un magasin de sport**
- **une pâtisserie**

Many will also offer services, such as **pressing, clés-minute, ressemelage rapide.** There will sometimes be movie theaters or book stores. While there are no "restaurants" properly speaking, you can usually find a variety of places to eat, either in the **centre** (pizzerias, cafeterias, snack bars) or nearby (fast-food restaurants).

A recent trend is to advertise them as **centres de vie,** in an effort to attract the whole family. It is not usual for a working-class French family to spend a good part of a Saturday afternoon at a **centre commercial.** However, they are closed on Sundays.

### ● Structure: L'adjectif interrogatif *quel*
Students often confuse **quel** with other question forms. For example, it is very common to hear them say: **Qu'est-ce que votre profession?** (instead of **Quelle est votre profession?**). Consequently, you may wish to contrast specifically the use of **quel** and **qu'est-ce que,** reminding students that **qu'est-ce que** is always followed by a subject and a verb. It may also be helpful to point out the expression **Qu'est-ce que c'est?**

## QUATRIÈME ÉTAPE

### ● Ex. F

As an alternative version of Ex. F, you can create a series of shopping lists (perhaps a set of four or five) so that students are more likely to go to different stores at different times. You can also add stores from the **centre commercial,** if you wish. Provide the shopkeepers with a list of items and prices that they are to sell. (You can also vary the prices for identical items—i.e., have more than one **épicerie** with different specials.)

## CHAPITRE 7

## PREMIÈRE ÉTAPE

### ● Point de départ: L'université

Instead of doing Ex. A and B, have students (in groups of two) prepare a description of their university that parallels the two descriptions in the **Point de départ.** Encourage them to use expressions from the text when appropriate, but to adapt the information to their particular situation. When they have finished, ask some groups to read their descriptions or have groups exchange descriptions for comparison and correction.

### ● Structure: L'accord des adjectifs

Many of the adjectives presented in this chapter are cognates and are therefore readily understandable. However, it should be noted that not all students necessarily need to learn *every* adjective. The important thing is for each person to have enough vocabulary to work with the people and things he/she will want to describe.

Colors can be introduced using TPR (Total Physical Response). Assemble different colored pens and pieces of paper. Then have students pick up and give someone else the color pen or paper you specify: **John, prenez le stylo rouge et donnez-le à Mary.** Don't worry about the use of the direct object pronoun. Students will obey the command rather than worry about the exact words being used. Once students know the names of the colors, show them pictures of different colored cars and bikes (or any other object whose name is masculine in French). Ask them questions such as: **De quelle couleur est cette voiture-ci? Avez-vous une voiture? Elle est (blanche) aussi?**

## DEUXIÈME ÉTAPE

### ● À vous!, Ex. B

For more variation, bring in photos of your family (or have students bring in photos of their own families), and have people describe whom they see. Students can also ask questions about the people in the photographs. This type of activity is best done in small groups.

As an additional activity, you can ask students to play a psychological portrait game. Pose the following situation: **Je vous donne un billet et tout l'argent que vous voudrez; vous allez passer un mois en France. Tous vos besoins seront satisfaits. Nommez trois choses que vous voudriez apporter avec vous.** Students write down the three objects and share the results with the class. Based on what is said, the class characterizes the person, using as many adjectives as possible. For example, Jeanne says: **Je vais apporter mon dictionnaire, une photo de ma famille et mon ordinateur.** The class concludes: **Jeanne est très pratique, elle est sentimentale et elle est travailleuse.**

## TROISIÈME ÉTAPE

### ● Point de départ: Les cours

As an alternate approach to this **Point de départ,** begin with the list of courses and disciplines. First, ask students how courses in their school are organized. Get them to talk about academic divisions (for example, humanities, natural sciences, etc.). Then, write on the board the basic French disciplinary divisions:

- **sciences humaines**
- **sciences naturelles**
- **sciences exactes**
- **études professionnelles**
- **beaux-arts**
- **lettres**

Using primarily subjects that are cognates of English terms, have students place them in the appropriate categories:

- **biologie**
- **mathématiques**
- **philosophie**
- **histoire**
- **journalisme**
- **musique**
- **sociologie**
- **littérature**
- **physique**

Then add some of the more "modern" disciplines: **informative, marketing,** etc.

When these divisions are clear, have students listen to the recording of the dialogue on the Instructor's Tape. Possible comprehension questions: **Sommes-nous à une université française ou américaine? Qu'est-ce que les deux étudiantes font comme études? Qui a le plus grand nombre de cours?**

● **Structure: Les verbes réguliers en -*ir***

We would recommend *not* devoting a lot of time to **-ir** verbs. Although it is necessary to recognize them and know their meaning, their frequency is relatively low. They are used most frequently in the **passé composé.**

## QUATRIÈME ÉTAPE

● **Point d'arrivée**

Additional activity: If you have exchange students from France or French-speaking countries on your campus or in your area, this would be an excellent time to invite them to come to class and talk about their educational experiences. You might want to invite students to prepare some simple questions with which to begin the interview. After students and visitors have conversed in French for a while, you could then invite them to switch to English in order to ask more sophisticated questions.

## CHAPITRE 8

## PREMIÈRE ÉTAPE

● **À vous!, Ex. A**

The parts of the body lend themselves nicely to a TPR (Total Physical Response) type activity. After presenting the parts of the body using yourself and/or students as models, ask them to point to the parts of the body you name. If you wish, divide the vocabulary into sections (the head, the upper body, the lower body), thus reducing the amount to be repeated and pointed to each time.

● **Structure: L'imparfait**

To present the imperfect inductively, begin with a monologue about what you used to do (for example, when you were in school): **Quand j'étais à l'université, j'habitais dans une résidence universitaire. J'avais trois camarades de chambre ma première année. Notre chambre n'était pas très grande, mais il y avait assez de place pour nous quatre. Moi, je me levais toujours la première. Je prenais une douche. Je m'habillais. Je me dépêchais pour aller à mon premier cours. J'avais souvent cours à 8h.** Ask students if they noticed you were using a different tense and if they can figure out why you weren't using the **passé composé.** Once you have established the name of the tense and the basic reason for its existence, you may want to continue in one of two ways:

• Proceed with a description of how the imperfect is formed (see margin notes) or
• continue the inductive presentation by asking students questions about when they were younger.

If you choose the second option, use a verb that can involve several members of a student's family. For example: **Quand vous étiez plus jeune... le samedi matin... à quelle heure vous leviez-vous?** (If necessary, model the correct form by talking about what time you got up when you were little). **Vous étiez le premier à vous lever? Votre sœur se levait avec vous? Ah, vous vous leviez tous les deux à 7h? Et vos parents, à quelle heure est-ce qu'ils se levaient?** When all or most of the forms have been elicited, summarize the formation of the imperfect.

The imperfect is presented in two different **étapes.** In this initial presentation, we concentrate on the forms of the imperfect and on its use with habitual actions. In the next **étape,** the exercises are aimed at demonstrating the other frequent uses of this tense.

● **Structure: Le verbe irrégulier *pouvoir***

For a more extensive inductive presentation of **pouvoir,** begin by telling a story about the trouble you had getting someone to do something with or for you. For example, *Je veux aller au cinéma, donc je téléphone à une amie.* **—Allô! Cécile? Tu veux aller au cinéma? —Oh, je voudrais bien, mais je ne peux pas. Je dois travailler ce soir.** *Elle ne peut pas, elle doit travailler. Je téléphone donc à mon frère.* **— Dis donc, Henri. Monique et toi, vous pouvez aller au cinéma? —Non, ce n'est pas possible. Nous ne pouvons pas. Nous sommes invités à dîner ce soir.** *Cécile ne peut pas aller au cinéma; mon frère et sa femme, ils ne peuvent pas y aller non plus.* Then ask some students if they want to go. Indicate by gestures that they are to refuse. When students have practiced most of the forms, review the spellings briefly. Then quickly show the imperfect and the **passé composé,** explaining the special meaning of the latter.

## DEUXIÈME ÉTAPE

● **Note culturelle**

When traveling in France, most medical needs can be taken care of at a pharmacy. Every town has at least one pharmacy open all night; the local paper will list this as **la pharmacie de nuit.** In Paris, the **Drugstores** have pharmacies open until 2 A.M. For more serious medical problems in Paris, you can find English-speaking doctors at the **Hôpital Américain de Paris** in Neuilly (**métro** stop: **Sablons**) as well as the **Hôpital Britannique de Paris** in Levallois (**métro** stop: **Anatole-France**).

While discussing the differences between American and French pharmacies, you may also wish to talk briefly about health care in general. In France, there is a unified and nationalized system of health care. Up to 80% of all medical expenses are covered under Social Security.

Moreover, this is true for anyone spending more than three months in the country; thus, you need not be a citizen to benefit from this system. As a cultural exercise, you might ask students to describe the system of health care in the United States and then to discuss the advantages and disadvantages of each system. This discussion would probably be in English. Students often ask instructors how to say in French the names of common illnesses. Here is a short list of some diseases:

- **une migraine**
- **une angine** (*strep throat, tonsillitis*)
- **une bronchite**
- **une pneumonie**
- **la mononucléose**
- **les oreillons** (*mumps*)
- **la rougeole** (*measles*)
- **la varicelle** (*chicken pox*)
- **la rubéole** (*German measles*)
- **un cancer**
- **le Sida** (*Aids*)

## TROISIÈME ÉTAPE

### ● Note culturelle
Given that much of the interest in physical fitness originated in the United States, it is not surprising that many of the French terms come from English. The following entries for health clubs in *Pariscope* and *L'Officiel des spectacles* contain some of these terms:

---

CENTRE AQUABUILDING, 6 rue St-Paul (4e) 42.71.66.69. Gyms aquatiques, danse classique, kinégyne, stretching, musculation, sauna, hammam, piscine.

---

TOP-FORME, 80, rue Traversière (12e). 43.07.09.09. Du Lun au Ven de 12h à 20h; Sam de 9h à 14h; Dim de 10h à 14h. Gym, aérobic, yoga, modern'jazz, boxe française, escrime, musculation, golf.

---

ESPACE VIT/HALLES, Place Beaubourg, 48, rue Rambuteau. 42.77.21.71. Ouvert 7 heures sur 7. Gym aquatique, harmonic, afro-brésilien, samba, modern'jazz, danses contemporaines, jazz débutant, aérobic, jogging, stretching, relaxation, gymnastique, cours musculation collectifs, programme individuel, 50 appareils, UVA hte pression, sauna, hammam, jacuzzi, boutique, restaurant diététique, piscine.

---

As a prereading exercise for the **Cinq groupes d'aliments** selection, have students discuss what they know about nutrition in general and food groups in particular. Encourage students, when working with the chart, to use their knowledge of cognates and their ability to guess from context. If students have true difficulty, choose certain expressions to work on as a class—for example:

- **renouveler les tissus du corps**
- **le tonus musculaire**
- **le rythme cardiaque**
- **le transit intestinal**
- **la vue nocturne**
- **le travail musculaire**

Students should be able to use cognates, word families, and logical associations to arrive at an approximate meaning in each case.

### ● Structure: Le verbe irrégulier *savoir*
To present **savoir** inductively, ask students whether or not they know how to do a particular sport, such as skiing. **Moi, je ne sais pas faire du ski. Et vous, vous savez faire du ski? Est-ce que Peter sait faire du ski?** By this point in the semester, at least some of the students will be able to deduce the various forms of **savoir** from the forms you provide in the questions.

## QUATRIÈME ÉTAPE

### ● Lecture: «Une consultation gratuite»
Jules Romains (1885–1972) was a poet and novelist as well as a playwright. His doctrine of **unanimisme,** the idea that the crowd exists as a distinct entity with its own collective soul and qualities, received a humorous and ironic demonstration in his famous farce, *Knock* (1923). In this play, a clever scoundrel, having established himself as a doctor in a village in the French Alps, proceeds to persuade the inhabitants that they are very ill and desperately need medical care. The scene featured in the excerpt in the text occurs during the second act and illustrates the psychological techniques Knock uses to unite the community in fear and concern. The play was later made into a movie starring the famous actor Louis Jouvet as Doctor Knock.

# INSTRUCTOR'S TAPE SCRIPT

## ÉTAPE PRÉLIMINAIRE

**Allons au café!** (text, p. 7)

## CHAPITRE 1

**Une scène au café** (text, p. 12)

**Parlons!** (text, p. 22)

**L'heure du déjeuner** (text, p. 31)

**Portrait: Mireille Loiseau, Paris** (text, p. 46)

### Conversation supplémentaire
— Tiens, Farid! Bonjour! Comment vas-tu?
— Bonjour.
— Bonjour, Nellie. Ça va, et toi?
— Ça va. Laurent, je veux te présenter Farid Azize. Il est marocain; il est architecte à Casablanca.
— Enchanté, Farid. Comment allez-vous?
— Enchanté, Laurent. Très bien, merci.
— Voulez-vous manger avec nous?
— Oh, oui, bien sûr, je veux bien, ouais.
— Mademoiselle, s'il vous plaît?
— Bonjour, Messieurs-dames, qu'est-ce que je peux vous servir?
— Nellie?
— Une salade niçoise et un Vittel, s'il vous plaît.
— Oui, d'accord. Et vous, Monsieur?
— Heum, un steak-frites?
— Je suis désolée, Monsieur, la maison ne sert que des sandwiches, des omelettes ou des salades.
— Heum, vous avez des croque-monsieur?
— Oui, Monsieur.
— Bien, donnez-moi un croque-monsieur. Vous avez des croque-madame?
— Oui.
— Donnez-moi aussi un croque-madame.
— D'accord. Et pour boire?
— Heum, donnez-moi un demi.
— Oui, entendu. Et vous, Monsieur?
— Je prendrai une omelette au fromage avec des frites.
— Et comme boisson?
— Ah, comme boisson je prendrai une limonade, s'il vous plaît.
— Très bien.

## CHAPITRE 2

**Moi, j'aime beaucoup...** (text, p. 62)

**Voici ma famille!** (text, p. 70)

**Portrait: Michel Kerguézec, Locmariaquer, (Bretagne), France** (text, p. 85)

### Conversations supplémentaires

— Je m'appelle Chantal Duprès. Je suis mariée. J'habite à Boston. J'ai trois enfants. Je suis professeur de langues dans une université américaine. J'enseigne le français. J'aime beaucoup le ski.
— Je suis Suzanne Boulanger. Je suis comédienne. J'habite un petit appartement à Paris. Ma famille habite à Lyon. Je travaille dans un atelier de théâtre. J'aime surtout l'opéra et le cinéma.
— Je m'appelle Farid Azize. Je suis marocain. J'habite à New York. Mais ma famille habite à Casablanca, au Maroc. Je travaille beaucoup. Je suis architecte. J'aime beaucoup le jazz et le ski.
— Je suis Mireille Roche. J'habite à New York. Je suis célibataire. Je suis professeur de danse et j'aime beaucoup la musique.
— Je m'appelle Alain Robert. Je suis célibataire. Je suis né à Quimper, mais j'habite à Rouen. Je suis psychologue. J'aime la gymnastique et le théâtre.

## CHAPITRE 3

**Où se trouve...** (text, p. 99)

**Véronique et ses amis font des projets.** (text, p. 109)

**Portrait: Véronique Béziers, Tarascon (Provence), France** (text, p. 123)

### Conversations supplémentaires

**Numéro 1**
— Allô, Elizabeth?
— Oui?
— Salut, c'est Laurent!
— Salut, Laurent. Comment vas-tu?
— Ça va, et toi?

— Très bien.

— Bon, euh, tu veux venir à une soirée chez Michel ce soir?

— Oh oui, avec plaisir!

— Euh, tu sais où il habite?

— Non.

— Il habite tout près de chez toi, ah, rue Voltaire.

— La rue Voltaire, c'est pas la rue qui est derrière la cathédrale?

— Si, exactement, juste en face du cinéma l'Odéon.

— Très bien.

— Bon, à ce soir!

— Au revoir, à ce soir!

— Au revoir!

### Numéro 2

— Pardon, Madame, savez-vous où est l'Hôtel de la Vigne, s'il vous plaît?

— Ah oui, l'Hôtel de la Vigne, c'est entre le boulevard Raspail et le jardin du Luxembourg, je crois bien. Oui, alors voilà, vous êtes sur le boulevard Montparnasse.

— D'accord.

— Descendez, et prenez votre première rue à droite.

— La première à droite?

— La première à droite, c'est le boulevard Raspail.

— D'accord.

— Ensuite la deuxième à gauche et vous y êtes.

— Ah, très bien. Merci beaucoup!

— Je vous en prie.

— Au revoir!

— Au revoir!

## CHAPITRE 4

**Vous allez en ville?** (text, p. 128)

**Prenons le metro!** (text, p. 136)

**Je veux prendre un taxi** (text, p. 147)

**Portrait: Massyla Fodéba, Dakar, Sénégal** (text, p. 162)

### Conversation supplémentaire

— Il y a un très bon film de Woody Allen ce soir, au cinéma des Champs-Élysées. Alors, on y va?

— Ah oui? Quel est le titre du film?

— *Hanna et ses trois sœurs.*

— Oui, j'aime beaucoup Woody Allen!

— Moi aussi!

— Bon, alors on y va?

— Euh, on prend le métro?

— Non, j'ai ma voiture, je peux passer vous prendre.

— Ha, très bien, on se donne rendez-vous alors...

— Rendez-vous, euh, au café Chez Paul.

— C'est où ça?

— C'est sur l'avenue de la République, juste en face de la bibliothèque municipale.

— Ha, d'accord, je vois bien!

— Bon, à ce soir?

— À ce soir!

— À ce soir!

## CHAPITRE 5

**Quel temps fait-il?** (text, p. 174)

**Tu veux voir le nouveau film au Gaumont les Halles?** (text, p. 185)

**On pourrait faire une excursion!** (text, p. 196)

**Déjeuner du matin** (text, p. 202)

**Portrait: Claire Maurant, Strasbourg, France** (text, p. 206)

### Conversations supplémentaires

### Numéro 1

— Quel mauvais temps aujourd'hui, dis donc, hein!

— Oui, c'est vrai, aujourd'hui il pleut, il fait du vent, oui, c'est vrai, aujourd'hui.

— Vous savez, moi, je n'ai pas l'habitude car dans le Midi il fait toujours beau, il fait du soleil, le temps est sec, le ciel est clair.

— Ah, la Côte d'Azur, bien sûr...

— Ouais, ce n'est pas comme en Bretagne où il pleut souvent et il fait assez frais, sans parler du brouillard!

— Oui, mais enfin ça, c'est normal, la Bretagne, euh... En ce qui concerne Paris, euh, hier il a fait un soleil magnifique, n'est-ce pas?

— Oui, c'est vrai.

— Et je pense que demain... demain il va faire... encore beau. Alors Paris, c'est magnifique, non?

— Oui, d'accord!

### Numéro 2

— Alors qu'est-ce qu'on fait ce soir, on va au cinéma?

— Oui.

— Oui, allons au cinéma, d'accord?

— D'accord!

— Oui, mais bon, j'ai le journal là, euh, qu'est-ce qu'on va voir ce soir, alors?

— Écoute, qu'est-ce qu'il y a, euh...

— A Montparnasse ils jouent un classique, *Les Vacances de Monsieur Hulot.* Ça vous dit rien?

— C'est une comédie, ça?

— Oui!

— Ouais, peut-être...

— Qu'est-ce que tu penses, toi, Jean-Louis?

— J'aimerais plutôt aller à l'Odéon. Je vois qu'il y a un film américain. Je crois que ça m'intéresserait. Ça s'appelle *Razor's Edge.*

— Ouais, c'est en anglais ça?

— Oui, c'est en anglais mais je crois que c'est un très, très bon film policier américain.

— Oui, mais je comprends pas l'anglais!

— Moi non plus, hein, moi non plus.

— Alors à quoi tu pensais pour le moment?

— Ben, écoute, il y a un film de science fiction là, *2001 Odyssée de l'espace.* C'est un vieux film mais c'est très bon.

— Moi, j'ai horreur des films de science fiction.

— Ah bon, ben, j'sais pas moi, alors!

— Peut-être une comédie, c'est pas mal après tout?

— A quoi est-ce que tu pensais comme comédie?

— *Les Vacances de Monsieur Hulot.*

— C'est un vieux film français, ça?

— Oui.

— Bien, ben, oui, moi j'aimerais bien, en fin de compte.

— Oui, d'accord, bonne idée, ouais, bonne idée.

— Bon, à huit heures, on se donne rendez-vous à huit heures?

— Huit heures, oui, devant le cinéma?

— Euh, non, non, plutôt au café des Saints-Pères.

— OK!

— D'accord!

— Oui, c'est bon.

— Au café des Saints-Pères. Puis on pourra sortir après!

— Exactement, prendre un pot...

— On prendra un pot, bon, d'accord!

— OK.

— Parfait.

— À ce soir!

— À ce soir!

— À ce soir!

## Numéro 3

— Ah, quelle belle journée j'ai passée aujourd'hui. Oh, c'était merveilleux. J'ai rencontré quelqu'un qui avait un bateau et ensuite il m'a emmenée faire du ski nautique.

— Ouh!

— Ah, c'était merveilleux. Oui, oui il n'est pas mal non plus!

— Ouh!

— Ah, ah!

— Pas mal!

— Et toi Laurent, qu'est-ce que t'as fait?

— Moi, aujourd'hui j'ai fait de la planche à voile pour la première fois, hein, c'est pas du gâteau, hein, c'est pas facile.

— Il y avait du vent?

— Non, mais, ah, c'est assez difficile même sans vent. J'ai pas réussi à tenir sur la planche plus d'une minute. Laisse-moi le dire, ça c'est difficile!

— Ah, ça a l'air compliqué, d'ailleurs, tu as beaucoup de courage de faire ça!

— Ouais, c'est dangereux, hein!

— Même sans vent!

— Ouais, même sans vent!

— Mais alors est-ce qu'il y avait, euh, un moniteur, là-bas, quelqu'un qui te montrait comment faire ou tu as fait tout seul?

— Non, j'ai rencontré une fille qui m'a appris à faire, ah, la planche à voile.

— Ah!

— Ah, toi aussi alors!

— Et ben oui, écoute, c'est les vacances.

— Et Élisabeth, tu as quelque chose à nous raconter, toi?

— Oh, moi je me suis fait bronzée toute la journée, et puis j'ai nagé, c'était formidable.

— Oui, dans l'étang?

— Non, dans la mer, il n'y avait pas de vagues, c'était merveilleux.

— Oui, tu es bronzée maintenant, ouais.

— Oui, ça commence!

— Et Jean-Mi?

— Et bien moi, j'ai joué, devinez à quoi? À la pétanque.

— Ouh!

— Ah, c'est bien!

— Avec mes amis de Marseille que j'ai retrouvés ici.

— C'est pas vrai, ils sont nombreux, là?

— Oh oui, il y a un bon groupe, oui. On a fait trois ou quatre, quatre parties.

— Et qui a gagné, alors?

— Eh, devinez, c'est moi!

— Ah, bravo!

— Mais oui! Alors devinez, ils m'ont payé le pastis.

— Ah, ah, ah!

— Ils m'ont payé l'apéritif!

— Tiens, à propos d'apéritif, si on allait dîner ensemble?

— Ah, oui, il y a un restaurant de fruits de mer au port.

— Ah, très bien, comment s'appelle-t-il ce restaurant?

— Je ne sais pas.

— Je crois que c'est Chez Nénette.

— Oui, je crois aussi.

—Chez Nénette?

—Oui, c'est Chez Nénette.

—Ah, d'accord! D'accord, alors on y va tout de suite?

—D'accord!

—Oui, si vous voulez, j'ai une petite faim, moi.

—D'accord et, euh, j'ai donné rendez-vous à des amis à la disco qui n'est pas très loin d'ici. Vous voulez venir?

—Après le repas, après le dîner, oui...

—Oui, on peut faire ça, très bonne idée.

—D'accord!

—Oh, très bien, quelle journée!

—Oui!

—Oh, oui!

## CHAPITRE 6

**Chez les petits commerçants** (text, p. 212)

**Au centre commercial** (text, p. 234)

**Portrait: Madame Thibaudet, Bordeaux (Gironde), France** (text, p. 248)

**Conversations supplémentaires**

**Numéro 1**

—Bonjour, Madame Vincent!

—Bonjour, Monsieur!

—Comment ça va aujourd'hui?

—Très bien. Je viens pour vous commander un gâteau d'anniversaire.

—Ah bon. Pour qui?

—Pour Patrick!

—Ah bon. Quel âge a-t-il?

—Quarante ans.

—Quarante ans! Oh, bien, il lui faut un beau gâteau.

—Oui!

—Qu'est-ce qui vous intéresserait? Je peux vous faire un très bon, un très bon gâteau au chocolat?

—Non, il n'aime pas le chocolat! Vous ne pourriez pas lui faire un gâteau au moka?

—Ah, oui, bien sûr! Avec de la crème, de la Chantilly?

—Ouais, très bien. Ça serait parfait.

—Pour quand est-ce que vous le voulez?

—Ah, il me le faut pour vendredi!

—Vendredi, bien. Écoutez, passez vendredi à onze heures.

—Entendu.

—Bien, ben, ce sera prêt.

—Merci, Monsieur, au revoir!

—Au revoir!

**Numéro 2**

—Bonjour, Monsieur!

—Bonjour, Madame. Qu'est-ce que vous désirez aujourd'hui?

—Alors voilà, je n'ai pas beaucoup de temps. Alors qu'est-ce que vous pouvez me proposer? J'ai besoin de servir le dîner dans une heure et demie.

—Bon, nous avons des plats tous prêts, hein. Heum, nous pouvons vous offrir une soupe à l'oignon. . .

—Ah, non pas de soupe pour commencer, c'est trop lourd! Vous avez des salades?

—Oui, nous avons une très belle salade de pommes de terre.

—Oui, très bien, d'accord.

—D'accord, je vous mets une salade, alors. Nous avons aussi de belles quiches.

—Ah oui, qu'est-ce que vous avez comme quiche?

—Une quiche à la tomate.

—Oui? Vous avez quelque chose au jambon peut-être ou au fromage?

—Oui, nous en avons aussi une au jambon et au fromage, si vous désirez.

—Bon, d'accord, je prendrais plutôt la quiche au jambon.

—D'accord, donc, une belle quiche et, aussi, oh, nous avons de beaux cœurs d'artichaut en salade aujourd'hui.

—Ah, oui, ça j'aimerais bien, s'il vous plaît. Euh, bon, alors c'est pour quatre personnes, hein?

—Quatre personnes, bon, d'accord! Voilà, Madame!

—Merci, Monsieur!

—Au revoir.

—Au revoir.

Vous allez entendre deux conversations ayant lieu au centre commercial, d'abord à la Fnac, ensuite à la papeterie.

**Numéro 1**

—Pardon, Monsieur. Vous travaillez ici n'est-ce pas?

—Oui, oui, bien sûr. Je peux vous aider, Madame?

—Oui, s'il vous plaît, euh, je voudrais acheter, euh, un disque compact de... de chansons folkloriques françaises. Est-ce que vous pouvez m'indiquer où se trouvent ces disques?

—Oui, oui, la section folklorique, c'est, euh, au fond à droite. Mais... écoutez, je vous amène. Suivez-moi.

—Merci beaucoup. Est-ce que vous avez un grand choix de... de ces chansons?

—Bien sûr, regardez. C'est classé par région. Donc, vous pouvez choisir.

—D'accord. Très intéressant. Bon, je vais prendre ces deux disques-là.

— Très bien. Et vous pouvez aller les payer à la caisse. C'est juste à droite.
— D'accord. Merci beaucoup.
— Je vous en prie.

## Numéro 2

— Bonjour, Mademoiselle. Est-ce que vous auriez des enveloppes, s'il vous plaît?
— Bonjour, Monsieur. Oui, nous en avons tout un stock, là sur le rayon derrière.
— Bien, alors, des enveloppes—j'aurai besoin d'enveloppes. J'aurai également besoin d'un petit cahier.
— Oui, euh, de combien de pages, à peu près?
— Oh, cent, cent cinquante, deux cents?
— Oui, très bien. Alors, voici.
— Un carnet, c'est très bien. Également, attendez... de quoi ai-je besoin? Ah oui, de papier à lettres. Est-ce que vous auriez du papier à lettres?
— Oui, alors, nous avons différents modèles. Euh... en voici un qui n'a pas beaucoup de décoration. Est-ce que vous voulez quelque chose de sobre?
— Oui, je préfère quelque chose de sobre.
— Très bien. Alors, voici.
— Bien, ce sera tout.
— Très bien. Alors, pour le papier à lettres, ce sera trente-cinq francs, le petit cahier vingt-cinq, et, ou les enveloppes huit francs. Voilà.
— Ça fait soixante-huit francs. Bien, voilà, Madame.
— Merci beaucoup, Monsieur.
— Au revoir, Madame.
— Au revoir, Monsieur.

## CHAPITRE 7

**L'université** (text, p. 254)

**Les profs et les étudiants** (text, p. 267)

**Les cours** (text, p. 279)

**Portrait: Jean Hébert, Lyon (Rhône-Alpes), France** (text, p. 294)

**Conversations supplémentaires**

### Numéro 1

— Bonjour, est-ce que cette place est prise?
— Non, non, vas-y, assieds-toi, je t'en prie!
— Merci. Euh, je me présente, je suis Hélène Leureux.
— Ah, très bien, je m'appelle Laurent.

— Je m'appelle Élisabeth.
— Bonjour, Élisabeth.
— Bonjour. Je viens du Canada et je suis étudiante étrangère, ici, à la faculté cette année.
— Oh, très bien, enchanté!
— Ça me plaît beaucoup, oui. Et toi, qu'est-ce que tu fais?
— Ben écoute, moi je viens juste d'arriver, je viens de passer le Bac A4, le Bac littéraire, hein, l'année dernière, et puis je commence juste mes années, heum, ma première année de lettres ici.
— Ah, bon...
— À l'université, oui.
— Qu'est-ce que tu veux faire plus tard?
— Ah, probablement devenir enseignant, devenir enseignant à l'université, oui.
— Oui, très bien, et dans quelle spécialité?
— Le roman moderne.
— Ah, très bien.
— Et toi, qu'est-ce que tu fais?
— Moi, je prépare un DUES de mathématiques.
— Et qu'est-ce que c'est un DUES?
— C'est un Diplôme universitaire d'études scientifiques.
— Ah, tu fais des sciences, alors?
— Oui, oui.
— Ah, très bien!
— Je suis en deuxième année de deuxième cycle.
— Très bien. Alors il faut faire combien d'années pour avoir le...
— Le DUES?
— Oui.
— Il faut faire trois ans.
— Trois ans.
— Mmmhmm.
— Donc il te faut encore un an?
— C'est ça.
— Eh, très bien.
— Et toi, qu'est-ce que tu fais, Hélène?
— Alors moi, je suis venue ici pour faire des études de philosophie.
— Ah, très bien!
— Oui, oui. Ça m'intéresse beaucoup, et il y a tellement de choix ici, en France pour les différents cours de philo. J'espère terminer cette année le troisième cycle.
— Très bien. Qu'est-ce que tu veux faire, après?
— Je voudrais devenir professeur également ou peut-être, je ne sais pas, écrivain. Enfin, je ne suis pas très sûre encore de ce que je veux faire.
— Très bien.

### Numéro 2

Écoutez cette conversation dans laquelle une étudiante

française fait des comparaisons entre les universités aux États-Unis et les universités en France.

— Tiens, Patricia, justement, je voulais te parler. Tu viens de rentrer des États-Unis, n'est-ce pas?

— Oui, oui, oui, juste, euh, il y a, il y a deux jours.

— Oui. Et tu as étudié là-bas?

— Oui, pendant, euh, quatre ans.

— Écoute, ça m'intéresse d'aller étudier aussi aux États-Unis. Est-ce que je peux te poser, euh, quelques questions, là?

— Oui, oui, vas-y, Laurent, bien sûr.

— Oui. Écoute, ce qui m'inquiète le plus, c'est le prix. Est-ce que c'est cher là-bas?

— Ah, oui, ça, c'est sûr, et c'est sans doute une grosse différence avec la France, je crois. C'est vrai que les universités aux U.S.A. sont très, très chères. On paie énormément pour les frais d'inscription.

— Ah oui.

— Mais en échange, il y a plus de bourses.

— Ah bon, les étrangers peuvent avoir des bourses aussi?

— Euh oui, je crois que c'est possible, oui, oui, oui.

— Ah, très bien. Eh ben, en France, on paie pas grand-chose, hein, comparé à ça.

— Ah oui? Est-ce qu'il y a une grosse différence?

— Ben oui, tu sais, ça, ça coûte presque rien ici, hein. Environ mille francs par an, et c'est pas grand-chose, hein.

— Ah oui, en effet.

— Oui, et au niveau de l'organisation, euh, est-ce que c'est clair comme système?

— Ah oui, alors là, ils sont vraiment forts pour l'organisation. C'est très simple. C'est très clair. En plus, tu trouves partout des documents, des brochures qui expliquent tout ce qu'il faut faire. Et donc, c'est très facile à comprendre.

— Ah, ça, c'est mieux qu'en France, parce qu'ici avec tous les formulaires qu'on a à remplir à droite et à gauche, ça, c'est, c'est vraiment compliqué, ça.

— Ah oui.

— Bien. Hum. Comment c'est au niveau des droits des étudiants? Est-ce que vous avez beaucoup de droits, de, de... ?

— Oui, oui, beaucoup. Mais tu sais, c'est logique, hein, parce que ils paient tellement d'argent pour leurs études que c'est un peu normal qu'ils aient beaucoup de droits.

— C'est vrai. Ici on n'en a pas tellement, mais on paie pas très cher non plus, hein.

— Oui.

— Bon, qu'est-ce que je voulais savoir aussi? Ben oui, alors, les profs, alors, est-ce qu'ils sont sympas en général? Comment ça marche?

— Ah ouais ouais, ils sont très gentils. Et puis, surtout, tu peux aller leur parler très facilement. C'est-à-dire, qu'ils ont une heure de bureau chaque semaine, tu vois, par exemple, le mercredi de deux heures à quatre heures. Tu vas frapper à la porte, et tu leur poses des questions sur n'importe quoi, sur des problèmes que tu as en cours, sur quelque chose que t'as pas compris, et, euh, ils te répondent comme ça. Donc, c'est très, très facile. Tu sais vraiment qui ils sont, et ils arrivent à te connaître.

— Ah, ça c'est bien, parce qu'ici, hein, les profs, ils sont un peu anonymes, quand même. On est tous dans l'amphithéâtre, etc. On n'arrive pas vraiment à bien les connaître, hein.

— Est-ce qu'ils ont, ils ont... Ils ont pas d'heures de bureau en France?

— Ben non, tu te souviens bien, hein. Non, ils n'ont pas d'heures de bureau, hein.

— Oui. Oui, c'est vrai. Ça a pas changé, hein.

— Ben non, ça a toujours pas changé, hein. Et au niveau des notes, alors, comment ça marche, ça?

— Très différent là-bas. Ils utilisent le système par lettres, tu sais, par exemple, A, A moins, B, B plus, B moins, etc.

— Ah oui?

— Tandis qu'en France, c'est toujours, euh... les, ah, sur vingt, c'est ça?

— C'est toujours la même chose, bien oui.

— Ah oui.

— Toujours c'est noté sur vingt, oui. Bien. Et hum, et au niveau des absents et des présents, comment est-ce qu'ils, euh, comment est-ce qu'ils contrôlent ça là-bas? C'est strict?

— Oui.

— Ou bien c'est comme ici, quoi? Si on veut venir, on vient, et puis euh, tu sais, en amphithéâtre, si on ne veut pas venir, ben, personne ne le sait, quoi.

— Ah oui, non, là-bas, t'as pas le choix. T'as pas le choix, parce que les profs font l'appel tous les jours au début de chaque cours. Ils ont une liste.

— Ah ouais?

— Avec les noms de tous les élèves, de tous les étudiants, et euh, ils contrôlent comme ça tous les jours. Et si jamais t'as trop d'absences, euh, ta note finale s'en ressent. Donc, il faut faire attention, ça fait vraiment partie de ta note.

— Ah, c'est un peu plus strict, alors.

— Ah oui, beaucoup plus.

— Et, et si t'as besoin d'aide, si t'as des questions, euh, je sais pas, sur l'administration ou des choses comme ça, comment est-ce que tu te débrouilles? Est-ce qu il y a un bureau où on peut aller ou... ?

— Oui, oui, toujours. Euh, là, là encore, hein, ils sont bien organisés. Leur système administratif est très clair. Ils sont là pour aider les étudiants, et pareil, tu n'hésites pas à aller leur poser des questions. Et ils te répondent simplement.

— Ben, c'est un peu comme chez nous aussi. On a quand même un service administratif qui est pas mauvais, hein.

— Oui, c'est vrai. C'est vrai.

— Oui. Et euh, et au niveau des devoirs, c'est dur? Y en a beaucoup?

— Oui, il y en a beaucoup. Par exemple, des devoirs à faire à la maison le soir quand tu rentres. T'es crevé, et t'en... tu te dis que tu aimerais bien faire autre chose, mais non, c'est pas possible, t'as au moins pour trois heures de travail chaque soir.

— Ouais, ben ça c'est pas vraiment différent d'ici, hein. Le boulot, on en a beaucoup aussi, hein.

— Ouais, ouais, ça se vaut.

— Bon, ben, écoute, je vais réfléchir, et puis je vais voir ce que, ce que je vais pouvoir faire.

— OK. Mais, si tu as encore des questions, appelle-moi, hein.

— C'est sympa. Salut!

— Salut.

## CHAPITRE 8

**Ça va? Ça ne va pas?** (text, p. 300)

**À la pharmacie** (text, p. 308)

**Santé passe richesse** (text, p. 319)

**Une consultation gratuite** (text, p. 330)

**Portrait: M. Ahmed Abdiba, Fès, Maroc** (text, p. 336)

### Conversation supplémentaire

— Bonjour, Madame, j'ai rendez-vous avec le docteur Roussin à quatre heures.

— Oui, Monsieur. Votre nom, s'il vous plaît?

— Carrer. C-A-deux R-E-R.

— C-A-deux R-E-R. Oui, en effet, euh, et vous êtes déjà venu voir le docteur Roussin, Monsieur?

— Non, c'est la première fois.

— Ah, bon, très bien. Euh, qu'est-ce que vous avez exactement?

— Eh, écoutez, je ne sais pas exactement. Je crois que j'ai la grippe ou quelque chose comme ça. Ça ne va pas très bien.

— Oui, ça fait longtemps que vous vous sentez mal?

— Ça fait une semaine, environ.

— Une semaine, d'accord. Est-ce que vous avez peut-être de la fièvre?

— Oui, j'ai de la fièvre.

— Bon, alors ne quittez pas. Asseyez-vous, un petit instant. Le docteur Roussin sera avec vous.

— D'accord, merci bien.

— Monsieur Carrer, entrez par ici, s'il vous plaît.

— Oui, merci.

— Bonjour, Monsieur!

— Bonjour, docteur! Monsieur... Carrer?

— Carrer, c'est exact!

— Bien, qu'est-ce qui vous amène, Monsieur?

— Eh bien, écoutez, ça fait une semaine que ça va pas du tout. Je, je, j'ai mal à la tête, j'ai mal à la gorge, je tousse....?

— Vous toussez. Vous avez de la fièvre en ce moment?

— Oui, j'ai trente-huit, trente-huit de fièvre.

— Et ça fait combien de temps que vous avez de la fièvre?

— Eh, écoutez, ça fait environ trois jours que j'ai de la fièvre, ça fait une semaine que je suis malade mais trois jours que...

— Heum, trois jours seulement. OK, vous pouvez ouvrir la bouche que...

— Ah...

— Oui, heum. Ça vous fait mal si j'appuie ici, juste au dessus des yeux?

— Oui, un petit peu, oui.

— Heum, ça c'est une sinusite, je pense. C'est une sinusite. Vous vous baignez souvent dans l'océan?

— Ah, oui, très souvent, oui.

— Oui, j'ai bien peur que.. j'ai bien peur que ce soit une sinusite. Bien, écoutez, je vais vous donner de l'aspirine et des gouttes à mettre dans le nez, et si ça ne va pas, heum, d'ici une semaine, vous reviendrez me voir, hein?

— Très bien. Donc pas d'antibiotiques?

— Non, pas d'antibiotiques. Je pense que ce sera suffisant et surtout, naturellement, ne vous baignez pas pendant une semaine et ne vous exposez pas au soleil. Ne vous mettez pas au soleil, pas de bain de soleil.

— D'accord, et les gouttes, combien de fois par jour?

— Ça sera marqué sur la boîte, cela sera deux fois par jour. Euh, matin et soir.

— D'accord.

— Voilà.

— Merci, docteur.

# STUDENT TAPE SCRIPT

## ÉTAPE PRÉLIMINAIRE

WORKBOOK, P. 7

**Exercice 1. The sounds of French.** The French equivalents of the five basic English vowels *(a, e, i, o, u)* are [a], [ə], [i], [o], [y]. Listen and repeat.

[a] Madame   Coca   garçon
[ə] de   demi   Monsieur
[i] merci   limonade   kir
[o] au   eau   rose
[y] nature   une   étudiante

There are in French, however, six other vowels that are close to these basic vowel sounds. They are [e], [ɛ], [ø], [œ], [ɔ], [u]. Listen and repeat.

[e] café   thé   lait
[ɛ] express   verre   bière
[ø] Monsieur   bleu   Europe
[œ] moteur   acteur   neuf
[ɔ] Coca   Orangina   limonade
[u] pour   vous   rouge

French also has three nasal vowels, that is, the sound is pushed through the nose rather than through the mouth: [ã], [ɛ̃], [ɔ̃]. Listen and repeat.

[ã] française   blanc   menthe
[ɛ̃] un   vin   pain
[ɔ̃] allons   citron   non

While practicing the preceding vowels sounds, you probably noticed that many French consonants are pronounced very much like their English counterparts. Consequently, you should have little trouble with the following phonemes. Listen and repeat.

[b] bière   blanc
[p] pressé   étape
[d] demi   Madame
[t] Vittel   citron
[m] menthe   crème
[n] nature   limonade
[g] garçon   guitare
[k] crème   kir
[s] pressé   citron
[z] fraise   Mademoiselle

[v] Vittel   vous
[l] lait   allemande
[r] rouge   merci

There are, however, a few consonant sounds that are not as easily recognizable. Listen and repeat the following.

[ʃ] chapitre   douche
[ʒ] je   rouge
[ɲ] espagnol   signe
[j] bière   Perrier
[ɥ] Suisse   huit
[w] oui   boisson

WORKBOOK, P. 8

**Exercice 2. Des boissons.** Now that you have heard and repeated all the basic sounds of French, practice them by listening to and repeating some of the drinks you might want to order in a café.

| | | |
|---|---|---|
| une limonade | une menthe à l'eau | un verre de blanc |
| un demi | un Coca | un thé nature |
| un verre de rouge | un thé citron | un Perrier |
| un express | un Orangina | un kir |
| un café crème | une bière allemande | un citron pressé |
| un Vittel | un lait fraise | une bière française |

WORKBOOK, P. 8

**Exercice 3. Au café.** Now that you are a little more familiar with these sounds, let's practice listening to some spoken French. Imagine that a large group of people arrive at a café. As the waiter struggles to get their orders, you "keep score" on the checklist provided in your workbook.

— Bonjour, Messieurs-dames, qu'est-ce que vous désirez?
*(tous en même temps):*
— Je voudrais un café-crème!
— Un thé nature!
— Une menthe à l'eau!
— Un thé au lait.
— Attendez, je ne comprends rien. Alors Monsieur, euh, vous désirez?
— Un express, s'il vous plaît.
— Et pour Mademoiselle?

— Un demi, s'il vous plaît.
— Mademoiselle, pour vous?
— Un thé au lait.
— Pour moi aussi, un thé au lait.
— Monsieur, qu'est-ce que je vous sers?
— Un café-crème.
— Bien, et Mademoiselle?
— Une limonade.
— Moi, je voudrais un demi.
— Et Monsieur, vous désirez?
— Un Vittel.
— Qu'est-ce que vous prenez, Mademoiselle?
— Une menthe à l'eau, s'il vous plaît.
— Bon, et enfin vous, Monsieur.
— Donnez-moi un demi, s'il vous plaît.
— Très bien, merci.

## CHAPITRE 1

### SEGMENT 1

**Prononciation: Les consonnes finales non-prononcés**
(text, p. 18)

**Prononciation: Les consonnes finales prononcées**
(text, p. 27)

**Prononciation: Les consonnes finales + *e***
(text, p. 36)

## CHAPITRE 1

### SEGMENT 2

WORKBOOK, P. 33

**I. Dans la rue et au café** You will hear some conversations that take place in the street or at a café. Match each conversation with the appropriate description. In some instances, more than one answer may be possible.

1. — Salut, Xavier.
   — Tiens. Bonjour, Jeannette. Ça va?
   — Oui, ça va. Et toi?
   — Oui, ça va très bien.
2. — Bonjour, Madame Rouquin. Comment allez-vous?
   — Très bien, merci. Et vous?
   — Très bien. Vous connaissez M. Gerval? Non? Mme Rouquin, M. Gerval.
   — Enchanté, Madame.

— Enchantée, Monsieur.
3. — Qu'est-ce que tu prends, Sophie?
   — Un lait fraise.
   — Et toi, Dominique?
   — Un express.
   — Bon. Deux express et un lait fraise, s'il vous plaît.
4. — Vous partez?
   — Oui.
   — À tout à l'heure.
   — Allez, au revoir.
   — Oui, c'est ça. À tout à l'heure.
5. — S'il vous plaît, Monsieur. Un demi.
   — Bon, un demi... Oui, Madame. Vous désirez?
   — Un café crème.
   — C'est ça. *(Il crie:)* Un café crème, un demi.
   — Pardon. Vous êtes américain?
   — Oui. Je m'appelle Bill Thomson. Je suis de Chicago.
   — Bonjour, Bill. Je m'appelle Françoise Valentin. J'habite ici à Paris.
6. — Tiens. Voilà Nicole... Salut, Nicole.
   — Bonjour, Didier. Comment vas-tu?
   — Très bien, merci. Et toi?
   — Oh, ça va bien.
   — Écoute. Tu connais Chantal? Non? Chantal Portès, Nicole Martineau.
   — Bonjour.
   — Bonjour.

WORKBOOK, P. 34

**II. Distinguez!** *(Distinguish!)* In each part of this activity, try to discriminate between the similar sounding words you will hear. Although some of the words will be unfamiliar, you should concentrate on making the appropriate distinctions.

**A. *Un* ou *une*?** Listen to each statement and tell whether the drink that is ordered is masculine (**un**) or feminine (**une**).

*MODÈLE:* You hear:   Un diabolo menthe, s'il vous plaît.
          You circle: *un*

1. Moi, je vais prendre une bière allemande.
2. Pour moi, une limonade, s'il vous plaît.
3. Qu'est-ce que je vais prendre? Oh, peut-être un kir... Oui, c'est ça.
4. S'il vous plaît, Monsieur. Je voudrais un whisky.
5. Moi, je voudrais bien prendre une tisane.
6. Pour moi... Oh, je ne sais pas... peut-être un petit chocolat chaud.

**B.** *Le, la* **ou** *les?* Listen to each statement and tell whether the food or drink mentioned is masculine singular (**le**), feminine singular (**la**), or masculine or feminine plural (**les**).

*MODÈLE:* You hear:   Je n'aime pas du tout le fromage.
You circle:   *le*

1. Moi, j'aime beaucoup la bière d'Alsace.
2. Oh, oui, j'aime bien le lait.
3. Non, non. Je n'aime pas beaucoup les frites.
4. Mon amie Suzanne, elle adore les champignons.
5. Mon amie Chantal, elle n'aime pas du tout la Chantilly.
6. Nous, on aime beaucoup la tarte à l'oignon.
7. Vous autres, vous n'aimez pas la crème fraîche?
8. Comment! Tu n'aimes pas les poires? Mais elles sont délicieuses!
9. Tu aimes le Calvados? Tiens. Moi, aussi.

**C.** *Il, elle, ils* **ou** *elles?* Listen to each statement and tell whether the subject pronoun is masculine singular (**il**), masculine plural (**ils**), feminine singular (**elle**), or feminine plural (**elles**).

*MODÈLE:* You hear:   François? Mais il ne parle pas chinois.
You circle:   *il*

1. Jeanne et Mireille, elles ne sont pas là?
2. Où est-ce qu'elle est, Françoise?
3. Je cherche Jean-Luc. Il est chez toi?
4. Les autres étudiants, où sont-ils?
5. Martine et Véronique, est-ce qu'elles parlent vraiment trois langues?
6. Mon amie Yvette, elle voyage beaucoup.
7. Tu connais Jean-Jacques, non? Il habite a Lyon.
8. Les amies de Chantal? Elles étudient l'allemand.
9. Georges et son ami, ils habitent au Quartier latin.
10. Éric ne fume pas. Il n'aime pas les cigarettes.

**D. Masculin ou féminin?** Listen to each statement and tell whether the person whose nationality is given is male or female.

*MODÈLE:* You hear:   Mathilde est française.
You circle:   *f*

1. Francis est anglais.
2. Dominique est canadienne.
3. Suimei est chinoise.
4. Gabriella est portugaise.
5. Kyo est japonais.

6. Helmut est allemand.
7. Rhoda est anglaise.
8. Claude est française.
9. Gina est italienne.
10. Jean-Marie est canadien.

WORKBOOK, P. 35

**III. Cette valise est à vous?** *(Does this suitcase belong to you?)* You are working as the representative of an American tour group in Paris. One of your jobs is to meet arriving flights and help people find their luggage. On this occasion, you are stuck with several pieces of luggage that have not been claimed. Based on the short conversations you overhear, try to match the person and the baggage tag. If a conversation does not match any of the tags, mark an X.

1. — Vous parlez très bien le français pour un Américain.
   — Mais je ne suis pas américain, moi. Je suis canadien-québécois.
2. — Vous connaissez ce monsieur-là?
   — Oui, je travaille avec lui. C'est un excellent ingénieur.
   — Il parle français?
   — Pas très bien. Il est chinois. Il parle mieux l'anglais.
3. — Bonjour, Madame.
   — Bonjour, Monsieur.
   — Ah, vous n'êtes pas française, Madame?
   — Non, je suis américaine. Je suis du sud des États-Unis.
4. — Regarde! Tu vois cette femme là-bas? Elle a l'air allemande, non?
   — Oh, je ne sais pas. Pour moi, elle a l'air plutôt anglaise. Je vais lui demander. Excusez-moi, Mademoiselle. Vous êtes allemande ou anglaise?
   — Moi, je suis allemande. Je suis de Berlin. J'habite à Berlin depuis des années.
5. — Votre passeport, s'il vous plaît.
   — Voilà, Monsieur.
   — Vous êtes de nationalité brésilienne, Mademoiselle?
   — Oui, mais j'habite en Italie, à Rome.
   — Et comment s'écrit votre nom de famille?
   — S-I-L-V-E-I-R-A, Silveira.
   — Merci, Mademoiselle. Passez.

WORKBOOK, P. 36

**IV. Mini-dictée: Deux étudiants étrangers à Paris** Listen to this short text about two foreign students in

Paris. It will be read first at normal speed, then more slowly, so that you can fill in the missing words. You may listen again, if necessary.

Jacques et Marisa sont étudiants. Ils ne sont pas français et ils n'habitent pas à Paris. Jacques est suisse. Il mange souvent au café. Marisa est italienne. Elle préfère les fast-foods.

## CHAPITRE 1

### SEGMENT 3

WORKBOOK, P. 36

**I. Quatre conversations**
A. You will hear four short conversations (Dialogues one to four). Listen to each conversation and try to match its number with the appropriate description. You will not understand all of what is being said; however, use the French you have already learned and any other clues you can pick up to identify the context for each conversation.

**Dialogue 1**
GABRIELLE:  Alors, qu est-ce que tu désires?
ANNIE:  Oh, je prendrais bien un sandwich.
GABRIELLE:  Oh oui, un sandwich.
ANNIE:  Voyons, un sandwich au jambon, fromage... oh, un sandwich au jambon.
GABRIELLE:  Ah, très bien, et pour moi une omelette. Une omelette au fromage ou au jambon? Non, je préfère une omelette au fromage. Monsieur!
GARÇON:  Oui, Mesdemoiselles, vous désirez?
GABRIELLE:  Pour moi, Monsieur, ça sera une omelette au fromage, s'il vous plaît.
GARÇON:  Bien, une omelette au fromage, et vous, Mademoiselle?
ANNIE:  Et pour moi, ce sera un sandwich au jambon.
GARÇON:  Un sandwich au jambon. Très bien. Et comme boissons?
GABRIELLE:  Oh, je ne sais pas, euh...
GARÇON:  Ben, un Coca, un Orangina, un diabolo citron...
ANNIE:  Un Coca pour moi.
GARÇON:  Bien, un Coca pour mademoiselle... et vous?
GABRIELLE:  Euh, vous dites, Monsieur?
GARÇON:  Oui, une limonade, un lait-fraise, un diabolo-citron, une thé, un café...
GABRIELLE:  Euh non. Un orangina s'il vous plaît.
GARÇON:  Et un Orangina pour mademoiselle.
GABRIELLE:  Merci, Monsieur.
ANNIE:  Merci.

**Dialogue 2**
MARC:  Bonjour Suzanne, ça va?
SUZANNE:  Ça va très bien, et toi?
MARC:  Ça va bien. Tu veux boire quelque chose?
SUZANNE:  Ah, volontiers, oui.
MARC:  Bien, qu'est-ce que tu veux boire?
SUZANNE:  Hmmm, un thé citron.
MARC:  Un thé citron, très bien. Mademoiselle, s'il vous plaît!
SERVEUSE:  Oui, Monsieur.
MARC:  Un thé citron s'il vous plaît, et un café noir.
SERVEUSE:  Très bien!
MARC:  Oh, voici Hélène. Bonjour, Hélène, ça va?
HÉLÈNE:  Bonjour, Marc. Ça va bien, et toi?
MARC:  Oui, très bien. Je te présente Suzanne. Suzanne, Hélène.
SUZANNE:  Oh, enchantée.
HÉLÈNE:  Bonjour, Suzanne, tu habites à Paris?
SUZANNE:  Oui, j'habite le dix-septième.
HÉLÈNE:  Tiens, quelle surprise! Moi aussi.
SUZANNE:  Vraiment?
HÉLÈNE:  Oui, et tu vas au lycée...?
SUZANNE:  Je vais au lycée Condorcet, oui, depuis trois ans.
MARC:  Quelle coincidence!
HÉLÈNE:  Moi aussi.
MARC:  Tu veux boire quelque chose, Hélène?
HÉLÈNE:  Oh oui, merci. Un café.
MARC:  Un café, très bien. Mademoiselle! Un café s'il vous plaît.
SERVEUSE:  Oui, Monsieur!

**Dialogue 3**
MIREILLE:  Bon, alors, on va au Quick pour déjeuner?
LAURENT:  Oh non, pas au Quick, hein, ça c'est pas très bon la nourriture, là-bas.
JEAN-MICHEL:  Oh oui, on y va toujours au Quick. Non, allons au café plutôt.
MIREILLE:  Mais non, on n'a pas le temps, on n'a que quarante cinq minutes. C'est beaucoup plus rapide, écoute.
LAURENT:  Oui, mais c'est moins sympa le Quick, enfin! n y a pas d'atmosphère là-bas.
JEAN-MICHEL:  Oui, il y a pas d atmosphère, et puis, je crois qu'on peut trouver un petit café, juste à côté d'ici.
LAURENT:  Ben écoute, moi je connais le café de la Perse, j'ai... j'ai... je connais quelqu'un qui est serveuse, là-bas. Elle s'appelle Sophie, elle est très sympa et si on n'a pas beaucoup de temps, eh bien, elle peut nous servir peut-être un peu avant les autres, quoi, enfin...
MIREILLE:  Tu es sûr?
LAURENT:  Ah, oui, oui, oui, c'est vraiment sympa.
JEAN-MICHEL:  Bon, allez, les copains, on va, on va au café.

MIREILLE: OK.

*(au café)*

SOPHIE: Bonjour, Laurent. Vous m'avez amené des copains aujourd'hui?

LAURENT: Ben oui, voilà! Vous vous rendez compte, ils voulaient aller au Quick! Alors, je me suis dit quand même, c'est pas possible, ça, donc, je vous ai amené de nouveaux clients.

SOPHIE: Bon, ça veut dire que vous êtes pressés.

LAURENT: Ah oui, on est assez pressés. Vous pouvez nous servir assez rapidement?

SOPHIE: Oui, d 'accord . Bon, vous avez vu le menu affiché, là?

LAURENT: Oui.

SOPHIE: Vous savez ce que vous voulez?

JEAN-MICHEL: Oui, moi je prendrai une omelette au fromage et aussi un café au lait si c'est possible.

SOPHIE: D'accord, et mademoiselle?

MIREILLE: Moi, je voudrais un sandwich au pâté avec un Perrier.

SOPHIE: Très bien, et Laurent?

LAURENT: Ben, moi je vais prendre un petit croque-monsieur avec beaucoup de fromage, comme d'habitude, hein, et...

SOPHIE: Vous voulez un croque-madame pour changer?

LAURENT: Euh, non, un croque-monsieur, c'est vraiment bon, hein...

SOPHIE: D'accord.

LAURENT: ...et puis un petit lait fraise avec, alors.

SOPHIE: D'accord, ben je vous apporte ça très vite.

**Dialogue 4**

FLORENCE: Si on allait manger au McDonald?

THIBEAULT: Oui, j'ai très faim!

FLORENCE: Regarde! Une amie de maman. Bonjour, Madame Launay.

MME LAUNAY: Bonjour, Florence, comment vas-tu?

FLORENCE: Très bien, et vous-même?

MME LAUNAY: Très bien, merci.

FLORENCE: Je vous présente Thibeault, un ami.

THIBEAULT: Bonjour, Madame.

MME LAUNAY: Bonjour, Thibeault, comment vas-tu?

THIBEAULT: Ça va bien, merci.

MME LAUNAY: Bien. Alors, qu'est-ce que vous faites tous les deux?

FLORENCE: On va manger au McDonald.

MME LAUNAY: Ah, très bien. Alors, bon appétit!

FLORENCE: Merci!

THIBEAULT: Merci!

GARÇON: Au suivant, s'il vous plaît.

FLORENCE: Un cheeseburger et un jus d'orange, s'il vous plaît.

GARÇON: D'accord, cheeseburger et un jus d'orange... et vous Monsieur?

THIBEAULT: Un grand Coca et des frites, s'il vous plaît.

GARÇON: D'accord, grand Coca et des frites.

**CHAPITRE 2**

**SEGMENT 1**

**Prononciation: La combinaison *qu*** (text, p. 59)

**Prononciation: La combinaison *ch*** (text, p. 67)

**Prononciation: Les consonnes *c* et *g*** (text, p. 76)

**CHAPITRE 2**

**SEGMENT 2**

WORKBOOK, P. 58

**I. L'alphabet**

**A.** You will have probably notaiced that many of the names of letters in French are quite similar to those in English. For example: a, b, c, d, f, l, m, n, o, p, q, r, s, t, v. Now repeat the following letters, which are different:

h, k, u, w, x, y, z.

Finally, there are two pairs of letters that can be confusing to speakers of English. Repeat each pair several times:

ei, gh.

To spell in French, you need to know several other expressions. For double letters, say **deux** *(two)* before the letters: **deux l, deux p, deux s, deux t.** If a letter has an accent mark, say the name of the accent after the letter: **e accent aigu (é), e accent grave (è), i accent circonflexe (î), c cédille (ç).** The same is true for a capital letter **(majuscule)** and a small letter **(minuscule): F majuscule, d minuscule.**

**B. Comment s'écrit...?** *(How is it written?)* Knowing the alphabet will come in handy, particularly when someone gives you names or addresses over the telephone. In this exercise, a French friend is telling you about two people you could contact while traveling in the south of France. Your friend spells out the last names, the street names, and the names of the towns. (Your friend assumes you can spell the first names and cognate words such as **avenue** and **boulevard**.) Write the names and addresses.

Georges FORESTIER. Avenue JAURÈS. ANTIBES.

Madeleine CHARRAT. Boulevard BLAZY. FRÉJUS.

WORKBOOK, P. 59

**I. Dans mon sac à dos. Dans ma chambre.** Two students, Mireille and Vincent, are going to describe what can be found in their backpacks. Write **M** under the picture of each item Mireille has in her backpack and **V** under the picture of each item that Vincent has. Not everything in the picture is mentioned on the tape. Mireille will begin.

—Dans mon sac à dos, j'ai des livres, des cahiers, un crayon et mon portefeuille. Je n'ai pas de calculatrice.

—Dans mon sac à dos à moi, j'ai des livres et des cahiers aussi. Je n'ai pas de crayon, mais j'ai deux stylos, un carnet et une calculatrice.

Now Vincent and Mireille will describe what they have in their dorm rooms. Once again, write **V** or **M** under the picture of each possession. Not everything in the picture is mentioned on the tape. This time Vincent will speak first.

—Dans ma chambre il y a un lit et deux chaises. Je n'ai pas de bureau. Au mur il y a des posters. J'ai une chaîne stéréo. J'ai beaucoup de cassettes, mais je n'ai pas de disques compacts.

—Dans ma chambre à moi il y a un lit, un bureau avec une chaise et beaucoup de plantes. Au mur il y a, bien sûr, des posters. J'ai aussi une chaîne stéréo et une grande quantité de disques compacts. J'ai aussi un petit ordinateur. J'ai un radio-réveil, mais je n'ai pas de téléviseur.

WORKBOOK, P. 60

**III. Une famille** The names of several members of the same family are listed below. One of the children is going to explain how these people are related to each other. As you listen to her explanation, fill in the family tree with the initials of the people she talks about.

Bonjour. Je m'appelle Pauline Clément et j'habite à Tours. Je vais vous parler de ma famille. Mon père s'appelle François Clément. Il est ingénieur agricole. Ma mère, qui s'appelle Marguerite, travaille dans une banque. J'ai un frère et une sœur. Mon frère est étudiant à l'université de Tours; il s'appelle Raymond. Ma petite sœur a quatre ans. Elle s'appelle Sylvie.

Mes grands-parents sont tous vivants. Mon grand-père Nicolas, c'est le père de mon père. Il habite avec ma grand-mère, Cécile, à Rouen. Mon grand-père maternel— le père de ma mère s'appelle Henri Favier. Il est avocat. Sa femme, ma grand-mère, s'appelle Ghislaine Favier.

Mon père a un frère. C'est mon oncle Alfred. Il n'est pas marié.

Ma mère, elle, a une sœur, ma tante Michèle. Son mari s'appelle André—André Truchet. Ils ont deux enfants: mon cousin Francis et ma cousine Céline. Et voilà ma famille.

WORKBOOK, P. 60

**IV. *Avoir ou être?*** Certain forms of the verbs **avoir** and **être** resemble each other closely. For each of the following sentences, circle which of the two forms you hear and then write the corresponding infinitive (**avoir** or **être**). You may not recognize every word in the sentence; listen carefully for the verb.

*MODÈLE:* You hear:  Vraiment? Il est avocat?
  Quelle surprise!
 You circle: *il est*
 You write: *être*

1. Tu cherches Martine? Ah, elle n'est pas là.
2. Comment! Tu as une nouvelle voiture? Formidable.
3. Georges et Michèle? Ils ont un joli appartement.
4. Tiens! Voilà Éric. Est-ce qu'il a son nouvel ordinateur?
5. Comment, Marie-Louise! Tu es étudiante!
6. Véronique et ma sœur te cherchent. Elles sont au café.

WORKBOOK, P. 61

**V. Mini-dictée** Complete the following conversation by writing the missing words. The conversation will be read twice.

—Ah, voilà <u>l'amie</u> de Bernard. Elle s'appelle Yvonne. Salut, Yvonne.

—Salut, Stéphane. Où sont <u>tes frères?</u>

—Comment? Moi, je <u>n'ai pas de</u> frères, mais j'ai deux sœurs.

—Ah, oui. Elles <u>ont</u> un appartement dans la rue Mauclair.

—Qu'est-ce qu'elles <u>aiment faire</u> comme distractions?

—Ma sœur Denise <u>adore les sports.</u> elle <u>fait</u> du tennis; ma sœur Isabelle <u>aime beaucoup</u> la politique.

—Moi, j'aime mieux la musique. Je suis pianiste.

—Ah, bon. <u>Qu'est-ce que</u> tu aimes comme musique?

—Je <u>préfère</u> la musique classique.

WORKBOOK, P. 61

**VI. Un portrait** Claire Turquin, a young French woman, talks about herself and her family during a radio interview. Listen to her self-description. Then answer the questions.

—Chers auditeurs, nous avons aujourd'hui dans notre studio une, euh, jeune, euh, Française qui va répondre à nos questions. Euh, bonjour, Mademoiselle.

—Bonjour.

—Comment vous appelez-vous, alors?

—Je m'appelle Claire Turquin.

—Très bien. Et vous êtes, euh, vous êtes de quelle région?

—Euh, je suis française. J'habite dans la région parisienne.

—Très bien. Parlez-nous un petit peu de votre famille.

—Oui, j'ai une très grande famille dont je suis très fière. Euh, j'habite avec mes parents. Et puis, j'ai deux frères, trois sœurs, ma grand-mère, qui habite avec nous, et puis aussi un chat.

—Ah! Très bien. Alors, ce, c'est une famille nombreuse, donc. Est-ce, est-ce que vous devez partager votre chambre avec vos frères et sœurs?

—Non, non, non. Euh, c'est une chambre personnelle. Il y a plein de choses dans ma chambre, d'ailleurs. Il y a une chaîne stéréo, des livres, des, des photos, des disques et plein de cartes postales.

—Très bien. Comment est-ce que vous allez, euh, à l'université alors? Est-ce que vous allez en voiture, euh?

—Non, malheureusement, je n'ai pas de voiture. J'ai seulement un vélo.

—Ah.

—Mais enfin, c'est pratique.

—Très bien. Parlez-moi un peu de, de, de vos loisirs.

—J'adore la nature. Euh, et j'aime, euh, à peu près tous les sports qu'on pratique en plein air, par exemple, le camping, le ski, et le vélo, bien sûr.

—Oui, est-ce que vous aimez, euh, la musique?

—Oui, beaucoup, beaucoup... surtout la musique classique et le jazz.

—Bien, nous savons donc que vous êtes étudiante et, où, où est-ce que vous étudiez, alors?

— À Paris.

—Et qu'est-ce que vous étudiez?

—Euh, principalement l'histoire, la géographie et les langues aussi.

—Ah très bien! Quelles langues est-ce que vous parlez?

—L'anglais et l'espagnol.

—Très bien. Est-ce qu'il y a des matières que vous n'aimez pas particulièrement?

—Ah oui, je déteste les maths et les sciences en général.

## CHAPITRE 2

### SEGMENT 3

WORKBOOK, P. 61

**I. Deux étudiants** Listen now to a short conversation between two students—Henri and Janine. Tell whether the characteristics below apply to Henri, to Janine, or to neither one.

HENRI:  Alors, moi, je suis de Rennes. Et toi?

JANINE:  Moi, je viens de Neuilly.

HENRI:  Tes parents habitent à Neuilly?

JANINE:  Oui, mes parent habitent à Neuilly, ainsi que mon frère et mes trois sœurs.

HENRI:  Qu'est-ce qu'ils font dans la vie?

JANINE:  Mon frère est avocat et mes trois sœurs sont encore à l'université.

HENRI:  Moi, je suis fils unique. Mes parents sont médecins.

JANINE:  Ah! Et qu'est-ce que tu aimes faire comme activités?

HENRI:  Moi, j'aime le karaté et aussi la musique de jazz.

JANINE:  D'accord.

HENRI:  Et toi?

JANINE:  Moi, j'aime beaucoup le tennis et la danse moderne.

## CHAPITRE 3

### SEGMENT 1

**Prononciation: La combinaison *gn*** (text, p. 97)

**Prononciation: La consonne *s*** (text, p. 105)

**Prononciation: La consonne *t*** (text, p. 115)

## CHAPITRE 3

### SEGMENT 2

WORKBOOK, P. 84

**I. L'intonation** Intonation refers to pitch, the rising and falling of the voice within the speaking range. Rising intonation indicates continuation—that there is more to follow. Falling intonation signals closure—that is, the end of a sentence or idea. French intonation patterns are determined by word groups and by the type of utterance. Listen to the following examples:

1. In the basic intonation pattern, voice pitch rises and falls:

Nous habitons à Paris.

Ma sœur et moi, nous habitons à Paris.

Ma sœur et moi, nous habitons à Paris depuis trois ans.

Notice that the voice rises at the end of each group except the last.

2. Short phrases and sentences as well as commands and short information questions are all marked by falling intonation:

Bonjour, Madame.

Je ne sais pas.

Dépêche-toi, mon petit!

Comment allez-vous?

3. Questions that can be answered by **oui** or **non** are marked by rising intonation:

Tu aimes danser?

Elle a des frères et des sœurs?

C'est ton livre?

Take a few minutes to practice these basic intonation patterns by saying the following sentences aloud. In each case, when you hear the number of the sentence, read the word groups, listen to the model intonation, and then repeat the word groups.

First practice the basic sentence pattern with rising and falling intonation.
1. Elle a deux frères.
2. Elle a deux frères et une sœur.
3. Dans ma chambre j'ai une chaîne stéréo et des cassettes.
4. Dans ma chambre j'ai un téléviseur, un frigo, un bureau et un lit, mais je n'ai pas de chaîne stéréo.
5. Je n'aime pas danser.
6. Je n'aime pas chanter, mais j'adore écouter des cassettes de musique classique.

Now practice some short utterances with falling intonation.
7. Très bien, merci.
8. Quelle heure est-il?
9. Merci beaucoup.
10. Un moment, s'il vous plaît.

And finally, practice some yes-no questions with rising intonation.
11. Tu as faim?
12. Est-ce qu'elles habitent à Paris?
13. Ce sont vos clés, Madame?
14. Vous voulez prendre quelque chose?

WORKBOOK, P. 85

**II. Les renseignements** People frequently need to ask for directions. Match each conversation you hear with the appropriate drawing.

**Conversation 1**
—S'il vous plaît, Madame, où se trouve le syndicat d'initiative?
—Le syndicat d'initiative? Mais c'est tout près, Monsieur. Vous continuez dans la rue Carnot jusqu'à une grande place. C'est la place Marmont. Vous traversez la place... Attention! Ne tournez pas tout de suite, mais traversez la place. Puis vous tournez à droite dans la rue de Seine et le syndicat d'initiative est là, en face du jardin municipal.
— Merci bien, Madame.
— Oh, je vous en prie, Monsieur.

**Conversation 2**
— Quand on arrive au centre-ville, il est facile de trouver un parking ?
— Oh, oui. Très facile. Écoute, tu prends l'avenue des Bénédictins, tu passes devant la place Jourdan, qui est sur ta gauche, tu continues, tu traverses l'avenue Garibaldi et tu vas un peu à droite. Tu es maintenant sur le boulevard Carnot. Alors, tu continues et il y a un parking sur ta gauche, juste à côté du Royal Limousin. D'accord?
— D'accord.

**Conversation 3**
— Monsieur, Monsieur. La rue de l'Abbaye, s'il vous plaît?
— Alors, continuez dans la rue de Seine, traversez la place Marmont et allez tout droit dans la rue Marmont. Allez jusqu'au bout, puis tournez à gauche. C'est là, la rue de l'Abbaye.
— Merci bien, Monsieur.
— De rien.

## Conversation 4

— Tiens! Henri! Qu'est-ce que tu fais là?

— Ben, je cherche une pharmacie. Il y en a une par ici?

— Oui, oui. Bien sûr. Il y a une pharmacie dans la rue Maupas.

— La rue Maupas? Où c'est? Je ne connais pas très bien le quartier.

— Alors, tu vas jusqu'au coin et tu tournes à droite.

— C'est pas à gauche?

— Non, non. À gauche, c'est le boulevard Carnot. Toi, tu veux l'avenue des Bénédictins. Continue tout droit et tu vas voir sur ta droite une grande place. C'est la place Jourdan. Tu traverses la place et voilà la rue Maupas. D'accord?

— Oui, oui. Merci. À bientôt.

— À bientôt, Henri.

WORKBOOK, P. 86

**III. À quelle heure?** In each conversation that you will hear, a time is mentioned. Match each conversation to the appropriate clock.

## Conversation 1

— S'il vous plaît, Madame. Pourriez-vous me dire quelle heure il est?

— Mais oui, Monsieur. Il est quatre heures moins le quart.

— Je vous remercie, Madame.

— Je vous en prie, Monsieur.

## Conversation 2

— Alors, Étienne, tu vas en ville ce soir?

— Oui, je vais retrouver les copains au centre commercial.

— À quelle heure est-ce que tu vas rentrer?

— J'sais pas. Vers onze heures, peut-être.

— Bon, d'accord. Mais pas plus tard que ça.

— Oui, Maman.

## Conversation 3

— Allô! Janine? C'est Mireille. Tu n'aurais pas le temps de déjeuner.

— Si. Où est-ce qu'on va?

— Il y a un nouveau restaurant algérien, près de la cathédrale. On pourrait l'essayer, si tu veux?

— Oui, je veux bien. Il est quelle heure maintenant?

— Midi et demi.

— Bon. Rendez-vous dans une demi-heure devant la cathédrale.

— Parfait. À tout à l'heure, Janine.

— À tout à l'heure.

## Conversation 4

— Écoute, Chantal. Ça te dirait quelque chose d'aller voir un film ce soir?

— Ah, oui. Ce serait sympa. On pourrait prendre quelque chose avant d'y aller, si tu veux.

— D'accord. À quelle heure est-ce qu'on se retrouve?

— Entre sept heures et sept heures et demie. Disons, sept heures et quart, au café Mably.

— D'accord. À ce soir, Chantal.

— À ce soir.

WORKBOOK, P. 86

**IV. Une journée chargée** *(A busy day)* Christiane Barbey is an executive in an advertising firm in Quimper. In addition to her regular work, she is also one of the organizers of the Festival de Cornouaille. Listen to her conversation with her secretary. Then fill in her appointment schedule for the busy day just before the opening of the festival.

— Patricia, pouvez-vous me donner une idée de mon emploi du temps aujourd'hui?

— Oui, bien sûr. Vous commencez à 10 heures. Oui, vous avez un rendez-vous avec Monsieur Souchon.

— D'accord. Et ensuite?

— Ensuite, une heure plus tard, c'est-à-dire à 11 heures précisément, vous verrez Monsieur Antoine et Madame Vittel.

— Mm mm, c'est bien.

— Alors, par contre après, vous n'avez plus rien de prévu excepté à 16 heures où vous visiterez la cathédrale pour voir si tout est vraiment bien prêt pour le concert.

— D'accord. Et ensuite?

— Ensuite, voyons, à 17 heures, ah oui, à 17 heures vous vouliez faire une promenade pour vérifier l'itinéraire du défilé.

— Bon. Euh, je sais qu'à 19 heures je dois retrouver mon mari au café...

— Mm, mm.

— ... et ensuite nous allons au théâtre à 21 heures.

— Mm mm.

— Oh, j'ai oublié! Est-ce que j'ai quelque chose à 15 heures?

— Ah oui, en effet. Vous avez raison. Vous allez chez le dentiste à 15 heures. N'oubliez pas.

— Bon, d'accord. Oui. Et, euh, je suis libre pour le déjeuner?

— Oui oui, absolument.

— Bon, et bien alors, à 12 heures 30 je retrouverai les autres organisateurs de la fête au restaurant Le St-Mathieu.

WORKBOOK, P. 86

**IV. Mini-dictée: Le quartier de l'université** Listen to this description of the area around the University of Nancy and fill in the missing words. The description will be read three times.

Le quartier de l'université est <u>loin de</u> la gare. Pour aller à l'université, vous prenez <u>la rue</u> Chabot <u>jusqu'au</u> boulevard de l'Université. La bibliothèque municipale est <u>tout près de</u> l'université. <u>À côté de la bibliothèque</u> il y a un restaurant et <u>en face du</u> restaurant se trouve une librairie. La librairie est <u>dans la rue de</u> l'École. Pour s'amuser, les étudiants vont au café <u>sur le</u> boulevard de l'Université et aussi <u>au cinéma</u> Royal, qui se trouve <u>dans l'avenue</u> de Bourgogne.

WORKBOOK, P. 87

**VI. Des messages** You find yourself alone in the apartment of the French family with which you are staying. The parents (**M. et Mme Loridon**) and your French "brother" (**Mathieu**) are all out, so you have to answer the phone. Listen to each conversation and fill in the time, place, and any other relevant information on the message pad by the phone.

**Conversation 1**

— Allô! Euh, je pourrais parler avec Mathieu, s'il vous plaît?
— Je suis désolée. Mathieu n'est pas là. Je peux prendre un message?
— Oui. C'est Jean-Jacques qui téléphone. Dites-lui qu'on va se retrouver à 8h15 devant le cinéma.
— 8h15, devant le cinéma.
— C'est ça. Merci bien. Au revoir.
— De rien. Au revoir.

**Conversation 2**

— Bonjour. Je voudrais parler avec Anne-Louise, s'il vous plaît.
— Je suis désolée, Madame. Mme Loridon n'est pas à la maison.
— Est-ce que vous pourriez lui dire que Nicole Favert a téléphoné et que nous allons jouer aux cartes demain après-midi à la maison de Mme Vervaine? Je vais vous donner son adresse; c'est 52, avenue Isabelle.
— Madame sait l'heure où vous allez jouer?
— C'est l'heure normale... 2h.
— Très bien. Je lui donnerai votre message.
— Merci beaucoup.
— Je vous en prie, Madame.

**Conversation 3**

— Allô! Mathieu?
— Non. Mathieu n'est pas là.
— Ah, il n'est pas encore rentré. C'est Jean-Jacques encore une fois. Vous voudriez bien lui dire que nous avons changé de projets? Nous n'allons pas au cinéma ce soir. On organise une soirée chez la copine de Mireille.
— Alors, vous n'allez pas au cinéma. Vous allez chez la cousine de Mireille.
— C'est ça. Oh là là. Mathieu ne sait pas où elle habite. Eh bien, dites-lui que c'est le 43, rue Grimaud. C'est derrière la cathédrale. Dites-lui de tourner à gauche dans l'avenue Poincaré et de continuer jusqu'au bout de l'avenue et de tourner à droite.
— Attendez. Tourner à gauche dans l'avenue Poincaré. Continuer jusqu'au bout, ensuite tourner à droite dans la rue Grimaud. Bon, d'accord.
— On y va vers 9h. Merci. Au revoir.
— Au revoir.

WORKBOOK, P. 88

**VII. Où êtes-vous?** You will be given three sets of directions, either by a stranger or by a friend. Follow each set of instructions, tracing your route on the map below and indicating where you end up. If you get lost, listen to the directions again.

— Vous dînez dans le restaurant à côté de l'hôtel du Chapeau Rouge. Après le dîner vous faites une promenade dans le parc, puis vous passez derrière l'hôpital psychiatrique, vous tournez à gauche dans l'avenue de Bourgogne, vous continuez dans l'avenue. En face de la pharmacie, vous tournez à droite et vous allez tout droit. Ensuite vous tournez à gauche et vous allez au coin de la rue de l'école et de la rue Chabot. Où êtes-vous?

— Tu es devant le théâtre. Tu tournes à gauche. Tu vas tout droit, tu traverses la place, tu ne tournes pas dans la rue Gabriel, mais, tu continues jusqu'à l'avenue Albert Premier. Tu tournes à droite, tu vas jusqu'à l'hôtel et ensuite tu traverses la rue. Où es-tu?

— Tu es au lycée Beaumarchais. Tu traverses l'avenue de Bourgogne et tu continues dans la rue qui est directement en face du lycée. Tu vas jusqu'au bout de la rue et tu tournes, d'abord à gauche, et ensuite à droite. Sur ta gauche, il y a un café. Qu'est-ce qu'il y a sur ta droite?

## CHAPITRE 3

### SEGMENT 3

WORKBOOK, P. 90

**I. Dans la rue**
A. You will hear four short conversations in which people ask for directions. Match the number of the conversation (1, 2, 3, 4) with the appropriate brief description. You will not understand most of each conversation in detail; simply listen for the general context.

**Numéro 1**
— Monsieur, s'il vous plaît, la rue Saint-Jacques?
— Oui, oui, c'est très simple, hein. Vous êtes maintenant sur l'avenue Lafayette, vous continuez tout droit, puis vous prenez la deuxième rue à gauche. Ça, c'est le boulevard Saint-Germain.
— Pardon, Monsieur, c'est la deuxième à gauche?
— Oui, c'est ça, la deuxième à gauche, oui.
— Oui?
— Vous êtes donc sur le boulevard Saint-Germain maintenant, vous continuez tout droit et la première à droite, c'est la rue Saint-Jacques.
— Très bien. Merci, Monsieur.
— Je vous en prie.

**Numéro 2**
— Merci Laurent, pour la bière. Excuse-moi, je dois partir. J'ai rendez-vous avec Michelle. Euh, nous avons rendez-vous à la librairie Hachette. Tu sais où ça se trouve?
— Oui, oui, c'est au coin de la rue Saint-Michel et de la rue Duprès, juste en face de la pharmacie Longchamps. Tu sais ou c'est?
— Ah, oui! La pharmacie derrière l'église?
— Ouais, c'est ça, exactement!
— Bon, très bien. Merci beaucoup. Au revoir!
— Je t'en prie. Au revoir!

**Numéro 3**
— Pardon, Madame, savez-vous où se trouve le bureau de poste près d'ici?
— Oh, voyons, oh, non enfin, excusez-moi, Mademoiselle, je ne suis pas d'ici. Je ne pourrais pas vous aider. Mais demandez à l'agent, au coin de la rue.
— D'accord. Merci, Madame.
— Je vous en prie. Au revoir!
— Au revoir!

**Numéro 4**
— Allô, bonjour.

— Allô, Élisabeth?
— Oui!
— Bonjour, comment ça va?
— Très bien, et toi?
— Bien, merci.
— Qu'est-ce que tu fais cet après-midi?
— Rien. On va au cinéma?
— Oui, c'est une bonne idée!
— Très bien. Je viens te chercher alors?
— Oui, je veux bien.
— Tu es à la maison?
— Non, je suis chez mes grands-parents.
— Quelle est l'adresse?
— C'est la rue des Hautes-Feuilles.
— Oui, euh, comment est-ce qu'on s'y rend?
— Tu vas jusqu'à la rue des Petits Fours....
— Oui.
— Tu tournes à droite.
— Oui.
— Ensuite, tu traverses le boulevard Haussmann, et tu prends la première rue à droite.
— La première rue à droite, d'accord! Et c'est quel numéro?
— C'est au numéro 3.
— Très bien, merci. À tout à l'heure!
— À tout de suite. Au revoir!
— Au revoir!

## CHAPITRE 4

### SEGMENT 1

**Prononciation: Les consonnes finales *m* et *n***
(text, p. 133)

**Prononciation: Les consonnes finales *m* et *n* au milieu d'un mot** (text, p. 144)

**Prononciation: Les consonnes finales *m* et *n* suivies de la voyelle *e*** (text, p. 155)

## CHAPITRE 4

### SEGMENT 2

WORKBOOK, P. 116

**I. Pourquoi est-ce qu'ils vont en ville?** Listen to the four conversations. Then write the number of each conversation under the appropriate drawing.

1. — Tu as envie d'aller au cinéma?
   — Oui, je voudrais bien. Mais j'ai une course à faire pour ma mère.
   — Où est-ce que tu dois aller?
   — À la banque.
   — Rien de plus facile. Tu vas à la banque et puis on va au cinéma. D'accord?
   — Oui, d'accord.

2. — Salut, Henri. Tu vas en ville?
   — Oui. Toi aussi?
   — Oui, je vais retrouver Jean-Jacques devant le cinéma.
   — Pourquoi ne pas y aller avec nous?
   — Ben oui, je veux bien. On y va à pied?
   — Non, on prend l'autobus. C'est plus rapide et nous avons rendez-vous à sept heures et demie.

3. — Eh bien, François, où est-ce qu'on va?
   — J'sais pas. En ville, peut-être?
   — Pour quoi faire?
   — J'sais pas. On peut aller au cinéma?
   — Non, je n'ai pas envie d'aller au cinéma
   — Eh bien. Allons prendre quelque chose au café.
   — Ben, d'accord. On va au café alors.

4. — OK. Qu'est-ce qu'on va faire demain après-midi?
   — Si on allait en ville? Moi, je voudrais acheter quelque chose.
   — Ah, oui. Qu'est-ce que tu veux acheter?
   — Quelque chose pour mon petit frère. Il va avoir cinq ans mardi.
   — On prend l'autobus?
   — Non, moi, je préfère y aller à pied. C'est plus amusant.

## WORKBOOK, P. 116

**II. Comment est-ce qu'ils vont en ville?** Listen to the four conversations. Then match the number of each conversation with the appropriate form of transportation.

1. — Dis, donc, comment est-ce qu'on va y aller, la-bàs? C'est à l'autre bout de Paris.
   — Oh, je sais pas. On a plusieurs possibilités. Euh, est-ce qu'on des tickets?
   — Ben oui, euh, je crois que tu en as. Tu en as plus, toi?
   — Non, moi, j'en ai plus du tout. Il faut que j'en achète.
   — Ben oui. Moi, je crois que j'ai ma... oui, j'ai ma carte orange, hein. Donc, on peut y aller comme ça.
   — Oh ben alors, moi, je vais acheter un carnet, parce que je vais m'en servir souvent après.

2. — Ouf, dis donc, on est fatigués, hein?
   — Oh oui, ça va, ça doit bien faire deux heures qu'on pédale, hein, je crois.

— Ouais, on a fait combien de kilomètres, tu crois?
— Oh, je pense qu'on en a bien fait une quinzaine, hein!
— Une quinzaine, hein! Ben dis donc, on pédale sans s'arrêter, quoi, hein?
— Oui.
— Dis donc, euh, tu as soif, toi?
— Oui. Pourquoi est-ce qu'on s'arrête pas dans un café?
— Très bonne idée, hein. Moi, je boirai bien une petite limonade.
— Oui, moi, je meurs de soif.

3. — Oh, regarde, c'est ma voisine, Madame Thibault. Elle est en train de faire ses courses. Tu la vois, par la fenêtre?
   — Ah oui, je la vois effectivement! Oui, oui, je la connais, cette dame. Elle est gentille.
   — Oui, elle est adorable. Dis donc, où est-ce qu'on descend déjà? J'ai oublié.
   — Écoute, non, c'est pas le prochain arrêt, mais c'est le deuxième.
   — Tu es sûr?
   — Oui, oui, je suis sûr parce que là, on peut pas y aller à partir d'ici. Non, non, c'est le deuxième.
   — Bon alors, fais attention aux marches, hein, quand on descend.
   — D'accord.

4. — Monsieur, pouvez-vous m'arrêter ici? C'est juste au coin de la rue, là.
   — Oui, bien sûr. Juste au coin de la rue.
   — D'accord. Euh, combien je vous dois?
   — Oui, eh bien, c'est—attendez, je regarde le compteur—trente-cinq francs, s'il vous plaît.
   — Trente-cinq francs. Voilà un, un billet de cent francs. Euh, rendez-moi, euh, rendez-moi cinquante francs.
   — Ah, merci beaucoup. Voilà, Madame.
   — Merci. Bonne journée, Monsieur.
   — Vous aussi.

## WORKBOOK, P. 117

### III. Les verbes pronominaux
**A.** Tell whether each thing said is a question, a statement, or a command.

1. Comment? Tu ne veux pas te lever?
2. Ne t'inquiète pas!
3. Je vais m'acheter un nouvel ordinateur.
4. Amuse-toi bien, mon garçon!
5. Elle se repose cet après-midi?
6. Ils ne vont pas s'amuser à Londres.
7. Mesdames! Messieurs! Asseyez-vous, je vous prie!
8. Nous allons nous renseigner à l'hôtel de ville.

**B.** Now, tell whether each of the following is in the present (**présent**) or the future (**futur).**

1. Oh, nous allons vraiment nous amuser au festival.
2. Normalement elle se couche vers 11 heures.
3. Nous espérons nous retrouver dans quelques semaines.
4. Je me lève rarement avant 9 heures.
5. Pourquoi est-ce qu'ils se lèvent de si bonne heure?
6. Mais non. Tu ne vas pas t'inquiéter. Tout va s'arranger.

WORKBOOK, P. 117

### IV. Les nombres
**A. Combien? Quel numéro?** Write the number you hear in each of the following statements.

*MODÈLE:*   You hear:   Marie-Louise habite quarante-et-un, rue de Fleurus.
            You write:   *41*

1. Bon, tu prends le 24 et tu descends avenue de la Reine,
2. Jean-Jacques habite 58, avenue Clémenceau.
3. C'est combien? 35 francs. Voilà, Monsieur.
4. Pardon, Madame. Le 61, il va jusqu'à la gare d'Austerlitz?
5. Quand on compte les cousins et les cousines, nous sommes 27 dans la famille.
6. Je vous dois combien? 48 francs. D'accord. Voilà et merci.

**B. C'est combien?** Write the final amount involved in each transaction you hear.

*MODÈLE:*   You hear:   — C'est combien, ce livre?
                    — Vingt-deux francs cinquante.
                    — Vingt-deux francs cinquante? C'est pas cher.
      You write: À la librairie, *22,50 (22F50)*

1. — Oui, est-ce que vous pouvez m'arrêter là bientôt? Vous voyez le bâtiment avec les colonnades? Juste, juste devant, devant le bâtiment de l'ambassade.
  — Très bien. Certainement, Madame. Alors...
  — Combien, combien je vous dois?
  — Euh, je regarde le compteur. Soixante mm... soixante-cinq francs, Madame.
  — Soixante-cinq francs. Alors, tenez, je vous donne... je vous donne soixante-dix francs. Vous pouvez garder le tout.

— Bien. Je vous remercie, Madame. Au revoir, Madame.
— Au revoir, Monsieur. Bonne journée.
— Merci.

2. — Bonjour, Madame.
  — Bonjour, Monsieur. Je voudrais une carte orange, euh, et un billet de trois jours. Je crois qu'il y a un tarif touristique, n'est-ce pas?
  — C'est ça, oui. C'est un peu moins cher. Pour trois jours, c'est, attendez, je regarde mes tarifs ici, c'est soixante-cinq francs.
  — Soixante-cinq francs! C'est quand même beaucoup pour trois jours. M'enfin.
  — Ah, c'est le prix, Madame.
  — Enfin, c'est pas de votre faute. Euh, voilà. Merci.
  — Merci beaucoup.

3. — Bonjour, Madame.
  — Bonjour, Monsieur.
  — Alors, je voudrais, euh, des timbres.
  — Oui. Combien de timbres, Monsieur?
  — Euh, cinq timbres pour la France.
  — Alors, cinq timbres à deux francs cinquante chacun pour la France, ça vous fait donc douze francs cinquante.
  — Oui, et je voudrais également un timbre pour le Maroc pour lettre.
  — Alors, une lettre pour le Maroc, ce sera quatre francs. OK? Donc, le total sera seize francs cinquante, Monsieur.
  — Voilà, je vous donne seize francs cinquante.
  — Merci beaucoup.

4. — Garçon, s'il vous plaît!
  — Oui, Madame.
  — Est-ce que je pourrais avoir un sandwich saucisson beurre et une limonade?
  — Très bien, un saucisson beurre et une limonade pour Madame.
  — Euh, et combien ça va faire?
  — Attendez.
  — Vous pouvez me dire?
  — Oui, ben, j'additionne. Ça nous fait quarante-cinq francs pour les deux.
  — Quarante-cinq francs, d'accord. J'ai assez d'argent. Ça va. Merci.
  — Merci.

5. — Monsieur, vous désirez?
  — Oui, euh, je voudrais des cigarettes. Donnez-moi deux paquets de gauloises, s'il vous plaît.
  — Alors, deux paquets de gauloises...
  — Filtre.
  — ... filtre. Alors, c'est dix francs chaque paquet. Donc, ça vous fait vingt francs.

—Et donnez-moi également *Le Monde,* s'il vous plaît.

—Oui, *Le Monde,* six francs. Donc, le total, vingt-six francs, Monsieur.

—Voilà, je vous donne trente francs.

—Oui, alors, pour vingt-six francs, je vous rends quatre francs.

—Bien. Merci, Madame.

—Au revoir.

WORKBOOK, P. 118

**V. Vous voulez prendre un message?** You are alone in the home of some French friends. The parents (**M. et Mme Roche**) and the children (**Christine et Mathieu**) are all out for the evening. When the phone rings, you answer and take messages for the absent family members. Fill in the message slips with the vital information. You may write in French or in English; the important thing is to get the basic message.

—Allô? M. Jean Roche, s'il vous plaît. Ah, bon. Il n'est pas là. Est-ce que vous voulez bien prendre un message pour lui? Ici, Georges Charvet à l'appareil. Charvet—C-H-A-R-V-E-T. Bon. Nous avons rendez-vous demain à huit heures du matin. Mais je dois aller à la gare demain matin. Est-ce qu'on peut se retrouver demain après-midi—oui, demain après-midi, disons, à deux heures? Demain après-midi à deux heures, c'est ça. Merci. Au revoir.

—Allô. Allô. Christine? Elle n'est pas là? Oh là là. C'est sa copine Isabelle. Oui, Isabelle. J'organise une soirée pour samedi soir et je voudrais inviter Christine. Oui, samedi soir huit heures, huit heures et demie. Toi aussi, tu es invité(e). Mais oui. Est-ce qu'Isabelle et toi, vous voudriez apporter des cassettes—des cassettes de rock ou de punk? Merci. C'est très gentil. Bon. À samedi. Au revoir.

WORKBOOK, P. 118

**VI. Samedi soir à Paris** Listen to the following conversation between Claire, who is French, and her American friend David. Then answer the questions by circling the letter of the correct response.

*Claire et David sont dans l'appartement de Claire.*

—Alors, David. Qu'est-ce qu'on fait ce soir?

—Je voudrais voir un film.

—Bonne idée. On passe un très bon film italien au ciné-club de la rue d'Ulm. On y va?

—D'accord. On prend ta voiture?

—Mais non. Prenons le métro. C'est plus rapide.

*Dans la station de métro Wagram...*

—Je vais prendre un billet.

—Non, j'ai un carnet. Voici un ticket pour toi. Tu vas acheter les billets pour le film.

—Quelle direction est-ce qu'on prend?

—Galliéni. C'est là. À gauche.

—Voilà un train qui arrive. Dépêchons-nous!

*Dans le métro...*

—Tout juste. Où est-ce qu'on change?

—À Opéra. Nous avons le temps. On peut se reposer un peu.

*Quelques moments après...*

—C'est ici que nous descendons?

—Oui. Maintenant nous prenons la direction Mairie d'Issy. Tourne à droite. Oui... là où ça dit «correspondance». C'est ça.

*Quelques moments après...*

—Nous descendons à la prochaine.

—Quel est le nom de la station?

—Monge. Puis nous allons à pied jusqu'au ciné-club.

*Claire et David descendent du métro et se trouvent dans la rue Monge. Un touriste allemand les arrête devant le plan du métro à l'entrée de la station.*

—Pardon, Monsieur. Je voudrais aller à la place de l'Étoile.

—Alors, David, tu vas expliquer à ce monsieur comment aller à la place de l'Étoile.

—Mais non. C'est toi, la Parisienne.

—D'accord. Vous prenez la direction Église de Pantin, vous changez au Châtelet, direction Pont de Neuilly.

—Merci, Mademoiselle.

—Je vous en prie, Monsieur. Allons-y, David! Le film commence dans dix minutes.

## CHAPITRE 4

### SEGMENT 3

WORKBOOK, P. 119

**I. Le métro de Paris** In this chapter, you are going to learn about the Paris subway system. Part of using that system is recognizing the many station names. To familiarize yourself with some of the most frequently used proper names, listen to the short conversations between people talking about using the metro. In each conversation, two stations will be mentioned by name: find each station in the list on page 120 and put the number of the conversation next to it.

### Numéro 1
— Pardon, Monsieur, savez-vous aller à la Gare du Nord?
— Oui, c'est très simple. Vous prenez la direction Porte de Clignancourt et vous changez à Châtelet.
— Je prends la Porte de Clignancourt et je change à Châtelet?
— C'est ça, exactement!
— Merci beaucoup, Monsieur.
— De rien.

### Numéro 2
— Suzanne, je dois aller à la rue de Varenne. Quelle est la direction en métro?
— C'est la direction Saint-Denis-Basilique.
— Oui.
— Et il faut changer à Montparnasse-Bienvenue. Saint-Denis-Basilique et je dois changer à Montparnasse-Bienvenue?
— C'est ça.
— Très bien, merci!
— De rien!

### Numéro 3
— Bon, les enfants, on va au Petit Palais. Alors, nous allons prendre la direction Pont-de-Neuilly et nous changeons à la Nation. Vous avez bien compris? Direction Pont-de-Neuilly et on change à la Nation.

### Numéro 4
— Excusez-moi, Madame, ah, je voudrais aller à l'Opéra.
— Oui, vous devez prendre la direction Porte-de-la-Chapelle et vous changez à la Concorde.
— Alors, direction Porte-de-la-Chapelle je change à la Concorde?
— C'est ça.
— D'accord, merci!
— De rien!

### Numéro 5
— Mesdames et Messieurs, nous allons nous retrouver à la Gare de l'Est. Alors prenez la direction Église de Pantin et changez à République.
— Qu'est-ce qu'elle a dit?
— Elle a dit direction Église de Pantin et changez à République.
— Ah! d'accord.

WORKBOOK, P. 119

#### II. Samedi soir
**A.** Listen to three friends discussing their plans for Saturday evening. Then answer the following questions by circling the letter of the correct response.

— Dis donc, Hélène, tu veux venir à un concert de jazz ce soir?
— Oh, non! Je n'aime pas du tout le jazz. Peut-être un film?
— Tu crois?
— Non, moi, j'ai envie de voir le concert de jazz!
— Bon, alors, allez-y tous les deux!
— Tu es sûre que tu ne veux pas venir?
— Oui, oui, oui, ça va, ça va, allez-y!
— Bon, tu as ta voiture?
— Non.
— On prend un taxi alors? Oh, non! C'est trop cher!
— Un bus, peut-être?
— C'est plus simple de prendre le métro.
— D'accord, bonne idée.
— Alors rendez-vous à la station Sèvres-Babylone.
— D'accord, à ce soir!
— À ce soir!

## CHAPITRE 5

### SEGMENT 1

**Prononciation: Les voyelles *a* et *i*** (text, p. 180)

**Prononciation: La voyelle *u*** (text, p. 192)

**Prononciation: Les combinaisons *ai* et *au*** (text, p. 200)

## CHAPITRE 5

### SEGMENT 2

WORKBOOK, P. 139

**I. Les loisirs** (*Leisure-time activities*) Listen as each person describes his/her favorite leisure-time activity and match the name with the drawing of that activity.

1.  — Serge, qu'est-ce que tu aimes faire, quand tu as du temps libre?
    — Moi? Euh, tu sais, je, j'aime me baigner surtout. Je vais nager, je...
    — Et où est-ce que tu vas normalement?
    — Oh, ben, moi, je vais dans la mer! Je nage dans la mer, la mer Méditerranée.
    — Et tu fais ça... euh, tu y vas tous les étés?
    — Ah, tous les étés, ça, c'est certain! Tous les mois, chaque fois que je peux, j'y vais. Oui, oui.
    — Et avec qui est-ce que tu te baignes?

— En général, je vais me baigner avec mon frère. On fait de la natation ensemble.

— Mmm, c'est sympathique.

2. — Et toi, Catherine, quel est ton passe-temps favori?

— Moi, j'adore faire des promenades, des randonnées en montagne, par exemple.

— Ah bon. Et tu fais ça où?

— En général, je vais dans les Alpes de Haute-Provence, tu sais. C'est très joli là-bas.

— Oui, je sais, c'est ravissant. Et, euh, est-ce que tu y vas toute seule ou... ?

— En général, j'y vais, j'y vais toujours avec mon chien qui adore ça.

— Ah, ça doit être très sympathique.

3. — Et toi, Philippe, qu'est-ce que tu aimes faire?

— Moi, j'adore aller à la pêche.

— Ah vraiment, tu aimes être pêcheur. Et tu es pêcheur en eau douce ou en eau salée?

— Ah, toujours en eau douce, moi, oui.

— Et où est-ce que tu pêches?

— Et bien, euh, en général, j'aime aller au, au lac d'Annecy, moi.

— Et tu y vas souvent?

— Oui, oh, j'y vais deux ou trois fois par an.

— Moi, je déteste la pêche. Et avec qui est-ce que tu y vas?

— Ah, j'aime bien y aller tout seul. Tu sais, c'est très tranquille quand tu pêches. J'aime faire ça tout seul.

— Oui, c'est pour ça que j'aime pas trop ça.

4. — Dis donc, Martine, c'est quoi, ton activité préférée?

— Ah moi, j'adore faire du jogging.

— Du jogging? Et bien, dis donc, c'est bien! Ça te garde en forme.

— Oui.

— Tu en fais souvent?

— J'en fais à peu près deux ou trois fois par semaine, euh, avant d'aller, euh, travailler.

— Ah oui, c'est bien. Et tu vas où, euh, pour en faire? Tu fais le tour de Paris?

— Euh, non, pas exactement, mais j'ai la chance d'habiter près du bois de Boulogne. Alors, euh, je vais au bois de Boulogne tôt le matin.

— Bien, c'est bien. Et tu en fais tout seul, toute seule, pardon?

— Euh, non. Enfin, quelquefois j'en fais toute seule, mais souvent j'y vais avec une copine.

5. — Salut, Yves. C'est quoi ton passe-temps favori en, en hiver?

— Alors, moi, mon passe-temps favori, c'est le ski de piste, hein.

— Ah bon! Mais c'est un, un bon exercice, ça!

— Oui oui, ça fait beaucoup de bien, beaucoup d'oxygène, etc. C'est très bon.

— Et tu vas où pour faire de, du ski de piste?

— J'adore skier sur les, les pistes autrichiennes, moi.

— Ouh! Ben dis donc, tu es un peu snob, hein?

— Ah oui, mais elles sont vraiment supérieures, écoute.

— Bien, c'est bien. Et tu y vas avec qui?

— Et bien, j'y vais avec mon frère d'habitude.

— Bien, d'accord. Et vous en faites souvent?

— Oui, on essaie d'aller, euh, assez régulièrement tous les ans et on reste environ une semaine!

— Bravo! C'est bien.

6. — Salut, Annie! C'est quoi, ton activité préférée? J'ai oublié.

— Oh moi, j'aime bien faire de la voile.

— Tu fais de la voile?

— Oui. On a un petit bateau. C'est, c'est super.

— Tu fais de la voile toute seule?

— Non non non, j'y vais, euh, avec mon mari, parfois les enfants, quand ils en ont envie, mais surtout mon mari.

— Ah bon, et vous faites de la voile en Méditerranée?

— Euh, pas exactement. Tu sais. On va à Arcachon, euh, sur le bassin d'Arcachon. C'est plus calme.

— Ah oui, à côté de Bordeaux. C'est très bien.

— Voilà.

— Et vous y allez en général pour combien de temps?

— Oh, tu sais, on y va tous les étés, euh, au mois de juillet, pour un mois à peu près.

— D'accord. Vous avez beau temps.

— Voilà.

— Ben, bravo!

WORKBOOK, p. 140

**II. Qu'est-ce que vous recommandez comme film?**
Listen to some young people talk about the types of films they prefer. Then write each person's name under the film you think he or she would like best.

1. Mon prenom, c'est Pierre. J'adore le cinéma. Je vois un ou deux films toutes les semaines. J'aime beaucoup les films étrangers—japonais, allemands, italiens.
2. Je m'appelle Ghislaine. Moi, j'adore les films policiers.
3. Je m'appelle Bertrand. Je vais rarement au cinéma. Quend je vois un film, c'est normalement une comédie.
4. Je suis Christine. Ce que j'aime voir, c'est un bon film d'épouvante. Je n'ai pas peur, moi.
5. Je m'appelle Éric. Je suis fanatique de science-fiction.

WORKBOOK, P. 140

**III. Passé? Présent? Futur?** Listen to the following sentences and, based on the verbs and other time words, tell whether they refer to the past, the present, or the future.

**A.** First, distinguish between past and present.

*MODÈLE:* You hear:   Elle a beaucoup mangé hier.
   You circle: *passé*

1. Elle regarde souvent les actualités à la télé.
2. Est-ce qu'elle a regardé le film sur la première chaîne hier soir?
3. Tu es sortie avec Jean-Patrice!
4. Tu es dans mon cours de science politique, non?
5. Moi, j'ai rendez-vous avec le professeur après le cours.
6. Moi, j'ai préparé tous mes devoirs.
7. Ils sont à la banque, je crois.
8. Ils sont allés à la banque, non?

**B.** Now distinguish between past and future.

*MODÈLE:* You hear:   Elle va regarder la télé ce soir.
   You circle: *futur*

1. Regarde! Elle a tout mangé!
2. Attention! Elle va tout manger.
3. Nous allons écouter la radio ce soir.
4. Nous avons écouté la météo à la radio.
5. Tu as acheté quelque chose?
6. Tu vas acheter quelque chose?
7. Ils ont très bien joué.
8. Quand est-ce qu'ils vont jouer?

**C.** Finally, distinguish between past, present, and future.

*MODÈLE:* You hear:   Est-ce qu'elles sont allées au concert?
   You circle: *passé*

1. Ils ne vont pas aller au concert.
2. Ils ne vont jamais au concert.
3. Mon ami et moi, nous nous sommes disputés.
4. Lui et moi, nous sommes de très bons amis.
5. Mais non. C'est moi qu'elle cherche.
6. Elle s'est couchée de bonne heure.
7. Elle va se coucher de bonne heure.
8. Elle n'a pas trouvé son cahier.

WORKBOOK, P. 141

**IV. Mini-dictée: Mon voyage en Californie** Chantal is a foreign student at your university. She has just spent Christmas vacation traveling around California with friends. Now she's telling your French class about her experiences. As she talks, fill in the blanks. Her comments will be read twice.

J'ai passé quinze jours en Californie. Nous <u>avons commencé</u> notre voyage à San Diego où nous <u>avons visité</u> Marineland. Nous <u>avons quitté</u> San Diego le 22 décembre. Nous <u>sommes montés</u> vers Los Angeles par la route nationale. J'ai un ami qui a un appartement à Oceanside. Là, nous <u>nous sommes reposés</u> trois jours. Je <u>suis allée</u> à la plage, j'<u>ai fait</u> des promenades en ville et nous a<u>vons mangé</u> de très bonnes choses. Après trois jours nous <u>sommes allés</u> à Los Angeles. Là j'<u>ai eu</u> l'occasion de <u>visiter</u> le quartier mexicain et j'<u>ai visité</u> Hollywood. Ça <u>a été</u> formidable!

À Los Angeles nous <u>avons pris</u> l'avion pour aller à San Francisco. Quelle belle ville! On <u>a fait</u> des promenades sur les quais, on <u>a</u> beaucoup <u>mangé</u> et j'<u>ai acheté</u> des souvenirs. Après San Francisco, nous <u>sommes rentrés</u> à la maison.

Je <u>suis</u> très contente de ce voyage. J'<u>ai pris</u> beaucoup de photos. L'année prochaine mes parents et moi nous <u>allons visiter</u> les États-Unis. Nous <u>allons retourner</u> en Californie, mais nous <u>allons</u> aussi <u>visiter</u> la Floride et la ville de New York.

WORKBOOK, P. 142

**V. Le samedi de Clotilde** Listen while Clotilde Vautier talks about what she did last Saturday. Then answer the questions in French.

Je m'appelle Clotilde Vautier. J'ai 16 ans. J'habite dans un appartement à Paris avec mes parents, mon frère et ma sœur. Je suis élève dans un lycée à Paris. Je vais vous décrire ce que j'ai fait samedi dernier.

Comme vous le savez peut-être, nous avons des cours en France le samedi matin. Par conséquent, je me suis levée à 7h15. J'ai pris une douche et je me suis préparée pour aller à l'école. J'ai pris le petit déjeuner avec ma sœur, parce que nous sommes à la même école. Mon père et mon frère (qui est à l'université), eux, ils sont restés au lit. Mais ma mère s'est levée avec nous. Ma sœur et moi avons quitté la maison vers 8h pour aller prendre le métro. Nous sommes donc arrivées à l'école pour notre premier cours, qui commence à 9h. Moi, j'ai cours jusqu'à 11h30 le samedi.

Après les cours, ma copine Pascale et moi, nous sommes allées manger au Macdo qui est près du lycée.

Ensuite nous avons fait les boutiques. Nous n'avons pas acheté grand-chose parce que nous n'avions pas beaucoup d'argent. Mais nous avons fait du lèche-vitrine. C'était chouette. Je suis rentrée vers cinq heures.

Le soir je suis sortie avec Pascale et son frère Didier. Nous sommes allés au cinéma et après, nous avons pris quelque chose à boire au café. Je suis rentrée vers 11h et je me suis couchée. Et voilà ce que j'ai fait samedi dernier, un samedi assez typique pour moi.

WORKBOOK, P. 142

**VI. Des projets de vacances** Listen while Luc and his family discuss their plans for spring vacation. Then answer the questions on your worksheet.

PÈRE: Les enfants, si on parlait des vacances... C'est bientôt.
LUC ET SOPHIE: Ah, oui.
MÈRE: C'est une idée ça, oui.
SOPHIE: Ah... oui, moi, j'ai des projets. J'ai été invitée chez Marie-Claire.
MÈRE: Comment?
SOPHIE: Ses parents ont une maison en Normandie et elle m'a dit qu'on pourrait faire de l'équitation et tout. C'est super.
LUC: Oui, ouais. Sophie veut aller chez sa copine. Moi aussi, moi je veux aller dans les Alpes, avec mes copains, Jean-Claude et Roger.
MÈRE: Oh, écoutez, les enfants, vous savez très bien qu'à cette époque de l'année maman nous attend dans sa maison à Aix.
LUC: Ah, non! Quelle barbe!
SOPHIE: C'est pas très rigolo. On y est déjà allé à Noël.
LUC: On y va tout le temps; c'est tout le temps la même chose. On s'ennuie là-bas, on s'ennuie.
MÈRE: Ça, je comprends bien. Mais soyez un peu patients avec votre grand-mère, quand même.
PÈRE: Écoutez, votre grand-mère vous adore. Je ne vous permets pas de parler sur ce ton.
SOPHIE: Qu'est ce que t'en penses, toi, papa? Tu as envie d'aller chez Mémé?
PÈRE: Oh, ça ne me dérangerait pas.
LUC: Oh, non, non. Moi, j'veux pas. Vous pourriez pas trouver quelque chose de plus amusant, non?
MÈRE: C'est vrai que ce n'est pas très passionnant. Qu'est-ce que tu en penses?
PÈRE: Eh, bien. Voyons voir. J'aimerais qu'on puisse rester ensemble.
MÈRE: Ah, oui, ça, je suis tout à fait d'accord.
LUC: Oui...
MÈRE: Alors, on peut peut-être voir quelque chose, non?
PÈRE: Écoutez, j'ai une petite surprise pour vous.
LUC ET SOPHIE: Ah?

PÈRE: J'ai déjà organisé un petit voyage.
LUC ET SOPHIE: Ah?
SOPHIE: Ben, pourquoi tu le disais pas? Où?
PÈRE: Ah, ah, à vous de deviner. C'est au sud. On va se diriger vers le sud.
LUC: En Provence.
PÈRE: À l'étranger.
LUC: En Italie!
PÈRE: Non.
SOPHIE: En Espagne.
PÈRE: Plus au sud.
MÈRE: Plus chaud, oui.
SOPHIE: Au bord de la mer?
PÈRE: Au bord de la mer. Au bord de l'océan.
LUC: Au Maroc!
PÈRE: Au Maroc! Très bien, Luc!
MÈRE: Voilà! T'as gagné!
PÈRE: J'ai réservé, et tenez-vous bien, un voyage pour nous quatre, au Club Med, à Agadir.
LUC: Agadir!
SOPHIE: Super! Alors, on pourra nager? La mer est assez chaude?
PÈRE: La mer sera très bonne à cette période de l'année. On pourra nager, on pourra faire de la voile. Tu pourras faire de l'équitation.
LUC: Et moi? Je pourrai faire du ski?
PÈRE: Et Luc, tu pourras faire du ski nautique.
MÈRE: Du ski nautique, bien sûr. Et moi, mes enfants, je vais avoir des vacances pour une fois. Pas de vaisselle, pas de ménage, rien du tout. Je vais avoir mon temps. Nous allons avoir notre temps pour nous, n'est-ce pas, chéri?
PÈRE: Absolument. Et je ne m'inquiète pas pour les vacances de votre maman.
MÈRE: Ah!
LUC: Allez! On y va!
SOPHIE: Super! Merci, papa. T'es super!
PÈRE: Bon, très bien, les enfants. Je vous adore.

## CHAPITRE 5

### SEGMENT 3

WORKBOOK, P. 143

**I. La météo**
**A.** You will hear four short conversations in which people talk about the weather as predicted by the reports on the radio. Based on what you hear, decide what clothing you'll bring on your vacation. Match the number of the report (1, 2, 3, 4) with the clothing description. (You will not understand everything in the reports in detail; listen for the gist of each conversation.)

## Numéro 1

Demain les températures vont varier entre moins deux degrés et plus trois degrés. Skieurs, attention aux chutes de neige et avalanches en montagne. Automobilistes, attention aux routes bloquées et risque de verglas.

## Numéro 2

Aujourd'hui, mistral sur le Midi. Beau temps sur l'ensemble du territoire à l'exception de la Bretagne. Températures variant entre vingt et vingt-cinq degrés.

## Numéro 3

Demain, le temps sera frais sur l'ensemble du pays. Le ciel sera couvert et il y aura possibilité de précipitation. N'oubliez pas votre parapluie. Les températures vont varier entre neuf et douze degrés. Automobilistes, attention, les routes seront glissantes.

## Numéro 4

Prévisions pour aujourd'hui et la nuit prochaine. Le temps sera variable mais frais, faisant place après des orages à de belles éclaircies sur l'ensemble du territoire. Les températures devraient varier entre treize degrés et vingt degrés. La nuit sera fraîche, avec dix degrés. Automobilistes, attention, les routes seront glissantes et il y aura des zones dispersées de brouillards matinaux.

WORKBOOK, P. 144

### II. Les amis

**A.** Listen to some friends trying to make plans together. Then answer the questions.

LAURENT: Alors, qu'est-ce qu'on fait, ce week-end? Vous voulez faire de la chute libre avec moi?
MIREILLE: Ah oui! C'est exaltant!
LAURENT: Ah ça te plaît! Et toi, alors?
JEAN-MICHEL: Oh mais non! La chute libre, c'est dangereux!
LAURENT: Mais non, c'est pas dangereux, et puis c'est en pleine nature, ça va nous faire du bien!
JEAN-MICHEL: Oui, non, mais moi, ça ne me plaît pas, je... je... je... très franchement j'ai peur de l'altitude.
LAURENT: Ah bon, ah bon.
JEAN-MICHEL: J'ai le vertige.
MIREILLE: Bon, et si on allait au cinéma, alors?
LAURENT: Oh ben non, on y est allés les deux derniers week-ends, on va pas recommencer encore, enfin!
JEAN-MICHEL: Ça dépend du film qu'ils ont...
LAURENT: Oh mais non!
JEAN-MICHEL: Mais tu sais, en fin de compte, je crois que samedi, il va faire beau temps, alors on pourrait peut-être aller faire un tennis, tous ensemble.

LAURENT: Oh ça, c'est une bonne idée, alors! Moi, ça me plairait, moi!
MIREILLE: Non, j'ai pas envie parce que, il y a l'exposition de Matisse.
LAURENT: Ben oui, mais... on pourrait y aller dimanche à l'expo?
JEAN-MICHEL: Ben oui, d'autant plus que dimanche, ils ont prévu du mauvais temps. On prévoit de la pluie.
LAURENT: Ah ouais?
JEAN-MICHEL: Oui.
LAURENT: Ben écoute, j'ai une idée. Nous, on va ensemble faire un tennis samedi et puis tous les trois, on va ensemble à l'expo....
MIREILLE: Au musée?
LAURENT: Oui, au musée, c'est ça, le dimanche.
MIREILLE: Bon, ben, c'est parfait. Moi, ça me convient parfaitement.
JEAN-MICHEL: Super! Ça tombe bien!

---

## CHAPITRE 6

### SEGMENT 1

**Prononciation: La voyelle é** (text, p. 218)

**Prononciation: Les voyelles è et ê** (text, p. 229)

**Prononciation: La voyelle e** (text, p. 239)

---

## CHAPITRE 6

### SEGMENT 2

WORKBOOK, P. 161

**I. Où?** Listen to the following short conversations and identify the store in which each takes place (**charcuterie, boucherie, boulangerie, pâtisserie**).

*MODÈLE:* You hear:  — Bonjour, Madame.
          — Madame Ferrier. Comment ça va?
          — Pas trop mal, merci. Et vous?
          — Très bien. Qu'est-ce que vous prenez aujourd'hui?
          — Donnez-moi six tranches de jambon et 500 grammes de salade de tomates.
          — Voilà. Et avec ça?
          — C'est tout pour aujourd'hui.
      You write: *charcuterie*

1. — Bonjour, Monsieur Grandier.
   — Bonjour, Madame. Qu'est-ce que je peux faire pour vous?
   — D'abord, j'ai besoin de quatre biftecks.
   — Très bien. Et avec ça?
   — Donnez-moi aussi un poulet, assez gros.
   — Voilà. Quatre biftecks et un poulet. Et avec ça?
   — C'est tout. Merci.

2. — Ah, bonjour, Madame Rivolet. Comment ça va?
   — Pas trop mal, Madame Michaut. Et vous?
   — Comme toujours. Vous désirez?
   — Voyons... je voudrais deux baguettes et une douzaine de petits pains.
   — Voilà. J'ai aussi des belles tartelettes pour le dessert.
   — Merci, non. Mais je prends une tarte aux pommes.
   — Un bon choix! Et c'est tout pour aujourd'hui?
   — Oui. Merci bien.

3. — Bonjour, Jean-Claude. Qu'est-ce que je peux faire pour toi aujourd'hui?
   — Maman m'a demandé d'acheter du pâté pour cinq personnes.
   — Bon. Voilà un bon morceau de pâté de campagne. C'est tout?
   — Non. Il me faut aussi de la salade de thon. Assez pour cinq personnes.
   — Voilà. Et avec ça?
   — Je pense que c'est tout.

4. — Qu'est-ce que vous désirez aujourd'hui, Monsieur Fernand?
   — Il me faut six croissants et un pain de campagne.
   — Et avec ça?
   — Donnez-moi aussi ce gâteau au chocolat.
   — Très bien. Et avec ça?
   — Euh... deux religieuses et quatre éclairs. Et c'est tout.
   — D'accord. Merci, Monsieur.

WORKBOOK, P. 162

**II. Qu'est-ce qu'ils ont acheté?** In the following conversations, young people are talking about their shopping trips. As you listen to each conversation, identify the store the person went to (**Fnac, bijouterie, magasin de jouets, magasin de sport**) and what he or she bought.

*MODÈLE:* You hear: — J'ai dépensé trop d'argent aujourd'hui.
— Qu'est-ce que tu as acheté?
— Eh bien... regarde ces deux cassettes. Super, non? J'ai aussi acheté une vidéo et disque compact.
— Tu as raison. C'est cher, tout ça. Mais c'est sensationnel. Écoutons d'abord le disque compact.

You write: Magasin: *Fnac*
Achats: *cassettes, vidéo, disque compact*

1. — Enfin. J'ai assez d'argent pour acheter un magnétophone.
   — Oui, mais est-ce que tu ne préfères pas ce radio-cassette?
   — Je ne sais pas. Je n'ai pas de Walkman non plus.
   — Regarde, ce radio-cassette est en solde.
   — C'est vrai. Si je l'achète, je peux aussi acheter quelques cassettes vierges et une cassette de Sting.
   — Alors, c'est décidé?
   — Oui, allons à la caisse.

2. — Tu exagères! C'est beaucoup trop cher!
   — Oui, mais Papa, tous mes amis ont ce jeu vidéo.
   — Alors, tu peux jouer à ce jeu chez tes amis. Je vais t'acheter quelque chose, mais il faut être raisonnable.
   — Et ces deux robots pour ma collection?
   — Voyons... euh... oui... c'est possible.
   — S'il te plaît, Papa, achète-moi ces robots.
   — Bon. D'accord. On les achète.

3. — Tes parents sont très généreux.
   — Oui, ils m'ont donné assez d'argent pour acheter une raquette.
   — Quelle raquette est-ce que tu vas prendre?
   — Une Wilson, je pense.
   — Oui, c'est pas mal. Voilà exactement ce qu'il faut.
   — Oui, et j'ai besoin de balles aussi.
   — Tu as raison. Il est difficile de jouer au tennis sans balles!

WORKBOOK, P. 162

**III. Mini-dictée: Les villages de Provence** There are many small towns in southern France. Write the population of each town in figures. You will hear each number three times.

1. Les Baux: quatre cent trente-trois
2. Cadenet: deux mille six cent quarante
3. Gordes: mille six cent sept
4. Ménerbes: mille vingt-sept
5. St-Rémy-de-Provence: huit mille quatre cent trente-neuf
6. Viviers: trois mille deux cent quatre-vingt-sept

WORKBOOK, P. 162

**IV. Annonces au supermarché** As you're walking through the supermarket, you hear a series of announcements about today's specials. As you hear the prices, write them down for reference while you shop.

*MODÈLE:* You hear: Mesdames et Messieurs, visitez notre boulangerie. Nous avons aujourd'hui des tartes aux fraises superbes à 36F50 la tarte.

You write: tarte aux fraises *36F60*

1. Mesdames et Messieurs. Spécial a la boulangerie-pâtisserie. Un gâteau moka délicieux à 89F.
2. Achetez des pains au chocolat. Aujourd'hui seulement, 30F la douzaine.
3. Pour votre dessert, achetez des petits fours. Prix spécial, 18F la douzaine.
4. Vous aimez les pâtisseries? Achetez des religieuses à 7F50 la pièce.
5. Mesdames et Messieurs, visitez notre charcuterie. Une délicieuse salade de thon à 29F la livre.
6. Vous aimez le pâté? Achetez notre pâté de campagne à 39F95 le kilo.
7. Pour un hors-d'œuvre, considérez notre jambon à 54F le kilo.
8. Des saucisses délicieuses pour votre dîner. Seulement 62F le kilo.

WORKBOOK, P. 163

**V. Mini-dictée: Notre journée au centre commercial**
Two friends are comparing their day at the mall. As they talk, fill in the blanks. The passage will be read twice.

— Je suis très fatiguée. J'ai passé toute la journée au centre commercial et j'ai acheté beaucoup de choses. D'abord, je suis allée à la Fnac. J'ai trouvé une vidéo de Sting, j'ai acheté des cassettes pour mon frère et j'ai aussi acheté un disque compact.
— Quel disque compact est-ce que tu as acheté?
— Un disque de U2.
— Moi, je me suis arrêté au magasin de jouets où j'ai trouvé un robot pour mon petit frère. J'ai regardé beaucoup de jouets, mais je sais que mon frère aime surtout les robots.
— Moi aussi, je suis allée au magasin de jouets. J'ai acheté un jeu vidéo et un camion pour mes cousins. Après, je suis allée au magasin de sport où j'ai trouvé une raquette de tennis qui était en solde.
— J'adore aller au centre commercial, mais je dépense toujours trop d'argent.
— Moi aussi, j'aime faire du shopping.

WORKBOOK, P. 163

**VI. Un cadeau pour mon petit frère** Cédric is in a toy store, looking for a present for his little brother. As you listen to his conversation with the salesperson, find out the following information.

— Bonjour, Monsieur.
— Bonjour, mon petit. Tu as choisi quelque chose?
— Non, pas encore. Je voudrais acheter un jouet pour mon petit frère.
— Bon. Qu'est-ce qu'il aime, ton petit frère?
— Oh... il aime beaucoup les trains électriques.
— Bon. Les trains électriques, ça coûte très cher. Combien d'argent as-tu?
— J'ai 80F.
— 80F. Pour 80F tu peux acheter un jeu vidéo, un robot ou un ballon de foot.
— Il n'y a rien d'autre?
— Si, si. Tu peux acheter un camion ou des petits soldats.
— Ah, ça, c'est pas terrible. Je pense que je vais prendre le jeu vidéo, parce qu'on jouera tous les deux comme ça.
— Ça, c'est une bonne idee.

**CHAPITRE 6**

**SEGMENT 3**

WORKBOOK, P. 164

**I. Des achats**
**A.** You will hear four short conversations between customers and shopkeepers. Match the number of the conversation (1, 2, 3, 4) with the brief descriptions below. (You will not understand everything in each conversation in detail; listen for the general context.)

**Numéro 1**
— Tiens, bonjour, Madame. Comment ça va?
— Très bien, merci!
— Qu'est-ce que vous voulez prendre?
— Je vais prendre du saucisson, s'il vous plaît.
— Oui, une quinzaine de tranches?
— C'est ça.
— Quelque chose d'autre?
— Oui, il me faudrait du pâté...
— Du pâté. Un morceau comme ça?
— Euh, un petit peu plus.
— Bien. C'est pour un pique-nique?
— Oui, c'est pour un pique-nique. Nous allons à la plage.

—Heum, j'ai un excellent jambon de Parme. Ça vous intéresse?

—Ah, oui! Donnez-m'en cinq tranches, s'il vous plaît.

—Bien, voilà!

—Merci!

—Alors ça fait, heum, heum, 85 francs.

—D'accord, voilà!

—Bien, merci, et voici votre monnaie, Madame.

—Merci!

—Au revoir, bonne journée!

—Merci, vous aussi!

### Numéro 2

—Bonjour, Monsieur. Qu'est-ce que vous désirez?

—Bonjour, Madame. Je voudrais, ah, cinq oranges...

—Cinq oranges, oui.

—Et... est-ce que vous avez des bananes?

—Oh oui, nous avons beaucoup de bananes ici. Combien vous en voulez?

—J'en prendrais trois, s'il vous plaît.

—Trois bananes. Oui, et avec ça?

—Heum...

—Oh, nous avons de beaux légumes aujourd'hui. Regardez ces haricots verts!

—Oui, très bien. Donnez-m'en... une livre.

—Une livre d'haricots verts, très bien. Et, euh, des tomates peut-être?

—Ouais. Donnez-moi un demi-kilo.

—Un demi-kilo de tomates, voilà. Alors c'est tout?

—C'est tout!

—Voilà, très bien. Alors ça fait, euh... 74 francs, Monsieur.

—D'accord, voilà 80.

—Voilà, et voilà votre monnaie.

—Merci beaucoup.

—Je vous en prie. Au revoir, Monsieur.

—Au revoir.

### Numéro 3

—Bonjour, Monsieur. Qu'est-ce que vous désirez aujourd'hui?

—Eh, bien, j'hésite. Qu'est-ce que vous avez? Qu'est-ce que vous me recommandez?

—Nous avons un beau rôti de bœuf. Nous avons aussi du veau, du porc...

—Heum, parlez-moi du veau. Combien coûte le veau?

—C'est 140 francs le kilo.

—Heum, et le porc?

—Oui, c'est 70 francs le kilo.

—Ah, ha! Écoutez, donnez-moi huit côtelettes, huit côtelettes de porc, s'il vous plaît.

—D'accord, huit belles côtelettes pour Monsieur. Eh, voilà, et avec ça?

—Oh, c'est tout. Ce sera tout, merci.

—D'accord. Au revoir, Monsieur.

### Numéro 4

—Bonjour, Madame!

—Bonjour, Madame!

—Euh, alors, qu'est-ce que vous pouvez me recommander? Euh, nous avons un déjeuner de famille et j'aimerais un bon dessert.

—Ah, nous avons beaucoup de gâteaux aujourd'hui. Nous avons des savarins, des gâteaux au chocolat, des tartes aux fraises et des tartes Tatin.

—Euh, et la tarte aux fraises, c'est combien?

—C'est 70 francs le gâteau.

—Et c'est bien frais, n'est-ce pas?

—Très frais, Madame. C'est d'aujourd'hui.

—Très bien. Je crois que je prendrai bien la tarte aux fraises.

—Parfait.

—Et peut-être, euh, je ne sais pas. Euh, vous avez des gâteaux pour les enfants?

—J'ai des mille-feuilles...

—Oui.

—J'ai des meringues.

—Oh, des meringues! Oui, alors, donnez-moi, euh, quatre meringues.

—Parfait, voilà.

—Très bien, merci. Au revoir!

—Au revoir!

### SEGMENT 1

**Prononciation: La voyelle *o*** (text, p. 263)

**Prononciation: La combinaison *ou*** (text, p. 274)

**Prononciation: La combinaison *oi*** (text, p. 284)

### SEGMENT 2

Workbook, p. 179

**I. De quoi est-ce qu'ils parlent?** You're listening to a series of commercials on the radio. Look at the drawings and put a check below the item or place talked about in each commercial.

*MODÈLE:* You see:   a VCR, a small TV, and a computer

You hear:   Noir et blanc portable avec écran de 31 cm. Livré avec antenne. Le prix avantageux de 899F. Idéal pour les enfants et comme télé secondaire.

You check: the drawing of the small TV

1. Système VHS d'enregistrement de haute qualité. Mémorisation de deux programmes sur une période de deux semaines ou répétitif du lundi au vendredi. Prix avantageux de ce magnétoscope de 5590F. Avec ce système, vous ne manquerez plus vos émissions préférées.

2. C'est la dernière rage chez les enfants. Il marche, il produit des sons, il bouge les bras et la tête. Le tout en plastique qui ne présente aucun danger même pour les plus jeunes. Si vous voulez faire vraiment plaisir à votre enfant, garçon ou fille, achetez ce robot. Il stimulera l'imagination et ne perdra pas son intérêt.

3. Vous n'avez qu'une heure pour prendre le déjeuner? Venez chez Simone et goûtez nos quiches, nos pizzas et nos tartes à l'oignon. Rien de plus facile. Situé tout près du parc Monceau, vous pouvez manger votre repas en plein air. Pour le dessert, nous vous offrons des tartelettes aux fraises ou des chaussons aux pommes.

4. Qu'est-ce qu'il vous faut pour la rentrée? Chez nous, vous trouverez non seulement vos manuels de classe, mais également tout ce qu'il vous faut pour vos devoirs: cahiers, stylos, gommes, règles. Tous les étudiants sérieux passent chez nous pour tous leurs besoins scolaires.

5. Mesdames, Messieurs. Fatigués de faire la cuisine après une longue journée de travail? Nous avons tout ce qu'il vous faut: jambon, saucisson, pâté, salades de toutes sortes. Laissez-nous faire le travail pour vous et rendez-nous visite au 54 de la rue Rousseau.

WORKBOOK, P. 181

**II. De qui est-ce que tu parles?** Your friends give descriptions of some people whose names they have forgotten. Listen to each description, look at the drawings, and identify the person you think is being described.

*MODÈLE:* You see:   two men

You hear:   Cet homme est assez âgé. Il est petit et costaud. Il a un grand nez et une barbe et il a très peu de cheveux. Qui est-ce?

You circle: *M. Lecasier.*

1. Elle est grande et tres bronzée. Elle a les cheveux courts et noirs. Elle a un petit nez. Qui est-ce?

2. Il est petit et costaud. Il a les cheveux noirs. Il a un très grand nez. Qui est-ce?

3. Elle est grande et mince. Elle a un petit nez et elle a les cheveux noirs. Qui est-ce?

4. Il est très bronzé. Il est grand et mince et il a les cheveux blonds. Il a un petit nez. Qui est-ce?

WORKBOOK, P. 182

**III. Féminin ou masculin?** Listen to each statement and indicate whether the adjective you hear is feminine or masculine.

*MODÈLE:* You hear:   C'est un jeune homme très naïf.

You circle: *masculin*

1. Quelle tarte délicieuse!
2. Mon frère n'est pas très discret.
3. C'est un vélo tout neuf.
4. Chantal est brune.
5. Si on veut participer aux Jeux olympiques il faut être très sportif.
6. C'était une émission très courte.
7. Pourquoi est-ce qu'elle est toujours impatiente?
8. C'est un bouquin ennuyeux.
9. C'est son petit ami.
10. Cest la première fois que je vais dans ce restaurant.

WORKBOOK, P. 183

**IV. Philippe et Martine** Claire is telling about her two friends, Philippe and Martine. Listen to the the description and decide which of the following adjectives apply to Philippe and which to Martine. Some adjectives may apply to both friends; others, to neither. Circle the appropriate adjectives in each list.

Mes amis, Philippe et Martine, ont tous les deux 24 ans. Ils habitent dans un vieil appartement au centre d'Avignon. Avignon se trouve dans le sud de la France. Leur appartement n'est pas grand, mais il est très confortable. Ils ont une voiture allemande—un minibus Volkswagen. Ils ont un grand chien brun et un petit chat noir.

Philippe est assez petit, mais musclé. Il a les cheveux et les yeux bruns. Il a une barbe. Martine est grande et mince. En fait, elle est plus grande que Philippe. Elle a les cheveux très longs. Ses yeux sont verts. Je trouve qu'elle est très belle.

Philippe a beaucoup d'énergie. Il adore la nature et les sports. Il voit l'avenir avec optimisme. Il est sérieux quand c'est nécessaire, mais en général il aime s'amuser. Il n'a pas beaucoup d'ambition.

Martine est moins sportive que Philippe. Elle aime rester à la maison. Elle adore les livres, la peinture et la musique. Elle espère être artiste un jour. Elle a plus de patience et moins d'énergie que Philippe.

Philippe et Martine sont frère et sœur. Mais ils sont très différents du point de vue apparence et personnalité. J'aime passer mon temps avec eux parce qu'il se passe toujours quelque chose d'intéressant.

WORKBOOK, P. 183

**V. Mini-dictée: Des rêves** You will hear a series of people tell what they would like to have or be or do. Complete their statements by writing the missing words that you hear. Each sentence will be read three times.

1. Je voudrais habiter dans <u>une jolie petite maison</u>.
2. Je voudrais avoir <u>une auto neuve allemande</u>.
3. Je voudrais être <u>une belle femme indépendante</u>.
4. Je voudrais visiter <u>un grand musée moderne</u>.
5. Je voudrais descendre dans <u>un nouvel hôtel français</u>.
6. Je voudrais acheter <u>des vieux livres intéressants</u>.

WORKBOOK, P. 183

**VI. Qui est le coupable?** You're at the airport, listening to your radio while waiting for a plane. You hear a report about a crime that has just been committed. A witness describes the criminal. You see a person in the airport who looks like the accused. Look at the drawing and put a check next to the person who looks like the criminal. Then write your own description of the person.

— Alors, Madame, vous me dites que vous avez vu le criminel?
— Mais oui. Je l'ai vu et j'ai bien noté son apparence.
— Pouvez-vous nous donner une description?
— Je vais essayer. C'est un homme avec les cheveux noirs, je pense.
— Vous n'êtes pas sûre?
— Si, si. Il a les cheveux noirs. Et ils sont courts et frisés.
— Est-ce qu'il est grand ou petit?
— Attendez. Il est... voyons... grand. Et il doit aimer le soleil.
— Pourquoi vous dites ça?
— Parce qu'il est très bronzé. Moi aussi, j'aime le soleil. C'est pour ça que j'ai remarqué...
— Madame... je vous en prie... continuez votre description.
— Oui. Bon... où est-ce que j'en étais. Voilà... il a le visage très rond, comme un ballon, un peu bizarre... et

un grand nez. Il n'est pas beau du tout. Et une moustache. Moi, je n'aime pas les moustaches.
— Et c'est tout?
— Euh... voyons... Il est grand, je vous ai dit ça? Et il est très mince. Comme une asperge!

WORKBOOK, P. 184

**VII. L'argot des étudiants** French students, like students of all nations, use slang (**argot**) to talk about school and university life. Listen to the following conversation between two French university students and try to pick out the slang expressions listed below. Following the conversation, the expressions will be explained. Write each term's equivalent in "standard" French in the space provided.

Deux étudiants, Patrick et Annie, se retrouvent dans le hall de l'université. Écoutons leur conversation.

— Hé, Patrick! Bonjour!
— Tiens, Annie. Salut, ça va? Qu'est-ce que tu deviens? Ça fait longtemps que je ne t'ai pas vue.
— Mon pauvre, j'ai un de ces boulots! Je passe mes journées le nez dans les bouquins. J'ai un examen demain en histoire. Et toi, comment vas-tu?
— Oh, j'ai un cours de philosophie qui est vachement dur.
— Qui est ton prof? C'est Duvigny, n'est-ce pas? On dit qu'il fait vraiment bosser ses étudiants.
— C'est exact. J'ai deux mémoires à remettre la semaine prochaine. Écoute. J'ai rendez-vous à midi trente avec Bruno au restau U. Tu veux bouffer avec nous?
— Je voudrais bien, mais il faut que j'aille à la librairie. À propos, est-ce que je peux te taper un peu d'argent? J'ai un bouquin à acheter et j'ai oublié de toucher un chèque.
— Combien tu veux? J'ai 50 francs sur moi.
— Vingt francs, c'est suffisant. Merci. Je te les rendrai demain. Allez, au revoir.
— Salut.

Maintenant traduisons en bon francais l'argot de Patrick et d'Annie. Le «boulot», c'est le «travail». Quand on dit qu'on a du boulot, ça veut dire qu'on a beaucoup de travail à faire. Un «bouquin», c'est un «livre». Quand on a le nez dans les bouquins, on étudie beaucoup. «Vachement» a le sens de «très»,. Si quelque chose est vachement bien, c'est très bien. Si c'est vachement dur, c'est très difficile. «Bosser», c'est un verbe qui veut dire «travailler beaucoup». S'il faut bosser, il est nécessaire de travailler dur. Le «restau U», c'est le «restaurant universitaire». Les étudiants peuvent y prendre des repas à des prix raisonnables. «Bouffer» veut dire «manger». On peut inviter quelqu'un à déjeuner ou à dîner en disant: «Tu veux bouffer?» «Taper», c'est pareil qu'«emprunter». Quand on veut qu'un copain nous prête quelque chose, on demande si on peut lui taper ce dont on a besoin.

## CHAPITRE 7

### SEGMENT 3

WORKBOOK, P. 184

**I. Quatre étudiants**
**A.** You will hear French students talk about their studies and their lives as students in France. Listen to the tape, then indicate (1) whether each student goes to school in Paris or in a regional university, and (2) whether (in American terms) each student specializes in fine arts, humanities, natural sciences, or social sciences.

—Je suis étudiante à l'Université de Jussieu, à Paris. Je fais des études de sciences physiques. Alors, j'ai des cours d'optique, de thermodynamique, d'électricité. Je vis dans un studio à Montparnasse et plus tard, j'aimerais donner des cours de physique.

—Je suis étudiant en musique au Conservatoire de Paris. Évidemment, je prends des cours de piano avec un professeur célèbre. Je prends aussi des cours d'orchestration et aussi des cours de solfège. Dans l'avenir, j'aimerais faire des tournées avec le célèbre Orchestre National de Paris.

—Je suis étudiante à l'Université de Nice. J'habite à la résidence universitaire et je fais des études littéraires. Je travaille surtout sur Balzac. Je prépare un mémoire sur le thème de Paris dans les romans de Balzac. Plus tard, j'aimerais bien devenir prof de français, c'est-à-dire enseigner surtout la littérature dans le lycée; et ben, j'espère réussir. Pour le moment, j'aime beaucoup ce que je fais. Mes cours m'intéressent, les professeurs sont vraiment très intéressants. Je suis très contente de ma vie actuelle.

—Je suis étudiante à Strasbourg. J'habite dans une famille et je me spécialise en lettres. Mais tout particulièrement, je fais des cours d'histoire et de dialectes, car l'alsacien est très populaire dans cette région. Éventuellement, j'aimerais étudier toutes les différentes régions en France.

## CHAPITRE 8

### SEGMENT 1

**Prononciation: La consonne *l*** (text, p. 305)

**Prononciation: La combinaison *ll*** (text, p. 316)

**Prononciation: La combinaison *ill* après une voyelle** (text, p. 326)

## CHAPITRE 8

### SEGMENT 2

WORKBOOK, P. 209

**I. Un accident** Listen to the story of Michel's accident. Then circle the drawing that best represents what happened.

Tu sais... Michel a eu un accident. Non, non, ce n'était pas trop grave. Mais tout de même, il a eu bien peur. Vendredi dernier il allait à l'école, il a commencé à traverser la rue quand il a été renversé par un motocycliste qui allait très vite. Michel a été blessé à la tête et au bras. On l'a transporté à l'hôpital où on s'est occupé de ses blessures. Non, non, il n'y a pas passé la nuit. Il est chez lui maintenant et il doit retourner à l'école demain ou après-demain.

WORKBOOK, P. 210

**II. Quel verbe?** Listen for the verb *that is conjugated* in each of the sentences. Then identify it by writing its infinitive.

*MODÈLE:* You hear:   Est-ce que tu vas sortir ce soir?
            You write: *aller*

1. Je ne peux pas sortir ce soir.
2. Ils doivent aller à la banque et à la charcuterie.
3. Je voudrais bien voir ce film avec vous.
4. Vous savez utiliser cet ordinateur?
5. Tu vas nous retrouver au stade, d'accord?
6. Comment? Elle ne veut pas y aller?
7. Elle a dû avoir des problèmes à la maison.
8. Je ne savais pas le nom du directeur.
9. Ils devaient arriver avant nous.
10. Pourquoi est-ce qu'elle ne voulait pas lui parler?
11. Malheureusement je n'ai pas pu les voir.
12. De toute façon, nous n'avions pas l'intention de l'acheter.

WORKBOOK, P. 210

**III. Pouvez-vous les identifier?** You will hear physical descriptions of six people. As you listen to each description, write the person's initials under the appropriate drawing.

NAMES:
Sophie Delpoux
Ahmed Fazoul
François Gélin
Roger Grignet
Juliette Marchand
Marcelle Waggonner

Juliette Marchand est une jeune femme de 25 ans. Quand elle était jeune, elle mangeait beaucoup et les autres enfants se moquaient d'elle. Mais elle a suivi un régime, elle a beaucoup maigri et elle est maintenant très jolie.

Quand Roger Grignet était jeune, il jouait beaucoup au football. Mais il s'est fait mal au dos, il ne peut plus travailler et depuis quelque temps il mange beaucoup et il grossit.

François Gélin est un homme d'affaires qui a réussi. Il travaille très dur—de 8h du matin jusqu'à 10h du soir. Il a 45 ans, mais il a l'air d'un homme de 60 ans—c'est-à-dire qu'il a beaucoup vieilli.

Marcelle Waggonner a 65 ans, mais elle fait de l'exercice tous les jours. Par conséquent, elle garde la ligne et elle a l'air beaucoup plus jeune que son âge.

Ahmed Fazoul habite un pays très pauvre. Comme ses frères et sœurs, il a très peu à manger et il maigrit. C'est vraiment tragique de voir maigrir les enfants.

Sophie Delpoux a 18 ans. Quand elle est née, elle était toute petite. Mais à l'âge de deux ans, elle a commencé à grandir... et elle a continué à grandir. Aujourd'hui, elle est plus grande que ses parents.

WORKBOOK, P. 211

**IV. Dictée: Discussion à table** The Cazenave family is eating dinner when they notice that the youngest child, Bernard, is not acting like his usual self. Write their conversation. The conversation will be read once at normal speed. Then each sentence will be read twice.

— Maman, Bemard ne mange pas.
— Bemard, qu'est-ce qu'il y a? Tu ne te sens pas bien, mon petit?
— Non, Maman. J'ai mal à la gorge. Je vais me coucher.
— C'est bien. Va te coucher. J'arrive tout de suite pour prendre ta température.
— Ce garçon est toujours malade. On téléphone au médecin?

— Non. C'est une petite grippe. Ce n'est pas grave.
— Je vais aller à la pharmacie chercher des pastilles pour la gorge.
— Si tu veux.
— Moi, je me sens très bien, Maman. Je peux manger le dessert de Bernard?

WORKBOOK, P. 212

**V. Que dit le médecin?** You are traveling in France with your brother and sister when they become ill. Because they don't speak French, you have explained their symptoms to the doctor. As you listen to the doctor's advice and instructions, take notes in English. You will probably not understand every word; the important thing is to get the gist of the information.

J'ai examiné votre sœur. Je peux vous rassurer. Ce n'est pas très grave, pas grave du tout. Elle a eu une crise de foie. Vous ne savez pas ce que c'est? Eh bien, ça veut dire qu'elle a eu un petit problème digestif. Elle n'a sans doute pas l'habitude de la cuisine française. Vous allez dire à votre sœur de boire de l'eau minérale et de ne pas manger de matières grasse—pas de saucisses et de saucisson, pas de jambon, pas de beurre, pas de fromage. Elle se sentira mieux dans deux ou trois jours.

Ne vous inquiétez pas. Votre frère, il est enrhumé. Rien de grave. Je vais lui donner quelque chose pour la gorge—des pastilles, peut-être. Je lui conseille de l'aspirine aussi. Non, non, il vaut mieux prendre un antihistaminique. C'est ça. Je lui donne un antihistaminique. Il doit prendre un cachet le matin et un autre le soir.

WORKBOOK, P. 212

**VI. Vous êtes témoin d'un accident** You are one of four witnesses (**témoins**) to an accident. When the police arrive, the three other witnesses, who are native speakers of French, explain what happened; however, their versions do not agree. Compare the three stories with the picture and circle the number of the most accurate description. Although there will be words you do not recognize, you should be able to tell the police which witness to rely on.

— Je m'appelle Claude Berger. Ma profession? Je suis avocat. Oui, j'ai vu l'accident. Je parlais avec des amis au café et j'ai vu une auto qui allait lentement. Elle avait le feu vert, mais elle roulait très lentement. Je ne sais pas pourquoi. Tout à coup, un vélomoteur est arrivé. Il allait très rapidement. Un jeune homme et une femme, oui. Ils s'embrassaient, je crois, ou ils parlaient. Mais de toute façon ils avaient le feu rouge et ils ne se sont pas arrêtés. C'est ça, ils ne se sont pas arrêtés, et ils ont brûlé le feu rouge. Oui, oui. Combien de blessés? Trois, je crois... oui, trois: le jeune homme s'est cassé le bras, son amie s'est fait mal à la jambe, je pense, et l'automobiliste, lui, il semblait avoir mal au cou.

— Je m'appelle Jean-Pierre. Mon nom de famille? Dupassage. 19 ans. Étudiant. Oui, j'ai vu l'accident. J'sais pas, moi. Je ne faisais pas vraiment attention, mais... Je pense que ce monsieur-là, lui, il ne regardait pas, je n'sais pas ce qu'il faisait, mais il n'a pas vu le feu rouge. Il a foncé... oui, il a brûlé le feu rouge... et il a renversé le vélomoteur. Oui, oui, y avait deux personnes—un mec et sa nana. Comment? Oh, un jeune homme et sa petite amie. Bien sûr qu'ils ont été blessés. Le type, je veux dire, le jeune homme, il s'est fait mal au cou, la fille s'est cassé le bras. L'automobiliste? Non, il n'avait rien, lui, rien du tout. Mais il était furieux! Comment? Ah, oui, y avait une femme qui traversait la rue et qui est tombée... elle s'est foulé la cheville, je crois.

— Mon nom? Hélène Doublet. Je suis professeur de philosophie. Oui, j'ai bien vu l'accident. Je sais exactement ce qui s'est passé. Les deux jeunes étudiants à vélomoteur attendaient que le feu passe au vert. Au feu vert, ils ont commencé à traverser et un monsieur qui conduisait une grosse voiture les a renversés. Oui, j'en suis certaine. Eux, ils avaient le feu vert. C'est le monsieur qui ne s'est pas arrêté. Il y a eu trois blessés: la jeune femme s'est cassé le bras, le jeune homme s'est fait mal au cou et l'automobiliste, lui, était en état de choc. Il n'est pas descendu de sa voiture. Il est resté là à répéter: «Oh, qu'est-ce que j'ai mal au dos... Qu'est-ce que j'ai mal au dos... »

## CHAPITRE 8

### SEGMENT 3

Workbook, p. 213

#### I. Deux conversations

**A.** You will first hear a conversation about health. Three people are involved, directly or indirectly—Catherine, Michèle, and Catherine's brother. Indicate which person matches each of the following descriptions.

### Dialogue 1

A: Bonjour, Catherine! Comment vas-tu?

B: Salut, Michèle. Ça va. Et toi?

A: Oh... Moi, ça va pas très bien tu sais. J'ai mal dans le dos, j'ai mal à la tête, j'ai mal dans le ventre, beuh... j'ai vraiment mal partout. Je me sens... constamment fatiguée. Mais... et toi, tu as l'air vraiment en pleine forme, dis donc!

B: Ah oui, moi c'est la pleine forme. Je fais un régime. Je fais du sport, je mange beaucoup de légumes frais et... j'ai mal nulle part. Ça va très bien.

A: Oh, quelle chance tu as! Mais comment va ton frère?

B: Alors lui, c'est la catastrophe totale! Il y a deux semaines il a eu un accident de voiture et il est resté pendant une semaine à l'hôpital. Mais... je crois que ça va aller mieux maintenant.

A: Ah bon! Mais qu'est-ce qu'il a eu exactement?

B: Oh, il s'est blessé à la jambe.

A: Oh! Mais j'espère qu'il va aller beaucoup mieux maintenant.

B: Oui, j'espère.

**B.** Now listen to the second conversation, which takes place in a pharmacy. Tell where the customer's main medical problem is situated.

### Dialogue 2

— Bonjour, Madame, est-ce que je peux vous aider?

— Oh, oui, je me sens très mal!

— Ah bon, qu'est-ce qui ne va pas?

— J'ai mal à la tête. J'ai le vertige. J'ai envie de vomir...

— Oh, oh, on dirait une grippe intestinale, hein!

— C'est possible, je crois que j'ai mangé quelque chose de mauvais hier soir.

— Bon, ben écoutez, hein, on va vous donner une tisane de tilleul, hein. On va vous donner aussi de l'aspirine évidemment, si vous avez mal à la tête. Euh, un peu de vitamine C pour vous donner de l'énergie, hein, et surtout, surtout pendant quarante-huit heures ne buvez pas d'alcool ni de café, ni de lait.

— Est-ce que je peux boire des jus de fruits?

— Oui, pas de problème avec le jus de fruits. Oui, oui, vous pouvez.

— Bon.

— D'accord?

— D'accord, merci, Monsieur.

— Au revoir, Madame.

# NOTES

FOURTH EDITION

ALLONS-Y!
LE FRANÇAIS PAR ÉTAPES

▼ ▼ ▼ ▼ ▼ ▼ ▼ ▼ ▼ ▼ ▼ ▼ ▼ ▼ ▼ ▼ ▼ ▼ ▼ ▼ ▼ ▼ ▼ ▼ ▼

**JEANNETTE D. BRAGGER**
The Pennsylvania State University

**DONALD B. RICE**
Hamline University

**HH** Heinle & Heinle Publishers
I T P An International Thomson Publishing Company
Boston, Massachusetts 02116 USA

The publication of **Allons-y! Fourth Edition** was directed by the members of the Heinle & Heinle French, German, and Russian Publishing Team:

Elizabeth Holthaus and Stan Galek, Team Leaders
Wendy Nelson, Editorial Director
Amy R. Terrell, Market Development Director
Gabrielle B. McDonald, Production Services Coordinator

Also participating in the publication of this program were:

| | |
|---|---|
| Publisher: | Stan Galek |
| Director of Production: | Elizabeth Holthaus |
| Managing Developmental Editor: | Amy Lawler |
| Project Manager: | Anita L. Raducanu/A+ Publishing Services |
| Photo/Video Specialist: | Jonathan Stark |
| Associate Editor: | Diana Bohmer |
| Associate Market Development Director: | Melissa Tingley |
| Production Assistant: | Lisa Winkler |
| Manufacturing Coordinator: | Barbara Stephan |
| Photo Coordinators: | Jerry Christopher |
| | Martha Leibs-Heckly |
| Illustrators: | Devera Ehrenberg |
| | Jane O'Conor |
| | Len Shalansky |
| Interior Designers: | Marsha Cohen |
| | ImageSet Design |
| Cover Illustrator: | Nicole Hupin-Otis |
| Cover Designer: | Mark E. Caleb |

Library of Congress Cataloging-in-Publication Data

Bragger, Jeannette D.
    Allons-y! : le français par étapes / Jeannette D. Bragger, Donald
Rice. -- 4th ed.
      p.   cm.
    ISBN 0-8384-6449-1
    1. French language--Textbooks for foreign speakers--English.
I. Rice, Donald, 1937–    . II. Title.
PC2129.E5B65   1995
448.2'421--dc20                                    95-42316
                                                   CIP

Manufactured in the United States of America

ISBN: 0-8384-6449-1 (student text)
ISBN: 0-8384-6454-8 (instructor's annotated edition package: 2-volume set)

10  9  8  7  6  5  4  3  2  1

# TABLE DES MATIÈRES

## PREMIÈRE PARTIE

*Mireille Loiseau*
*Paris, France*

*Michel Kerguézec*
*Locmariaquer, France*

*Véronique Béziers*
*Tarascon, France*

## CHAPITRE QUATRE • Allons en ville!     126

*Masslya Fodéba*
*Dakar, Sénégal*

## DEUXIÈME PARTIE

**Intégration culturelle • PARIS EN IMAGES**                                  168

## CHAPITRE CINQ • Amusons-nous!                                              172

*Claire Maurant*
*Strasbourg, France*

*Madame Thibaudet*
*Bordeaux, France*

*Jean Hébert*
*Lyon, France*

## CHAPITRE HUIT • Soignons-nous!     298

*M. Ahmed Abdiba*
*Fès, Maroc*

## TROISIÈME PARTIE

## Intégration culturelle • LA FRANCE EN IMAGES — 340

## CHAPITRE NEUF • Faisons des études à l'étranger! — 344

*Peter Robidoux*
*Baton Rouge, Louisiane*

## CHAPITRE DIX • Installons-nous!                            388

*Anne et Yves Coron*
*Caen, France*

*Marie-Claude Étienne*
*Pointe-à-Pitre, Gaudeloupe*

*François Maillet
Toulouse, France*

*Isabelle et Martine Moix*
*Lausanne, Suisse*

*René Délavenne*
*Trois Rivières, Québec*

## MAPS

# PREFACE TO THE STUDENT EDITION

▼▼▼▼▼▼▼▼▼▼▼▼▼▼▼▼▼▼▼▼▼

*ALLONS-Y! Le français par étapes,* Fourth Edition, is an integrated learning system designed to provide beginning-level students with immediately useful language skills in French. It is comprised of a mutually supporting network of learning components:

- a textbook (with student edition annotations)
- a workbook
- student audio tapes and CDs
- a special Instructor's Annotated Edition (conveniently divided into two paperback booklets)
- instructor's audio tapes
- a new culture-based video program
- a testing program in two formats: printed and computerized
- computer software: *Système-D 2.1: Writing Assistant for French*
- multimedia computer software: *Nouvelles dimensions*
- a resource manual for instructors
- an Instructor's Resource Kit

Together, these components provide students with unprecedented opportunities for listening to, speaking, reading, and writing French. They also open up the classroom and language lab to the sights and sounds of the French-speaking world.

Because we are convinced that creative use of language is possible from the outset, we have developed a program that allows for maximum interaction among students and between students and instructors, beginning with the preliminary lessons. Interaction is based on tasks to be accomplished and on effective linguistic functioning in the types of situations likely to be encountered in real life. We have tried to put into practice the principles set forth in the ACTFL Proficiency Guidelines so that we may help students function as accurately as possible in a variety of contexts.

By retaining the best of the Third Edition, and by making changes on the basis of the suggestions of numerous users, we have tried to insure that the Fourth Edition of *ALLONS-Y!* will be even more useable and exciting than the first.

## To the Student

As you begin to use the French language, you will quickly discover that your interaction with French speakers or your classmates need not be postponed to some unspecified point in the future. It might help convince you of this to know that of the 80,000 words found in the French language, the average French person uses only about 800 on a daily basis. *Therefore, the most important task ahead of you is not to **accumulate** as much knowledge as possible about French grammar and vocabulary, but to **use** what you do know as effectively and as creatively as you can.*

Communication in a foreign language means understanding what others say and transmitting your own messages in such a way as to avoid misunderstandings. As you learn to do this, you will make the kinds of errors that are necessary to language learning. Consequently, errors should be seen by you as a positive step toward effective communication. They advance rather than hinder you in your efforts.

In using the Fourth Edition of *ALLONS-Y!*, you may be interested to learn about the capabilities of version 2.1 of the award-winning software program **Système-D:** *Writing Assistant for French,* since it is with this software in mind that we constructed the open-ended composition exercises found in the Workbook. **Système-D'**s array of on-line tools include:

- a bilingual dictionary of more than 8,000 entries complete with examples of usage
- a verb conjugator that can call up over 500,000 conjugated verb forms
- an on-line reference grammar
- an index to functional phrases
- sets of thematically related vocabulary items

An on-line word processor enables you to capture the fruits of your labors in an electronic file that, when printed out, provides both you and your instructor with a legible product.

## Acknowledgments

We would like to thank the following people at Heinle & Heinle Publishers who worked closely with us on the Fourth Edition of *ALLONS-Y!*: Charles H. Heinle, Stan Galek, Elizabeth Holthaus, Wendy Nelson, Amy Lawler, and Diana Bohmer. We would also like to thank: Gabrielle B. McDonald, Production Coordinator; Lisa Winkler, Production Assistant; Amy Terrell, Market Development Director; Melissa Tingley, Associate Market Director; and Jonathan Stark, Photo/Video Specialist.

In addition, we would like to thank: our project manager, Anita Raducanu of A+ Publishing Services: the artists Devera Ehrenberg, Jane O'Conor, and Len Shalansky; and the photographer Stuart Cohen.

We would like to acknowledge the contributions of the following colleagues who reviewed the Third Edition and made excellent suggestions for revisions:

- Elizabeth T. Blount, University of South Carolina
- Mary Ellen Scullen, University of Louisville
- Kenneth H. Rogers, University of Rhode Island
- Amber Landis, Illinois State University
- Wendy Pfeffer, University of Louisville
- Denise Phillippe, Ohio State University
- Catherine Marin, Georgia Tech University
- Susan Hendrickson, Arizona State University

Finally, our special thanks, as always, go to Baiba and Mary, who continue to support and encourage us during the many hours spent in front of the computers. As for Alexander, whose arrival on the scene preceded that of the First Edition by only a few months, he's now working on Chapter 12. He has been joined by Hilary who is making her way through Chapter 7. At this pace, they will both finish *ALLONS-Y!* in time to go to college!

J.D.B.
D.B.R.

# Première Partie

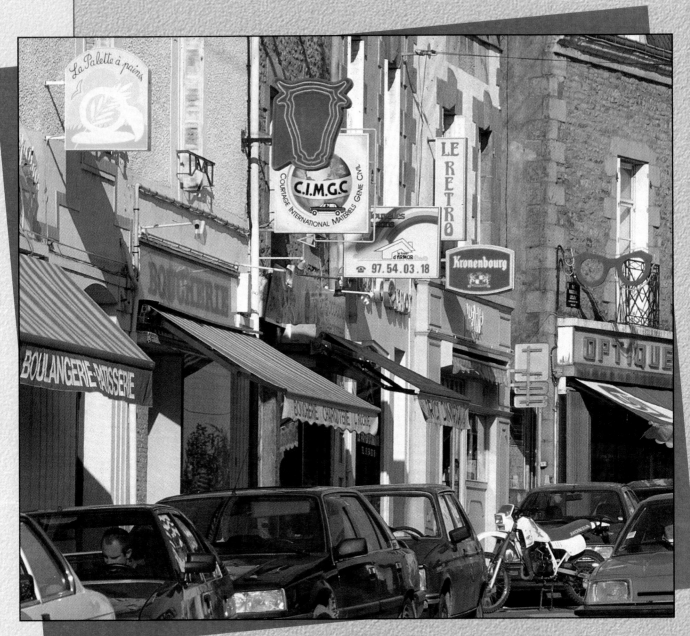

*Although you are just beginning to study French, can you already understand any of the signs shown on the stores in this typical French city?*

# Étape préliminaire

**ÉTAPE SUPPORT MATERIALS** (STUDENT)

**Cahier:** pp. 1–8

 **Student Tape:**
Étape préliminaire

---

ÉTAPE SUPPORT
MATERIALS (INSTRUCTOR)

 Transparencies:
EP-1a, 1b, 2a, 2b

Resource Manual:
The Resource Manual
includes a series of alternative
Étapes préliminaires that
may be used in place of or in
addition to the one in the textbook. See the Instructor's
Guide in this Instructor's
Annotated Edition for more
detailed information.

 Instructor's Tape:
Étape préliminaire,
Student Text, p. 7

 Multimedia:
See the Resource
Manual for correlation
to our multimedia
product.

Like the learning of most skills, the learning of French requires *attention, practice,* and *patience.* It also requires that you abandon any general misconceptions you may have and change certain habits associated with speaking English. The following introductory exercises will demonstrate some basic language principles involved in learning French.

**A.** Draw the picture suggested by each word.

1. a window

2. a loaf of bread

3. a washcloth

You probably drew a picture of a window that slides up and down; a French person would more likely draw a window that opens out. Your bread probably had the form of a rectangular loaf; the French person's bread would be a long, thin **baguette** or a round **pain de campagne.** And you would probably not be able to slide your hand *into* the washcloth you drew as you could with a French **gant de toilette** *(wash glove).*

- *Basic principle 1: Languages are culture-specific. Words exist to express notions relevant to a particular culture.*

**B.**   Give an idiomatic version of each awkward phrase.

1.  You can me see?
2.  I me brush the teeth.
3.  I have shame to it admit.
4.  She is mounted into the bus.

Each of the preceding sentences is a word-for-word translation of a French sentence. Although it is possible to convey the same idea in both French and English, word order and word choice differ.

- *Basic principle 2: It is not possible to translate word for word from French to English or from English to French. You must find the equivalent structure in each language.*

**C.**   Listen to your instructor say each sentence.

1.  Je ne sais pas pourquoi.
2.  Est-ce que vous avez un stylo?
3.  Ce ne sont pas mes gants.
4.  Il est déjà parti, non?

You will notice that, although each written sentence has at least five words, the spoken sentence sounds almost like one long word. You will also notice that certain sounds "slide together" with the sounds that follow them and that other sounds are dropped entirely.

- *Basic principle 3: French is spoken in groups of words. You should learn to listen for the group rather than for isolated words. If you try to listen in English (that is, translate as you go), you will rapidly get lost. Try hard to listen in French.*

**D.**   Repeat the English vowels *a, e, i, o, u.* Watch other people in the class repeat the same vowels. Now watch your instructor pronounce the French vowels **a, e, i, o, u.** Say this English sentence: "What are you going to do next summer?" Now watch your instructor say the equivalent French sentence: **Qu'est-ce que tu vas faire l'été prochain?** You will probably have noticed that your instructor's mouth moves more distinctly in pronouncing French than do the mouths of people speaking English.

- *Basic principle 4: You cannot speak French with a "lazy" mouth. Learn to open and close your mouth, to spread and round your lips as a particular sound requires.*

**E.**   Pronounce each English word.

roof / aunt / tomato / either / route

There is probably a certain amount of variation in the way you and your classmates pronounce these words. Yet whether you say [rŏof] or [rōof], the word remains comprehensible. However, if you were to allow the same vowel variation in *full* and *fool,* there would certainly be confusion.

- *Basic principle 5: Certain sounds, called phonemes, contrast with each other to create the distinctions necessary to form meaning. Learn to articulate the phonemes of French as correctly as possible.*

The first twelve chapters of this book will give you practice in recognizing and articulating the phonemes of French. In addition, the preliminary exercises on the Student Tape provide a quick introduction to the basic sounds you will need.

**F.**   Pronounce each English word.

night / through / knave / knowledge / doubt

In each case, certain letters are not pronounced. This situation occurs even more frequently in French. Listen to your instructor pronounce the following French words.

mais / champ / lisent / prend / peine

Very often a letter is silent in French when it falls at the end of a word. In addition, the letter **h** is never pronounced.

homme / honnête / hôtel

■   *Basic principle 6: There is no one-to-one correspondence between spoken and written French. As a general rule, the spoken form is shorter and simpler than the written.*

The pronunciation exercises in the first eleven chapters of the book will also help you to learn to recognize the relationships between sound and spelling in French.

**G.**   Try to guess the English meanings of the following French words.

| | | | | |
|---|---|---|---|---|
| imaginer | important | vérifier | catholique | délicieux |
| musicien | pharmacie | optimiste | naturel | profession |

Now do the same with these French words.

wagon / lecture / car / figure / rester / demander

You were undoubtedly able to guess almost all of the words in the first group; these are called *cognates.* Thanks to the large number of cognates between French and English, you begin your study of French with a considerable vocabulary. However, the words in the second group are *false cognates* (the French call them **faux amis,** or *false friends*). A **wagon** is not a wagon, but a *railroad car;* a **lecture** is a *reading,* not a lecture; a **car** is a *bus,* not an automobile. Your **figure** is your *face,* not your figure. **Rester** does not mean to rest, but rather *to stay,* and **demander** means *to ask for,* not to demand. Therefore, although there are hundreds of cognates, beware of false friends.

■   *Basic principle 7: There are many similarities between French and English vocabulary. However, always check an apparent cognate to see if it makes sense in its context.*

**H.**   Point out the spelling differences between these cognates.

theater / **théâtre**    facade / **façade**    premier / **première**

Although the letters of the French alphabet are the same as those of the English alphabet, French uses *diacritic marks* (sometimes called accent marks), which have two basic purposes:

1.   to distinguish between words that are pronounced the same but have different meanings (example: **ou** = *or,* **où** = *where*);
2.   to identify the different pronunciations of the same letter (example: the **c** of **local** is pronounced [k]; the **ç** of **français** is pronounced [s]).

The most frequently used diacritics are:

| | |
|---|---|
| **Accent aigu** (*acute accent*) | Used above the letter **e** to signal the closed vowel [e]: **été** |
| **Accent grave** (*grave accent*) | Used above the letter **e** to signal the open vowel sound [ɛ]: **père;** used above the vowels **a** and **u** to distinguish between like-sounding words—**la, là; ou, où** |
| **Accent circonflexe** (*circumflex*) | Used above a vowel to indicate the disappearance of an **s** from the earlier form of the word: **château, fête, maître, hôte, coût** |
| **Cédille** (*cedilla*) | Used below the letter **c** before **a, o,** or **u** when the consonant is pronounced [s]: **leçon** |

■ *Basic principle 8: A French word is not spelled correctly unless its diacritic marks are in place.*

Now that you have these principles in mind, it's time to begin learning some French. **Allons-y!**

# P R E M I È R E   É T A P E

## Point de départ

▼▼▼▼▼▼▼▼▼▼▼▼▼

*Allons au café!*

—**S'il vous plaît,** *Monsieur...*
—*Un moment, Madame... Oui, Madame,*
   *vous désirez?*
—*Un express, s'il vous plaît.*

—*Voilà... Un express **pour** Madame.*
—*Merci, Monsieur.*
—**Je vous en prie,** *Madame.*

please / for

you're welcome

### LES BOISSONS CHAUDES

un café crème
un thé nature

un express    un café au lait
un thé citron    un thé au lait

### LA BIÈRE ET LE VIN

une bière française
un kir

un demi     une bière
allemande
un verre
de rouge    un verre
de blanc

Instructor's Tape:
Allons au café!

Suggestion, Point de départ:
Dramatize the mini-dialogue;
have students repeat, books
closed; have students repeat,
looking at text; have students
read, then recreate the dialogue. Present beverage alternatives, using the transparency of hot and cold drinks.

*Allons au café!:* Let's go to
   the café!

Transparencies:
EP-1a, 1b, 2a, 2b
(hot and cold bever-
ages)

**Culture:** If you order simply **un café,** you will get **un
express**—black, fairly
strong coffee. If you want a
cup of coffee with cream,
order **un café crème. Un
café au lait,** normally
served at breakfast, con-
tains roughly equal parts of
coffee and steamed milk.

This vocabulary is further
explained on p. 8.

LES BOISSONS FROIDES NON-ALCOOLISÉES

un Coca • un Orangina • une limonade • un Perrier • un Vittel • un lait fraise • une menthe à l'eau • un citron pressé • un diabolo citron

**Vocabulary:** Like **Coca,** the words **Orangina, Perrier,** and **Vittel** are registered trademarks and thus must be capitalized.

**allemande**   German
**au lait**   with milk
**blanc**   white
**un citron pressé**   lemonade; **une orange pressée**   orangeade
**un demi**   draught beer
**un diabolo citron**   **limonade** mixed with lemon-flavored syrup;
   **limonade** may also be mixed with other flavors—**un diabolo menthe**
   (mint), **un diabolo fraise** (strawberry)
**un kir**   white wine with black currant liqueur
**un lait fraise**   milk with strawberry syrup
**une limonade**   sweet, carbonated lemon-tasting soft drink
**une menthe à l'eau**   water with mint syrup
**nature**   plain, unflavored
**un Orangina**   brand of carbonated orange-flavored soft drink
**un Perrier**   brand of carbonated mineral water
**rouge**   red
**un thé citron**   tea with lemon
**un verre**   glass
**un Vittel**   brand of non-carbonated mineral water

## À VOUS! (Exercices de vocabulaire)

Ex. A: ⇄

**Variation,** Ex. A: Books closed; use the transparency of hot and cold drinks with overlay; point to choices.

**A.**   Order the suggested beverages.

> *Modèle:*      un café crème
>    —*Vous désirez, Mademoiselle (Monsieur, Madame)?*
>    —*Un café crème, s'il vous plaît.*

1. un Coca   2. un thé citron   3. un kir   4. une limonade
5. un Orangina   6. un thé nature   7. un express   8. un verre de rouge
9. une bière allemande   10. un demi   11. un citron pressé   12. un Perrier
13. un lait fraise   14. un verre de blanc   15. une orange pressée
16. une menthe à l'eau   17. une bière française   18. un thé au lait
19. un diabolo citron

**B.** Get the waiter's attention and order a drink of your choice.

*Modèle:*   —*S'il vous plaît, Monsieur (Madame).*
—*Oui, Monsieur (Mademoiselle, Madame), vous désirez?*
—*Un demi (un express, un diabolo fraise), s'il vous plaît.*

**C.** Play the role of waiter or customer in the following situation. The customer orders what he or she wishes to drink; the waiter brings the wrong beverage.

*Modèle:*   GARÇON:   *Vous désirez?*
CLIENTE:   *Un thé au lait, s'il vous plaît.*
GARÇON:   *Voilà, Mademoiselle... un thé citron.*
CLIENTE:   *Non, Monsieur... un thé au lait.*
GARÇON:   *Ah, pardon, Mademoiselle, un thé au lait.*
CLIENTE:   *Merci, Monsieur.*
GARÇON:   *Je vous en prie, Mademoiselle.*

## L · E · X · I · Q · U · E

Ex. B: ⇄
**Suggestion,** Ex. B: You play the role of waiter; each student must get the waiter's attention and order a drink. Students are not allowed to repeat an order until all drinks have been mentioned.
**Follow-up,** Ex. B: If your students have already learned numbers (alternative **Étape préliminaire**), allow them to order what they wish. Ask everyone to keep track of orders, then summarize at end: **trois limonades, cinq diabolos citron,** etc.
Ex. C: ⇄
**Follow-up,** Ex. C: Students do the exercise in pairs, alternating roles.

**À faire chez vous** *(To do at home):* **CAHIER / Étape préliminaire**

At the end of each chapter you will find the **Lexique,** a list of words and expressions in the chapter. Each list is divided into three parts: **Pour se débrouiller** *(To get along)*—expressions used to accomplish the communicative acts emphasized in the chapter; **Thèmes et contextes**—words related to the context of the chapter and organized into thematic groups; and **Vocabulaire général**—other nouns, verbs, adjectives, etc., presented in the chapter.

To review chapter vocabulary, read each word and expression aloud and see if you can associate the correct meaning with it. Mark each word or expression whose meaning you do not know and consult the glossary at the end of the book.

**Pour se débrouiller**

*Pour s'adresser à une personne*
Madame
Mademoiselle
Monsieur

*Pour commander une boisson*
S'il vous plaît...
Vous désirez?

*Pour être poli*
Je vous en prie.
Merci.
Pardon.

**Thèmes et contextes**

*Les boissons alcoolisées*
une bière allemande
une bière française
un demi
un kir
un verre de blanc
un verre de rouge

*Les boissons chaudes*
un café
un café au lait
un café crème
un express
un thé au lait
un thé citron
un thé nature

*Les boissons froides non-alcoolisées*
un citron pressé
un Coca
un diabolo citron
un diabolo fraise
un diabolo menthe
un lait fraise
une limonade
une menthe à l'eau
une orange pressée
un Orangina
un Perrier
un Vittel

*Le café*
Allons au café!
un(e) client(e)
un garçon (de café)

Mireille Loiseau
Paris (Île de France),
France

—On va prendre quelque chose?
—Oui, je voudrais bien un Coca.

# Allons prendre quelque chose!

## OBJECTIVES

**In this chapter, you will learn:**

- to meet and greet people;
- to get something to eat and drink;
- to ask for and give information about basic activities;
- to hesitate in order to gain time to think;
- to read a café and a fast-food menu;
- to understand a simple conversation upon meeting someone for the first time.

### ALLONS-Y!
#### Video Program

**ACTE 1**
**FÊTE D'ANNIVERSAIRE**

Première étape   Commandons!

Deuxième étape   Parlons!

Troisième étape   Tu aimes les fast-foods?

Quatrième étape  Lecture: La Dauphine vous propose

---

**CHAPTER SUPPORT MATERIALS** (STUDENT)

**Cahier:** pp. 9–38

 **Student Tape:** Chapitre 1 Segments 1, 2, 3

---

CHAPTER SUPPORT MATERIALS (INSTRUCTOR)

 **Transparencies:** 1-1 through 1-6

 **Instructor's Tape:** Chapitre 1, Text, pp. 12, 22, 31, 46

Resource Manual: Activity Cards for Ex. H, p. 45

 **SYSTÈME-D software:** Writing activities for this chapter are found in the **Cahier:** Rédigeons! (p. 36).

 Multimedia: See the Resource Manual for correlation to our multimedia product.

---

Objectives: Note that the objectives include statements about speaking, listening, and reading. The main grammar points of the chapter are embedded within these objectives.

# PREMIÈRE ÉTAPE
## Point de départ

▼ ▼ ▼ ▼ ▼ ▼ ▼ ▼ ▼ ▼ ▼ ▼ ▼ ▼

*Commandons!* Let's order!

breakfast

## Commandons!

### Le petit déjeuner

un café au lait     un thé au lait

un croissant     un chocolat

lunch

### Le déjeuner

with pâté (meat spread) / with cheese / open-faced grilled ham and cheese sandwich

un sandwich **au pâté**     une omelette **au fromage**     **un croque-monsieur**

with ham

un sandwich **au jambon**     une omelette au jambon

with mixed herbs / open-faced grilled ham and cheese with egg sandwich

un sandwich au fromage     une omelette **aux fines herbes**     **un croque-madame**

### Une scène au café

uh (hesitation)

Let's see (hesitation) / I'll have
also (too)

| | |
|---|---|
| ANTOINE: | S'il vous plaît, Monsieur. |
| GARÇON: | Oui. Vous désirez? |
| HÉLÈNE: | Je voudrais... **euh**... un sandwich au jambon et un thé citron. |
| GARÇON: | Et pour vous, Monsieur? |
| ANTOINE: | **Voyons**... moi, **je vais prendre** une omelette aux fines herbes... et un thé citron **aussi.** |
| GARÇON: | Merci. |

## Note culturelle

In France, people of all ages and from all walks of life frequent **cafés.** They go there for breakfast or a light lunch, to chat with friends after school and work, or simply to spend an hour or two reading the newspaper or a book and watching people walk by. In the summertime, the tables on the sidewalk in front of the café (**la terrasse**) are full. In the winter, most of the activity moves inside.

There are different kinds of cafés. On exclusive avenues such as the Champs-Élysées, you will find elegant cafés that cater primarily to tourists. There you can eat exotic ice cream or pay 30F ($7.00) for a Coke as you watch a constant parade of passersby. In the business centers of French cities, the cafés attract primarily workers and shoppers, who stop by for lunch or to relax for a moment on their way home. Near every school and university, you are sure to find cafés filled with students discussing their classes and arguing ideas. Finally, every town and city has its **cafés du coin** (neighborhood cafés). There you will find, seated at little tables or standing at the counter, a mixture of customers—factory workers discussing politics, retirees playing cards, teenagers trying their luck at pinball (**le flipper**) and other electronic games.

**Question:** What places are the equivalent of cafés in the United States?

**Le savez-vous?**
▲▲▲▲▲▲▲▲▲▲▲▲▲▲
**Approximately how many cafés are there in the city of Paris?**
a. 1,000
b. 5,000
c. 12,000

Réponse ▲▲▲

## À VOUS! (Exercices de vocabulaire)

**A.** **Qu'est-ce que tu prends?** *(What are you having?)* You and a friend are in a café. Using the words suggested, discuss what to have for lunch.

*Modèle:*   un sandwich au fromage  /  un sandwich au jambon
—*Qu'est-ce que tu prends?*
—*Euh... je voudrais un sandwich au fromage. Et toi?*
—*Voyons... moi, je vais prendre un sandwich au jambon.*

1. un sandwich au jambon  /  un croque-monsieur
2. une omelette au fromage  /  un sandwich au fromage
3. un sandwich au pâté  /  une omelette aux fines herbes
4. un croque-monsieur  /  une omelette au jambon

**B.** **Le petit déjeuner.** Order the breakfast of your choice in a café.

*Modèle:*   —*Vous désirez?*
—*Un café au lait et un croissant, s'il vous plaît.*

**Reminder,** Ex. A: In this and following exercises, if you have to pause, remember to use a filler expression (**euh, voyons**).

Ex. A: ⇄

**Variation,** Ex. A: After looking at the model, students close books and you give cues from transparency.

**Implementation,** Exs. B and C: You play the role of **garçon.**

**Expansion,** Ex. B: Give students the option of saying **Pas de croissants.**

▲▲▲   b

C.  **Le déjeuner.** With a friend, order the lunch of your choice in a café. One of your classmates will play the role of the server.

> *Modèle:*     —*Oui, Mademoiselle (Madame, Monsieur). Qu'est-ce que vous désirez?*
> —*Un sandwich au jambon et... euh... un express.*
> —*Et pour Monsieur (Mademoiselle, Madame)?*
> —*Je vais prendre une omelette au fromage et... voyons... un Perrier.*

## S·T·R·U·C·T·U·R·E

### *L'article indéfini* (**un, une, des**)

| | |
|---|---|
| **un** garçon | **une** femme *(woman)* |
| **un** café | **une** bière |
| **un** citron | **une** orange |

The English equivalents of the above nouns would be preceded by the indefinite article *a* (or *an*). In French, however, one must distinguish between the *masculine* indefinite article **un** and the *feminine* indefinite article **une.**

For an English speaker, there is nothing surprising about the fact that a waiter (**un garçon**) is masculine and a woman (**une femme**) is feminine. But it is much more startling to learn that a cup of coffee (**un café**) is masculine and a beer (**une bière**) is feminine, or that a lemon (**un citron**) is masculine while an orange (**une orange**) is feminine. All nouns in French have gender, even those that do not refer to people. Since there are no infallible rules for determining gender, it is best to associate each noun with the appropriate article from the very beginning. For example, remember **un café,** not just **café.**

Ordinarily, the **n** of **un** is not pronounced. However, when the word that follows **un** begins with a vowel or a silent **h,** the **n** is pronounced: **un‿Orangina, un‿homme** *(man)*, but **un thé.** The **n** of **une** is always pronounced.

The plural form of the indefinite articles **un** and **une** is **des. Des** is the equivalent of the English word *some:*

| | |
|---|---|
| Un café au lait, un chocolat et **des** croissants, s'il vous plaît. | A coffee with hot milk, a hot chocolate, and *some* croissants, please. |
| Moi, je voudrais une salade et **des** frites. | I'd like *a* salad and *some* french fries. |

▲  ▲  ▲

# APPLICATION

**Suggestion,** Ex. D: For structural exercises of this sort, either (1) do with whole class or (2) model with class (group or individual response), then have students work in pairs.

**Variation,** Exs. D and/or E: Books closed; use transparency of hot and cold drinks without overlay for cues.

**D.** Remplacez les mots en italique. *(Replace the italicized words.)*

1. *Un café,* s'il vous plaît. (un thé au lait / un Orangina / une limonade / un demi / une omelette au jambon / un croque-monsieur / une bière / un Coca / un kir / une menthe à l'eau / un diabolo citron)
2. Voilà, Mademoiselle... *un Perrier.* (un express / une orange pressée / un sandwich au pâté / un Vittel / un thé nature / un verre de blanc / une bière allemande / un croque-madame / une omelette aux fines herbes)
3. Pour moi, *des frites et un Coca.* (des croissants et un café au lait / une salade et des frites)

**E. Moi, je voudrais... Et toi?** Say that you would like one or some of the following items. Then ask another student about his/her choice; he/she will respond with a drink or a food item not on the list.

   *Modèle:*     café
                     —*Moi, je voudrais un café. Et toi, (Peter)?*
                     —*Moi, je vais prendre un chocolat.*

1. thé citron    2. Vittel    3. limonade    4. kir    5. frites    6. diabolo fraise
7. express    8. menthe à l'eau    9. Coca    10. croissants    11. salade
12. bière allemande    13. omelette au fromage    14. sandwich au jambon
15. croque-monsieur

# S·T·R·U·C·T·U·R·E

## Le présent des verbes réguliers en -er (1ère et 2e personnes)

| | |
|---|---|
| **Je fume** rarement. | *I rarely smoke.* |
| **Tu travailles** beaucoup. | *You work a great deal.* |
| **Nous parlons** anglais. | *We speak English.* |
| **Vous chantez** bien. | *You sing well.* |

### Subject pronouns

| English | French |
|---|---|
| *I* | **je** |
| *you* | **tu** (one person, known well) |
| *we* | **nous** |
| *you* | **vous** (one person, not known well, or two or more people) |

1. Verbs consist of two parts: a *stem,* which carries the meaning, and an *ending,* which indicates the subject.
2. In English, verb endings seldom change (with the exception of the third-person singular in the present tense—*I read,* but *she reads*). In French, verb endings are very important, since each verb ending must agree in person and number with the subject.
3. Most French verbs are regular and belong to the first conjugation—that is, their infinitive (unconjugated form) ends in **-er.** The stem is found by dropping the **-er** from the infinitive:

| *Infinitive* | *Stem* |
|---|---|
| **travailler** *(to work)* | **travaill-** |
| **parler** *(to speak)* | **parl-** |
| **voyager** *(to travel)* | **voyag-** |
| **visiter** *(to visit a place)* | **visit-** |
| **manger** *(to eat)* | **mang-** |
| **habiter** *(to live)* | **habit-** |
| **étudier** *(to study)* | **étudi-** |
| **chanter** *(to sing)* | **chant-** |
| **fumer** *(to smoke)* | **fum-** |
| **nager** *(to swim)* | **nag-** |

4. To conjugate a regular **-er** verb, add the right endings to the stem:

| Subject | Ending | Conjugated verb form | | |
|---|---|---|---|---|
| je | **-e** | je parl**e** | je mang**e** | j'habit**e** |
| tu | **-es** | tu parl**es** | tu mang**es** | tu habit**es** |
| nous | **-ons** | nous parl**ons** | nous mang**eons** | nous habit**ons** |
| vous | **-ez** | vous parl**ez** | vous mang**ez** | vous habit**ez** |

▲  ▲  ▲

## APPLICATION

**F.** Remplacez les sujets en italique et faites les changements nécessaires. *(Replace the italicized subjects and make the necessary changes.)*

1. *Je* parle anglais. (tu / nous / vous / je)
2. *Nous* travaillons beaucoup. (je / vous / tu / nous)
3. *Tu* habites à Paris. (vous / nous / je / tu)
4. *Vous* étudiez beaucoup. (nous / je / tu / vous)
5. *Je* voyage rarement. (tu / vous / nous / je)

### Note grammaticale

#### Quelques adverbes

Here are some frequently used French adverbs. Adverbs modify verbs and are usually placed directly *after* the conjugated verb.

| | | | | | |
|---|---|---|---|---|---|
| **bien** | well | **souvent** | often | **beaucoup** | a lot |
| **mal** | poorly | **rarement** | rarely | **un peu** | a little |

Nous étudions **beaucoup.**   We study *a lot.*
Tu chantes **bien.**   You sing *well.*
Nous voyageons **souvent.**   We travel *often.*

The adverbs **très** *(very)* and **assez** *(rather, enough)* can be used in combination with all of these adverbs except **beaucoup.** When they are used with **un peu, très** and **assez** take the place of **un: très peu, assez peu:**

Vous parlez **assez bien.**   You speak *fairly well.*
Je travaille **très peu.**   I work *very little.*

**Suggestion,** Subject pronouns: Using gestures and yourself as the subject, establish the difference between singular **(je, tu)** and plural **(nous, vous).** Have students perform gestures, using themselves as subjects. Then add **tu/vous** distinctions. Have students repeat gestures, using **vous** when pointing to you or to a group of students and **tu** when pointing to one other student.

**Suggestion,** Verb conjugation: (1) Establish orally the link between subject and verb ending; use several verbs. (2) Introduce orally the sound changes (elision, liaison) for **étudier** and **habiter.** (3) Write on board the four forms of **parler** and **étudier.** (4) Explain the notion of infinitive and the English equivalents of **le présent.**

**G. On pose des questions aux nouveaux arrivés.** *(The new arrivals are asked some questions.)* Patrick and Laura have just arrived at the home of the French family with whom they will be spending the year. The children of the family start by asking Patrick about himself. Play the role of Patrick and answer the questions, using the expressions in parentheses.

*Modèle:*      Tu nages beaucoup? (non / très peu)
                      *Non, je nage très peu.*

1. Tu parles français? (oui / un peu)
2. Tu étudies beaucoup? (non, mais *(but)* / assez)
3. Tu chantes bien? (non, mais / assez bien)
4. Tu voyages souvent? (non / rarement)
5. Tu manges beaucoup? (non, mais / assez)
6. Tu travailles beaucoup? (non / très peu)

Then they ask Laura about her and her friends. Play the role of Laura and answer the questions, using the expressions in parentheses.

*Modèle:*      Vous chantez bien? (non / faux [*off-key*])
                      *Non, nous chantons faux.*

7. Vous nagez? (oui / très souvent)
8. Vous voyagez rarement? (non / assez souvent)
9. Vous parlez anglais? (oui)
10. Vous étudiez beaucoup? (oui)
11. Vous travaillez? (oui / beaucoup)
12. Vous mangez beaucoup? (non, mais / assez)

**H. On vous pose des questions.** *(You are asked some questions.)* You are seated in a café with some French university students. They ask you questions—first, about yourself **(tu)**; then, about you and your friends **(vous)**. Answer their questions on the basis of your own experience.

1. Tu habites à Paris?
2. Tu étudies beaucoup?
3. Tu travailles?
4. Tu chantes bien?
5. Tu manges beaucoup?
6. Vous habitez à Paris?
7. Vous voyagez beaucoup?
8. Vous nagez?
9. Vous parlez français?
10. Vous visitez souvent New York?

**Pronunciation:** Can you think of some French words used in English in which the final consonant is not pronounced? Suggestions: *ballet, rapport, coup d'état.*

**Student Tape:**
Chapitre 1
Segment 1

You will find the **Pronunciation** section of each **étape** on your Student Tape.

# PRONONCIATION      *Les consonnes finales non-prononcées*

As a general rule, final consonants in French are silent. Because speakers of English are accustomed to pronouncing most final consonants, you will have to pay close attention to final consonants when speaking French:

| ENGLISH: | part | uncles | mix | cup |
|---|---|---|---|---|
| FRENCH: | part | Georges | prix | coup |

**I.** Read each word aloud, being careful *not* to pronounce the final consonant.

désirez / travailler / français / un thé au lait / Paris / bien / assez / garçon / beaucoup / vous / je voudrais / s'il vous plaît / tu parles / nous mangeons / Monsieur

## S·T·R·U·C·T·U·R·E

**Structure:** Since **est-ce que** and intonation are the most common interrogative forms in conversation and since they present little structural difficulty, they are introduced before inversion. **N'est-ce pas,** another simple form, has also been included; however, it should be stressed that **n'est-ce pas** is used much less frequently.

### Les formes interrogatives

—**Tu étudies** beaucoup?
—**Oui, j'étudie** beaucoup.

—*Do you study* a lot?
—*Yes, I study* a lot.

—**Est-ce que vous parlez** espagnol?
—**Non, nous ne parlons pas** espagnol.

—*Do you speak* Spanish?
—*No, we don't speak* Spanish.

—**Tu habites** à Lyon, **n'est-ce pas?**

—*You live* in Lyon, *don't you?*

—**Oui, j'habite** à Lyon.

—*Yes, I live* in Lyon.

A great many questions can be answered by *yes* or *no.* There are three basic ways to ask such questions in French:

**Suggestion,** Yes/no questions and answers: (1) Write an affirmative statement on the board, such as **Tu voyages beaucoup.** Point out intonation (voice falling at end of phrase) and have students repeat the statement. (2) Transform the statement into a question using each of the three question forms and pointing out the change in intonation; have students repeat. (3) Have students answer affirmatively and negatively (if necessary, go from **très peu** to **ne... pas beaucoup).** (4) Repeat step 3 with **Tu habites à Paris?**

1.  Make your voice rise at the end of a group of words:

    **Vous habitez** à Bordeaux?

2.  Place the expression **est-ce que** before a group of words and make your voice rise at the end:

    **Est-ce que tu voyages** souvent?

3.  Add the phrase **n'est-ce pas** to the end of a group of words and make your voice rise:

    Je chante bien, **n'est-ce pas?**

    To answer a yes/no question negatively, place **ne** before and **pas** immediately after the conjugated verb:

    Je **ne** parle **pas** espagnol.
    Tu **ne** chantes **pas** très bien.
    Nous **ne** mangeons **pas** assez.

If the verb begins with a vowel or a silent **h, ne** becomes **n':**

    Nous **n'**habitons **pas** à Paris.
    Je **n'**étudie **pas** assez.

**Grammar:** The phrase **n'est-ce pas?** is the equivalent of *don't you?, aren't you?, isn't that right?,* and assumes a *yes* answer.

▲ ▲ ▲

## APPLICATION

**J. Posez des questions.** *(Ask questions.)* Now it's the turn of the American students (Patrick and Laura) to ask questions of their French "brothers" and "sisters." Using the expressions suggested below, play the roles of Patrick and Laura. Change the infinitive to agree with the subject and vary the question form you use. Begin by asking questions of all the young people.

*Modèle:*    vous / parler anglais
*Vous parlez anglais?* or *Est-ce que vous parlez anglais?*

1. vous / travailler
2. vous / étudier beaucoup
3. vous / fumer
4. vous / chanter bien
5. vous / nager

Then ask questions of individuals.

*Modèle:*    Marie-Laure, tu / manger beaucoup
*Marie-Laure, tu manges beaucoup?* or
*Marie-Laure, est-ce que tu manges beaucoup?*

6. Éric, tu / parler anglais
7. Nicole, tu / voyager souvent
8. Martine, tu / habiter à Paris aussi
9. Didier, tu / manger bien
10. Véronique, tu / étudier beaucoup

**K. Mireille et François.** Mireille Loiseau tends to disagree a lot with her brother François. Whenever one of them answers a question affirmatively, the other contradicts the answer. Play the roles of Mireille and François in answering the following questions.

*Modèle:*    Mireille, tu chantes bien, n'est-ce pas?
MIREILLE:  *Oui, je chante très bien.*
FRANÇOIS:  *Mais non, tu ne chantes pas bien!*

1. François, tu parles allemand, n'est-ce pas?
2. Mireille, tu manges très peu, n'est-ce pas?
3. François, tu travailles beaucoup, n'est-ce pas?
4. Mireille, tu voyages souvent, n'est-ce pas?
5. François, tu fumes rarement, n'est-ce pas?
6. Mireille, tu nages, n'est-ce pas?

Ex. K: △ Have one student play the role of Mireille, another the role of François, and a third the person who asks the question. Then have students rotate roles.

**Follow-up,** Ex. K: Ask similar questions of individual students; other students react by agreeing or disagreeing.

## Débrouillons-nous!

▲ ▲ ▲ ▲ ▲ ▲ ▲ ▲ ▲ ▲ ▲ ▲ ▲ ▲ ▲ ▲ ▲ ▲ ▲ ▲

The **Débrouillons-nous!** section reviews and integrates the material from the **étape.** One or both exercises may be used at the end of class (when you have time), at the start of the next class (as a warm-up), or as part of the **Reprise** section the next day.

Ex. L: ⇄

### Petite révision de l'étape

**L.  Toi...** Using the expressions given below and asking only yes/no questions, find out as much information as possible about one of your classmates. He/she will then ask for information about you.

> *Modèle:*    habiter à Chicago
> —*Toi, tu habites à Chicago?* or *Est-ce que tu habites à Chicago, toi?*
> —*Non, je n'habite pas à Chicago. J'habite à...*

1.  habiter à New York
2.  parler anglais / espagnol / allemand *(German)*
3.  étudier beaucoup
4.  chanter bien
5.  manger beaucoup
6.  nager souvent
7.  travailler
8.  voyager beaucoup

**M.  Au café.** Two students, who have just met in class, go to a café for lunch. They place their order and then ask each other questions to get acquainted.

Ex. M: ⇄

**À faire chez vous: CAHIER, Chapitre 1^{er} / 1^{ère} étape**

**Instructor's Tape: Parlons!**

# DEUXIÈME ÉTAPE

## Point de départ

▼▼▼▼▼▼▼▼▼▼▼▼▼▼▼▼▼

 **ALLONS-Y!** Video Program

### ACTE 1
**FÊTE D'ANNIVERSAIRE**

**QUESTIONS DE FOND**
1. Why is the family all together?
2. What drink does Xavier request?
3. What does Aude's mother hope for?

Hi / How're you doing? / So long / Good-bye / See you soon.

**Suggestion, Point de départ:** Use the recorded dialogues from the Instructor's Tape. Explain in English the context for each dialogue; then have students listen and repeat with books closed. Finally, introduce alternative expressions.

**Variation, Point de départ:** Act out each dialogue, have students repeat and/or read; then have them practice with original expressions and alternatives. Vary the number of people and their degree of acquaintance.

How are you?

I'm fine
I would like you to meet (to introduce you to)

Delighted (to meet you)

*Parlons!*

—**Salut,** *Jean-Marc.* **Comment ça va?**
—*Ça va bien. Et toi, Martine, ça va?*
—*Oh, oui. Ça va.*
—*Martine Fortier, Suzanne Lecaze.*
—*Bonjour, Suzanne.*
—*Bonjour, Martine.*

—**Allez, au revoir,** *Jean-Marc.*
—**Au revoir,** *Martine.* **À bientôt.**
—*Au revoir, Suzanne.*
—*Au revoir, Martine.*

—*Bonjour, Madame.* **Comment allez-vous?**
—*Très bien, Isabelle. Et toi?*
—**Je vais bien** *aussi, merci. Madame,* **je voudrais vous présenter** *Jean-Claude Merrien. Jean-Claude, Madame Duvalier.*
—**Enchanté,** *Madame.*
—*Enchantée, Monsieur.*

—*Au revoir, Madame.*
—*Au revoir, Isabelle. Au revoir, Monsieur.*
—*Au revoir, Madame.*

| ***Les salutations*** | ***Les réponses*** | |
|---|---|---|
| Bonjour. ——————————→ | Bonjour. | *salutations:* greetings |
| Salut. ——————————————→ | Salut. | |
| Comment ça va? ⎫ | (Oui,) ça va bien. ⎫ | |
| Ça va? ⎬ ——————→ | (Oui,) ça va. ⎬ ———→ Et toi? | |
| Ça va bien? ⎭ | (Oui,) **pas mal.** ⎭ | not bad |
| Comment allez-vous? ————→ | Je vais très bien, merci. Et vous? | |

| ***On prend congé*** | ***Les présentations*** | |
|---|---|---|
| Au revoir. | Je te présente (Thierry). | *On prend congé:* Saying good-bye |
| Allez, au revoir. | (Thierry, Michel.) | |
| Salut. | Je voudrais vous présenter (Caroline | |
| **À tout à l'heure.** | Mercier). | See you in a while. |
| À bientôt. | Enchanté(e), Madame (Monsieur, | |
| | Mademoiselle). | |
| | (Caroline Mercier, Jacques Merlot.) | |

## Note culturelle

In France, custom requires that you shake hands when you greet people and when you take leave of them. This social rule is followed by men and women, young and old. If the two people are related or are very good friends, instead of shaking hands they often kiss each other on both cheeks. In formal situations, **Monsieur, Madame,** or **Mademoiselle** always accompanies **bonjour** and **au revoir.**

**Question:** How do Americans greet each other and say good-bye? When do they shake hands?

Le savez-vous?
▲▲▲▲▲▲▲▲▲▲▲▲▲▲
**French young people often use expressions from a foreign language when they are taking leave of someone. What do they say?**
a. Bye-bye!
b. Ciao!
c. Adios!

Réponse ▲▲▲

## À VOUS! (Exercices de vocabulaire)

A. **Répondons!** *(Let's answer!)* Complete the dialogues with an appropriate expression. In the first group of exchanges, you are speaking with people you know well or with fellow students.

*Modèle:*     (Martine) Salut, Georges.
            *Salut, Martine.*

1. (Pierre) Salut, Sandrine.
2. (Véronique) Comment ça va, Jean-Patrice?
3. (Éric) Ça va, Yvonne?
4. (Gérard) Salut, Chantal. Ça va bien?
5. (Marianne) Robert, Sylviane.
6. (Dominique) Allez, au revoir, Nicole.
7. (Francine) À bientôt, Caroline.

Now you are speaking with older people whom you do *not* know very well.

*Modèle:*          (M. Legard) Bonjour, Jeannette.
                   *Bonjour, Monsieur.*

8.   (Mme Michaud) Bonjour, Édouard.
9.   (M. Dupont) Comment allez-vous, Étienne?
10.  (Mme Maire) Madame Piquet, je voudrais vous présenter Annick et Vincent.
11.  (M. Alviez) Au revoir, Mademoiselle.
12.  (Mme Guérin) À bientôt, Philippe.

Ex. B: ○ Before students work in groups, do a model conversation for each situation.

**B.   Faites des présentations.** *(Make introductions.)*

1.   Introduce another student to the instructor.
2.   Introduce two students to each other.

Ex. C: △

**C.   Dans la rue.** You are walking down the street with a friend when you run into a second friend. Greet him/her and make introductions. The two people who have been introduced ask each other questions about where they live. Then your second friend says good-bye to you and your first friend.

▲▲▲   a, b

# R·E·P·R·I·S·E

*Première étape*

Ex. D: △ Vary the groups so that students work with different partners.

**D.   Qu'est-ce que tu prends?** *(What are you having?)* Three friends order lunch in a café. Imitate their conversation, substituting your own food and drink choices. Rotate until everyone has played each role.

**Reminder,** Ex. D: The model is designed to show you a possible form for this conversation. It is *not* necessary to repeat it word for word.

*Modèle:*      PIERRE:      *Qu'est-ce que tu prends, Hélène?*
               HÉLÈNE:      *Voyons... moi, je vais prendre une omelette au fromage et un demi.*
               PIERRE:      *Et toi, Chantal?*
               CHANTAL:     *Moi, je voudrais un croque-monsieur.*
               HÉLÈNE:      *Et un demi?*
               CHANTAL:     *Non, un Perrier. Et toi, Pierre, qu'est-ce que tu prends?*
               PIERRE:      *Un sandwich au jambon et un Perrier.*

**E. Posons des questions.** Use the verbs and expressions below to find out some personal information about other people in the class. Ask each question twice: first, of one fellow student; then, of a pair of students or of your instructor. The person(s) to whom you address each question will give you an answer.

*Modèle:* fumer (beaucoup)
*Henri, tu fumes? Tu fumes beaucoup? Et*
*Madame (Jacqueline et Sarah), vous fumez?*

1. habiter à *(city)*
2. travailler (beaucoup)
3. étudier (assez)
4. voyager (beaucoup)
5. nager (bien)
6. chanter (bien)
7. parler français (allemand, espagnol)
8. fumer (beaucoup)

## S·T·R·U·C·T·U·R·E

### *Le présent des verbes réguliers en -er (3^e personne)*

Jacques? **Il voyage** beaucoup.
Hélène? **Elle parle** espagnol.
Paul et Philippe? **Ils chantent** bien.
Marie et Jeanne? **Elles** n'**étudient** pas beaucoup.
Claire et Vincent? **Ils visitent** Paris.

~~~~~~~~~~ **Subject pronouns** ~~~~~~~~~~

| English | French |
|---------|--------|
| *he* | **il** |
| *she* | **elle** |
| *they* | **ils** (two or more males, group of males and females) |
| *they* | **elles** (two or more females) |

To form the present tense of an **-er** verb in the third person, add the appropriate ending to the stem. Recall that the stem is found by dropping the **-er** ending from the infinitive (**étudier → étudi-**):

| Subject | Ending | Conjugated verb form | | |
|---------|--------|----------------------|---|---|
| il | **-e** | il parle | il mange | il habite |
| elle | **-e** | elle parle | elle mange | elle habite |
| on | **-e** | on parle | on mange | on habite |
| ils | **-ent** | ils parl**ent** | ils mang**ent** | ils habit**ent** |
| elles | **-ent** | elles parl**ent** | elles mang**ent** | elles habit**ent** |

Remember to make a liaison between the **s** of **ils** or **elles** and a verb beginning with a vowel or a silent **h: ils‿étudient, elles‿habitent.**

▲ ▲ ▲

**Usage:** In French, there is another third-person pronoun, **on.** It is used to refer to a *general, undefined* group of people. The English equivalent is *one* or *people* (in general). **On** is also the equivalent of *you* or *they* when these pronouns do not refer to anyone in particular: *You drink white wine with fish,* or *They say that Chicago is very windy.* Even though **on** usually refers to a number of people, from a grammatical point of view it is a singular pronoun, acting just like **il** or **elle: À Paris on parle français.**

## APPLICATION

**F.** Remplacez les sujets en italique et faites les changements nécessaires.

1. *Je* chante bien. (Marie / Jean et Yvette / Patrick / François et Jacques / tu / vous)
2. *Il* habite à Montréal. (elle / ils / elles / tu / vous / je)
3. *Hervé* travaille rarement. (Annick / Chantal et Geneviève / Pierre et Marc / on / je / vous)
4. *Elle* ne mange pas assez. (ils / il / nous / on / vous / je / elles)
5. *Georges et Sylvie* fument beaucoup. (vous / tu / elles / on / il / je / nous)

**G. Un peu plus tard.** *(A little later.)* Your new French friends ask you questions about some of the other American students in your group. Answer according to the suggestions in parentheses.

1. Est-ce que Robert habite à Chicago? (à Denver)
2. Est-ce qu'on parle français à Denver? (anglais)
3. Est-ce qu'on fume beaucoup à Denver? (très peu)
4. Est-ce que Nancy et Susan parlent allemand? (non)
5. Est-ce que Beverly travaille? (oui)
6. Est-ce que George et Bill voyagent souvent? (rarement)
7. Est-ce que Mark chante bien? (faux)
8. Est-ce que Carol mange beaucoup? (non, mais / assez)
9. Est-ce que Frank étudie souvent? (non)
10. Est-ce que Frank et Carol habitent à Denver? (Dallas)

Ex. H: ☐

**H. La ronde des questions.** *(The question circle.)* Using one of the suggested cues, each student in the group asks four questions—one corresponding to each of the following pronouns: **tu, vous, il/elle, ils/elles.** The other members of the group respond according to what they know or hear.

*Modèle:*     parler espagnol
LISA:     *Bill, tu parles espagnol?*
BILL:     *Oui, je parle espagnol.*
LISA:     *Diane et James, vous parlez espagnol?*
DIANE:     *Non, nous ne parlons pas espagnol.*
LISA:     *James, est-ce que Bill parle espagnol?*
JAMES:     *Oui, il parle espagnol.*
LISA:     *Bill, est-ce que Diane et James parlent espagnol?*
BILL:     *Non, ils ne parlent pas espagnol.*

1. travailler
2. fumer
3. manger beaucoup
4. habiter à ____

# PRONONCIATION   *Les consonnes finales prononcées*

**Student Tape:**
Chapitre 1
Segment 1

The major exceptions to the rule of unpronounced final consonants are **c, r, f,** and **l.** These four consonants are usually pronounced when they are the last letter of a word. It may be helpful to use the English word **CaReFuL** as a memory aid.

| | | | |
|---|---|---|---|
| par**c** | bonjou**r** | acti**f** | ma**l** |
| chi**c** | au revoi**r** | che**f** | espagno**l** |

This rule does *not* apply to the infinitives of **-er** verbs: **parler, chanter, voyager.**

**I.**  Read each word aloud, being careful to pronounce the final consonant unless the word is an infinitive.

Marc / kir / bref / mal / étudier / bonjour / sec / espagnol / amour / Montréal / manger / Jean-Luc / il / tarif

**J.**  Read each word aloud, being careful to decide whether or not the final consonant should be pronounced.

au revoir / bientôt / chocolat / professeur / mal / n'est-ce pas / souvent / nager / un Vittel / bar / café au lait / anglais / beaucoup / actif / salut

# S·T·R·U·C·T·U·R·E

## *L'article défini (le, la, l', les)*

J'aime **le** vin, mais je préfère **la** bière.

I like wine, but I prefer beer.

Elle n'aime pas beaucoup **l'**eau minérale et elle n'aime pas du tout **les** boissons gazeuses.

She doesn't like mineral water and she doesn't like carbonated beverages at all.

The French definite article has three singular forms and one plural form:

| | | |
|---|---|---|
| MASCULINE SINGULAR | **le** | **le** vin, **le** thé, **le** jambon |
| FEMININE SINGULAR | **la** | **la** bière, **la** limonade, **la** salade |
| MASCULINE OR FEMININE SINGULAR BEFORE A VOWEL OR A VOWEL SOUND | **l'** | **l'**eau minérale, **l'**Orangina |
| PLURAL (MASCULINE OR FEMININE) | **les** | **les** boissons gazeuses, **les** omelettes |

The definite article is often used to designate a noun in a general or collective sense. For example, **Michel n'aime pas la bière** means that Michel dislikes all kinds of beer; **Anne préfère les sandwiches** means that Anne prefers sandwiches as a type or kind of food. Notice that in English the noun is used *without* an article to express these ideas. The definite article is frequently used in French after the following expressions:

**Grammar:** The written forms of **préférer** change the accent on the *second* e from acute (**é**) to grave (**è**) when the ending is silent (**-e, -es, -ent**): **je préfère, tu préfères, il/elle/on préfère, ils/elles préfèrent.** When the ending is pronounced (**-ons, -ez**), the acute accent remains: **nous préférons, vous préférez.**

| | |
|---|---|
| **aimer** | to like, to love |
| **aimer beaucoup** | to like a lot |
| **adorer** | to love, to really like |
| **ne pas aimer** | to dislike |
| **ne pas aimer du tout** | not to like at all, to dislike |
| **préférer** | to prefer |
| **aimer mieux** | to like better, to prefer |

▲  ▲  ▲

## APPLICATION

**K.** Replace the indefinite article with the appropriate definite article **(le, la, l', les).**

*Modèles:*    un Coca          *le Coca*
              une limonade     *la limonade*

1. un café   2. une eau minérale   3. une salade   4. un thé   5. des sandwiches   6. une bière   7. un lait   8. des omelettes   9. un Orangina   10. une limonade   11. un chocolat   12. des boissons alcoolisées

**L.  Les goûts.** You learn that Mireille Loiseau and her friends have differing tastes. In each category, you discover what the first person likes **(aimer, aimer beaucoup),** what the second person prefers **(aimer mieux, préférer),** and what the third person dislikes **(ne pas aimer, ne pas aimer du tout).**

*Modèle:*    Éric (bière) / Mireille (vin) / Roger (boissons alcoolisées)
             *Éric aime (beaucoup) la bière, mais Mireille aime mieux (préfère) le vin. Roger n'aime pas (du tout) les boissons alcoolisées.*

1.  Mireille (thé) / Sylvie (café) / Geneviève (boissons chaudes)
2.  Henri (fromage) / Didier (jambon) / Jean-Jacques (sandwiches)
3.  Colette (Vittel) / Yvonne (Perrier) / Jeanne (eau minérale)
4.  Robert (vin) / Marie (bière) / Christine (boissons alcoolisées)
5.  Annick (limonade) / Jacques (Orangina) / Guy (boissons gazeuses)

**M.  Tu voudrais...?** *(Would you like. . . ?)* Offer each of the following items of food and drink to at least two of your classmates. They will accept or ask for something else, depending on their personal preferences.

*Modèle:*    bière
             —*Tu voudrais une bière?*
             —*Ah, oui. J'aime beaucoup la bière.*
             —*Toi aussi, tu voudrais une bière?*
             —*Non, merci. Je n'aime pas la bière.* or *Je préfère le vin. Je voudrais un verre de rouge.*

1.  un verre de vin
2.  un Perrier
3.  une omelette au fromage
4.  un sandwich au pâté
5.  un thé au lait

**Reminder,** Ex. M: When offering or asking for something to eat or drink, use an indefinite article **(un, une, des);** when indicating your likes, dislikes, or preferences, use a definite article **(le, la, l', les).**

Ex. M: △ or ○

## ▲▲▲▲▲▲▲▲▲▲▲ Débrouillons-nous! ▲▲▲▲▲▲▲▲▲▲

*Petite révision de l'étape*

Ex. N: ⇄

**N.  Échange.** Ask questions of another student, who will answer you and find out similar information about you.

> *Modèle:*  —*Est-ce que tu habites à Richfield?*
> —*Non, j'habite à Duluth. Et toi?*
> —*Moi, j'habite à Denver.* or *Moi aussi, j'habite à Duluth.*

Ex. O: △ You play the role of **garçon** and go from group to group taking orders.

**À faire chez vous: CAHIER, Chapitre 1er / 2e étape**

**O.  Une scène au café.** You and a friend are going to a café to have lunch. Just as you arrive, you see another friend. You greet each other, make introductions, sit down, and order. The three of you have a short conversation (including a discussion of your likes and dislikes in food and drink). Then the friend you met at the café leaves.

# TROISIÈME ÉTAPE

## Point de départ

▼▼▼▼▼▼▼▼▼▼▼▼

Instructor's Tape:
L'heure du déjeuner

*Tu aimes les fast-foods?*

**L'heure du déjeuner**

Mireille, Angélique et Thierry **sont en ville.**

| | |
|---|---|
| MIREILLE: | On mange quelque chose? |
| ANGÉLIQUE: | Oui, **pourquoi pas? On va** au Quick? |
| THIERRY: | **D'accord.** J'aime bien les fast-foods. |

*L'heure du déjeuner:*
Lunchtime

are downtown

why not? / Shall we go . . . ?

OK.

**Vocabulary: Un fast-food**
(singular) refers to a fast-food restaurant; **les fast-foods** (plural) refers to the type of food served there.

Transparency:
1-2 (Quick menu board)

Suggestion, Point de départ: Have students first look at picture and menu board. Ask them to point out similarities and differences with American fast-food restaurants. Then use the recorded dialogue on the Instructor's Tape to present the conversation.

Au Quick.

| | |
|---|---|
| MIREILLE: | Qu'est-ce que tu manges? |
| ANGÉLIQUE: | Pour moi, un Giant, des frites et un milkshake au chocolat. |
| THIERRY: | Moi, je voudrais un Big, des frites et un Coca. |

| | | |
|---|---|---|
| two / three<br>vanilla | MIREILLE: | D'accord. Mademoiselle, **deux** Giants, un Big, **trois** frites, un Coca, un milkshake au chocolat et un milkshake **à la vanille.** |
| Hey! | THIERRY: | **Tiens!** Voilà Jeanne. |
| is | ANGÉLIQUE: | Elle **est** américaine, n'est-ce pas? |
| from | THIERRY: | Non, non, elle est canadienne. Elle est **de** Montréal. Elle chante très bien—en français et en anglais. |
| That's great (neat)! | MIREILLE: | **C'est chouette, ça.** |

### Note culturelle

In 1920, France had more than 500,000 cafés. Today, there are fewer than 175,000. A major cause of this decline is the growth of the fast-food industry in France. Fast-food restaurants are becoming almost as popular in France as they are in the United States. The best known is McDonald's, sometimes called **Macdo** in French. The major French fast-food restaurant chain is called **Le Quick,** run by a supermarket corporation called **Casino.** In addition to soft drinks and milk shakes, many of these fast-food restaurants serve wine and/or beer.

**Questions:** Study the menu and the picture of the Quick restaurant. In what ways do French fast-food restaurants seem similar to their American counterparts? Do you notice any differences?

## À VOUS! (Exercices de vocabulaire)

Ex. A: ⇄

**A.   On va au Quick?** Suggest to a friend that you go to the following places for a bite to eat. Your friend may either agree or suggest a different place.

*Modèle:*    au Quick
—*On mange quelque chose?*
—*Oui, pourquoi pas?*
—*On va au Quick?*
—*D'accord.* or *Non, je n'aime pas beaucoup le Quick. Allons*
(let's go) *au Macdo.*

1. au Macdo    2. au Burger King    3. au Café Minet    4. au Love Burger

**B.  Un, deux, trois... au Quick.** Based on the drawings below, order food for yourself and your friends.

**Follow-up,** Ex. B: Have students give their own orders from the Quick menu on p. 31.

*Modèle:*    *Deux cheeseburgers, deux frites, un Coca et un milk-shake à la vanille, s'il vous plaît.*

# R·E·P·R·I·S·E

*Deuxième étape*

**C.  Bonjour!... Salut!...** Play the roles of the people in each of the following situations. Pay attention to the level of language—formal or informal.

Ex. C: ⇄ and △

*Modèle:*    Henri, Jean-Jacques (greetings)
—*Salut, Jean-Jacques.*
—*Salut, Henri. Ça va?*
—*Oui, ça va. Et toi?*
—*Oui, ça va bien.*

1.   Henri, Jean-Jacques *(greetings)*
2.   M. Ventoux, Chantal *(greetings)*
3.   Claude, Angèle, Henri *(greetings, introductions)*
4.   Martine, Annick, Mme Leroux *(greetings, introductions)*
5.   Mme Didier, Gérard *(good-byes)*
6.   Ahmed, Jean *(good-byes)*

Ex. D: ○

**D.** **Mon ami(e).** *(My friend.)* Mention the name of one of your friends to some of your classmates. They will ask you questions about this friend, using the following verbs: **habiter, parler, étudier, chanter, fumer, manger, voyager, travailler, aimer, préférer.**

*Modèle:*          mon amie Carole
          —*Est-ce qu'elle habite à Boston?*
          —*Non, elle habite à...*

## S·T·R·U·C·T·U·R·E

**Suggestion, Être:** (1) Have students repeat conjugation of a regular **-er** verb while you write pronouns in two groups: **je, tu, il, elle, on, ils, elles / nous, vous.** (2) Have students repeat conjugation of **être** while you write pronouns in five groups: **je / tu, il, elle / ils, elles / nous / vous.** (3) Have students repeat in negative. (4) Add written verb forms to pronouns. You may wish to combine this presentation with an inductive introduction (see Instructor's Guide).

### Le présent du verbe irrégulier *être*

| | |
|---|---|
| Sylvie **est** de New York. | Sylvie *is* from New York. |
| Ils ne **sont** pas ici. Ils **sont** à Québec. | They *aren't* here. They*'re* in Quebec City. |
| —Vous **êtes** américains? | —*Are* you American? |
| —Non, nous **sommes** canadiens. | —No, we *are* Canadian. |

Some French verbs do not follow the pattern of conjugation you have learned for regular **-er** verbs. They are called *irregular verbs* because they do not fit into a fixed category. One of the most frequently used irregular verbs is **être** *(to be)*:

| **être** *(to be)* | |
|---|---|
| je **suis** | nous **sommes** |
| tu **es** | vous **êtes** |
| il, elle, on **est** | ils, elles **sont** |

The interrogative and negative forms follow the same patterns as **-er** verbs:

—Est-ce que **tu es** française?
—Non, je **ne** suis **pas** française, je suis américaine.

▲  ▲  ▲

## APPLICATION

**E.** Remplacez le sujet en italique et faites les changements nécessaires.

1. *Éric* est à Bordeaux. (je / Hélène et moi, nous / tu / elles)
2. *Monique* est de Paris. (Jean-Jacques / je / vous / ils / nous / tu)
3. Est-ce que *Mathieu* est au Macdo? (Nathalie / Monsieur et Madame Ledoux / vous / tu / on / nous)
4. *Yves et Mathilde* ne sont pas au café. (Jean-Luc / je / Denise / vous / elles / on / tu)

**F.** **Martine n'est pas là. Elle est à Nice.** You notice that, just two days before a vacation break, many of your new friends are not around. When you ask Mireille where everybody is, she explains that they are in other cities. Reproduce Mireille's answers.

*Modèle:*     Renée / Strasbourg
              *Renée? Elle n'est pas là. Elle est à Strasbourg.*

1. Georges / Toulouse
2. Chantal et Marcel / Grenoble
3. Michèle et Jeanne / Cannes
4. Vincent / Orléans
5. Brigitte / Bordeaux
6. Jean-Pierre et Henri / Rennes

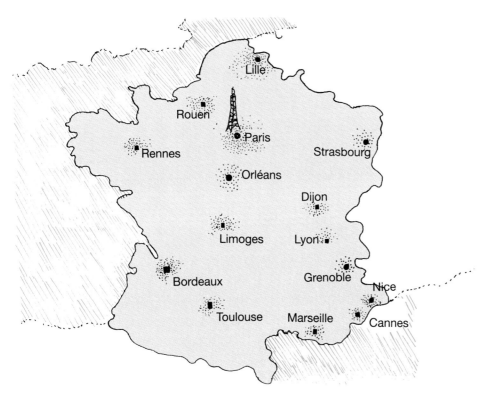

Ex. G: ⇄

**G. Ils ne sont pas de Paris.** Even though many of your French friends live in Paris, they were not born there. When you ask them if they are from Paris, they tell you where they are originally from. Using the cities below, ask and answer questions according to the model.

> *Modèle:*    vous / Marseille
> —*Vous êtes de Paris?*
> —*Non, nous ne sommes pas de Paris. Nous sommes de Marseille.*

1. vous / Lyon
2. tu / Nice
3. Étienne et Dominique / Lille
4. vous / Rouen
5. Édouard / Limoges
6. tu / Dijon

**Student Tape:**
Chapitre 1
Segment 1

# PRONONCIATION   *Les consonnes finales + e*

If a word ends in a mute **e** (an **e** without a diacritic mark), the preceding consonant is pronounced. The mute **e,** as its name implies, remains silent:

| | | |
|---|---|---|
| chant**e** | femm**e** | fromag**e** |
| parl**e** | salad**e** | omelett**e** |

**H.** Read each pair of words aloud, being careful not to pronounce the consonant at the end of the first word and making sure to pronounce the consonant before the final **e** of the second word.

français, française / allemand, allemande / italien, italienne / américain, américaine / Denis, Denise / François, Françoise

▲▲▲  a

**I.** Say each word aloud, being careful to pronounce a consonant before a final **e** and not to pronounce a final consonant alone (with the exception of **c, r, f, l**).

Madame / bien / limonade / Rome / chocolat / Vittel / tu es / canadienne / jambon / pour / croissant / chose / voudrais / kir / chef

# S·T·R·U·C·T·U·R·E

## *Les adjectifs de nationalité*

Jacques est **français**.
Claire est **française**.

Bernard et Yves sont **canadiens**.
Yvette et Simone sont **canadiennes**.

In French, adjectives agree in *gender* (masculine or feminine) and *number* (singular or plural) with the person or thing to which they refer.

1.   Some adjectives have identical masculine and feminine forms:

Il est **belge** *(Belgian)*.
Il est **russe** *(Russian)*.
Il est **suisse** *(Swiss)*.

Elle est **belge.**
Elle est **russe.**
Elle est **suisse.**

2.   Many adjectives have a feminine form that consists of the masculine form + **-e:**

Il est **français**.
Il est **anglais**.
Il est **américain**.
Il est **mexicain**.
Il est **allemand**.
Il est **espagnol**.
Il est **japonais**.
Il est **chinois** *(Chinese)*.
Il est **sénégalais** *(Senegalese)*.

Elle est **française.**
Elle est **anglaise.**
Elle est **américaine.**
Elle est **mexicaine.**
Elle est **allemande.**
Elle est **espagnole.**
Elle est **japonaise.**
Elle est **chinoise.**
Elle est **sénégalaise.**

3.   Finally, some adjectives have a feminine form that consists of the masculine form + **-ne:**

Il est **italien**.
Il est **canadien**.
Il est **égyptien**.

Elle est **italienne.**
Elle est **canadienne.**
Elle est **égyptienne.**

4.   To form the plural of all these adjectives, simply add **-s** to the masculine or feminine singular form. If the singular form already ends in **-s,** the singular and the plural are the same.

Ils sont **allemands**.
Ils sont **français**.

Elles sont **chinoises.**
Elles sont **italiennes.**

▲  ▲  ▲

**Supplementary Vocabulary:** Here are some additional adjectives of nationality. You are not expected to know all of these; pick out those that apply to you or that have some importance for you.

**algérien(ne), argentin(e), australien(ne), autrichien(ne)** *(Austrian),* **danois(e), grec(-que), indien(ne), iranien(ne), israélien(ne), libanais(e)** *(Lebanese),* **marocain(e), norvégien(ne), polonais(e)** *(Polish),* **suédois(e)** *(Swedish),* **tunisien(ne), turc(-que).** Ask your instructor for other nationalities you may want to say.

## APPLICATION

**J. Et Roger?** Answer the questions according to the model. In the first six items, the first person is female and the second is male. In the last six items, the first person is male and the second female.

*Modèle:*    Jacqueline est française. Et Roger?
*Il est français aussi.*

1. Janet est américaine. Et Stan?
2. Sophia est italienne. Et Vittorio?
3. Olga est russe. Et Boris?
4. Fatima est égyptienne. Et Ahmed?
5. Miko est japonaise. Et Yoshi?
6. Isabela est mexicaine. Et José?
7. Harold est anglais. Et Priscilla?
8. Maurice est canadien. Et Jeanne-Marie?
9. Gunther est allemand. Et Helga?
10. Tchen est chinois. Et Sun?
11. Alfred est suisse. Et Jeannette?
12. Yves est français. Et Mireille?

**Variation,** Ex. K: Teach students the expression **Je suis d'origine** + feminine adjective. Then have students tell you and/or each other about their nationalities and ethnic backgrounds.

**Follow-up,** Ex. K: Have each student choose a new nationality and city of origin. Have other students try to find out by asking, **Tu es italienne? Tu es de Berlin?,** etc.

**K. Les nationalités.** You are with a group of young people from all over the world. Find out their nationalities by making the indicated assumption and then correcting your mistake.

*Modèle:*    Marguerite—portugais / New York
*—Est-ce que Marguerite est portugaise?*
*—Mais non, elle est de New York.*
*—Ah, bon. Elle est américaine.*
*—C'est ça. (That's it.) Elle est américaine.*

1. Monique—suisse / Paris
2. Lin-Tao *(m.)*—japonais / Beijing
3. Francesca—mexicain / Rome
4. Jean-Pierre—belge / Québec
5. Verity—américain / Londres *(London)*
6. Fumiko et Junko *(f.)*—égyptien / Tokyo
7. Carlos et Pablo—espagnol / Guadalajara
8. Natasha et Svetlana *(f.)*—canadien / Moscou
9. Eberhard *(m.)* et Heidi—suisse / Berlin
10. Gina et Sofia—vénézuélien / Madrid

## Note grammaticale

### Les noms de profession

Most nouns that refer to work or occupation follow the same pattern as adjectives of nationality.

1.  Some nouns have identical masculine and feminine forms:

Il est **secrétaire.**          Elle est **secrétaire.**
Il est **médecin** *(doctor).*          Elle est **médecin.**
Il est **professeur** *(teacher).*          Elle est **professeur.**
Il est **ingénieur** *(engineer).*          Elle est **ingénieur.**

2.  Some nouns have a feminine form that consists of the masculine form + **-e:**

Il est **avocat** *(lawyer).*          Elle est **avocate.**
Il est **étudiant** *(college student).*          Elle est **étudiante.**
Il est **assistant** *(teaching assistant).*          Elle est **assistante.**

3.  Other nouns have a feminine form that consists of the masculine form + **-ne:**

Il est **mécanicien** *(mechanic).*          Elle est **mécanicienne.**
Il est **pharmacien** *(pharmacist).*          Elle est **pharmacienne.**

4.  Nouns of profession, like adjectives of nationality, form the plural by adding **-s** to the masculine or feminine singular:

Ils sont **avocats.**          Elles sont **professeurs.**
Ils sont **mécaniciens.**          Elles sont **étudiantes.**

**Grammar:** Notice that French, unlike English, does *not* require an indefinite article **(un, une, des)** when identifying someone's profession after the verb **être.** Thus, the equivalent of *I am a lawyer* is **Je suis avocat(e).**

**L.** **Voilà M. Chevalier. Il est avocat.** You and a French friend are attending a function with his/her parents. Your friend points out various acquaintances of his/her parents and states their professions. Recreate the statements of your friend.

*Modèles:*    M. Chevalier / avocat
*Voilà M. Chevalier. Il est avocat.*

M. et Mme Richard / pharmacien
*Voilà M. et Mme Richard. Ils sont pharmaciens.*

1. M. et Mme Aubert / médecin
2. Mme Forestier / professeur
3. Mme Longin / avocat
4. M. Cordier / cadre *(executive)*
5. M. Dumoulin / avocat
6. Nicole et Suzanne Martineau / étudiant
7. Patrick Desnoyers / étudiant
8. Georges Denis / secrétaire
9. Mme Beaujour / ingénieur
10. Mlle Jacquier / mécanicien
11. M. Gautier / mécanicien
12. Catherine Raymond et Jeanne Duval / assistant à l'université

**Variation,** Ex. M: Have students ask each other: **Tu voudrais être...?** Then you ask them about what they have learned: **Est-ce que _____ voudrait être dentiste? Qu'est-ce que _____ voudrait être? Qui voudrait être _____?** (Have them answer for themselves and for others.)

**M.** **Est-ce que tu voudrais être ingénieur?** From the following list, choose several careers or jobs that you would like and several that you would not like.

*Modèle:*    *Je voudrais être architecte, mais je ne voudrais pas être avocat(e).*

**architecte** / **comptable** *(accountant)* / **dentiste** / **avocat(e)** / **journaliste** / **professeur** / **secrétaire** / **cadre** / **pharmacien(ne)** / **mécanicien(ne)** / **ingénieur** / **musicien(ne)** / **agriculteur(-trice)** *(farmer)* / **acteur (actrice)** / **astronaute** / **vendeur(-euse)** *(salesperson)* / **homme (femme) d'affaires** *(businessman, businesswoman)* / **fonctionnaire** *(civil servant)* / **commerçant(e)** *(small business owner)* / **instituteur(-trice)** *(grade-school teacher)* / **programmeur(-euse)**

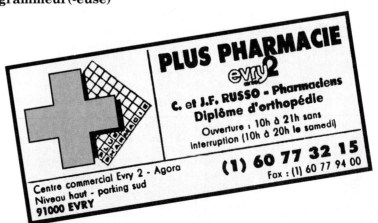

## ▲▲▲▲▲▲▲▲▲ Débrouillons-nous! ▲▲▲▲▲▲▲▲▲

*Petite révision de l'étape*

**N. Échange.** Posez les questions suivantes à un(e) camarade de classe, qui va vous répondre.

Ex. N: ⇄

1. Quelle *(what)* est ta nationalité?
2. Tu es d'origine italienne (allemande, ____)?
3. Tu es professeur?
4. Tu habites à ____, n'est-ce pas?
5. Tu es de ____ aussi?
6. Tu travailles?
7. Tu parles espagnol? allemand? chinois? russe?
8. Tu aimes les boissons alcoolisées? Les boissons chaudes?
9. Tu voudrais être astronaute?
10. Qu'est-ce que tu voudrais être?

**O. Au Quick.** You and two friends decide to have lunch at a nearby Quick. You talk about what you will eat. Then one of you places the order. While eating, each of you notices an acquaintance from another country. You each point out this person to your friends and tell them something about him/her.

Ex. O: △ Model this dialogue with three students before dividing class into groups.

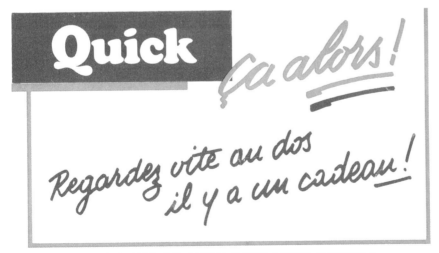

**LES IDEES DE QUICK POUR VOUS EPATER !**

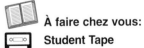 **À faire chez vous: CAHIER, Chapitre 1ᵉʳ / 3ᵉ étape**

**À faire chez vous: Student Tape**

Now that you've completed the first three **étapes** of **Chapitre 1ᵉʳ,** do Segment 2 of the STUDENT TAPE. See **CAHIER, Chapitre 1ᵉʳ,** *Écoutons!,* for exercises that accompany this segment.

# QUATRIÈME ÉTAPE

## L·E·C·T·U·R·E

### *La Dauphine vous propose*

*Here is a list of items served in a café called* **La Dauphine.** *Because you would rarely order more than two or three items to eat and drink, it is not really necessary to understand every item when you try to read the menu. What you* can *do, however, is to use the French you already know as well as your general knowledge to try to recognize or figure out as many items as you can. Study the menu below, then do the exercises that follow.*

**Prereading:** Discuss possible reactions to a café menu: Do you just go ahead and order **un hot dog** and **un Coca?** Do you take a wild guess? What strategies might you use to figure out unfamiliar words (such as cognates, grouping of like items)?

**Transparency: 1-3** (menu from La Dauphine)

---

## La Dauphine vous propose

### Plats Chauds

| | |
|---|---|
| CROQUE-MONSIEUR | 30F |
| CROQUE-MADAME | 36F |
| OMELETTE JAMBON OU FROMAGE | 36F |
| OMELETTE MIXTE | 40F |
| HOT DOG | 30F |
| FRANCFORT FRITES | 44F |

### Sandwiches

| | |
|---|---|
| JAMBON OU GRUYÈRE OU PÂTÉ | 18F |
| AMÉRICAIN: crudités et jambon | 44F |

### Salades

| | |
|---|---|
| SALADE NATURE | 30F |
| SALADE DE TOMATES | 44F |
| CAROTTES RÂPÉES | 32F |
| SALADE DE CONCOMBRES | 44F |

### Boissons

| | | | |
|---|---|---|---|
| 33 EXPORT | 20F | CAFÉ | 11F |
| 33 RECORD | 18F | CRÈME | 24F |
| HEINEKEN | 24F | CHOCOLAT | 24F |
| KREICK BELLEVUE | 50F | THÉ LAIT OU | |
| COCA-COLA | 24F | CITRON | 24F |
| JUS DE FRUITS | 24F | THÉS AROMATISÉS | 24F |
| JUS PRESSÉS | 28F | CAFÉ VIENNOIS | 40F |
| EAUX MINÉRALES | 20F | CAPPUCCINO | 18F |

# COMPRÉHENSION

**A.** Your traveling companions do *not* speak French at all. They tell you what they would like to eat or drink, and you tell them what they should order and how much it will cost.

1. I'm not very hungry; all I want is a cup of espresso.
2. I can't eat meat. I want something with cheese.
3. I'm really thirsty; I'd like a nice glass of lemonade.
4. Can I have a ham and cheese omelet?
5. Is it possible to get just a plain lettuce salad?
6. All I want is a beer.

**B. Devinez!** *(Guess!)* You are more adventuresome than your friends, so you decide to try an item whose name you don't recognize. If you were to order each of the following, what do you think you would get?

1. un sandwich américain   2. une Kreick Bellevue   3. un crème   4. un francfort frites   5. une salade de concombres   6. des carottes râpées   7. un café viennois

## R·E·P·R·I·S·E

*Troisième étape*

**C. Le déjeuner au Surf.** You and two classmates go to the **Surf**, a small fast-food restaurant in Avignon. Discuss with your friends what you and they will have to eat. Then go to the counter and order.

**SURF PIZZABURGER**

**PLATS CHAUDS**

| | | |
|---|---|---|
| Pizza René | | 20F |
| Hot Dog | simple 14F   double 20F | |
| Brochette de Dinde | | 34F |

**HAMBURGERS**

| | | | | |
|---|---|---|---|---|
| Freeburger | 16F | Fishburger | | 20F |
| Big Free | 24F | Big Fish | | 28F |
| Surfburger | 20F | | | |
| Big Surf | 28F | Frites | simple 14F | double 20F |
| Cheeseburger | 20D | Salade du jour | | 10F |
| Big Cheese | 28F | Croque-Monsieur | | 18F |

| **DESSERTS** | | **BOISSONS FRAÎCHES** | | | |
|---|---|---|---|---|---|
| Apple Pie | 14F | Coca-Cola | 14F | 18F | 28F |
| Sundae | 18F | Limonade | 10F | 14F | 24F |
| Pavé au chocolat | 14F | Jus d'orange | 12F | 16F | 26F |
| | | Milk Shake | 20F | | |

**D.** **Des photos.** While traveling in Europe, you met people from several different countries. Upon your return to France, you are showing photographs of these people to your French family. Using the information given below, give each person's profession, tell where he/she lives, and indicate his/her nationality. Remember to make all adjectives agree with the person to whom they refer.

▲▲▲ a

> *Modèle:*     M. Cordero / professeur / Madrid
> *M. Cordero est professeur. Il habite à Madrid. Il est espagnol.*

1. Michael Frye / avocat / Londres
2. Mme Sebastiani / médecin / Rome
3. Natasha Fedchenko / mécanicien / Moscou
4. Jean-Yves Péronnet / étudiant / Bordeaux
5. M. Dalbach / ingénieur / Munich
6. Janine Néel / cadre / Toulouse
7. Li Ping *(f.)* / dentiste / Shangaï
8. Susan Yaeger / professeur / Pittsburgh

**À faire chez vous:**
**Student Tape**

**CAHIER, Chapitre 1ᵉʳ:**
*Rédigeons! / Travail de fin de chapitre* (including STUDENT TAPE, Chapitre 1ᵉʳ, Segment 3)

# Point d'arrivée

*Activités orales*

## Exprimons-nous!

When French speakers pause to think of what to say next, two conversation fillers they frequently use are **euh** and **voyons.**

| | |
|---|---|
| Martine parle anglais et... **euh...** allemand, oui, allemand. | Martine speaks English and...*uh*...German, yes, German. |
| **Voyons...** moi, je voudrais une omelette au fromage et un demi. | *Let's see*...I'd like a cheese omelet and a draught beer. |

Ex. E: △

**Implementation,** Ex. E: You play the role of **garçon,** circulating from table to table.

**Transparencies:**
**1-5, 1-6** (menu from a second café, menu board from a third fast-food restaurant)

**E.** **Au café.** You and a friend meet at a café for a drink **(un verre)** or for breakfast or lunch. After you greet each other, another friend arrives. Introduce him/her to your first friend. The two people who have just met try to get better acquainted by asking each other questions about their nationality, residence, work, languages, and the like. Don't forget to order something for the new arrival.

F.  **On mange quelque chose?** While downtown on a Saturday afternoon, you and a friend run into one or more classmates. You are hungry. Therefore, you try to get people interested in going somewhere (café, fast-food restaurant) for something to eat. When you have decided, go to the place and order your food. (If you can't all agree, split into smaller groups, say good-bye, and go off to the place of your choice.)

G.  **Une présentation.** Question another student in order to introduce him/her to the class. Find out (1) his/her nationality, (2) where he/she is from, (3) where he/she lives now, (4) what languages he/she speaks, (5) whether he/she likes to sing, travel, swim, etc., and (6) what kinds of snack food and beverages he/she prefers. When you have finished, present the student to the class.

H.  **En attendant à l'aéroport.** While waiting for a plane at an international airport, you and your friends take turns guessing the nationalities and professions of various people. After making your guesses, one of you goes up to each person and finds out the correct information. Use the cards provided by your teacher. The person holding a card plays the role of the person(s) pictured.

**Variation,** Exs. E and F: May be presented as semi-improvised skits in class. Give students time to work out basic details.

Ex. F: △ or ○

**Implementation,** Ex. F: Assign students to different corners of the room to play the roles of **garçon** or **employé(e)** at different cafés and fast-food restaurants. Make copies of menus and menu boards from the transparencies.

**Implementation,** Ex. G: If class is large, have students work in groups of six (three pairs) for presentations.

**Reminder,** Ex. G: Don't try to translate your questions directly from English to French. Instead, use the French you have learned to find a way to get the needed information.

Ex. H: ○

**Implementation,** Ex. H: Cards are available in the Resource Manual.

**Portrait:** At the end of each chapter, you will find a short monologue by the character(s) featured in that chapter. You will not know all the words in the monologue; however, by using your reading strategies, you will be able to get the gist of what the characters have to say.

**Instructor's Tape: Mireille Loiseau, Paris**

**Portrait:** After students have listened to the Instructor's Tape or read the **Portrait,** ask questions to verify comprehension: **Où est-ce que Mireille habite? Est-ce qu'elle est originaire de Paris? Est-ce qu'elle est étudiante à l'université? Est-ce qu'elle aime les fast-foods? Qu'est-ce qu'elle préfère?**

**Suggestion, Profil:** Have students silently read through the information in the **Profil.** Then ask them (in English) to give some facts about Paris to verify their comprehension of the reading. Continue to the discussion questions. You might point out to students that France is a much more highly centralized country than the United States, with Paris being the focal point. Ask them the advantages and disadvantages of such centralization.

# PORTRAIT
*Mireille Loiseau, Paris*

Je suis parisienne. Mes parents, mon frère François et moi, nous habitons à Paris depuis six ans. Je suis née à Strasbourg et j'ai encore de la famille en Alsace. Je suis élève au lycée Victor Duruy. Mes amis et moi, nous déjeunons souvent dans le quartier. Ils aiment les fast-foods, mais moi, je préfère aller au café. J'adore les omelettes et les boissons à la menthe.

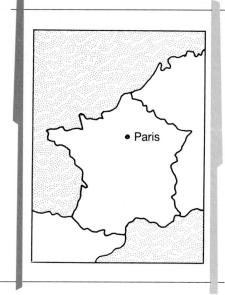

# Profil
*Paris*

**SITUATION:** sur la Seine, en Île-de-France

**POPULATION:** 2 200 000 habitants

**IMPORTANCE:** capitale de la France

**LIEUX D'INTÉRÊT:** la tour Eiffel, la cathédrale de Notre-Dame, l'avenue des Champs-Élysées, le Louvre

**HISTOIRE:** habitée par les Gaulois, conquise par les Romains en 52 avant Jésus-Christ *(B.C.)*

**COMMENTAIRE:** Malgré *(in spite of)* des efforts vers la décentralisation, Paris demeure *(remains)* le centre politique, commercial, culturel et symbolique de la France.

**À discuter:** What cities play the role of Paris in the lives and minds of the American people?

# L·E·X·I·Q·U·E

## Pour se débrouiller

*Pour saluer*
Bonjour.
Salut.
Comment allez-vous?
Comment ça va?
Ça va (bien)?

*Pour répondre à une salutation*
Bonjour.
Salut.
Je vais (très) bien.
Ça va (bien).
Pas mal.

*Pour faire les présentations*
Je vous présente...
(Michel, Suzanne; Suzanne,
Michel.)
Enchanté(e).

*Pour prendre congé*
Au revoir.
Allez, au revoir.
À bientôt.
À tout à l'heure.
Salut.

*Pour proposer quelque chose à
manger ou à boire*
Tu prends quelque chose?
Tu voudrais...?
Qu'est-ce que tu prends?
On mange quelque chose?
On va au...?

*Pour commander*
Je vais prendre...
Je voudrais...

## Thèmes et contextes

*Les fast-foods*
un fast-food
un double
un simple
un milk shake au chocolat
à la vanille

*Le petit déjeuner*
un croissant

*Le déjeuner*
un croque-madame
un croque-monsieur
des frites *(f.pl.)*
une omelette aux fines herbes
au fromage
au jambon
une (part de) pizza
une quiche
une salade
un sandwich au fromage
au jambon
au pâté

*Les nationalités*
allemand(e)
américain(e)
anglais(e)
belge
canadien(ne)
chinois(e)
égyptien(ne)
espagnol(e)
français(e)
italien(ne)
japonais(e)
mexicain(e)
portugais(e)
russe
sénégalais(e)
suisse
vénézuélien(ne)

*Les professions*
un acteur (une actrice)
un(e) agriculteur(-trice)
un(e) architecte
un(e) assistant(e)
un(e) astronaute
un(e) avocat(e)
un cadre
un(e) commerçant(e)
un(e) comptable
un(e) dentiste
un(e) étudiant(e)
un(e) fonctionnaire
un homme (une femme)
d'affaires
un ingénieur
un(e) instituteur(-trice)
un(e) journaliste
un(e) mécanicien(ne)
un médecin
un(e) musicien(ne)
un(e) pharmacien(ne)
un professeur
un(e) programmeur(-euse)
un(e) secrétaire
un(e) vendeur(-euse)

## Vocabulaire général

*Verbes*
chanter         nager
être            parler
étudier         travailler
fumer           visiter
habiter         voyager
manger

*Adverbes*
assez           un peu
beaucoup        rarement
bien            souvent
mal             très

Michel Kerguézec
Locmariaquer (Bretagne),
France

—C'est à toi, ça, Michel?
—Oui. Tu as un ordinateur, toi?

# Faisons connaissance!

## OBJECTIVES

**In this chapter, you will learn:**

- to talk about possessions;
- to express likes and dislikes;
- to describe your family;
- to have someone repeat what you have not heard or understood;
- to read a short descriptive text about people;
- to understand people talking about themselves and their families.

**CHAPTER SUPPORT MATERIALS** (STUDENT)

**Cahier:** pp. 39–62

**Student Tape:**
Chapitre 2
Segments 1, 2, 3

**CHAPTER SUPPORT MATERIALS (INSTRUCTOR)**

**Transparencies:**
2-1 through 2-7

**Instructor's Tape:**
Chapitre 2,
Text, pp. 62, 70, 85

**SYSTÈME-D software:**
Writing activities for
this chapter are found
in the **Cahier:**
*Rédigeons!* (p. 61).

**Multimedia:**
See the Resource
Manual for correlation
to our multimedia
product.

## ALLONS-Y!
### Video Program

**ACTE 2**
**SCÈNE 1: LES COUPLES**
**SCÈNE 2: UNE FAMILLE**
**À LA GUADELOUPE**

▶ Première étape  C'est à toi, ça?
▶ Deuxième étape  Moi, j'aime beaucoup...
▶ Troisième étape  Voici ma famille!
▶ Quatrième étape  Lecture: **Mon identité**

# P R E M I È R E   É T A P E

## Point de départ

▼ ▼ ▼ ▼ ▼ ▼ ▼ ▼ ▼ ▼ ▼ ▼ ▼ ▼ ▼

*C'est à toi, ça?*

**J'habite dans...**

une maison

un appartement
**un immeuble**

une chambre
**une résidence
universitaire**

apartment building /
dormitory

To go into town, I have

**Pour aller en ville, j'ai...**

une voiture (une auto)

une motocyclette
(une moto)

un vélomoteur

une bicyclette
(un vélo)

At our house, there is

**Chez nous, il y a...**

un Walkman
(un baladeur)

une chaîne stéréo
des cassettes *(f.pl.)*
des compacts disques *(m.pl.)*

un téléviseur
**un magnétoscope**

VCR

Dans **ma** chambre, il y a                                    my

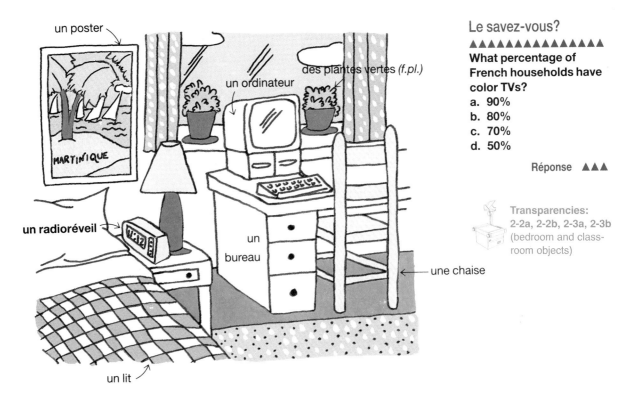

Pour aller en classe, j'ai...

Vocabulary: Some additional vocabulary that you may need when talking about objects you own or use includes: **un appareil-photo** *(camera)*, **une caméra** *(movie camera or camcorder)*, **un frigo** *(refrigerator)*, **un téléphone, un transistor, des coussins** *(m.pl., cushions)*, **une lampe, une affiche** *(poster)*, **une armoire** *(dresser)*, **un miroir** *(mirror)*, **une serviette** *(briefcase)*, **une machine à écrire** *(typewriter)*, **des disques** *(m.pl., records)*, **un réveil-matin** *(alarm clock)*.

## À VOUS! (Exercices de vocabulaire)

**A. Qu'est-ce que c'est?** Answer the questions according to the drawings.

*Modèles:*     Qu'est-ce que c'est?
*C'est un cahier.*
*Ce sont des cassettes.*

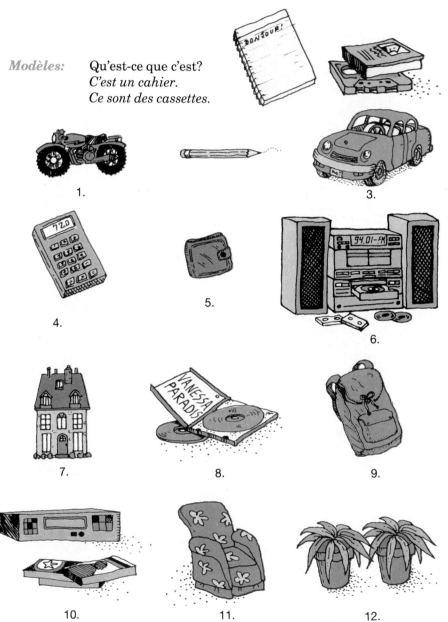

**B.   Christine, Bertrand, Antoinette et René.** On the basis of the drawings, complete each person's description of where he/she lives.

1.   Je m'appelle *(my name is)* Christine Devise. J'habite dans _____ .
     J'ai _____ et _____ , mais je n'ai pas de (d') _____ . Pour aller en ville, j'ai
     _____ .

2.   Je m'appelle Bertrand Perreaux. J'habite dans _____ . J'ai _____ et _____ .
     Pour aller à l'université, j'ai _____ .

3.   Je m'appelle Antoinette Salanches. Moi, j'habite dans _____ . Chez nous,
     il y a _____ , mais nous n'avons pas de (d') _____ . Pour aller en classe, j'ai
     _____ .

4.  Moi, je m'appelle René Poulain. J'habite dans ___ . Dans ma chambre il y a ___ et ___ et ___ , mais il n'y a pas de (d') ___ . Pour aller en classe, j'ai ___ .

# S·T·R·U·C·T·U·R·E

*Le présent du verbe irrégulier* **avoir** *et quelques expressions avec* **avoir**

**Michel Kerguézec a** une Renault Clio.

Et vous, est-ce que **vous avez** une voiture?

Non, **nous** n'**avons** pas de voiture.

Ça ne fait rien. **Chantal et Mireille ont** une moto.

*Michel Kerguézec has* a Renault Clio.

How about you? *Do you have* a car?

No, *we do* not *have* a car.

It doesn't matter. *Chantal and Mireille have* a motorcycle.

The verb **avoir** *(to have)* is irregular:

| **avoir** *(to have)* | |
|---|---|
| j'**ai** | nous **avons** |
| tu **as** | vous **avez** |
| il, elle, on **a** | ils, elles **ont** |

In a negative sentence, the indefinite articles **un, une,** and **des** change to **de** (**d'** before a vowel or a vowel sound). This often occurs with the verb **avoir:**

J'ai un portefeuille.

Bruno a un ordinateur.

Nous avons des posters.

Je **n'**ai **pas de** portefeuille.

Bruno **n'**a **pas d'**ordinateur.

Nous **n'**avons **pas de** posters.

Many common French expressions use the verb **avoir.** Among the most frequently used are:

| **avoir besoin de** | to need |
| **avoir faim** | to be hungry |
| **avoir soif** | to be thirsty |

**J'ai besoin d'**un stylo.

**Je n'ai pas faim,** mais **j'ai** très **soif.**

*I need* a pen.

*I'm not hungry,* but *I'm* very *thirsty.*

▲  ▲  ▲

**Grammar:** Note that **avoir besoin** is followed by **de** (not **des**) when it precedes a *plural* noun: **Ils ont besoin *de* plantes vertes.**

# APPLICATION

**C.** Remplacez le sujet et faites les changements nécessaires.

1. *Luc* a soif, mais *il* n'a pas faim. (Chantal / je / nous / Irène et Claude / tu / vous)
2. Est-ce que *François* a une chaîne stéréo? (tu / Mireille Loiseau / Michèle et Francine / vous / Michel Kerguézec)
3. *Ils* n'ont pas d'ordinateur. (elle / tu / nous / je / elles / Éric)
4. *Nous* avons besoin d'un lit et de chaises. (je / vous / ils / tu / Nicole)

Ex. D: ⇄

**Follow-up,** Ex. D: Using transparencies from **Point de départ,** ask students if they have various items.

**D.** **Non, mais j'ai...** Each time you ask about someone's possessions, you learn that he/she does not have the object you mention, but something else instead.

*Modèle:*     Philippe / ordinateur / calculatrice
—*Est-ce que Philippe a un ordinateur?*
—*Non, il n'a pas d'ordinateur, mais il a une calculatrice.*

1. Nathalie / motocyclette / vélo
2. tu / stylo / crayon
3. Monique et Didier / maison / appartement
4. vous / radioréveil / Walkman
5. tu / sac / portefeuille
6. Madeleine / plantes vertes / posters
7. vous / faim / soif
8. elle / besoin de / cassettes / compacts disques

**Suggestion, Il y a** and **voilà:**
(1) Place several items (books, notebooks, pen, backpack, etc.) on a desk. Ask: **Qu'est-ce qu'il y a sur le bureau? Est-ce qu'il y a des livres? Un magnétoscope?** Get yes/no answers. (2) Ask students to point out objects scattered around the classroom:
—**Est-ce qu'il y a une calculatrice?**
—**Voilà une calculatrice.**
(3) Introduce **voici** as part of the same activity.

The negative of **il y a un (une, des)** is **il n'y a pas de: Il n'y a pas de** plantes vertes dans la chambre. **Il n'y a pas de** stylos ici *(here).* **Voilà** and **voici** do not have a negative form.

## Note grammaticale

### *Il y a, voilà et voici*

The expressions **il y a** and **voilà** both are the equivalent of *there is* or *there are* in English. **Il y a** is used to state that a person, place, or thing exists. It does not necessarily mean that the item in question can be seen from where you are standing. **Voilà** is used to point out the location of a person, place, or thing. It is usually intended to get someone to look in that direction.

**Voici** is the equivalent of the English *here is* or *here are.* It is used to point out the location of a person, place, or thing that is near the speaker.

| | |
|---|---|
| Dans ma chambre **il y a** un lit, un bureau et des chaises. | In my room, *there are* a bed, a desk, and some chairs. (They exist.) |
| **Voilà** les chaises. | *There are* the chairs. (They are located away from me, the speaker. Look at them.) |
| **Voici** le bureau. | *Here is* the desk. (It is located near me, the speaker. Look at it!) |

**E.** **La chambre de Michel.** First tell whether each item is or is not found in Michel Kerguézec's room.

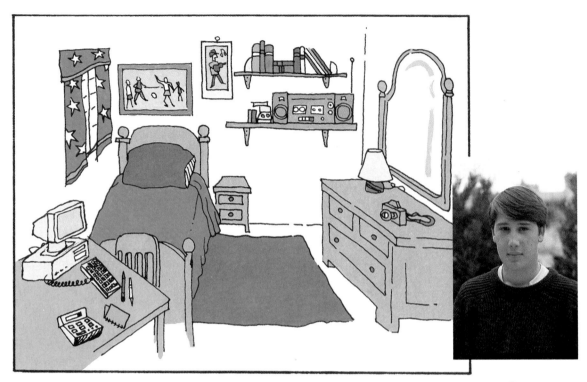

*Modèles:*   une lampe
*Dans la chambre de Michel il y a une lampe.*

des compacts disques
*Il n'y a pas de compacts disques.*

> **Reminder:** Use an indefinite article **(un, une, des)** after **il y a.** Use a definite article **(le, la, l', les)** after **voilà** and **voici.**

un lit / une chaise / un bureau / des cassettes / un ordinateur / des posters / un téléviseur / une chaîne stéréo / des livres / des crayons et des stylos / des plantes vertes / un radioréveil / un vélo / des cahiers / une calculatrice / un sac à dos

Now point out to another student those items that are in the room.

*Modèle:*   *Voilà la lampe.*

**F.** **Dans ta chambre est-ce qu'il y a...?** Find out from several classmates what they have and do not have in their rooms at home or in the dormitory.

Ex. F: ○

*Modèle:*   —*Dans ta chambre* (in your room) *est-ce qu'il y a des posters?*
—*Comment?* (What did you say?)
—*Tu as des posters dans ta chambre?*
—*Oui, il y a des posters dans ma chambre* (in my room). or
*Non, je n'ai pas de posters dans ma chambre.*

Suggestion, Le, la, les: Pick up objects in the classroom, identifying them by owner: **Voici le livre de Mark. Voici la calculatrice d'Hélène. Voici les cahiers de Marie.** Then continue, asking students:

—**Qu'est-ce que c'est?**

—**C'est le sac de Priscilla.** and/or

—**Ce sont les livres de Michel?**

—**Non, voilà les livres de Michel.**

If you present this structure in this way, you may omit Ex. H.

# S·T·R·U·C·T·U·R·E

### L'article défini *(le, la, l', les)* (suite)

Où est **la** lampe?     Where is *the* lamp?
Ce sont **les** clés **de** Pierre.     Those are Pierre's keys.

You have already learned that the definite article **(le, la, l', les)** is used in French to designate a noun in a general or collective sense. In this case, it often has no English equivalent: **Tu aimes le fromage?** *(Do you like cheese?)* The definite article may also designate a noun in a specific sense. The question **Où est la lampe?** asks for the location of a particular lamp (one that has already been mentioned in the conversation). The phrase **les clés de Pierre** refers to the particular keys that belong to Pierre. Notice in the latter example that the definite article can be used with **de** to indicate possession *(Pierre's keys)*.

▲   ▲   ▲

## APPLICATION

**Reminder:** Remember to use **c'est** with a singular noun and **ce sont** with a plural noun.

**G.  Ça, c'est...** *(That's . . .)* When you and a friend stay after class one day, you notice that your other classmates have left behind several of their belongings. You show these objects to your friend, who identifies the owners.

*Modèles:*     —Voici un livre. (Béatrice)
—*Ça, c'est le livre de Béatrice.*

—Voici des crayons. (Marc)
—*Ça, ce sont les crayons de Marc.*

1.  Voici un cahier. (Vincent)
2.  Voici une calculatrice. (Sylviane)
3.  Voici un sac. (Anne-Marie)
4.  Voici des cassettes. (Martine)
5.  Voici des livres. (Jean-Pierre)
6.  Voici des cahiers. (Yvonne)
7.  Voici un stylo. (Michel)
8.  Voici des clés. (Gérard)
9.  Voici un sac à dos. (Mireille)
10.  Voici une cassette. (Claude)

**H.  Voilà les livres de...** Point out objects belonging to other members of the class.

*Modèles:*     *Voilà les livres de Robert.*
*Voilà la calculatrice de Marthe.*

# PRONONCIATION   *La combinaison* **qu**

 **Student Tape:**
Chapitre 2
Segment 1

In English, the combination *qu*, except at the end of a word *(unique)*, is pronounced [kw]: *quote, quick, request.* In French, the combination **qu** is always pronounced [k]; the **u** is silent. Notice the difference between:

| *English* | *French* |
|-----------|----------|
| *Qu*ebec | **Qu**ébec |
| se*qu*ence | sé**qu**ence |

**I.**   Read each word aloud, being careful to pronounce the **qu** combination as [k].

est-ce que / croque-monsieur / qu'est-ce que / quelque chose / Jacqueline / Véronique / critique / Québec / disque

# S·T·R·U·C·T·U·R·E

## *Les adjectifs possessifs (1^{ère} et 2^{e} personnes)*

—Tu aimes **ton** ordinateur?
—Oui, j'aime beaucoup **mon** ordinateur.

—Do you like *your* computer?
—Yes, I like *my* computer a lot.

—Où est **ta** chambre?
—Voilà **ma** chambre.

—Where is *your* room?
—There's *my* room.

—Tu aimes **mes** amis?
—Oh, oui. J'aime bien **tes** amis.

—Do you like *my* friends?
—Oh, yeah. I like *your* friends.

—C'est **votre** maison?
—Non, ce n'est pas **notre** maison.

—Is that *your* house?
—No, it's not *our* house.

—Où sont **nos** clés?
—Voici **vos** clés.

—Where are *our* keys?
—Here are *your* keys.

Possessive adjectives in French agree with the noun they modify, *not* the possessor. Consequently, French has three forms for both *my* and "familiar" *your* and two forms for *our* and "formal or plural" *your*. The following chart summarizes the first- and second-person possessive adjectives:

| *Subject* | *Masculine singular* | *Feminine singular* | *Masc. and fem. plural* | *English equivalent* |
|-----------|----------------------|---------------------|-------------------------|----------------------|
| je | **mon** | **ma** | **mes** | *my* |
| tu | **ton** | **ta** | **tes** | *your* |
| nous | **notre** | **notre** | **nos** | *our* |
| vous | **votre** | **votre** | **vos** | *your* |

▲   ▲   ▲

## APPLICATION

**J.**  Remplacez le mot en italique et faites les changements nécessaires.

1.  Voilà mon *vélo*. (crayon / bureau / immeuble / Walkman)
2.  Voilà ma *calculatrice*. (maison / chaîne stéréo / résidence)
3.  Voilà mes *cassettes*. (plantes vertes / clés / amis)
4.  Où est ta *résidence?* (maison / chambre / cahier / sac à dos / porte-feuille / calculatrice)
5.  Où sont tes *compacts disques?* (cassettes / posters / livres / amis)
6.  Nous aimons notre *maison*. (voiture / ordinateur / posters / magnétoscope / amis / professeur)
7.  Est-ce que vous avez votre *stylo?* (voiture / calculatrice / cahiers / clés / carnet / vélo)

**K.  Non, non, non!** All of a sudden everyone seems confused about who certain things belong to. When a stranger tries to take your school things, you politely set him/her straight.

*Modèle:*     Ah, voici mon crayon.
              *Je m'excuse. Ce n'est pas votre crayon, c'est mon crayon.*

1.  Ah, voici mon cahier.
2.  Et ma calculatrice.
3.  Et mes livres.
4.  Et mes stylos.

Then your neighbors confuse their possessions with those belonging to your family.

*Modèle:*     C'est notre voiture?
              *Non, ce n'est pas votre voiture, c'est notre voiture.*

5.  C'est notre téléviseur?
6.  Ce sont nos chaises?
7.  C'est notre magnétoscope?
8.  Ce sont nos clés?

Finally, your friend thinks your possessions are his/hers.

*Modèle:*     Eh bien, donne-moi *(give me)* ma clé.
              *Mais non, ce n'est pas ta clé, c'est ma clé.*

9.   Eh bien, donne-moi mon crayon.
10.  Eh bien, donne-moi mes cahiers.
11.  Eh bien, donne-moi ma cassette.
12.  Eh bien, donne-moi mon sac à dos.

**L.  Vous avez faim? Vous avez soif?** When you ask some classmates whether they are hungry or thirsty, they respond by telling you what they would like to eat or drink. You get what they ask for and then distribute the items, using the appropriate possessive adjectives or definite articles + **de.**

BOISSONS:          **un Coca, une limonade, une eau minérale, une bière, un verre de vin, un citron pressé**

CHOSES À MANGER:   **un sandwich au ____ , une omelette au ____ , des frites, des croissants**

*Modèle:*          —*Vous avez soif?*
                   —*Oui, je voudrais un Coca.*
                   —*Pour moi, une limonade.*
                   —*Et moi, je vais prendre une eau minérale.*
                   —*Voilà ton Coca.*
                   —*Merci.*
                   —*Marie, c'est ta limonade?*
                   —*Non, ça, c'est la limonade de Sarah. Moi, j'ai une eau minérale.*
                   —*Oh, pardon! Voilà ton eau minérale.*

## ▲ ▲ ▲ ▲ ▲ ▲ ▲ ▲ ▲ Débrouillons-nous! ▲ ▲ ▲ ▲ ▲ ▲ ▲ ▲ ▲ ▲

*Petite révision de l'étape*

**M.  Échange.** Posez les questions à un(e) autre étudiant(e), qui va vous répondre.

Ex. M: ⇄

1.  Est-ce que tu habites dans un appartement?
2.  Qu'est-ce que tu as pour aller en ville? Une voiture? Un vélo?
3.  Est-ce que tu étudies beaucoup? Est-ce que tu as un stylo? Des livres? Un ordinateur? Une calculatrice?
4.  Est-ce que tu as une chaîne stéréo? Un radioréveil? Un Walkman?
5.  Dans ta chambre est-ce qu'il y a des livres? Des plantes vertes? Des posters? Un bureau?
6.  Tu as besoin d'un stylo? D'une calculatrice? De crayons?
7.  Tu as faim? (Qu'est-ce que tu voudrais?) Tu as soif? (Qu'est-ce que tu voudrais?)

**N.  Qu'est-ce qu'il y a dans ta chambre?** *(What's in your room?)* You have an important paper to write and need a quiet place to work, but there's a party going on where you live. Therefore, you would like to borrow someone else's room or apartment. Ask your classmates questions in order to find the most comfortable and best equipped place to work.

Ex. N: ○

**Follow-up,** Ex. N: Ask students: **Chez qui est-ce que vous voudriez étudier? Pourquoi?**

**À faire chez vous: CAHIER, Chapitre 2 / 1ère étape**

**Instructor's Tape:
Moi, j'aime
beaucoup...**

**Suggestion, Point de départ:**
Go over expressions on the
like/dislike continuum. Begin
with **aimer,** working up to
**adorer** and down to **détester.**
Then use the Instructor's Tape
to present the dialogue.

**ALLONS-Y!**
*Video Program*

ACTE 2: SCÈNE 1
LES COUPLES

**QUESTIONS DE FOND**
1. How long has the
   third couple known
   each other?
2. Which couple tells
   the most romantic
   story?
3. Compare American
   couples with those
   you see here.

# DEUXIÈME ÉTAPE

## Point de départ

▼▼▼▼▼▼▼▼▼▼▼▼▼▼▼

*Moi, j'aime beaucoup...*

Bonjour. Je m'appelle Christine. Et voici Robert. C'est mon **petit ami,** mais nous avons des **goûts** différents.

| Christine | Robert |
|---|---|
| J'aime les **chats.** | Moi, j'aime mieux les **chiens.** |
| J'aime beaucoup le camping. | Moi, je déteste la nature. |
| Je n'aime pas les sports. | Moi, j'adore le tennis. |
| Je n'aime pas du tout la télévision. | Moi, j'aime bien **regarder** la télé. |
| J'aime la musique classique. | Moi, je préfère la musique populaire. |
| J'aime le cinéma et le théâtre. | Moi, je n'aime pas le cinéma et je n'aime pas le théâtre **non plus.** |
| J'adore la **peinture.** | Moi, j'aime beaucoup la sculpture. |
| J'étudie les **langues** et les maths. | Moi, j'étudie les sciences et la littérature. |
| Je n'aime pas travailler. | Ah, moi, j'aime bien mon **travail.** |
| **Pourtant,** j'aime bien Robert. | Et moi, j'aime bien Christine. |

*Glossary (margin):*
boyfriend
tastes
cats / dogs
to look at, to watch
either
painting
languages
work
Nevertheless

## À VOUS! (Exercices de vocabulaire)

**A. Est-ce que vous aimez...?** Give your reactions to each item. If you agree with a positive reaction by the previous person, use the expression **aussi** *(also);* if you agree with a negative reaction by the previous person, use the expression **non plus** *(either).*

> *Modèle:*     —*Est-ce que vous aimez le tennis?*
> —*Oui, j'aime le tennis.* or *J'aime bien le tennis.* or *J'adore le tennis.* or *Je n'aime pas le tennis.*
> —*Et vous?*
> —*Moi aussi* (I, too), *j'aime le tennis.* or *Je n'aime pas le tennis non plus.*

1. le cinéma   2. la bière   3. les maths   4. le camping   5. la musique classique   6. la politique   7. les sports   8. les chats   9. regarder la télé   10. nager   11. danser   12. travailler   13. voyager   14. manger

**B. Qu'est-ce que vous aimez mieux?** Indicate your preferences. Use both the expression **aimer mieux** and the verb **préférer.**

> *Modèle:*     le football ou le basket
> —*J'aime mieux le football. Et toi?*
> —*Moi aussi, je préfère le football.* or *Moi, je préfère le basket.*

1. le football américain ou le base-ball
2. les chiens ou les chats
3. la peinture ou la sculpture
4. le cinéma ou le théâtre
5. la musique populaire ou le rock
6. la musique classique ou le jazz
7. écouter *(to listen to)* la radio ou regarder la télé
8. chanter ou danser
9. étudier ou travailler
10. aller en ville ou rester *(to stay)* à la maison

**Grammar:** You may use an infinitive as well as a noun after verbs such as **aimer: J'aime beaucoup regarder la télé.**

**Vocabulary:** You may also express varying degrees of liking and disliking. The following list goes from the strongest positive reaction to the strongest negative reaction—**j'adore / j'aime beaucoup / j'aime / j'aime bien / j'aime assez / j'aime un peu / je n'aime pas / je n'aime pas du tout / je déteste.**

Ex. B: ⇄

**Vocabulary:** In French, **le football** refers to soccer; football as played in the United States is called **le football américain.**

Ex. C: △

**C.** **Qu'est-ce que vous aimez le mieux?** When asking someone to compare more than two items, you must add the article **le** to **aimer mieux—aimer le mieux.** However, in the answer, the **le** is not needed. No change is made with **préférer.** Ask two of your classmates to choose from the following sets of items.

*Modèle:*     la musique classique, le jazz ou le rock
     —*Qu'est-ce que tu aimes le mieux—la musique classique, le jazz ou le rock?*
     —*Moi, j'aime mieux le rock.*
     —*Et toi?*
     —*Moi, je préfère la musique classique.*

1. le football, le football américain ou le basket
2. la peinture, la sculpture ou l'architecture
3. la musique, la danse ou le cinéma
4. la musique populaire, le funk ou le rock
5. les chiens, les chats ou les hamsters
6. écouter la radio, regarder la télé ou aller au cinéma
7. parler, chanter ou danser

# R·E·P·R·I·S·E

*Première étape*

Ex. D: ⇄

**D.** **Ma famille et moi, nous...** *(My family and I . . .)* Tell a classmate where you and your family live and what you own.

*Modèle:*     *Ma famille et moi, nous sommes de New York, mais nous habitons à Minneapolis dans une maison. Dans la maison il y a une chaîne stéréo, mais il n'y a pas d'ordinateur. Etc.*

**Implementation,** Ex. E: Give objects from the classroom (**stylo, cahier,** etc.) and/or visuals (photos, drawings) to students. Distribute items so that some belong to one student and others to two students. After a while, let students play the role of questioner.

**E.** **C'est à qui, ça?** *(Who does that belong to?)* Your instructor will point to objects and ask you who they belong to. He/she will then verify your answer.

*Modèle:*     —*C'est à qui, ça?*
     —*C'est le livre de Paul.*
     —*Paul, c'est votre livre?*
     —*Oui, c'est mon livre.* or *Non, c'est le livre de (Nancy).*

# S·T·R·U·C·T·U·R·E

Suggestion, Information questions: Make a statement, then ask students to verify the information: **Jean-Pierre habite à Rouen. Où est-ce qu'il habite?** Write question form on board. Other models: **Rouen se trouve en Normandie. Jean-Pierre a trois frères. Il aime manger les choses sucrées. Il n'étudie pas beaucoup parce qu'il n'aime pas les sciences.**

## *Les questions d'information **qui, où, que** et **pourquoi***

You have already learned how to ask questions that take *yes* or *no* as an answer. Frequently, however, you ask a question because you are seeking specific information:

—**Qui** regarde la télé?      —*Who* is watching TV?
—Claudine regarde la télé.      —Claudine is watching TV.

To find out *who* is doing something, use **qui.**

—**Où est-ce que** Claudine habite?      —*Where* does Claudine live?
—Elle habite à Bordeaux.      —She lives in Bordeaux.

To find out *where* something or someone is located, use **où + est-ce que (qu').**

**Grammar:** When **qui** is the subject of a sentence, the verb always takes the third-person singular form:—**Qui aime les sports?—Jean, Philippe et moi, nous aimons les sports.**

—**Où est** Bordeaux?      —*Where is* Bordeaux?
—Pardon?      —What did you say?
—**Où se trouve** la ville de Bordeaux?      —*Where is* the city of Bordeaux *located?*
—Bordeaux est au sud-ouest de Paris.      —Bordeaux is southwest of Paris.

When a question with **où** contains the verb **être** or the expression **se trouver, est-ce que** is not usually used.

—**Qu'est-ce qu'**elle regarde?      —*What* is she watching?
—Elle regarde un film.      —She's watching a movie.

To find out *what* someone wants or is doing, use **qu' est-ce que.**

—**Pourquoi est-ce qu'**elle ne regarde pas le match de foot?      —*Why* isn't she watching the soccer match?
—**Parce qu'**elle n'aime pas les sports.      —*Because* she doesn't like sports.

To ask *why,* use **pourquoi + est-ce que (qu').** The answer to this question usually begins with **parce que (qu').**

▲ ▲ ▲

## APPLICATION

**F.**  Remplacez les mots en italique et faites les changements nécessaires.

1. Qui *regarde la télé?* (écoute la radio / parle / mange / travaille / étudie le français)
2. Où est-ce que vous *habitez?* (travaillez / étudiez / aimez voyager / mangez)
3. Où est *Bordeaux?* (Toulouse / ta maison / mon crayon / mes clés / mes livres)
4. Qu'est-ce que tu *cherches?* (regardes / manges / écoutes / étudies)
5. Pourquoi est-ce qu'elle *n'étudie pas?* (ne travaille pas / regarde le match de foot / a besoin d'un ordinateur / n'a pas de cassettes)

Ex. G: ○

**G.  Faisons connaissance de Michel Kerguézec.** You have just met some friends of Michel Kerguézec. When they say something about Michel, you ask a follow-up question to keep the conversation going.

*Modèle:*    Michel n'habite pas à Rennes.
             *Où est-ce qu'il habite?*

1. Il étudie beaucoup. (qu'est-ce que)
2. Il n'aime pas les mathématiques. (pourquoi)
3. Il travaille. (où)
4. Il mange beaucoup. (qu'est-ce que / aimer)
5. Il passe l'été *(spends the summer)* à Cassis. (où)
6. Il a des chiens et des chats. (qu'est-ce que / aimer mieux)
7. Il y a des gens qui *(people who)* n'aiment pas Michel. (qui / pourquoi)

**H.  Faisons connaissance!** Ask a classmate questions in order to get to know him/her better. In some cases, you can get the information with a yes/no question; other times, you will need to use a question word (**qui, où, qu'est-ce que, pourquoi**). Find out . . .

*Modèle:*    where he/she lives
             —*Où est-ce que tu habites?*
             —*J'habite à Clarksburg.*

1. whether he/she is originally from the city where he/she now lives.
2. whether he/she works.
3. where he/she works.
4. why he/she works (or doesn't work). (Possible answer: **avoir besoin d'argent** [*money*].)
5. why he/she is studying French.
6. whether he/she has a dog or a cat. (Why or why not?)
7. what he/she likes more—music, sports, or politics.
8. who likes to travel more, you or he/she.
9. whether he/she likes to dance. (What? Where?)

# PRONONCIATION *La combinaison ch*

In English, the combination *ch* is usually pronounced with the hard sounds [tch] or [k]: *chicken, reach; character, architect.* In French, the combination **ch** usually has a softer sound, much like the *sh* in the English word *sheep.* Notice the difference in the following pairs:

| **English** | **French** |
|---|---|
| *ch*ief | **ch**ef |
| tou*ch* | tou**ch**e |
| ar*ch*itect | ar**ch**itecte |

**I.** Read each word aloud, being careful to pronounce **ch** as [sh]:

chante / chose / Chantal / chinois / chien / chambre / machine / chat / chaîne / chercher / chef / chic / chinois

**Prononciation:** There are a few words in French, mainly of Greek origin, in which **ch** is pronounced with a hard sound [k]: **orchestre, écho, chrétien, Christian(e).**

# S·T·R·U·C·T·U·R·E

## *Le présent du verbe irrégulier **faire** et quelques expressions avec **faire***

—Qu'est-ce qu'**on fait** aujourd'hui?

—Moi, **je fais** du tennis. Et vous?

—**Nous faisons** un tour à vélo.

—Jean-Louis aussi?

—Non, **il fait** des devoirs.

—What *are we doing* today?

—*I'm playing* tennis. What about you?

—*We're going* for a bike ride.

—Jean-Louis too?

—No, *he's doing* homework.

| **faire** *(to do, to make)* | |
|---|---|
| je **fais** | nous **faisons** |
| tu **fais** | vous **faites** |
| il, elle, on **fait** | ils, elles **font** |

The verb **faire** is used in idiomatic expressions where the English equivalent is not the basic meaning of the verb. The following are a few of these expressions. You will encounter additional expressions in future chapters:

| **faire un voyage** | to take (go on) a trip |
|---|---|
| **faire une promenade** | to take (go for) a walk |
| **faire du sport** | to participate in sports |
| **faire du ski** | to go skiing |
| **faire du tennis** | to play tennis |
| **faire un tour (à vélo, en voiture, à moto)** | to go for a ride (on a bike, in a car, on a motorcycle) |

**Nous faisons une promenade.**
**Tu fais du ski?**

*We are going for a walk.*
*Do you ski (go skiing)?*

**Suggestion, Faire:** (1) Have students repeat the conjugation of **faire** while you write pronouns in four groups: **je, tu, il, elle, on / ils, elles / nous / vous.** (2) Repeat in negative. (3) Write verb forms in five groups: **je, tu / il, elle, on / ils, elles / nous / vous.** (4) Act out the various activities expressed with **faire** while saying: **Je fais du ski. Je fais une promenade.** Then ask students: **Qui aime faire du ski? Qui aime faire un tour à vélo?**, etc.

**Grammar:** The verb **faire** is often used in questions. In such cases, the answer frequently involves a verb other than **faire:**
—**Qu'est-ce que tu fais?**
—**Je travaille.**
—**Qu'est-ce qu'ils aiment faire?**
—**Ils adorent voyager.**

▲  ▲  ▲

## APPLICATION

**J.**    Remplacez le sujet et faites les changements nécessaires.

1. *Jean-Luc* fait du ski dans les Alpes. (Béatrice / nous / les amis de Sylvie / je / vous / tu)
2. *Marie-Claire* ne fait pas du ski. (Stéphane / je / vous / mon ami / tu / nous / mes camarades de chambre)
3. Qu'est-ce que *Pierre* fait? (tu / vous / les autres / on / nous / Chantal)

Ex. K: ○

**K.**    **Qu'est-ce qu'on fait ce week-end?** Michel Kerguézec calls up a friend to see what everyone is doing this weekend. The friend in turn asks the person(s) in question what he/she/they are doing. Play the role of Michel and use the suggested activities.

> *Modèle:*    Martine / travailler
> MICHEL:    *Qu'est-ce que Martine fait ce week-end?*
> L'AMI(E):    *Martine, qu'est-ce que tu fais ce week-end?*
> MARTINE:    *Je travaille ce week-end.*
> MICHEL:    *Hein? Qu'est-ce qu'elle fait?*
> L'AMI(E):    *Elle travaille.*

1. Jean-Pierre / étudier
2. Maurice et Vincent / rester à la maison
3. Bernadette / faire du ski
4. Paul / faire du tennis
5. Gérard et Yvette / travailler
6. René / voyager

Ex. L: ○ To encourage variety, assign activities or have students pick them from a hat.

**L.**    **Qu'est-ce qu'on fait ce soir?** Ask several people what they would like to do tonight. They will answer using one of the possibilities listed below. In each case, tell whether their idea coincides with yours.

> *Modèle:*    VOUS:    *Qu'est-ce qu'on fait ce soir?*
> ÉTUDIANT(E):    *Moi, je voudrais aller danser.*
> VOUS:    *Moi aussi, je voudrais aller danser.* or *Moi, je voudrais faire une promenade.*

faire du tennis / faire une promenade / faire un tour en voiture (à vélo, à moto) / parler / manger / aller danser / aller nager / regarder la télé / écouter des cassettes / rester à la maison

▲ ▲ ▲ ▲ ▲ ▲ ▲ ▲ ▲ ▲ **Débrouillons-nous!** ▲ ▲ ▲ ▲ ▲ ▲ ▲ ▲ ▲ ▲

*Petite révision de l'étape*

**M. Échange.** Posez les questions à un(e) autre étudiant(e), qui va vous répondre.

Ex. M: ⇄

1. Est-ce que tu aimes la nature? La politique? Les sports?
2. Est-ce que tu aimes mieux le thé, le café ou le lait?
3. Est-ce que tu as besoin d'une calculatrice? Pourquoi ou pourquoi pas?
4. Où est-ce que tu aimes passer l'été? Où est ___ ?
5. Qui aime mieux le football américain, toi ou ___ ?
6. Est-ce que tu fais du ski? Du tennis?
7. Qu'est-ce que tu aimes faire pendant *(during)* le week-end?

**N. Moi, je suis...** Imagine that it is your first day in an international school where the common language is French. Go up to another student and introduce yourself. Tell who you are, what you do, where you are from. Then try to give the other person an idea of what you like and dislike, giving examples (where appropriate) of what you own or don't own.

Ex. N: ⇄

📖 **À faire chez vous: CAHIER, Chapitre 2 / 2e étape**

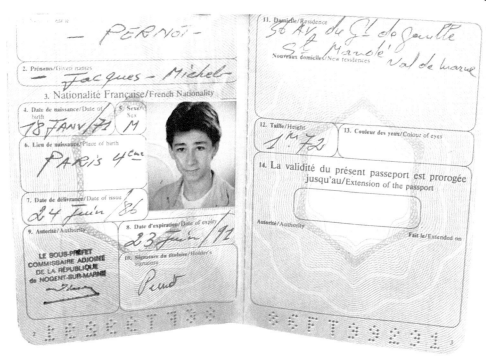

**Instructor's Tape:**
**Voici ma famille!**

**Transparency:**
**2-7** (Michel
Kerguézec's
family tree)

ALLONS-Y!
Video Program

ACTE 2: SCÈNE 2
UNE FAMILLE À
LA GUADELOUPE

**QUESTIONS DE FOND**
1. What is Christine's
   mother's name and
   profession? And her
   father's?
2. Name two of Chris-
   tine's other relatives
   and their professions.
3. What is Christine's
   profession?

# TROISIÈME ÉTAPE

## Point de départ

*Voici ma famille!*

first name
last name
father / mother / sister /
   brothers / is named
fairly tall / brown hair /
   brown eyes / grandfather /

grandmother

Bonjour. Je m'appelle Michel Kerguézec. Michel, c'est mon **prénom.** Kergué-zec, c'est mon **nom de famille.** Nous sommes quatre dans ma famille. J'ai un **père,** une **mère** et une **sœur.** Je n'ai pas de **frères.** Ma sœur **s'appelle** Sophie. Elle est **assez grande.** Elle a les **cheveux bruns** et les **yeux bruns** aussi. Nous habitons dans une maison à Locmariaquer avec mon **grand-père** et ma **grand-mère.**

**Variation:** If you have not done
the alternative **Étape préliminaire** that introduces numbers,
do the **Structure** section on p.
74 (numbers from 1–69) before
presenting the **Point de
départ,** thus enabling students
to respond to questions about
the size of their families.

**Suggestion, Point de départ:**
Present vocabulary with
student books closed, using
the transparency and the
Instructor's Tape.

who / uncle
married / His wife
son / fairly short / blond hair
blue eyes / wears glasses /
   aunt
Her husband

J'ai aussi de la famille **qui** n'habite pas en Bretagne. Voilà mon **oncle** Jacques. C'est le frère de mon père. Il est **marié. Sa femme** s'appelle Élise. Ils ont un **fils**—c'est mon cousin André. Il est **assez petit.** Il a les **cheveux blonds** et les **yeux bleus.** Il **porte des lunettes.** Ma **tante** Élise a aussi une fille, Jacque-line, d'un premier mariage. Jacqueline est mariée. **Son mari** s'appelle René.

# À VOUS! (Exercices de vocabulaire)

**A.  Vous et votre famille.** First, complete the following sentences with information about you and your family.

1.  Je m'appelle...
2.  Mon prénom, c'est...
3.  Mon nom de famille, c'est...
4.  Mon père s'appelle...
5.  Ma mère s'appelle...
6.  J'ai ____ frères. Il(s) s'appelle(nt)... (Je n'ai pas de frères.)
7.  J'ai ____ sœurs. Elle(s) s'appelle(nt)... (Je n'ai pas de sœurs.)
8.  Mes grands-parents habitent (n'habitent pas) avec nous.

**B.  Du côté de votre mère... Du côté de votre père...** *(On your mother's side . . . On your father's side . . .)* Answer the following questions about family members on both sides of your family.

1.  Est-ce que votre mère est d'une petite famille ou d'une famille nombreuse *(a big family)?*
2.  Est-ce que vous avez des oncles? Comment est-ce qu'ils s'appellent? Est-ce qu'ils sont mariés? Est-ce qu'ils ont des enfants? des fils? des filles?
3.  Comment s'appellent vos cousins? Où est-ce qu'ils habitent?
4.  Est-ce que vous avez des tantes aussi du côté de votre mère? Est-ce qu'elles travaillent? Elles sont avocates?
5.  Et votre père, il est d'une famille nombreuse?
6.  Est-ce que vous avez des tantes du côté de votre père? Est-ce qu'elles sont mariées? Est-ce qu'elles ont des enfants?
7.  Comment s'appellent vos cousines du côté de votre père?
8.  Est-ce que votre père a aussi des frères? Où est-ce qu'ils habitent? Est-ce qu'ils travaillent? Ils sont architectes?

**Variation,** Ex. B: Have students work in pairs; remind them to change **vous** to **tu.**

**Vocabulary:** Some additional words that may prove useful in describing a particular family situation are: **un beau-père** *(stepfather, father-in-law),* **une belle-mère** *(stepmother, mother-in-law),* **un beau-frère** (stepbrother, brother-in-law), **une belle-sœur** *(stepsister, sister-in-law).*

   If one of your parents is dead, you may say: **Mon père est mort. Ma mère est morte.** If your parents are divorced, you may say: **Mes parents sont divorcés.**

## Note grammaticale

### *L'apparence*

To describe hair and eyes in French, use the verb **avoir** and a definite article.

| | |
|---|---|
| **J'ai les cheveux roux.** | *I have red hair.* |
| **Mon grand-père a les cheveux gris.** | *My grandfather has gray hair.* |

To say that someone is short or tall, use the adjectives **petit** and **grand**. If the person is female, add an **e.** If you are talking about more than one person, add an **s**:

| | |
|---|---|
| **Ma sœur est très petite.** | *My sister is very short (small).* |
| **Mes frères sont assez grands.** | *My brothers are fairly tall (big).* |

**Implementation,** Ex. C: Describe yourself, some of your family members, and several students in the class to clarify vocabulary and structures for describing physical traits. Then ask questions about other students and a few family members before dividing the class into small groups to describe themselves and their families.

**C. Ma famille.** Describe each member of your immediate family, telling whether he/she is short or tall and indicating the color of his/her hair and eyes. Also mention whether or not he/she wears glasses. Remember to include yourself!

*Modèle:*     *Mon père est très grand. Il n'a pas de cheveux. Il est chauve (bald). Il a les yeux bruns et il ne porte pas de lunettes.*

## R·E·P·R·I·S·E

Ex. D: ⇄

**Reminder:** Be sure to distinguish between nouns that require an indefinite article **(un, une, des)** and nouns that require a definite article **(le, la, l', les).** Remember that the negative of **un, une, des** is usually **de;** however, **le, la, l', les** do not change after a negated verb.

### *Deuxième étape*

**D. Faisons connaissance!** To get to know one of your classmates better, ask him/her a series of yes/no questions. Use the elements suggested below.

*Modèles:*     avoir / voiture
            —*Tu as une voiture?*
            —*Oui, j'ai une voiture.* or *Non, je n'ai pas de voiture.*

                aimer / sports
            —*Tu aimes les sports?*
            —*Oui, j'aime les sports.* or *Non, je n'aime pas les sports.*

1. habiter / dans / appartement
2. aimer / animaux

3.   aimer mieux / chiens / ou / chats
4.   avoir / chien (chat)
5.   aimer / musique
6.   avoir / chaîne stéréo
7.   aimer le mieux / rock / funk / jazz / musique classique
8.   faire / ski
9.   aimer / étudier
10.  faire / devoirs

**E.   Un nouvel ami.** *(A new friend.)* A French exchange student whom you have just met is telling you about his family and his life in France. Each time he makes a statement, ask a follow-up question using **qui, où, qu'est-ce que,** or **pourquoi.**

*Modèle:*        Nous sommes de Paris, mais nous n'habitons pas à Paris.
                  *Où est-ce que vous habitez?*

1.   Nous habitons à Aix-en-Provence.
2.   Mes parents travaillent à Aix.
3.   Moi, je fais des études à l'université. J'étudie les mathématiques et les sciences.
4.   Je n'étudie pas les langues.
5.   J'aime mes profs et les autres étudiants, mais le week-end j'aime mieux être avec mes amis. Je fais beaucoup de choses avec mes amis.
6.   Nous faisons du ski.
7.   Je regarde très peu la télé.
8.   Mais je connais quelqu'un qui *(know somebody who)* regarde beaucoup la télé.

**Le savez-vous?**
▲▲▲▲▲▲▲▲▲▲▲▲▲▲▲▲
**Brittany** (La Bretagne) **is the _____ part of France.**
**a. northernmost**
**b. southernmost**
**c. easternmost**
**d. westernmost**

Réponse  ▲▲▲

When a number precedes a noun beginning with a vowel or a vowel sound, liaison occurs and the final consonant is pronounced: **cinq étudiants, huit appartements.** In liaison, **x** and **s** are pronounced **z: deux appartements, trois amis, dix omelettes, vingt-six ordinateurs.**

The **t** of **vingt** is not pronounced, except in liaison: **vingt livres,** but **vingt étudiants.** However, in the numbers from 21 through 29, the **t** of **vingt** is always pronounced: **vingt-cinq.**

# S·T·R·U·C·T·U·R·E

## *Les nombres de 0 à 69*

The French equivalent of the number *one* agrees with the noun it introduces: **un livre, une orange.** Zero and the numbers from two on always stay the same.

| | | | | | |
|---|---|---|---|---|---|
| 0 | **zéro** | 7 | **sept** | 14 | **quatorze** |
| 1 | **un, une** | 8 | **huit** | 15 | **quinze** |
| 2 | **deux** | 9 | **neuf** | 16 | **seize** |
| 3 | **trois** | 10 | **dix** | 17 | **dix-sept** |
| 4 | **quatre** | 11 | **onze** | 18 | **dix-huit** |
| 5 | **cinq** | 12 | **douze** | 19 | **dix-neuf** |
| 6 | **six** | 13 | **treize** | 20 | **vingt** |

The numbers from twenty-one through sixty-nine follow a regular pattern. 21, 31, 41, 51, and 61 all use **et;** other numbers use only a hyphen.

| | | | | | |
|---|---|---|---|---|---|
| | | 30 | **trente** | 40 | **quarante** |
| 21 | **vingt et un** | 31 | **trente et un** | 41 | **quarante et un** |
| 22 | **vingt-deux** | 32 | **trente-deux** | 42 | **quarante-deux** |
| 23 | **vingt-trois,** etc. | 33 | **trente-trois,** etc. | 43 | **quarante-trois,** etc. |
| 50 | **cinquante** | 60 | **soixante** | | |
| 51 | **cinquante et un** | 61 | **soixante et un** | | |
| 52 | **cinquante-deux** | 62 | **soixante-deux** | | |
| 53 | **cinquante-trois,** etc. | 63 | **soixante-trois,** etc. | | |

▲   ▲   ▲

# APPLICATION

**F.   Pour compter...**

1.   Comptez de 0 à 10, de 10 à 0, de 11 à 20, de 20 à 11, de 0 à 20, de 20 à 0.
2.   Comptez de 21 jusqu'à 69, de 69 à 21.
3.   Comptez de 10 jusqu'à 60 par 10.
4.   Donnez les nombres impairs *(odd)* de 1 jusqu'à 69.
5.   Donnez les nombres pairs *(even)* de 2 jusqu'à 68.
6.   Lisez les numéros de téléphone suivants: 45. 31.47.54 / 55. 62.17.41 / 61. 33.14.68 / 20. 55.15.61 / 30. 29.12.66 / 21. 57.44.13 / 48. 32.19.51 / 66. 39.11.16.

**G. Calculons!** Do the following arithmetic problems.

**Follow-up,** Ex. G: Speed math drill. Write on board problems such as: **6 × 10 − 9 − 3 + 16 = ?** Students give results of each calculation: **60, 51, 48, 64.**

*Modèle:*   2 + 2
—*Combien font* (how much is) *deux et deux?*
—*Deux et deux font quatre.*

1. 3 + 6       5. 8 + 12       9. 42 + 23       13. 27 + 39
2. 7 + 9       6. 10 + 30       10. 28 + 9       14. 24 + 27
3. 11 + 4       7. 25 + 35       11. 19 + 42
4. 14 + 3       8. 16 + 18       12. 21 + 18

*Modèle:*   3 × 20
—*Combien font trois fois vingt?*
—*Trois fois vingt font soixante.*

15. 2 × 15       17. 3 × 19       19. 4 × 10       21. 3 × 7       23. 5 × 5
16. 4 × 9       18. 7 × 8       20. 6 × 11       22. 2 × 24       24. 9 × 7

## Note grammaticale

**Suggestion,** Age and **combien de:** Give your age, then guess a student's age and have him/her agree or correct you. Also ask students about numbers of brothers and sisters and their ages.

### *Combien de...?  /  Quel âge avez-vous?*

The expression **combien** is the equivalent of both *how much* and *how many*. When **combien** precedes a noun, it must be followed by **de.**

—**Combien de** frères avez-vous?
—J'ai trois frères.

—*How many* brothers do you have?
—*I have three brothers.*

—**Combien de** voitures est-ce qu'ils ont?
—Ils ont deux voitures.

—*How many* cars do they have?
—*They have two cars.*

To ask someone's age in French, use the verb **avoir** and the expression **quel âge:**

—**Quel âge as-tu?**
—**J'ai dix-neuf ans.**
—**Quel âge a ton père?**
—**Il a quarante-sept ans.**

—*How old are you?*
—*I am 19.*
—*How old is your father?*
—*He's 47.*

When stating age, note that the word **ans** *(years)* must be included in French even though the word *years* may be omitted in English.

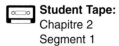 **Student Tape:**
Chapitre 2
Segment 1

**H.  Toi et ta famille.** Ask several of your classmates the following questions.

1.  Quel âge as-tu?
2.  Quel âge a ton père? et ta mère?
3.  Combien de frères est-ce que tu as? Quel âge ont-ils (a-t-il)?
4.  Combien de sœurs est-ce que tu as? Quel âge ont-elles (a-t-elle)?
5.  Combien d'oncles et de tantes est-ce que tu as du côté de ton père (ta mère)?

# PRONONCIATION  *Les consonnes c et g*

Depending on the sound that follows it, the French consonant **c** may represent the hard sound [k], as in the English word *car,* or the soft sound [s], as in the English word *nice.* Similarly, the consonant **g** may represent either the hard sound [g], as in *gun,* or the soft sound [ʒ], as in *sabotage.*

The hard sounds [k] and [g] occur before another consonant and before the vowels **a, o,** and **u:**

[k]: **c**lasse, **c**ar, **c**orps, é**c**u

[g]: **g**rand, **g**are, mé**g**ot, **g**uide

The soft sounds [s] and [ʒ] occur before the vowels **e, i,** and **y. C** is also soft when it has a cedilla (**ç**):

[s]: fa**c**e, ra**c**ine, Saint-**C**yr, fran**ç**ais

[ʒ]: â**g**e, ri**g**ide, **g**ymnase

Ex. I: ○

**I.**  Read each word aloud, being careful to give the appropriate hard or soft sound to the consonants **c** and **g.**

café / citron / croissant / ça / cahier / pièces / combien / Françoise / Orangina / goûts / rouge / fromage / portugais / belge / langue / Roger / égyptienne

# S·T·R·U·C·T·U·R·E

## Les adjectifs possessifs (3ᵉ personne)

—C'est le vélo de Bénédicte?
—Oui, c'est **son** vélo.

—It's Bénédicte's bike?
—Yes, it's *her* bike.

—Où est la chambre de Mathieu?
—**Sa** chambre est là-bas.

—Where is Mathieu's room?
—*His* room is over there.

—Tu aimes les amis de ta sœur?

—Do you like your sister's friends?

—Oui, en général, j'aime **ses** amis.

—Yes, generally I like *her* friends.

—Où sont les cassettes de Jeanne et de Monique?
—Voici **leurs** cassettes.

—Where are Jeanne and Monique's cassettes?
—Here are *their* cassettes.

Suggestion, Possessive adjectives: Present as in **Étape 1.** This time do not speak directly to the owner: **Voici un livre. C'est le livre de Paul? Oui, c'est son livre.** Visually reinforce use of **son, sa, ses** for masculine and feminine and **leur(s)** for singular and plural.

The third-person singular forms of the possessive adjectives are **son, sa,** and **ses.** Like the first- and second-person possessive adjectives (**mon, ta, nos, votre,** etc.), these adjectives agree in gender with the noun they modify, *not* with the person who possesses the noun. The third-person plural of the possessive adjective has only two forms: **leur** (with singular nouns) and **leurs** (with plural nouns).

| Subject | Masculine singular | Feminine singular | Masc. and fem. plural | English equivalent |
|---------|--------------------|--------------------|-----------------------|--------------------|
| je | **mon** | **ma** | **mes** | *my* |
| tu | **ton** | **ta** | **tes** | *your* |
| il, elle, on | **son** | **sa** | **ses** | *his, her* |
| nous | **notre** | **notre** | **nos** | *our* |
| vous | **votre** | **votre** | **vos** | *your* |
| ils, elles | **leur** | **leur** | **leurs** | *their* |

▲  ▲  ▲

**Grammar:** Because a possessive adjective agrees with the noun it modifies and *not* with the possessor, the gender of a possessor in the third person must be determined from the context, not from the adjective:
**son** père *(his father* or *her father)*
**son** vélo *(her bike* or *his bike)*
**sa** mère *(his mother* or *her mother)*
**sa** chambre *(her room* or *his room)*
**ses** amis *(her friends* or *his friends)*

**Grammar:** When a feminine noun begins with a vowel or a vowel sound, the masculine form (**son**) is used: **son‿auto, son‿amie.**
  The **s** of **ses** and **leurs** is silent, except before a noun beginning with a vowel or a vowel sound. Then liaison takes place: **leurs‿avocats.**

Découvrez la France... et l'Europe! avec...

**T**OURING **C**AMPING **C**ARISTE **C**ARAVANING **F**RANCE

TCCF
*Votre Club*

## APPLICATION

**J.**  Remplacez les mots en italique et faites les changements nécessaires.

1. Voilà son *stylo.* (cahier / appartement / amie / vélo)
2. Où est sa *chambre?* (maison / calculatrice / clé / télévision)
3. Ce sont ses *clés?* (cassettes / cahiers / amis / stylos)
4. Où est leur *ordinateur?* (transistor / voiture / appartement / maison)
5. Voici leurs *livres.* (clés / amies / crayons / compacts disques)
6. Voici son *crayon.* (maison / appartement / ami / amie / cassettes / amis / chaîne stéréo / cahier)
7. Voilà leur *maison.* (chambre / voiture / clés / amis / ordinateur / appartement / livres)

Ex. K: ⇄

**K.  C'est la chambre d'Anne-Marie, n'est-ce pas?** You are showing a friend around a dormitory. As you point out different places, people, and objects, he/she tries to identify them. You confirm the identification, using the appropriate possessive adjective **(son, sa, ses, leur, leurs).**

*Modèle:*    chambre / Anne-Marie
—*Voici une chambre.*
—*C'est la chambre d'Anne-Marie, n'est-ce pas?*
—*Oui, c'est sa chambre.*

1. chambre / Robert
2. chambre / Guy et Jacques
3. clés / Éric
4. clés / Annick et Pascale
5. clés / Véronique

6. amie / Claire
7. amie / Jean-Luc
8. amis / Yvonne
9. bureau / Roger
10. bureau / Nicole

Ex. L: ⇄

**L.  À qui est (sont)...?** *(Whose . . . ?)* Find out to whom the following objects belong.

Dominique

M. Allard

M. et Mme Lehmann

*Modèles:*   la chaîne stéréo
—*À qui est la chaîne stéréo?*
—*C'est la chaîne stéréo de Dominique.*
—*Ah, bon. C'est sa chaîne stéréo.*

les cassettes
—*À qui sont les cassettes?*
—*Ce sont les cassettes de Dominique.*
—*Ah, bon. Ce sont ses cassettes.*

**Follow-up,** Ex. L: Choose four students to play the roles of Dominique, M. Allard, M. and Mme Lehmann. Then repeat the items in Ex. L:—**À qui est la chaîne stéréo?**—**C'est la chaîne stéréo de Dominique.**—**Dominique, c'est ta chaîne stéréo?**—**Oui, c'est ma chaîne stéréo.**—**Oui, c'est sa chaîne stéréo.**

1. le cahier   2. la voiture   3. les chiens   4. le vélo   5. les livres
6. l'appareil-photo *(camera)*   7. la maison   8. les clés   9. la chambre

## ▲▲▲▲▲▲▲▲▲ Débrouillons-nous! ▲▲▲▲▲▲▲▲▲▲

*Petite révision de l'étape*

**M.   Échange.** Posez les questions suivantes à un(e) autre étudiant(e), qui va vous répondre.

Ex. M: ⇄

1. Vous êtes combien dans ta famille?
2. Comment s'appelle ton père? Et ta mère?
3. Est-ce qu'ils travaillent tous les deux *(both)?* Où? Qu'est-ce qu'ils font?
4. Combien de sœurs est-ce que tu as? Quel âge ont-elles? Est-ce que tu as aussi des frères? Quel âge ont-ils?
5. Est-ce qu'ils (elles) sont étudiant(e)s aussi?
6. Où est-ce que tes grands-parents habitent—dans une maison? dans un appartement?
7. Quel est le prénom de ton (ta) meilleur(e) *(best)* ami(e)?
8. Quel âge a-t-il (elle)?
9. Où est-ce qu'il (elle) habite?
10. Est-ce que ses parents travaillent aussi?
11. Combien de frères et de sœurs est-ce qu'il (elle) a?
12. Est-ce qu'ils (elles) sont marié(e)s?

Ex. N: ⇄

**N.   Ta famille.** Find out as much as you can about another student's family. Begin by getting information about the size and composition of the family. Then choose one member of the family (mother, father, brother, sister, or grandparent) and ask more detailed questions.

**À faire chez vous: CAHIER, Chapitre 2 / 3e étape**

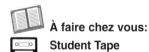

**À faire chez vous: Student Tape**

Now that you've completed the first three **étapes** of **Chapitre 2,** do Segment 2 of the STUDENT TAPE. See **CAHIER, Chapitre 2,** *Écoutons!,* for exercises that accompany this segment.

# QUATRIÈME ÉTAPE

## L·E·C·T·U·R·E

### Mon identité

*The ability to read in French develops more rapidly than the skills of speaking, listening, and writing. One reason is the large number of cognates (similar words) shared by French and English. Use the many cognates in the paragraphs below to get the general idea* without *consulting the definitions that follow.*

Je suis présidente d'une grande[1] entreprise. J'ai une grande maison, quatre téléviseurs couleur et trois voitures. Mon mari et moi, nous voyageons beaucoup. Nous avons un chalet en Suisse et un appartement à Paris. Mes enfants[2] sont dans une école[3] privée et chacun[4] a une chaîne stéréo, une grande quantité de disques compacts et de vidéos et une voiture. Ma vie[5] est très intéressante; je n'ai pas de problèmes.

Je suis étudiante. Je travaille comme serveuse[6] et j'habite dans une petite chambre en ville. J'aime les sports, surtout[7] le tennis. J'adore la musique classique. Je n'ai pas de disques compacts, mais j'écoute[8] souvent la radio. J'étudie les langues, la littérature et la linguistique parce que ce sont des sujets fascinants. J'aime ma vie; je n'ai pas de problèmes.

Je suis père de famille. J'ai deux enfants: un fils et une fille. Nous n'avons qu'une[9] petite maison, mais elle est confortable. Ma femme et moi, nous faisons beaucoup de choses[10] avec[11] nos enfants. Nous aimons le camping et les sports. Ma femme fait du ski; moi, j'aime mieux le football. Nous célébrons les jours de fête[12] en famille —oncles, tantes, cousins, cousines et grands-parents, nous dînons ensemble.[13] Ma vie est très agréable; je n'ai pas de problèmes.

Je suis à la retraite.[14] Ma femme est morte en 1990. J'habite avec mon fils Michel à Rennes. Il est marié. Sa femme s'appelle Renée. Ils ont deux filles. Je ne travaille pas. J'aime beaucoup la nature et je fais souvent des promenades. Le soir[15] je mange avec la famille et après le dîner je regarde la télévision. Ma vie est assez agréable; je n'ai pas de problèmes.

Je suis professeur de psychiatrie. Je travaille dans une clinique à Bordeaux. J'ai un mari très sympathique.[16] Nous aimons aller[17] au théâtre et au cinéma. Nous avons beaucoup d'amis et nous aimons discuter ensemble. Nous parlons des crises d'identité, du matérialisme, des goûts, de la famille, des influences sociales sur la personnalité. Au travail, je passe mon temps[18] à analyser les personnes «qui n'ont pas de problèmes».

1. large   2. children   3. school   4. each one   5. life   6. waitress   7. especially   8. listen (to)
9. only a   10. things   11. with   12. holidays   13. together   14. retired   15. in the evening
16. nice (friendly)   17. to go   18. spend my time

## COMPRÉHENSION

**A.   Les mots apparentés.** *(Cognates.)* What do you think each of the following cognates means?

la présidente / couleur / voyager / privé(e) / la quantité / intéressant(e) / le problème / la linguistique / fascinant / confortable / dîner / agréable / la nature / la psychiatrie / la clinique / l'identité / le matérialisme / l'influence / social(e) / la personnalité / analyser

**B.   Vrai ou faux?** Reread the **Lecture** using the definitions at the end. Then decide which statements are true **(vrai)** and which are false **(faux).** Support your answers.

1.   La présidente d'entreprise

     a.  Je suis matérialiste.
     b.  J'ai une grande maison à Paris.
     c.  Je suis riche.
     d.  Je passe les vacances avec mes enfants.

2.   L'étudiante

     a.  Je travaille dans un restaurant.
     b.  J'adore le tennis.
     c.  J'habite dans un appartement.
     d.  Je fais des sciences.
     e.  J'ai une chaîne stéréo et beaucoup de cassettes.

3.   Le père de famille

     a.  J'ai cinq enfants.
     b.  J'ai trois filles.
     c.  Je n'aime pas le camping.
     d.  Je fais du sport, surtout du ski.
     e.  Je passe les jours de fête en famille.

4.   L'homme à la retraite

     a.  J'habite avec la famille de mon fils à Rennes.
     b.  Je fais souvent des promenades avec ma femme.
     c.  Je prends le déjeuner dans un restaurant fast-food avec mes amis.
     d.  Le soir je suis à la maison.

5.   Le professeur de psychiatrie

     a.  J'aime bien mon mari.
     b.  J'aime les films.
     c.  J'aime mieux les idées que les actions.
     d.  J'adore les discussions.
     e.  J'analyse les problèmes des présidentes d'entreprise, des étudiantes, des pères de famille et des retraités.

# R·E·P·R·I·S·E

*Troisième étape*

**C. Qui a le plus grand nombre de...?** *(Who has the most . . . ?)* Go around the class asking other students how many brothers, sisters, aunts, uncles, and cousins they have. Based on your findings, your instructor will try to determine **qui a le plus grand nombre de frères, de sœurs,** etc.

**D. Qui est-ce?** *(Who is it?)* Give a short description of someone in your class. The others will try to guess who it is. Include in your description size, color of hair and eyes, and whether or not the person wears glasses. If no one guesses, add another detail (something the person has, something you know about the size of the person's family, what he/she likes to do, etc.).

Implementation, Ex. C: Allow students to circulate for a short time. Then ask the five questions, comparing answers from different parts of the classroom (i.e., students will not have had time to talk to everyone).

Ex. D: ◯

## Point d'arrivée

*Activités orales*

### Exprimons-nous!

When French speakers do not hear or understand what someone says, they use expressions such as **Comment? Pardon? Quoi? Hein?** to ask for repetition. The latter two expressions are informal.

—Ils n'aiment pas le vin.
—**Comment? (Pardon?)**

—They don't like wine.
—*Excuse me. What did you say?*

—M. et Mme Verlay, ils n'aiment pas le vin.

—M. et Mme Verlay don't like wine.

—Tu veux une boisson?

—Do you want something to drink?

—**Hein? (Quoi?)**
—Est-ce que tu voudrais une boisson?

—*Huh? What'd you say?*
—Would you like something to drink?

📖 À faire chez vous:
📼 **Student Tape**

**CAHIER, Chapitre 2:**
*Rédigeons! / Travail de fin de chapitre* (including STUDENT TAPE, Chapitre 2, Segment 3)

Le savez-vous?
▲▲▲▲▲▲▲▲▲▲▲▲▲▲
Mémé **et** Pépé **are terms often used by French children when talking to or about their** ____ .
a. mother and father
b. grandmother and grandfather
c. brother and sister
d. uncle and aunt

Réponse ▲▲▲

▲▲▲   b

Ex. E: ⇄ Pair students who
have not worked together on
an **Échange** in this chapter.

**E.** **Faisons connaissance!** Get to know another student by trying to discover the indicated information. He/she will ask the same things about you. Find out his/her name; where he/she is from; where he/she lives now; the size and makeup of his/her family; his/her interests (sports, politics, etc.); his/her possessions; his/her likes and dislikes (activities).

**F.** **Je suis...** Present yourself to the class. Give as much information as you can (within the limits of the French you have learned) about your family, your interests, your activities, and your possessions.

**G.** **Le déjeuner en ville.** *(Lunch in town.)* You go to a café or a fast-food restaurant for lunch with a student you have just met. When you arrive, you see a friend. Along with two other members of the class, play the roles of the students in this situation. During the conversation, make introductions, order lunch, and find out as much as possible about each other.

**H.** **L'arbre généalogique.** *(Family tree.)* Construct your family tree and explain to the class (or to a small group of students) the relationships between you and the other family members. (Bring in a family picture, if possible.) For each person mentioned, give several pieces of information.

**I.** **Contrastes.** Imagine that you and another student are like the two people in the picture on page 62. The two of you are very different: you come from different families (one large, one small) and you have different possessions and interests. Invent the personal details of your lives and present them to the class in the form of a dialogue of opposites.

*Locmariaquer, France*

 Instructor's Tape:
Michel Kerguézec,
Locmariaquer
(Bretagne), France

# PORTRAIT

*Michel Kerguézec, Locmariaquer
(Bretagne), France*

Comme l'indique mon nom (Kerguézec),
je suis de Bretagne. Mes parents, ma
sœur, Sophie, et moi, nous parlons français, bien sûr, mais mes grands-
parents, ils parlent aussi breton. Je
suis né dans la ville où j'habite. Locmariaquer est une ville de 56 000 habitants à l'entrée du golfe du Morbihan,
près de Vannes. J'ai dix-sept ans et je
suis élève au lycée. J'ai les cheveux
bruns et les yeux bleus. J'aime la musique rock et le tennis. Alors, bien sûr,
dans ma chambre j'ai une raquette de tennis, un poster de Sting et beaucoup de
cassettes.

# Profil

*La Bretagne*

**SITUATION:** l'ouest de la France
**POPULATION:** 2 707 886 habitants
**VILLES PRINCIPALES:** Rennes, Brest,
Quimper, Vannes, Saint-Malo
**CLIMAT:** doux, mais pluvieux *(rainy)*
**ÉCONOMIE:** pêche, agriculture (arti-
chauts, choux-fleurs, haricots verts),
industrie (automobile)
**LIEUX D'INTÉRÊT:** Carnac (monu-
ments préhistoriques), la Pointe du
Raz (extrémité occidentale de la
France)

**Suggestion, Profil:** Begin by
asking students about particular states in the United States
and their particular characters
(Texas, California, a New
England state, etc.). Make sure
that they conclude that different regions have different characteristics, i.e., point to the
multi-cultural aspects of the
United States. Then have them
read the information on
Bretagne, verify their comprehension in English, and
proceed to the discussion
questions.

**COMMENTAIRE:** Les Bretons sont très fiers *(proud)* de leur héritage celtique. Il
y a beaucoup de Bretons qui continuent à parler breton et à suivre *(to follow)*
les coutumes de leurs ancêtres.

**À discuter:** Are there any regions in the United States where the people
cling to their own language and customs? If so, where? If not, why do you
think there are none?

## L·E·X·I·Q·U·E

### Pour se débrouiller

*Pour indiquer ses goûts et ses
préférences*
    adorer
    aimer (assez, bien, beaucoup,
      mieux, le mieux)
    détester,
    ne pas aimer (du tout)
    préférer

*Pour se présenter*
    je m'appelle...
    je suis...

*Pour se renseigner*
    comment s'appelle...
    où
    pourquoi
    qu'est-ce que
    qui

*Pour faire répéter*
    Comment?
    Hein?
    Pardon?
    Quoi?

*Pour décrire une personne*
    avoir ＿＿ ans
    avoir les cheveux blonds (bruns, gris,
      noirs, roux)
    avoir les yeux bleus (bruns, verts)
    être chauve

*Pour demander et indiquer l'âge*
    Quel âge avez-vous (as-tu)?
    J'ai ＿＿ ans.

*Pour établir la possession*
    À qui est...?
    C'est à qui,...?
    C'est le (la, l', les) de...
    C'est (ce sont) son (sa, ses)...
              leur (leurs)...

*Pour identifier le possesseur*
    À qui est (sont)...?
    C'est ton (votre)...?
    C'est à qui, ça?

### Thèmes et contextes

*Les habitations*
    un appartement
    une chambre
    un immeuble
    une maison
    une résidence
      (universitaire)

*Les matériaux scolaires*
    un cahier
    une calculatrice
    un carnet
    un crayon
    un livre
    un sac à dos
    un stylo

*Les moyens de transport*
    une auto
    une bicyclette
    une moto(cyclette)
    un vélo
    un vélomoteur
    une voiture

*Les possessions*
- un appareil-photo
- un bureau
- une cassette
- une chaîne stéréo
- une chaise
- un chat
- un chien
- une clé
- un disque compact
- une lampe
- un lit
- un magnétoscope
- un ordinateur
- une plante verte
- un portefeuille
- un poster
- un radioréveil
- un sac (à main)
- un téléviseur (couleur)
- un Walkman (un baladeur)

*Les activités*
- faire du ski
- faire du sport
- faire du tennis
- faire une promenade
- faire un tour (en voiture, à vélo, à pied)
- faire un voyage

*Les goûts et les préférences*
- l'art *(m.)*
- le camping
- le cinéma
- les langues *(f.pl.)*
- la littérature
- les mathématiques *(f.pl.)*
- la musique
- la nature
- la politique
- les sciences *(f.pl.)*
- la sculpture
- les sports *(m.pl.)*
- la télévision
- le tennis
- le théâtre

*La famille*
- un(e) cousin(e)
- une femme
- une fille
- un fils
- un frère
- une grand-mère
- un grand-père
- un mari
- une mère
- un oncle
- un père
- une sœur
- une tante

**Vocabulaire général**

*Verbes*
- avoir
- avoir besoin de
    - faim
    - soif
- chercher
- écouter
- faire
- regarder
- rester

---

**ALLONS-Y!**
Video Program

**ACTE 2**

**VOCABULAIRE**

Scène 1: les couples
le coup de foudre
*love at first sight*
l'aboutissement
*the outcome*

Scène 2: une famille à
   la Guadeloupe
la restauratrice
*the restaurant owner*
l'institutrice
*the teacher*
la secrétaire-comptable
*the secretary-accountant*
la boîte privée
*the private office*
sur les genoux
*on the lap*
la sucette   *the lollipop*

Véronique Béziers
Tarascon (Provence),
France

—Allons-y! Faisons connaissance de la ville!

# Renseignons-nous!

## OBJECTIVES

**In this chapter, you will learn:**

- to identify and locate places in a city;
- to ask for and give directions;
- to give orders and suggest activities;
- to tell time;
- to make plans;
- to indicate possession;
- to read a tourist brochure;
- to understand discussions of plans and activities.

**CHAPTER SUPPORT MATERIALS** (STUDENT)

**Cahier:** pp. 63–92

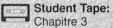 **Student Tape:** Chapitre 3 Segments 1, 2, 3

CHAPTER SUPPORT MATERIALS (INSTRUCTOR)

Transparencies: 3-1 through 3-7

Instructor's Tape: Chapitre 3, Text, pp. 99, 109, 123

SYSTEME-D *software:* Writing activities for this chapter are found in the **Cahier:** Ex. VI (p. 78), Ex. VII (p. 83).

Multimedia: See the Resource Manual for correlation to our multimedia product.

## ALLONS-Y!
### Video Program

**ACTE 3**
**LA VILLE**

Première étape   Faisons connaissance de la ville!
Deuxième étape   Où se trouve... ?
Troisième étape   Rendez-vous à 10 heures
Quatrième étape  Lecture: Visitez Fougères!

**Suggestion, Point de départ:** Use the transparency to present the buildings. Have students repeat the terms and ask them about places they don't recognize: **Qu'est-ce que c'est, un bureau de tabac?**

# PREMIÈRE ÉTAPE
## Point de départ

▼ ▼ ▼ ▼ ▼ ▼ ▼ ▼ ▼ ▼ ▼ ▼ ▼ ▼

*Faisons connaissance de la ville!*

**ALLONS-Y!** Video Program

### ACTE 3
### LA VILLE

**QUESTIONS DE FOND**
1. What does the woman teach the young man?
2. Where does the young man's trip start? Where will it end?

Dans une ville il y a souvent

| | | |
|---|---|---|
| library | un aéroport | une cathédrale | **une bibliothèque** |
| railroad station / church / post office | **une gare** | **une église** une synagogue | **un bureau de poste** |
| school (general or elementary) / town (city) hall / high school / police station | **une école** **un lycée** | une université un hôpital | **un hôtel de ville** **un commissariat de police** |
| bookstore | un hôtel | **une librairie** | |
| tobacco store (also sells stamps, newspapers) | une banque | **un bureau de tabac** une pharmacie | |

Pour s'amuser, il y a souvent

| | | |
|---|---|---|
| | un café | un cinéma | un parc |
| stadium | un restaurant | un théâtre | **un stade** |
| museum / swimming pool | un fast-food | **un musée** | **une piscine** |

# À VOUS (Exercices de vocabulaire)

**Transparencies:**
**3-1, 3-2** (Ex. A, public buildings)

**A.   Qu'est-ce que c'est?** Identify each place or building.

**Implementation,** Ex. A: Do with books closed, using the transparency.

*Modèle:*       *C'est une cathédrale.*

1.

2.

3.

4.

5.

6.

7.

8.

9.

10.

11.

12.

Ex. B: ⇄

**B.  Est-ce qu'il y a un(e) ____ dans le quartier?** *(Is there a ____ in the neigh-borhood?)* Ask a passerby if the following places are in the area. The passerby will answer yes and name the street where each can be found.

*Modèle:*     restaurant / dans la rue Clemenceau
              —*Pardon, Madame (Monsieur). Est-ce qu'il y a un restaurant*
              *dans le quartier?*
              —*Oui. Il y a un restaurant dans la rue Clemenceau.*

1.  parc / dans la rue Bellevue
2.  théâtre / dans l'avenue Jean Mermoz
3.  synagogue / dans la rue d'Orléans
4.  musée / dans l'avenue de la Libération
5.  pharmacie / dans l'avenue Aristide Bruant
6.  cinéma / dans la rue Mazarin
7.  église / dans la rue de Strasbourg
8.  piscine / dans la rue Jean-Jacques
9.  fast-food / dans l'avenue de Paris
10. bureau de tabac / dans la rue Vauban
11. hôtel / dans la rue de la Montagne
12. une école / dans l'avenue du Maréchal Joffre

Ex. C: ⇄ This exercise, simple in appearance, is designed to introduce and reinforce the notion that **il** and **elle** may refer to things as well as people.

**C.  Il est là.** *(It is there.)* You are looking at a map of the town where you are staying in France. A stranger comes up and asks you where certain buildings and places are located. Using **il est** or **elle est** and the expression **là,** indicate the various locations on the map.

*Modèle:*     la gare
              —*Où est la gare?*
              —*La gare? Elle est là.*

1.  la cathédrale
2.  le bureau de poste
3.  l'université
4.  l'hôpital
5.  le parc
6.  la gare
7.  l'aéroport
8.  le commissariat de police
9.  le stade
10. l'hôtel de ville
11. la bibliothèque
12. le musée

## Note culturelle

Most French towns and cities date from the Middle Ages, a period when the major concern in city planning was protection. Often, the town grew up around a castle (**un château**) or a church, with the houses crowded together within defensive walls. As a result, the streets were narrow and winding and did not follow any predetermined pattern.

In the center of French cities today, the basic street pattern has changed very little since the fifteenth century. Most of the walls have come down, and the towns have expanded. However, you still find a central square (**une place**) with its **château** or church. In larger cities, each **quartier** may have its own **place centrale.**

**Questions:** Compare the layout of the town or city where you live with that of a typical French town or city. What differences do you notice? How might you explain these differences?

## S·T·R·U·C·T·U·R·E

### *Le verbe irrégulier* **aller**

| | |
|---|---|
| Comment **vas-tu?** | How *are you?* |
| **Marie va** à Paris. | *Marie is going* to Paris. |
| **Ils ne vont pas** à Nice. | *They are not going* to Nice. |

Suggestion, Aller: (1) Have students repeat conjugation while you write pronouns on board in four groups: je / tu, il, elle, on / ils, elles / nous, vous. (2) Repeat with the negative. (3) Add written forms to pronouns on board.

The verb **aller** (*to go* and, in some expressions dealing with health, *to be*) is irregular:

| **aller** *(to go)* | |
|---|---|
| je **vais** | nous **allons** |
| tu **vas** | vous **allez** |
| il, elle, on **va** | ils, elles **vont** |

▲   ▲   ▲

## APPLICATION

**D.**  Remplacez le sujet en italique et faites les changements nécessaires.

1. *Henri* va à Londres. ( je / nous / M. et Mme Duplessis / Chantal)
2. Est-ce que *Jeanne* va en ville? (tu / Éric / vous / Paul et son frère)
3. *Ils* ne vont pas à la bibliothèque. (Michèle / je / nous / on)

Ex. E: ⇄

**E.** **À la gare.** You are at the railroad station with a group of friends who are all leaving to visit cathedrals in different French cities. Each time you ask if someone is going to a certain cathedral town, you find out that you are wrong. Ask and answer questions following the model.

> *Modèle:*  Alex / à Paris (à Rouen)
> —*Alex va à Paris?*
> —*Mais non, il ne va pas à Paris, il va à Rouen.*

1. Thérèse / à Strasbourg (à Bourges)
2. tu / à Poitiers (à Chartres)
3. Jean-Paul et François / à Marseille (à Albi)
4. vous / à Angers (à Reims)
5. Michel / à Metz (à Lyon)

---

### Note grammaticale

**Suggestion,** Adverbs: Put on board a continuum running from **toujours** to **ne . . . jamais.** Use **aller à la bibliothèque** with different people and frequencies.

#### Quelques adverbes

The following adverbs are often used with **aller:**

| | |
|---|---|
| **toujours**  *(always)* | **de temps en temps**  *(from time to time)* |
| **souvent**  *(often)* | **quelquefois**  *(sometimes)* |
| **rarement**  *(rarely)* | **ne . . . jamais**  *(never)* |

**De temps en temps** and **quelquefois** usually begin or end the sentence. The shorter adverbs directly follow the verb. **Ne . . . jamais** is a negative expression. **Ne** precedes the verb and **jamais** follows it, just as with **ne . . . pas.**

| | |
|---|---|
| **De temps en temps** nous allons en ville. | *From time to time* we go into town. |
| Il va **souvent** à l'église. | He *often* goes to church. |
| Je **ne** vais **jamais** à la bibliothèque. | I *never* go to the library. |

Ex. F:  This and succeeding exercises avoid **au,** which will be introduced in the next **Structure.**

When a negative answer using **jamais** contains no verb, it is used without **ne:** —**Tu vas souvent au musée? —Jamais.**

**F.** **Une enquête.** *(A survey.)* Ask three other students the questions below and take note of their answers. The students do not need to answer with complete sentences.

> *Modèle:*  —*Est-ce que tu vas souvent à l'aéroport?*
> —*Rarement.*
> —*De temps en temps.*
> —*Jamais.*

1. Est-ce que tu vas souvent à la bibliothèque?
2. Est-ce que tu vas souvent à l'église ou à la synagogue?
3. Est-ce que tu vas souvent à l'hôpital?
4. Est-ce que tu vas souvent à l'hôtel de ville?

**G.  Les résultats.** *(The results.)* Now report your findings from Exercise F to other members of your class. This time use complete sentences.

Ex. G: ○

*Modèle:*   *De temps en temps Éric va à la bibliothèque. Janine va rarement à la bibliothèque, et Martine va très souvent à la bibliothèque.*

## S·T·R·U·C·T·U·R·E

*La préposition **à** et l'article défini*

Nous sommes **à la** piscine.
Mon frère travaille **à l'**aéroport.
Nous allons **au** cinéma
    ensemble.
Elle parle **aux** médecins.

We're *at the* swimming pool.
My brother works *at the* airport.
We're going *to the* movies
    together.
She's talking *to the* doctors.

Suggestion, À + definite article: Use the transparency of buildings; begin with à la, then proceed to au. Switch to people: **parler à la mère de** _____ , **l'oncle de** _____ , then **le père de** _____ and **les frères (sœurs) de** _____ .

When followed by **la** or **l'**, the preposition **à** *(to, at, in)* does not change. However, **à** followed by **le** contracts to form **au**, and **à** followed by **les** contracts to form **aux:**

à + la → **à la**          **à la** maison
à + l' → **à l'**          **à l'**église
à + le → **au**            **au** café
à + les → **aux**          **aux** professeurs

The **x** of **aux** is silent, except when it precedes a vowel or a vowel sound. Then, in liaison, it is pronounced as a **z: aux‿étudiants.**

▲  ▲  ▲

**Le savez-vous?**
▲▲▲▲▲▲▲▲▲▲▲▲▲▲
**When the French use the term** le foot, **what are they referring to?**
a.  a part of the body
b.  American football
c.  soccer

Réponse  ▲▲▲

## APPLICATION

**H.**  Remplacez les mots en italique et faites les changements nécessaires.

1. Il va à la *cathédrale.* (maison / bibliothèque / gare / piscine)
2. Elles sont à l'*hôpital.* (université / église / aéroport / hôtel de ville)
3. Est-ce que tu vas au *café*? (restaurant / musée / bureau de poste / fast-food)
4. Je parle aux *professeurs.* (médecins / avocats / ingénieurs)

**I.**    Remplacez les mots en italique et faites les changements nécessaires.

1.  Ma sœur travaille au *musée*. (bureau de poste / hôtel / gare / théâtre)
2.  Nous allons souvent au *café*. (église / parc / hôtel de ville / gare / piscine)
3.  Est-ce que nous sommes déjà au *restaurant?* (cathédrale / hôpital / musée / bureau de poste / stade)
4.  Il parle au *garçon*. (professeur / avocat / étudiants / médecins)

Ex. J: ○

**J.**    **Tu vas au musée, toi?** A group of young people join you in front of a map of the town where you are staying. Find out where each one is headed, being careful to use the appropriate form of **à** + the definite article.

*Modèle:*    musée / hôpital
          —*Tu vas au musée, toi?*
          —*Non, je vais à l'hôpital.*

1.  église / cathédrale              5.  bureau de poste / parc
2.  librairie / piscine              6.  café / pharmacie
3.  gare / aéroport                  7.  banque / restaurant
4.  théâtre / cinéma                 8.  hôtel de ville / commissariat de police

Ex. K: ○

**K.**    **D'abord... ensuite...** *(First . . . then . . .)* After lunch, you and your friends are discussing your plans. Using the verb **aller** and the appropriate form of **à** + the definite article, find out where each person is headed.

*Modèle:*    Anne-Marie (piscine / bibliothèque)
          —*Anne-Marie, où est-ce que tu vas?*
          —*D'abord, je vais à la piscine et ensuite je vais à la bibliothèque.*

▲▲▲  C

1.  Élisabeth (banque / théâtre)
2.  Pierre et Sylvie (restaurant / cinéma)
3.  Monique (bureau de poste / pharmacie)
4.  Jean-Jacques (hôtel / gare)
5.  Simone (musée / parc)
6.  Henri et Alain (bureau de tabac / stade)

**Supplementary vocabulary:** Additional games that can be used with **jouer à** include **le golf, le hockey (sur glace,** *on ice*), **les cartes** *(cards)*, **les dames** *(checkers)*, **le Monopoly, le Scrabble.**

**L.**    **Après les cours, nous jouons...** *(After classes, we play . . . )* What sports and games do you and your friends play? How about you and your family? Choose games from the following list to complete the sentences. Notice that the verb **jouer** *(to play)* is followed by **à** before the name of a sport or game. Be sure to make the appropriate contraction.

| | | |
|---|---|---|
| **le basket** | **le volley** | **les échecs** *(m.pl.) (chess)* |
| **le football** | **le base-ball** | **le flipper** *(pinball)* |
| **le football américain** | **le tennis** | **le Nintendo** |

*Modèle:*          Mes amis et moi, nous jouons...
                   —*Mes amis et moi, nous jouons au basket.*

1. Mes amis et moi, nous aimons jouer...
2. Quelquefois nous jouons...
3. Nous jouons rarement...
4. Nous ne jouons jamais...
5. Ma famille et moi, nous jouons...
6. Nous ne jouons jamais...

## PRONONCIATION   *La combinaison* **gn**

**Student Tape:**
Chapitre 3
Segment 1

In French, the combination **gn** is pronounced as [ɲ]—much like the *ny* in the English word *canyon:* **gagner, ligne.**

**M.** Read each word aloud, being careful to pronounce the **gn** combination as [ɲ].

espagnol / renseignons-nous / magnifique / magnétique / signe / Agnès / Champagne / montagne / champignon

## S·T·R·U·C·T·U·R·E

### *Le futur immédiat*

Qu'est-ce que **vous allez faire** ce soir?
Moi, **je vais aller** au concert.
**Georges et moi, nous allons faire** un tour en voiture.
**Mathilde ne va pas quitter** la maison.

What *are you going to do* tonight?
*I'm going to go* to the concert.
*Georges and I are going to go* for a ride.
*Mathilde isn't going to leave* the house.

To express a future action, especially one that will occur in the not-too-distant future, use a present tense form of **aller** and an infinitive. This structure is the equivalent of the English phrase *going to* + verb.

Note that in the negative **ne . . . pas** is placed around the conjugated form of **aller: Mathilde** *ne va pas* **quitter la maison.**

**Suggestion,** Immediate future: (1) Review conjugation of **aller.** (2) Have students generate conjugation of **aller travailler ce soir (demain).** (3) Repeat in negative. (4) Have one student give the present **(je travaille)** and another the future **(je vais travailler)** of several verbs.

▲   ▲   ▲

## APPLICATION

**N.** Remplacez le sujet en italique et faites les changements nécessaires.

1. *Suzanne* va faire une promenade ce soir. (Jean-Paul / nous / je / les Mauclair / tu / vous)
2. *Marc* ne va pas quitter la maison. (Annick / je / mes amis / vous / tu / nous)
3. Est-ce que *Nicolas* va aller en ville? (tu / Georges et sa sœur / vous / on / Paulette / nous)

**O. Qu'est-ce qu'on va faire ce soir?** You find out from some of your friends what they are going to do tonight.

*Modèle:*      Charles, qu'est-ce que tu vas faire ce soir? (aller au cinéma)
*Je vais aller au cinéma (ce soir).*

1. Marcelle, qu'est-ce que tu vas faire ce soir? (travailler)
2. Et Jean-Pierre, qu'est-ce qu'il va faire? (aller au théâtre)
3. Et Michèle et son amie? (étudier)
4. Sylvie, qu'est-ce que tu vas faire ce soir? (regarder la télé)
5. Et Gérard, qu'est-ce qu'il va faire? (aller en ville)
6. Et Jacques et Isabelle? (rester à la maison)
7. Et vous deux? (faire un tour à vélo)

**Follow-up,** Ex. O: Ask students to talk about their plans for **ce soir, ce week-end,** etc.

**P. Et toi, qu'est-ce que tu vas faire?** Now find out from several of your classmates what they are going to do tonight **(ce soir),** tomorrow night **(demain soir),** and over the weekend **(pendant le week-end).** Then report your findings to the class.

▲ ▲ ▲ ▲ ▲ ▲ ▲ ▲ ▲ ▲ **Débrouillons-nous!** ▲ ▲ ▲ ▲ ▲ ▲ ▲ ▲ ▲

*Petite révision de l'étape*

Ex. Q: ⇄

**Q. Échange.** Ask another student the following questions. He/she will respond on the basis of his/her knowledge and personal situation.

1. Est-ce qu'il y a un aéroport dans notre ville? Une gare? Un hôpital? Un bureau de poste? Une cathédrale? Un stade? Une piscine? Un musée?
2. Est-ce que tu vas souvent au cinéma? À l'église ou à la synagogue? À l'hôtel de ville? À la bibliothèque? Au fast-food? Au théâtre? À la banque?
3. Est-ce que tu vas regarder la télé ce soir? Écouter la radio? Rester à la maison (dans ta chambre)? Étudier? Aller en ville? Parler au professeur?

Ex. R: ⇄ Students choose destinations, then circulate.

**R. Dans la rue.** While heading for a place in town (your choice), you bump into a friend. Greet your friend, find out how he/she is and where he/she is going. If you are going to the same place, suggest that you go there together **(On y va ensemble?).** He/she will agree **(Oui. Allons-y!).** If not, find out what he/she is going to do tomorrow night **(demain soir).** Either suggest that you do it together or tell what different plans you have. Then say good-bye and continue on your way.

**À faire chez vous:** CAHIER, Chapitre 3 / 1ère étape

# DEUXIÈME ÉTAPE

## Point de départ

▼ ▼ ▼ ▼ ▼ ▼ ▼ ▼ ▼ ▼ ▼ ▼

*Où se trouve...?*

Instructor's Tape:
Où se trouve...?

*se trouve:* is (located, found)

Transparency:
3-3 (map of Tarascon)

**Suggestion, Point de départ:**
(1) Use the transparency to present spatial relationships. Then do Ex. A. (2) Have students listen to the dialogue on the Instructor's Tape as you trace the route on the map. Then do Exs. B and C.

---

Véronique Béziers habite à Tarascon, dans le **sud** de la France. À Tarascon il y a un **château fort** qui date du XV[e] **siècle.** Regardez le **plan** de la ville.

south

fortified castle / century / map (of city)

Le château est **près de** l'église Sainte-Marthe, mais il est **loin de** la gare.

near / far from

**Devant** le château il y a le boulevard du Château. **Derrière** le château se trouve le **Rhône.** Le château est situé **entre** le boulevard du Château et le Rhône.

in front of / behind

river in southern France that flows from the Alps into the Mediterranean Sea / between

L'hôtel de ville de Tarascon se trouve **au coin de** la rue Monge et de la rue des Halles.

on the corner of

Le commissariat de police se trouve **en face de** l'hôpital.
Il y a une pharmacie **à côté de** l'hôtel St-Jean.
Il y a un **pont au bout de** l'avenue de la République.
À Tarascon on **stationne** les voitures **dans** un garage ou sur un grand parking qui se trouvent **sur** le boulevard Gambetta.

across from

next to

bridge / at the end of

park / in

on

passerby / asks for
information

Véronique visite le château de Tarascon avec des amis. Un **passant demande** des **renseignements.**

—S'il vous plaît, Mademoiselle. Est-ce qu'il y a une banque près d'ici?
—Oui, Monsieur. Dans la rue des Halles.
—La rue des Halles? Où se trouve la rue des Halles?

cross / straight ahead
until / turn right
on your left

—Bon, vous **traversez** le boulevard du Château et vous allez **tout droit** dans la rue Monge. Continuez **jusqu'à** la rue des Halles et **tournez à droite.** Il y a une banque en face de l'hôtel de ville, **sur votre gauche.**
—Merci bien, Mademoiselle.
—Je vous en prie, Monsieur.

## À VOUS! (Exercices de vocabulaire)

Ex. A: This exercise avoids the
contraction **du,** which will be
presented in the next
**Structure.**

**A. La ville de Tarascon.** When someone asks you about Tarascon, you first answer using the suggested expressions.

> *Modèle:*    Où est le château? (près de l'église Sainte-Marthe)
> *Elle est près de l'église Sainte-Marthe.*

1. Où est l'hôtel Saint-Jean? (à côté de la pharmacie)
2. Où est la banque? (en face de l'hôtel de ville)
3. Où est le château? (loin de la gare)
4. Où est le bureau de poste? (près de l'hôtel Terminus)
5. Où est le pont? (au bout de l'avenue de la République)
6. Où est le boulevard du Château? (entre le château et l'église Sainte-Marthe)

Now correct the erroneous statements that you hear about Tarascon by looking at the map on page 99 and using the appropriate expressions to locate each place.

*Modèle:*        Le château est près de la gare, n'est-ce pas?
                 *Mais non, il est (assez) loin de la gare.*

7.  La pharmacie est à côté de l'hôtel Terminus, n'est-ce pas?
8.  Le stade est près de la gare, n'est-ce pas?
9.  Le stade est en face de l'hôpital, n'est-ce pas?
10. Le Rhône est devant le château, n'est-ce pas?
11. L'hôtel de ville est au bout de l'avenue Guynemer, n'est-ce pas?
12. La rue Amy est entre le boulevard Gambetta et le boulevard Victor Hugo, n'est-ce pas?

## Note culturelle

Many American cities are laid out in fairly regular patterns: streets often meet at right angles, run north and south or east and west, and have numbers (Second Avenue, Seventeenth Street). As you have seen, in French cities, streets rarely form regular patterns and they are usually given the name of a landmark (**le boulevard du Château**), a famous person (**le boulevard Victor Hugo**), or an historical reference (**l'avenue de la République**).

Americans often express distance in terms of city blocks and compass points: "Go three blocks east and turn left." The French indicate the cross street on which to turn: **Vous allez jusqu'à la rue Monge et vous tournez à gauche.**

**Questions:** What is the origin of the street names in your town or neighborhood? Is it possible to direct people around the area where you live using blocks and compass points?

**B.** Remplacez les mots en italique.

1.  Traversez *la rue.* (la place / le boulevard / l'avenue)
2.  Vous tournez à droite *dans l'avenue Mitterrand.* (dans la rue Sainte-Catherine / sur le boulevard des Italiens / sur la place Notre-Dame)
3.  Vous continuez tout droit *jusqu'à la rue Jean-Baptiste.* (jusqu'à la place de la Révolution / jusqu'à l'avenue Clemenceau / jusqu'au boulevard Garibaldi)
4.  Allez tout droit *jusqu'à l'avenue de la Gare.* (jusqu'au coin / jusqu'au bout de la rue Balzac / jusqu'à la cathédrale)
5.  Tournez à gauche *dans la rue Sainte-Anne.* (dans l'avenue de la Marine / sur le boulevard Masséna / sur la place Stanislas)

**Vocabulary:** Notice that French uses the preposition **sur** to talk about a square or a boulevard (**sur la place, sur le boulevard**) and the preposition **dans** to talk about streets and avenues (**dans la rue, dans l'avenue**).

**Implementation,** Ex. C: Do the first destination with the class, using the transparency. Then have students work in pairs, using the map in the book. Quickly review one or two items with the transparency before continuing.

**C.  Pardon, Monsieur/Madame.** You are standing in front of the château in Tarascon. Explain to passersby how to get to the following places.

> *Modèle:*        l'hôtel de ville
> —*Pardon, Monsieur (Madame). L'hôtel de ville, s'il vous plaît?*
> —*Vous traversez le boulevard du Château. Vous continuez dans la rue Monge jusqu'à la rue des Halles. L'hôtel de ville est au coin de la rue Monge et de la rue des Halles, sur votre droite.*

1.  le stade
2.  le commissariat de police

3.  le bureau de poste
4.  l'hôtel Saint-Jean

# R·E·P·R·I·S·E

## *Première étape*

**D.  Les parents de vos amis.** While talking with some of your new friends, you have learned about their parents. Tell about their work and their leisure activities.

> *Modèle:*        le père de Janine (hôtel / les livres / bibliothèque)
> *Le père de Janine travaille à l'hôtel. Il aime beaucoup les livres; il va souvent à la bibliothèque.*

1.  le père de Mireille (gare / les films / cinéma)
2.  la mère de Michel (aéroport / la nature / parc)
3.  le père de Véronique (bureau de poste / l'art / musée)
4.  la mère de Jean-Alex (hôpital / la littérature / librairie)
5.  le père de Jacqueline (bureau de tabac / voyager / aéroport)
6.  la mère de Philippc (université / chanter / théâtre)
7.  le père de Denise (banque / l'art gothique / cathédrale)
8.  la mère de Marielle (hôtel de ville / manger / restaurant)

**Reminder:** You must listen carefully to distinguish between general questions that require the present tense and questions about a future time that call for **aller** + infinitive.

**E.  Questions.** Your instructor will play the role of an exchange student who has just arrived at your university. Answer his/her questions, paying close attention to the time frame.

1.  Est-ce que vous étudiez beaucoup? Est-ce que vous allez étudier ce soir?
2.  D'habitude, qu'est-ce que vous faites le soir *(in the evening)?* Qu'est-ce que vous allez faire ce soir?
3.  Où est-ce que vous allez dîner ce soir—à l'université, au restaurant ou à la maison? Où est-ce que vous dînez d'habitude *(usually)?*
4.  Est-ce que vous étudiez le français? Le russe? Le chinois? Est-ce que vous allez étudier une autre langue?
5.  Est-ce que vous faites souvent des promenades? Est-ce que vous allez faire une promenade pendant le week-end?

## S·T·R·U·C·T·U·R·E

### La préposition *de* et l'article défini

| | |
|---|---|
| Elle arrive **de la** gare. | She is arriving *from the* station. |
| Quelle est l'adresse **de l'**hôtel? | What is the address *of the* hotel? |
| Voilà la voiture **du** professeur. | There is the teacher's car. |
| Nous parlons **des** étudiants. | We are talking *about the* students. |

When followed by **la** or **l'**, the preposition **de** *(of, about, from)* does not change. However, **de** followed by **le** contracts to form **du,** and **de** followed by **les** contracts to form **des:**

| | |
|---|---|
| de + la → **de la** | **de la** pharmacie |
| de + l' → **de l'** | **de l'**hôtel |
| de + le → **du** | **du** musée |
| de + les → **des** | **des** étudiants |

The **s** of **des** is silent, except when it precedes a vowel or a vowel sound. Then, in liaison, it is pronounced as a **z: des églises.**

▲   ▲   ▲

## APPLICATION

**F.** Remplacez les mots en italique et faites les changements nécessaires.

1. Quel est le nom du *restaurant?* (banque / hôtel / librairie / musée)
2. Où est l'entrée *(entrance)* du *lycée?* (parc / bibliothèque / bureau de poste / église / gare)
3. Est-ce que tu as l'adresse de l'*avocat?* (hôtel / restaurant / bureau de tabac / librairie / professeur / pharmacie)
4. Non, elle ne parle pas du *professeur.* (médecin / avocats / ingénieurs / assistante / professeurs)

**Le savez-vous?**

▲▲▲▲▲▲▲▲▲▲▲▲▲

**The Rhône is the ____ of the major French rivers.**
a. **busiest**
b. **longest**
c. **shortest**
d. **most dangerous**

Réponse ▲▲▲

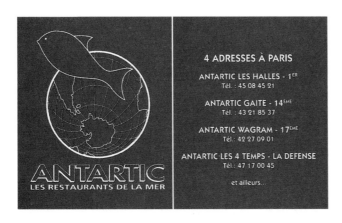

4 ADRESSES À PARIS

ANTARTIC LES HALLES - 1ᴱᴿ
Tél.: 45 08 45 21

ANTARTIC GAITE - 14ᴱᴹᴱ
Tél.: 43 21 85 37

ANTARTIC WAGRAM - 17ᴱᴹᴱ
Tél.: 42 27 09 01

ANTARTIC LES 4 TEMPS - LA DEFENSE
Tél.: 47 17 00 45

et ailleurs...

ANTARTIC
LES RESTAURANTS DE LA MER

## Note grammaticale

### *De et les prépositions de lieu*

Many of the prepositions of place presented in the **Point de départ** of this **étape** are followed by **de**:

| | |
|---|---|
| **près de**   *(near)* | **à côté de**   *(next to)* |
| **loin de**   *(far from)* | **au bout de**   *(at the end of)* |
| **en face de**   *(across from)* | **au coin de**   *(at the corner of)* |

This **de** follows the usual rules for contraction:

La voiture est en face **de la** maison.
Tu habites à côté **de l'**hôtel?

Nous sommes près **du** musée.
Le parc est au bout **du** boulevard.

**G.   Remplacez les mots en italique et faites les changements nécessaires.**

1. La banque est *près* de la gare. (à côté / en face / loin)
2. Nous habitons *en face* de l'avenue Leclerc. (près / au bout / loin)
3. Est-ce que la pharmacie est *loin* du restaurant? (en face / près / à côté)
4. L'hôtel est près de la *cathédrale*. (université / musée / parc / gare)
5. Le café est en face de l'*église*. (théâtre / boulangerie / bureau de poste / hôtel de ville / commissariat de police)

**Grammar:** Remember that some of the place prepositions are not followed by **de: devant, derrière, entre, dans, sur.** Example: **devant l'église.**

**H.   La ville.** Using the drawing on p. 105, answer the questions that a stranger might ask you about the city. Be as precise as possible.

*Modèle:*      Pardon, Monsieur. Le théâtre, s'il vous plaît?
            —*Le théâtre? Il est dans l'avenue de la République, en face de l'hôtel.*

▲▲▲   b

1. Pardon, Madame. Le restaurant, s'il vous plaît?
2. Pardon, Monsieur. Où se trouve l'église, s'il vous plaît?
3. Pardon, Mademoiselle. Où est la pharmacie?
4. S'il vous plaît, le musée?
5. La banque, s'il vous plaît?
6. Où est le bureau de poste, s'il vous plaît?
7. Est-ce qu'il y a un bureau de tabac près d'ici?
8. Pardon, Monsieur. L'hôtel, il est près de l'aéroport?

**I.  Moi, je joue du...** What musical instruments do you, your friends, and your relatives play? Choose instruments from the list below and talk about the people mentioned. Notice that the verb **jouer** is followed by **de** before a musical instrument. (The preposition **à** is used only with games.) Be sure to make the appropriate contraction.

**Supplementary Vocabulary:** Additional musical instruments that can be used with **jouer de** include **le hautbois** *(oboe)*, **le violoncelle** *(cello)*, **le tuba**, **l'harmonica** *(m.)*, **l'orgue** *(m.)*.

*Modèle:*    *Je joue du saxophone.*

| | | |
|---|---|---|
| **le piano** | **la flûte** | **la trompette** |
| **le violon** | **le saxophone** | **la batterie** *(drums)* |
| **la guitare** | **la clarinette** | **le trombone** |

1. vous
2. votre père
3. votre mère
4. vos frères et vos sœurs
5. votre ami...
6. votre amie...

# PRONONCIATION  *La consonne s*

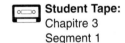

**Student Tape:** Chapitre 3 Segment 1

Depending on the sounds that surround it, the letter **s** may represent the sound [s], as in the English word *rinse,* or the sound [z], as in the English word *rise.*

The consonant **s** represents the sound [s] when it is the first letter in a word or when it is followed by a second **s** or by another consonant: **sœur, masse, disque.**

The consonant **s** represents the sound [z] when it occurs between two pronounced vowels or when it is followed by a mute **e: visage, rose.**

**J.**  First, read each pair of words aloud, being careful to distinguish between the [s] of the first word and the [z] of the second.

dessert, désert  /  poisson, poison  /  coussin, cousin  /  russe, ruse

Now read each word aloud, being careful to distinguish between [s] and [z].

désirez  /  souvent  /  croissant  /  Mademoiselle  /  brésilien  /  suisse  / classique  /  église  /  maison  /  professeur  /  musée  /  passer  /  ensuite

## S·T·R·U·C·T·U·R·E

### L'impératif

**Écoute!**                                *Listen!*
**Faites** attention!                     *Be* careful! (*Pay* attention!)
**Allons** en ville ensemble!            *Let's go* downtown together!

Imperative or command forms of verbs are used to give orders, directions, and suggestions. The three forms of the imperative—**tu** (familiar), **vous** (formal or plural), and **nous** (plural, including yourself)—are based on the present tense. The subject pronoun is omitted and the verb is used alone. In written French, the **s** of the **tu** form is dropped for regular **-er** verbs and for **aller:**

| *Present tense* | *Imperative* | *Present tense* | *Imperative* |
|---|---|---|---|
| tu travailles | **travaille!** | tu vas | **va!** |
| vous travaillez | **travaillez!** | vous allez | **allez!** |
| nous travaillons | **travaillons!** | nous allons | **allons!** |

To form the negative imperative, place **ne** before the verb and **pas** after it:

**Ne parlez pas** anglais!               *Don't speak* English!
**Ne mange pas!**                        *Don't eat!*

**Suggestion,** Imperative: Using the verb **regarder,** establish the three forms of the imperative: (1) speak to one student; (2) speak to several students; (3) involve the whole class. Repeat in the negative. Then show on the board the relationship between **tu regardes, vous regardez, nous regardons,** and the imperative forms.

**Grammar:** The verbs **avoir** and **être** have irregular imperative forms: **avoir: aies! ayez! ayons!; être: sois! soyez! soyons!** These forms are used relatively infrequently.

## APPLICATION

**K.** Give the three imperative forms of the following verbs.

> *Modèle:*     regarder     *Regarde! Regardez! Regardons!*

1. chanter   2. ne pas parler anglais   3. aller au bureau de poste   4. avoir de la patience   5. être sage *(be good, said to a child)*

**L.   Dites à...** *(Tell . . .)* Use the appropriate command forms to get the following people to do what you want.

> Dites à votre petit frèrc...d'écouter.   *Écoute!*

1. de ne pas regarder la télé.   2. d'aller à l'école.   3. de faire attention.
4. d'être sage.

Dites à vos amis...de chanter.   *Chantez!*

5. de regarder.   6. de ne pas écouter.   7. de faire attention.   8. d'aller au commissariat de police.

Proposez à vos amis...de danser.   *Dansons!*

9. d'aller au cinéma.   10. de faire une promenade.   11. de ne pas avoir peur *(to be afraid).*   12. de ne pas rester à la maison.

**M. Allez-y!** *(Go on and do it!)* Using the suggested verbs, tell one or two of your classmates to do something. They are obliged to obey you!

VERBES: **regarder, écouter, chanter, danser, parler, aller, faire des devoirs, chercher**

*Modèles:*   *Charles et Henri, chantez!*
*Anne, parle à Monique!*
*Éric, dansons!*

Ex. M: ⇄ or △ Encourage students to vary the form **(tu, vous, nous).**

# ▲▲▲▲▲▲▲▲▲▲ Débrouillons-nous! ▲▲▲▲▲▲▲▲▲▲

*Petite révision de l'étape*

**N. Échange.** Answer the questions, referring to the city or town where your school is located.

Ex. N: ⇄

1. Est-ce que tu vas à l'aéroport de temps en temps? Est-ce qu'il est près de la ville? Près de l'université?
2. Est-ce que tu vas souvent au cinéma? Est-ce qu'il y a un cinéma près de l'université? Qu'est-ce qu'il y a en face du cinéma?
3. Est-ce qu'il y a un restaurant près de l'université? Quel est le nom du restaurant? Est-ce que tu dînes au restaurant de temps en temps?
4. Est-ce qu'il y a un hôtel près de l'université? Quel est le nom de l'hôtel? Qu'est-ce qu'il y a à côté de l'hôtel?
5. Comment est-ce qu'on va de ___ à ___ ? *(Choose places on campus or in town; get directions.)*

**O. Je vous en prie.** A group of French-speaking visitors is on your campus. Each person wants to see a different place—either on campus or in town. Help these visitors by giving them directions on how to get where they want to go.

Implementation, Ex. O: Divide class into guides and visitors. Have visitors choose a place to visit on or off campus; agree on where the conversation is taking place (e.g., in front of classroom building or elsewhere on campus). Do a model conversation for the whole class before having students pair off. If time allows, have guides and visitors reverse roles, using a different destination.

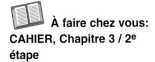

**À faire chez vous: CAHIER, Chapitre 3 / 2e étape**

# TROISIÈME ÉTAPE
## Point de départ

▼▼▼▼▼▼▼▼▼▼▼▼▼▼▼▼

*Rendez-vous à 10 heures*

Every year / Flowers
poster / this year

**Tous les ans,** à Tarascon, il y a un festival, la fête des **Fleurs.** Véronique Béziers et ses amis regardent une **affiche** annonçant le festival de **cette année.**

### FÊTE DES FLEURS
*Tarascon*

Saturday

**samedi** 27 juin

| | | |
|---|---|---|
| Parade | 10h30 | **Défilé:** la Grande Cavalcade (bd Victor Hugo, bd Gambetta, bd Itam) |
| | 11h–12h | Danses folkloriques (place de la Mairie) |
| (Food) tasting / on the banks of | 12h–14h | **Dégustation:** spécialités de la région (**au bord du** Rhône) |
| | 13h–15h | Concert de rock: Louis Bertgani et «Les Visiteurs» (place de la Mairie) |
| | 14h–18h | Sports: tennis, judo, volley-ball (stade municipal) |
| | 16h–18h | Exposition de peintures (musée des Beaux-Arts) |
| organ | 19h–21h | Concert d'**orgue** (église Sainte-Marthe) |
| | 19h–21h | Dégustation: spécialités de la région (au bord du Rhône) |
| sound and light | 21h30 | Spectacle **son et lumière** (devant le château) |
| Fireworks | 22h30 | **Feux d'artifice** (au bord du Rhône) |
| Dance | 23h | **Bal** populaire (devant le château) |

Véronique et ses amis font des **projets.**

plans

| | |
|---|---|
| VÉRONIQUE: | **Alors,** qu'est-ce qu'on fait? |
| JEAN-LOUP: | Allons **voir** le défilé! |
| CÉCILE: | **D'accord. Bonne idée!** |
| PATRICIA: | Oui. Pourquoi pas? |
| DAVID: | Mais moi, je voudrais faire du tennis. |
| VÉRONIQUE: | Pas de problème! D'abord, on va voir le défilé et ensuite on va au stade faire du tennis. Ça va? |
| LES AUTRES: | Oui, ça va. |
| CÉCILE: | Où est-ce qu'**on se retrouve?** |
| DAVID: | Et **à quelle heure?** |
| VÉRONIQUE: | Sur le boulevard Gambetta, devant le parking, à 10 heures. D'accord? |
| LES AUTRES: | D'accord. |
| PATRICIA: | Alors, **c'est décidé.** Rendez-vous à 10 heures devant le parking sur le boulevard Gambetta. |

So
see
OK / Good idea!

Instructor's Tape:
Véronique et ses
amis font des projets

do we meet
what time

it's settled

## À VOUS! (Exercices de vocabulaire)

**A.  Où? À quelle heure?** You are staying in Tarascon at the time of the festival. You run into a group of American tourists who do not speak French and are confused by the schedule of events. Answer their questions.

> *Modèle:*   Where are the fireworks? And when?
> *On the banks of the Rhone river. They start at 10:30 P.M.*

1.  Where are the folk dances? What time?
2.  When does the parade start? What route will it take?
3.  If we get hungry, is there food to eat? Where? When?
4.  My husband and I love classical music. Are there any concerts? When? Where?
5.  Our children hate classical music. Is there anything for them? When? Where?
6.  What time does the dancing begin?
7.  My children would like to watch some sporting events. Where can they go? All day?
8.  We heard there was an historical pageant with music and lights. What time does that start? Where do we go to see it?

**Culture:** In France, many public events are listed in official time—that is, using a 24-hour clock rather than the 12-hour clock used to express time in conversation. For times after 12 noon, subtract 12 from the official time. Example: **14h** = 2:00 P.M.

Ex. B: ⇄

**B.** **Qu'est-ce qu'on fait?** You and your friend are planning to attend the **fête des Fleurs** in Tarascon. Ask your friend what he/she wants to do at the festival. In the first part of the exercise, when your friend suggests an activity, you indicate your agreement by saying: **D'accord. Bonne idée!** or **Oui. Pourquoi pas?**

*Modèle:*      aller voir le défilé
—*Alors, qu'est-ce qu'on fait?*
—*Allons voir le défilé!*
—*D'accord. Bonne idée!* or *Oui. Pourquoi pas?*
—*Bon. C'est décidé. On va voir le défilé.*

1. écouter le concert de rock
2. manger des spécialités de la région
3. aller au bal populaire
4. aller voir le son et lumière
5. regarder le tennis
6. aller voir les feux d'artifice

In the second part of the exercise, when you propose an activity, your friend has a different idea. Settle the disagreement by suggesting that first (**d'abord**) you do one activity and then (**ensuite**) you do the other.

*Modèle:*      aller voir les danses folkloriques / écouter le concert de jazz
—*Alors, qu'est-ce qu'on fait?*
—*Allons voir les danses folkloriques!*
—*Mais moi, je voudrais écouter le concert de jazz.*
—*D'abord, on va voir les danses folkloriques et ensuite on écoute le concert de jazz. D'accord?*
—*Bon. D'accord.*

7. aller voir le défilé / manger des spécialités de la région
8. écouter le concert de rock / regarder le judo
9. regarder le tennis / écouter le concert d'orgue
10. manger des spécialités de la région / aller voir le son et lumière
11. aller voir les feux d'artifice / aller au bal populaire

Ex. C: ⇄

**C.** **À quelle heure est-ce qu'on se retrouve? Et où?** You and your classmate have decided where to go. Now you need to arrange a time and place to meet.

*Modèle:*      10h / devant le parking sur le boulevard Gambetta
—*À quelle heure est-ce qu'on se retrouve?*
—*À 10 heures.*
—*Et où?*
—*Devant le parking sur le boulevard Gambetta.*
—*D'accord. Rendez-vous à 10 heures devant le parking sur le boulevard Gambetta.*

1. 11h / à la place de la Mairie
2. 3h / au stade
3. 4h / à l'église Sainte-Marthe
4. 9h / devant le château
5. 10h / derrière le château
6. 2h / au musée des Beaux-Arts

**A VOIR DE TOUTE FAÇON
A TARASCON
BEAUCAIRE · BARBENTANE :**
- Château de Tarascon
- Château de Beaucaire
- Eglise Sainte-Marthe
- Le vieux Tarascon
  et le vieux Beaucaire
- Hôtels de Ville de Tarascon
  et de Beaucaire
- Porte Condamine
- Cordeliers
- Musée Souleïado
- La maison de Tartarin
- Barrage de Vallabrègues
- La Montagnette
  et l'Abbaye de Frigolet
- Le village de Barbentane

*Emblème de Tarascon, la Tarasque
est un monstre imaginaire dont la
représentation est promenée dans
les rues pendant les fêtes de la
Tarasque.*

*TARASCON*

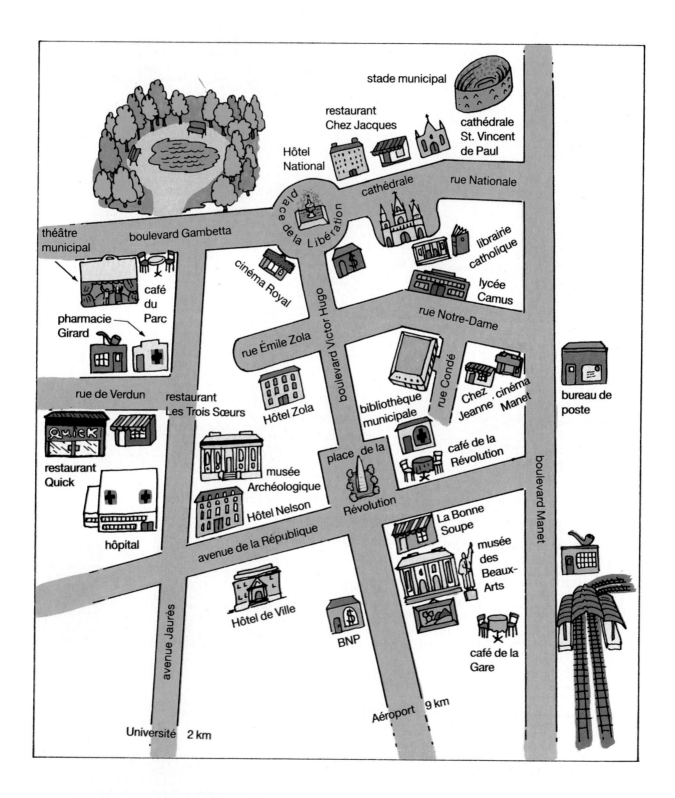

## R·E·P·R·I·S·E

Transparency:
3-5 (map of imaginary
French city shown on
p. 112)

*Deuxième étape*

Suggestion, Ex. D: Do the
first destination with the class,
using the transparency of the
city map. Then have students
work in pairs. You may wish to
go over their work, using the
transparency again.

**D.   S'il vous plaît...?** You are at the place de la Libération when some tourists stop you and ask how to get to certain places. Using the map on p. 112, give them as precise directions as possible.

> *Modèle:*   le lycée Camus
> —*Le lycée Camus, s'il vous plaît.*
> —*Le lycée Camus? Il est dans la rue Notre-Dame, en face de la bibliothèque municipale.*
> —*C'est loin d'ici?*
> —*Non, non. Vous traversez la place de la Libération et vous continuez sur le boulevard Victor Hugo jusqu'à la rue Notre-Dame. Tournez à droite et le lycée est sur votre gauche.*

1. la gare   2. le restaurant Chez Jeanne   3. l'hôtel Nelson   4. l'hôtel de ville

Now you are standing in front of the St. Vincent de Paul Cathedral. Continue using the map on p. 112 to help tourists find where they want to go.

> *Modèle:*   un bureau de poste
> —*Excusez-moi, Monsieur (Madame). Est-ce qu'il y a un bureau de poste près d'ici?*
> —*Oui. Il y a un bureau de poste sur le boulevard Manet.*
> —*Le boulevard Manet? C'est à gauche ou à droite?*
> —*Vous allez à gauche et vous continuez jusqu'au bout de la rue Nationale. Là, vous tournez à droite et vous continuez tout droit. Le bureau de poste est en face du cinéma Manet.*

5. une pharmacie   6. un bureau de tabac   7. une banque   8. un fast-food

**E.   Un petit exercice.** Guide one of your classmates through the following exercise, using the imperative and the map on p. 112.

Ex. E: ⇄ Have one student
look at the exercise and the
other at the map. The command giver should act out unfamiliar words.

1. regarder le plan de la ville
2. chercher le musée
3. faire attention (Il y a deux musées: vous préférez l'art moderne.)
4. expliquer où se trouve le musée
5. aller au tableau (*chalkboard*)
6. faire une peinture ou une statue
7. retourner à sa place

# S·T·R·U·C·T·U·R·E

## *Le présent du verbe irrégulier* **prendre**

| | |
|---|---|
| **Je prends** le petit déjeuner. | *I eat (have)* breakfast. |
| **Tu ne prends pas** ton temps. | *You're not taking* your time. |
| **Elle prend** le métro. | *She takes* the subway. |
| **Nous prenons** un café. | *We're having* a cup of coffee. |
| **Prenez** la rue Monge. | *Take* Monge Street. |
| **Ils prennent** un billet. | *They are buying* a ticket. |

The irregular verb **prendre** has several English equivalents: *to take; to have* or *to eat* or *to drink* when talking about meals, food, or beverages; and *to buy* when referring to tickets.

| **prendre** *(to take, to have; to eat, to drink; to buy)* | |
|---|---|
| je **prends** | nous **prenons** |
| tu **prends** | vous **prenez** |
| il, elle, on **prend** | ils, elles **prennent** |

Two other verbs conjugated like **prendre** are **apprendre** *(to learn)* and **comprendre** *(to understand).*

| | |
|---|---|
| **Elle apprend** l'italien. | *She is learning* Italian. |
| **Je ne comprends pas.** | *I don't understand.* |

▲　▲　▲

## APPLICATION

**F.** Remplacez les sujets et faites les changements nécessaires.

1. *Marie-Hélène* prend le déjeuner. (Jacques / tu / nous / vous / Hervé et son cousin / je)
2. *Gérard* ne prend pas le métro d'habitude. (je / nous / Chantal / Michèle et ses amis / tu)
3. Est-ce que *vous* apprenez l'italien? (nous / tu / Jean-Pierre / M. et Mme Beauchamp / Jacqueline)
4. *Émilie* ne comprend pas la question. (tu / nous / les étudiants / je / vous / Vincent)

**G. Dis-moi!** *(Tell me!)* While traveling together on the bus in Paris, you find out some things about Mireille Loiseau and her friends.

*Modèle:*    Dis-moi! Est-ce que tu prends souvent l'autobus? (de temps en temps)

*Je prends l'autobus de temps en temps.*

1. Dis-moi! Est-ce que Stéphane prend souvent l'autobus? (rarement)
   a. Et tes parents? (assez souvent)
   b. Et ta sœur? (ne . . . jamais)
2. Dis-moi! Qu'est-ce que Martine prend pour aller à l'université? (le métro)
   a. Et toi et ton frère? (l'autobus)
   b. Et Jean-Jacques? (le métro)
   c. Et tes professeurs? (le métro aussi)
3. Dis-moi! Quelle route est-ce que Didier prend pour rentrer à la maison? (la rue du Bac)
   a. Et toi? (l'avenue de l'Armée)
   b. Et tes parents? (le boulevard de l'Ouest)
   c. Et Geneviève? (la rue Champollion)
4. Dis-moi! Est-ce que Jean-Luc apprend l'anglais? (l'italien)
   a. Et Michèle? (l'espagnol)
   b. Et vous deux? (le russe)
   c. Et les autres? (le chinois)

**H. La ronde des questions.** Posez quatre questions **(tu, vous, il/elle, ils/elles)** aux autres membres de votre groupe.      Ex. H: ☐

1. prendre le petit déjeuner d'habitude   2. apprendre l'espagnol   3. bien comprendre les hommes *(men)* ou les femmes *(women)*   4. prendre souvent l'autobus

# PRONONCIATION   *La consonne t*

📼 **Student Tape:** Chapitre 3 Segment 1

The **t** in French is usually pronounced like the *t* in the English word *stay:* **hôtel, Vittel, hôpital.** The **th** combination in French is also pronounced [t]. Compare:

| *English* | *French* |
|-----------|----------|
| *th*eater | **th**éâtre |
| Ca*th*olic | ca**th**olique |

When the combination **ti** occurs in the middle of a word, there is no hard-and-fast rule for pronunciation: the **t** may be pronounced [t] or [s]. In general, if an English cognate of the word has a [t] sound, its French counterpart has a [t] sound also. If an English cognate has a [sh] or a [s] sound, its French counterpart is usually pronounced [s].

| *English* | *French* |
|-----------|----------|
| pi*t*y | pitié |
| na*t*ion | nation |
| democra*c*y | démocratie |

**Le savez-vous?**
▲▲▲▲▲▲▲▲▲▲▲▲▲▲
**Why would someone go to a** syndicat d'initiative?
a. **to get tourist information**
b. **to obtain a business loan**
c. **to ask for protection**

Réponse ▲▲▲

**I.**    Read each word aloud, being sure to pronounce **th** as [t] and to distinguish between [t] and [s] when necessary.

thé / tes / tabac / national / menthe / étudiant / cathédrale / partie / habiter / question / bibliothèque / omelette / à côté / Athènes / aristocratie / mythe

## S·T·R·U·C·T·U·R·E

**Suggestion,** Time: Use a model clock. Begin by having students repeat the hours from **une heure** to **midi** (contrast with **minuit**). Then have them repeat the time every five minutes from **trois heures** to **quatre heures.**

**Grammar:** The word **heure** is feminine; consequently, the word **demie** ends in **-e** in times such as **deux heures et demie** and **trois heures et demie.** The words **midi** and **minuit** are masculine; consequently, no **-e** is added to **demi: midi et demi, minuit et demi.**

▲▲▲   a

### Quelle heure est-il?

Il est une heure.

Il est deux heures.

Il est deux heures dix.

Il est deux heures et quart.

Il est deux heures et demie.

Il est trois heures moins vingt.

Il est trois heures moins le quart.

Il est midi.

Il est minuit et demi.

To distinguish between A.M. and P.M., use the expression **du matin** *(in the morning),* **de l'après-midi** *(in the afternoon),* or **du soir** *(in the evening).*

| | |
|---|---|
| 9:12 A.M. | neuf heures douze **du matin** |
| 2:30 P.M. | deux heures et demie **de l'après-midi** |
| 8:40 P.M. | neuf heures moins vingt **du soir** |

▲   ▲   ▲

## APPLICATION

Transparency:
3-6 (clock faces with times different from those in the text)

**J.**   Give the time for every three minutes between **9h** and **10h.**

**K.**   **Quelle heure est-il?** Find out the time from a classmate. Tell whether it is morning **(du matin),** afternoon **(de l'après-midi),** or evening **(du soir).**

**Follow-up,** Ex. K: Use the transparency to practice additional times. Begin and end the exercise by asking the actual time.

*Modèle:*        2h20 P.M.
                   —*Quelle heure est-il? (Vous avez l'heure? Tu as l'heure?)*
                   —*Il est deux heures vingt de l'après-midi.*

1.  8:20 A.M.      3.  10:55 P.M.      5.  7:45 P.M.      7.  12:00 A.M.      9.  11:45 A.M.
2.  10:25 A.M.     4.  3:10 P.M.       6.  4:15 P.M.      8.  1:30 A.M.      10.  6:35 A.M.

## Note grammaticale

### *Quelques expressions pour parler de l'heure*

To ask someone *what time* something happens, use **À quelle heure...?** The response to this question requires either the preposition **à** (if you give an exact time) or the preposition **vers** (if you give an approximate time):

**Suggestion,** Time expressions: Tell students in French at what time you have classes, eat lunch, go home; explain when you work. Then ask: **À quelle heure est-ce que vous avez des cours aujourd'hui? . . . vous déjeunez? . . . rentrez? Quand est-ce que vous étudiez? . . . travaillez?**

—**À quelle heure** est-ce qu'on         —*What time* do we eat?
   mange?
—**À 6h15.**                              —*At 6:15.*
—**Vers 6h.**                             —*Around 6 o'clock.*

To ask someone *when* something occurs, use **quand.** To indicate that something happens *between* two times, use either **entre ___ et ___** or **de ___ jusqu'à ___ :**

—**Quand** est-ce que tu fais            —*When* do you do your French
   ton français?                             (homework)?
—**Entre 8h et 9h.**                     —*Between 8 and 9.*

—**Quand** est-ce que ta mère           —*When* does your mother
   travaille?                                work?
—Elle travaille **de 4h jusqu'à**        —She works *from 4 until
   **minuit.**                               midnight.*

**L.   Au festival de Tarascon.** You want to find out when you and your friends will do certain things the day of the festival. Answer the questions, using the information provided.

*Modèle:*    Quand est-ce qu'on va à l'exposition de peinture? (vers 3h)
*On va à l'exposition vers 3h.*

1.   À quelle heure est-ce qu'on va au défilé? (vers 10h)
2.   À quelle heure commence le concert de rock? (à 1h)
3.   Quand est-ce qu'on mange? (entre 12h et 2h)
4.   Quand est-ce qu'il y a du judo? (de 2h jusqu'à 6h)
5.   À quelle heure est-ce qu'on va au son et lumière? (vers 9h)
6.   À quelle heure commence le feu d'artifice? (à 10h30)
7.   À quelle heure est-ce qu'il y a des danses folkloriques? (entre 11h et 12h)
8.   À quelle heure est-ce que le bal commence? (vers 11h)

▲ ▲ ▲ ▲ ▲ ▲ ▲ ▲ ▲ ▲ **Débrouillons-nous!** ▲ ▲ ▲ ▲ ▲ ▲ ▲ ▲ ▲ ▲

*Petite révision de l'étape*

Ex. M: ⇄

**M.   Échange.** Posez des questions à un(e) camarade de classe, qui va vous répondre.

1.   Est-ce que tu prends l'autobus pour aller à l'université? Pour aller en ville?
2.   Est-ce que tu apprends le russe? Quelle autre langue est-ce que tu voudrais apprendre?
3.   Est-ce que tu comprends toujours tes parents? Est-ce que tes parents comprennent bien les jeunes *(young people)*?
4.   En semaine *(during the week),* où es-tu d'habitude à 9h du matin? À midi? À 5h de l'après-midi? À 8h du soir?
5.   Pendant le week-end, où es-tu d'habitude à 11h du matin? À 2h de l'après-midi? À 9h du soir?

Ex. N: ○

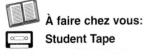   **À faire chez vous: CAHIER, Chapitre 3 / 3ᵉ étape**

**À faire chez vous: Student Tape**

Now that you've completed the first three **étapes** of **Chapitre 3,** do Segment 2 of the STUDENT TAPE. See **CAHIER, Chapitre 3,** *Écoutons!,* for exercises that accompany this segment.

**N.   Qu'est-ce qu'on fait?** Make plans with one or more of your classmates to do something. Agree on an activity. Then arrange a time and place to meet. If necessary, give directions on how to get to the meeting place.

ACTIVITÉS: **aller au cinéma, aller à un concert, faire une promenade, regarder une vidéo, écouter des disques, faire du tennis**

# QUATRIÈME ÉTAPE

## L·E·C·T·U·R·E

### Visitez Fougères!

*Read the following tourist brochure published by the tourist office of Fougères, a city in eastern Brittany. Use the many cognates to do Exercise A without looking at the definitions that follow the brochure.*

FOUGÈRES

"Nulle part en France
le voyageur ne rencontre
de contraste aussi grandiose ...
La Bretagne est là
dans sa fleur"

*Balzac.*

## FOUGÈRES Ville d'Art
### Citadelle du Duché de Bretagne

Visitée et chantée par les grands écrivains de l'époque romantique, FOUGÈRES offre aux touristes, aux historiens, aux peintres, avec le souvenir vivant de son passé et de son site incomparable, le spectacle de ses monuments d'architecture militaire avec son château et ses fortifications urbaines, de foi médiévale avec ses magnifiques églises.

Riche de son passé, FOUGÈRES est de nos jours un centre industriel et agricole très important.

*écrivains:* writers     *foi:* faith     *de nos jours:* nowadays

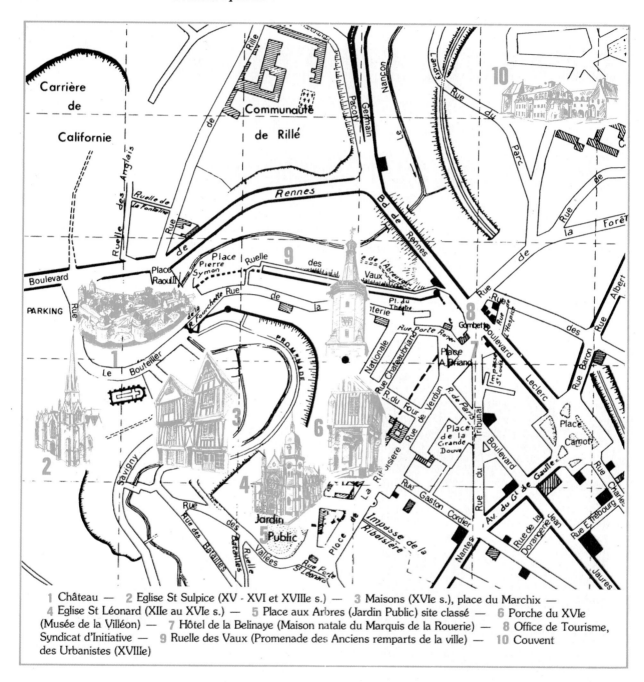

1 Château — 2 Eglise St Sulpice (XV - XVI et XVIIIe s.) — 3 Maisons (XVIe s.), place du Marchix — 4 Eglise St Léonard (XIIe au XVIe s.) — 5 Place aux Arbres (Jardin Public) site classé — 6 Porche du XVIe (Musée de la Villéon) — 7 Hôtel de la Belinaye (Maison natale du Marquis de la Rouerie) — 8 Office de Tourisme, Syndicat d'Initiative — 9 Ruelle des Vaux (Promenade des Anciens remparts de la ville) — 10 Couvent des Urbanistes (XVIIIe)

## COMPRÉHENSION

**Postreading:** Have students imagine a poster for Fougères, using the format **Fougères— son château, ses . . . , ses . . . , son . . .** , etc. They should use both the brochure and the map for ideas. Then ask them to design a similar poster to attract French-speaking tourists to their area.

**A.   La brochure.** After your first reading of the brochure, list as many facts about the city of Fougères as you can. Then read the brochure again, this time consulting the definitions at the end, and add to your list any attractions or ideas that you missed.

**B.   Le plan de la ville.** Study the map of Fougères and pick out five sites you would like to visit.

## *Troisième étape*

**C.  Pourriez-vous me dire...?** *(Could you tell me . . . ?)* You are at the American Embassy in the African city of Bamako, the capital of Mali. Find out where certain places are located and get directions on how to go there.

Ex. C: ⇄

Among the places you might be looking for are: **une pharmacie, un bureau de tabac, un bureau de poste, le commissariat de police, une boulangerie** *(bakery),* **un café, un restaurant, une banque, un hôtel, l'hôpital**

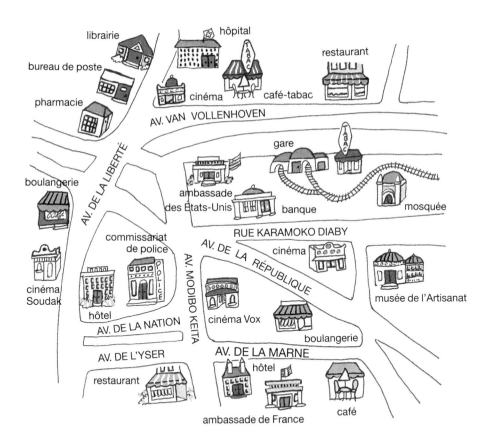

**D.  Quelle heure est-il?** Answer according to the cues.

> *Modèle:*     2h30
> —*Quelle heure est-il?*
> —*Il est deux heures et demie.*

1. 7h25   2. 11h52   3. 10h15   4. 3h30   5. 8h10   6. 1h45   7. 4h40
8. 12h05   9. 8h33   10. 9h16   11. 0h05   12. 4h20

**À faire chez vous:**
**Student Tape**
**CAHIER, Chapitre 3:**
*Rédigeons! / Travail de*
*fin de chapitre* (including
STUDENT TAPE, Chapitre
3, Segment 3)

# Point d'arrivée

*Activités orales*

## Exprimons-nous!

When stopping a stranger to ask for directions or other information, French speakers use expressions such as **pardon, s'il vous plaît, excusez-moi,** and **pourriez-vous me dire:**

**S'il vous plaît,** la rue du Pirou?

*Would you please direct me to the rue du Pirou?*

**Pardon,** Madame. **Pourriez-vous me dire** où se trouve la rue Sully?

*Pardon me,* Madam. *Could you tell me where the rue Sully is located?*

**Excusez-moi,** Monsieur. **Pourriez-vous me dire** s'il y a une pharmacie près d'ici?

*Excuse me,* Sir. *Could you tell me if there is a drugstore near here?*

Ex. E: ⇄

**Suggestion,** Ex. E: Students should distinguish between asking for a specific place (**Où est l'hôtel Zola?**) and a generic place (**Est-ce qu'il y a un restaurant près de...?**).

**E.   Renseignons-nous!** *(Let's get some information!)* You have been living in the town on p. 112 for several months. A stranger (who does not speak English) stops you in the street and asks directions. Help the stranger find the desired destination.

| You are at the: | The stranger is looking for: |
| --- | --- |
| ■ railroad station | ■ the Hotel Zola |
| ■ Hotel Nelson | ■ the Catholic bookstore |
| ■ cathedral | ■ a restaurant (near the hospital) |
| ■ archeological museum | ■ a bank |

**Suggestion,** Ex. F: Have students give presentations in small groups. Then choose a limited number to present their friends to the class.

**F.   Mon ami(e).** Make a presentation to the class about a friend. Include such information as name, where he/she lives in relation to you, family, possessions, interests, likes, and dislikes.

Ex. G: ⇄

**G.   À Bamako.** You and an Austrian student (whom you have just met) are newly arrived in Mali. You are having lunch at the café on avenue Van Vollenhoven (see map on p. 121). After ordering, you talk about your families, your interests, etc. Then you look at the map and help each other decide the best way to get to the places you wish to go to. Your destination is the Cinéma Soudak; your friend is looking for a bank.

**H.   Au festival de Tarascon.** You and one or more of your classmates are in Tarascon for the festival. Using the poster on p. 108
and the map on p. 99, plan your activities for the day. You will
probably want to do some things together. However, each person
should have one activity that he/she will do alone. You can then
make plans to meet again later in the day.

Ex. H: ⇄

# PORTRAIT

*Véronique Béziers, Tarascon
(Provence), France*

J'habite dans la ville de Tarascon, dans
le sud de la France, non loin d'Avignon.
Notre appartement se trouve dans la
rue des Halles, en face de l'hôtel de ville
et tout près du château. J'y habite avec
mes parents et ma sœur Danielle. Tous
les ans je participe à la fête des Fleurs;
cette année je vais faire des danses
folkloriques.

 **Instructor's Tape:**
Véronique Béziers,
Tarascon (Provence),
France

**Portrait:** Have students listen
to the recording on the
Instructor's Tape. Then ask
questions to check comprehension.

# Profil

*Tarascon*

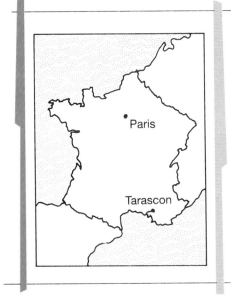

**SITUATION:**  dans le sud de la France,
au bord du Rhône
**POPULATION:**  11 024 habitants
**IMPORTANCE:**  centre expéditeur de
fruits et de légumes *(vegetables)*
**LIEUX D'INTÉRÊT:** château,   église
romane
**HISTOIRE:**  ville natale du Tartarin de
Tarascon, personnage *(character)* in-
venté par l'auteur Alphonse Daudet
**COMMENTAIRE:** Comme beaucoup de
petites villes de France, Tarascon
s'anime une fois par an à l'occasion de

**Suggestion, Profil:** Begin by
having students contrast their
town to other towns in the
region or the country in terms
of festivals. Have them point
out similarities and differences.
Then have them silently read
the information in the **Profil.**
Ask some questions in English
to verify comprehension and
then proceed to the discussion
question.

sa fête. Des habitants de la région et des touristes d'autres régions de la France
rejoignent les Tarasconnais pour une journée de culture populaire.

**À discuter:** Do small towns and cities in the United States have their own
popular festivals? Is this widespread or is it more typical of certain regions?

# L·E·X·I·Q·U·E

## Pour se débrouiller

*Pour demander un renseignement*
Pardon,...
S'il vous plaît,...
Excusez-moi,...

Pourriez-vous me dire...?
Où est (se trouve)...?
Est-ce qu'il y a un(e) ___ près d'ici
(dans le quartier)?

*Pour situer un endroit*
à côté de
au bord de
au bout de
au coin de
derrière

devant
en face de
entre
loin de
près de

*Pour expliquer comment aller quelque part*
tourner à droite (à gauche)
dans l'avenue
dans la rue
sur le boulevard
sur la place

continuer tout droit
jusqu'à...
traverser

*Pour organiser une activité*
Qu'est-ce qu'on va faire?
Je voudrais voir...
Allons...
Faisons...

On y va ensemble?
D'accord. Bonne idée.
Oui. Pourquoi pas?
Oui. Allons-y!

*Pour fixer un rendez-vous*
À quelle heure est-ce qu'on se retrouve?
Où est-ce qu'on se retrouve?
On se retrouve à...
Rendez-vous à...

*Pour demander et indiquer l'heure*
Quelle heure est-il?
Il est une heure.
une heure et quart.
une heure et demie.
deux heures moins le quart.
midi.
minuit.
À quelle heure?
à (vers) ___ h
Quand?
entre ___ h et ___ h
de ___ h jusqu'à ___ h

## Thèmes et contextes

*Les bâtiments et les lieux publics*

l'aéroport *(m.)*
la bibliothèque
le bureau de poste
une cathédrale
un château
le commissariat de police
une école
une église
la gare
l'hôpital

l'hôtel de ville
un lycée
un musée
un parc
un parking
une piscine
un pont
un stade
une synagogue
une université

*Les bâtiments commerciaux*

une banque
une boulangerie
un bureau de tabac
un cinéma
une épicerie

un hôtel
une librairie
une pharmacie
un restaurant
un théâtre

*Les jeux*

le base-ball
le basket
le flipper

le football (américain)
le tennis
le volley

*Les instruments de musique*

la batterie
la clarinette
la flûte
la guitare
le piano

le saxophone
le trombone
la trompette
le violon

*Un festival*

un bal
un concert d'orgue
          de rock
les danses folkloriques *(f.pl.)*
un défilé

les feux *(m.pl.)* d'artifice
déguster
     une spécialité de la région
un spectacle son et lumière

## Vocabulaire général

*Verbes*

aller
jouer à (de)
stationner
voir

*Adverbes*

d'abord
de temps en temps
ensuite
là-bas
ne . . . jamais
quelquefois
rarement
souvent
toujours

ALLONS-Y!
Video Program

**ACTE 3**
LA VILLE

**V O C A B U L A I R E**
une fois que vous êtes
*once you are*
longer   *to go along*
la direction   *the last*
   *station of a Paris*
   *Metro line*
Gare de Lyon, Bastille,
Gare d'Austerlitz,
Maubert-Mutualité, La
Défense, Place d'Italie
   *names of Paris*
   *Metro stations*

*Massyla Fodéba*
*Dakar, Sénégal*

—Tu voudrais aller en ville avec moi?
—Oui, j'ai une course à faire.

# Chapitre 4

## Allons en ville!

### OBJECTIVES

**In this chapter, you will learn:**

- to make plans to do various activities in town;
- to talk about various means of urban transportation;
- to use the Paris subway;
- to talk about future plans;
- to read short informational texts about transportation;
- to understand conversations about making plans.

### ALLONS-Y!
Video Program

**ACTE 4**
SCÈNE 1: AU CAFÉ
SCÈNE 2: PRENONS LE MÉTRO

▷ Première étape  Vous allez en ville?
▷ Deuxième étape  Prenons le métro!
▷ Troisième étape  Je veux prendre un taxi!
▷ Quatrième étape  Lecture: Histoire de billets

**CHAPTER SUPPORT MATERIALS** (STUDENT)

**Cahier:** pp. 93–120

 **Student Tape:** Chapitre 4 Segments 1, 2, 3

CHAPTER SUPPORT MATERIALS (INSTRUCTOR)

 Transparencies: 4-1 through 4-7

 Instructor's Tape: Chapitre 4, Text, pp. 128, 136, 147, 162

SYSTÈME-D *software:* Writing activities for this chapter are found in the **Cahier:** Ex. IV (p. 98), Ex. V (p. 98), Ex. VII (p. 116) *Rédigeons!* (p. 119).

 Multimedia: See the Resource Manual for correlation to our multimedia product.

**Instructor's Tape:**
**Vous allez en ville?**

**Transparencies:**
**4-1, 4-2** (people and activities)

# PREMIÈRE ÉTAPE
## Point de départ

**ALLONS-Y!**
Video Program

**ACTE 4: SCÈNE 1**
AU CAFÉ

**QUESTIONS DE FOND**
1. Why did Sébastien arrive late?
2. What are the two suggested activities for tonight?
3. What do they finally settle on?

*Vous allez en ville?*

text audio
CD 1-26

today
to meet (arranged in advance)
subway

—*Tu vas en ville **aujourd'hui?***
—*Oui, je vais **retrouver** des amis. Nous avons rendez-vous à 2h.*
—*Tu prends l'autobus?*
—*Non, je vais prendre le **métro.***

**Suggestion, Point de départ:**
Have students look at the transparency while listening to the conversations on Instructor's Tape. After each conversation, ask students questions, moving from the drawings **(Où est-ce qu'il va retrouver ses amis? Il va prendre l'autobus pour y aller?)** to personal questions **(Où est-ce que vous retrouvez vos amis? Est-ce que vous avez rendez-vous avec un[e] ami[e] après le cours?)**

feel like

—*Tu **as envie d'**aller au cinéma ce soir?*
—*Ah, oui. Bonne idée. On prend le métro?*
—*Non. Prenons l'autobus.*

—Je **dois** aller en ville aujourd'hui pour **faire des achats**. Tu voudrais m'accompagner?
—Oui. Moi aussi, j'ai besoin d'**acheter** quelque chose. On y va **à pied?**
—Non. J'ai la voiture de ma sœur.

must, have to  /  to go shopping
to buy  /  on foot

—Je vais en ville **faire une course**. Je dois aller au bureau de poste.
—Moi aussi, **j'ai une course à faire**.
—C'est parfait. On y va **ensemble** et ensuite on **fait du lèche-vitrines**.

**Grammar:** With the verb **aller**, it is usually necessary to specify where one is going—that is, you can't use the verb all by itself (as is done in English). When the place is not indicated, the pronoun **y** *(there)* is used: **Allons-y! On y va? Tu voudrais y aller aussi? Claude y va à pied.**

to do an errand
have an errand to do
together  /  to go window
   shopping

## À VOUS! (Exercices de vocabulaire)

**A.  Je dois..., mais j'ai envie de...** In each case, tell what you have to do (**je dois**) and what you feel like doing (**j'ai envie de**).

*Modèle:*      aller au bureau de poste / retrouver mes amis
               *Je dois aller au bureau de poste, mais j'ai envie de*
               *retrouver mes amis.*

1. aller à la banque  /  faire du lèche-vitrines
2. acheter quelque chose pour ma mère  /  aller au cinéma
3. retrouver mes amis  /  faire des achats
4. faire des courses pour mon père  /  retrouver mes amis au café
5. prendre l'autobus  /  prendre le métro
6. rester à la maison avec ma petite sœur  /  aller chez mon ami Jean-Pierre
7. y aller à pied  /  prendre la voiture de mes parents
8. faire mes devoirs  /  aller voir l'exposition de peintures au musée

**Grammar:** In the verb **acheter**, **è** replaces **e** in forms where the ending following the **t** is not pronounced: **j'achète, tu achètes, elle achète, ils achètent.** But: **nous achetons, vous achetez.**

**B.** **Pourquoi (comment) est-ce qu'ils vont en ville?** Based on the drawings, tell why and how each student is going downtown.

1. Chantal

*Modèle:*   *Elle va en ville pour retrouver une amie.* or *Elle va retrouver une amie (en ville).*
*Elle prend l'autobus.*

2. Vincent

3. Michèle

4. Monique

5. Liliane

6. Marc et Christian

**C.** **Tu voudrais aller en ville?** You are going downtown and invite a friend to come along. When you explain your reason for going, he/she agrees and suggests a way of getting there. You have a different idea, which your friend accepts.

Ex. C: ⇄

*Modèle:*   aller au bureau de poste / métro / à pied
  —*Tu voudrais aller en ville avec moi?*
  —*Pour quoi faire?*
  —*Je dois (je vais) aller au bureau de poste.*
  —*D'accord. On prend le métro?*
  —*Non, non. Allons à pied.*
  —*D'accord. On y va à pied.*

**Reminder:** The first-person plural imperative form may be used to make a suggestion: **Prenons l'autobus! Allons à pied!** Notice that in this case you need not use **y** with **aller.**

Prenons (lets take)

1. faire des achats / autobus / voiture
2. aller au cinéma / voiture / métro
3. faire du lèche-vitrines / vélo / à pied
4. faire une course / à pied / autobus
5. voir une exposition au musée / métro / vélos
6. prendre quelque chose au café / autobus / à pied

# S·T·R·U·C·T·U·R·E

## *Les jours de la semaine*

—**Quel jour sommes-nous aujourd'hui?**
—**Nous sommes mercredi.**

—*What day is it today?*

—*It's Wednesday.*

**Mardi** je vais au théâtre.     *Tuesday* I'm going to the theater.

In French, the days of the week are:

| | |
|---|---|
| **lundi** *(Monday)* | **vendredi** *(Friday)* |
| **mardi** *(Tuesday)* | **samedi** *(Saturday)* |
| **mercredi** *(Wednesday)* | **dimanche** *(Sunday)* |
| **jeudi** *(Thursday)* | |

The days of the week are not usually accompanied by either an article or a preposition. Thus, **jeudi** is the equivalent of *on Thursday* as well as just *Thursday.* To indicate a repeated occurence, the French use the definite article **le.** Thus, **le dimanche** is the equivalent of *on Sundays* or *every Sunday:*

J'ai rendez-vous avec M. Didier **jeudi.**
**Le dimanche,** ma famille et moi aimons faire une promenade après le dîner.

I have a meeting with M. Didier *(on) Thursday.*
*On Sundays,* my family and I like to take a walk after dinner.

Suggestion, Days of the week: (1) Have students repeat the days of the week. (2) Write today's date plus the dates for the next six days. Ask: **Quel jour est-on aujourd'hui? Aujourd'hui, on est le (lundi 9). Et le 10, c'est mercredi? Mais non, c'est mardi.** (3) Finally, illustrate the difference between **samedi** and **le samedi.**

▲  ▲  ▲

## APPLICATION

**D. Quel jour sommes-nous?** *(What day is it?)* Your friend is forgetful and never knows what day it is. Answer his/her questions, using the day *following* the day mentioned in the question.

*Modèle:*    lundi
—*Nous sommes lundi aujourd'hui?*
—*Non, nous sommes mardi aujourd'hui.*

1. jeudi   2. samedi   3. mercredi   4. dimanche   5. vendredi   6. mardi

**E. Ah, il arrive jeudi.** Some students from France are coming to visit your university. They have been visiting different U.S. cities and will arrive on different days. Using the calendar below, tell on what day of the week each student will arrive.

### JANVIER

| L | M | M | J | V | S | D |
|---|---|---|---|---|---|---|
| 1 | 2 | 3 | 4 | 5 | 6 | 7 |
| 8 | 9 | 10 | 11 | 12 | 13 | 14 |
| 15 | 16 | 17 | 18 | 19 | 20 | 21 |
| 22 | 23 | 24 | 25 | 26 | 27 | 28 |
| 29 | 30 | 31 | | | | |

*Modèle:*    Jean-Michel Tilorier va arriver le 18.
*Ah, il arrive jeudi.*

1. Renée Musigny va arriver le 15.
2. Maurice Alard et Olivier Basset vont arriver le 17.
3. Bruno Monteil va arriver le 21.
4. Marie et Jeanne Cottet vont arriver le 20.
5. Henri Vergnaud va arriver le 16.
6. Tous les autres *(all the others)* vont arriver le 19.

**Vocabulary:** Students in France often use the expression **avoir cours** without the indefinite article **(un, des): Tu as cours cet après-midi?** *(Do you have class today?)* **Je n'ai pas cours aujourd'hui.**

**F. Quels jours?** *(What days?)* The French exchange students, having arrived on your campus, are curious to know about life in the United States. Answer their questions about when you and your family do certain things.

*Modèle:*    Quel jour est-ce que tu vas au cinéma?
*D'habitude, je vais au cinéma le vendredi ou le samedi.*

1. Quels jours est-ce que tu as des cours?
2. Quels jours est-ce qu'il n'y a pas de cours à ton université?
3. Tu travailles? Quel(s) jour(s)?
4. Quel(s) jour(s) est-ce qu'on fait les courses chez toi?

5.   Quel(s) jour(s) est-ce que tes parents sont à la maison?
6.   Quel(s) jour(s) est-ce qu'on mange un grand *(large)* dîner chez toi?

## PRONONCIATION   *Les consonnes finales m et n*

**Student Tape:**
Chapitre 4
Segment 1

Like most final consonants in French, **m** and **n** are not pronounced at the end of a word. However, the presence of **m** or **n** frequently signals that the vowel preceding the **m** or **n** is nasalized—that is, that air passes through the nose as well as the mouth during pronunciation. Depending on which vowel precedes the final **m** or **n**, three different nasal sounds are possible:

**Pronunciation:** Modern usage no longer distinguishes between **im, in** and **um, un**. The same phonetic symbol, [ɛ̃], is used for both sounds.

| [ã] | [ɛ̃] | [ɔ̃] |
|---|---|---|
| **-am** (champ) | **-aim** (faim) | **-om** (nom) |
| **-an** (tant) | **-ain** (saint) | **-on** (sont) |
| **-em** (temps) | **-ien** (bien) | |
| **-en** (gens) | **-éen** (européen) | |
| | **-um** (parfum) | |
| | **-un** (un) | |

**G.**   Read each word aloud, being careful to nasalize the vowel without pronouncing the final consonant(s).

citron / allemand / Jean / appartement / boisson / vin / Verdun / demain / blanc / canadien / souvent / jambon / combien / nous avons / prend / vingt

**Le savez-vous?**
▲▲▲▲▲▲▲▲▲▲▲▲▲▲▲
**Senegal is found at the _____ tip of Africa.**
a.  **northern**
b.  **southern**
c.  **eastern**
d.  **western**

Réponse ▲▲▲

# S·T·R·U·C·T·U·R·E

## *Le présent du verbe irrégulier vouloir*

**Tu veux** un Coca?                      *Do you want* a Coke?
**Elle ne veut pas** de café.             *She doesn't want* any coffee.
**Ils veulent** aller chez Marie.         *They want* to go to Marie's.
**Est-ce que vous voulez** faire          *Do you want* to take a walk?
   une promenade?

The verb **vouloir** is used to indicate something one wants to have or do:

| vouloir *(to want)* | |
|---|---|
| je **veux** | nous **voulons** |
| tu **veux** | vous **voulez** |
| il, elle, on **veut** | ils, elles **veulent** |

**Suggestion, Vouloir:** (1) Review ordering in a café, substituting **vouloir** for **désirer** and **prendre:—Qu'est-ce que vous voulez?—Une limonade.—Ah, vous voulez une limonade. Georges veut une limonade.** Etc. (2) Write pronouns on board in three groups: **je, tu, il, elle, on / ils, elles / nous, vous.** (3) Write forms in four groups: **je, tu / il, elle, on / ils, elles / nous, vous.** (4) To review verb + infinitive, ask students: **Vous voulez aller à Paris?**

▲  ▲  ▲

## APPLICATION

**H.** Remplacez les sujets en italique et faites les changements nécessaires.

1. *Je* veux habiter à Paris. (nous / mes sœurs / Jacques / tu)
2. Est-ce que *Michel* veut aller en ville? (tu / Martine / vos parents / vous)
3. *Anne-Marie* ne veut pas de frites. (je / les autres / nous / Michel / on)

Ex. I: ⇄

**I. Ils veulent tous faire autre chose.** *(They all want to do something else.)* Your brother/sister asks if you're going to the movies with your friends or relatives. Explain that they all seem to have other plans.

▲▲▲ d

*Modèle:*     Suzanne / aller au concert
                   *—Est-ce que tu vas au cinéma avec Suzanne?*
                   *—Non, elle veut aller au concert.*

1. Alain / faire du ski
2. les parents / dîner au restaurant
3. Geneviève / aller à la bibliothèque
4. nos cousins / faire un tour en voiture
5. Denise / faire des achats
6. Jean et Catherine / regarder la télé

### Note grammaticale

*Quelques expressions avec* **vouloir**

You are already familiar with **je voudrais** and **tu voudrais.** The **nous** and **vous** forms of this polite expression can also be used to offer or request something:

| | |
|---|---|
| **Vous voudriez** y aller aussi? | *Would you like* to go too? |
| **Nous voudrions** parler à Yves. | *We would like* to talk to Yves. |

The idiomatic expression **vouloir bien** is an informal way of saying *OK, gladly, with pleasure:*

| | |
|---|---|
| —**Tu veux** faire un tour à vélo? | —*Do you want* to take a bike ride? |
| —Oui, **je veux bien.** | —Yes, *I'd like to.* |

Ex. J: ⇄

**J. Des invitations.** Invite a friend to go somewhere or to do something with you. When your friend accepts, suggest a way of getting there. Use the appropriate forms of **vouloir** and **vouloir bien.**

*Modèle:*    aller en ville / autobus
—*Tu veux aller en ville?*
—*Oui, je veux bien.*
—*Prenons l'autobus.*
—*D'accord. C'est une bonne idée.*

1. aller au cinéma / métro
2. faire un tour en voiture / ma voiture
3. dîner en ville / autobus
4. visiter la cathédrale / à pied
5. faire des courses en ville / nos vélos

Now invite some people you know less well to do something or go somewhere. When they accept, suggest a day. This time, instead of **vouloir bien** (which is appropriate for more informal situations), use **avec plaisir.**

*Modèle:*    aller au théâtre / samedi
—*Est-ce que vous voudriez aller au théâtre?*
—*Oui, avec plaisir.*
—*Samedi, c'est possible?*
—*Oui, samedi, c'est très bien.*

6. aller au concert / jeudi
7. dîner chez nous / mardi
8. faire une promenade avec nous / dimanche
9. aller voir l'exposition au musée / samedi

**Follow-up,** Ex. J: Have students invite *you* to do something. Then have them invite a friend to do the same thing.

▲ ▲ ▲ ▲ ▲ ▲ ▲ ▲ ▲ ▲ **Débrouillons-nous!** ▲ ▲ ▲ ▲ ▲ ▲ ▲ ▲ ▲

*Petite révision de l'étape*

**K.   Échange.** Posez les questions suivantes à un(e) autre étudiant(e), qui va vous répondre.

Ex. K: ⇄

1. Où est-ce que tu voudrais aller un jour *(someday)?*
2. Quelle autre langue est-ce que tu voudrais apprendre un jour?
3. Qu'est-ce que tu vas faire ce soir? Est-ce que tu as envie de ____ ? (Non? Qu'est-ce que tu voudrais faire?)
4. Quels jours est-ce que tu n'as pas de cours?
5. Qu'est-ce que tu fais le samedi? Le dimanche?
6. Quel jour de la semaine est-ce que tu préfères? Pourquoi?

Ex. L: ⇄

**L.   Tu voudrais y aller?** Invite a classmate to do something with you. When you get an affirmative response, arrange a day and a time and agree on a means of transportation.

**À faire chez vous: CAHIER, Chapitre 4 / 1ère étape**

**Instructor's Tape:**
**Prenons le métro!**
**Suggestion, Point de départ:**
Begin by discussing (in English) the major points of the
**Note culturelle** on p. 139.
Then have students listen to
the conversation on the Instructor's Tape. On the
map, show them the places and
route mentioned.

**ALLONS-Y!**
**Video Program**

ACTE 4: SCÈNE 2
PRENONS LE MÉTRO

**QUESTIONS DE FOND**
1. Where is Xavier
   now? Where does
   he want to go? How
   will he get there?
2. What is the difference between **la
   Carte orange** and
   a single ticket?

**Transparency:**
4-4 (Paris metro)

**Transparency:**
4-5 (map of Montreal
metro, for additional
practice)

**Grammar: Descendre** is a
regular **-re** verb, a category that you will not meet
formally until Chapter 11.
For the moment, learn the
following verb forms: **je
descends, tu descends,
nous descendons, vous
descendez.**

it is necessary to change
  trains

get off

# DEUXIÈME ÉTAPE

## Point de départ

▼▼▼▼▼▼▼▼▼▼▼▼▼▼▼▼▼

*Prenons le métro!*

Massyla Fodéba et son ami belge, Stéphane, vont prendre le métro pour aller
au musée Rodin. Massyla habite près de la place d'Italie, où il y a une station
de métro. Les deux garçons regardent un plan de métro.

| | |
|---|---|
| MASSYLA: | Bon. Nous sommes là, place d'Italie. |
| STÉPHANE: | Où est le musée Rodin? |
| MASSYLA: | Il est près de la station Invalides. Là. Alors, nous prenons la direction Charles de Gaulle–Étoile. |
| STÉPHANE: | C'est direct? |
| MASSYLA: | Non, **il faut prendre une correspondance.** Nous changeons à La Motte-Picquet, direction Créteil. Et nous **descendons** à la station Invalides. |
| STÉPHANE: | Bon. Allons-y! |

Massyla et Stéphane entrent dans la station et vont **au guichet.**          to the ticket window

| STÉPHANE: | Je prends un billet? |
|---|---|
| MASSYLA: | Non, tu prends **un carnet** de dix billets. C'est **moins cher.** |

book (of tickets) / less expensive

| STÉPHANE: | Et toi, tu ne prends pas de billet? |
|---|---|
| MASSYLA: | Non, j'ai **une Carte orange.** C'est bon un mois entier dans le métro ou dans l'autobus. |

orange card

| STÉPHANE: | C'est bien, ça. *(Au guichet)* S'il vous plaît, Madame. Un carnet de dix. |
|---|---|
| L'EMPLOYÉE: | Trente-quatre francs cinquante, Monsieur. *Sept euros* |

*CD 1-28*

A map showing the locations of the various monuments in Paris appears on p. 168 (Intégration culturelle «Paris»).

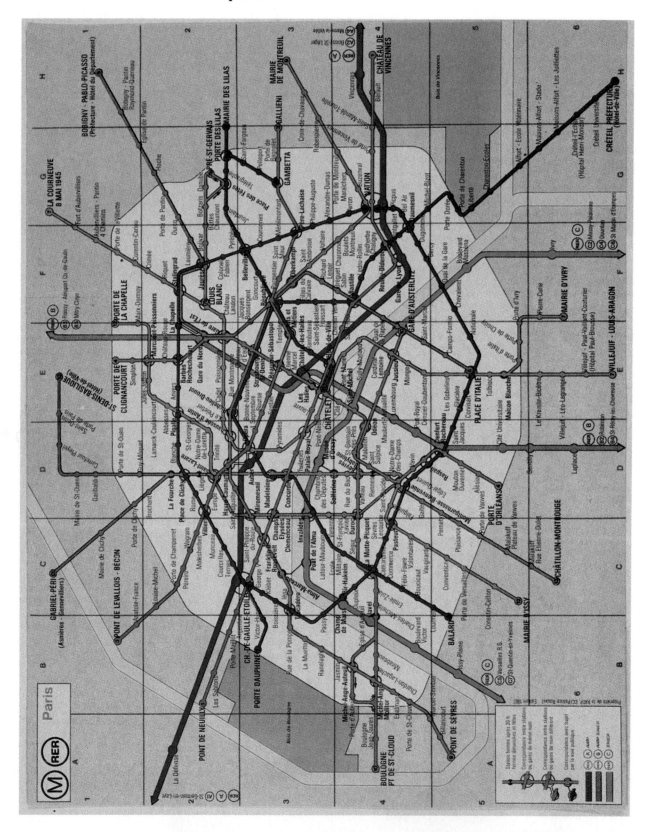

## Note culturelle

**Le métro** is one of the best-developed subway systems in the world. There are fifteen lines, organized so that one can go almost anywhere in Paris with a minimum number of **correspondances** (changes of line). Each line has a number. However, most often the lines are designated by the **directions** (stations at each end of the line). Thus, Line 1 is called **Château de Vincennes–Pont de Neuilly** (sometimes abbreviated to **Vincennes-Neuilly),** Line 4 is **Porte d'Orléans–Porte de Clignancourt (Orléans-Clignancourt),** and so forth.

To determine your route, you look at **un plan de métro** (map) like the one on p. 138. On the map, find the station where you want to get off and the station at the end of the line beyond it (for example, **la direction Orléans).** Then follow the signs for that **direction.** If you need to change trains, find the new **direction** (from the map) and look for signs indicating **correspondance** and **direction.** Do not confuse subway lines with the **RER** lines (trains that run between Paris and its suburbs).

**Métro** tickets can be bought singly **(un billet)** or in groups of five **(un carnet de cinq)** or ten tickets **(un carnet de dix).** You can also buy special tickets: unlimited one-day travel **(formule 1),** unlimited travel for three or five days **(Paris Visite),** unlimited travel for six days **(un Coupon jaune),** and a full-month commuter ticket **(une Carte orange).** These tickets can all be used on buses as well as on the subway.

| **Questions:** What American cities have subway systems? What other means of public transportation are available in American cities?

### Le savez-vous?

▲▲▲▲▲▲▲▲▲▲▲▲▲▲▲▲
**The Paris** métro **has a worldwide reputation. Many people do not know, however, that there is more than one subway system in France. What other cities have a metro?**
a. **Toulouse**
b. **Marseille**
c. **Lyon**
d. **Lille**

Réponse   ▲▲▲

## À VOUS! (Exercices de vocabulaire)

**A.   Au guichet.** Buy the indicated metro tickets.

*Modèle:*     a book of ten tickets
         *Un carnet de dix, s'il vous plaît.*

1.   one ticket
2.   a ticket that allows you unlimited travel for a single day     " un Paris Visite pour un jour "
3.   a book of five tickets
4.   a ticket that allows you unlimited travel for three days
5.   a ticket that allows you to travel for a month     un mois
6.   a ticket that allows you to travel for almost a week     une semaine

**B.** **Prenons le métro!** Following the models and using the metro map on p. 138, explain how to use the subway. The number-letter combinations (shown in parentheses after the name of each station) correspond to the grid coordinates on the map and will help you locate the stations.

*Modèles:*   Alain / Saint-Lazare (D2) → Bastille (F4)
*Alain, tu prends la direction Mairie d'Issy, tu changes à Concorde, direction Château de Vincennes, et tu descends à Bastille.*

M. Genois / Montparnasse-Bienvenüe (D4) → Opéra (D3)
*M. Genois, vous prenez la direction Porte de Clignancourt, vous changez à Châtelet, direction La Courneuve, et vous descendez à Opéra.*

1. Jacqueline / Charles de Gaulle-Étoile (C3) → Raspail (D4)
2. Albert / gare du Nord (E2) → gare de Lyon (F4)
3. Mme Fantout / Louvre (E3) → Trocadéro (C3)
4. Isabelle et Jean-Luc / Odéon (D4) → place de Clichy (D2)

**C.** **Prenons le métro! (suite)** Explain to each person how to take the subway. Specify the kind of ticket to buy. Consult the metro map on p. 138. (Map coordinates are in parentheses.)

▲▲▲  a, b, c, d

*Modèle:*   *Tu vas (vous allez) à la station Monceau, tu prends (vous prenez) un carnet de dix, tu prends la direction..., etc.*

1. Olga, your German friend, is in Paris for four or five days. Her hotel is near the Odéon station (D4). She wants to go to church near the Madeleine station (D3).
2. Mr. and Mrs. Van D'Elden, some Dutch friends of your family, are spending three weeks in Paris. Their hotel is near the Palais-Royal station (D3). Their first day in the city they want to go to a store near the Montparnasse-Bienvenüe station (D4).
3. A stranger passing through Paris is trying to get from the airline terminal at Porte Maillot (B2) to the gare du Nord (E2).

# R·E·P·R·I·S·E

## Première étape

Transparency:
4-6 (drawings for
Ex. D)

**D.** **D'habitude,...** Some members of your family follow a regular routine. On a certain day of the week, they always go downtown. Based on the drawings, tell why they go downtown and how they go.

*Modèle:*   votre mère
*Le lundi ma mère va en ville pour
faire des courses.* or *Le lundi
ma mère fait des courses en ville.
Elle y va à pied.*

1. votre grand-père

2. votre cousin

3. votre sœur

4. votre tante et votre oncle

5. vos cousines

**E.   Demande aux autres.** *(Ask the others.)* Tell the person next to you to ask   Ex. E: ○
the other members of your group the following questions. After asking each
group member individually, the questioner will report back to you.

1. Demande aux autres s'ils veulent aller à la bibliothèque.
   *Est-ce que tu veux aller à la bibliothèque? Et toi,...?*
2. Demande aux autres ce qu'ils veulent acheter.
   *Qu'est-ce que...?*
3. Demande aux autres la ville qu'ils veulent visiter un jour.
   *Quelle ville...?*
4. Demande aux autres ce qu'ils veulent faire samedi.
   *Qu'est-ce que...?*

**Suggestion,** Time adverbs:
Use a (French) calendar to introduce adverbs of time.
Begin with the present and
move to the future.

### S·T·R·U·C·T·U·R·E

*Les adverbes désignant le présent et le futur*

| | |
|---|---|
| Ma mère travaille **aujourd'hui.** | My mother is working *today.* |
| **Demain** elle ne va pas travailler. | *Tomorrow* she's not going to work. |
| Où est-ce qu'ils sont **maintenant?** | Where are they *now?* |
| **Lundi matin** je vais aller à mon cours de maths. | *Monday morning* I'm going to my math class. |
| Elles vont arriver **la semaine prochaine.** | They are going to get here *next week.* |

You have already learned a few adverbs that express present or future time. Here is a list of these and other expressions:

**maintenant** *(now)*
**aujourd'hui** *(today)*
**ce matin** *(this morning)*
**cet après-midi** *(this afternoon)*
**ce soir** *(tonight)*
**cette semaine** *(this week)*
**cette année** *(this year)*

**bientôt** *(in a little while)*
**demain** *(tomorrow)*
**demain matin** *(tomorrow morning)*
**demain après-midi** *(tomorrow afternoon)*
**demain soir** *(tomorrow evening)*
**la semaine prochaine** *(next week)*
**l'année prochaine** *(next year)*

In addition, **matin, après-midi, soir,** and **prochain** can be combined with the days of the week: **lundi matin, samedi après-midi, dimanche soir, mardi prochain.** Time expressions are usually placed at the very beginning or end of a sentence.

le + lendemain (following day after tomorrow) ▲ ▲ ▲

## APPLICATION

**F.**  Remplacez les mots en italique et faites les changements nécessaires.

1.  Où est-ce que tu vas *aujourd'hui?* (maintenant / cet après-midi / vendredi soir / cette semaine)
2.  *Cet après-midi* je vais aller au cinéma. (ce soir / aujourd'hui / samedi matin / jeudi après-midi / demain)
3.  Elles vont être à Paris *mercredi prochain.* (cette année / la semaine prochaine / bientôt / l'année prochaine / vendredi prochain)

**G. Pas ce soir...** When you are at home, your mother is always asking about your and other people's activities; however, she usually gets them all confused. Correct her statements, using the information given.

*Modèle:*   Jean et toi, vous allez au cinéma ce soir? (demain soir)
*Pas ce soir. Nous allons au cinéma demain soir.*

1. Jean et toi, vous allez en ville mercredi soir? (mercredi après-midi)
2. Ton père va faire les courses demain matin? (samedi matin)
3. Marcel va faire du ski cette semaine? (la semaine prochaine)
4. Ton frère apprend l'espagnol cette année? (l'année prochaine)
5. Marie et toi, vous allez au cinéma ce soir? (vendredi soir)
6. Ta sœur va prendre la voiture cet après-midi? (dimanche après-midi)
7. Tes grands-parents vont arriver aujourd'hui? (jeudi prochain)
8. Est-ce que tu vas faire tes devoirs maintenant? (ce soir)

**H. L'emploi du temps des Verdun.** *(The Verduns' schedule.)* Use the calendar to answer questions about the Verdun family's activities during the month of February. Choose the appropriate time expressions, assuming that today is the morning of October 15.

| LUNDI | MARDI | MERCREDI | JEUDI | VENDREDI | SAMEDI | DIMANCHE |
|---|---|---|---|---|---|---|
| 1 | 2 | 3 | 4 | 5 Restaurant | 6 | 7 église |
| 8 | 9 | 10 | 11 | 12 Restaurant | 13 | 14 église |
| 15 M. et Mme. en théâtre ville (soir) | 16 M. jouer au tennis | 17 M. travail (soir) | 18 Mme. Musée | 19 Mme. travail (matin) restaurant | 20 Mme. (cours de russe (après-midi) | 21 église |
| 22 Cathédrale | 23 Les Michaud | 24 Les Michaud | 25 Les Michaud | 26 Restaurant Les Michaud | 27 | 28 église |

*Modèle:*   Quand est-ce que Mme Verdun va aller au musée?
*Jeudi.*

1. Quel soir est-ce que M. Verdun va travailler?
2. Quand est-ce que les Verdun vont visiter la cathédrale?
3. Quand est-ce que les Verdun dînent au restaurant?
4. Quand est-ce qu'ils vont avoir la visite des Michaud?
5. Quand est-ce que M. Verdun va jouer au tennis?
6. Quel matin est-ce que Mme Verdun va travailler?

Student Tape:
Chapitre 4
Segment 1

# PRONONCIATION   *Les consonnes* **m** *et* **n** *au milieu d'un mot*

When **m** or **n** is followed by a consonant other than **m** or **n**, the preceding vowel is nasalized and the **m** or **n** is not pronounced: **chanter, impossible, monde.** When **m** or **n** is followed by another **m** or **n,** and when **m** or **n** falls between two vowels, the **m** or **n** is pronounced and the preceding vowel is *not* nasalized: **dommage, ami, imiter.**

**I.**   Read each word aloud, being careful to distinguish between **m** or **n** followed by a consonant, **m** or **n** between vowels, and **m** or **n** in combination with another **m** or **n.**

Londres / camping / banque / sandwich / japonais / oncle / cinéma / immédiatement / limonade / tante / Orangina / caméra / nombres / omelette / changer / sciences / inutile

## S·T·R·U·C·T·U·R·E

*Les expressions* **espérer** *et* **avoir l'intention de**

**Suggestion, Espérer** and **avoir l'intention de:** (1) Have students discuss in English the difference between **je veux aller** and **je vais aller.** (2) Introduce **j'espère aller** and **j'ai l'intention d'aller.** Have students differentiate them from the first two expressions. (3) Have students react with one of the four expressions to **faire mes devoirs, aller au cinéma, avoir une Fiat,** etc. You may wish to include **avoir envie de** in the list of expressions for discussing future plans.

**J'espère** acheter une Renault l'année prochaine.

*I hope* to buy a Renault next year.

**J'ai l'intention de** demander de l'argent à mon père.

*I intend* to ask my father for some money.

You have already learned two ways to talk about future actions: what you *want* to do (**vouloir**) and what you *are going* to do (**aller**). You can make the exact state of your plans more specific by telling what you *hope* to do (**espérer**) or what you *intend* to do (**avoir l'intention de**). In all four expressions, the action verb is in the infinitive form.

In the following examples, note how the meanings of these expressions progress from the least certain to the most certain:

**Grammar:** In the verb **espérer, è** replaces **é** in forms where the ending following the **r** is not pronounced: **j'espère, tu espères, il espère, elles espèrent.** But: **nous espérons, vous espérez.**

**vouloir** + infinitive

**Je voudrais aller** en France.
*I would like to go* to France.

**espérer** + infinitive

**J'espère aller** en France.
*I hope to go* to France.

**avoir l'intention de** + infinitive

**J'ai l'intention d'aller** en France.
*I intend to go* to France.

**aller** + infinitive

**Je vais aller** en France.
*I am going to go* to France.

These expressions can also be used in the negative:

**Je n'ai pas l'intention d'aller** en France.

*I don't intend to go* to France.

▲   ▲   ▲

## APPLICATION

**J.** Remplacez le verbe en italique et faites les changements nécessaires.

1. Je *veux* aller en France. (vais / espère / n'ai pas l'intention / voudrais)
2. Nous *allons* faire un voyage. (voudrions / avons l'intention / espérons / voulons)
3. Est-ce que tes parents *vont* voyager en Afrique? (espèrent / ont l'intention / veulent)

**K.** **Un jour.** Tell how each person feels about doing the following activities someday.

*Modèle:*       voyager en Europe (votre père / vos amis / vous)
*Mon père ne veut pas voyager en Europe.*
*Mes amis espèrent voyager en Europe un jour.*
*Moi, j'ai l'intention de voyager en Europe l'année prochaine.*

1. aller à Paris (votre mère / vos frères [sœurs, amis] / vous)
2. voyager en Asie (votre amie / vos parents / vous)
3. être président(e) (vous et vos amis / votre père / votre sœur [frère, ami])
4. avoir une Mercédès (votre père / vos amis / vous)

**L.** **Tu voudrais habiter en Europe un jour?** Ask your classmates how they feel about doing the following things at the times indicated. Then tell them how you feel.     Ex. L: ◯

*Modèle:*       habiter en Europe un jour
—*Tu voudrais habiter en Europe un jour?*
—*Ah, oui. Je veux habiter à Paris ou à Londres.*
—*Moi, j'espère habiter à Madrid.*
—*Moi, je n'ai pas envie d'habiter en Europe.*

1. habiter en Europe un jour
2. faire un long voyage l'année prochaine
3. aller au cinéma vendredi soir
4. avoir une famille un jour
5. aller au match de ____ samedi après-midi
6. dîner au restaurant la semaine prochaine

## ▲▲▲▲▲▲▲▲▲ Débrouillons-nous! ▲▲▲▲▲▲▲▲▲

*Petite révision de l'étape*

Ex. M: ⇄

**M. Échange.** Posez les questions à un(e) autre étudiant(e), qui va vous répondre.

1. Est-ce que tu espères être à l'université l'année prochaine?
2. Est-ce que tu as l'intention de continuer à étudier le français?
3. Est-ce que tu voudrais apprendre une autre langue?
4. Qu'est-ce que tu as l'intention de faire ce soir?
5. Qu'est-ce que tu vas faire samedi après-midi?
6. Qu'est-ce que tu veux faire dimanche?
7. Qu'est-ce que tu as l'intention de faire la semaine prochaine?
8. Qu'est-ce que tu espères être un jour?

Ex. N: ⇄ You will probably want to model this exercise first. Alternative problem: going from a hotel near Saint-Sulpice to the airline terminal at Porte Maillot.

**N. Il faut prendre quelle direction?** You are staying in Paris at a hotel near the place de l'Odéon (D4). You need to go to the American Express office near the Opéra (D3). You have recently arrived in Paris and don't understand the subway system yet, so you ask the desk clerk for help. When he/she explains how to get there, you repeat the instructions to make sure you have understood. (Another student will play the role of the desk clerk.)

**À faire chez vous:**
**CAHIER, Chapitre 4 / 2ᵉ étape**

# T R O I S I È M E   É T A P E

## Point de départ

▼▼▼▼▼▼▼▼▼▼▼▼▼▼▼

Instructor's Tape:
Je veux prendre un
taxi!

### *Je veux prendre un taxi!*

*Taxi!   Taxi!*

Suggestion, Point de départ:
(1) Do a mini-planning strategy
about taking a taxi. Have students generate that passen-
gers need to know their destination, how long the trip will
take, how much it will cost. (2)
Then have them listen to the
recording on the Instructor's
Tape.

La sœur de Mireille Loiseau, Andrée, et son amie Gabrielle ont des billets pour le concert de Sting à Paris. Elles quittent la maison de Gabrielle pour aller au concert.

| | |
|---|---|
| ANDRÉE: | Alors, on prend l'autobus? |
| GABRIELLE: | Mais non. On n'a pas **le temps**. Il est **déjà** 8h40. Le concert commence dans vingt minutes. Il faut prendre un taxi. |
| ANDRÉE: | Bon. D'accord. Ah, voilà un taxi. Taxi! Taxi! |
| LE CHAUFFEUR: | Mesdemoiselles? Où est-ce que vous allez? |

time / already

Elles **montent dans** le taxi.

get in

| | |
|---|---|
| GABRIELLE: | Au **Zénith**, s'il vous plaît. **Il faut combien de temps pour y aller?** |
| LE CHAUFFEUR: | Vingt minutes... vingt-cinq au maximum. |
| GABRIELLE: | Eh, bien. **Dépêchez-vous!** Nous sommes **pressées**. |

Paris auditorium where
many rock concerts are
held / How long does it
take to go (get) there?

Hurry up! / in a hurry

Elles arrivent au Zénith. Gabrielle descend. C'est Andrée qui va payer.

| | |
|---|---|
| ANDRÉE: | **Je vous dois combien,** Monsieur? |
| LE CHAUFFEUR: | Quarante-quatre francs, Mademoiselle. |
| ANDRÉE: | Voilà **un billet de 50. Gardez la monnaie,** Monsieur. |
| LE CHAUFFEUR: | Merci, Mademoiselle. Au revoir. |

How much do I owe you?

a 50-franc bill / Keep the
change.

CD1-30
text audio

## Note culturelle

French money, like currency in the United States, is based on the decimal system. The main unit, the **franc,** is divided into 100 **centimes.** Coins **(les pièces de monnaie)** are issued by the French government. Bills **(les billets)** are issued by the **Banque de France.** Here are examples of French money:

| une pièce de | 5 centimes | un billet de | 20 francs |
|---|---|---|---|
| | 10 centimes | | 50 francs |
| | 20 centimes | | 100 francs |
| | 50 centimes | | 200 francs |
| | 1 franc | | 500 francs |
| | 2 francs | | |
| | 5 francs | | |
| | 10 francs | | |
| | 20 francs | | |

Prices in French are written either with a comma (**22,50 [vingt-deux cinquante]**) or with an **F (22F50 [vingt-deux francs cinquante]).**

**Question:** Check the financial pages of your local newspaper. What is the current value of the French franc against the American dollar?

# À VOUS! (Exercices de vocabulaire)

**A.** **Il faut combien de temps pour y aller?** As you make plans with a friend, discuss how long it will take to get to your destination. The answer will depend on the means of transportation you choose.

*Ex. A:* ⇄

*Modèle:*      au parc / en autobus (10 minutes) / à pied (30 ou 35 minutes)
           *—Il faut combien de temps pour aller au parc?*
           *—Pour y aller en autobus, il faut dix minutes.*
           *—Et pour y aller à pied?*
           *—À pied? Il faut trente ou trente-cinq minutes.*

> **Vocabulary:** In French the preposition **en** is used in **en voiture, en autobus, en métro,** and **en taxi,** but **à** is used in **à pied** and **à vélo.**

1. à la bibliothèque / à pied (25 minutes) / à vélo (10 minutes)
2. à la cathédrale / en métro (20 minutes) / en autobus (25 ou 30 minutes)
3. à l'aéroport / en taxi (45 minutes) / en métro (30 ou 35 minutes)
4. à la gare / en voiture (20 minutes) / en autobus (20 ou 25 minutes)
5. en ville / à pied (35 minutes) / en autobus (15 minutes)

**B.** **Je vous dois combien?** Ask the taxi driver how much you owe and give him/her money (French bills in denominations of 10F, 20F, and 50F). Then either tell him/her to keep the change **(Gardez la monnaie)** or take the change and give a tip **(Et voilà pour vous).**

*Ex. B:* ⇄

*Modèle:*      36F
           *—Je vous dois combien?*
           *—Trente-six francs, Monsieur (Madame).*
           *—Voilà un billet de cinquante... Et voilà pour vous.*
           *—Merci, Monsieur (Madame). Au revoir.*

1. 18F    2. 42F    3. 27F    4. 31F    5. 48F

## Le savez-vous?

▲▲▲▲▲▲▲▲▲▲▲▲▲▲▲

**Berlioz, Racine, Delacroix, and Voltaire have their pictures on various denominations of French paper money. What do these four men have in common?**

a. **They were all well-known political figures.**
b. **They were all famous scientists.**
c. **They were all associated with the arts (literature, music, painting, etc.).**
d. **They were all famous generals.**

**Réponse** ▲▲▲

# R·E·P·R·I·S·E

*Deuxième étape*

**C. Ils sont très actifs!** Michel Kerguézec, his sister Sophie, and his parents lead very busy lives. Based on their activity calendar, tell what will be happening on each day shown. Give your answers from Michel's point of view (that is, Michel = **je**) and use **aller** plus an infinitive to tell what is going to happen. Today is May 10.

*Modèle:*    Ce soir mes parents vont dîner au restaurant.
Demain je vais manger au Quick.

matin          après-midi          soir

▲▲▲ C

**D.  Pourquoi est-ce qu'ils font ça?** Using the cues provided, suggest the reasons for people's actions. Use an appropriate form of **aller, vouloir, espérer,** or **avoir l'intention de** plus an infinitive in each answer.

*Modèle:*      Pierre va rester à la maison. (faire ses devoirs)
                *Il va rester à la maison parce qu'il veut (a l'intention de) faire*
                *ses devoirs.*

1.  Isabelle fait ses devoirs vendredi soir. (faire du ski samedi)
2.  Claude et Michèle apprennent l'anglais. (aller à New York l'année prochaine)
3.  Louis va à la librairie. (acheter un livre intéressant)
4.  Frédérique étudie les sciences. (être médecin un jour)
5.  Juliette va en ville ce soir. (retrouver des amis)
6.  Gérard travaille beaucoup. (acheter une moto)

# S·T·R·U·C·T·U·R·E

## Le présent des verbes pronominaux

**Je me lève** de bonne heure.
**Ma petite amie Chantal se lève** de bonne heure aussi.
**Nous nous téléphonons** tous les samedis et tous les dimanches.
Mais **nous ne nous parlons pas** en semaine.
Ton petit ami et toi, **est-ce que vous vous téléphonez** souvent?

*I get up* early.
*My girlfriend Chantal gets up* early too.
*We call each other* every Saturday and Sunday.

But *we don't talk to each other* during the week.
You and your boyfriend, *do you call each other* often?

*reciproc-l*

Pronominal verbs are verbs that require a pronoun in addition to the subject. Pronominal verbs may have two different meanings. They may express:

1.  An action that reflects back on the subject:

**Je me lève.**           *I get up.* (Literally, *I get myself up.*)
**Elle se renseigne.**   *She gets information.* (Literally, *she informs herself.*)

2.  An action in which two or more subjects interact:

**Nous nous téléphonons.**        *We call each other.*
**Elles se retrouvent** au café.   *They meet (each other) at the café.*

**Grammar:** The verb **se lever** requires an **è** instead of an **e** whenever the vowel following the **v** is not pronounced: **il se lève,** but **nous nous levons.**

In either case, the subject (noun or pronoun) is accompanied by its corresponding reflexive or reciprocal pronoun (**me, te, se, nous, vous**). This pronoun usually comes directly before the verb:

| **se lever** *(to get up)* | |
|---|---|
| je **me lève** | nous **nous levons** |
| tu **te lèves** | vous **vous levez** |
| il, elle, on **se lève** | ils, elles **se lèvent** |

To ask a question with a pronominal verb, use intonation, **est-ce que,** or an interrogative expression + **est-ce que:**

Vous vous amusez?     *Je m'amuse.*

**Est-ce qu'**ils se retrouvent souvent en ville?    *Ils se retrouvent souvent.*

**Pourquoi est-ce que** tu ne t'amuses pas?    *Je me ne m'amuse pas parceqn*

     To make a negative statement with a pronominal verb, put **ne** in front of the reflexive or reciprocal pronoun and **pas** immediately after the verb:

Je **ne** me lève **pas** de bonne heure.
Nous **ne** nous parlons **jamais**.

     Here is a list of some frequently used pronominal verbs:

If a verb begins with a vowel or a vowel sound, the pronouns **me, te,** and **se** become **m', t',** and **s':** **je m'amuse, tu t'amuses, elle s'amuse.** The **s** of **nous** and **vous** (normally silent) is pronounced in liaison with a vowel or a vowel sound: **nous nous_amusons, vous vous_amusez.**

| | |
|---|---|
| **se lever** | *to get up* |
| **se coucher** | *to go to bed* |
| **se renseigner** | *to get information*    *renseignements* |
| **s'amuser** | *to have a good time* |
| **se promener** | *to take a walk* |
| **se reposer** | *to rest* |
| **se préparer (pour/à)** | *to get ready (to)* |
| **se dépêcher** | *to hurry* |
| | |
| **se téléphoner** | *to call each other* |
| **se parler** | *to speak (talk) to each other* |
| **se retrouver** | *to meet (each other) (by prearrangement)* |

*se trompe*

*Je m'ennuie*

*je m'excuse*

*se réveiller (wake up)*
*se raser*
*se maquiller*
*s'énerver (upset)*
*s'ennuyer (bored)*
*s'inquiéter (worry)*
*s'excuser (pardon)*

▲ ▲ ▲

*se calmer*
*s'appeler   je m'appelle   tu t'appelle*
*se laver (wash oneself)*
*se brosser*
*s'asseoir (Asseyez vous)*
*s'amuser*
*s'habiller (get dressed)*

Carte France Télécom

**Renseignez-vous en appelant gratuitement le** 05 202 202

**France Telecom**

## APPLICATION

**E.** Remplacez le sujet en italique et faites les changements nécessaires.

1. *Je* me repose. (Jeanne / nous / vous / les autres / tu)
2. *Ils* se téléphonent souvent. (vous / mes sœurs / on / nous / nos cousins)
3. Est-ce que *tu* t'amuses bien? (vous / elles / Patrick / on)
4. *Elle* ne se dépêche jamais. (nous / je / tu / vous / mes parents)

**F.   Le dimanche.** Véronique Béziers explains what she does on Sundays. Use the cues to create her explanation. Be careful: Not all the verbs are pronominal.

*Modèle:*    d'habitude / s'amuser bien / le dimanche
           *D'habitude je m'amuse bien le dimanche.*

1. se lever / vers 10h
2. prendre / un café et des croissants
3. téléphoner à / mon amie Patricia
4. (nous) se parler au téléphone / pendant une heure
5. déjeuner *(to have lunch)* / avec ma famille ⟵ ———— don't say the "e"
6. quelquefois / (Patricia et moi) se retrouver en ville / pour aller voir un film          ville — say the "e"
7. quelquefois / (nous) se promener au jardin public
8. le soir / se préparer pour la semaine
9. se coucher / vers 10h30 ou 11h          je ne me dépêche pas
10. le dimanche, c'est le jour où / ne pas se dépêcher

*Véronique
Béziers en ville*

## Note grammaticale

### Le futur immédiat des verbes pronominaux

| | |
|---|---|
| **Ma sœur et moi, nous allons nous retrouver** en ville. | *My sister and I are going to meet downtown.* |
| **Tu vas t'acheter** quelque chose? | *Are you going to buy yourself something? (Are you going to buy something for yourself?)* |
| Oui, **je voudrais m'acheter** un jean. | *Yes, I would like to buy myself some jeans.* |
| Ensuite, **on va se balader** un peu. | *Afterwards, we're going to take a little stroll.* |

The immediate future of a pronominal verb is formed in the same way as the immediate future of any other verb—that is, with **aller** and an infinitive. The reflexive or reciprocal pronoun that accompanies the verb agrees with the subject of **aller** and is placed immediately before the infinitive.

The negative of the immediate future is formed by putting **ne . . . pas** around the conjugated form of **aller:**

Je **ne** vais **pas** me coucher de bonne heure.

The same rules for agreement and placement apply to pronominal verbs preceded by other conjugated verbs such as **vouloir** and **espérer:**

Moi, **je veux me reposer** un peu.
**Nous espérons nous amuser** pendant le voyage.

**G.** Remplacez le sujet en italique et faites les changements nécessaires.

1. *Je* vais me reposer. (nous / Marc / tu / mes parents / on / vous)
2. Est-ce que *tu* vas t'acheter quelque chose? (elle / Marc / tes parents / vous / nous / on)
3. *Ils* ne veulent pas se dépêcher. (elle / nous / je / tu / on / les autres)

**H.** **Samedi prochain.** Next Saturday is a special day. Consequently, Véronique Béziers is not planning to follow her usual weekend routine. Using the cues, describe what she normally does on Saturday morning and then tell how next Saturday is going to be different.

*Modèle:*     rester à la maison / se balader avec des amis à la campagne
*Normalement je reste à la maison le samedi. Mais samedi prochain je vais me balader avec des amis à la campagne.*

1. ne pas se lever de bonne heure  /  se lever à 7h30   *Je ne me lève pas de bonne heure.*
2. ne pas se dépêcher  /  se dépêcher
3. (mon amie Cécile et moi) se téléphoner  /  ne pas se parler au téléphone   *nous n'allons pas nous parler*
4. rester à la maison  /  (Cécile et moi) se retrouver en ville   *nous allons nous retrouver*
5. ne pas faire d'achats  /  s'acheter quelque chose   *je vais m'acheter*
6. se reposer un peu  /  ne pas se reposer
7. se coucher de bonne heure  /  se coucher vers minuit
8. ne pas s'amuser  /  s'amuser   *je vais m'amuser*

**I.   Et toi?** You and your classmates are discussing your daily lives. Use the suggested verbs to tell what you usually do (or don't do) and what you are planning to do in the near future. VERBES: **se lever, se coucher, se reposer, se promener, se téléphoner, se retrouver.**

*Modèle:*    se lever
—*Moi, je me lève d'habitude vers 7h30 en semaine.*
—*Moi, je n'aime pas me lever de bonne heure. Je me lève vers 9h ou 9h30 en semaine.*
—*Et le week-end, à quelle heure est-ce que tu te lèves?*
—*Vers onze heures et demie ou midi.*

# PRONONCIATION   *Les consonnes **m** et **n** suivies de la voyelle **e***

**Student Tape:**
Chapitre 4
Segment 1

The presence of a mute **e** at the end of a word causes the preceding consonant, which in many cases would be silent, to be pronounced. In the case of **m** and **n,** pronouncing the consonant denasalizes the preceding vowel:

| | | | |
|---|---|---|---|
| Sim**on** | améric**ain** | **un** | **an** |
| Sim**one** | améric**aine** | **une** | **âne** |

**J.**  Read each pair of words aloud, being careful to pronounce the **m** or **n** in the first word and keep the **m** or **n** silent in the second.

américaine, américain  /  mexicaine, mexicain  /  cousine, cousin  /  prochaine, prochain  /  Christiane, Christian  /  une, un  /  Jeanne, Jean

**K.**  Now read each word aloud, distinguishing between words in which the final consonant is silent (nasal vowel) and those in which it is pronounced.

madame  /  marine  /  vin  /  direction  /
fume  /  chaîne  /  garçon  /  machine  /
Rome  /  Lyon  /  crème  /  italien

**Reminder:** The final **s** of the **tu** form is dropped in the imperative of **-er** verbs: **Tu te lèves. Lève-toi! Ne te lève pas!**

**Suggestion,** Imperative of pronominal verbs: (1) Have students stand up and sit down on command: **Levez-vous! Asseyez-vous!** Then vary the commands: **Levez-vous! George, as-seyez-vous! Betsy, asseyez-vous! Brian, ne vous asseyez pas!** (2) Ask students to generate the **vous** forms (affirmative and negative) for **se dé-pêcher.** (3) Then expand to **nous** and, finally, **tu** (pointing out the change to **toi).**

# S·T·R·U·C·T·U·R·E

## *L'impératif des verbes pronominaux*

| **Dépêche-toi!** | *Hurry up!* |
|---|---|
| **Ne vous levez pas!** | *Don't get up!* |

The command forms of pronominal verbs follow the same pattern as the other command forms you have learned—that is, the subject pronoun is simply dropped. In an affirmative command, the reflexive or reciprocal pronoun is placed *after* the verb. When written, this pronoun is attached to the verb with a hyphen. Notice that, for ease of pronunciation, **te** becomes **toi** when it follows the verb. In a negative command, the reflexive or reciprocal pronoun remains *before* the verb.

Here are some common expressions involving the imperative of pronominal verbs:

| **Dépêche-toi! Dépêchez-vous!** | *Hurry up!* |
|---|---|
| **Amuse-toi bien! Amusez-vous bien!** | *Have a good time!* |
| **Lève-toi! Levez-vous!** | *Get up! Stand up!* |
| **Assieds-toi! Asseyez-vous!** | *Sit down!* |
| **Calme-toi! Calmez-vous!** | *Take it easy!* |

| **Ne te dépêche pas! Ne vous dépêchez pas!** | *Don't hurry!* |
|---|---|
| **Ne te lève pas! Ne vous levez pas!** | *Don't get up!* |
| **Ne t'inquiète pas! Ne vous inquiétez pas!** | *Don't worry!* |
| **Ne t'énerve pas! Ne vous énervez pas!** | *Don't get upset!* |

▲ ▲ ▲

## APPLICATION

**L.** Give the **vous** forms of the following imperatives.

1. Dépêche-toi!   2. Amuse-toi bien!   3. Ne t'inquiète pas!   4. Ne t'énerve pas!   5. Assieds-toi!   6. Calme-toi!

Now give the **tu** forms of the following imperatives.

7. Levez-vous!   8. Calmez-vous!   9. Ne vous dépêchez pas!   10. Ne vous inquiétez pas!   11. Amusez-vous bien!   12. Asseyez-vous!

**M.  Dialogues à compléter.** Complete each dialogue with an appropriate expression using the imperative (affirmative or negative) of a pronominal verb.

> *Modèle:*  —André! André! *Lève-toi! (Dépêche-toi!)*
> —Comment? Qu'est-ce qu'il y a?
> —Il est déjà 8h. Tu as cours dans cinq minutes.

1. —Tu vas en ville ce soir?
   —Je vais au cinéma avec Anne-Marie.
   —C'est formidable! _____
2. —Oh, là là! Qu'est-ce que je vais faire? Où est mon sac à dos? Où sont mes livres? J'ai un examen ce matin et je ne trouve pas mon sac à dos.
   —_____ Jacques et moi, nous allons chercher ton sac à dos.
3. —Jean-Jacques! Il est déjà 19h30!
   —Et alors?
   —Ben, le film commence à 20h. _____
4. —Bonjour, Monsieur. Est-ce que vous avez le temps de parler avec moi?
   —Certainement, Mademoiselle. _____
5. —Où est Chantal? Il est 6h. Elle devait *(was supposed to)* être là à 5h30.
   —_____ Elle va arriver dans un instant.

## ▲▲▲▲▲▲▲▲▲▲ Débrouillons-nous! ▲▲▲▲▲▲▲▲▲

Ex. N: ⇄

*Petite révision de l'étape*

**N. Échange.** Posez les questions à un(e) camarade de classe, qui va vous répondre.

1. À quelle heure est-ce que tu te lèves d'habitude en semaine? Et le week-end?
2. À quelle heure est-ce que tu vas te lever demain matin? Pourquoi?
3. Est-ce que tu te dépêches pour aller à ton premier *(first)* cours? Pourquoi (pas)?
4. Est-ce que tu te reposes pendant la journée *(during the day)*? Quand?
5. Est-ce que tes parents et toi, vous vous téléphonez souvent?
6. Où est-ce que tes amis et toi, vous vous retrouvez d'habitude?
7. Est-ce que tu t'énerves facilement *(easily)*?   je m'énerve pas
8. Est-ce que tu t'amuses quand tu es avec ta famille?

**O. Il faut prendre un taxi.** You are in Paris with your parents, who don't speak French. They want to go from their hotel (the Paris Sheraton) to Notre-Dame Cathedral. They don't like the subway, so they ask you to go with them in a taxi. Hail a taxi and tell the driver where you want to go. Then ask if it's nearby and how long the trip will take. Remember to pay for the ride when you reach your destination. (A classmate will play the role of the driver.)

Ex. O: ⇄ Divide the class into pairs and have each pair choose a card. Students playing the role of the American look at side 1 of the card for the address, then give the card to their partner, who looks at side 2 for time of trip and price. Model the dialogue before students begin work in pairs.

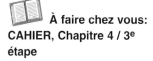

**À faire chez vous: CAHIER, Chapitre 4 / 3e étape**

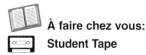

**À faire chez vous: Student Tape**

Now that you've completed the first three **étapes** of **Chapitre 4**, do Segment 2 of the STUDENT TAPE. See **CAHIER, Chapitre 4, *Écoutons!,*** for exercises that accompany this segment.

# QUATRIÈME ÉTAPE

## L·E·C·T·U·R·E

### Histoire de billets

*Read the following cartoon sequence, taken from a brochure distributed by the* **RATP (Régie Autonome des Transports Parisiens)** *for people who are unfamiliar with the transportation system in Paris. Do **not** look at the definitions at the end. Once you have a sense of the passage's general meaning, do the first comprehension exercise, which deals with guessing from context.*

John Busy est arrivé à Paris sans sa "Rolls" parce qu'il préfère voyager, comme disent les Parisiens, dans sa "deuxième voiture."

Avec un seul ticket, John Busy peut aller à toutes les stations dans le métro.

Le métro est en service de l'aube jusqu'à après minuit. Son réseau consiste en 359 stations facilitant le déplacement entre tous les musées, les monuments et d'autres points d'intérêt.

20 km en dehors de Paris, le métro devient le RER avec des correspondances, par exemple, aux stations Châtelet — Les Halles, Charles de Gaulle — Étoile et Gare du Nord.

1. *disent:* say   2. *déplacement:* movement   3. *lui permettra:* will allow him   4. *environs:* surrounding area   5. *magasins:* stores

# COMPRÉHENSION

**A.   Devinez!** *(Guess!)* For each boldfaced word, choose the meaning that best fits the context. In items 1 through 3, you will be given several choices. In the remaining items, it is up to you and your classmates to suggest the possibilities and then select the best one.

1.   John Busy est arrivé à Paris **sans** sa «Rolls» parce qu'il préfère voyager dans sa «deuxième voiture» (le métro). *(with / without / in / on)*
2.   Avec un **seul** ticket, John Busy peut aller à toutes les stations dans le métro. *(special / only / lonely / single)*
3.   Le métro est en service de **l'aube** jusqu'après minuit. *(east / dawn / weekdays / twilight)*
4.   Son **réseau** consiste en 359 stations.
5.   20 km **en dehors de** Paris, le métro devient le RER.
6.   Dans certaines stations du RER, il peut même **louer** un vélo.
7.   Pour **rentrer** à son hôtel, John Busy prend le bus à un des 5 658 **arrêts d'autobus.**
8.   John Busy a déjà fait ses **projets** pour demain.

**B.**   **Vous allez à Paris?** Reread the text, this time looking at the definitions found at the end. Pick at least five items of information that would be very useful to an American tourist going to Paris for the first time.

### R·E·P·R·I·S·E

*Troisième étape*

Ex. C: ⇄

**C.**   **Combien?** You and your friends are going over how much money you have paid for certain things or services. Each time you say the price, your friend asks for confirmation, so you repeat more clearly.

> *Modèle:*      12,50
>          —*Douze cinquante.*
>          —*Combien?*
>          —*Douze ~~francs~~ euros cinquante.*

1. 3,25    2. 16,40    3. 51,65    4. 39,15    5. 47,30    6. 13,60    7. 26,50    8. 65,45

Ex. D: ⇄

*Comment rester de glace devant de tels délices!*
Café ou chocolat liégeois
Banana split      L'Iceberg

**D.**   **Échange.** Posez les questions à un(e) camarade de classe, qui va vous répondre.

1. À quelle heure est-ce qu'on se lève chez toi d'habitude? Qui se lève le premier (la première)? Qui se lève le dernier (la dernière)? En semaine? Le week-end?
2. Qui se couche le premier chez toi? À quelle heure? Et le dernier?
3. Quand est-ce que tu te dépêches? (Je me dépêche pour...)
4. Quand est-ce que tu t'amuses?
5. Est-ce que tu t'énerves souvent? Quand?
6. Est-ce que tu aimes te promener? Quand? Où? Comment? (à pied, en voiture, à vélo)
7. Tes parents et toi, vous vous parlez souvent?
8. Tes amis et toi, vous vous retrouvez souvent après les cours?

*Je m'énerve rarement.*

▲ ▲ ▲ ▲ ▲ ▲ ▲ ▲ ▲ ▲ ▲ ▲ ▲ ▲ ▲ ▲ ▲ ▲ ▲ ▲ ▲

# Point d'arrivée

À faire chez vous:
**Student Tape**

**CAHIER, Chapitre 4:**
*Rédigeons! / Travail de*
*fin de chapitre* (including
STUDENT TAPE, Chapitre
4, Segment 3)

*Activités orales*

## Exprimons-nous!

In French, to suggest an activity to someone, you can use expressions such as **Tu voudrais? Tu veux? Tu as le temps de?**

**Tu voudrais** aller en ville?
**Tu veux** aller voir un film?
**Tu as le temps de** faire du lèche-vitrines?

| *To accept a suggestion* | *To refuse a suggestion* |
|---|---|
| **Bien sûr. Pourquoi pas?** | **Je ne peux pas.** |
| **Oui. C'est une bonne idée.** | **Je dois** travailler. |
| **Oui. Je veux bien.** | Non, **je n'ai pas le temps.** |

**E.   Une visite-éclair de Paris.** *(A lightning-fast visit to Paris.)* You and a friend have only a few hours between planes in Paris. Discuss how you will manage to see the following sights. Use such expressions as **Nous allons à la station... Nous prenons la direction... Nous changeons à... Nous descendons à... Ensuite nous allons...** Begin and end your tour at the gare du Nord (E2), which has trains connecting with the airport. To answer, refer to the metro map on p. 138.

1.   la cathédrale de Notre-Dame (métro: Cité—E4)
2.   l'arc de Triomphe (métro: Charles de Gaulle–Étoile—C3)
3.   la tour Eiffel (métro: Trocadéro—C3)
4.   Montmartre (métro: place de Clichy—D2)

**F.   Au café.** Your Brazilian friend, who speaks no English, has joined you in Paris. You are in a café on the rue Dauphine. Greet your friend and order a drink. Discuss your families, activities, etc. Then, using the map of this section of Paris (see p. 168) and the metro map (see p. 138), explain how to get from the café to the St-Germain-des-Prés subway station (D4), how to buy a ticket, and how to take the subway to the place d'Italie (E5).

Ex. E: ⇄

**Variation,** Ex. E: Have each
pair of students write out the
directions. Then exchange the
directions with another group
and try to follow on the **métro**
map the instructions given.

Ex. F: ⇄

**G. Allons en ville!** You and a friend are making plans to do something downtown over the weekend. Decide what you want to do, when you want to do it, and how you will get there. Then try to persuade two other friends to join you.

**H. Mes projets.** *(My plans.)* Discuss your future plans with some friends. Talk about next year **(l'année prochaine)** and the years following **(dans deux ans, dans cinq ans, dans dix ans,** etc.). Suggestions: Consider what you definitely intend to do **(J'ai l'intention de chercher un travail),** what you would like to do **(Je voudrais voyager),** and what you hope to do **(J'espère avoir une famille).**

# PORTRAIT
*Massyla Fodéba, Dakar, Sénégal*

Je suis né à Dakar et j'y ai habité jusqu'à l'âge de 19 ans. Après avoir fini mes études au lycée Senghor à Dakar, je suis venu en France où j'ai fait un DEUG avant d'entrer à une école d'ingénieurs. Quand j'étais à Dakar, je prenais l'autobus pour aller en ville. Mais quand je suis à Paris, je prends le métro. Il est très efficace et il ne coûte pas cher.

En gros, j'aime bien Paris. Avec mes amis, pour passer le temps, on joue au foot, on va au cinéma. Mais je garde toujours un très bon souvenir de mon pays natal et j'espère retourner au Sénégal pour y travailler un jour.

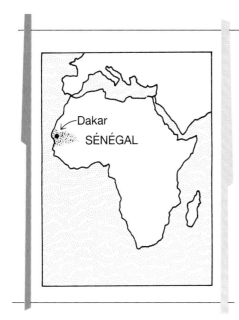

# Profil

*Le Sénégal*

A detailed map of the French speaking world appears on pp. 478–479.

**SITUATION:** sur la côte ouest de l'Afrique, entre la Mauritanie et la Guinée-Bissau

**POPULATION:** 6 700 000 habitants

**CAPITALE:** Dakar

**LANGUE OFFICIELLE:** français

**RELIGIONS:** musulmans (80–90%), chrétiens, animistes

**ÉCONOMIE:** arachides *(peanuts),* coton, mil *(millet),* riz, pêche *(fishing),* mines de fer *(iron),* industries chimiques

**HISTOIRE:** Ancienne colonie de la France; indépendance—1960

**COMMENTAIRE:** Léopold Sédar Senghor, le premier président du Sénégal (1960–1980), est aussi un poète très important. C'est un chef du mouvement nommé **la négritude**—effort de revalorisation de la culture africaine.

**À discuter:** The African poet Léopold Senghor becomes president of his country; the Caribbean poet Aimé Césaire serves as a representative from Martinique to the French Assembly. French presidents, such as De Gaulle and Mitterand, are also writers. Do we find a similar interplay between politics and the arts in the United States? Why (not)?

*Dakar, Sénégal*

# L·E·X·I·Q·U·E

## Pour se débrouiller

*Pour organiser une sortie*
On prend l'autobus.
    le métro.
    un taxi.
    sa voiture.
    son vélo.
On y va à pied.
Il faut combien de temps pour y aller en autobus?
            en métro?
            à pied?
            en taxi?
            en voiture?
            à vélo?

Quand est-ce qu'on y va?
 aujourd'hui
 ce matin
 cet après-midi
 ce soir
 demain (matin, après-midi, soir)
 lundi (mardi, mercredi, jeudi, vendredi, samedi, dimanche) (matin, après-midi, soir)
 cette semaine
 la semaine prochaine
 cette année
 l'année prochaine
Qu'est-ce qu'on va faire?
 avoir rendez-vous avec
 avoir une course à faire
 faire des achats
 faire du lèche-vitrines
 faire une course
 n'avoir rien à faire
 retrouver quelqu'un

*Pour parler de ses projets*
 aller + *infinitif*
 avoir envie de + *infinitif*
 avoir l'intention de + *infinitif*
 espérer + *infinitif*
 vouloir + *infinitif*

*Pour demander le jour qu'il est*
    C'est aujourd'hui...?
    Quel jour est-ce aujourd'hui?
    Quel jour sommes-nous?
      C'est aujourd'hui...

*Pour faire, accepter ou refuser une proposition*
    Tu veux (tu voudrais)...?
    Vous voulez (vous voudriez)...?
      Mais oui.
      Bien sûr.
      Avec plaisir.
      C'est une bonne idée.
      Pourquoi pas?
      Je veux bien.

      C'est impossible.
      Je ne peux pas.
      Je dois + *infinitif*

*Pour se débrouiller dans le métro*

| | |
|---|---|
| changer | prendre |
| descendre | Quelle direction? |

*Pour payer*

| | |
|---|---|
| C'est combien? | Voilà pour vous. |
| Je vous dois combien? | Gardez (la monnaie). |

**ALLONS-Y!**
**V**ideo **P**rogram

---
**ACTE 4**
---

**V O C A B U L A I R E**

Scène 1: au café
content   *happy*
en retard   *late*
pas grave   *not serious*
une orange pressée
   *an orange juice*
une carafe d'eau
   *a pitcher of water*
Comme ça, ça roule.
   *That's cool.*

Scène 2: prenons le
    métro
me rendre = aller
ticket à l'unité
   *one regular ticket*
environ = à peu près
autant de   *as many as*
à tout de suite
   *see you in a minute*

**Thèmes et contextes**

*Le métro*
    un billet
    une bouche de métro
    un carnet de cinq (dix)
    une Carte orange
    une correspondance
    un Coupon jaune
    formule 1
    le guichet
    les heures *(f.pl.)* de pointe
    Paris Visite
    un plan de métro
    une station de métro

*L'argent* (m.)
    un billet
    un centime
    un franc
    une pièce de monnaie

**Vocabulaire général**

*Verbes*

| | |
|---|---|
| (s')acheter | monter (dans) |
| s'amuser | se parler |
| apprendre | prendre |
| arriver | se préparer |
| se balader | se promener |
| comprendre | quitter |
| se coucher | se renseigner |
| se dépêcher | se reposer |
| s'énerver | (se) retrouver |
| entrer (dans) | se téléphoner |
| s'inquiéter | vouloir |
| se lever | |

# Deuxième Partie

**Transparencies:**
**P-1** through **P-18**

**Intégration culturelle:** For suggestions, information, and activities to go with this section. see the Resource Manual.

fontaine Tinguely

SPECTACLES

L'ATELIER
JEANNE MOREAU
LE RÉCIT DE LA SERVANTE

OFFREZ-VOUS PARIS

PARIS

Centre Pomp

INTEGRATION

★ CULTURELLE

5.me ARRt

RUE DU POT DE FER

**carte inter–musées museums pass**

musées et monuments de ris avec une seule **carte coupe-file** e pass for 60 museums and onuments in paris : **stop queueing**.

ait pour 1, 3 ou 5 jours consécutifs. ailable for 1, 3 or 5 nsecutifs days.

vente : musées, monuments, métro et office de tourisme de paris.

on sale : museums, monuments, metro and paris tourist office.

la **V**illette
parc de la Villette

# PARIS ★ EN IMAGES

musée du Louvre, à l'intérieur

musée du Louvre, à l'extérieur

musée d'Orsay

1 – **Cité des Sciences et de l'Industrie**
2 – **géode**
3 – **parc**
4 – **folies**
5 – **zénith**
6 – **grande halle**
7 – **théâtre Paris-Villette**
8 – **cité de la Musique**

la Villette, Cité des Sciences et de l'Industrie

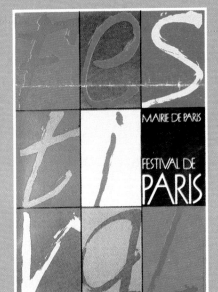

MAIRIE DE PARIS

FESTIVAL DE PARIS

Festival de Paris

parc EuroDisney

AVENUE VICTOR HUGO

Obélisque
de Louksor

arc de Triomphe

rue Saint Honoré

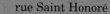

découvrir PARIS

Montmartre, place
du Tertre

tour Eiffel

la Défense

avenue des
Champs-Élysées

**PARIS CANAL**

Bassin de la Villette
11 Quai de la Loire - 75019 PARIS
☎ (1) 42.40.96.97
Télex : 642248 QUIZTOUR
Fax : (1) 42.40.77.30

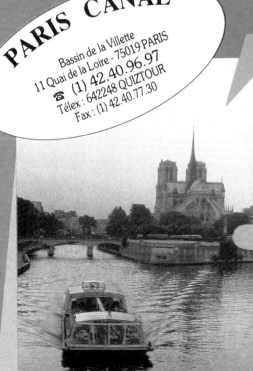

bateau-mouche sur la Seine

Notre Dame de Paris

Claire Maurant
Strasbourg (Alsace),
France

—Moi, j'ai envie de m'amuser un peu.
—Moi aussi. Qu'est-ce qu'on va faire?

# Amusons-nous!

## OBJECTIVES

**In this chapter, you will learn:**

- to organize leisure-time activities;
- to talk about events in the past;
- to talk about the weather;
- to read informational materials about leisure-time activities;
- to understand conversations about leisure-time activities.

**CHAPTER SUPPORT MATERIALS** (STUDENT)

**Cahier:** pp. 121–144

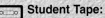 **Student Tape:** Chapitre 5 Segments 1, 2, 3

**CHAPTER SUPPORT MATERIALS (INSTRUCTOR)**

**Transparencies:** 5-1 through 5-5

**Instructor's Tape:** Chapitre 5, Text, pp. 174, 185, 196, 202, 206

**SYSTÈME-D** *software:* Writing activities for this chapter are found in the **Cahier:** Ex. V (p. 131), *Rédigeons!* (p. 131).

**Multimedia:** See the Resource Manual for correlation to our multimedia product.

## ALLONS-Y!
### Video Program
**ACTE 5**
**UNE EXCURSION**

Première étape  Quel temps fait-il?
Deuxième étape  Tu veux voir le nouveau film au Gaumont les Halles?
Troisième étape  On pourrait faire une excursion!
Quatrième étape  Lecture: Déjeuner du matin

Instructor's Tape:
Quel temps fait-il?

Transparencies:
5-1a, 5-1b (weather
symbols)

# PREMIÈRE ÉTAPE

## Point de départ

*Quel temps fait-il?:* What is
  the weather like?
company

in the process of / plans

## Quel temps fait-il?

En semaine Claire Maurant travaille comme comptable pour une **société** textile à Strasbourg. Mais le week-end elle aime s'amuser avec ses amis. C'est
samedi après-midi. Claire et ses amis sont **en train de** faire des **projets.**

| | |
|---|---|
| CLAIRE: | Bon. Qu'est-ce qu'on va faire? |
| ANDRÉ: | Moi, je voudrais bien jouer au tennis. J'ai besoin de faire un peu d'exercice. |
| THIERRY: | Moi aussi. Mais **il ne fait pas très beau** maintenant. |
| CLAUDETTE: | Et la **météo** annonce de la **pluie** pour **toute la journée.** |
| CLAIRE: | Et qu'est-ce qu'**elle prévoit** pour demain? |
| CLAUDETTE: | Oh, il va **faire du soleil** demain. |
| THIERRY: | Eh bien, on va faire du sport demain. Et ce soir **on pourrait** aller au cinéma. **Vous avez vu** le film de Belmondo, *Le Solitaire?* |
| CLAIRE: | Oui, **je l'ai vu** à Paris avec ma cousine. |
| ANDRÉ: | Bon, alors, on va voir un autre film ou on va trouver autre chose à faire. |

it's not very nice out
weather report / rain / the
  whole day
it predicts

to be sunny

we could / Have you seen

I saw it

*C'01-34*

### Quel temps fait-il?

Il fait du soleil.
Il fait beau.
Il fait chaud.

Il y a un orage.
Il fait mauvais.

Il pleut.

*la pluie*
*un parapluie*

Il fait bon.
Pas trop froid,
  pas trop chaud.

Il neige.
Il fait froid.

Le ciel est couvert.
Le temps est nuageux.

**Suggestion, Point de départ:**
(1) Begin with weather expressions. Show students transparency. Ask: **Quel temps
fait-il?** Point to first symbol
and say: **Il fait du soleil. Il fait
beau. Il fait chaud.** Use gestures to reinforce meaning.
Have students repeat each
statement. After practicing all
captions, remove overlay and
have students make state-
ments about symbols you indicate. (2) Have students listen to the conversation on the
Instructor's Tape.

*Il y a des éclaircies.*
*Le ciel se dégage.*

*Il fait un froid de canard!*

Il fait du vent. (Il y a du vent.)
Il fait frais.

Il fait du brouillard.

Il y a du verglas.

*Quel temps de chien!*

## Note culturelle

Temperatures in France and other European countries are given on the Celsius (centigrade) scale. Here is a comparison of Celsius temperatures and their Fahrenheit equivalents:

| C: | 30° | 25° | 20° | 15° | 10° | 5° | 0° | −5° |
|---|---|---|---|---|---|---|---|---|
| F: | 86° | 77° | 68° | 59° | 50° | 41° | 32° | 23° |

To convert from Celsius to Fahrenheit, divide by 5, multiply by 9, and add 32. To convert from Fahrenheit to Celsius, subtract 32, multiply by 5, and divide by 9. To tell a temperature, a French person would say, **La température est de cinq degrés** or **Il fait cinq degrés dehors** *(outside)*.

**Question:** What is today's temperature in both Fahrenheit and Celsius?

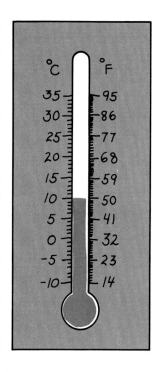

## À VOUS! (Exercices de vocabulaire)

**A.  Quel temps fait-il?** Tell what the weather is like in each drawing.

*le climat*
*(weather) la météo, le temps*
*(wind) le vent*
*Quel temps fait-il?*
*le climat peut etre*
*sec*
*humide*
*doux (mild)*
*frais / frisquet*
*(cool)*

*Il fait beau*
*mauvais*
*froid*
*chaud, bon*

*un orage (storm)*

*Modèle:*                *Il fait chaud. (Il fait du soleil.  /  Il fait très beau.)*

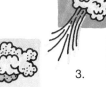

1.

2.

3.

4.

5.

6.

7.

**B.  Est-ce qu'il fait beau aujourd'hui?** You're traveling around the United States with your friend's family. Each time you call home, your parents want to know what the weather is like. Answer their questions negatively. Then give the indicated weather condition.

*Modèle:*  —Est-ce qu'il fait beau aujourd'hui? (mauvais)
—*Non, il ne fait pas beau (aujourd'hui). Il fait mauvais.*

1.  Est-ce qu'il fait chaud aujourd'hui? (froid)
2.  Est-ce qu'il pleut aujourd'hui? (il neige)
3.  Est-ce que le ciel est couvert? (du soleil)
4.  Est-ce qu'il y a un orage? (beau)
5.  Est-ce qu'il fait frais? (très froid)
6.  Est-ce qu'il fait chaud? (du vent)
7.  Est-ce qu'il fait du soleil? (nuageux)
8.  Est-ce qu'il fait froid? (assez chaud)

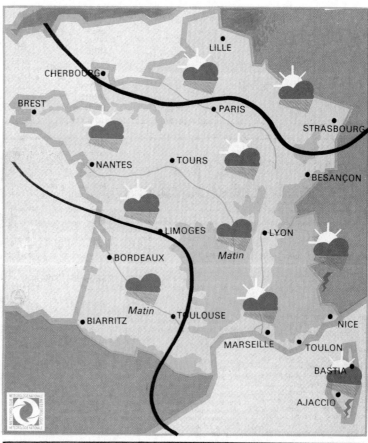

Un tremblement de terre

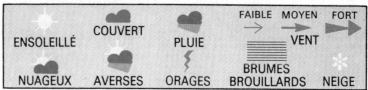

downpour

**C.** **Quel temps est-ce qu'il va faire le 16 février?** Below is a list of predicted temperatures for various French and European cities. The first
number is the high during the day and the second number is the low during
the night. Based on the high temperature, say whether it will be warm **(Il
va faire bon)**, cool **(Il va faire frais)**, cold **(Il va faire froid)**, or very cold
**(Il va faire très froid)** on February 16.

*Transparency:*
5-2 (Ex. C, alternative
weather map)

*Modèle:*     Bordeaux
             *Il va faire frais. Le maximum va être de 14 degrés.*

**Mardi 16 février**

TEMPÉRATURES (le premier chiffre indique le
maximum enregistré dans la journée du
16 février, le second le minimum dans la
nuit du 16 au 17 février):

Ajaccio, 14 et 5 degrés; **Biarritz**, 20 et
11; **Bordeaux**, 14 et 7; **Bréhat**, 7 et 4;
**Brest**, 7 et 4; **Cannes**, 14 et 7; **Cherbourg**, 5 et 2; **Clermont-Ferrand**, 12 et 4;
**Dijon**, 2 et 0; **Dinard**, 8 et 2; **Embrun**, 8
et −1; **Grenoble-St-Geoirs**, 11 et 1;
**Grenoble-St-M.-H.**, 11 et 2; **La Rochelle**,
12 et 5; **Lille**, 2 et −4; **Limoges**, 10 et 5;
**Lorient**, 6 et 5; **Lyon**, 8 et 2; **Marseille-**

**Marignane**, 12 et 8; **Nancy**, 1 et −5;
**Nantes**, 10 et 4; **Nice**, 13 et 7; **Paris-
Montsouris**, 6 et 1; **Paris-Orly**, 7 et 0;
**Pau**, 17 et 7; **Perpignan**, 15 et 4;
**Rennes**, 6 et 3; **Rouen**, 6 et 2; **Saint-
Étienne**, 10 et 3; **Strasbourg**, 0 et −6;
**Toulouse**, 15 et 2; **Tours**, 6 et 3.

TEMPÉRATURES RELEVÉES À L'ÉTRANGER:
**Alger**, 21 et 11; **Genève**, 4 et 0;
**Lisbonne**, 15 et 9; **Londres**, 2 et 0;
**Madrid**, 14 et 3; **Rome**, 12 et 1;
**Stockholm**, −6 et −16.

**Grammar:** To talk about
what the weather is
going to be in the near future, use **aller** + an infinitive: **Il va faire froid. Le
ciel va être nuageux. Il va
neiger.** The infinitive of **il
pleut** is **pleuvoir: Il va
pleuvoir.** The immediate
future of **il y a** is **il va y
avoir: Il va y avoir du
verglas.**

## S·T·R·U·C·T·U·R·E

*Les mois de l'année*

| | |
|---|---|
| **janvier** | **juillet** |
| **février** | **août** |
| **mars** | **septembre** |
| **avril** | **octobre** |
| **mai** | **novembre** |
| **juin** | **décembre** |

*l'hiver*
*le printemps*
*l'été*
*l'automne*

All the months of the year are masculine and are used without articles.
They are not capitalized. To express the idea of *in* a month, use **en** or **au
mois de (d')**:

**En janvier,** il neige beaucoup.          *In January,* it snows a lot.
Il fait chaud **au mois d'août.**           It's hot *in August.*

▲  ▲  ▲

## APPLICATION

**D. Quel temps fait-il chez vous?** For each month, describe what the weather is like in your area.

*Modèle:*     septembre
         *En septembre, il fait frais et il y a du vent.*

1. janvier    2. juillet    3. mars    4. novembre    5. mai    6. août
7. décembre    8. juin

**E. Je suis né(e) au mois de...** (*I was born in . . .* ) Tell your classmates what month you were born in and what the weather is usually like.

*Modèle:*     *Je suis né(e) au mois de juillet. Il fait toujours* (always) *très chaud en juillet.*

### Note grammaticale

#### La date

| | |
|---|---|
| **Nous sommes le combien aujourd'hui?** | |
| **Quelle date sommes-nous?** | *What is today's date?* |
| → **Quelle est la date aujourd'hui?** | |

| | |
|---|---|
| **Nous sommes le 5 avril.** | |
| **Aujourd'hui c'est le 5 avril.** | *Today is April 5.* |
| **C'est aujourd'hui le 5 avril.** | |

To express the date in French, use the definite article **le,** a cardinal number (**trente, dix, cinq**), and the name of the month. The one exception is the first of the month, expressed by **le premier:**

C'est **le premier février.**      It's *February 1.*

**F. C'est quelle date?** Give the following dates in French.

*Modèle:*     le 23 mars
         *le vingt-trois mars*

| | | |
|---|---|---|
| 1. le 8 janvier | 4. le 16 septembre | 7. le 31 mai |
| 2. le 15 août | 5. le 4 juillet | 8. le 12 juin |
| 3. le 1<sup>er</sup> octobre | 6. le 14 juillet | 9. aujourd'hui |

## Note grammaticale

*Les saisons de l'année*

le printemps

l'été

l'automne

l'hiver

All the nouns for the seasons are masculine. To express the idea of *in* a particular season, use **en** with **hiver, automne,** and **été,** and **au** with **printemps.**

**En automne** on joue au football.
**En hiver** il fait froid.
Il pleut beaucoup **au printemps.**
On va à la plage **en été.**

Soccer is played *in the fall.*
It's cold *in the winter.*
It rains a lot *in the spring.*
People go to the beach *in the summer.*

**G.  Chez vous.** Explain what the weather is like during the various seasons in the region where you live.

*Modèle:*  Quel temps fait-il chez vous en hiver?
*Chez nous, en hiver, il neige et il fait très froid.*

1.  Quel temps fait-il chez vous en hiver?   2.  Et en automne?   3.  En été?
4.  Et au printemps?

**H.  Des questions, encore des questions, toujours des questions!** You're working with small children who are always curious about something. Answer their questions.

1.  Combien de saisons est-ce qu'il y a dans une année?
2.  Quels sont les mois de l'été?
3.  En quelle saison est-ce qu'on fait du ski?
4.  En quelle saison est-ce qu'on va à la plage?
5.  En quelles saisons est-ce qu'on joue au football? Au basket?
6.  En quelle saison est-ce qu'on célèbre Thanksgiving? Pâques *(Easter)?*
7.  Quelle est la date aujourd'hui?
8.  Quelle est la date du premier jour des vacances?

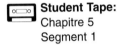

**Student Tape:**
Chapitre 5
Segment 1

# PRONONCIATION   *Les voyelles **a** et **i***

In French, the letters **a** and **i**, when not combined with another vowel or with the consonants **m** or **n,** are pronounced as follows:

The French **a** sound is between the *a* sounds in the English words *fat* and *father*. It is pronounced with the mouth rounded.

The French **i** sound is similar to the *i* sound in the English word *machine*. It is pronounced with the lips spread wide, as in a smile.

**I.**  Read each word aloud, being careful to open your mouth to pronounce **a** and to spread your lips (smile!) when saying **i.**

la / Ça va? / gare / papa / ici / livre / dîne / ville / Paris / mari / Italie / pharmacie / capitale / politique / rive / île / divisé / habiter / film / tennis

## S·T·R·U·C·T·U·R·E

**Suggestion, Passé composé**
with **avoir:** (1) Present using
**D'habitude je quitte la maison à 8h.** Substitute: **Demain matin je vais aussi quitter la maison à 8h.** Then, **Exceptionnellement, ce matin j'ai quitté la maison à 7h30.** (2) Review conjugation of **avoir.** (3) Explain past participles of regular **-er** verbs. (4) Have students conjugate several verbs in **passé composé** using past participles you give them. (5) Repeat one or two conjugations in the negative. (6) Have students contrast present and past, then immediate future and past.

### *Le passé composé avec **avoir***

Samedi dernier **il a fait** très beau.

**J'ai travaillé** dans le jardin et **mes parents ont joué** au golf.

Dimanche **il a plu** et **nous avons visité** le Louvre.

Qu'est-ce que **vous avez fait** pendant le week-end?

Last Saturday *the weather was* beautiful.

*I worked* in the garden and *my parents played* golf.

Sunday *it rained* and *we visited* the Louvre.

What *did you do* over the weekend?

In French, to talk about actions that were carried out in the past, you use the past tense called the **passé composé** *(compound past)*. This tense is called "compound" because it is made up of two parts: a helping verb, which agrees with the subject, and a past participle. For most French verbs, the helping verb is **avoir:**

| helping verb **(avoir)** | past participle |
|---|---|
| ↓ | ↓ |

Nous   **avons**        **visité**   Paris.

Thus, the **passé composé** of the verb **visiter** is as follows:

| *visiter* | |
|---|---|
| j'**ai visité** | nous **avons visité** |
| tu **as visité** | vous **avez visité** |
| il, elle, on **a visité** | ils, elles **ont visité** |

The key to using the **passé composé** is learning the past participles. The past participle of an **-er** verb sounds exactly like the infinitive; however, the written form ends in **-é:**

| *Infinitive* | *Past participle* |
|---|---|
| chanter | chant**é** |
| étudier | étudi**é** |
| manger | mang**é** |
| parler | parl**é** |

*[handwritten notes in margin:]* prendre - pris · mettre - mis · venir - venu · revenir - revenu

The past participles of irregular verbs often do not follow the same pattern. Among the verbs you have already learned, the following have irregular past participles:

| *Infinitive* | *Past participle* |
|---|---|
| faire | **fait** |
| pleuvoir | **plu** |
| prendre | **pris** |
| voir | vu |

*[handwritten note:]* avoir ... eu

To form the negative of the **passé composé,** simply insert **ne** and **pas** around the helping verb. Remember that **ne** becomes **n'** before a vowel:

Ils **n'**ont **pas** trouvé le musée.        They did*n't* find the museum.

▲   ▲   ▲

*[handwritten notes in right margin:]* Verbs: past part / er → é / ir → i / re → u

## APPLICATION

**J.** Replace the past participle in italics with those given in parentheses.

1. Est-ce que tu as *voyagé?* (travaillé / écouté la radio / visité Paris / pris l'autobus)
2. J'ai *trouvé* le livre. (acheté / commencé / aimé / regardé)
3. Hier soir nous avons beaucoup *dansé.* (parlé / mangé / étudié / travaillé)
4. Elles n'ont pas *chanté.* (mangé / fait le voyage / appris les verbes / quitté la maison)

**K.** Remplacez le sujet en italique et faites les changements nécessaires.

1. *J'*ai regardé la télé. (nous / elle / tu / ils / vous / je / on)
2. *Paul* a déjà visité Paris, n'est-ce pas? (Chantal / tu / vous / elles / nous / je)
3. *Elles* n'ont pas fait les devoirs. (tu / nous / il / je / vous / elles)
4. Quand est-ce que *tu* as quitté la maison? (vous / elles / il / tu / on)

**L. Oui et non.** You spent the evening at a friend's house. The next day your other friends want to know all about it. Tell them what you did and did not do.

*Modèles:*     Est-ce que tu as parlé à Simone? Et à Francine?
               *J'ai parlé à Simone, mais je n'ai pas parlé à Francine.*

               Est-ce que vous avez dansé? (étudier)
               *Nous avons dansé, mais nous n'avons pas étudié.*

1. Est-ce que vous avez téléphoné à Paul? Et à Marie?
2. Est-ce que vous avez écouté la radio? (danser)
3. Est-ce que tu as mangé un sandwich? Et des fruits?
4. Est-ce que tu as regardé la télé? (étudier)
5. Est-ce que tu as parlé aux parents de Sylvie? Et à sa sœur?
6. Est-ce que vous avez fait une promenade? (prendre la voiture)

▲▲▲ C

CLIP'S SUR ÉCRANS GÉANTS.

**M.  Pourquoi est-ce que vous êtes en retard?** *(Why are you late?)* You and your friend arrive late at a party. Use the drawing and the verbs to explain what happened.

**Variation,** Ex. M: Another student explains why the people in the drawing were late (**Ils ont quitté la maison...** Etc.).

*Modèle:*     *Nous avons quitté la maison à 8h15...*

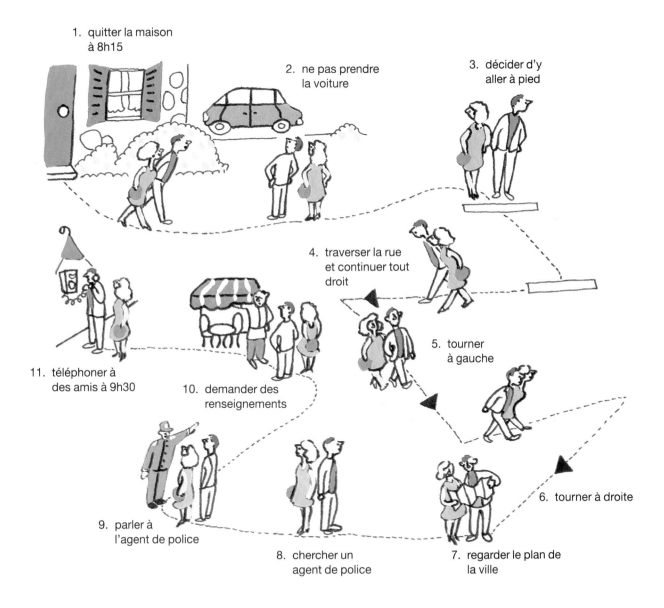

1. quitter la maison à 8h15
2. ne pas prendre la voiture
3. décider d'y aller à pied
4. traverser la rue et continuer tout droit
5. tourner à gauche
6. tourner à droite
7. regarder le plan de la ville
8. chercher un agent de police
9. parler à l'agent de police
10. demander des renseignements
11. téléphoner à des amis à 9h30

## Débrouillons-nous!

▲ ▲ ▲ ▲ ▲ ▲ ▲ ▲ ▲ ▲ **Débrouillons-nous!** ▲ ▲ ▲ ▲ ▲ ▲ ▲ ▲ ▲ ▲

*Petite révision de l'étape*

Ex. N: ⇄

**N.  Échange.** Posez les questions suivantes à un(e) camarade de classe, qui va vous répondre.

1.  Est-ce que tu aimes mieux la neige ou la pluie? Qu'est-ce que tu fais quand il neige? Quand il pleut?
2.  Est-ce que tu supportes mieux *(better tolerate)* le froid ou la chaleur? Qu'est-ce que tu aimes faire quand il fait froid? Quand il fait chaud?
3.  Quelle saison est-ce que tu préfères? Pourquoi?
4.  Quelle est la date de ton anniversaire *(birthday)*? Quel temps fait-il en général le mois de ton anniversaire?
5.  Est-ce que tu as étudié hier soir? Tu as fait tes devoirs de français?
6.  Est-ce que tu as quitté la maison (ta chambre) de bonne heure ce matin? Tu as pris l'autobus pour aller à l'université?
7.  Est-ce que tu as déjà visité Paris? Rome? Québec?
8.  Est-ce que tu as téléphoné à tes amis récemment? Tes amis et toi, vous vous téléphonez souvent?
9.  Est-ce que tu as mangé quelque chose au petit déjeuner? Est-ce que tu prends le petit déjeuner d'habitude?

Ex. O: ⇄

**O.  Mon week-end.** It's Monday morning and you and your friend are discussing what you did (or did not do) over the weekend. Begin by reminding each other of Saturday's and Sunday's weather. Then use some of the following verbs to tell about your activities.

VERBES: **travailler, regarder la télé (une vidéo), parler à, téléphoner à, danser, manger, visiter, prendre (l'autobus) pour..., écouter la radio, faire une promenade (un tour)**

**À faire chez vous: CAHIER, Chapitre 5 / 1ère étape**

LA PETITE VENISE

Pont de la Courtille
Parc des Bords de l'Eure
CHARTRES
Tél. 37.91.03.65

PEDALOS
BARQUES
CANOES

*Dans un cadre agréable*
*Promenade ombragée sur l'Eure*

Instructor's Tape:
**Tu veux voir le nouveau film au Gaumont les Halles?**

Suggestion, Point de départ:
(1) As a prereading exercise, have students talk about where to find movie information and what information is in newspaper listings. (2) Have them look at the excerpt from *L'Officiel des spectacles* and do Ex. A. (3) Have them listen to the dialogue on the Instructor's Tape.

# D E U X I È M E   É T A P E

## Point de départ

▼ ▼ ▼ ▼ ▼ ▼ ▼ ▼ ▼ ▼ ▼ ▼ ▼

*Tu veux voir le nouveau film au Gaumont les Halles?*

**Il y a** trois semaines Claire Maurant **est allée** à Paris pour voir sa cousine Mireille Loiseau. Un jour les deux jeunes femmes **ont eu** la conversation suivante avec Jean-Francis, le frère de Mireille.

ago / went
had

textaudio
CD 1-36

| | |
|---|---|
| MIREILLE: | Alors, qu'est-ce qu'on fait ce soir? |
| CLAIRE: | Pourquoi pas nous balader un peu? |
| JEAN-FRANCIS: | Non, ce n'est pas très intéressant, ça. |
| CLAIRE: | Eh bien, qu'est-ce que tu veux faire, toi? |
| JEAN-FRANCIS: | On pourrait **louer** une vidéo. |
| CLAIRE: | Non. Moi, j'ai envie de **sortir.** |
| MIREILLE: | Moi, j'ai une idée. Allons voir le nouveau film au Gaumont les Halles. |
| CLAIRE: | J'espère que ce n'est pas un film **d'épouvante.** **J'ai horreur** de ça. |
| MIREILLE: | Non, non, non. C'est une comédie dramatique **polonaise** qui s'appelle *La Double Vie de Véronique.* |
| JEAN-FRANCIS: | **Ça passe** à quelle heure? |
| MIREILLE: | Voyons! Je vais regarder dans le **journal**. Elle passe à 20h. |
| JEAN-FRANCIS: | Écoute! Moi, j'ai une course à faire. On se retrouve devant le Gaumont les Halles à 19h45. D'accord? |
| MIREILLE: | À huit heures moins le quart devant le Gaumont les Halles. D'accord, Claire? |
| CLAIRE: | Oui. D'accord. |

to rent
to go out

horror
I hate
Polish

It is showing
newspaper

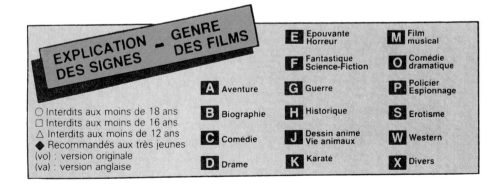

## À VOUS! (Exercices de vocabulaire)

**A.** **Renseignons-nous!** Each week in Paris you can purchase entertainment guides at newsstands **(kiosques).** Answer the questions about the following excerpt from one of these guides, *L'Officiel des spectacles.*

**⓪ DOUBLE VIE DE VERONIQUE (LA).** — Norvégien-polonais, coul. (90). Comédie dramatique, de Krzysztof Kieslowski : Deux jeunes filles en tous points semblables. L'une est Polonaise, l'autre, Française. Elles ne se connaissent pas et cependant un lien surnaturel semble les unir. Prix d'interprétation Cannes 1991. Avec Irène Jacob, Halina Gryglaszewska, Kalina Jedrusik, Aleksander Bardini, Wladyslaw Kowalski. **Gaumont les Halles 1er** (vo), **Gaumont Opéra 2e** (vo), **Saint-André-des-Arts 6e** (vo), **Pagode 7e** (vo), **Gaumont Ambassade 8e** (vo), **Bastille 11e** (vo), **Gaumont Alésia 14e** (vo), **Gaumont Parnasse 14e** (vo).

**GAUMONT LES HALLES,** rue du Forum, Pte Rambuteau (Niveau - 3), M° Châtelet-Les Halles, 40 26 12 12. (H). Pl. 40F. CB. TR. 31F : lun + ET, CV et FN du dim 20h au ven 18h et - 18 ans (dim 20h au mar 18h). TU. 26F : de 11h à 12h45.

**1)** *Séances 11h40, 13h45, 15h50, 17h55, 20h, 22h05. Film 20 mn après :*
    **LA DOUBLE VIE DE VERONIQUE** (vo)

**2)** *Séances: 11h10, 13h45, 16h20, 18h55, 21h30. Film 15 mn :*
△ **LES ANGES DE LA NUIT** (vo) (Dolby stéréo)

**3)** *Séances 11h10, 13h45, 16h20, 18h55, 21h30. Film 15 mn après :*
    **JUNGLE FEVER** (vo)

**4)** *Séances 11h20, 13h25, 15h30, 17h35, 19h40, 21h45. Film 25 mn après :*
    **TOTO LE HEROS**

**5)** *Séances 11h30, 14h, 16h30, 19h, 21h30. Film 25 mn après :*
□ **LE SILENCE DES AGNEAUX** (vo)

**6)** *Séances 11h40, 14h10, 16h40, 19h10, 21h40. Film 25 mn après :*
    **CE CHER INTRUS** (vo)

1. What kind of film is *La Double Vie de Véronique?* When was it made? Who directed it? How many movie theaters is it playing at?
2. One place where *La Double Vie de Véronique* is being shown is the **Gaumont les Halles.** Where is this movie house located? Where do you get off the subway when you go there?
3. You are meeting a friend, who is not free until after 8:30 P.M. Which show will you attend?
4. There are usually short subjects before the main feature. At what time will *La Double Vie de Véronique* start?
5. How much will it cost to see the film? Does everyone pay the same price?

**B.** **Qu'est-ce qu'on va voir?** Using the information from *L'Officiel des spectacles* on pages 187 and 188, recommend films for your friends. They will tell you what kinds of films they like and will ask you questions about where and when the films are playing as well as where (in what countries) the films were made.

*Modèle:*     — *Moi, j'adore les films policiers.*
              — *Va voir* Miller's Crossing.
              — *Où est-ce qu'il passe?*
              — *Au Saint-Lambert.*
              — *À quelle heure est la première séance?*
              — *À 14h (à 2 heures de l'après-midi).*
              — *C'est un film français?*
              — *Non, c'est un film américain.*

▲▲▲   a

**Afin d'en faciliter la lecture, voici une liste des abréviations qui accompagnent les renseignements concernant les salles.**

○ Films interdits aux moins de 18 ans.
□ Films interdits aux moins de 16 ans.
△ Films interdits aux moins de 12 ans.
◆ Recommandés aux très jeunes.
(H) Salles accessibles aux handicapés physiques.
Les numéros attribués aux salles multiples ne constituent qu'un repère pour la lecture des programmes, mais ne correspondent pas nécessairement à l'ordre donné par les exploitants.
DESIGNATION DES CARTES EN USAGE :
CB : Carte bleue Visa acceptée.
CP : Carte Pathé (300 F - 10 entrées)
        Possibilité de réservation.

C UGC : Cartes UGC « Privilège » I et II (112 F - 4 entrées) ou 168 F (2 personnes - 6 entrées). Rens. : 47 47 12 34.
TR : Tarif réduit appliqué aux catégories indiquées, sauf le vendredi soir, samedi, dimanche, fêtes et veilles de fêtes.
CF : Carte fidélité de la salle.
CV : Carte Vermeil.
FN : Familles nombreuses.
MI : Militaires appelés.
ET : Etudiants.
CH : Chômeurs.

**Culture:** Foreign films in France are shown both in the original language with subtitles (**version originale**) and dubbed in French (**version française**).

---

Ⓞ **DISCRETE (LA).** — Franç., coul. (90). Comédie dramatique, de Christian Vincent : Un homme qui voulait se venger de la trahison d'une femme à l'encontre du beau sexe, s'éprend de celle qu'il avait choisie, au hasard, pour en faire sa victime. Avec Fabrice Luchini, Judith Henry, Maurice Garrel, Marie Bunel, François Toumarkine, Yvette Petit, Nicole Félix, Olivier Achard. **Latina 4e, Bretagne 6e, Balzac 8e.**

Ⓒ **JOUR DES ROIS (LE).** — Franç., coul. (90). Comédie, de Marie-Claude Treilhou : Trois sœurs âgées, très différentes, sont marquées malgré elles par la personnalité extravagante de l'artiste de la famille qui échappe à leur univers et au poids des années. Avec Danielle Darrieux, Micheline Presle, Paulette Dubost, Robert Lamoureux, Michel Galabru, Manuela Gouary, Sherif Scouri. **Epée de Bois 5e.**

Ⓞ **JUNGLE FEVER.** — Amér., coul. (91). Comédie dramatique, de Spike Lee : Flipper, Noir américain, croit mettre une clef de voûte à sa réussite en ayant une maîtresse blanche, Américaine d'origine italienne. Le couple se heurtera aux préjugés racistes. Avec Wesley Snipes, Annabella Sciorra, Spike Lee, Anthony Quinn, Ossie Davis, Ruby Dee, Samuel Jackson, Lonette McKee, John Turturro, Frank Vincent. **Gaumont les Halles 1er (vo), Gaumont Opéra 2e (vo), 14 Juillet Odéon 6e (vo), Gaumont Ambassade 8e (vo), Bastille 11e (vo), Bienvenue Montparnasse 15e (vo).**

Ⓚ **KICKBOXER N°2 (Le successeur - Kickboxer II : the road back).** — Amér., coul. (90). Arts martiaux, de Albert Pyun : Adepte de la non violence, le frère de Kurt Sloan, mort à l'issue de son brillant combat contre Tong Po, est amené à affronter ce sauvage lutteur assoiffé de vengeance. Avec Sasha Mitchell, Peter Boyle, Cary Hiroyuchi Tagawa, Dennis Chan, Michel Qissi, John Diehl, Matthias Hues. **(Voir rubrique « Nouveaux films »).**

Ⓞ **LABYRINTHE DES PASSIONS (Laberinto de pasiones).** — Espagnol, coul. (82). Comédie dramatique, de Pedro Almodovar : Une jeune érotomane, membre d'un sauvage groupe musical féminin, l'héritier d'un empereur arabe déchu, passionné par les cosmétiques et les hommes : un cocktail explosif dans un Madrid survolté. Avec Cecilia Roth, Imanol Arias, Helga Line, Antonio Banderas, Marta Fernandez-Muro, Fernando Vivanco. **Studio des Ursulines 5e (vo).**

Ⓒ **LADY FOR A DAY (Grande dame d'un jour).** — Amér., noir et blanc (33). Comédie, de Frank Capra : Une clocharde de New York, avec la complicité de ses amis, se fait passer pour une femme du monde aux yeux de sa fille, fiancée à un noble Espagnol. Inédit en France depuis sa sortie en 1935. Avec May Robson, Guy Kibbee, Glenda Farrell, Warren Williams, Jean Parker, Walter Connolly, Nat Pendleton, Barry Norton, Ned Sparks. **14 Juillet Odéon 6e (vo), 14 Juillet Bastille 11e (vo), 14 Juillet Beaugrenelle 15e (vo).**

Ⓜ **LAST WALTZ.** — Amér., coul. (78). Film musical, de Martin Scorsese : Le concert d'adieu du groupe « The Band » en novembre 1976 au Winterland de San Francisco en compagnie de prestigieux invités. Avec The Band, Bob Dylan, Joni Mitchell, Neil Diamond, Emmylou Harris, Neil Young, Ringo Starr, Van Morrison, Ron Wood, Eric Clapton, Muddy Waters. **14 Juillet Odéon 6e (vo).**

Ⓓ **LIAISONS DANGEREUSES, (LES) (Dangerous liaisons).** — Amér., coul. (88). Drame, de Stephen Frears : Au XVIIIe siècle, deux libertins s'amusent à bafouer l'innocence amoureuse, par victimes interposées, avant de s'affronter à visage découvert. D'après le roman de Choderlos de Laclos. Avec John Malkovich, Glenn Close, Michelle Pfeiffer, Swoosie Kurtz, Keanu Reeves, Uma Thurman, Peter Capaldi, Joe Sheridan, Valerie Gogan, Laura Benson. **Cinoches 6e (vo).**

Ⓓ **LIFEBOAT.** — Amér., noir et blanc (43). Drame, de Alfred Hitchcock : Neuf rescapés du naufrage d'un paquebot se retrouvent à bord d'un canot de sauvetage. Parmi eux, un nazi, le seul capable de diriger l'embarcation.... Avec Tallulah Bankhead, William Bendix, Walter Slezak, Mary Anderson, John Hodiak, Hume Cronyn. **Action Ecoles 5e (vo).**

Ⓞ **LISTE NOIRE (LA) (Guilty by suspicion).** — Amér., coul. (90). Comédie dramatique, de Irwin Winkler : En 1951, un célèbre réalisateur de Hollywood est poursuivi par la Commission des activités antiaméricaines. Il lui faudra choisir entre dénoncer ses amis ou perdre son travail. Avec Robert De Niro, Annette Bening, George Wendt, Patricia Wettig, Sam Wanamaker, Luke Edwards, Chris Cooper, Ben Piazza. **Cinoches 6e (vo).**

Ⓓ **LOLITA.** — Brit., noir et blanc (62). Drame passionnel, de Stanley Kubrick : La passion obsessionnelle d'un homme de lettres pour une nymphette ingénue et perverse. D'après le roman de Vladimir Nabokov. Avec Sue Lyon, James Mason, Shelley Winters, Peter Sellers. **Républic Cinémas 11e (vo), Denfert 14e (vo).**

Ⓒ □ **LUNE FROIDE.** — Franç., noir et blanc (91). Comédie, de Patrick Bouchitey : A 40 ans, Dédé et Simon, éternels adolescents, cèdent la nuit venue aux rêves fous auxquels ils n'osent aspirer le jour. Vient la nuit de la pleine lune, fertile en sortilèges. D'après Charles Bukowski. Avec Jean-François Stévenin, Patrick Bouchitey, Jean-Pierre Bisson, Laura Favali, Marie Mergey, Silvana de Faria. **Saint-André-des-Arts 6e.**

Ⓓ **MADAME BOVARY, de Claude Chabrol.** — Franç., coul. (91). Drame, de Claude Chabrol : Mariée à un brave médecin de campagne, Emma, par insatisfaction et vanité, fait le malheur de cet homme et le sien propre. D'après le roman de Gustave Flaubert. Avec Isabelle Huppert, Jean-François Balmer, Christophe Malavoy, Jean Yanne, Lucas Belvaux, Christiane Minazzoli, Jean-Louis Maury, Florent Gibassier. **14 Juillet Parnasse 6e.**

Ⓕ △ **MALEDICTION N°4 (LA) (Omen IV).** — Amér., coul. (91). Fantastique, de Jorge Montesi, et Dominique Othenin-Gérard : Manifestant dès son baptême un pouvoir diabolique terrifiant, la petite fille adoptée par un jeune couple d'avocats serait-elle l'Antéchrist ?. Avec Faye Grant, Michael Woods, Michael Lerner, Madison Mason, Ann Hearn, Jim Byrnes, Don S. Davis, Asia Vieira. **George V 8e (vo), Hollywood Boulevard 9e.**

Ⓒ **MAMAN, J'AI RATE L'AVION ! (Home alone).** — Amér., coul. (90). Comédie, de Chris Columbus : Oublié à Chicago, dans la fièvre du départ de la famille pour Paris, un petit garçon se fait le gardien vigilant et imaginatif de la maison menacée par d'inquiétants visiteurs. Avec Macaulay Culkin, Catherine O'Hara, John Heard, Joe Pecsi, Daniel Stern, Roberts Blossom. **Saint-Lambert 15e.**

Ⓟ **MANIERE FORTE (LA) (Hard way).** — Amér., coul. (91). Comédie policière, de John Badham : Un flic new-yorkais reçoit pour mission de servir de baby-sitter à une vedette de cinéma cherchant à capter sur le terrain, en vue d'un prochain rôle, « l'essence » même de l'expérience policière. Avec James Woods, Michael J. Fox, Stephen Lang, Annabella Sciorra, Delroy Lindo, Luis Guzman, Mary Mara, Christina Ricci, John Capodice, Penny Marshall, Conrad Roberts. **Forum Horizon 1er (vo), Rex 2e, 14 Juillet Odéon 6e (vo), George V 8e (vo), Pathé Marignan Concorde 8e (vo), Pathé Français 9e, Nation 12e, UGC Lyon Bastille 12e, Fauvette 13e, Pathé Montparnasse 14e, 14 Juillet Beaugrenelle 15e (vo), Gaumont Convention 15e, Pathé Clichy 18e.**

Ⓕ ◆ **MARRRTIENS ! (LES).** — Amér., coul. (90). Science-fiction, de Patrick Read Johnson : Attirés sur notre terre par un canular radiophonique, cinq Martiens, confrontés à l'hostilité de la population d'une bourgade américaine, voudraient rejoindre leur planète. Avec Douglas Barr, Royal Dano, Ariane Richards, Jimmy Briscoe, Kevin Thomson, Tony Cox, Debbie Lee Carrington, Tommy Madden. **Saint-Lambert 15e.**

Ⓞ **MERCI LA VIE.** — Franç., noir et blanc, couleur (90). Comédie dramatique, de Bertrand Blier : Deux filles face à elles-mêmes, aux « mecs », à leurs souvenirs. S'agit-il de la réalité, ou du tournage d'un film ? De toute façon, c'est moche. « Merci la vie... ». Avec Charlotte Gainsbourg, Anouk Grinberg, Gérard Depardieu, Michel Blanc, Jean Carmet, Catherine Jacob, François Perrot, Jean-Louis Trintignant, Annie Girardot, Thierry Frémont. **Epée de Bois 5e.**

Ⓟ △ **MILLER'S CROSSING (Un cadavre sous le chapeau).** — Amér., coul. (90). Policier, de Joel et Ethan Coen : Un parieur malchanceux, bras droit d'un caïd irlandais dont il partage - à son insu - la maitresse, se trouve mêlé à une nouvelle guerre des gangs sur fond de Prohibition. Avec Gabriel Byrne, Albert Finney, Jon Polito, Marcia Gay Harden, J.E. Freeman, Mike Starr, Al Mancini. **Saint-Lambert 15e (vo).**

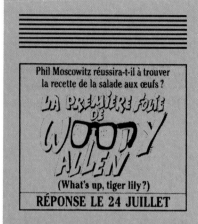

Phil Moscowitz réussira-t-il à trouver la recette de la salade aux œufs ?

**LA PREMIÈRE FOLIE DE WOODY ALLEN**

(What's up, tiger lily ?)

**RÉPONSE LE 24 JUILLET**

**ACTION ECOLES**, 23, rue des Ecoles, M° Maubert-Mutualité ou Cardinal Lemoine, 43 25 72 07. (H). Pl. 36F. TR. 26F (week-end compris) : lun + ET, CV et - 20 ans. CF : 6ème ent. gratuite.
1) *Séances 14h, 15h40, 17h20, 19h, 20h40, 22h20. Film 10 mn après :*
**LIFEBOAT** (vo)

2)
**\*FESTIVAL WOODY ALLEN** (vo)
*Mer 14h, 16h, 18h, 20h, 22h :* **Quoi de neuf, Pussy Cat ?.** — *Jeu 14h, 16h, 18h, 20h, 22h :* **Stardust memories.** — *Ven 14h, 16h, 18h, 20h, 22h :* **Tout ce que vous avez toujours voulu savoir sur le sexe....** — *Sam, mar 14h, 16h, 18h, 20h, 22h :* **Manhattan.** — *Dim 14h, 16h, 18h, 20h, 22h :* **Bananas.** — *Lun 14h, 16h, 18h, 20h, 22h :* **Guerre et amour\***

**EPEE DE BOIS**, 100, rue Mouffetard, M° Censier-Daubenton, 43 37 57 47. Pl. 35F. TR. 25F : lun + ET, CV, - 20 ans, FN, MI et CH. TU. 24F : à 12h.
1) *Ven, sam 22h :* △ **Hot spot.**
*Tlj 12h :* **Aux yeux du monde.**
*Tlj (sf dim) 16h, 20h05, mn 0h05 :* **Merci la vie.**
*Mer 14h30 :* ◆ **Robinson et cie.**
*Tlj 18h15 :* **Hors la vie.**
*Mer 20h15. tlj (sf mer) 14h, 20h15 :* **Cheb**

2) *Tlj 16h :* **Halfaouine** (vo).
*Dim 16h :* **Le jour des rois.**
*Tlj 18h :* **Cellini** (vo).
*Tlj 14h :* **Toujours seuls.**
*Tlj 22h15 :* **Chuck Berry** (vo).
*Tlj 12h :* **Acte d'amour** (vo)
*Mer, jeu, dim, lun, mar 22h :* **Les Doors** (vo)

**SAINT-ANDRE-DES-ARTS**, 30, rue Saint-André-des-Arts, M° Saint-Michel, 43 26 48 18. (H). Pl. 38F. TR. 28F : lun + ET, CV, - 25 ans et CH.
1) *Film 14h15, 16h15, 18h10, 20h05, 22h05 :*
**LA DOUBLE VIE DE VERONIQUE** (vo)

2) *Film 14h25, 16h25, 18h20, 20h15, 22h15 :*
□ **LUNE FROIDE**

**14 JUILLET ODEON**, 113, bd Saint-Germain, M° Odéon, 43 25 59 83. Pl. 40F. TR 31F : lun + ET, CV (jusqu'à 18h30), FN, MI et - 18 ans. 22F : groupes scolaires (rés. 43 25 19 71).
1) *Séances 13h10, 15h, 16h50, 18h40, 20h30, 22h20. Film 10 mn après :*
**LADY FOR A DAY** (vo)

2) *Séances 13h10, 15h30, 17h50, 20h10, 22h30. Film 10 mn après :*
**JUNGLE FEVER** (vo)

3) *Séances 13h40, 15h50, 18h, 20h10, 22h20. Film 10 mn après :*
**LAST WALTZ** (vo) (Dolby stéréo)

4) *Séances 14h, 16h30, 19h, 21h30. Film 10 mn après :*
△ **LES ANGES DE LA NUIT** (vo)

5) *Séances 13h30, 15h40, 17h50, 20h, 22h10. Film 10 mn après :*
**LA MANIERE FORTE** (vo) (Dolby stéréo)

**14 JUILLET PARNASSE**, 11, rue Jules-Chaplain, M° Vavin, 43 26 58 00. Pl. 39F. TR. 29F : lun + ET, CV, FN, MI et - 18 ans. 22F : groupes.
1) *Séances 13h55, 16h30, 19h, 21h45. Film 10 mn après :*
**MADAME BOVARY, de Claude Chabrol**

2)
**\*INTEGRALE NANNI MORETTI** vo
*Mer, dim 14h, 16h, 18h, 20h, 22h :* **La messe est finie.** — *Jeu 14h, 16h, 18h, 20h, 22h :* **Sogni d'oro.** — *Ven 14h, 16h, 18h, 20h, 22h :* **Bianca.** — *Sam 14h, 16h, 18h, 20h, 22h :* **Palombella rossa.** — *Lun 14h, 16h, 18h, 20h, 22h :* **Je suis un autarcique.** — *Mar 14h, 16h, 18h, 20h, 22h :* **Ecce homo\***

3) *Tlj 14h10. (- 14 ans : 15F) :* ◆ **Crin blanc et** ◆ **Le ballon rouge.**
*Tlj 16h10, 18h10, 20h10, 22h10 :* **Alice** (vo)

**STUDIO DES URSULINES**, 10, rue des Ursulines, M° Luxembourg ou Port-Royal, 43 26 19 09 et 43. Salle climatisée. Pl. 34F. TR. 25F : lun + ET, MI, CV, FN, - 18 ans, CH et Cte Jeunes.
*Mer 22h10 :* **Sexe, mensonges et vidéo** (vo)
*Dim 16h :* **Barry Lyndon** (vo).
*Sam 21h50 :* △ **Qui a peur de Virginia Woolf ?** (vo).
*Mar 19h15 :* △ **Casanova, de Fellini** (vo).
*Sam 20h10 :* △ **La nuit du chasseur** (vo).
*Jeu 22h10 :* **The element of crime** (vo).
*Ven 20h, lun 20h15 : 1984** (vo).
*Mer, jeu, ven 12h :* **Outremer.**
*Mer, sam, dim 14h :* **La gloire de mon père.**
*Mer, sam, dim 16h :* **Le château de ma mère.**
*Jeu, ven, lun, mar 14h :* ◆ **Sa majesté des mouches** (vo).
*Ven 22h10 :* **Big time** (vo).
*Lun 22h10, mar 17h30 :* **Labyrinthe des passions** (vo).
*Dim 17h50 :* **Don Giovanni, de Joseph Losey** (vo).
*Mer, jeu, ven 17h45, sam, dim 12h, mar 22h :* **L' Atalante** (vo).
*Mer, mar 19h30, sam, lun 17h45 :* **Macbeth, de Roman Polanski** (vo).
*Jeu, ven, lun, mar 15h45 :* **Veraz** (vo).
*Lun, mar 12h :* **Sale comme un ange**

**SAINT-LAMBERT**, 6, rue Péclet, M° Vaugirard, 45 32 91 68 et 48 28 78 87. Pl. 32F. TR. 25F : lun + ET, CV, CH et - 15 ans. 16F : groupes.
**Salle 1 :**
*Mer, ven 13h30 :* ◆ **Les voyages de Gulliver, de Dave Fleischer.**
*Mer 17h, mar 13h30 :* ◆ **L' histoire sans fin n°2.**
*Jeu 13h30 :* ◆ **Tintin et le lac aux requins.**
*Jeu, sam, lun 15h, mar 17h :* ◆ **Les tortues ninja n°1.**
*Jeu, dim 16h45 :* ◆ **Mary Poppins.**
*Ven 15h, sam, lun 17h :* ◆ **Les Marrrtiens !.**
*Sam, lun 13h30 :* ◆ **Les 12 travaux d'Astérix.**
*Dim 13h30 :* ◆ **La flûte à 6 schtroumpfs.**
*Mer, mar 19h :* **Alexandre Nevski** (vo).
*Mer, dim 21h, sam 19h :* △ **Miller's crossing** (vo).
*Jeu, dim 19h15, mar 21h :* **Arizona junior** (vo).
*Jeu 21h :* **La mort aux trousses** (vo).
*Ven 18h45, lun 21h15 :* **Dersou Ouzala** (vo).
*Ven 21h15 :* **Gatsby le magnifique** (vo).
*Sam 21h, lun 18h45 :* **Excalibur** (vo)

*Mer, dim, mar 15h, ven 17h :*

**MAMAN, J'AI RATE L'AVION !**

**Salle 2 :**
*Mer, dim 13h30, ven 15h :* ◆ **Le triomphe de Babar.**
*Mer 17h, sam 13h30, mar 15h :* **Allo maman, c'est encore moi.**
*Jeu 13h30, sam 17h :* ◆ **La guerre des boutons.**
*Jeu, dim 17h :* **Chérie, j'ai rétréci les gosses.**
*Ven, lun 13h30 :* ◆ **Crin blanc et** ◆ **Le ballon rouge.**
*Ven, lun 17h :* ◆ **Fantasia.**
*Dim 15h, mar 13h30 :* ◆ **Tintin et le temple du soleil.**
*Mar 17h :* ◆ **L' histoire sans fin n°1.**
*Mer 19h, lun 21h :* **Quand Harry rencontre Sally** (vo).
*Mer 21h :* **La règle du jeu.**
*Jeu 19h :* □ **L' important, c'est d'aimer.**
*Jeu 21h :* **Hôtel du Nord.**
*Ven, mar 19h :* **L' équipée sauvage** (vo).
*Sam, mar 21h :* **Arsenic et vieilles dentelles** (vo).
*Dim 19h :* **Agent X 27**

*Mer, sam, lun 15h, jeu 15h15 :*

**CINOCHES**, carrefour de l'Odéon, 1, rue de Condé, M° Odéon, 46 33 10 82. (H). Pl. 35F. TR. 25F : lun + ET, CV et - 18 ans (sf sam, dim et fêtes).
1) *Tlj 19h20 :* **Green card** (vo).
*Tlj 21h30 :* **L' insoutenable légèreté de l'être** (vo).
*Jeu, sam, dim, mar 13h40 :* **Le mystère von Bulow** (vo).
*Tlj 16h :* ◆ **Cendrillon.**
*Tlj 19h55. Sam séance suppl. à 0h10 :* **La liste noire** (vo).

2) *Tlj 15h50 :* ◆ **Fantasia.**
*Tlj 17h30. Sam séance suppl. à 0h10 :* △ **Easy rider** (vo).
*Tlj 13h40 :* **Les liaisons dangereuses, de Frears** (vo).
*Mer, lun 13h40 :* **Le cercle des poètes disparus** (vo).
*Tlj 18h :* △ **Misery** (vo).
*Tlj 21h30 :* **The two Jakes** (vo)

---

**Grammar:** In official time, the hour is treated as a 60-minute whole: **14h15 = quatorze heures quinze, 17h30 = dix-sept heures trente, 22h45 = vingt-deux heures quarante-cinq.** Expressions such as **et quart, moins,** and **et demi(e)** are not used.

**C. Rendez-vous à 18h.** Invite a friend to go to the movies with you. Then make arrangements about where and when to meet.

*Modèle:*    *La Discrète* / devant le cinéma / 18h20
— *Est-ce que tu veux (voudrais) voir* La Discrète?
— *Mais oui. On dit* (people say) *que c'est un très bon film. À quelle heure est-ce que tu veux y aller?*
— *Il y a une séance à 18h20. On pourrait se retrouver devant le cinéma, vers 18 heures (six heures).*
— *D'accord. Rendez-vous à 18h (6h), devant le cinéma.*

1. *Le Silence des agneaux* / à la station de métro Denfert-Rochereau / 20h15
2. *Uranus* / devant le cinéma / 19h30
3. *Cinéma Paradiso* / au Café Royal / 18h
4. *La Vie des morts* / en face du cinéma / 21h

Ex. C: ⇄ Have two students model the conversation before dividing the class into pairs.

R·E·P·R·I·S·E

## Première étape

**D.** **Quel temps est-ce qu'il a fait?** Match the headlines with the weather descriptions.

Joie chez les agriculteurs

Trois maisons inondées!

Aéroport fermé

Accident de bateau à voile

35°! La France transpire!

Les skieurs se réjouissent!

Pas de soleil depuis 15 jours

*inondées:* flooded

*fermé:* closed

*bateau à voile:* sailboat

*transpirer:* to sweat

*se réjouir:* to be delighted

*depuis:* for

1. Il a fait du vent.
2. Il a fait du brouillard.
3. Il y a eu un orage.
4. Il a fait chaud.
5. Il a neigé.
6. Il a plu.
7. Le temps a été nuageux.

**E.   Un séjour à Paris.** *(A stay in Paris.)* Here is a paragraph from a letter you wrote to a friend last year explaining your plans for a visit to Paris. Now that you've returned from your trip, you want to tell your friend that you fulfilled your plans. Redo the paragraph by changing the italicized verbs to the **passé composé.** Start your story with **L'année dernière, j'ai visité Paris** *(Last year I visited Paris).*

L'année prochaine je *vais visiter* Paris. Avant de quitter les États-Unis, mes parents et moi, nous *allons étudier* le plan de la ville et mon père *va acheter* les billets d'avion. Je *vais* aussi *chercher* des renseignements sur Paris à la bibliothèque de mon université. Ma famille et moi, nous *allons quitter* New York le 25 juin et nous *allons traverser* l'Atlantique en avion. À Paris nous *allons commencer* notre visite par l'avenue des Champs-Élysées. Moi, je *vais visiter* le quartier des étudiants (le Quartier latin). Le soir, mon père et ma mère *vont visiter* Saint-Germain-des-Prés et moi, je *vais regarder* la télévision française. Nous *allons* aussi *manger* beaucoup de choses délicieuses. Nous *allons* beaucoup *aimer* Paris.

**F.   Et vous?** Répondez aux questions.

1.   Est-ce que vous étudiez beaucoup? Est-ce que vous avez étudié hier soir? Est-ce que vous allez étudier ce soir?
2.   D'habitude, est-ce que vous dînez à l'université, au restaurant ou à la maison? Où est-ce que vous avez dîné hier soir? Où est-ce que vous allez dîner ce soir?
3.   Est-ce que vous aimez voyager? Est-ce que vous avez fait un voyage récemment? Est-ce que vous allez faire un voyage l'année prochaine?
4.   Est-ce que vous prenez le petit déjeuner d'habitude? Est-ce que vous avez pris le petit déjeuner ce matin? Est-ce que vous allez prendre le petit déjeuner dimanche matin?

# S·T·R·U·C·T·U·R·E

## *Les adverbes et les prépositions désignant le passé*

| | |
|---|---|
| **La semaine dernière** j'ai visité Montmartre. | *Last week* I visited Montmartre. |
| Nous avons déjeuné ensemble **hier**. | We had lunch *yesterday*. |

The following time expressions are used to talk about an action or a condition in the past.

> **hier**   *yesterday*
> **hier matin (après-midi, soir)**   *yesterday morning (afternoon, evening)*
> **mercredi (samedi) dernier**   *last Wednesday (Saturday)*
> **le week-end dernier**   *last weekend*
> **la semaine dernière**   *last week*
> **le mois dernier**   *last month*
> **l'année dernière**   *last year*

avant hier  (day before yesterday)

The following expressions will enable you to express for how long you did something and how long ago something happened.

> **pendant une heure (deux jours, six ans)**   *for an hour (two days, six years)*
> **il y a une heure (deux mois, cinq ans)**   *an hour (two months, five years) ago*

Notice that time expressions are usually placed either at the beginning or at the end of the sentence.

▲  ▲  ▲

## APPLICATION

**G.** Remplacez les mots en italique et faites les changements nécessaires.

1. *Hier* nous avons eu un accident. (la semaine dernière / jeudi dernier / hier soir / l'année dernière)
2. Qu'est-ce que tu as fait *samedi dernier*? (hier après-midi / le mois dernier / la semaine dernière / il y a huit jours)
3. Ils ont été à Paris *la semaine dernière*. (il y a trois ans / le mois dernier / pendant deux semaines / il y a quinze jours)

**Follow-up,** Ex. H: Question-answer drill based on **pour-quoi/parce que.**
MODÈLE:—**Pourquoi est-ce que vous n'allez pas visiter la cathédrale?**
— **Parce que nous avons visité la cathédrale hier (la semaine dernière, il y a trois jours,** etc.). Suggestions: **acheter du chocolat, étudier à la bibliothèque, visiter le musée, prendre le déjeuner, parler à votre ami(e), télé-phoner à vos grands-parents.**

**H.** **Mais non!** Claire Maurant often contradicts what her brothers and sisters try to tell her parents. Use the expressions in parentheses to play the role of Claire.

*Modèles:*     Gérard a habité à Paris pendant deux ans. (un an)
*Mais non! Il a habité à Paris pendant un an.*

Claire va visiter la cathédrale demain. (hier)
*Mais non! J'ai visité la cathédrale hier.*

1. Hervé a été à Paris il y a quatre jours. (trois semaines)
2. Françoise va parler à ses parents cette semaine. (la semaine dernière)
3. Nous avons travaillé pendant cinq heures. (trois heures)
4. M. et Mme Beaulieu vont acheter une maison. (l'année dernière)
5. Nos cousins vont visiter le musée demain. (mardi dernier)
6. Claire va travailler ce soir. (hier soir)
7. Ses copines ont téléphoné hier. (il y a huit jours)
8. Les Leroux ont acheté leur voiture la semaine dernière. (le mois dernier)

**Student Tape:**
Chapitre 5
Segment 1

# PRONONCIATION   *La voyelle **u***

In French, the letter **u,** when not followed by another vowel or by the consonants **m** or **n** at the end of a word or before another consonant, is always pronounced in the same fashion. To learn to make the sound represented by the letter **u,** first pronounce the letter **i** (remember to spread your lips in a smile). Then, keeping the interior of your mouth in the same tense position, move your lips forward as if to whistle. There is no equivalent sound in English.

**I.** Read each word aloud, being careful to pronounce the **u** sound with your lips positioned as far forward as possible.

une / tu / fume / autobus / bureau / portugais / salut / vue / russe / musique / musée / sur / architecture / d'habitude

*musée d'Orsay, Paris*

*Verbs that move your body*

# S·T·R·U·C·T·U·R·E

## Le passé composé avec *être*

**Je suis sorti** hier soir.
**Nous sommes allés** au concert et ensuite à un café.
**Vous êtes restés** longtemps au café?
Non, **nous sommes rentrés** vers 11h30.

*I went out* last night.
*We went* to the concert and then to a cafe.
*Did you stay* at the cafe a long time?
No, *we got home* about 11:30.

To talk about past events, you have already learned to use the **passé composé** with the auxiliary verb **avoir**. In addition, some verbs use **être** as their auxiliary verb in the **passé composé.** The past participles of many of these verbs are formed in the regular manner (that is, **-er** becomes **-é**). Note, however, that the past participles of **descendre** and **sortir** are **descendu** and **sorti.** Here are some verbs conjugated with **être:**

| Infinitive | Past participle |
|---|---|
| aller | **allé** |
| arriver | **arrivé** |
| descendre | **descendu** |
| entrer | **entré** |
| monter | **monté** |
| rentrer *(to go home, to come home)* | **rentré** |
| rester | **resté** |
| retourner | **retourné** |
| sortir | **sorti** |

The past participle of a verb conjugated with **être** acts like an adjective. This means that it agrees in gender (masculine or feminine) and in number (singular or plural) with the subject of the verb. Notice the various possibilities in the first and second persons:

je **suis allé** / je **suis allée**
tu **es allé** / tu **es allée**
nous **sommes allés** / nous **sommes allées**
vous **êtes allé** / vous **êtes allée** / vous **êtes allés** / vous **êtes allées**

In the third person, each past participle has one possible form:

il **est allé**
elle **est allée**

ils **sont allés**
elles **sont allées**

▲  ▲  ▲

*Venir → venu*

## APPLICATION

**J.** Remplacez le sujet en italique et faites les changements nécessaires.

1. *Hervé* est allé au cinéma. (Jeanne / je / nous / les autres / vous / tu)
2. *Yvonne* n'est pas sortie. (Marc / Sylvie et Alain / nous / je / tu / vous)
3. Est-ce que *vous* êtes descendus à Châtelet? (Monique / vos amis / elles / tu / Éric)

**K. Oui ou non?** You're part of a student group on a tour of Paris. All of the students have dispersed, leaving you the only one to answer the group leader's questions. Answer **oui** or **non** according to the cues in parentheses.

1. Est-ce que Nicole et Marie-Claire sont sorties? (oui)
2. Est-ce que Madeleine est allée à la tour Eiffel? (non / au Louvre)
3. Est-ce que Didier est resté dans sa chambre? (oui)
4. Est-ce que Bénédicte est déjà rentrée? (non / pas encore [*not yet*])
5. Est-ce que Philippe et sa sœur sont arrivés? (oui)
6. Est-ce qu'Anne et Chantal sont montées dans leur chambre? (non)
7. Est-ce que Sylvie est allée au théâtre? (oui)
8. Est-ce que tu es allé(e) au Quartier latin? (non)

**L. Les cousins.** Each time that Claire Maurant asks her cousins, Mireille and Jean-Francis Loiseau, a question, they say that the activities were already carried out.

*Modèle:*     Est-ce que vous voulez aller à la piscine aujourd'hui? (hier)
*Non, nous sommes allés à la piscine hier.*

1. Mireille, tu veux aller à Montmartre ce soir? (hier soir)
2. Est-ce que tes parents vont rentrer de leur voyage demain? (mardi dernier)
3. Est-ce que nos cousins suisses vont arriver demain? (il y a trois jours)
4. Est-ce que vous voulez aller au théâtre cette semaine? (la semaine dernière)
5. Jean-Francis, tu veux sortir ce soir? (tous les soirs la semaine dernière)
6. Mireille, est-ce que ton ami américain Jim va bientôt retourner à New York? (déjà)
7. Est-ce que nous allons au Louvre cet après-midi? (déjà / trois fois cette semaine)
8. Est-ce que votre père va bientôt rentrer? (il y a une heure)

**M. La journée de Claire.** Use the verbs to tell what Claire Maurant did last Wednesday. Be careful to distinguish verbs conjugated with **être** from those conjugated with **avoir.**

*Modèles:*     quitter la maison
*Elle a quitté la maison.*

aller au bureau de tabac
*Elle est allée au bureau de tabac.*

1. aller à la station de métro
2. prendre le métro
3. descendre à l'île de la Cité
4. visiter le Palais de Justice
5. rester au musée jusqu'à deux heures et demie
6. rentrer à la maison
7. monter dans sa chambre
8. téléphoner à une amie
9. retrouver l'amie près du Grand Rex
10. aller voir *La Mouche*

## ▲ ▲ ▲ ▲ ▲ ▲ ▲ ▲ ▲ Débrouillons-nous! ▲ ▲ ▲ ▲ ▲ ▲ ▲ ▲ ▲

*Petite révision de l'étape*

**N. Mon week-end.** Using the verbs you have already learned, describe to another student what you did during a memorable weekend. (If you prefer, you may describe the weekend of a friend or a family member.) Use both verbs conjugated with **avoir** and verbs conjugated with **être.**

**O. Allons au cinéma!** Using *L'Officiel des spectacles (pp. 187–188),* make arrangements with another student to go to the movies. Be sure to discuss the kind of film you would like to see, to choose a film, and to arrange where and when you will meet.

Ex. N: ⇄

**Reminder:** The following verbs you know are conjugated with **être: aller, arriver, descendre, entrer, monter, rentrer, rester, retourner, sortir.**

Ex. O: ⇄

Transparency:
5-3 (alternative excerpt from *Pariscope*)

**À faire chez vous:**
**CAHIER, Chapitre 5 / 2e** étape

text audio
CD1-38

# TROISIÈME ÉTAPE

## Point de départ

▼▼▼▼▼▼▼▼▼▼▼▼▼▼▼

**Transparencies:**
5-4, 5-5 (sports and activities)

**Instructor's Tape:**
On pourrait faire une excursion!

*On pourrait:* We could

split up / Some (of them) . . . , the others . . . / singer

they all met (again)

**Suggestion, Point de départ:** (1) Use the transparency to present sports. Do. Ex. A with the transparency. (2) Have students listen to the conversation on the Instructor's Tape.
have a game of tennis

to win

reconstructed castle on a mountain peak about 50 km southwest of Strasbourg

crazy

difficult

go for a hike

mountain range in eastern France

outdoors

### On pourrait faire une excursion!

Samedi soir Claire et ses amis **se sont séparés. Les uns** sont allés écouter du jazz, **les autres** sont allés voir un **chansonnier** à un café-théâtre. Puis **ils se sont tous retrouvés** dimanche matin pour refaire des projets.

CLAIRE: Il fait un temps splendide aujourd'hui! Qu'est-ce qu'on va faire?

ANDRÉ: Vous voulez jouer au golf? Je peux téléphoner pour réserver.

THIERRY: Ou, si vous préférez, pourquoi ne pas **faire une partie de tennis?**

CLAUDETTE: Non, non, non. Vous autres garçons, vous voulez toujours **gagner.** Moi, je veux m'amuser.

CLAIRE: Écoutez! J'ai une idée. On va faire une excursion... au **Haut-Kœnigsbourg.**

CLAUDETTE: Voilà. Une jolie petite promenade à vélo.

THIERRY: Mais vous êtes **folles!** À vélo! C'est loin. C'est très **difficile.**

CLAIRE: Eh bien, si vous voulez, on prend la voiture, on apporte un pique-nique, on visite le château, puis on **fait une randonnée** dans les **Vosges.**

ANDRÉ: Ah! Super! Allons-y!

### Les activités **en plein air**

ALLONS-Y!
Video Program

**ACTE 5**
UNE EXCURSION

**QUESTIONS DE FOND**
1. Nommez quatre activités qu'on peut pratiquer au Club Med.
2. Quelle est l'activité la plus pratiquée au Club Med?
3. Qui choisit les activités pour les clients?

faire du ski (de piste)

faire du patinage

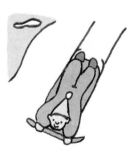

faire de la luge

nager, se baigner

faire de la planche à voile

faire du ski nautique

faire de la voile

jouer au tennis

jouer au foot(ball)

faire des randonnées *(f.pl.)*

aller à la pêche

**Le savez-vous?**

▲▲▲▲▲▲▲▲▲▲▲▲▲▲▲▲

**Which of the following is the most popular partici- pant sport in France?**
a. bicycling
b. aerobics
c. skiing
d. swimming

Réponse ▲▲▲

*ennouleu*
*dangereaux*
*amusant  amusant*

*heureaux   heureuse*

*facile*
*dificile*
*intéressant  intéressante.*

Et aussi...

faire du **ski de fond**    cross country skiing
jouer au golf
jouer au basket
faire du jogging
faire de l'aérobic *(m.)*

**Vocabulary:** Some addi- tional outdoor activities in- clude: **aller à la chasse** *(to go hunting),* **faire de la plongée sous-marine** *(to go scuba diving),* **faire de l'alpinisme** *(to go moun- tain climbing),* **jouer aux boules ou à la pétanque** *(to play bocce ball),* **faire du canoë / du kayak** *(to go canoeing / kayaking).*

## À VOUS! (Exercices de vocabulaire)

**A.  Vous et les sports.** Give your personal reactions to or experiences with each of the activities mentioned below.

*Modèle:*   faire de l'aérobic
*Je fais souvent de l'aérobic.* or *Je voudrais bien faire de l'aéro- bic un jour.* or *J'ai fait de l'aérobic ce matin.* or *Je n'ai jamais fait de l'aérobic.*

1.  faire du jogging   2.  nager   3.  aller à la pêche   4.  faire des randonnées
5.  faire du ski (de piste, de fond)   6.  faire de la planche à voile   7.  jouer au golf   8.  faire du ski nautique   9.  jouer au basket   10.  faire de la voile

Ex. B: ○

*je n'ai pas le temps*

**B.** **Alors, qu'est-ce qu'on va faire?** Make plans with some of your class-mates to do one of the activities mentioned for each type of weather. Express your feelings about the possibilities. Then come to an agreement about which activity, when, and where.

1. Il fait très chaud: nager, faire de la voile, faire de la planche à voile, faire du ski nautique
2. Il a neigé: faire du ski (de piste, de fond), faire de la luge
3. Il fait beau: jouer au golf, jouer au tennis, jouer au basket
4. Il fait frais: faire du jogging, aller à la pêche, faire une randonnée

▲▲▲ C

# R·E·P·R·I·S·E

*Deuxième étape*

**C.** **Je suis allé(e) en ville hier après-midi.** Using the verbs in the drawing, describe what these people did yesterday.

*Modèle:*      je      *J'ai quitté l'hôtel à 12h30, je suis allé(e)...*

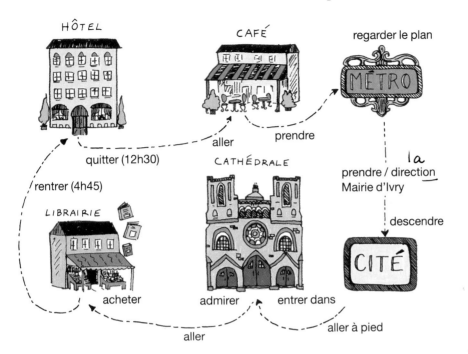

*etre vs. avoir*

*nous avons admiré*
*nous sommes allé*
*nous avons acheté*
*nous sommes rentré*

1. je   2. Jean-Jacques   3. ma sœur et moi, nous   4. mes amis

*Ils ont quitté*
*"E" Ils sont allé*

**D. Le calendrier de Massyla Fodéba.** Look at Massyla Fodéba's calendar for last week and answer the questions about his activities. Today is Monday the fifteenth.

*Modèle:*  Quand est-ce que Massyla a déjeuné avec sa famille?
*Il a déjeuné avec sa famille hier après-midi (hier à midi).*

| | | |
|---|---|---|
| Lundi | 8 | chez le dentiste |
| Mardi | 9 | cinéma avec Raoul |
| Mercredi | 10 | |
| Jeudi | 11 | bibliothèque (3h–7h) |
| Vendredi | 12 | rendez-vous avec le professeur Arnault |
| Samedi | 13 | dîner chez les Piéron |
| Dimanche | 14 | déjeuner en famille |
| | | cinéma avec Maryse |

1. Quand est-ce qu'il est allé à la bibliothèque?
2. Pendant combien de temps est-ce qu'il est resté à la bibliothèque?
3. Quand est-ce qu'il a dîné avec les Piéron?
4. Quand est-ce qu'il a eu rendez-vous avec son professeur? (il y a ___ jours)
5. Combien de fois *(times)* est-ce qu'il est allé au cinéma la semaine dernière?
6. Quand est-ce qu'il est allé au cinéma avec Maryse?
7. Quand est-ce qu'il est allé chez le dentiste?

*Il y a deux jours.*
*Avant hier.*

# PRONONCIATION    *Les combinaisons **ai** et **au***

The combinations **ai** and **au** are pronounced as single vowel sounds in French. The letters **ai** sound like the *e* in the English word *melt*. The combination **au** is always pronounced like the *o* in the English word *hope*.

**E.**  Read each word aloud, being careful to pronounce the **ai** combination as a single sound.

j'aime / française / anglais / frais / je vais / maître / semaine / il fait

**F.**  Now read each word aloud, being careful to pronounce the **au** combination as a single sound.

au / aussi / auto / autobus / de Gaulle / gauche / aujourd'hui / haut

# S·T·R·U·C·T·U·R·E

*Le passé composé des verbes pronominaux*

| | |
|---|---|
| **Je me suis trompée.** | *I made a mistake. (I was mistaken.)* |
| **Hélène ne s'est pas disputée** avec son frère. | *Hélène did not have a fight (an argument) with her brother.* |
| **Ils se sont parlé** au téléphone hier soir et tout va bien. | *They spoke (to each other) on the phone last night and everything is OK.* |

In the **passé composé**, *all* pronominal verbs are conjugated with the auxiliary verb **être**. The reflexive or reciprocal pronoun is placed directly in front of the auxiliary verb:

| *se tromper* | |
|---|---|
| je **me suis trompé(e)** | nous **nous sommes trompés(es)** |
| tu **t'es trompé(e)** | vous **vous êtes trompé(e)(s)(es)** |
| il, on **s'est trompé** | ils **se sont trompés** |
| elle **s'est trompée** | elles **se sont trompées** |

The past participle usually agrees in gender and number with the reflexive or reciprocal pronoun (which stands for the subject).

To form the negative, place **ne . . . pas** around the auxiliary verb:     *and reflexive pronoun*

Je **ne** me suis **pas** bien amusé hier soir.
Elles **ne** se sont **pas** disputées.

▲  ▲  ▲

# APPLICATION

**G.** Remplacez le sujet en italique et faites les changements nécessaires.

1. *Je* me suis bien amusé hier soir. (Marie / nous / les garçons / vous / tu / on)
2. *Elle* ne s'est pas trompée. (tu / les autres / je / vous / Henri / nous)
3. *Ils* se sont disputés? (vous / nous / les autres / Jeanne et ses parents)

**H. Pourquoi (pas)?** Say that if the following people are or are not doing something, it is because of what they have previously done, as indicated in parentheses.

*Modèle:*   Ton frère est toujours au lit? (se coucher à 1h du matin)
*C'est parce qu'il s'est couché à 1h du matin.*

1. Tu te couches déjà? (se coucher à minuit hier soir)   Je me suis coucher
2. Martine et Charles ne se parlent pas? (se disputer la semaine dernière)   Ils se sont disputé
3. Tu ne téléphones pas à Robert ce matin? (se parler hier)   nous nous sommes parlé hier
4. Tes frères ne veulent pas aller au festival? (ne pas s'amuser l'année dernière)   ne se sont pas s'amuser
5. Tu as envie d'aller danser ce soir? Tu n'es pas fatigué(e)? (se reposer cet après-midi)   je me suis reposé
6. Comment! Jean-Pierre n'est pas à Lyon? Il est à Grenoble! (se tromper de train)   il s.'est trompé
7. Tu veux te reposer un peu? (se lever de très bonne heure ce matin)   Je me suis levé
8. Comment! Anne-Marie aime faire du jogging? (s'acheter un Walkman)   elle s'est acheté

**I. Ils se sont bien amusés.** Using the verbs suggested, recount the day that Michel Kerguézec spent with his friend François. Fill in appropriate details, such as times, food, etc.

*Modèle:*   s'amuser bien
*Michel et son ami François se sont bien amusés (vendredi dernier). Michel...*

s'est levé                        ils se sont parlé
1. se lever   2. téléphoner à   3. se parler pendant   4. inviter ____ à aller
5. se retrouver   6. décider de   7. se tromper de jour *(to go on the wrong day)*   8. décider de   9. aller   10. retourner chez   11. jouer aux cartes
12. rentrer   13. manger   14. se coucher                   ils ont joué
ils sont rentré   Il a mangé   il s'est couché

Now recount the day's activities from Michel's point of view.

*Modèle:*   *François et moi, nous nous sommes bien amusés (vendredi dernier). Je...*

# ▲▲▲▲▲▲▲▲▲▲▲ Débrouillons-nous! ▲▲▲▲▲▲▲▲▲▲▲

*Petite révision de l'étape*

Ex. J: ⇄

**J.   Échange.** Compare what you did yesterday with another student's activities. Use both pronominal and nonpronominal verbs.

> *Modèle:*      —*Hier matin je me suis levé(e) à 7h. Et toi?*
> —*Moi, je suis resté(e) au lit jusqu'à 9h. Etc.*

Ex. K: △ or ☐

**K.   Et s'il pleut? Et s'il fait superbeau?** With two or three classmates, plan some outdoor activities for the coming weekend. In your discussion, consider various weather possibilities. Work out as many details as you can.

**À faire chez vous:
CAHIER, Chapitre 5 / 3ᵉ étape**

**À faire chez vous:
Student Tape**

Now that you've completed the first three **étapes** of **Chapitre 5,** do Segment 2 of the STUDENT TAPE. See **CAHIER, Chapitre 5, *Écoutons!,*** for exercises that accompany this segment.

# QUATRIÈME ÉTAPE

▼▼▼▼▼▼▼▼▼▼▼▼▼

## L·E·C·T·U·R·E

Instructor's Tape:
Déjeuner du matin

**Prereading:** Have students free-associate feelings, thoughts, images about breakfast. Encourage them to imagine a variety of moods.

## Déjeuner du matin

*There is more to reading a poem than just understanding the meaning of the words. The full meaning of a poem depends on the relationship between what is said and what is not said, and it is up to the reader to complete the unsaid part with his or her own thoughts and feelings. Here is a poem in very simple language about an ordinary event—breakfast. Read it several times, then do the two exercises that follow: the first deals with what is said; the second, with what is unsaid.*

## Déjeuner du matin

Il a mis[1] le café
Dans la tasse[2]
Il a mis le lait
Dans la tasse de café
Il a mis le sucre
Dans le café au lait
Avec la petite cuiller[3]
Il a tourné
Il a bu le café au lait
Et il a reposé[4] la tasse
Sans me parler

Il a allumé[5]
Une cigarette
Il a fait des ronds
Avec la fumée[6]
Il a mis les cendres[7]
Dans le cendrier[8]
Sans me parler
Sans me regarder
Il s'est levé
Il a mis
Son chapeau[9] sur sa tête

Il a mis
Son manteau de pluie[10]
Parce qu'il pleuvait[11]
Et il est parti
Sous[12] la pluie
Sans une parole[13]
Sans me regarder
Et moi j'ai pris
Ma tête dans ma main
Et j'ai pleuré.[14]

Jacques Prévert, *Paroles* © 1949, Éditions Gallimard

1. put   2. cup   3. spoon   4. put down again   5. lit   6. smoke   7. ashes   8. ashtray   9. hat
10. raincoat   11. was raining   12. in   13. word   14. cried

# APPRÉCIATION

**A.   Qu'est-ce qui s'est passé?** *(What happened?)* Using the expressions suggested below, summarize the "events" of the poem.

*Modèle:*     prendre le petit déjeuner
              *On a pris le petit déjeuner. Il…*

*ils ne se sont pas parlé      il est parti*

prendre du café au lait / fumer / se parler / se regarder / partir *(to leave,* conjugated with **être)** / pleurer *elle a pleuré*

**B.   Qui? Pourquoi?** In English, discuss with your classmates the story behind this breakfast. Who are these two people? Where are they? What has happened? What is happening? Why? Does more than one explanation make sense?

*Le Petit-déjeuner Buffet
La Soupière*

*à partir de 7 heures*

*24 F Prix net*

*homework*

## R·E·P·R·I·S·E

*Troisième étape*

**C. Il y a quelques semaines.** (*A few weeks ago.*) Claire Maurant describes one of the days she spent in Paris with her cousins Mireille and Jean-Francis Loiseau. Use the **passé composé** to recreate her sentences, making sure to distinguish between pronominal and nonpronominal verbs.

*Modèle:*    Jean-Francis et Mireille / se lever à 7h
*Ce jour-là* (that day) *Jean-Francis et Mireille se sont levés à 7h.*

1. je / se lever à 7h30    *je me suis levé*
2. je / prendre une douche (*shower*)    *j'ai pris*
3. Jean-Francis / faire du jogging    *il a fait*
4. Mireille et moi / faire du yoga    *nous avons fait*
5. Jean-Francis et Mireille / se préparer pour aller au travail    *ils se sont préparé*
6. nous / déjeuner ensemble    *Nous avons de déjeuné*
7. ils / se dépêcher pour prendre leur autobus    *ils se sont dépêché*
8. je / rester à leur appartement jusqu'à 10h    *je suis resté chez eux*
9. je / faire des courses    *j'ai fait des courses*
10. je / s'acheter un nouveau maillot de bain (*bathing suit*)    *je me suis acheté*
11. Mireille et moi / se retrouver à 12h30 pour déjeuner    *nous nous sommes retrou*
12. Jean-Francis / aller chercher sa fiancée Jocelyne à la gare    *il est allé*
13. Jean-Francis et Jocelyne / s'embrasser    *ils se sont embrassé*
14. ils / rentrer chez Jean-Francis    *ils sont rentré*
15. Mireille et moi / retrouver les deux amoureux vers 6h    *nous avons retrouvé*
16. nous / dîner ensemble au restaurant    *nous avons dîné*
17. Mireille et moi / s'amuser à écouter des disques compacts    *nous nous sommes amusé*
18. Jean-Francis et Jocelyne / se parler    *ils se sont parlé*
19. je / se coucher vers 11h    *je me suis couché*
20. les autres / ne pas se coucher avant minuit    *ils ne se sont pas couché*

Ex. D: ⇄ or ◯

**D. Un jour de pluie... un jour de neige... un jour de soleil...** Tell your classmate(s) about a particularly enjoyable day you remember (or imagine). Choose a day in which you participated in one or more outdoor activities. In your description, include the weather and your routine activities as well as sports.

*Modèle:*    *Il a fait très froid ce jour-là et il a neigé. Je me suis levé(e)...*

▲ ▲ ▲ ▲ ▲ ▲ ▲ ▲ ▲ ▲ ▲ ▲ ▲ ▲ ▲ ▲ ▲ ▲ ▲ ▲ ▲ ▲ ▲ ▲ ▲ ▲

# Point d'arrivée

**À faire chez vous:**
**Student Tape**

**CAHIER, Chapitre 5:**
*Rédigeons! / Travail de fin de chapitre* (including STUDENT TAPE, Chapitre 5, Segment 3)

*Activités orales*

## Exprimons-nous!

For recounting a sequence of activities, the following expressions are useful:

**d'abord (premièrement)**      **ensuite (puis)**      **enfin**

**D'abord,** j'ai fait des courses: je suis allé au bureau de poste, j'ai acheté un livre pour mon cours d'histoire et je suis allé chercher de l'argent à la banque. **Ensuite,** je me suis promené dans le parc, **puis** j'ai pris quelque chose à boire au café. **Enfin,** je suis rentré à la maison.

E.   **Ma journée.** Describe your activities, from the time you got up to the time you went to bed, on a recent school day or on a day when you didn't have any classes.

F.   **Au café.** You and some friends meet downtown in a cafe. Greet each other, order something to drink and eat, and then use **L'Officiel des spectacles** listing on pages 187 and 188 to decide on a movie to see and when to see it.

G.   **Un week-end.** Tell your classmates about one of your favorite weekends. If possible, bring in photos and describe your activities and those of your friends (or family members).

H.   **Un jour de fête.** You and your friends are making plans for an upcoming holiday. Plan a busy schedule of activities, including sports, movies, and the like. Be detailed in your plans—determine time, place, etc.

Suggestion, Ex. E: Have students work in pairs. Then create new pairs so that on the second round each student compares his/her routine to that of the partner in the first round.

Ex. F: △ or □

Ex. G: ○

Ex. H: ○

# PORTRAIT

*Claire Maurant*
*Strasbourg, France*

Je suis alsacienne. J'habite à Strasbourg avec mes parents, mes deux frères et ma sœur. Je travaille comme comptable pour une société textile. J'aime bien mon travail, mais j'adore passer les week-ends avec mes amis. Je suis assez sportive. Je joue un peu au tennis, mais je préfère les sports moins compétitifs. Il y a quelques week-ends, par exemple, on est allé faire du camping en Allemagne. On a amené nos vélos. Il a fait très beau: on a fait des randonnées à pied et à vélo, on s'est baigné et on a fait du canoë. On s'est bien amusé.

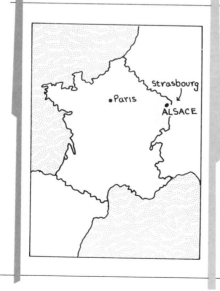

# Profil

*L'Alsace*

**SITUATION:** à l'est de la France, sur le Rhin, près de l'Allemagne
**POPULATION:** 1 566 000 habitants
**VILLES PRINCIPALES:** Strasbourg, Mulhouse, Colmar
**CLIMAT:** hivers froids, étés chauds, beaucoup de pluie
**ÉCONOMIE:** centre commercial et industriel
**LIEUX D'INTÉRÊT:** les Vosges (montagnes), Obernai et Riquewihr (villages avec des maisons sculptées)

**HISTOIRE:** Objet de dispute entre pays voisins, l'Alsace est tour à tour française (1681–1871), allemande (1871–1919), française (1919–1940), allemande (1940–1944), française (1944– ).

**COMMENTAIRE:**   L'Alsace est une province très pittoresque, célèbre pour ses nids de cigogne *(stork nests)*, son architecture et ses particularités linguistiques (à cause de son histoire, beaucoup de gens parlent alsacien, un dialecte germanique).

**À discuter:** Have any regions of the United States had a history similar to that of Alsace? If so, which ones and how? If not, why not?

## L·E·X·I·Q·U·E

### Pour se débrouiller

*Pour parler du temps qu'il fait*

Quel temps fait-il?                     Il fait du soleil.
Il est nuageux.                         Il fait du vent.
Il fait beau.                           Il y a un orage.
Il fait bon.                            Il y a du verglas.
Il fait chaud.                          Il neige.
Il fait frais.                          Il pleut.
Il fait froid.                          Le ciel est couvert.
Il fait mauvais.                        La température est de ___ degrés.
Il fait du brouillard.                  Il fait ___ degrés dehors.

*Pour exprimer ses préférences à propos du temps*

J'aime (je n'aime pas) la pluie (la neige).
Je supporte bien (mal, mieux) le froid (la chaleur).

*Pour demander et donner la date*

Nous sommes le combien aujourd'hui?     Nous sommes le 5 avril.
Quelle date sommes-nous?                Aujourd'hui, c'est le 5 avril.
Quelle est la date aujourd'hui?         C'est aujourd'hui le 5 avril.
Quelle est la date de ___?              Je suis né(e) au mois de ___.

*Pour énumérer une suite d'actions*

d'abord                                 puis
ensuite                                 enfin

*Pour situer des actions dans le passé*

lundi (mardi, etc.) dernier
lundi (mardi, etc.) après-midi
la semaine dernière
le mois dernier
l'année dernière
le lendemain

### Thèmes et contextes

*Les mois de l'année*

janvier                                 juillet
février                                 août
mars                                    septembre
avril                                   octobre
mai                                     novembre
juin                                    décembre

*Les saisons de l'année*

le printemps (au printemps)          l'automne (en automne)
l'été (en été)                       l'hiver (en hiver)

*Les films*

une comédie                          un film de science-fiction
un drame psychologique               un film fantastique
un film d'aventure                   un film policier
un film d'épouvante                  une séance

*Les activités sportives*

aller à la pêche                     jouer au basket
se baigner                              au foot(ball)
faire de l'aérobic (*m.*)               au golf
   du jogging             au tennis
   de la luge          nager
   du patinage
   de la planche à voile
   des randonnées (*f.pl.*)
   du ski (de piste)
   du ski de fond
   du ski nautique
   de la voile

## Vocabulaire général

*Verbes*

avoir horreur de                     sortir
se disputer                          se tromper
gagner

ALLONS-Y!
Video Program

ACTE 5
UNE EXCURSION

**VOCABULAIRE**
la planche à voile
  *windsurfing board*
la voile   *sailing*
le tennis   *tennis*
le golfe   *golf*
le trapèze volant
  *the flying trapeze*

*Madame Thibaudet*
*Bordeaux (Gironde),*
*France*

—Ah, Madame Thibaudet. Quel plaisir de vous voir! Vous allez en ville?
—Oui, j'ai des courses à faire. Vous aussi, Monsieur Monnet?

# Allons faire les courses!

## OBJECTIVES

**In this chapter, you will learn:**

- to ask for information and make purchases in stores;
- to choose the right store when making a purchase;
- to express quantities;
- to use a variety of expressions to say what you want to buy;
- to understand information presented by salespeople;
- to read ads about a variety of products.

**CHAPTER SUPPORT MATERIALS** (STUDENT)

**Cahier:** pp. 145–164

 **Student Tape:** Chapitre 6 Segments 1, 2, 3

**CHAPTER SUPPORT MATERIALS** (INSTRUCTOR)

 **Transparencies:** 6-1 through 6-6

 **Instructor's Tape:** Chapitre 6, Text, pp. 212, 234, 248

 **SYSTÈME-D** *software:* Writing activities for this chapter are found in the **Cahier:** Ex. V (p. 154).

 **Multimedia:** See the Resource Manual for correlation to our multimedia product.

## ALLONS-Y!
### Video Program

**ACTE 6**
SCÈNE 1: LES COURSES
SCÈNE 2: AU CENTRE COMMERCIAL

▶ Première étape    Chez les petits commerçants
▶ Deuxième étape    Au supermarché
▶ Troisième étape    Au centre commercial
▶ Quatrième étape    Lecture: Des produits alimentaires

**Instructor's Tape:**
Chez les petits
commerçants

**Transparencies:**
6-1a, 6-1b, 6-2a, 6-2b
(drawings of items
found in a **boulan-
gerie,** a **pâtisserie,**
and a **charcuterie**)

**Vocabulary:** To enable you
to state your personal likes
and dislikes, this chapter
contains a great deal of
vocabulary. From each
major category of words,
select the ones that you
are likely to use most
often. For example, you
are not expected to learn
the vocabulary for every
kind of vegetable, but you
should learn to say the
items that you particularly
like and dislike.

to do her shopping
bread

was it better

# PREMIÈRE ÉTAPE

## Point de départ

*Chez les petits commerçants*

Ce matin, Mme Thibaudet est allée en ville **faire ses courses.** À la boulangerie, elle a acheté du **pain**—une baguette et un pain de campagne.

Ensuite, elle a traversé la rue pour aller à la pâtisserie. Là, elle a hésité:
est-ce qu'**il valait mieux** acheter une tarte, des tartelettes ou des gâteaux?
Après quelques instants elle a pris sa décision. Elle a acheté une tartelette au
citron et une religieuse pour son dessert.

À la boulangerie, on peut acheter:

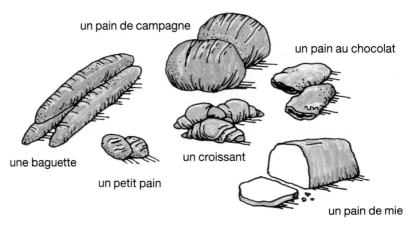

un pain de campagne

un pain au chocolat

une baguette

un petit pain

un croissant

un pain de mie

À la pâtisserie, on peut acheter:

un millefeuille   une religieuse   une tarte aux abricots

une tartelette au citron   une tarte aux pommes   un éclair

un gâteau au chocolat   une tarte aux fraises

**Vocabulary:** The word **pâtisserie** may refer to either a pastry shop or the pastries made and sold there.

**Supplementary Vocabulary, Pâtisserie: un baba au rhum** *(rum pastry)*, **un gâteau aux amandes** *(almond cake)*, **un gâteau moka, des petits fours** *(small pastries of all flavors)*, **une tarte aux cerises** *(cherry pie).*

Après la pâtisserie, Mme Thibaudet est allée à **la charcuterie.**

delicatessen

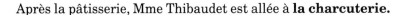

de la salade de thon

de la salade de tomates

du saucisson   du pâté   du jambon   des saucisses *(f.pl.)*   de la salade de concombres

32F LE KILO   39F95 LE KILO   54F50 LE KILO   29F LE KILO   15F LE KILO   49F LE KILO   17F LE KILO

**Vocabulary:** Note that **saucisson** means *salami* and **saucisse** means *sausage.*

—Bonjour, Madame Thibaudet. Comment allez-vous aujourd'hui?
—Bonjour, Madame Fernand. Ça va pas mal, et vous?
—Assez bien, merci. Qu'est-ce que vous désirez aujourd'hui?
—D'abord, **il me faut** du pâté—**assez** pour trois personnes.
—Très bien. Voilà. Et avec ça?
—**Donnez-moi** six **tranches** de jambon. Ce jambon-ci.
—Et avec ça?
—**Je prends** aussi une douzaine de tranches de saucisson. Des tranches très **fines.** C'est tout.
—Bon. Le pâté, 12F; le jambon, 25F; et le saucisson, 15F. Ça fait 52F. Merci bien et au revoir, Madame.
—Au revoir, Madame.

I need / enough

give me / slices

I'll take
thin

# Note culturelle

In France, it is still common for people to shop for food in small neighborhood stores where each shopkeeper **(le petit commerçant)** specializes in a particular kind of food.

Bakery shops often specialize either in bread **(une boulangerie)** or in pastry **(une pâtisserie).** However, many stores combine both **(une boulangerie-pâtisserie).** Since the French are known for their excellent bread and pastries, several of these shops are usually found in every neighborhood. Bakery shops are typically open from 7 or 8 A.M. until 1 P.M. and then again from 4 P.M. until 7 P.M. They are often closed on Monday morning. Most French people buy their bread fresh every morning.

**La charcuterie** is somewhat like an American delicatessen because you can buy a variety of prepared foods, particularly salads and some hot dishes. The **charcuterie** also sells ham and other cooked pork products, such as sausages, salami, ham, and pâté. When shopping in a **charcuterie,** you may buy meats by the slice **(une tranche)** or you may simply specify the number of people you're planning to serve **(du pâté pour quatre personnes).** The **charcutier (charcutière)** will then help you determine how much you should buy.

**Questions:** How frequently do you buy bread? What is the difference between French and American bread? What kinds of stores do you go to when you want to buy prepared foods?

# À VOUS! (Exercices de vocabulaire)

**A.   C'est combien?** You play the role of a shopkeeper and one of your class-mates plays a customer. Tell how much he/she has to pay for each item in the drawings.

Ex. A: ⇄

*Modèle:*

—*Une baguette, s'il vous plaît.*
—*Une baguette? Ça fait deux francs cinquante.*

1.   2.   3.   4.

5.   6.   7.   8.

9.   10.   11.   12.

Ex. B: ⇄

**B.   Il me faut...** *(I need . . .)* Use the cues to tell the shopkeeper what you need.

*Modèle:*     1 livre / salade de concombres
              *Il me faut une livre de salade de concombres.*

1.   1 livre / salade de tomates
2.   4 tranches / jambon
3.   10 tranches / saucisson
4.   6 saucisses
5.   1 livre / salade de thon
6.   3 tranches / pâté

**Vocabulary,** Ex. B: France uses the metric system of weights and measures. The basic unit of weight is the kilogram **(un kilo),** which equals one thou-sand grams **(un gramme).** Half a kilogram **(un demi-kilo)** is also called **une livre** *(a pound)*. However, because a kilogram is approximately 2.2 American pounds, a French **livre** is a little more than an American pound. The basic unit of measurement for liquids is the liter **(un litre),** which is roughly equivalent to a quart.

**C.  Chez les petits commerçants.** Use the cues to roleplay making purchases with one of your classmates. One of you is the customer; the other is the shopkeeper.

*Modèles:*     1 pain de campagne  /  2F50
—*Vous désirez?*
—*Je voudrais un pain de campagne. C'est combien?*
—*Un pain de campagne, c'est deux francs cinquante.*

1 livre  /  salade de thon  /  15F
—*Vous désirez?*
—*Je voudrais une livre de salade de thon. C'est combien?*
—*La salade de thon, c'est quinze francs la livre.*

1.  3 millefeuilles  /  8F la pièce
2.  1 baguette  /  2F50
3.  1 gâteau au chocolat  /  49F
4.  5 éclairs  /  6F50 la pièce
5.  1 tarte aux abricots  /  64F
6.  1 livre  /  jambon  /  26F la livre
7.  1 livre  /  salade de tomates  /  8F
8.  3 saucisses  /  5F30 la saucisse

## S·T·R·U·C·T·U·R·E

### Les adjectifs démonstratifs *(ce, cet, cette, ces)*

| | |
|---|---|
| Je vais prendre **ce** pain de campagne. | I'll take *this* round loaf of bread. |
| Et aussi **cette** baguette et **ces** croissants. | And also *this* bread and *these* croissants. |

The demonstrative adjective is used to point out specific things. It has three singular forms that are equivalent to the English words *this* or *that:*

**ce**      masculine singular before a pronounced consonant (**ce livre**)

**cet**     masculine singular before a vowel or vowel sound (**cet͜ hôtel**)

**cette**   feminine singular (**cette maison**)

The demonstrative adjective has only one plural form, which is equivalent to the English words *these* or *those:*

**ces**     plural (**ces fraises, ces fruits**)

The **s** of **ces** is silent, except before a vowel or a vowel sound (**ces͜ amis, ces͜ hôtels**).

## APPLICATION

**D.** Replace the definite article with the demonstrative adjective.

*Modèle:*   la tartelette au citron
*cette tartelette au citron*

1. le pâté
2. les petits pains
3. l'hôtel
4. les saucisses
5. la baguette
6. le gâteau
7. l'étudiante
8. la tarte
9. l'étudiant
10. les croissants
11. le jambon
12. l'appareil-photo
13. l'église
14. les éclairs
15. le pain de campagne

**E.   C'est combien?** Find out the price of each item. Use the demonstrative adjective in your question.

*Modèle:*   pain de campagne
*C'est combien, ce pain de campagne?*

**À la boulangerie-pâtisserie**

1. baguette
2. pain de campagne
3. éclairs
4. croissants
5. gâteau

**À la charcuterie**

6. saucisses
7. salade de thon
8. jambon
9. saucisson
10. pâté

**À la Fnac**

11. magazine
12. disques compacts
13. radio-cassette
14. magnétoscope
15. chaîne stéréo

### Note grammaticale

#### Les adjectifs démonstratifs (suite)

Sometimes it may be important to distinguish between *this* and *that* or between *these* and *those*. When you have a lot of choices and want to be precise about the object or people you're referring to, use the demonstrative adjective with the noun and add **-ci** (*this, these*) or **-là** (*that, those*) to the noun:

Donnez-moi **ces** tartes-**ci**.          Give me *these* pies (*over here*).
Et je prends **ce** pain-**là**.          And I'll take *that* bread (*over there*).

Remember to use **-ci** and **-là** only if the distinction is necessary to make the meaning clear for someone else.

**Le savez-vous?**

▲▲▲▲▲▲▲▲▲▲▲▲▲▲▲

In France, the crusty French bread is eaten
a. only at breakfast
b. only at lunch as part of sandwiches
c. only at dinner
d. with every meal

Réponse ▲▲▲

**F.  À la Fnac.** You're shopping at the **Fnac** with a friend. Because there are so many things to choose from, you always have to explain which object you're referring to. Use **-ci** or **-là** in your answer, depending on the cue in parentheses.

*Modèle:*     Quels livres est-ce que tu vas acheter? *(those)*
              *Ces livres-là.*

1.  Quelle calculatrice est-ce que tu préfères? *(this one)*
2.  Quel magazine est-ce que tu vas acheter? *(that one)*
3.  Quels compacts disques est-ce que tu préfères? *(those)*
4.  Quels livres est-ce que tu aimes mieux? *(these)*
5.  Quel magnétoscope est-ce que tu vas acheter? *(this one)*
6.  Quelle télévision est-ce que tu aimerais acheter? *(that one)*

**Student Tape:** Chapitre 6 Segment 1

▲▲▲  d

# PRONONCIATION  *La voyelle é*

The letter **é** (as in the word **été**) is pronounced like the vowel sound in the English word *fail;* however, the French vowel is not a diphthong. In other words, it is a single, steady sound, whereas the English vowel tends to slide from one sound to another.

**G.**  Read each word aloud, being careful to pronounce **é** with enough tension to avoid a diphthong.

Réponse ▲▲▲

thé / café / église / métro / éclair / cathédrale / été / écouté / désiré / allé / hésité / acheté / étudié / stéréo / Hervé / téléphone / préféré / pâté / Québec / université / aéroport / lycée / télévision

# S·T·R·U·C·T·U·R·E

## *Les expressions de quantité*

| | |
|---|---|
| **Combien de** disques compacts est-ce que tu as? | *How many* compact discs do you have? |
| **Combien de** jambon est-ce que tu as acheté? | *How much* ham did you buy? |
| **Combien d'**argent est-ce que tu as? | *How much* money do you have? |

To ask *how much* or *how many* of something someone has, use **combien de.** A variety of expressions, either specific or general, may be used to answer. Note that all the expressions listed below are followed by **de,** regardless of the gender and number of the noun they modify.

**Structure:** When **combien de** and a noun are followed by the **passé composé,** the past participle must agree in gender and number with the noun: **Combien de disques compacts est-ce que tu as achetés?**

~~~~~~~~~~~~~ **General quantities** ~~~~~~~~~~~~~

J'ai **beaucoup de** disques compacts, mais j'ai **très peu de** cassettes.

I have *a lot of* compact discs, but I have *very few* cassettes.

| | |
|---|---|
| **beaucoup de** | a lot of, a great deal of, many, much |
| **ne . . . pas beaucoup de** | not many, not much |
| **un peu de** | a little, a little bit of |
| **très peu de** | very little, very few |

**Grammar:** The expression **un peu** can be used only with noncount nouns (nouns that are always singular). To express *a few* with a plural noun, French uses **quelques: un peu de thé,** but **quelques pommes.**

~~~~~~~~~~~~~ **Specific quantities** ~~~~~~~~~~~~~

J'ai acheté **un morceau de** pâté et six **tranches de** jambon.

I bought *a piece of* pâté and six *slices of* ham.

| | |
|---|---|
| **un kilo de** | a kilogram of |
| **un demi-kilo de** | a half-kilogram of |
| **une livre de** | a pound (French) of |
| **50 grammes de** | 50 grams of |
| **un litre de** | a liter of |
| **une bouteille de** | a bottle of |
| **une douzaine de** | a dozen |
| **un morceau de** | a piece of |
| **un bout de** | a piece of |
| **une tranche de** | a slice of |

~~~~~~~~~~~~~ **Expressions of sufficiency** ~~~~~~~~~~~~~

Je **n'**ai **pas assez d'**argent pour acheter un vélo.

I *don't* have *enough* money to buy a bike.

| | |
|---|---|
| **trop de** | too much, too many |
| **assez de** | enough |
| **ne . . . pas assez de** | not enough |

**Grammar:** Note that the preposition **pour** followed by an infinitive is used to say what one has (or does not have) enough for: **J'ai assez d'argent pour acheter une voiture.**

▲  ▲  ▲

## APPLICATION

**H.** Remplacez les mots en italique par les expressions entre parenthèses.

1. J'ai *trop de* patience. (assez de / trop de / pas assez de)
2. Il a *trop d'*argent. (assez de / pas assez de / trop de)
3. Elles ont *assez de* pâtisseries. (trop de / pas assez de / assez de)
4. Nous avons *trop de* jambon. (pas assez de / assez de / trop de)

Ajoutez les expressions entre parenthèses à chaque phrase et faites les changements nécessaires.

*Modèle:*     Georges a de la limonade. (beaucoup)
             *Georges a beaucoup de limonade.*

5. Nous avons des amis. (pas beaucoup / très peu / beaucoup)
6. Elles ont des disques. (beaucoup / très peu / pas beaucoup)
7. Mon oncle a de la patience. (pas beaucoup / beaucoup / très peu)

**I.** Use the cues to answer the salesperson.

*Modèle:*     Qu'est-ce que je peux faire pour vous? (1 kilo / abricots; 1 livre / salade de tomates)
             *Il me faut un kilo d'abricots et une livre de salade de tomates.*

1. Qu'est-ce que je peux faire pour vous? (1 litre / vin rouge; 8 tranches / saucisson)
2. Qu'est-ce qu'il vous faut? (1 bouteille / Perrier; 2 kilos / pommes)
3. Qu'est-ce que je vous donne? (50 grammes / pâté; 1 morceau / saucisson)
4. Qu'est-ce que vous désirez? (une douzaine / abricots; 1 livre / salade de thon)
5. Qu'est-ce qu'il vous faut? (un bout / pâté; 1 livre / jambon)

**J. Questions d'argent.** First, describe each person's financial situation, using the expressions **beaucoup, pas beaucoup, un peu,** and **très peu.**

**Monique:** 60F     **Sylvie:** 7 000F     **Edgar:** 2F     **Jean-Paul:** 25F

*Modèle:*     Est-ce que Monique a de l'argent?
             *Oui, mais elle n'a pas beaucoup d'argent.*

1. Est-ce qu'Edgar a de l'argent?
2. Et Sylvie?
3. Et Monique?
4. Et Jean-Paul?

Now decide if each person has too much, enough, or not enough money to buy the things indicated. Use the expressions **trop de, assez de,** and **pas assez de.**

*Modèle:*       Une calculatrice coûte 60 francs. (Monique)
              *Monique a assez d'argent pour acheter une calculatrice.*

5.  Un ordinateur coûte 12 000 francs. (Sylvie)
6.  Un ticket de métro coûte 3F50. (Monique)
7.  Un petit pain coûte 2 francs. (Edgar)
8.  Un vélo coûte 1 200 francs. (Sylvie)
9.  Un Walkman coûte 150 francs. (Jean-Paul)
10. Un disque coûte 45 francs. (Jean-Paul)
11. Un Coca coûte 8 francs. (Edgar)
12. Une tarte aux pommes coûte 55 francs. (Monique)

## Débrouillons-nous!

*Petite révision de l'étape*

**K.  Échange.** Posez les questions à un(e) autre étudiant(e), qui va vous répondre.

   1.  Est-ce que tu vas souvent à la boulangerie? Est-ce que tu aimes les croissants? Est-ce que tu as mangé des croissants récemment? Est-ce que tu aimes le pain français?
   2.  Est-ce que tu aimes les pâtisseries? Lesquelles *(which ones)* est-ce que tu préfères? Est-ce que tu manges souvent des desserts? Quel dessert est-ce que tu préfères? Qu'est-ce que tu prends avec ton dessert? Une tasse *(a cup)* de café? Une tasse de thé? Un Coca?
   3.  Est-ce que tu aimes le jambon? Qu'est-ce que tu préfères, la salade de thon ou la salade de concombres? Est-ce que tu aimes le saucisson? Est-ce que tu aimes le pâté?

Ex. K: ⇄

Ex. L: △

**L.  Un dîner.** You and your friends are organizing a dinner for your parents. You're in charge of buying some prepared foods and the dessert. First, you go to the **charcuterie** and then to the **boulangerie-pâtisserie.** Let the shopkeepers know what you need **(il me faut..., je prends..., donnez-moi...).** Two different classmates will play the roles of the shopkeepers.

**Reminder,** Ex. L: Remember to use **Madame** or **Monsieur** when you greet someone or say good-bye.

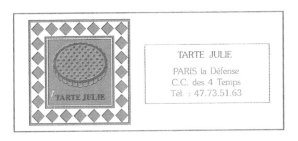

TARTE JULIE

PARIS la Défense
C.C. des 4 Temps
Tél. : 47.73.51.63

**À faire chez vous:**
**CAHIER, Chapitre 6 / 1ère étape**

# DEUXIÈME ÉTAPE

## Point de départ

▼ ▼ ▼ ▼ ▼ ▼ ▼ ▼ ▼ ▼ ▼ ▼ ▼ ▼ ▼ ▼

### Au supermarché

Après la charcuterie, Mme Thibaudet est allée au supermarché.

DES LÉGUMES

DES FRUITS

Qu'est-ce qu'on peut y acheter?

Transparencies:
6-3, 6-4, 6-5 (draw-
ings of food items
on pp. 222 and 223)

**Vocabulary:** The partitive, introduced lexically in the vocabulary items, is presented
fully later in this **étape**.

DES LÉGUMES *(m.)*
**des asperges** *(f.)*
**des champignons** *(m.)*
**des choux** *(m.)*
**des concombres** *(m.)*
**des courgettes** *(f.)*
**des haricots verts** *(m.)*
**des oignons** *(m.)*
**des petits pois** *(m.)*
**des pommes de terre** *(f.)*
**des radis** *(m.)*
**de la salade**
**des tomates** *(f.)*

DES FRUITS *(m.)*
**des abricots** *(m.)*
**des bananes** *(f.)*
**des cerises** *(f.)*
**des citrons** *(m.)*
**des fraises** *(f.)*
**des framboises** *(f.)*
**des melons** *(m.)*
**des oranges** *(f.)*
**des pêches** *(f.)*
**des poires** *(f.)*
**des pommes** *(f.)*

DES CONSERVES

DE LA VIANDE

DES PRODUITS LAITIERS

DES PRODUITS SURGELÉS

DES CONSERVES (f.)

| | |
|---|---|
| **de la choucroute** | sauerkraut |
| **de la confiture** | |
| **des sardines** (f.) | |
| **de la sauce tomate** | |
| **de la soupe** | |
| **du thon** | |

DE LA VIANDE

**du bifteck**
**du gigot** _ lamb
**du poulet**
**du rosbif**
**du rôti de porc**

DES PRODUITS LAITIERS

**du beurre**
**du brie**
**du camembert**
**de la crême**
**du gruyère**
**du lait**
**du yaourt**

*frozen*

DES PRODUITS SURGELÉS

**des pommes frites** (f.)
**du poulet**
**du poisson**
**de la glace**
**de la pizza**

D'AUTRES PRODUITS

D'AUTRES PRODUITS (m.)

| | |
|---|---|
| **de la farine** | flour |
| **de l'huile** (f.) | oil |
| **du ketchup** | |
| **de la mayonnaise** | |
| **de la moutarde** | |
| **des pâtes** (f.) | pasta |
| **du poivre** | pepper |
| **du riz** | rice |
| **du sel** | |
| **du sucre** | |
| **du vinaigre** | |

## Note culturelle

In France, one can buy fruits, vegetables, and staple food products in a variety of places. There is, of course, the supermarket **(le supermarché),** which is becoming more and more popular as the pace of life increases and more and more women take jobs away from home. The supermarket has become the most convenient way to shop for many French people, who rely increasingly on frozen and canned foods. Just like their American counterparts, French supermarkets provide bakery counters, extensive delicatessen sections, and sometimes seafood counters.

As convenient as the supermarket may be, many French people still prefer to patronize the general store **(l'épicerie)** that can be found in every neighborhood or an open-air market **(le marché en plein air).** Most families, however, divide their shopping among all of the available stores. The neighborhood **épicerie** caters to customers who have ample time to shop and those who shop on their way home from work. Supermarket shopping tends to be done less frequently and for larger quantities. The **marché en plein air** is still very popular because the prices are often better and the produce is particularly fresh. Besides appealing to family shoppers, the **marché en plein air** also attracts the chefs of exclusive restaurants, who buy only the freshest produce.

**Questions:** Do you think there is a difference between where older Americans shop and where younger people shop? Is there a difference in shopping habits between city and rural areas?

## À VOUS! (Exercices de vocabulaire)

**A. Qu'est-ce que c'est?** Identify the following foods.

*Modèles:*  *C'est une banane. Ce sont des fraises.*

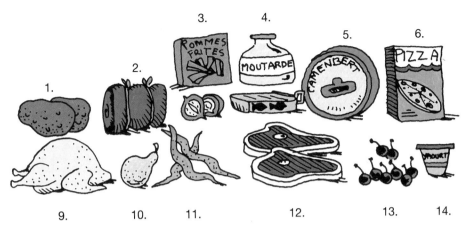

**B.  Dans le filet de Mme Thibaudet.** Calculate the cost of the items in Mme Thibaudet's shopping bag.

> *Modèle:*   2 kilos de tomates  /  6F50 le kilo
> *Deux kilos de tomates à six francs cinquante le kilo, ça fait treize francs.*

1. 2 kilos de pommes  /  10F50 le kilo
2. 3 bottes *(bunches)* de radis  /  4F la botte
3. 1 kilo d'abricots  /  16F90 le kilo
4. 1 livre de petits pois  /  19F90 le kilo
5. 3 biftecks (1 livre)  /  55F le kilo
6. 1 livre de champignons  /  19F20 le kilo
7. 2 kilos d'oranges  /  8F90 le kilo
8. 1 rôti de bœuf (1 kilo)  /  30F le kilo

**C.  Dans le chariot de Claire Maurant il y a...** *(In Claire Maurant's shopping cart there is . . .)* Claire's mother sent her to the supermarket. Since Claire forgot the shopping list, she buys things from memory. Look at the drawing and tell what she's buying.

> *Modèle:*   *Il y a une pizza.*

**D. Qu'est-ce que Claire a oublié?** When Claire gets home, her mother looks at the shopping list and tells her what she forgot to buy. Look at the drawings and name the things she forgot.

*Modèle:*    *Elle a oublié la mayonnaise.*

# R·E·P·R·I·S·E

*Première étape*

Ex. E: ⇄

**E.  À la charcuterie.** Ask the shopkeeper how much each of the following items costs.

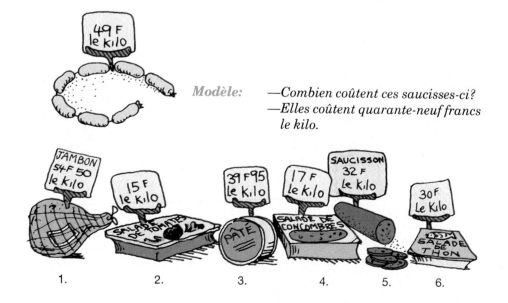

*Modèle:*    —*Combien coûtent ces saucisses-ci?*
             —*Elles coûtent quarante-neuf francs le kilo.*

▲▲▲  a

**F.   Des achats.** *(Purchases.)* Use the cues to roleplay scenes in a store.          Ex. F: ⇄

*Modèle:*      3 kg / pommes / beaucoup / 10F50 le kilo
            —*Je voudrais trois kilos de pommes.*
            —*Oui, nous avons beaucoup de pommes.*
            —*C'est combien?*
            —*À dix francs cinquante le kilo, ça fait trente et un francs
              cinquante.*

1.   2 kg / abricots / beaucoup / 17F le kilo
2.   1 livre / fraises / beaucoup / 18F le kilo
3.   2 kg / concombres / beaucoup / 7F50 le kilo
4.   3 bouteilles / Perrier / beaucoup / 5F50 la bouteille
5.   1 livre / jambon / beaucoup / 45F le kilo
6.   1 livre / salade de tomates / beaucoup / 19F le kilo

# S·T·R·U·C·T·U·R·E

## Le partitif

Quand je vais à la charcuterie, j'achète toujours

**du** pâté                 *some* pâté
**de la** salade de thon    *some* tuna salad
**des** saucisses           *some* sausages

—Est-ce que vous avez **du** jambon?
—Oui, et nous avons **des** saucisses aussi.

So far, you've learned two types of articles: the definite articles **le, la, l', les,** which mean *the* in English, and the indefinite articles **un, une, des,** which mean *a (an),* or *some.* A third type of article, the partitive article, expresses a certain amount or quantity, not the whole, of something. In English this idea is expressed either with the word *some* (I bought *some* vegetables) or without a modifier (I bought milk and cheese). The partitive article has three singular forms and one plural form:

| Le partitif | | |
|---|---|---|
| SINGULAR | Masculine | **du** |
| | Feminine | **de la** |
| | Masculine or feminine before a vowel or a silent **h** | **de l'** |
| PLURAL | Masculine or feminine | **des** |

**Reminder:** The **s** of **des** is silent, except in liaison.

▲  ▲  ▲

## APPLICATION

**G.**  Replace the definite article with the partitive article.

> *Modèle:*     le pain     *du pain*

1.  la salade
2.  le pâté
3.  les croissants
4.  la limonade
5.  la pâtisserie
6.  le thé
7.  les tartelettes
8.  la crème
9.  le lait
10. le café
11. l'eau minérale
12. les petits pains

**H.**  Remplacez les mots en italique et faites les changements nécessaires.

1.  Marie-Jeanne achète du *pâté*. (jambon / saucisson / salade de thon / saucisses)
2.  Je vais prendre du *thé*. (Coca / eau minérale / limonade / café)
3.  Elle a acheté des *tartelettes*. (croissants / baguettes / religieuses / éclairs)

---

### Note grammaticale

#### Le partitif (suite)

The partitive articles **du, de la, de l', des** become **de** or **d'** after a negative expression, regardless of the gender and number of the noun. In English, the negative partitive is expressed either with the word *any* (I don't have *any* money) or without a modifier (I'm not buying ice cream):

—Tu prends **du** café?
—Non, je **ne** prends **pas de** café.

—Are you having coffee?
—No, I'm *not* having coffee.

—Vous avez **de la** mayonnaise?
—Non, nous **n'**avons **pas de** mayonnaise.

—Do you have *any* mayonnaise?
—No, we do*n't* have *any* mayonnaise.

—Tu as acheté **des** sardines?
—Non, je **n'**ai **pas** acheté **de** sardines.

—Did you buy *(any)* sardines?
—No, I did*n't* buy *(any)* sardines.

**Reminder:** Students should consistently pronounce **pas de** as **pad,** regardless of the gender and number of the noun that follows.

**Reminder:** The definite articles **le, la, l', les** don't change after a negative expression.

**Reminder,** Ex. I and J: Change the partitive articles to **de** after a negative (**pas de**), but don't change the definite articles (**pas le**).

**I.**  **Merci, pas de...**  Each time someone offers you something, you refuse politely. Remember that the partitive and indcfinite articles become **de** after the negative.

> *Modèle:*     Du pain?     *Merci, pas de pain.*

1. De la moutarde?
2. Du pâté?
3. Du Perrier?
4. Des croissants?
5. De la soupe?
6. Des oranges?
7. De la limonade?
8. Du café?
9. De la salade?
10. Des pâtisseries?

**J.** Engage in short conversations based on the models.

> *Modèle:*   prendre / limonade / non / ne pas aimer
> —*Tu prends de la limonade?*
> —*Non, je ne prends pas de limonade.*
> —*Pourquoi pas?*
> —*Parce que je n'aime pas la limonade.*

1. prendre / pâté / non / ne pas aimer
2. vouloir / café / non / ne pas aimer du tout
3. aller acheter / jambon / non / détester
4. aller manger / soupe / non / ne pas aimer
5. prendre / eau minérale / non / ne pas aimer du tout

> *Modèle:*   café / express
> —*Vous désirez du café?*
> —*Oui, je voudrais un express.*

6. thé / thé citron
7. fruits / banane, orange
8. pâtisserie / religieuse, millefeuille
9. pain / baguette, pain de campagne
10. café / café au lait

> *Modèle:*   pain / baguette, pain de campagne
> —*Vous aimez le pain?*
> —*Oui, j'aime beaucoup le pain.*
> —*Est-ce que vous avez acheté du pain hier?*
> —*Oui, j'ai acheté une baguette et un pain de campagne.*

11. pâtisseries / tarte aux pommes, gâteau au chocolat
12. salade / salade de tomates, salade de concombres
13. eau minérale / bouteille de Vittel, bouteille de Perrier
14. pain / pain au chocolat, petit pain
15. viande / rôti de porc, gigot

Ex. J: The three parts of this exercise are designed to reinforce the differences between (1) **pas de** and **pas le (la, l', les)** (2) the partitive and the indefinite articles, and (3) the partitive, definite, and indefinite articles.

Reminder, Ex. J: Note the difference between **du café** (*some coffee*) and **un express** (*an expresso*).

**Reminder:** Note the differences between **le pain** (*bread in general*), **du pain** (*some bread*), and **un pain** (*a loaf of bread*).

# PRONONCIATION   *Les voyelles è et ê*

The letters **è** as in **mère** and **ê** as in **fête** are pronounced like the *e* in the English words *bed* and *belt*.

**Student Tape:** Chapitre 6 Segment 1

**K.** Read each word aloud, being careful to pronounce **è** and **ê** in the same way.

mère / frère / père / crème / achète / scène / bibliothèque / tête / êtes / fête

## *Les nombres de 70 à 100*

#### Les nombres de 70 à 100

| | | | |
|---|---|---|---|
| 70 | **soixante-dix** | 86 | **quatre-vingt-six** |
| 71 | **soixante et onze** | 87 | **quatre-vingt-sept** |
| 72 | **soixante-douze** | 88 | **quatre-vingt-huit** |
| 73 | **soixante-treize** | 89 | **quatre-vingt-neuf** |
| 74 | **soixante-quatorze** | 90 | **quatre-vingt-dix** |
| 75 | **soixante-quinze** | 91 | **quatre-vingt-onze** |
| 76 | **soixante-seize** | 92 | **quatre-vingt-douze** |
| 77 | **soixante-dix-sept** | 93 | **quatre-vingt-treize** |
| 78 | **soixante-dix-huit** | 94 | **quatre-vingt-quatorze** |
| 79 | **soixante-dix-neuf** | 95 | **quatre-vingt-quinze** |
| 80 | **quatre-vingts** | 96 | **quatre-vingt-seize** |
| 81 | **quatre-vingt-un** | 97 | **quatre-vingt-dix-sept** |
| 82 | **quatre-vingt-deux** | 98 | **quatre-vingt-dix-huit** |
| 83 | **quatre-vingt-trois** | 99 | **quatre-vingt-dix-neuf** |
| 84 | **quatre-vingt-quatre** | 100 | **cent** |
| 85 | **quatre-vingt-cinq** | | |

The **t** of **vingt** in **quatre-vingts, quatre-vingt-un,** etc., and the **t** of **cent** are not pronounced. **Quatre-vingts** is written with an **s** only when it is *not* followed by another number: **quatre-vingts francs.**

The two most important functions associated with numbers are understanding them and expressing them orally. Unless you write checks, it is unusual that numbers are spelled out.

▲  ▲  ▲

## APPLICATION

**L.** Do the following number exercises.

1. Count from 60 to 100.
2. Give the odd numbers from 1 to 99.
3. Give the even numbers from 0 to 100.
4. Count from 0 to 100 by tens.
5. Read the following phone numbers: 46 23 39 57; 64 83 92 42; 98 66 54 32; 34 52 76 97; 87 91 71 95.

## Note grammaticale

### *Les nombres de 100 à 1 000 000*

| | | | |
|---|---|---|---|
| 100 | **cent** | 200 | **deux cents** |
| 101 | **cent un** | 201 | **deux cent un** |
| 102 | **cent deux** | 202 | **deux cent deux** |

| | | | |
|---|---|---|---|
| 1 000 | **mille** | 2 000 | **deux mille** |
| 1 001 | **mille un** | 2 500 | **deux mille cinq cents** |
| 1 002 | **mille deux** | | |
| | | 2 550 | **deux mille cinq cent cinquante** |

| | | | |
|---|---|---|---|
| 1 000 000 | **un million** | 2 000 000 | **deux millions** |

**Deux cents, trois cents,** etc., are written with an **s** only when they are *not* followed by another number. **Mille** is invariable; it never takes an **s**. The commas used in English to write numbers in the thousands and millions are either omitted or replaced by a period: 3,560 = **3 560** or **3.560**. To express percentages, the French use a comma: 3.3 = **3,3** (**trois virgule trois**).

**Grammar:** When followed by a noun, **un million** is treated as an expression of quantity and therefore requires **de: un million de téléspectateurs, six millions de francs.**

**M.  Des statistiques.** Read the following statistics for various French cities.

| | *Habitants* | *Cinémas* | *Théâtres* | *Musées* |
|---|---|---|---|---|
| PARIS | 2 176 243 | 515 | 61 | 85 |
| LYON | 413 095 | 128 | 33 | 21 |
| MARSEILLE | 874 436 | 185 | 37 | 24 |
| LILLE | 168 424 | 120 | 9 | 7 |
| BORDEAUX | 208 159 | 163 | 14 | 9 |
| TOULOUSE | 347 995 | 167 | 17 | 13 |

*Modèle:*     *Paris a 2 176 243 habitants, 515 cinémas, 61 théâtres et 85 musées.*

**N. Faisons des calculs!** *(Let's do some math!)* Do the following math problems.

*Modèles:*     200 + 300 =
*Deux cents et trois cents font cinq cents.*

200 ÷ 50 =
*Deux cents divisé par cinquante fait quatre.*

25 × 3 =
*Vingt-cinq multiplié par trois fait soixante-quinze.*

30 − 15 =
*Trente moins quinze font quinze.*

| | | |
|---|---|---|
| 1.   5 000 − 3 000 = | 4.   600 ÷ 3 = | 7.   450 ÷ 5 = |
| 2.   225 × 4 = | 5.   608 − 16 = | 8.   950 + 250 = |
| 3.   90 + 60 = | 6.   155 × 6 = | 9.   1 000 ÷ 20 = |

 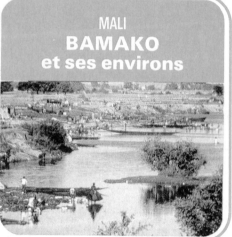

**O. Le Mali.** Mali is a French-speaking country in northwestern Africa. Its capital city is Bamako. Read aloud the following facts about Mali.

1. La superficie *(area)* du Mali est 1 240 km.
2. La population du Mali est 8 730 000 habitants.
3. La distance entre la capitale Bamako et les villes suivantes est:

| BAMAKO | → | ALGER | 2 878 km |
|---|---|---|---|
| BAMAKO | → | ROME | 3 793 km |
| BAMAKO | → | GENÈVE | 3 971 km |
| BAMAKO | → | PARIS | 4 169 km |
| BAMAKO | → | LONDRES | 4 378 km |
| BAMAKO | → | FRANCFORT | 4 430 km |
| BAMAKO | → | STOCKHOLM | 5 653 km |
| BAMAKO | → | NEW YORK | 7 065 km |

# Débrouillons-nous!

▲ ▲ ▲ ▲ ▲ ▲ ▲ ▲ ▲ ▲ ▲ ▲ ▲ ▲ ▲ ▲ ▲ ▲

*Petite révision de l'étape*

**P. Un pique-nique.** You and your friends are planning a picnic. You have to decide what you want to buy, and you don't always agree. For each suggestion one of you makes, a second person agrees but a third person disagrees.

Ex. P: △

> *Modèle:* jambon
> —*Est-ce que nous allons acheter du jambon?*
> —*Ah oui. J'adore le jambon.*
> —*Non, je ne veux pas de jambon. Je déteste le jambon.*

1. pâté
2. saucisson
3. eau minérale
4. salade de concombres
5. Coca
6. croissants
7. saucisses
8. poulet
9. tartelettes au citron
10. pâtisseries
11. bananes
12. salade de thon

**Q. Au supermarché.** Three of your friends are about to spend the weekend at your house. Since they are *your* guests, your family expects you to do the food shopping for everyone. Make your shopping list and then go to various stores to make your purchases. Your classmates will play the roles of the shopkeepers.

Ex. Q: ⇄

**À faire chez vous: CAHIER, Chapitre 6 / 2e étape**

*La charcuterie en libre-service*

*Les fruits et légumes*

MARCHÉ RICHELIEU

**JAMBON SEC D'AOSTE VIEILLE RÉSERVE**
Avec couenne,
le kg ___ **79**F**,90**

**JAMBON SUPÉRIEUR MADRANGE RUBAN BLEU**
Découenné, dégraissé, le kg ___ **49**F**,90**

**TOMATES**
Cat. 1. Orig. France
Cal. 47 et +, le kg ___ **4**F**,90**

**POMMES DE TERRE**
Espagne ou Maroc, cal. 35,
le filet de 2,5 kg ___ **9**F**,90**
soit le kg 3,96 F

**Instructor's Tape:**
Au centre commercial

**Transparency:**
6-6 (in the Fnac, the
toy store, the sporting
goods store [pp. 234
and 235])

# TROISIÈME ÉTAPE
## Point de départ

attracts
brings together
toys
department stores
meeting place

*Au centre commercial*

Le centre commercial **attire** des gens de tous les âges et de tous les intérêts. Il **réunit** une grande variété de magasins et de boutiques: des magasins de vête- ments, des magasins de **jouets,** des magasins de sport et même des **grands magasins.** En France, comme aux États-Unis, le centre commercial est devenu le **lieu de rencontre** pour les adolescents aussi bien que pour les adultes.

**ALLONS-Y!**
Video Program

ACTE 6: SCÈNE 2
AU CENTRE COMMERCIAL

**QUESTIONS DE FOND**
1. Avec quelle fréquence est-ce que les Français vont au centre commercial?
2. Comment leurs réponses différent- elles de celles que vous donneraient des Américains de votre région?

## À Paris

Mireille Loiseau et sa cousine, Claire Maurant, se trouvent à la Fnac. **De quoi** parlent-elles? Des **derniers** vidéoclips, bien sûr!

what
latest

**Suggestion, Point de départ:**
Use the transparencies of scenes in stores to have stu- dents roleplay the various characters.

**FORUM DES HALLES**
1 à 7, rue Pierre Lescot
75001 Paris - 40.26.81.18
**MONTPARNASSE**
136, rue de Rennes
75006 Paris - 45.44.39.12
**ETOILE**
26, avenue de Wagram
75008 Paris - 47.66.52.50

song
Of course! / saw / fantastic

—Est-ce que tu as entendu la dernière **chanson** de Madonna?
—**Bien entendu!** Et j'ai aussi **vu** son vidéoclip. Il est **extra!**

—**Je pense que** je vais acheter le disque compact. Et je vais aussi **louer** une vidéo.

I think that / to rent

—Moi, j'ai besoin de cassettes **vierges.**

blank

—Après, on va chez moi regarder la vidéo.

—D'accord.

## À Bordeaux

Madame Thibaudet et son amie se trouvent au magasin de jouets. Elles ne vont pas souvent au centre commercial, mais Madame Thibaudet cherche un cadeau pour sa petite fille.

—Regarde tous ces jouets! Tu vas acheter quelque chose pour ta petite fille?

—Je ne sais pas. Elle est **tellement gâtée...** Et puis il vaut peut-être mieux **lui** acheter un **vêtement.**

so spoiled / for her<br>article of clothing

—Oh, écoute. C'est son anniversaire et elle a assez de vêtements. Regarde cette **poupée.** Et ce **camion.** Pourquoi pas un robot ou un **ballon**?

doll / truck / ball<br>video game

—Non. Elle a déjà tout ça. Tiens... je vais lui acheter un **jeu vidéo.**

## À Marseille

Véronique Béziers et son frère sont au magasin de sport. Ils sont **tous les deux** très sportifs et ils adorent regarder tous les appareils modernes pour la gymnastique.

both

workout machine

—Je voudrais bien acheter un vélo ou un **appareil de gymnastique.** Mais c'est trop cher.

—Écoute... l'hiver dernier tu t'es déjà acheté des skis. Pourquoi pas prendre une raquette de tennis et des balles?

—T'as raison. C'est beaucoup moins cher et j'aime bien jouer au tennis. Ah, zut!

cash

Ils n'acceptent pas les chèques. Il faut payer **en espèces** ou par carte de crédit.

automatic teller machine

—Pas de problème! Il y a un **distributeur automatique de billets** tout près.

## À VOUS! (Exercices de vocabulaire)

**Reminder,** Ex. A: Be sure to include some of the vocabulary for objects from earlier chapters, particularly from Chapter 2, where you talked about things in a room.

**A.   Qu'est-ce qu'on peut y acheter?** Explain what one can buy in each store.

> *Modèle:*      Fnac
> *—Qu'est-ce qu'on peut acheter à la Fnac?*
> *—On peut y acheter des disques, etc.*

1.   Fnac
2.   magasin de sport

3.   magasin de jouets
4.   grand magasin

**B.   Des cadeaux d'anniversaire.** *(Birthday gifts.)* Say what you'll buy for      Ex. B: ○
each member of your family and for three of your best friends. Be sure to
tell in what kind of store you'll make each purchase.

   *Modèle:*      *Je vais aller au magasin de sport acheter un ballon de foot*
                  *pour mon père.*

**C.   Est-ce que vous acceptez les chèques?** You go to a variety of stores      Ex. C: ⇄
(small and large) to make purchases. Select one method of payment and
ask the cashier if you can use it. The cashier responds in the negative and
gives the alternative methods of payment. You may have to go to an automatic teller machine if you don't have cash.

R·E·P·R·I·S·E

*Deuxième étape*

**D.   Mon petit déjeuner.** Ask one of your classmates what he/she eats for      Ex. D: ⇄
breakfast. Follow the model.

   *Modèle:*      —*Est-ce que tu prends du café?*
                  —*Non, je ne prends pas de café. Je préfère le thé.* or *Oui, je*
                   *prends du café.*

| *Le petit déjeuner* | | |
| --- | --- | --- |
| le pain | le café | les œufs *(eggs)* |
| le pain au chocolat | le thé | le bacon |
| le croissant | le lait | le jambon |
| la confiture | le jus d'orange | les saucisses |
| le beurre | | |
| le toast (le pain grillé) | | |
| les céréales | | |

**E.   En quelle année?** Read the year of each event.

   1.   1776      la Révolution américaine
   2.   1789      la Révolution française
   3.   1492      Christophe Colomb en Amérique
   4.   1945      la fin de la Seconde Guerre mondiale
   5.   1815      la fin de l'empire de Napoléon
   6.   1963      l'assassinat du président Kennedy
   7.   1988      les élections présidentielles en France
   8.   1889      la construction de la tour Eiffel

**Grammar:** Note that dates
can be stated in one of two
ways: 1993 = **mille neuf
cent quatre-vingt-treize**
or **dix-neuf cent quatre-
vingt-treize.**

## S·T·R·U·C·T·U·R·E

*Le présent et le passé composé du verbe irrégulier **devoir***

**Tu dois** 20 francs à ta sœur.
**Nous devons** rentrer ce soir.
**Ils ont dû** aller en ville.
**Je dois** retrouver Jean au café.

Il n'est pas là? **Il doit** être
malade ou **il a dû** oublier.

*You owe* your sister 20 francs.
*We have to* go home tonight.
*They had to* go into town.
*I'm supposed to* meet Jean at the
    café.

He isn't there? *He must* be sick
    or *he must have* forgotten.

The verb **devoir** is irregular in the present tense and has an irregular past
participle:

| devoir | |
|---|---|
| je **dois** | nous **devons** |
| tu **dois** | vous **devez** |
| il, elle, on **doit** | ils, elles **doivent** |
| PAST PARTICIPLE: **dû** (avoir) | |

The present and **passé composé** of **devoir** have several meanings,
depending on the context of the sentence.

The verb **devoir** in the present tense may have two meanings:

1. owing (money or objects);
2. obligation (*I am supposed to . . . , I have to . . .* ).

The verb **devoir** in the **passé composé** may also have two meanings:

1. obligation or necessity (*I had to* call my family);
2. probability or speculation (*I must have* left the keys in the car).

▲  ▲  ▲

## APPLICATION

**F.**   Remplacez les sujets en italique et faites les changements nécessaires.

1. *Elle* doit beaucoup d'argent. (tu / Jacques / je / nous / vous / ils)
2. *Il* a dû aller en ville. (Marcelle / tu / ils / vous / je / nous)
3. *Nous* devons rentrer demain. (elles / ma sœur / Jules / je / tu)

**G. D'abord...** Each time someone is going to do something, you say that something else has to be done first. Use the present tense of **devoir** and the cues in parentheses.

*Modèle:*   Je vais aller au cinéma. (faire tes devoirs)
*D'abord tu dois faire tes devoirs.*

1. Ils vont regarder la télévision. (aller à l'épicerie)
2. Simone va aller au centre commercial. (manger quelque chose)
3. Je vais aller au café. (aller à la charcuterie)
4. Nous allons faire une promenade. (faire vos devoirs)
5. Jacques va faire du ski. (parler à son père)
6. Je vais écouter mes disques. (aller chercher ton frère)

**H. Mes obligations.** Explain to one of your classmates what you had to do last week and what you have to do next week. Use the **passé composé** of **devoir** to express the past and the present tense of **devoir** to express the future. SUGGESTED THINGS TO DO: **faire mes devoirs, travailler, téléphoner à, aller, parler à, acheter, apprendre, faire les courses.**

Ex. H: ⇄

*Modèle:*   *La semaine dernière j'ai dû aller chez le dentiste.*
*La semaine prochaine je dois travailler au supermarché.*

# PRONONCIATION   *La voyelle **e***

The letter **e** without a written accent may represent three different sounds in French:

[e]   the sound also represented by **é** (acute accent)
[ɛ]   the sound also represented by **è** (grave accent)
[ə]   the sound in the word **le**

At the end of a word, the letter **e** is pronounced [e] when it is followed by a silent consonant (**chanter, les**) except when this consonant is the letter **t** (**poulet**). The letter **e** is then pronounced [ɛ]. It is also pronounced [ɛ] when it is followed by a consonant in the same syllable (**elle, personne**). The letter **e** is pronounced [ə] at the end of a syllable in the middle of a word (**petit, cerise**). It is also pronounced [ə] in certain two-letter words (**le, ne, me**). Remember that **e** without an accent is usually silent at the end of a word.

**I.** Read each word aloud, being careful to distinguish among the three sounds of **e.**

[e]   des / mes / aller / il est / assez / manger / avez
[ɛ]   poulet / jouet / baguette / verre / appelle / hôtel / asperges / express
[ə]   de / le petit / demain / pamplemousse / retour / demande

**Student Tape:**
Chapitre 6
Segment 1

**Reminder,** Pronunciation: As a rule, French syllables end in a vowel: **vé-lo, bou-che-rie.** Two consonants next to each other in the middle of a word usually split into different syllables: **char-cu-te-rie.**

## Le savez-vous?
▲▲▲▲▲▲▲▲▲▲▲▲▲▲
Mammouth **is a**
a. **fast-food chain specializing in meats**
b. **wholesale food outlet**
c. **supermarket chain**
d. **stationery store**

Réponse  ▲▲▲

**J.**   Read the following words aloud. Each contains at least two different pronunciations of the letter **e.**

regarder / mercredi / chercher / elle est / se promener / traversez / demander / papeterie / de jouets / bracelet / quatre-vingt-sept

# S·T·R·U·C·T·U·R·E

## *L'adjectif interrogatif* **quel**

—**Quelles** pâtisseries est-ce que tu vas acheter?

*What (which) pastries are you going to buy?*

—Des éclairs et des religieuses.

The adjectives **quel, quelle, quels, quelles** *(which, what)* are used to ask someone to identify something (**Quel livre? Le livre de français.** *Which book? The French book.*). Because **quel** is an adjective, it must agree in gender and number with the noun it modifies. All forms are pronounced the same, regardless of their spelling.

   **Quel** may be used with both things and people, and it usually occurs in two types of questions:

1.   Immediately before a noun (**quel** + noun):

| | |
|---|---|
| **Quelle** pâtisserie? | *What (which) pastry?* |
| **Quel** livre est-ce que tu cherches? | *What (which) book are you looking for?* |
| **Quels** sports est-ce que tu aimes? | *What (which) sports do you like?* |
| **Quelles** jeunes filles est-ce que tu as invitées? | *What (which) girls did you invite?* |

2.   Separated from the noun by the verb **être** (**quel** + **être** + noun):

| | |
|---|---|
| **Quelle** est votre adresse? | *What's your address?* |
| **Quels** sont tes disques préférés? | *What are your favorite records?* |

▲   ▲   ▲

**Grammar:** When **quel** and the noun are followed by the **passé composé,** the past participle must agree in gender and number with the noun: **Quels disques as-tu achetés?**

## APPLICATION

▲▲▲   C

**K.**   Use **quel** to form a question with each noun. Then spell the form of **quel** that you used. Remember that each written form must agree in gender and number with the noun it modifies.

*Modèle:*   livre   *Quel livre? (Q-U-E-L)*

1. chien
2. magasin
3. appartement
4. portefeuilles
5. voiture
6. chambre
7. peintures
8. langue
9. vélo
10. filles
11. cahiers
12. chaîne stéréo
13. musique
14. appareil-photo
15. garçons

**L.   Qu'est-ce que tu cherches?** Your friend has misplaced a lot of things. For each lost item, ask a question with **quel** to get more information.

*Modèle:*   Je cherche mon stylo.
            *Quel stylo?*

1. Je cherche ma clé.
2. Je cherche mon cahier.
3. Je cherche mes livres.
4. Je cherche les cassettes.
5. Je cherche mon disque.
6. Je cherche une adresse.
7. Je cherche les posters.
8. Je cherche les plantes.

**M.   Des renseignements.** Ask one of your classmates questions with **quel** to get the required information. Use either **quel** + noun or **quel + être +** noun.

Ex. M: ⇄

*Modèles:*   son nom
            *Quel est ton nom?*

            les sports qu'il/elle préfère
            *Quels sports est-ce que tu préfères?*

1. son nom
2. sa saison préférée
3. son adresse
4. son numéro de téléphone
5. les cours qu'il/elle prend
6. la musique qu'il/elle préfère
7. les devoirs pour demain
8. son professeur préféré

**Reminder,** Ex. N: Remember to use verbs like **aimer, aimer mieux,** and **préférer** in your questions.

**Suggestion,** Ex. N: Since students have just done a series of exercises with **quel,** you may wish to save this exercise for use in starting the next class period.

Ex. O: ○

**Reminder,** Ex. O: Remember to use store name as you explain what you are going to do.

**À faire chez vous:**
**CAHIER, Chapitre 6 / 3ᵉ étape**

**À faire chez vous:**
**Student Tape**
Now that you've completed the first three **étapes** of **Chapitre 6,** do Segment 2 of the STUDENT TAPE. See **CAHIER, Chapitre 6,** *Écoutons!,* for exercises that accompany this segment.

## ▲ ▲ ▲ ▲ ▲ ▲ ▲ ▲ ▲ Débrouillons-nous! ▲ ▲ ▲ ▲ ▲ ▲ ▲ ▲ ▲

*Petite révision de l'étape*

**N.  Échange.** Posez les questions à un(e) autre étudiant(e), qui va vous répondre.

1.  which music he/she likes
2.  what his/her address is
3.  what his/her telephone number is
4.  what drink **(une boisson)** he/she prefers
5.  what day of the week he/she likes best
6.  what season he/she prefers
7.  which class **(un cours)** he/she likes best
8.  which professor he/she likes best

**O.  Au centre commercial.** You and your friends are going to the mall. When everyone gets there, each person tells what he/she is going to do. Then decide to meet again at a certain time so you can all go for a pizza.

**Les Centres Commerciaux :**
- Le Forum des Halles 1-7, rue Pierre Lescot - 1ᵉʳ - Ⓜ Les Halles - R.E.R. Châtelet-Les Halles.
- Le Centre Maine-Montparnasse 17, rue de l'Arrivée -15ᵉ - Ⓜ Montparnasse.
- Les Boutiques de Paris du Palais des Congrès - Porte Maillot - Ⓜ Porte Maillot.
- Les Galeries marchandes des Champs-Elysées : Lido, Passage des Champs, Berri, Claridge, Rond-Point des Champs-Elysées - 8ᵉ - Ⓜ George V et Franklin-Roosevelt.
- Les 4 Temps - Parvis de la Défense - Hauts-de-Seine - Ⓜ R.E.R. La Défense.

*Forum des Halles, Paris*

# QUATRIÈME ÉTAPE

▼▼▼▼▼▼▼▼▼▼▼▼

## L·E·C·T·U·R·E

### Des produits alimentaires

*When faced with reading a long list, as in the advertising brochures here and on p. 244, we often scan the text to focus on particular items. This means that we do not read every word, but rather look for key words. Some food lists use photos to catch our interest and help us identify the items. Whether illustrated or not, such lists are only partially read by potential customers, who focus exclusively on the items that meet their specific tastes and needs. Scan the two brochures and then do the comprehension exercises on p. 245.*

**Prereading:** Have students name the food sections found in American supermarkets and tell them what are the French equivalents.

# Bretagne-Normandie-Pays de Loire

1 - Assortiment biscuits bretons pur beurre "AÉR".
Le coffret métal 350 g **17,90 F.** Le kg 51,14 F
2 - *CHOUCHENN MELMOR hydromel.
La bouteille 75 cl **26,00 F.** Le litre 34,67 F
3 - *Liqueur de fraise de PLOUGASTEL 22% vol.
La bouteille 70 cl **43,80 F.** Le litre 62,58 F
4 - Bâton sucre de pomme de ROUEN
100 g **10,90 F** Le kg 109 F
Le lot de 3 bâtons (150 g) **19,90 F.** Le kg 132,67 F
5 - Biscuits galettes de PLEYBEN pur beurre.
Le lot 2 paquets de 130 g **9,90 F.** Le kg 38,08 F
6 - Biscuits bretons pur beurre "GUEL ATAO" ou
GALETTES AER.
Le lot 2 paquets de 200 g **9,95 F.** Le kg 24,87 F
7 - Gâteau de Bretagne pur beurre tourré pruneau
ou framboise "AÉR". 350 g **11,80 F.** Le kg 33,72 F
8 - Crêpes dentelle enrobées chocolat au lait
ou chocolat noir/menthe "SOUPÇONS" LOC
MARIA. La boîte 300 g **29,95 F.** Le kg 99,84 F
9 - Crêpes dentelle "LES GAVOTTES" LOC MARIA.
Le coffret métal 250 g **27,90 F.** Le kg 116,60 F
10 - Crêpes pur beurre "AÉR". Le sachet 300 g **7,40 F**
Le kg 24,67 F

11 - *Calvados du DUC D'AIGUILLON hors d'âge 40%
vol. La bouteille 70 cl **109,00 F.** Le litre 155,72 F
12 - *Whisky "W.B. BRETON" 40% vol.
La bouteille 70 cl **69,50 F.** Le litre 99,29 F
13 - *Eau de vie de cidre "FINE BRETAGNE" 40% vol.
La bouteille 70 cl **79,50 F.** Le litre 113,58 F
14 - *Cidre normand brut ou doux "DUCHE DE
LONGUEVILLE".
Le Pack de 4 boîtes 33 cl **13,50 F.** Le litre 10,23 F
15 - *Cidre bouché normand PAYS D'AUGE "LA CIDRAIE".
La bouteille 75 cl **9,50 F.** Le litre 12,67 F
16 - *Cidre bouché breton traditionnel "LOIC RAISON".
La bouteille 75 cl **9,00 F.** Le litre 12,00 F
17 - *SANCERRE blanc A.O.C. "CÔTES DE CHAVIGNOL"
1988. La bouteille 75 cl **49,00 F**
18 - *MUSCADET SUR LIE A.O.C. "DOMAINE DE LA
CROIX" 1989. La bouteille 75 cl **24,80 F**
19 - *TOURAINE MESLAND rouge A.O.C. "LES PETITS
FOUASONS" 1988. La bouteille 75 cl **16,50 F**
20 - *SAUMUR CHAMPIGNY rouge A.O.C. "CLOS DE
L'ÉGLISE" 1988. La bouteille 75 cl **29,50 F**

21 - *CHINON A.O.C. "DOMAINE LES MILLIARGES"
1988. La bouteille 75 cl **21,00 F**
22 - Grand-Pont 45% M.G. GRAINDORGE.
Le kg **59,80 F**
23 - Fromage du Pays Nantais dit "DU CURÉ"
40% M.G. La boîte 180 g **9,95 F.** Le kg 55,28 F
24 - Livarot 40% M.G. A.O.C. GRAINDORGE.
La boîte 500 g **27,80 F.** Le kg 55,60 F
25 - Camembert 45% M.G. A.O.C. LEPETIT.
La boîte 250 g **10,90 F.** Le kg 43,60 F
26 - Tripes bretonnes au beurre. Le kg **39,80 F**
27 - Rillettes du MANS. Le kg **36,90 F**
28 - Rillettes du MANS MIRBELL. Le pot 220 g **7,50 F**
Le kg 34,09 F
29 - Pâté breton CREIS KER. Le kg **29,80 F**
30 - Andouille de GUEMENE. Le kg **98,00 F**
31 - Petits Pois à l'étuvée extra-fins RÖDEL.
La 1/2 boîte (280 g) **9,50 F.** Le kg 33,91 F
32 - Thon blanc à l'huile d'arachide RÖDEL.
La boîte 1/5 (166 g) **26,50 F.** Le kg 159,64 F
33 - Sardines à l'huile d'olive RÖDEL.
La boîte 1/6 (115 g) **13,90 F.** Le kg 120,87 F

*A consommer avec modération

# À VOUS! (Exercices de compréhension)

**A.  Au Maxicoop.** Look at the advertisement on p. 243, and decide in which part of the supermarket you're going to find the following items.

*Modèle:*    shampooing ultra doux
*Au rayon hygiène entretien.*

1.  Bordeaux rouge A.C.
2.  papier toilette Ouaty
3.  pain grillé normal Pelletier
4.  pommes frites
5.  beurre laitier
6.  pizzas Paésa
7.  cônes Pilpa
8.  demi-jambon
9.  Pampers
10.  Orangina
11.  mayonnaise Bénédicta
12.  insecticide Catch
13.  œufs frais
14.  M. Propre

**B.  Ça coûte combien?** You're interested in the following items from the list of foods and drinks in the catalogue **Saveurs de nos Régions** on p. 244. Use the number to find the item in the picture. Say what it is. Then, indicate the cost. Work with a classmate to have these short conversations.

*Modèle:*    6
—*Qu'est-ce que c'est?*
—*Ce sont des biscuits bretons.*
—*Ça coûte combien?*
—*C'est 9F95 pour deux paquets.*

a.  item 1    c.  item 22    e.  item 3    g.  item 25    i.  item 7    k.  item 29
b.  item 10    d.  item 31    f.  item 12    h.  item 32    j.  item 20    l.  item 33

## R·E·P·R·I·S·E

*Troisième étape*

**C.  Au centre commercial.** Find out what your friends bought at the mall. Use the forms of **quel** in your questions.

*Modèle:*    disque / Madonna
—*Qu'est-ce que tu as acheté?*
—*J'ai acheté un disque.*
—*Quel disque?*
—*Le dernier disque de Madonna.*

1.  vidéo / Billy Idol
2.  cassette / U2
3.  disque / Europe
4.  poster / Sinead O'Connor
5.  disque compact / Téléphone
6.  cassette / Michel Polnareff
7.  vidéo / Paula Abdul
8.  disque / Les Avions

Ex. D: ⇄

**D. Échange.** Posez les questions à un(e) autre étudiant(e), qui va vous répondre.

1. Qu'est-ce que tu dois faire ce soir?
2. Quelles sont tes responsabilités à la maison? Qu'est-ce que tu dois faire?
3. Est-ce que tu dois beaucoup étudier pour ce cours?
4. Est-ce que tu dois de l'argent à quelqu'un? À qui? Pourquoi?
5. Qu'est-ce que tu as dû faire le week-end dernier?
6. Qu'est-ce que tu as dû faire pour réussir *(pass)* au dernier examen de français?

**À faire chez vous:**
**Student Tape**

**CAHIER, Chapitre 6:**
*Rédigeons! / Travail de fin de chapitre* (including STUDENT TAPE, Chapitre 6, Segment 3)

# Point d'arrivée

*Activités orales*

## Exprimons-nous!

When you're in a store in a French-speaking country, it's very important to know how to ask for what you need or want and to find out how much something costs.

*Pour indiquer ce que vous désirez dans un magasin*

> **Donnez-moi** deux biftecks, s'il vous plaît.
> **Il me faut** une livre de beurre et un litre de lait.
> **Est-ce que vous avez (avez-vous)** des cassettes de Paula Abdul?
> **Je voudrais** dix tranches de jambon.
> **J'ai besoin de** rosbif. Assez pour quatre personnes.
> **Je prends** un kilo de pommes de terre et deux concombres.

*Pour demander le prix de quelque chose*

> **C'est combien?**
> **Ça coûte combien?**
> **Ça fait combien?**
> **Je vous dois combien? (Combien est-ce que je vous dois?)**
> **Il (elle, ils, elles) vaut (valent) combien, ce (cet, cette, ces)...?**

**E.   Faisons un pique-nique.** You're going on a picnic and one of your friends is going to do the shopping for it. Explain to him or her where to go and what to buy.

> *Modèle:*   *D'abord tu vas à la boulangerie. Tu vas acheter une baguette et un pain de campagne. Ensuite tu vas aller...*

**F.   Bien sûr, Mme Thibaudet.** Mme Thibaudet is feeling a bit under the weather and you have agreed to do the weekly shopping for her. Using the list below, go the appropriate stores and make your purchases. She has given you 200 francs. Is it enough?

| | |
|---|---|
| rôti de bœuf (pour 4 personnes) | Vittel (2 bouteilles) |
| pommes de terre (1 kilo) | poulet (1) |
| salade de concombres (1 livre) | éclairs (2) |
| tomates (1 livre) | brie (250 grammes) |
| baguettes (2) | saucisson (16 tranches) |
| tarte (ou gâteau) (1) | jambon (4 tranches) |

**G.   Est-ce que vous avez oublié...?** When you come back from your shopping trip in Exercise F, Mme Thibaudet questions you about what you bought and what you forgot. You may have to explain that you didn't have enough money for everything.

**H.   À l'épicerie.** You're in an **épicerie,** buying food for a dinner you're making for your friends. Using a variety of expressions, explain what you need and want. Also ask how much the various items cost and how much you owe for everything. Be sure to use polite expressions of greeting, thanking, and leave-taking.

**I.   À la Fnac.** You're at the Fnac in Toulouse, buying a birthday present for your best friend. Explain what your friend likes to do in his/her leisure time and what his interests are. Ask about the latest records and music videos. Finally, make a selection, find out if you can pay for the item by check, thank the salesperson, and say good-bye.

Ex. E: ⇄

**Reminder,** Ex. E: Use the expressions **d'abord** or **premièrement** *(first),* **puis** or **ensuite** *(then),* and **enfin** or **finalement** when you enumerate the tasks.

Ex. F: ⇄ or ○

**Suggestion:** Since Exs. F and G are different versions of exercises done earlier in the chapter, they could be eliminated if you're short of time. Or, they can be expanded to involve the whole class (See Instructor's Guide.)

Ex. G: ⇄

Ex. H: ⇄

Ex. I: ⇄

# PORTRAIT

## *Madame Thibaudet, Bordeaux (Gironde), France*

Je suis née à Bordeaux et j'y ai toujours habité. J'adore ma ville et j'ai un grand nombre d'amis de mon âge. Maintenant que je suis à la retraite, j'ai beaucoup de temps à passer avec mes enfants et mes deux petites filles. Mon mari travaille encore, alors il n'est pas souvent à la maison. Nous menons une vie assez modeste, mais nous adorons manger des bonnes choses. C'est pour ça que je passe pas mal de temps dans la cuisine à préparer des bons repas. Je fais les courses une fois par semaine chez les petits commerçants dans le quartier. Bien sûr, j'achète mon pain frais tous les matins chez le boulanger. Je suis très contente de ma vie.

# Profil

## *Bordeaux*

**SITUATION:** dans le sud-ouest de la France, sur la Gironde (estuaire de la Garonne)

**DÉPARTEMENT:** Gironde (33)

**PROVINCE:** Aquitaine

**POPULATION:** 254 122 habitants (5$^e$ ville de France par sa population)

**AGGLOMÉRATION:** 640 012 habitants

**IMPORTANCE:** un des grands ports de France

**INDUSTRIE:** métallurgie, mécanique, alimentation, aéronautique

**AGRICULTURE:** vin (4$^e$ rang national pour la production), blé, tabac, lait

**LIEUX D'INTÉRÊT:** le Grand Théâtre, le port, la place de la Bourse, la cathédrale St-André, la tour St-Michel

**HISTOIRE:**  domination des Romains qui introduisent la vigne dite «le claret», domination des ducs d'Aquitaine, Éléonor d'Aquitaine (personnage important au 12ᵉ siècle), occupation anglaise pendant la guerre de Cent ans (1337–1453)

**À discuter:** Which state is the major wine producer in the United States? What do you know about it? What other U.S. states are known for their wine production?

*Vignobles dans la campagne près de Bordeaux*

## L·E·X·I·Q·U·E

### Pour se débrouiller

*Pour indiquer ce que vous désirez dans un magasin*
Donnez-moi...
Est-ce que vous avez...? (Avez-vous...?)
Il me faut...
Je voudrais...
J'ai besoin de...
Je prends... (Je vais prendre...)

*Pour demander le prix de quelque chose*
Ça coûte combien?
Ça fait combien?
C'est combien?
Je vous dois combien? (Combien est-ce que je vous dois?)
Il (elle, ils, elles) vaut (valent) combien, ce (cet, cette, ces)...?

*Pour indiquer la quantité*

assez de (pas assez de)
beaucoup de
une boîte de
une botte de
un bout de
une bouteille de

un demi-kilo de
une douzaine de
____ grammes de
un kilo de
un litre de
une livre de

un morceau de
une tasse de
une tranche de
trop de

## Thèmes et contextes

*Les magasins et les petits commerçants*

une boulangerie—un(e) boulanger(-ère)
une boucherie—un(e) boucher(-ère)
une charcuterie—un(e) charcutier(-ère)
un centre commercial
une épicerie—un(e) épicier(-ère)
un grand magasin
un magasin de jouets
un magasin de sport
un marché en plein air
une pâtisserie—un(e) pâtissier(-ère)
un supermarché

*L'argent* (m.)

une caisse
une carte de crédit
un chèque
un distributeur automatique de billets
en espèces

*La musique*

une cassette vierge
une chanson
un disque
une radio-cassette
une vidéo
un vidéoclip

*Un magasin de jouets*

un ballon
un camion
un jeu vidéo
un jouet
une poupée
un robot

*Un magasin de sport*

un appareil de gymnastique
un ballon (de foot)
une raquette (une balle) de tennis
un vélo

*La boulangerie-pâtisserie*

une baguette
un croissant
un éclair
un gâteau (au chocolat)
un millefeuille
un pain de mie
un pain au chocolat
un pain de campagne
une pâtisserie
un petit pain
une religieuse
une tarte (aux pommes,
    aux fraises, aux abricots)
une tartelette (au citron)

*La charcuterie*

le jambon
le pâté
un rôti de porc cuit
une salade (de tomates,
    de concombres, de thon)
une saucisse
un saucisson

*La boucherie*

un bifteck
le bœuf
le canard
le gigot
le mouton
le porc
le poulet
un rôti (de porc, de bœuf)
la viande

*Le petit déjeuner*
   le bacon
   les céréales *(f.pl.)*
   la confiture
   le jus d'orange
   le lait
   les œufs *(m.pl.)*
   le toast (le pain grillé)

*Les légumes* (m.pl.)
   une asperge
   une carotte
   un champignon
   un chou
   la choucroute
   un concombre
   une courgette
   un haricot vert
   un oignon
   un petit pois
   une pomme de terre
   un radis
   une salade
   une tomate

*Les fruits* (m.pl.)
   un abricot
   une banane
   une cerise
   un citron
   une fraise
   une framboise
   un melon
   une orange
   une pêche
   une poire
   une pomme

*Les produits laitiers* (m.pl.)
   le beurre
   la crème
   le fromage (le brie,
      le camembert, le gruyère)
   le yaourt

*Les produits surgelés* (m.pl.)
   la glace
   la pizza
   le poisson
   les pommes frites *(f.pl.)*

*Autres produits alimentaires*
   la farine
   l'huile *(f.)*
   le ketchup
   la mayonnaise
   la moutarde
   les pâtes *(f.pl.)*
   le poivre
   le riz
   le sel
   le sucre

## Vocabulaire général

*Verbes*
   accepter
   acheter
   chercher
   devoir
   faire les (des) courses
   louer
   penser
   rêver

ALLONS-Y!
Vídeo Program

### ACTE 6

**V O C A B U L A I R E**

SCÈNE 1: LES COURSES
les courgettes   *zucchini*
une laitue   *lettuce*
les champignons
   *mushrooms*

SCÈNE 2: AU CENTRE COM-
   MERCIAL
mes courses d'alimenta-
tion   *my food shop-
ping*
des cadeaux   *gifts*
des fringues = des vête-
ments *(familier)*
(la) consommation
   *consumer goods*
des lunettes   *glasses*
un magasin de bijoux
   *jewelry store*
la nourriture   *food*
sert (servir)   *to serve*
l'entretien   *the upkeep*

*Jean Hébert*
*Lyon (Rhône-Alpes),*
*France*

—Tu vas faire des études ici?
—Oui, je suis aux États-Unis pour toute l'année.

# Parlons des études!

## OBJECTIVES

**In this chapter, you will learn:**
- to talk about your university and your studies;
- to describe objects;
- to describe people;
- to react positively and negatively to what is said;
- to understand conversations about academic life;
- to read texts and documents about French education.

**CHAPTER SUPPORT MATERIALS** (STUDENT)

**Cahier:** pp. 165–186

 **Student Tape:** Chapitre 7 Segments 1, 2, 3

**CHAPTER SUPPORT MATERIALS (INSTRUCTOR)**

 Transparencies: 7-1 through 7-5

 **Instructor's Tape:** Chapitre 7, Text, pp. 254, 267, 279, 294

 **SYSTÈME-D** *software:* Writing activities for this chapter are found in the **Cahier:** Ex. IV, V, VI (p. 169), Ex. IV, V (p. 173), Ex. V (p. 178), *Rédigeons!* (p. 184).

 Multimedia: See the Resource Manual for correlation to our multimedia product.

**ALLONS-Y!**
Video Program

**ACTE 7**
SCÈNE 1: LES ÉTUDES
SCÈNE 2: LA VIE DES ÉTUDIANTS

Première étape    L'université
Deuxième étape    Les profs et les étudiants
Troisième étape   Les cours
Quatrième étape   Lecture: Demain la faculté

**Instructor's Tape:**
**L'université**

The **Points de départ** in
Chapter 7 present university
life from an American point of
view. They are designed to
give students the French
vocabulary to talk about their
educational experiences.

**Transparency:**
**7-1** (map of campus)

among

state

ALLONS-Y!
Vidéo Program

ACTE 7: SCÈNE 1
LES ÉTUDES

**QUESTIONS DE FOND**
1. Nommez quatre
   spécialités des étu-
   diants français à la
   Sorbonne.
2. Comparez-les à
   celles de votre
   propre université.

**Suggestion:** To introduce
vocabulary, lead students
through the map of a campus.
Give your own description first,
using some of the same words
used by Barbara and Susan.
Then follow up by asking questions about the campus.

Most of the

residence halls (dorms)

**Suggestion, Point de départ:**
Have students listen to the recording of the monologues.
The recording may also be
used as a listening comprehension exercise.

**Reminder:** Point out that **un
collège** is roughly equivalent
to middle school. It is therefore not a cognate of the
generic English word *college*.

# PREMIÈRE ÉTAPE

## Point de départ

### *L'université*

Jean Hébert arrive de Lyon pour faire des études dans une université aux États-Unis. En parlant avec deux étudiantes, Barbara et Susan, il est surpris d'apprendre qu'il y a des différences importantes **parmi** les universités améri-caines. Barbara et Susan comparent les campus où elles font leurs études. Barbara est étudiante dans une grande université **d'état,** son amie Susan étudie dans une petite université dans la même région.

**Barbara**

**Susan**

Moi, je suis étudiante dans une université d'état.

Mon université est située au centre d'une grande ville. Beaucoup d'étudiants habitent en ville—chez eux ou dans des appartements.

Sur le campus il y a un centre d'étudiants, un stade, deux grandes piscines, une grande librairie, un musée d'art, une salle de concert et un nombre limité de résidences. Mon campus est comme une petite ville où il y a même un hôtel.

Et moi, je fais mes études dans une petite université privée.

Mon université se trouve dans un petit village pas trop loin d'une grande ville. **La plupart des** étudiants habitent sur le campus dans des **résidences universitaires.**

Mon campus a beaucoup d'espaces verts, une bibliothèque, une piscine et quelques résidences universitaires.

Mon université **comprend** la **faculté** de sciences et de lettres, la faculté de **droit,** l'école des études commerciales, la faculté de médecine et l'école des sciences agricoles, **chacune** avec ses propres bâtiments. Chez nous, on peut préparer un diplôme «undergraduate» ou un diplôme avancé (la **maîtrise** ou le doctorat).

À mon université **il n'y a que** la faculté de sciences et de lettres. Toutes les salles de classe et tous les **bureaux** des profs se trouvent dans deux bâtiments au centre du campus. Tous les étudiants préparent un **diplôme** «undergraduate» qui se fait en quatre ans.

includes  /  there is only
school
law
offices

each one

degree

master's degree

Nos classes sont très grandes. D'habitude le professeur fait une **conférence,** ensuite nous nous divisons en petits groupes pour discuter avec ses assistants. Il y a un grand nombre d'étudiants qui **sèchent** leurs cours. Mais nos classes de langue et d'anglais sont petites et il faut toujours être là.

Nos classes sont généralement petites. Nous avons l'occasion de poser des questions au professeur. La plupart des étudiants **assistent à** leurs cours.

lecture

attend

cut (a class)

Notre année scolaire est divisée en trimestres. Nous **rentrons début** septembre. Nous passons des examens **au milieu** et à la fin de chaque trimestre. L'année se termine début juin.

Notre année est divisée en semestres. La **rentrée** est au début du mois de septembre. Nous passons des examens au milieu et à la fin de chaque semestre (en décembre et en mai). L'année se termine fin mai ou début juin.

go back to school  /  first day of classes
at the beginning of
in the middle

**Follow-up, Point de départ:**
Discuss in English the differences between Barbara's and Susan's schools.

## Note culturelle

There are some notable differences between the French and the American university systems. In France, education is nationalized, and therefore all schools, including universities, are controlled by the government (**ministère de l'éducation nationale**). French universities do not charge tuition and admission is open to anyone who has passed the **baccalauréat** exam (competitive national exam) at the end of secondary school (**lycée**). Although university admission is open, an exam at the end of the first year determines who may continue into the second year. About 60 percent of French university students do not pass this exam and must repeat their first year. Those who complete the first two years of college in a maximum of three years may then continue at their leisure. Because education is free, there are more "professional" students in France than there are in the United States.

**Questions:** In your opinion, what are the advantages and disadvantages of a tuition-free university system? (Think about such things as student rights and privileges, etc.) If you didn't have to pay tuition, do you think you would take longer to complete your degree?

## À VOUS! (Exercices de vocabulaire)

Implementation, Exs. A and B: Have students work in pairs; then verify with the entire class.

**A.  Mon université.** Complete the sentences with information about your personal educational situation.

1.  Je fais mes études à ____ .
2.  C'est une ____ université ____ .
3.  Elle est située ____ .
4.  La plupart des étudiants habitent ____ .
5.  L'université comprend ____ faculté(s): ____ .

6. Sur mon campus, il y a ___ .
7. Moi, je prépare un diplôme de ___ .
8. Un jour je voudrais préparer ___ de ___ . *Ou:* Je n'ai pas l'intention de ___ .
9. En général, les classes sont ___ .
10. L'année scolaire est divisée en ___ .
11. La rentrée des classes est ___ .
12. Nous passons des examens ___ .
13. L'année se termine ___ .
14. Dans ma région il y a ___ grande(s) université(s) et ___ petite(s) université(s) privée(s).

**B. Une autre université.** Redo Exercise A by giving information about a friend who is in a university that is very different from yours.

*Modèle:*     *Mon ami(e) ___ fait ses études à ___ . C'est une université ___ .*

## S·T·R·U·C·T·U·R·E

### L'accord des adjectifs

You've already learned some adjectives of nationality and profession, and you've seen a number of adjectives in your readings. Adjectives provide information about the nouns they modify. For example, they help to distinguish between two similar objects:

Ce bâtiment est grand.          Ce bâtiment est petit.
Ce bâtiment est **laid.**          Ce bâtiment est **beau (joli).**          ugly / beautiful (pretty)
Ce bâtiment est moderne.          Ce bâtiment est **vieux.**          old

**Suggestion,** Adjective agreement: (1) Remind students of need for agreement by using **américain.** Remind them that *things* have gender by recalling **le mois (vendredi) dernier** and **l'année (la semaine) dernière.** (2) Establish basic *oral* principle: feminine form ends in consonant sound, masculine form ends in vowel sound. (3) Establish basic *written* principle: feminine, **-e;** masculine, another letter. (4) Go through summary in text, pointing out examples that confirm both rules and exceptions.

Cette conférence est intéressante.
Cette conférence est **facile.**
Cette conférence est **bonne.**

easy
good

**Vocabulary:** Note that **conférence** is a false cognate that means *lecture,* not *conference.*

boring

bad

Cette conférence est **ennuyeuse.**
Cette conférence est difficile.
Cette conférence est **mauvaise.**

**Quelles sont les couleurs de votre université?**

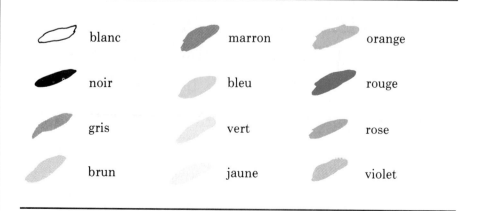

blanc          marron          orange

noir           bleu            rouge

gris           vert            rose

brun           jaune           violet

~~~~~~~~~~~~~~ **Adjective agreement** ~~~~~~~~~~~~~~

In French, adjectives must agree in gender with the nouns they modify. Therefore, if the noun is feminine, the adjective is also feminine. And if the noun is masculine, the adjective is also masculine.

~~~~~~~~~~~~~~ **Feminine forms of adjectives** ~~~~~~~~~~~~~~

1. The feminine form of most adjectives is created by adding **-e** to the masculine form. Note that when this happens, the last consonant is pronounced:

   Le musée est **grand.**      La bibliothèque est **grande.**

2. If the masculine form of an adjective ends in **-e,** the feminine form stays the same:

   Le cours est **difficile.**      La leçon est **difficile.**

3. Some adjectives undergo special changes:

   | | | | |
   |---|---|---|---|
   | **-er** | changes to | **-ère** | **cher → chère** |
   | **-x** | changes to | **-se** | **ennuyeux → ennuyeuse** |
   | **-et** | changes to | **-ette** | **violet → violette** |
   | **-et** | changes to | **-ète** | **secret → secrète** |
   | **-n** | changes to | **-nne** | **bon → bonne** |
   | **-el** | changes to | **-elle** | **sensationnel → sensationnelle** |
   | **-f** | changes to | **-ve** | **sportif → sportive** |

4. Adjectives of color that come from names of objects usually don't change in the feminine:

   Voilà un sac **marron.**      Voici une table **marron.**
   Voilà un livre **orange.**      Voici une auto **orange.**

5. Certain adjective forms are irregular and must be learned separately:

   Le campus est **beau.**      La ville est **belle.**
   Le quartier est **vieux.**      La maison est **vieille.**
   Le bâtiment est **blanc.**      La salle de classe est **blanche.**

▲  ▲  ▲

## APPLICATION

**C.** First give the feminine form of each adjective.

*Modèle:*    gris    *grise*

1. facile
2. suisse
3. français
4. petit
5. vert
6. premier

7. délicieux
8. dernier
9. blanc
10. ambitieux
11. vieux
12. italien

13. mauvais
14. intellectuel
15. ennuyeux
16. discret
17. actif
18. grand

Now give the masculine form of each adjective.

*Modèle:*    verte    *vert*

19. intéressante
20. française
21. blanche
22. première
23. mauvaise
24. ennuyeuse
25. belle

26. vieille
27. italienne
28. délicieuse
29. légère *(light)*
30. bonne
31. naïve
32. violette

**D.** **Comparaisons.** You and your friend are comparing where you live and what you own. For each statement, respond with another statement that uses the same adjective and the cue in parentheses. Remember to make the adjectives agree with the nouns.

*Modèle:*    Mon appartement est petit. (maison)
            *Ma maison est petite.*

**Vocabulary,** Ex. D, No. 1: Use the adjective **neuf** **(neuve)** when *new* means *brand new.* Use the adjective **nouveau** when *new* means *changed, no longer the same.*

1. Ma maison est neuve. (appartement)
2. Mon vélo est vieux. (voiture)
3. Ma vidéo est intéressante. (livre)
4. Ma chaîne stéréo est chère. (ordinateur)
5. Mon sac à dos est marron. (valise *[suitcase]*)
6. Mon vélomoteur est japonais. (voiture)
7. Mon appartement est grand. (chambre)
8. Mon appartement est blanc. (maison)

**E.** **De quelle couleur est...?** Choose the color that best describes each object.

1. De quelle couleur est le ciel?
2. De quelle couleur sont les pommes?
3. De quelle couleur sont les abricots?
4. De quelle couleur sont les bananes?
5. De quelle couleur sont les petits pois?
6. De quelle couleur sont les pommes de terre?

7.   De quelle couleur est la neige?
8.   De quelle couleur sont les nuages?
9.   De quelle couleur sont les arbres *(trees)* en automne?
10.   De quelle couleur sont les murs *(walls)* de votre chambre?

**F.   Comment est...?** Which adjectives in the list best describe each drawing?

grand / beau / difficile / moderne / ennuyeux / intéressant / facile /
laid / bon / mauvais / joli / petit / vieux / sensationnel / compliqué /
français / extraordinaire / fantastique / amusant / chouette / long

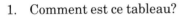

1.   Comment est ce tableau?

2.   Comment est cette ville?

3.   Comment est ce cours?

4.   Comment est ce livre?

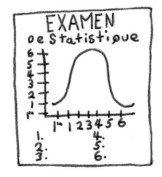

5.   Comment est cet examen?

6.   Comment est cette voiture?

**Grammar: Marron** and **orange** don't change form in the plural: **des cheveux marron, des crayons orange.**

## Note grammaticale

### *Le pluriel des adjectifs*

In addition to agreeing in gender, adjectives must agree in number with the nouns they modify. That means that if a noun is singular, the adjective must be singular. And if the noun is plural, the adjective must be plural.

1. The plural form of most adjectives is created by adding **-s** to the singular form. Note that there is no pronunciation change from singular to plural:

   Le stylo est **bleu.**          Les stylos sont **bleus.**
   La classe est **ennuyeuse.**    Les classes sont **ennuyeuses.**

2. If the masculine singular form of an adjective ends in **-s** or **-x,** the masculine plural form remains the same. Again, there is no change in pronunciation:

   Ce film est **mauvais.**    Ces films sont **mauvais.**
   Ce livre est **vieux.**     Ces livres sont **vieux.**

3. If the singular form of an adjective ends in **-eau,** the plural form adds **-x.** Again, there is no change in pronunciation:

   Ce livre est **beau.**    Ces livres sont **beaux.**

**G.** Give the plural form of each adjective and tell whether you added an **-s,** an **-x,** or nothing.

1.  petit
2.  laide
3.  ennuyeuse
4.  dernier
5.  noir

6.  gris
7.  vieille
8.  brun
9.  intéressant
10. beau

11. bon
12. blanche
13. vieux
14. mauvais
15. orange

**H.   Ma maison est...** Use an adjective to make a statement about each object. Then ask another student a question. Follow the model.

Ex. H: ⇄

*Modèle:*      ma maison
—*Ma maison est grande. Et ta maison?*
—*Ma maison est grande aussi.* or *Ma maison n'est pas grande.*
   *Elle est petite.*

mon livre
—*Mon livre est intéressant. Et ton livre?*
—*Mon livre est intéressant aussi.* or *Mon livre n'est pas inté-*
   *ressant. Il est ennuyeux.*

1. ma maison (mon appartement)   2. ma chambre   3. mes livres   4. mon vélo   5. mon auto   6. mes vidéos (mes disques)   7. ma ville   8. mon cours d'anglais (de mathématiques, de littérature, de français, etc.)

**Le savez-vous?**
▲▲▲▲▲▲▲▲▲▲▲▲▲▲▲
The strongly centralized nature of the French educational system dates from
a.  the Middle Ages
b.  the reign of Louis XIV
c.  the time of Napoleon
d.  The end of World War II

Réponse  ▲▲▲

# PRONONCIATION   *La voyelle o*

**Student Tape:**
Chapitre 7
Segment 1

The letter **o** represents two different sounds in French: [ɔ], which is similar to the vowel sound in the English word *lost,* and [o], which is similar to the vowel sound in the English word *go* (without a diphthong). The sound [o] is used when **o** is the last sound of a word (**métro, gigot),** before **s** plus a vowel (**rose),** and when the letter **o** has a circumflex (**hôtel).** In other cases, the letter **o** is pronounced [ɔ].

**I.**   Read each word aloud, being careful to clearly pronounce the [ɔ] of the first word and avoid making a diphthong with [o] in the second.

notre, nos  /  votre, vos  /  téléphoner, métro  /  sport, hôte  /  orage, chose  / octobre, prose  /  soleil, exposé

**J.**   Read each word aloud, being careful to distinguish between [ɔ] and [o].

pomme  /  rôti  /  promenade  /  chocolat  /  kilo  /  trop  /  roquefort  /  gigot  / Sorbonne  /  haricots  /  photo  /  monotone  /  chose  /  bonne

S·T·R·U·C·T·U·R·E

## La place des adjectifs

J'ai acheté un vélomoteur **neuf.**
C'est un film **japonais.**
J'ai trouvé des livres **intéressants** à la bibliothèque.

In French, unlike in English, an adjective is usually placed *after* the noun it modifies. However, the following adjectives are exceptions, because they are normally placed *before* the noun they modify: **grand, petit, vieux, jeune, bon, mauvais, nouveau, long, beau, joli, autre:**

Elle habite dans un **petit** appartement.
Nous avons eu une **mauvaise** journée.
J'ai rencontré des **jeunes** filles du Maroc.

When two adjectives modify the same noun, each adjective occupies its normal position, either before or after the noun:

J'ai acheté une **jolie petite** maison.
Nous avons visité une **belle** cathédrale **gothique.**
C'est une voiture **beige** et **marron.**

▲▲▲ C               ▲    ▲    ▲

## APPLICATION

**K.**   **Nous ne sommes jamais d'accord.** *(We never agree.)* No matter what you and your friends talk about, you never seem to agree. Contradict each statement by using an adjective with the opposite meaning.

> *Modèle:*     C'est un petit appartement.
>                 *Au contraire! C'est un grand appartement.*

1. C'est une voiture neuve.
2. C'est un grand musée.
3. C'est un exercice difficile.
4. C'est une belle maison.
5. Ce sont des livres intéressants.
6. Ce sont des vieilles églises.
7. Ce sont des mauvaises idées.
8. C'est un voyage ennuyeux.
9. C'est un bon restaurant.
10. Ce sont des bons ordinateurs.
11. C'est un beau tableau.

**L.  Quelle sorte de ___ avez-vous?** *(What kind of ___ do you have?)* Choose one or two adjectives from the list to answer each question.

allemand / américain / anglais / beau / blanc / chinois / difficile / facile / français / grand / gris / italien / japonais / jaune / joli / laid / long / moderne / nouveau / petit / rouge / vert / vieux

*Modèle:*　　Quelle sorte de maison avez-vous?
　　　　　　*Nous avons une petite maison blanche.*

1. Quelle sorte de maison avez-vous?
2. Quelle sorte d'auto avez-vous (voulez-vous avoir)?
3. Quelle sorte de restaurant préférez-vous?
4. Quelles sortes d'ami(e)s est-ce que vous avez?
5. Quelles sortes de devoirs faites-vous pour le cours de français?
6. Quelle sorte de voyage avez-vous fait?
7. Quelle sorte de vélo avez-vous?
8. Quelles sortes d'examens avez-vous dans le cours de français?

**M.  J'ai vu un film.** *(I saw a film.)* Pick a film you've seen recently and tell your classmate about it. Use as many adjectives as you can to describe the film and give your opinion about it. Your classmate will ask you questions.

Ex. M: ⇄

SUGGESTED ADJECTIVES: **bon, mauvais, beau, laid, intéressant, sensationnel, fantastique, long, historique, émouvant** *(moving),* **chouette, ennuyeux, amusant, triste** *(sad).*

*Modèle:*　　*Hier soir j'ai vu un très beau film. Il s'appelle* Napoléon. *C'est un film historique. Il est très émouvant mais un peu triste. C'est aussi un film très long. J'ai beaucoup appris. C'est un film intéressant.*

## Débrouillons-nous!

▲ ▲ ▲ ▲ ▲ ▲ ▲ ▲ ▲ **Débrouillons-nous!** ▲ ▲ ▲ ▲ ▲ ▲ ▲ ▲ ▲

*Petite révision de l'étape*

Ex. N: ⇄

**N. Échange.** Posez les questions à un(e) autre étudiant(e), qui va vous répondre.

1. Est-ce que ta famille habite dans une maison? De quelle couleur est la maison? C'est une grande maison? (Est-ce que ta famille habite dans un appartement? Est-ce que l'appartement est grand? C'est un joli appartement?)
2. Est-ce que tu as une auto? De quelle couleur est ton auto? C'est une auto neuve? C'est une auto américaine? (Est-ce que tu as un vélo? De quelle couleur est ton vélo? C'est un vélo neuf? C'est un vélo américain?)
3. Est-ce qu'il y a des restaurants près du campus? Comment sont-ils?
4. Depuis combien de temps fais-tu des études dans cette université?
5. Pourquoi est-ce que tu as choisi *(did you choose)* cette université?
6. Comment sont tes cours?
7. D'habitude, est-ce que tu assistes à tes cours?
8. Combien de fois as-tu séché ton cours de français?

Ex. O: △

**Suggestion,** Ex. O: Besides talking about the campus itself, you may talk about the surrounding area and things to do in your town. Remember to use some expressions of quantity, such as **assez de, beaucoup de, pas trop de,** etc.

**O. Mon université.** You're talking to some French friends of your parents. They're planning to send their son (daughter) to college in the United States for a couple of years. Describe your university in the most positive terms to persuade them that it's an excellent place to pursue one's studies.

*Jean Hébert et deux amis.*

**À faire chez vous: CAHIER,** Chapitre 7 / 1ᵉʳᵉ étape

# DEUXIÈME ÉTAPE
## Point de départ

▼▼▼▼▼▼▼▼▼▼▼▼▼▼▼

Instructor's Tape:
Les profs et les
étudiants

Suggestion, Point de départ:
Have students listen to the
monologues on tape. Play the
monologues in small seg-
ments and ask basic information questions about each
segment. Then play all four
monologues as students follow the text.

## *Les profs et les étudiants*

Dans ses discussions avec les profs et les étudiants, Jean Hébert découvre que les universités américaines se composent de gens qui ont des personnalités et des goûts très variés.

### Portraits de deux profs

**Le professeur Santerre**

**Le professeur Merlot**

ALLONS-Y!
Vidéo Program

ACTE 7: SCÈNE 2
LA VIE DES ÉTUDIANTS

**QUESTION DE FOND**
Nommez deux avantages et deux inconvénients de la vie d'un(e) étudiant(e) à la Sorbonne.

| | |
|---|---|
| Voici le professeur Santerre. Il est **d'un certain âge.** | Voici le professeur Merlot. Elle est assez jeune. |

Il a une moustache et une barbe. Il a les cheveux courts et gris et les yeux bleus. Il est **costaud,** mais il n'est pas **gros.**

Elle porte des **lunettes,** elle a les cheveux longs, les yeux bruns et elle est grande et **mince.**

middle-aged
glasses

heavyset / thin (slender)
fat

Le professeur Santerre est très énergique. Il adore **enseigner** et il est très à l'aise avec ses étudiants. Il fait des recherches pour ses cours, mais il **publie** très rarement. Pour lui, l'important c'est les étudiants **débutants** de **niveau** «undergraduate».

Le professeur Merlot est intellectuel et un peu timide. Elle préfère la **recherche** à l'**enseignement.** Elle adore passer son temps à la bibliothèque ou à la maison devant son ordinateur. Elle a déjà publié **plusieurs** articles et un livre. Pour elle, l'important, c'est la recherche et son travail avec les étudiants de niveau maîtrise ou doctorat.

to teach
research
teaching
publishes

beginning
level / several

| | | |
|---|---|---|
| rather | M. Santerre est idéaliste. | Mlle Merlot est **plutôt** réaliste. |
| | Il est patient. | Elle est impatiente. |
| | Il est généreux. | Elle est généreuse aussi. |
| | Il est actif. | Elle est ambitieuse. |
| | Il est indépendant. | Elle est indépendante aussi. |
| looks (seems) | Il est jovial. | Elle **a l'air** un peu triste. |
| single | Il est marié. | Elle est **célibataire.** |
| | Il est heureux. | Elle est satisfaite de ce qu'elle a accompli. |

### Portrait de deux étudiants

#### Serge Cazenave

#### Marie Orlan

| | | |
|---|---|---|
| | Serge est jeune. Il n'a que 18 ans. Il est grand et costaud. Il a les cheveux blonds et les yeux verts. Il | Marie est un peu plus âgée. Elle est petite et svelte. Elle a les cheveux noirs et les yeux bruns. |
| tanned | est très **bronzé.** | Elle est un peu pâle. |
| | Serge est optimiste. | Marie est quelquefois pessimiste. |
| lazy | Il est un peu **paresseux.** | Elle est très active. |
| dishonest | Il est honnête. | Elle n'est pas **malhonnête.** |
| | Il est un peu naïf. | Elle est très réaliste. |
| sometimes | Il est **parfois** indiscret. | Elle est toujours discrète. |
| | Il n'est pas marié. | Elle est divorcée et mère de deux enfants. |
| in a good mood | Il est presque toujours **de bonne humeur.** | Elle est un peu nerveuse et quelquefois elle est de mauvaise humeur. |
| | Serge est un très bon étudiant, mais il n'est pas toujours très sérieux. | Marie est contente de continuer ses études. C'est une excellente étudiante. |

## Note culturelle

In 1971, France passed a law that created a system of continuing education for adults who, for whatever reason, were not able to complete their education when they were younger. This system is called **la formation permanente** and is designed to diminish the educational inequalities that exist in France. Since 1971, millions of French people have taken advantage of continuing education programs to advance in their jobs. Just as important, those who don't complete the **bac** know that they can continue their education at a later time and that they always have a second chance to improve their work situation.

**Questions:** Have you ever taken a continuing education course? Which one(s)? Are you a returning adult student? Do you know someone who is a returning adult student?

## À VOUS! (Exercices de vocabulaire)

Transparency: 7-3 (Ex. A, scenes for practicing descriptions)

**A. Mme Rimadier et Marc Oursin.** Answer the questions based on what you see in the drawings.

Implementation, Ex. A: Have students work in pairs; then verify with the entire class.

Voici Madame Rimadier.

1. Comment est-elle? Est-elle petite? Est-ce qu'elle a les cheveux courts? Est-elle mince? Est-ce qu'elle est âgée ou plutôt jeune?
2. Combien d'enfants a-t-elle? Est-ce qu'ils sont jeunes? Quel âge ont-ils probablement?
3. Que fait Mme Rimadier dans sa vie professionnelle? Est-ce un bon ou un mauvais professeur? Est-ce qu'elle est enthousiaste ou ennuyeuse? Est-ce qu'elle aime enseigner?
4. Est-ce qu'elle fait aussi des recherches? Où est-ce qu'elle va pour faire ses recherches? Est-ce qu'elle est intellectuelle? Est-elle paresseuse?
5. Qu'est-ce qu'elle fait pour s'amuser? Est-ce qu'elle est sportive?
6. Est-ce qu'elle travaille beaucoup? Est-ce que vous pensez qu'elle est ambitieuse? Est-ce qu'elle a l'air satisfaite de sa vie? Est-ce qu'elle est optimiste ou pessimiste?

Voici Marc Oursin.

7. Comment est-il? Faites sa description physique.
8. Est-ce qu'il s'amuse beaucoup avec ses amis? Est-ce qu'il est paresseux? Est-ce qu'il est sportif? Qu'est-ce qu'il aime faire?
9. Est-ce qu'il est travailleur? Est-il studieux? Est-ce qu'il est intellectuel?
10. Est-il optimiste ou pessimiste? Est-ce qu'il est ambitieux?
11. En général, est-ce qu'il a l'air content?

**Vocabulary,** Ex. B: Note that **belle** and **jolie** are used to say that a woman is beautiful (pretty) and **beau** is used to say that a man is handsome.

Ex. B: ⇄

**B.   Deux portraits.** Describe the two people indicated below. Give a physical description first. Then describe their personality traits. Your classmate will respond by asking you two more questions about these people.

1.  a professor

2.  a student

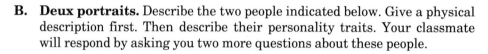

R·E·P·R·I·S·E

*Première étape*

Ex. C: △

**C.   Visitons le palais et le jardin du Luxembourg!** You're guiding your friends around the Luxembourg Palace and Gardens in Paris. Using the notes below, describe what you see. You may add to the description or change it, as long as you keep the main idea.

> *Modèle:*      parc / immense
> *C'est un parc immense.* or *C'est un très grand parc.* or *Nous sommes ici dans un parc immense.*

**Le jardin du Luxembourg**
1.  parc / intéressant
2.  touristes *(m.)* / américain
3.  théâtre de marionnettes / joli / petit
4.  allées *(paths [f.])* / serpentin
5.  statue *(f.)* de Delacroix / beau

**Le palais du Luxembourg**
6.  porte / monumental
7.  terrasse *(f.)* / beau
8.  bibliothèque / vieux
9.  peintures de Rubens / beau
10.  deux patios *(m.)* / élégant

**D. Des monuments.** Use two adjectives to describe each of the following Parisian monuments.

SUGGESTIONS: **petit, grand, moderne, vieux, intéressant, laid, beau, joli, affreux, sensationnel, fantastique**

*Modèle:*   la Conciergerie
*Elle est vieille et très grande.*

1.  la tour Eiffel

2.  l'arc de Triomphe

3. Notre-Dame de Paris

4. la tour Montparnasse

5. le musée du Louvre

6. l'obélisque de Louksor

# S·T·R·U·C·T·U·R·E

## Les adjectifs (suite)

Irregularities occur in two situations involving descriptive adjectives.

1. **Beau, nouveau, vieux**

   J'adore cet appartement. Il est très **beau.**
   Oui, tu as raison. C'est un **bel** appartement.

When the adjectives **beau, nouveau,** and **vieux** are used before a masculine singular noun beginning with a vowel or a vowel sound, each has a special form that allows liaison with the noun:

un **bel** hôtel        un **nouvel** ami        un **vieil** appartement

| *Summary of adjective forms:* **beau, nouveau, vieux** | | | |
| --- | --- | --- | --- |
| MASCULINE SINGULAR | beau | nouveau | vieux |
| MASCULINE SINGULAR<br>   before a vowel sound | bel | nouvel | vieil |
| MASCULINE PLURAL | beaux | nouveaux | vieux |
| FEMININE SINGULAR | belle | nouvelle | vieille |
| FEMININE PLURAL | belles | nouvelles | vieilles |

2. **Adjectives used with parts of the body**

   —Les yeux de ma mère **sont bleus.**
   —Comment?
   —Ma mère **a les** yeux **bleus** et **les** cheveux **blonds.**

In Chapter 2, you learned to use the verb **être** with adjectives to describe parts of the body. An even more common construction is to use the verb **avoir** with the definite article preceding the part of the body and the descriptive adjective.

▲   ▲   ▲

# APPLICATION

**E.**  Ajoutez les adjectifs et faites tous les changements nécessaires.

> *Modèles:*     C'est une maison. (beau)
> *C'est une belle maison.*
>
> Ce sont des arbres. (beau)
> *Ce sont des beaux arbres.*

1. C'est un livre. (beau)
2. Ce sont des maisons. (beau)
3. C'est un arbre. (beau)
4. C'est une église. (beau)
5. C'est un ami. (nouveau)
6. C'est une amie. (nouveau)
7. Ce sont des livres. (nouveau)
8. C'est un musée. (vieux)
9. C'est un hôtel. (vieux)
10. C'est une maison. (vieux)
11. Ce sont des églises. (vieux)
12. C'est un appareil-photo. (vieux)

**F.  Deux portraits.** Describe François and Yvette, using the elements provided. Use the verb **avoir** and the definite article in your sentences.

**François**
1. cheveux bruns
2. yeux bruns
3. cheveux très courts

**Yvette**
4. cheveux blonds
5. yeux bleus
6. cheveux longs

**G.  Ma famille et mes amis.** Tell one of your classmates about the people below. Give each person's age (if appropriate), physical description, and personality description. Select from the adjectives provided.

actif / ambitieux / beau / costaud / courageux / cruel / discret / dynamique / égoïste / énergique / frivole / généreux / grand / heureux / honnête / idéaliste / impatient / indépendant / indiscret / intelligent / jeune / joli / malhonnête / mince / naïf / optimiste / paresseux / patient / pessimiste / petit / réaliste / sérieux / sincère / sportif / svelte / triste / vieux

1. votre frère ou votre père
2. votre sœur ou votre mère
3. votre ami(e)
4. votre professeur (il ou elle)

# PRONONCIATION  *La combinaison **ou***

The combination **ou** in French is usually pronounced [u], as in the English word *boot* (without a diphthong): **nous, tourner.** However, when the **ou** combination is followed by a vowel sound, it is pronounced [w], as in the English word *will:* **oui.**

**H.**  Read each word aloud, being careful to distinguish between [u] and [w].

rouge / beaucoup / oui / poulet / couvert / ouest / jouer / tour / cousin / silhouette / Louvre / août / souvent / pirouette / moutarde

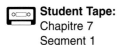

# S·T·R·U·C·T·U·R·E

## *Le comparatif*

In English, comparisons are made either by using a comparison word *(more, less, as)* or by adding the suffix *-er* to an adjective. In French, you must always use a comparison word.

### ~~~~ Comparison of adjectives and adverbs ~~~~

| | |
|---|---|
| Elle est **plus grande que** son frère. | She's *taller than* her brother. |
| Il est **aussi sérieux que** sa sœur. | He's *as serious as* his sister. |
| Ils travaillent **moins rapidement que** leurs amis. | They work *less rapidly than* their friends. |

The expressions **plus** *(more)*, **aussi** *(as)*, and **moins** *(less)* are used to compare adjectives and adverbs. They are followed by **que** *(than, as)*.

### ~~~~ Comparison of nouns ~~~~

| | |
|---|---|
| Nous avons **plus d'argent que** Paul. | We have *more money than* Paul. |
| J'ai **autant d'énergie que** lui. | I have *as much energy as* he (does). |
| Elle a **moins de tact que** moi. | She has *less tact than* I (do). |

The expressions **plus de** *(more)*, **autant de** *(as much)*, and **moins de** *(less)* are used to compare nouns and are also followed by **que.** If you want to use a pronoun rather than a noun in your comparison, use the stress pronouns **moi, toi, lui, elle, nous, vous, eux** *(they,* masculine), **elles.**

▲  ▲  ▲

**Suggestion,** Comparisons: Introduce by using students and traits or objects they possess: height **(grand)**, age **(âgé)**, speed **(marcher ou parler rapidement)**, skill in sports **(jouer bien)**, quality of books or films **(bon)**, quantity **(avoir des clés, des livres, des disques, des cassettes).**

**Reminder:** In French, most adverbs are formed by adding the suffix **-ment** to the feminine form of an adjective: *lente → lentement, sérieuse → sérieusement.*

## APPLICATION

**I.** Ajoutez les mots entre parenthèses et faites tous les changements nécessaires.

*Modèle:*     Philippe est jeune. (plus, son frère)
             *Philippe est plus jeune que son frère.*

1.  Francine est intelligente. (plus, sa sœur / aussi, son père / moins, son amie)
2.  Henri parle rapidement. (aussi, toi / moins, Jeanne / plus, moi)
3.  Nous avons beaucoup de disques. (plus, Philippe / autant, eux / moins, vous)
4.  Elles font beaucoup de progrès. (autant, Marie / plus, moi / moins, toi)

**J.   Les élèves du lycée Voltaire.** Make the comparisons indicated.

| Nom de l'élève | Examen de classement | Heures de préparation |
|---|---|---|
| Sylvie | $1^{\text{ère}}$ | 20 |
| Louis | $5^{\text{e}}$ | 15 |
| Yves | $19^{\text{e}}$ | 30 |
| Simone | $35^{\text{e}}$ | 15 |
| Gilbert | $60^{\text{e}}$ | 10 |

*Modèle:*     (intelligent) Yves et Simone
               *Yves est plus intelligent que Simone.*

1.   (intelligent) Sylvie et Yves / Louis et Simone / Gilbert et Louis / Simone et Sylvie / Gilbert et Sylvie

*Modèle:*     (faire des devoirs) Yves et Gilbert
               *Yves fait plus de devoirs que Gilbert.*

2.   (faire des devoirs) Yves et Simone / Louis et Simone / Gilbert et Sylvie / Louis et Gilbert / Gilbert et Yves

**K.   Géographie humaine: Les régions.** Compare the following regions in terms of their geographical size and population.

| Régions | Superficie (km²) | Population (millions) | Densité (hab./km²) |
|---|---|---|---|
| Afrique | 30 388 000 | 587 | 18,1 |
| Amérique | 42 081 000 | 803 | 15,9 |
| Asie | 27 580 000 | 3 036 | 102,6 |
| Europe | 4 937 000 | 492 | 99,7 |
| Océanie | 8 510 000 | 28 | 2,8 |
| U.R.S.S. | 22 402 000 | 278 | 12,4 |

*Modèles:*     (grand) l'Europe et l'Asie
               *L'Europe est moins grande que l'Asie.*

               (habitants) l'U.R.S.S. et l'Océanie
               *L'U.R.S.S a plus d'habitants que l'Océanie.*

               (habitants par km²) l'U.R.S.S. et l'Océanie
               *L'U.R.S.S. a plus d'habitants par kilomètre carré que l'Océanie.*

1.   (grand) l'Amérique et l'Océanie / l'U.R.S.S. et l'Afrique / l'Asie et l'Europe / l'Asie et l'Amérique / l'Océanie et l'Europe

2. (habitants) l'Asie et l'U.R.S.S. / l'Europe et l'Amérique / l'Afrique et l'Amérique / l'Europe et l'Océanie

3. (habitants par km²) l'Europe et l'Asie / l'Amérique et l'Afrique / l'Océanie et l'U.R.S.S. / l'Amérique et l'U.R.S.S.

---

### Note grammaticale

## Les comparatifs *meilleur* et *mieux*

| | |
|---|---|
| Mes notes sont **meilleures** **que** les notes de mon frère. | My grades are *better than* my brother's grades. |
| Il parle **mieux que** moi. | He speaks *better than* I (do). |

The adjective **bon** and the adverb **bien** have irregular comparative forms: **bon(ne)(s)** → **meilleur(e)(s), bien** → **mieux.** The English equivalent of **meilleur** and **mieux** is *better.* Be sure to distinguish between the adjective **meilleur,** which modifies a noun and agrees with it in gender and number, and the adverb **mieux,** which modifies a verb and is invariable. Notice that the comparative forms of **bon** and **bien** are regular when you want to indicate equality or inferiority:

Elle chante **aussi bien que** sa sœur.
Ces oranges-ci sont **moins bonnes que** ces oranges-là.

---

**L.** Add the words in parentheses and make all necessary changes.

1. Mes notes sont bonnes. (moins, tes notes / meilleur, les notes de Pierre / aussi, les notes de Micheline)
2. Marguerite chante bien. (mieux, moi / moins, Félicité / aussi, toi)

**M. Bon et bien.** Answer the questions according to the models. Be sure to distinguish between **bon** and **bien, meilleur** and **mieux.**

*Modèles:*   Quelle sorte d'étudiant est Georges? Comparez-le à Claire.
*Georges est un bon étudiant. C'est un meilleur étudiant que Claire.*

Comment Gérard chante-t-il? Comparez-le à Philippe.
*Gérard chante bien. Il chante mieux que Philippe.*

1. Quelle sorte d'étudiante est Valérie? Comparez-la à Denis.
2. Comment Annick chante-t-elle? Comparez-la à Mireille.
3. Comment Vincent parle-t-il? Comparez-le à Jean-Yves.
4. Quelle sorte d'assistante est Christiane? Comparez-la à Luce.
5. Quelle sorte de professeur est Antoine? Comparez-le à Robert.
6. Comment marche la Renault Clio? Comparez-la à la Peugeot.

**N. Les élèves du lycée Voltaire.** Make the indicated comparisons using **meilleur** and **mieux**.

| Nom de l'élève | Note en maths | Note en littérature |
|---|---|---|
| Sylvie | 14/20 | 16/20 |
| Louis | 16/20 | 10/20 |
| Yves | 12/20 | 12/20 |
| Simone | 8/20 | 11/20 |
| Gilbert | 8/20 | 6/20 |

*Modèle:*      (bon en littérature) Sylvie et Louis
            *Sylvie est meilleure en littérature que Louis.*

1.  (bon en littérature) Simone et Gilbert / Louis et Yves / Simone et Louis / Gilbert et Sylvie
2.  (bon en maths) Simone et Gilbert / Louis et Sylvie / Yves et Sylvie / Sylvie et Simone
3.  (travailler bien en littérature) Yves et Gilbert / Simone et Sylvie / Simone et Louis / Sylvie et Yves
4.  (travailler bien en maths) Gilbert et Simone / Yves et Gilbert / Louis et Sylvie / Yves et Sylvie / Sylvie et Gilbert

▲ ▲ ▲ ▲ ▲ ▲ ▲ ▲ ▲ **Débrouillons-nous!** ▲ ▲ ▲ ▲ ▲ ▲ ▲ ▲ ▲ ▲

*Petite révision de l'étape*

Ex. O: ⇄

**O. Vous et...** Compare yourself to your brother, sister, mother, father, friend, etc., using the following descriptive elements. Remember that the adjectives in the description must agree in gender and number with the nouns or pronouns they modify.

1.  être âgé(e)
2.  être intelligent(e)
3.  avoir des ami(e)s
4.  avoir du temps libre
5.  travailler sérieusement
6.  bien jouer au tennis
7.  bien chanter
8.  être optimiste
9.  être un(e) bon(ne) étudiant(e)
10. être ambitieux(-se)
11. dépenser de l'argent
12. avoir de l'imagination

Ex. P: ⇄

**P. Deux professeurs.** You and your classmate are discussing your professors. Each of you compares two professors you have had for a course. Compare physical and personality traits as well as teaching (**enseigner** = *to teach*).

**À faire chez vous:**
CAHIER, Chapitre 7 / 2e étape

# TROISIÈME ÉTAPE

## Point de départ

▼▼▼▼▼▼▼▼▼▼▼▼▼

*Les cours*

Jean Hébert retrouve Susan et Barbara au centre d'étudiants et il leur pose des questions à propos de leurs cours.

| | | |
|---|---|---|
| JEAN: | Quelle est votre spécialisation? | |
| BARBARA: | Moi, je suis étudiante en lettres; j'étudie la philosophie et les langues modernes. | |
| SUSAN: | Et moi, je suis en sciences naturelles. J'espère faire ma médecine l'année prochaine. | |
| JEAN: | Tu as un **emploi du temps** très **chargé,** non? | schedule / busy |
| SUSAN: | Ah, oui! J'ai cinq cours. | |
| JEAN: | Cinq cours! C'est beaucoup, mais tu n'as pas ces cours tous les jours? | |
| SUSAN: | Non, non. Le lundi, le mercredi et le vendredi j'ai trois heures de cours le matin et deux heures de **travaux pratiques** l'après-midi. Le mardi et le jeudi j'ai seulement deux heures de cours. | lab |
| BARBARA: | Moi, j'ai moins d'heures de cours. J'ai un cours d'espagnol, deux cours de philosophie et un cours de littérature française. Mais il y a beaucoup de devoirs et d'examens. | |
| JEAN: | Est-ce qu'il y a beaucoup d'étudiants qui **ratent** leurs examens? | fail |
| BARBARA: | Non, pas beaucoup. Il n'est pas difficile de réussir, mais il faut travailler dur pour avoir des bonnes notes. | |

**Les disciplines et les matières**

| | |
|---|---|
| *Les sciences humaines* (f.pl.) | *Les études professionnelles* (f.pl.) |
| l'anthropologie *(f.)* | le commerce |
| l'histoire *(f.)* | **la comptabilité** |
| la linguistique | le droit |
| la psychologie | **la gestion** |
| les sciences économiques *(f.pl.)* | le journalisme |
| les sciences politiques | le marketing |
| la sociologie | la médecine |
| | |
| *Les sciences naturelles* | *Les beaux-arts* (m.pl.) |
| la biologie | l'art dramatique *(m.)* |
| la botanique | **le dessin** |
| la géologie | la musique |
| | la peinture |
| | la sculpture |
| *Les sciences exactes* | |
| l'astronomie *(f.)* | *Les lettres* (f.pl.) |
| la chimie | les langues modernes *(f.pl.)* |
| **l'informatique** *(f.)* | les langues mortes |
| les mathématiques *(f.pl.)* | la littérature |
| **la physique** | la philosophie |
| | |
| *La gymnastique (la gym)* | |

accounting

management

drawing

computer science

physics

## Note culturelle

### *L'enseignement supérieur en France*

Higher education in France is organized somewhat differently from that in the United States. Before students enter college at 18 or 19 years old, they have passed the **baccalauréat (bac)** exam, which is considered roughly equivalent to the first two years of general education in an American university. French students therefore take only the first two years (or three, if they failed the exam after the first year) to obtain their general university diploma **(diplôme d'études universitaires générales).** In the following two years they may obtain a **licence** (roughly equivalent to the first year of a master's degree in the United States) and a **maîtrise** (equivalent to an American master's degree). If they continue, they spend three years or more getting one of two kinds of doctorate degrees **(doctorat du troisième cycle, nouveau doctorat).**

French students may also select to study in one of the prestigious professional schools (**École nationale d'administration, École polytechnique, École des mines,** etc.) called **les grandes écoles.** Admission to these schools usually requires three to four years of preparation and an additional two to four years of study.

Finally, French students have the option of getting a technology degree **(diplôme universitaire de technologie)** from a technology institute.

**Question:** What advantages and disadvantages do you see in the French educational system as compared to the American one?

### Le savez-vous?

▲▲▲▲▲▲▲▲▲▲▲▲▲▲▲

French students visiting the United States will probably be surprised by all *but one* of the following:

a.  intercollegiate athletics
b.  residence halls
c.  fraternities and sororities
d.  small private colleges located in small towns

Réponse  ▲▲▲

## À VOUS! (Exercices de vocabulaire)

**A.  Il est étudiant? En quoi?** Based on the courses they're taking, tell what majors the students are in.

> *Modèle:*    Mathieu / sociologie, sciences économiques, psychologie
> *Mathieu? Il est en sciences humaines.*

1.  Jeannette / physique, chimie, maths
2.  Hervé / philosophie, allemand, littérature anglaise
3.  Mireille / sculpture, peinture, dessin
4.  Jean-Jacques / anatomie, physiologie, psychologie
5.  Hélène / anthropologie, sciences politiques, sciences économiques
6.  Alain / biologie, génétique, botanique
7.  Anne-Marie / comptabilité, gestion
8.  Marc / informatique, mathématiques

**Vocabulary:** To state your major, use the verb **faire** or the expressions **être en...**, **faire des études de...**: Je fais du français. Je suis en sciences politiques. Je fais des études de droit.

**B.** **Qu'est-ce que vous étudiez?** Answer the questions according to your own academic situation.

1. Vous êtes étudiant(e) en quoi?
2. Combien de cours avez-vous ce semestre (trimestre)?
3. Est-ce que votre emploi du temps est très chargé?
4. À quelle heure avez-vous votre cours de français?
5. Combien de fois par semaine avez-vous votre cours de français?
6. Quels jours avez-vous votre cours de français?
7. Avez-vous des travaux pratiques pour le cours de français?
8. Quels autres cours avez-vous?
9. Est-ce que vous avez réussi à votre dernier examen de français ou est-ce que vous l'avez raté?
10. Est-ce que vous avez eu une bonne note? Une assez bonne note? Une note moyenne *(average)*? Une mauvaise note?

 b

R·E·P·R·I·S·E

*Deuxième étape*

**Transparency:**
**7-5** (chart for Ex. C)

**C.** **Les ouvriers de l'atelier Michelin.** Make the indicated comparisons among the workers at the Michelin plant.

| Nom de l'ouvrier | Âge | Minutes pour faire le travail | Qualité du travail | Salaire (par mois) |
|---|---|---|---|---|
| Jean-Loup | 22 | 15 min. | excellent | 10 000F |
| Mireille | 21 | 18 min. | bien | 7 500F |
| Albert | 40 | 18 min. | bien | 12 500F |
| Thierry | 55 | 20 min. | assez bien | 10 000F |
| Jacqueline | 18 | 25 min. | assez bien | 6 500 F |

*Modèle:*     (être âgé) Jacqueline et Albert
              *Jacqueline est moins âgée qu'Albert.*

1. (être âgé) Jean-Loup et Mireille / Albert et Thierry / Mireille et Jacqueline
2. (travailler rapidement) Jean-Loup et Thierry / Jacqueline et Thierry / Mireille et Albert
3. (le travail / être bon) Jean-Loup et Albert / Thierry et Mireille / Albert et Jacqueline
4. (travailler bien) Mireille et Albert / Thierry et Jean-Loup / Mireille et Thierry
5. (gagner de l'argent) Albert et Jacqueline / Thierry et Jean-Loup / Mireille et Thierry

**D.  Des comparaisons.** Compare your university to another university you know something about. Talk about the differences and similarities between the two campuses, the profs, the students, and other things.

Ex. D: ↵

## S·T·R·U·C·T·U·R·E

*Les verbes réguliers en* **-ir**

—**Je réussis** toujours à mes examens. Et toi?
—Moi aussi. **J'ai réussi** à mon examen de français hier.

—*I* always *pass* my exams. What about you?
—Me too. *I passed* my French exam yesterday.

**Vocabulary: Réussir à** *(to succeed)* in the context of exams means *to pass:* **J'ai réussi à l'examen.** The equivalent of *to take an exam* is **passer un examen.**

Here is the way to form the present tense of regular **-ir** verbs:

| **finir** *(to finish)* | |
| --- | --- |
| je fin**is** | nous fin**issons** |
| tu fin**is** | vous fin**issez** |
| il, elle, on fin**it** | ils, elles fin**issent** |
| PAST PARTICIPLE: **fini** (avoir) | |

Suggestion, -ir verbs: Initial presentation may be based on one -ir verb, such as **choisir.** Using visuals from Chs. 1 and 6 (food items), have students say what they generally choose when they're at a café or in a store: **Je choisis toujours une religieuse ou une tranche de tarte aux pommes.**

Some other **-ir** verbs that follow this pattern are:

| **choisir** | to choose |
| --- | --- |
| **grossir** | to gain weight |
| **maigrir** | to lose weight |
| **obéir (à** + noun) | to obey (someone or something) |
| **réfléchir (à** + noun) | to think, to reflect (about something) |
| **réussir (à un examen)** | to succeed (to pass an exam) |

▲  ▲  ▲

## APPLICATION

**E.**  Remplacez le sujet en italique et faites les changements nécessaires.

1. *Elle* ne réfléchit pas assez. (je / elles / tu / ils / nous / il / vous)
2. *Tu* grossis. (vous / elle / je / nous / ils / elles)
3. *Ils* finissent toujours leurs devoirs. (tu / nous / elle / vous / je)
4. *J'*ai réussi à l'examen. (nous / vous / il / elles / tu)
5. Est-ce que *tu* as fini l'exercice? (vous / elles / il / elle / ils)

Ex. F: ☐

**F.   Questions.** Use each cue to ask four questions (**tu, vous, il** or **elle, ils** or **elles**) of the other students in your group.

1.   réussir au dernier examen
2.   finir les devoirs
3.   réfléchir assez

4.   obéir toujours à ___ parents
5.   maigrir
6.   obéir au professeur

Ex. G: ⇄

**G.   Les deux dernières années.** You've just met a friend you haven't seen in two years. After saying hello, tell each other what you did during those two years. Use some of the **-ir** verbs you've just learned (such as **réussir, finir, maigrir, grossir, choisir**) along with other verbs you know.

*Modèle:*     —*Tiens! Bonjour, comment ça va?*
—*Ça va bien, et toi?*
—*Ça va. Dis-moi, qu'est-ce que tu as fait pendant les deux dernières années?*
—*Je suis allé(e) en Californie avec mes parents.*
—*Moi, j'ai réussi à mes examens et je commence à l'université en septembre. Etc.*

**Student Tape:**
Chapitre 7
Segment 1

# PRONONCIATION   *La combinaison oi*

The combination **oi** in French is pronounced [wa], as in the English word *watt:* **moi, boîte.** The one exception is the word **oignon,** in which **oi** is pronounced [ɔ], like **o** in the French word **octobre.**

**H.**   Read each word aloud, pronouncing the combination **oi** carefully.

toi / avoir / mois / trois / oignon / froid / étoile / Antoine / noir / poires / loi / droit / froid / Blois / roi / obligatoire / choisir

# S·T·R·U·C·T·U·R·E

## L'interrogation—l'inversion

Quel temps **fait-il**?           *What's* the weather like?
**Va-t-il** pleuvoir?              *Is it going* to rain?
**Voulez-vous** aller au parc?     *Do you want* to go to the park?

In addition to using the question forms you've already learned (intonation, **est-ce que, n'est-ce pas**), it is possible to ask a question by inverting the subject and the verb. Note that very often we do the same thing in English (*They are* going out tonight. *Are they* going out tonight?).

In French, inversion is most commonly seen in writing. It is therefore most important for you to recognize it when you read. In everyday conversation, either intonation or **est-ce que** are the preferred interrogative forms.

When you write an inverted verb and subject, connect the two words with a hyphen:

**voulez-vous?**          **vas-tu?**          **ont-ils?**

When a conjugated verb ends in a vowel and you want to invert it with **il, elle,** or **on,** place a **-t-** between the two words. This makes pronunciation easier:

Que cherche-**t**-elle?          *But:* Que cherchent-elles?
Où va-**t**-il?                  *But:* Où vont-ils?

In the **passé composé,** inversion takes place with the auxiliary verb (**avoir** or **être**) and the subject:

**As-tu fini** tes devoirs?          **Es-tu allé** au cinéma?

When the conjugated verb is followed by an infinitive, the inversion involves only the conjugated verb and the subject:

**Aimes-tu** aller au cinéma?          **Veut-il** aller avec nous?

▲  ▲  ▲

## APPLICATION

**I.   Comment?** *(What did you say?)* Each time you ask your friends a question, they ask you to repeat it. You ask the question again, using **est-ce que.**

> *Modèle:*      —*As-tu un Walkman?*
> —*Comment?*
> —*Est-ce que tu as un Walkman?*

1.   As-tu une chaîne stéréo?
2.   Prenez-vous souvent le métro?
3.   Avez-vous acheté un gâteau?
4.   As-tu pris l'autobus?
5.   Est-elle française?
6.   Où habites-tu?
7.   Pourquoi vont-ils en ville?
8.   Quel temps fait-il?
9.   Ont-elles réussi à l'examen?

**J.   Questionnaire.** Use inversion to ask another student the following questions. The other student will answer according to his/her personal experience.

> *Modèle:*      Demandez à un(e) autre étudiant(e) s'il (si elle) est américain(e).
> *Es-tu américain(e)?*

Demandez à un(e) autre étudiant(e)...

1.   s'il (si elle) parle espagnol.
2.   s'il (si elle) a une télévision dans sa chambre.
3.   s'il (si elle) aime faire du ski.
4.   s'il (si elle) a fait un voyage l'année dernière.
5.   où il (elle) est allé(e).
6.   s'ils (ses parents) ont beaucoup d'amis.
7.   quand ils (ses parents) vont visiter Paris.
8.   s'ils (ses parents) aiment jouer au tennis.

## Note grammaticale

### L'inversion (suite)

Although inversion is less frequently used in spoken French than are the other interrogative forms, some questions are routinely asked with inversion (fixed expressions) and some verbs (particularly short ones) are commonly inverted when they appear in a question.

~~~~~~~~~~~~~~ **Fixed expressions** ~~~~~~~~~~~~~~

Comment allez-vous? Comment vas-tu?
Comment vous appelez-vous? Comment t'appelles-tu?
Quel temps fait-il?
Quel jour sommes-nous?
Quelle date sommes-nous?
Quelle heure est-il?

~~~~~~~~~~~~~~ **Verbs often used with inversion** ~~~~~~~~~~~~~~

| | |
|---|---|
| **avoir** | As-tu une voiture? |
| **être** | Est-elle française? |
| **aller** | Vont-ils en France cet été? |
| **vouloir** | Veux-tu aller au cinéma? |

**K. Et toi?** For each statement, use the cue in parentheses to ask a question with inversion.

*Modèle:*    Je m'appelle Barbara. (s'appeler)
       *Et toi, comment t'appelles-tu?*

1. Moi, j'ai la voiture ce soir. (vouloir aller en ville)
2. Je vais aller à la plage ce week-end. (aller rester à la maison)
3. Je m'appelle Georges. (s'appeler)
4. Je vais très bien. (aller)
5. Je suis française. (être américain)
6. J'ai beaucoup de disques. (avoir des vidéos)
7. Je vais aller au centre commercial. (vouloir m'accompagner)
8. Je vais à Madrid cet été. (où / aller cet été)
9. C'est le 22 septembre. (être quelle date)
10. Il est 3h. (être quelle heure)

## ▲▲▲▲▲▲▲▲▲▲ Débrouillons-nous! ▲▲▲▲▲▲▲▲▲▲

*Petite révision de l'étape*

Ex. L: ⇄

**L. Échange.** Ask one of your classmates questions using the following elements. He/she will then ask the same information of you. Use inversion when appropriate.

Demandez...

1. le nombre de cours qu'il (elle) a.
2. le cours qu'il (elle) préfère.
3. combien de jours par semaine a lieu le cours de ___ .
4. sa spécialisation.
5. comment il (elle) a choisi ses cours.
6. s'il (si elle) a plus de devoirs que ses amis.
7. s'il (si elle) est un(e) meilleur(e) étudiant(e) que ses amis.
8. s'il (si elle) lit plus rapidement que ses amis.
9. s'il (si elle) comprend mieux le français que ses amis.
10. s'il (si elle) obéit toujours à ses professeurs.

Ex. M: ⇄

**Reminder,** Ex. M: The person asking the questions should remember to use inversion if it is appropriate.

**M. Mon emploi du temps.** A French person of college age is visiting your family. He/she asks you about your school week. After you explain about your major, your courses, and your schedule, your French visitor will ask you to compare your courses: Is history more interesting, more difficult than math? Is your English literature professor better, more serious than your chemistry professor? Etc.

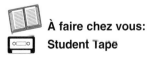

**À faire chez vous: CAHIER, Chapitre 7 / 3e étape**

**À faire chez vous: Student Tape**

Now that you've completed the first three **étapes** of **Chapitre 7,** do Segment 2 of the STUDENT TAPE. See **CAHIER, Chapitre 7,** *Écoutons!,* for exercises that accompany this segment.

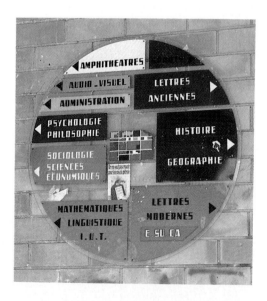

# Q U A T R I È M E   É T A P E

## L·E·C·T·U·R·E

*Demain la faculté*

*The following text is taken from the magazine* **Phosphore,** *which is intended primarily for secondary-school students. In this article, secondary-school students talk about what they imagine college life to be and college students talk about what their experience is. As you read the text, pay particular attention to the differences in attitude between the* **lycée** *and the university students.*

Vous l'avez décroché,[1] ce bac qui tournait à l'idée fixe. Les études supérieures s'ouvrent[2] à vous, une nouvelle vie commence. Troquer[3] le statut d'élève contre celui d'étudiant, c'est autre chose que de passer de l'école au collège[4] ou du collège au lycée. Vous allez quitter (un peu) l'adolescence pour entrer (un peu) dans l'âge adulte. Certains changeront de ville, beaucoup s'éloigneront[5] du toit familial. Ce sera le début de l'indépendance. Elle fait rêver[6] cette première année de fac, vous l'attendez depuis si longtemps! Tiendra-t-elle toutes ses promesses? C'est une autre affaire. Écoutez ce que racontent les lycéens et les étudiants et jugez vous-même.

## LES LYCÉENS RÊVENT

«Il n'y aura plus de contraintes.[7] Plus d'appel,[8] plus de profs autoritaires, plus d'emploi du temps imposé. C'est cette liberté qui me motive. Liberté de choisir ses matières, d'aller et venir quand on veut. Moi qui n'aime pas être forcée, je serai comblée.»[9] (Sabine A.)

«À la fac, on cumule les avantages du lycée et de la vie active. D'un côté on est autonome, responsable de soi-même, plus libre qu'au lycée. De l'autre, on garde ses copains et on ne se préoccupe pas encore de payer des impôts[10] et autres problèmes de ce genre.» (Denis D.)

«Je suis pressée de me spécialiser, de concentrer mes efforts sur ce que j'aime.» (Nathalie A.)

«Je crois que ce sera plus sympa. Mais il faudra être plus actif. Au lycée, on est toujours dans la même classe, les liens[11] se nouent[12] tout naturellement en deux ou trois semaines. À la fac, si je n'aborde[13] pas les autres étudiants, je resterai seule toute l'année. Je n'ai pas envie d'être une étudiante anonyme dans un amphi.»[14] (Sylvie B.)

«Les profs ont des centaines d'étudiants sous les yeux. Ils ne peuvent pas s'occuper de tout le monde. C'est ça qui m'inquiète. J'ai besoin de la pression du prof pour travailler...» (Patrice C.)

## LES ÉTUDIANTS EN PARLENT

«Ma première année de médecine, je suis allée deux fois au cinéma et une fois en boîte,[15] c'est tout. Heureusement, les choses s'arrangent par la suite. En deuxième année, tu travailles encore beaucoup, mais c'est plus relax. Et en troisième année, tu as un peu de temps pour toi.» (Nathalie, médecine)

«Je suis arrivé dans un hall immense. Pas un seul plan des lieux.[16] Où trouver l'amphi BR02? Dans la tour de vingt étages? Dans une des quatre ailes[17] de bâtiment? Un vrai rébus!...»[18] (Julien, DEUG sciences-éco)

«Je ne m'y habitue pas. On perd[19] un temps fou. En première année, on commence par un «semestre d'orientation». Ça signifie qu'on a des cours dans tous les sens[20] et qu'on ne fait à peu près rien. L'année commence effectivement en février, et se termine en mai. Ça ne fait pas lourd.» (Cécile, 2e année de DEUG lettres)

«La première semaine, on se sent toujours un peu seul,[21] mais ça vient vite. À la fac, c'est plus cool, donc les langues[22] se délient[23] plus vite.» (Bertrand, DEUG lettres modernes)

«Je suis arrivée dans un amphi de 600 places. Dès le deuxième jour, j'ai compris que pour un cours qui commençait à 8h30, il me fallait arriver à 7h30 si je voulais trouver de la place. Il y avait des gens assis[24] partout, même dans les escaliers.[25] Cette année-là, je n'ai connu personne à la fac. Il y a un concours[26] à la fin de l'année, et tout le monde voit dans son voisin un concurrent[27] possible... » (Florence, 2e année de médecine)

«Les DEUG première année ne sont jamais très bien vus.[28] Les enseignants[29] ne commencent vraiment à s'intéresser aux étudiants qu'à partir de la licence. Nous n'avons jamais de professeurs, ce sont les assistants qui doivent se faire[30] les «première année». Les rapports sont plutôt distants.» (Véronique, DEUG sciences-éco)

«D'un côté, le prof sur son estrade.[31] De l'autre, les étudiants massés dans les gradins.[32] La structure d'un amphi, ça explique tout. Au milieu, c'est le ravin.»[33] (Nicolas, DEUG droit)

1. got   2. open up   3. to exchange   4. intermediate school between elementary and secondary school   5. will go away   6. dream   7. constraints   8. roll-taking   9. have everything I wish for 10. taxes   11. ties   12. *here:* form   13. approach   14. short for **amphithéâtre,** a lecture hall 15. nightclub   16. building map   17. wings   18. puzzle   19. wastes   20. in every kind of subject 21. alone   22. tongues   23. loosen   24. sitting   25. stairs   26. competitive exam   27. competitor 28. seen   29. teachers   30. take on   31. rostrum   32. stepped rows of seats   33. ravine

# À VOUS! (Exercices de compréhension)

**A.   Que disent les élèves et les étudiants?** Answer the questions, using the information contained in the reading.

1.   What are some of the major advantages that secondary-school students mention about going to college?
2.   What do the college students say about being in college?
3.   In general, what is the difference in attitude between the statements made by the secondary school students and the college students?
4.   Do some of the college students' complaints sound familiar? What are some of the similarities and differences that you see between the French college experience and your own experience?
5.   What was your attitude about college before you started your first year? What is your attitude about college now?

## Troisième étape

**B.   Parlons des cours!** Talk to one of your classmates about your classes. Tell him/her which classes you're taking now, which ones you've taken in previous terms, which ones you want to take, and which ones you are never going to take. As you talk, your classmate will ask you questions for clarification. When you're done, get the same information from your classmate.

Ex. B: ⇄

**C.   Quand?** Explain to your classmate why or when you do the following things.

Ex. C: ⇄

*Modèle:*      Quand est-ce que tu maigris?
              *Je maigris quand je suis au régime. ou Je maigris quand j'ai mes examens de fin de semestre.*

1.   Quand est-ce que tu réussis à tes examens?
2.   Quand est-ce que tu grossis?
3.   Quand est-ce que tu maigris?
4.   Quand est-ce que tu ne réussis pas à un examen?

**D. Comment? Je ne t'ai pas entendu.** *(What did you say? I didn't hear you.)*
Each time you ask something, the other person doesn't hear you. Repeat
your question, using inversion.

*Modèle:*      Où est-ce que tu vas?
                 —*Comment? Je ne t'ai pas entendu.*
                 —*Où vas-tu?*

1. Quel temps est-ce qu'il fait?
2. Comment est-ce que tu t'appelles?
3. Est-ce que tu veux aller à la piscine?
4. Est-ce que tu as acheté ce disque?
5. Est-ce qu'ils ont pris le métro?
6. Est-ce qu'elle va avec nous?
7. Où est-ce que vous allez?
8. Est-ce que tu as un magnétoscope?

**À faire chez vous:**
**Student Tape**

**CAHIER, Chapitre 7:**
***Rédigeons! / Travail de***
***fin de chapitre*** (including
STUDENT TAPE, Chapitre
7, Segment 3)

# Point d'arrivée

*Activités orales*

## Exprimons-nous!

When you're asked to react to something, it's very important
to respond appropriately. Use the following expressions to
show your enthusiasm for or negative reaction to something.

*Pour montrer son enthousiasme*

| | |
|---|---|
| **Formidable!** | Fantastic! |
| **Sensationnel! (C'est sensass!)** | |
| **C'est épatant!** | That's great! |
| **C'est vachement bien!** | That's great! |
| **Quelle bonne nouvelle!** | Good news! |
| **C'est chouette!** | |
| **C'est super!** | |

*Pour réagir de façon négative*

| | |
|---|---|
| **C'est affreux!** | That's terrible! |
| **C'est barbant!** | It's boring! (It's a drag!) |
| **C'est rasant!** | It's boring! (It's a drag!) |

| | |
|---|---|
| **Ça, c'est malheureux!** | That's unfortunate! |
| | (That's too bad!) |
| **C'est pas marrant, ça!** | That's not fun! *(ironic)* |
| **C'est dommage!** | That's too bad! |

**E.   Mon université.** You've been asked to make a short presentation about your university to a French-speaking audience. Prepare the description of your school and university life.

**F.   L'université en France.** Prepare a series of questions you would like to ask a student from France about French universities and university life.

**G.   Visitons le campus!** You and another student are to take some visiting French students on a tour of your campus. Discuss what you're going to show them, where you're going to take them, etc. Then take this imaginary walking tour of your campus; two other students will play the roles of the French visitors.

Ex. G: ⇄

**H.   Mon frère (ma sœur) et moi.** Make a comparison between yourself and your brother (your sister, a friend, your mother, your father, your wife, or your husband). Use as many of the adjectives you've learned as possible. Your comparison should include both physical and personality traits.

Ex. H: ⇄

**I.   Un(e) nouvel (nouvelle) ami(e).** You've just met a new person at your university. Tell your classmate about this person, including physical and personality traits.

Ex. I: ⇄

**J.   Un album de famille.** Bring some photographs of family members to class. Tell your group about each person's physical and personality traits. Your classmates will ask you questions.

Ex. J: ◯

**K.   Une interview.** Pretend that you work at your university newspaper and that you're interviewing a visiting professor from France. Your classmate will play the role of the professor. Find out as much as you can about the person, about what he/she does, about university life in France, about students in France, etc. Don't forget to ask some of your questions with inversion, if appropriate.

Ex. K: ⇄

**L.   Des cadeaux d'anniversaire.** Describe some things you've bought for people for their birthdays. Be as precise as you can by using a variety of descriptive adjectives. Your classmate will ask you questions for clarification. When you're done, get the same type of information from your classmate.

Ex. L: ⇄

# PORTRAIT

*Jean Hébert, Lyon (Rhône-Alpes), France*

Je suis en deuxième année du DEUG lettres à l'université de Lyon. Mes cours sont assez difficiles, mais la vie est beaucoup plus facile qu'elle ne l'était en première année. Parce que j'ai raté mon examen de première année, j'ai dû redoubler. J'étais toujours très nerveux, je ne suis presque jamais sorti et je n'ai pas rencontré beaucoup de gens. Maintenant, je suis plus relax, je suis habitué à la vie universitaire et je suis beaucoup plus discipliné. J'ai l'intention de continuer mes études et de faire un doctorat de littérature américaine. Maintenant que j'ai visité les États-Unis, je comprends un peu mieux la culture et je parle beaucoup mieux l'anglais. Ça m'aide beaucoup avec mes cours. Je sais que les professeurs ne gagnent pas beaucoup d'argent, mais c'est la profession que j'ai choisie. Pour moi, la satisfaction du job compte beaucoup plus que l'argent.

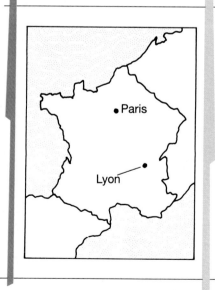

Paris

Lyon

# Profil

*Lyon*

**SITUATION:** dans le sud-est de la France, au confluent du Rhône et de la Saône

**DÉPARTEMENT:** Rhône (69)

**POPULATION:** 462 840 habitants (3ᵉ ville de France par sa population)

**AGGLOMÉRATION:** 1 220 844 habitants

**IMPORTANCE:** carrefour *(crossroads)* et centre commercial, centre de recherche sur le cancer

**INDUSTRIE:** construction mécanique, textile, mécanique de précision, chimie, alimentation, matériaux de construction

**AGRICULTURE:** blé, maïs, vin, lait, foire internationale

**LIEUX D'INTÉRÊT:** Vieux-Lyon avec le théâtre romain de Fourvière (le plus ancien théâtre de la Gaule), basilique Notre-Dame de Fourvière, musée des tissus

**GASTRONOMIE:** La région lyonnaise compte le plus grand nombre de cuisiniers (plusieurs centaines) de toutes les régions françaises. Il y a trois catégories de restaurants: «les grands restaurants» tenus par des chefs célèbres comme Paul Bocuse, «les restaurants classiques» qui servent des plats traditionnels et «les bouchons» qui offrent des spécialités régionales.

**HISTOIRE:** capitale de la Gaule romaine et chrétienne

**À discuter:** Lyon is considered by many to be the gastronomic capital of France. Why do you think this is probably the case? Is there one city or region in the United States that might be considered its gastronomic capital? Why or why not?

**Lexique:** This vocabulary section contains a long list of adjectives for describing people and things. Many are cognates (they look like English words and have the same meaning). Rather than trying to memorize the whole list, focus on the terms that you're most likely to use to describe people and things that are important to you.

# L·E·X·I·Q·U·E

## Pour se débrouiller

*Pour donner les traits physiques d'une personne*
  Il (elle) a les yeux bleus, verts, bruns.
  Il (elle) a les cheveux blonds, roux, bruns, gris, noirs, blancs.
  Il (elle) a les cheveux longs, courts, frisés.
  Il (elle) est grand(e), petit(e), mince, svelte.
  Il est beau.
  Elle est belle, jolie.
  Il a une barbe, une moustache.

*Pour faire des comparaisons*
  aussi . . . que
  autant de . . . que
  meilleur(e)(s) . . . que
  mieux . . . que
  moins (de) . . . que
  plus (de) . . . que

*Pour parler des programmes*
  avoir une spécialisation en
  être étudiant(e) en
  faire des études de
    (les) beaux-arts *(m.pl.)*
    (le) droit
    (les) lettres *(f.pl.)*
    (la) médecine
    (les) sciences exactes *(f.pl.)*
    (les) sciences humaines *(f.pl.)*
    (les) sciences naturelles *(f.pl.)*
  préparer un diplôme
          une licence
          une maîtrise
          un doctorat

*Pour parler des cours*
  s'inscrire à un cours
  prendre un cours
  assister à un cours
  sécher un cours
  un emploi du temps
  une faculté
  la rentrée (des classes)
  une conférence

*Pour parler des examens*
  un examen de classement
  passer un examen
  réussir à un examen
  rater un examen
  échouer à un examen
  une note

*Pour montrer son enthousiasme*
  Formidable!
  Quelle bonne nouvelle!
  Sensationnel!
  C'est sensass!
  C'est super!
  C'est épatant!
  C'est chouette!
  C'est vachement bien!

*Pour réagir de façon négative*
  C'est affreux!
  C'est barbant!
  C'est rasant!
  Ça, c'est malheureux!
  C'est pas marrant, ça!
  C'est dommage!

## Thèmes et contextes

*Les cours* (m.pl) *(les matières* [f.pl.])

l'anthropologie *(f.)*
l'art dramatique *(m.)*
l'astronomie *(f.)*
la biologie
la botanique
la chimie
la comptabilité
le dessin
la géologie
la gestion
l'histoire *(f.)*
l'informatique *(f.)*
le journalisme
les langues modernes *(f.pl.)*

les langues mortes *(f.pl.)*
la linguistique
la littérature
le marketing
les mathématiques *(f.pl.)*
la musique
la peinture
la philosophie
la physique
la psychologie
les sciences économiques *(f.pl.)*
les sciences politiques
la sculpture
la sociologie

## Vocabulaire général

*Verbes*

choisir
finir
grossir

maigrir
marcher
obéir (à)

publier
réfléchir (à)
réussir (à)

*Adjectifs*

actif(-ve)
ambitieux(-se)
beau, bel, belle
blanc(he)
bleu(e)
blond(e)
bon(ne)
brun(e)
célibataire
chargé(e)
chouette
content(e)
court(e)
cruel(le)
délicieux(-se)
difficile
discret(-ète)
ennuyeux(-se)
facile
frivole
généreux(-se)
grand(e)
gris(e)
gros(se)

heureux(-se)
honnête
idéaliste
impatient(e)
indépendant(e)
indiscret(-ète)
intellectuel(le)
intéressant(e)
jaune
jeune
joli(e)
laid(e)
long(ue)
malhonnête
marié(e)
marron
mauvais(e)
mince
moche
moderne
naïf(-ve)
neuf(-ve)
noir(e)
nouveau, nouvel,
nouvelle

occupé(e)
optimiste
orange
paresseux(-se)
pessimiste
petit(e)
premier(-ère)
privé(e)
réaliste
rose
rouge
roux, rousse
scolaire
secret(-ète)
sensationnel(le)
sérieux(-se)
sportif(-ve)
timide
triste
universitaire
vert(e)
vieux, vieil, vieille
violet(te)

**ALLONS-Y!**
Video Program

ACTE 7

**VOCABULAIRE**

SCÈNE 1: LES ÉTUDES
le cursus   *the curriculum, course of study, program*
le Moyen Âge   *the Middle Ages*

SCÈNE 2: LA VIE DES ÉTUDIANTS
en revanche   *however*
les loisirs   *leisure time, spare time activities*

M. Ahmed Abdiba
Fès, Maroc

—Vous prenez deux cachets, trois
fois par jour, avec de l'eau.

# Soignons-nous!

## OBJECTIVES

**In this chapter, you will learn:**

- to talk about your own and other people's health and physical fitness;
- to refer to habitual actions in the past;
- to tell what you can and cannot do;
- to tell what you do and do not know how to do;
- to understand conversations about health and physical fitness;
- to read documents and texts dealing with health and physical fitness.

**CHAPTER SUPPORT
MATERIALS** (STUDENT)

**Cahier:** pp. 187–214

 **Student Tape:**
Chapitre 8
Segments 1, 2, 3

**CHAPTER SUPPORT
MATERIALS** (INSTRUCTOR)

 Transparencies:
8-1 through 8-3

Instructor's Tape:
Chapitre 8,
Text, pp. 300, 308,
319, 330, 336

SYSTÈME-D *software:*
Writing activities for
this chapter are found
in the **Cahier:**
Ex. V (p. 193),
Ex. VII (p. 208),
*Rédigeons!* (p. 213).

 Multimedia:
See the Resource
Manual for correlation
to our multimedia
product.

## ALLONS-Y!
### Video Program

**ACTE 8**
**UNE VISITE DU MÉDECIN**

Première étape    Ça va? Ça ne va pas?
Deuxième étape    À la pharmacie
Troisième étape    Santé passe richesse
Quatrième étape   Lecture: Une consultation gratuite

**Instructor's Tape:**
Ça va? Ça ne va pas?

**Transparencies:**
8-1a, 8-1b (parts of
the body [drawing
from p. 301])

# P R E M I È R E   É T A P E

## Point de départ

▼▼▼▼▼▼▼▼▼▼▼▼▼▼▼▼▼

*Ça va? Ça ne va pas?*

**Suggestion, Point de départ:**
Have students listen to the dialogue on the Instructor's
Tape. Then use the transparency to practice parts of the
body.

ALLONS-Y!
Video Program

ACTE 8
UNE VISITE DU MÉDECIN

**QUESTIONS DE FOND**
1. Où est-ce que
   Ludgi a mal?
2. Est-ce qu'elle de la
   fièvre?
3. Qu'est-ce que le
   médecin prescrit
   pour Ludgi?

to play a trick on    Deux amies de Véronique Baudoux décident de **jouer un petit tour à** leur copine.

| | |
|---|---|
| FRANÇOISE: | Salut, Véronique. Ça va? |
| VÉRONIQUE: | Oh, oui. Ça va bien. |

Say! You don't look very good    GISÈLE: C'est vrai? **Mais dis donc. Tu n'as pas bonne mine** aujourd'hui.

I feel all right    VÉRONIQUE: Ah, non? Mais **je me sens assez bien.**

Don't you have a headache?    GISÈLE: Écoute. Tes yeux sont tout rouges. **Tu n'as pas mal à la tête?**

VÉRONIQUE: Non, mais j'ai un peu mal à la gorge.

face    FRANÇOISE: Et ton **visage** est très pâle.

VÉRONIQUE: Oui, en effet, je commence à avoir mal au cœur.

GISÈLE: Ma pauvre Véronique. Tu devrais rentrer.

are right    VÉRONIQUE: Vous **avez** peut-être **raison.** Je ne me sens pas bien du tout. Je vais rentrer me coucher. Au revoir. Et merci!

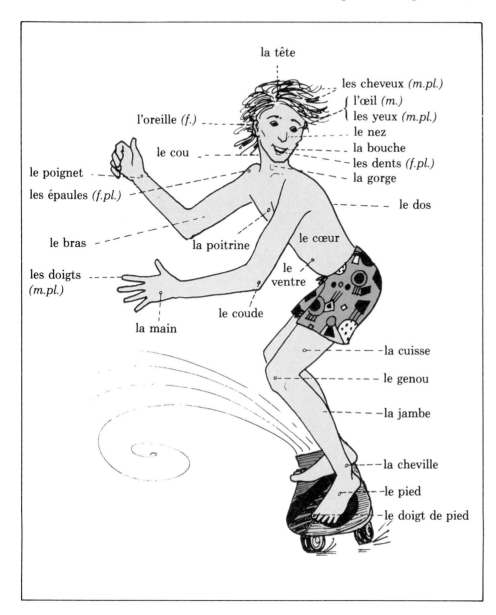

la tête

les cheveux *(m.pl.)*

l'œil *(m.)*

les yeux *(m.pl.)*

le nez

la bouche

les dents *(f.pl.)*

la gorge

l'oreille *(f.)*

le cou

le poignet

les épaules *(f.pl.)*

le dos

le bras

la poitrine

le cœur

les doigts *(m.pl.)*

le ventre

le coude

la main

la cuisse

le genou

la jambe

la cheville

le pied

le doigt de pied

**Le savez-vous?**

▲▲▲▲▲▲▲▲▲▲▲▲▲▲▲

**Children have their own language to describe things that are important to them. Which of the following expressions do French children use when talking about minor hurts and injuries?**

a. faire dodo

b. avoir un bobo

c. vouloir un bisou

d. none of the above

Réponse ▲▲▲

## À VOUS! (Exercices de vocabulaire)

**A.   J'ai mal partout.** *(I hurt everywhere.)* Utilisez les éléments suggérés pour indiquer où vous avez mal.

> *Modèle:*     la tête     *J'ai mal à la tête.*

1. la jambe   2. le bras   3. le dos   4. le ventre   5. les pieds   6. le cou
7. le genou   8. l'épaule   9. la cheville   10. les oreilles   11. le poignet
12. le cœur   13. les dents   14. la gorge

**Vocabulary:** The expression **avoir mal au cœur** *(to feel nauseated)* refers to the stomach, not to the heart.

Suggestion, Ex. B: Avoid discussing agreement with **se casser la jambe** and **se fouler la cheville** unless students specifically ask.

**B.**    **Des blessures.** *(Injuries.)* On utilise souvent l'expression **se blesser à** *(to injure)* et les verbes **se casser** *(to break)*, **se fouler** *(to sprain)*, **se faire mal à** *(to hurt)* avec les parties du corps pour décrire les résultats d'un accident. Utilisez les expressions données pour indiquer ce qui est arrivé aux personnes suivantes.

> *Modèle:*      Nadia et Mme Bernard se sont blessées (à)... le bras
> *Nadia et Mme Bernard se sont blessées au bras.*

1.   Elles se sont blessées (à)...

     a. la jambe
     b. la tête
     c. le dos

2.   Je me suis cassé...

     a. le bras
     b. la jambe
     c. le pied
     d. le nez
     e. une dent

3.   Ma sœur s'est foulé...

     a. la cheville
     b. le pied
     c. le poignet

4.   Je me suis fait mal (à)...

     a. le genou
     b. le dos
     c. l'épaule
     d. la main
     e. la poitrine
     f. le doigt
     g. le cou

Ex. C: ⇄

**C.**    **Dis donc! Tu n'as pas bonne mine aujourd'hui!** Parlez à un(e) camarade de classe au sujet de sa santé *(health)*. Suivez les modèles en variant les expressions que vous utilisez.

> *Modèles:*      —*Ça va?*
> —*Non, ça ne va pas. Je ne me sens pas très bien.*
> —*Qu'est-ce qui ne va pas? (Qu'est-ce qu'il y a?)*
> —*J'ai mal (à la tête, au ventre, etc.).*

▲▲▲ b

> —*Dis donc! Tu n'as pas bonne mine aujourd'hui.*
> —*C'est vrai. J'ai un peu mal (au dos, aux dents, etc.).*
>
> —*Mon (ma) pauvre. Tu devrais rentrer.*
> —*Tu as peut-être raison. Je vais rentrer tout de suite.*

# S·T·R·U·C·T·U·R·E

## L'imparfait

Comment est-ce que **tu t'amusais** quand **tu étais** petite?

**Je jouais** avec mes copains.
**Nous avions** un petit lapin et **nous** le **promenions** dans le quartier.

What *did you do for fun* when *you were* little?

I *played* with my buddies.
*We had* a little rabbit and *we used to walk* him around the neighborhood.

You have already learned to express actions in the past using the **passé composé.** Now you will learn a second past tense, the imperfect **(l'imparfait),** which will allow you to describe what you *used to do.*

To form the imperfect, begin with the **nous** form of the present tense, drop the **-ons** ending, and add the endings **-ais, -ais, -ait, -ions, -iez, -aient.** This rule applies to all French verbs except **être,** which has the irregular stem **ét-** (the endings remain the same, however):

| L'imparfait | | | | |
|---|---|---|---|---|
| *Infinitive* | **parler** | **finir** | **faire** | **être** |
| *Stem* | nous **parló̶ns̶** | nous **finissó̶ns̶** | nous **faisó̶ns̶** | **ét-** |
| je | parl**ais** | finiss**ais** | fais**ais** | ét**ais** |
| tu | parl**ais** | finiss**ais** | fais**ais** | ét**ais** |
| il, elle, on | parl**ait** | finiss**ait** | fais**ait** | ét**ait** |
| nous | parl**ions** | finiss**ions** | fais**ions** | ét**ions** |
| vous | parl**iez** | finiss**iez** | fais**iez** | ét**iez** |
| ils, elles | parl**aient** | finiss**aient** | fais**aient** | ét**aient** |

▲ ▲ ▲

**Suggestion,** Imperfect: (1) Ask students what fruits and vegetables they like now. Then ask if they liked those fruits and vegetables when they were children **(quand vous aviez 4 ou 5 ans).** (2) Have students repeat the imperfect forms of **aimer** while you write pronouns in three groups: **je, tu, il, elle, on, ils, elles / nous / vous.** (3) Contrast the pronounced forms with those of the present, then with those of the **passé composé.** (4) Write verb forms on board. (5) Show the relationship between the present-tense **nous** form and the imperfect stem of all verbs (except **être**). Have students conjugate some irregular verbs—for example, **faire, prendre, avoir,** and finally **être.**

## APPLICATION

**D.** Remplacez les sujets en italique et faites les changements nécessaires.

1. *Elle* aimait danser. (nous / tu / vous / ils / je)
2. *Je* ne faisais pas attention en classe. (nous / tu / elles / vous / il)
3. *Ils* se promenaient à pied. (elle / nous / tu / je / vous / on)
4. Est-ce que *tu* avais de l'argent? (vous / elle / ils / on)
5. *Il* était très fatigué. (je / nous / elles / vous / on / tu)

## Note grammaticale

### L'imparfait et les actions habituelles

| | |
|---|---|
| Tous les étés **nous allions** au bord de la mer. | Every summer *we used to go (would go)* to the seashore. |
| **Je restais** quelquefois au lit jusqu'à midi, mais **mon père se levait** toujours avant 7h. | Sometimes *I stayed (would stay)* in bed until noon, but *my father* always *got up* before 7 o'clock. |

The imperfect tense is used to describe what happened over and over again in the past. Certain adverbs and expressions often accompany the imperfect tense. They reinforce the idea of habitual actions, of things that *used to be done* or *would be done* repeatedly. Among these adverbs and expressions are:

| | |
|---|---|
| **autrefois** | in the past |
| **d'habitude** | usually |
| **fréquemment** | frequently |
| **quelquefois** | sometimes |
| **souvent** | often |
| **toujours** | always |
| **tous les jours** | every day |
| **une fois par jour** | once a day |
| **une fois par semaine** | once a week |
| **le lundi, le mardi...** | Mondays, Tuesdays,... |
| **le matin, l'après-midi, le soir** | mornings, afternoons, evenings |

**E.** **Pendant que nos parents étaient en Italie...** L'année dernière les parents de Jean Hébert ont passé deux mois en Italie. Utilisez les suggestions et l'imparfait pour décrire la vie de Jean et de sa sœur pendant l'absence de leurs parents.

*Modèle:*    en général / ma sœur et moi / s'occuper de tout *(to take care of everything)*
*En général, ma sœur et moi, nous nous occupions de tout.*

1. tous les matins / nous / se réveiller *(to wake up)* de bonne heure
2. quelquefois / elle / rester au lit pendant une heure ou deux
3. d'habitude / je / se lever tout de suite
4. je / prendre une douche / toujours
5. le matin / je / ranger *(to put in order)* la maison
6. ma sœur / faire les courses
7. nous / déjeuner ensemble / fréquemment

8. l'après-midi / nous / se séparer
9. elle / retrouver ses amies / au stade
10. je / aller en ville
11. le vendredi soir / ma sœur et ses amies / dîner en ville
12. le samedi soir / je / sortir avec mes copains

**F.   Quand tu avais sept ans...** Utilisez les expressions suggérées pour demander à un(e) camarade de classe ce qu'il (elle) faisait quand il (elle) avait sept ans.

Ex. F: ⇄

*Modèle:*   aimer aller à l'école
—*Est-ce que tu aimais aller à l'école?*
—*Oui, j'aimais aller à l'école.* ou *Non, je préférais jouer avec mes amis.*

1. habiter ici
2. se disputer avec ses frères et ses sœurs
3. aller à l'école
4. aimer aller à l'école
5. être paresseux(-se)
6. jouer souvent avec ses copains
7. se lever de bonne heure
8. se coucher tard
9. manger beaucoup

# PRONONCIATION   *La consonne l*

**Student Tape:**
Chapitre 8
Segment 1

The letter **l** in French represents either the consonant sound [l], as in the English word *lake,* or the semiconsonant sound [j], as in the English word *you.* In general, a single **l** is pronounced [l]—**la, Italie, hôtel.** At the end of a word, the combination **il** is pronounced [il] when preceded by a consonant—**avril**— and [j] when preceded by a vowel—**travail.**

**Pronunciation:** In a few words, the **l** in the **il** combination is silent: **gentil, fils.**

**G.**   Read each word aloud, being careful to pronounce the **l** in the first list [l], and the **il** in the second list [j].

[l]: les, librairie, quel, ciel, joli, parle, avril
[j]: travail, ail, détail, vieil, appareil, réveil

**35**^F00
**Réveil à quartz avec lumière, 3 aiguilles**
Sonnerie progressive et à répétition.
Pile non fournie, coloris assortis

**Grammar:** In the **passé composé,** the verb **pouvoir** is the equivalent of *to succeed in.* It is often used in the negative to explain why you were unable to do something: **Après avoir téléphoné plusieurs fois, j'ai pu parler au directeur.** *After telephoning several times, I succeeded in talking to the director.* **Ils n'ont pas pu aller au cinéma avec nous; leur fils était malade.** *They weren't able to go to the movies with us; their son was ill.*

# S·T·R·U·C·T·U·R·E

## *Le verbe irrégulier* **pouvoir**

—Est-ce que **tu peux** m'aider?
—Non, **je ne peux pas.**
—Tu ne m'as pas aidé mardi non plus.
—Non, **je ne pouvais pas.** Je n'avais pas la voiture.

—*Can you* help me?
—No, *I can't.*
—You didn't help me Tuesday either.
—No, *I couldn't.* I didn't have the car.

| **pouvoir** *(to be able to; may)* | |
|---|---|
| je **peux** | nous **pouvons** |
| tu **peux** | vous **pouvez** |
| il, elle, on **peut** | ils, elles **peuvent** |
| PAST PARTICIPLE: **pu** (avoir) | IMPERFECT STEM: **pouv-** |

The verb **pouvoir** is usually followed by an infinitive. It is the equivalent of both *can (to be able to)* and *may (to have permission to),* depending on the context.

J'ai du temps libre ce soir; **je peux** faire la cuisine.

I have some free time tonight; *I can (am able to)* do the cooking.

Ma mère dit que **mon frère peut** aller au cinéma.

My mother says that *my brother may (has permission to)* go to the movies.

▲   ▲   ▲

## APPLICATION

**H.** Remplacez les sujets en italique et faites les changements nécessaires.

1. *Nous* pouvons jouer au tennis demain? (je / elles / tu / il / vous)
2. *Je* ne peux pas rester. (nous / elle / tu / vous / ils)
3. *Elle* voulait les accompagner, mais elle ne pouvait pas. (je / ils / nous / on / vous)

**I.   Qui va m'aider?** Vous avez besoin d'aide, mais chaque fois que vous trouvez quelqu'un, vous apprenez qu'il (elle) ne peut pas vous aider. Utilisez le verbe **pouvoir** et les expressions suggérées pour faire des petites conversations.

Ex. I: ⇄

*Modèle:*      tu / avoir trop de devoirs
*—Est-ce que tu peux m'aider?*
*—Non, je ne peux pas.*
*—Tu ne peux pas? Pourquoi pas?*
*—J'ai trop de devoirs.*

1. tu / aller au ciné-club ce soir
2. tes parents / sortir ce soir
3. ta sœur / avoir mal au dos
4. ton cousin / vouloir se coucher de bonne heure
5. vous / ne pas avoir le temps

**J.   Des explications.** Quelqu'un vous rappelle *(reminds)* que vous et vos amis n'avez pas fait certaines choses. Utilisez le passé composé de **pouvoir** et les expressions suggérées pour expliquer pourquoi vous ne les avez pas faites.

*Modèle:*      Tu n'as pas téléphoné à Jacques. (trouver son numéro de téléphone)
*C'est que je n'ai pas pu trouver son numéro de téléphone.*

1. Tu n'as pas aidé Michèle hier après-midi. (finir mon travail)
2. Alain n'a pas réussi à l'examen de chimie. (finir la dernière partie)
3. Chantal et toi, vous n'êtes pas allés à la soirée chez Dominique? (trouver son appartement)
4. Éric et son cousin ne sont pas allés au concert samedi soir. (avoir des billets)
5. Tu n'as pas acheté de cadeau pour ton petit frère. (aller au magasin de jouets)

**K.   Des excuses.** Il y a un(e) étudiant(e) dans votre université que vous essayez d'éviter *(to avoid)*. Mais il (elle) vous demande constamment de faire quelque chose avec lui (elle). Utilisez le verbe **pouvoir** et des expressions de votre choix pour inventer vos excuses.

*Modèle:*      Allons au théâtre.
*Je ne peux pas (aller au théâtre). Je n'ai pas d'argent.* ou *Je ne peux pas sortir ce soir. J'ai mal à la tête.*

1. Faisons du jogging.
2. Allons au cinéma ce soir.
3. Voici les crêpes que j'ai préparées; tu vas les goûter.
4. Regardons quelque chose à la télé.
5. Allons en ville faire du lèche-vitrines.
6. Allons au centre commercial.

## ▲▲▲▲▲▲▲▲▲▲ Débrouillons-nous! ▲▲▲▲▲▲▲▲▲▲

*Petite révision de l'étape*

Ex. L: ⇄

**L.  Quand tu avais dix ans...** Posez des questions à un(e) camarade de classe pour vous renseigner au sujet de ce qu'il (elle) faisait quand il (elle) avait dix ans. Ne vous limitez pas aux expressions suggérées.

> *Modèle:*    où / habiter
> —*Où est-ce que tu habitais quand tu avais dix ans?*
> —*J'habitais à Grand Forks.*
> —*Ta famille avait une grande maison?*
> —*Non, à cette époque-là* (at that time) *nous habitions dans un appartement.*

1. où / habiter   2. avec qui / jouer   3. qu'est-ce que / aimer manger   4. à quelle heure / se lever / se coucher   5. tes parents / travailler   6. aller à l'école   7. tes grands-parents / être vivants   8. être heureux(-se)

Ex. M: ⇄

 **À faire chez vous: CAHIER, Chapitre 8 / 1ère étape**

**M.  Qu'est-ce qui ne va pas?** Two friends meet in the street. One is sick, the other has recently had an accident. Inquire about each other's health, tell about your problems, and show concern for the other person.

---

Instructor's Tape:
À la pharmacie

Transparency:
8-2 (medicines and bandages)

Suggestion, Point de départ:
Use the transparency to introduce medicines and bandages. Then have students listen to the dialogue on the Instructor's Tape.

# DEUXIÈME ÉTAPE
## Point de départ
▼▼▼▼▼▼▼▼▼▼▼▼▼

## *À la pharmacie*

Mme Thibaudet parle avec sa petite fille Cécile.

| MME THIBAUDET: | Mais dis donc, ma petite Cécile. Qu'est-ce qu'il y a? Tu as le nez tout rouge. |
| | |
| runny  CÉCILE: | J'sais pas. J'ai le nez **qui coule** et j'ai mal à la gorge. |
| cold  MME THIBAUDET: | Tu as sans doute un **rhume**. |

| | |
|---|---|
| CÉCILE: | Non, non. Je ne suis pas enrhumée. J'ai peut-être une allergie. |
| MME THIBAUDET: | Ah! Dans ce cas-là, tu devrais aller à la pharmacie. |

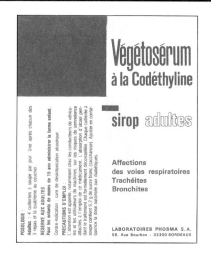

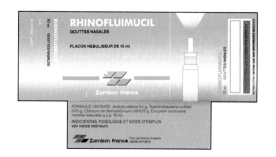

**Culture:** When you buy medicine in France, the pharmacist will often ask if you would like it in the form of a pill **(un cachet** or **un comprimé),** a capsule **(une gélule),** and in some instances a suppository **(un suppositoire).**

Cécile va à la pharmacie.

| | | |
|---|---|---|
| LA PHARMACIENNE: | Bonjour, Mademoiselle. Vous voulez? | |
| CÉCILE: | J'ai besoin de quelque chose, mais je ne sais pas de **quoi.** J'ai le nez qui coule et j'ai un peu mal à la gorge. Mais je ne tousse pas et je n'ai pas de fièvre. | what |
| LA PHARMACIENNE: | Ah, vous avez les yeux tout rouges. Vous avez peut-être une allergie? Vous êtes comme ça **depuis longtemps?** | for a long time |
| CÉCILE: | Depuis huit jours. | |
| LA PHARMACIENNE: | Ben, voilà. Vous avez sans doute **le rhume des foins.** Je vais vous donner des antihistaminiques. Si la gorge vous fait mal, vous pouvez prendre ces **pastilles.** | hay fever<br><br>lozenges |
| CÉCILE: | Très bien. Merci, Madame. Au revoir. | |

## Note culturelle

The French often consult their local pharmacist when they are not feeling well. If the pharmacist considers the illness to be serious, he or she will advise the customer to see a doctor. In case of a cold, flu, or minor accident, the pharmacist will recommend over-the-counter medicine and will do some first aid. Every city and town in France has at least one pharmacy that remains open all night. All other pharmacies have signs on their doors indicating which pharmacy has long hours.

When you go to a pharmacy, you may ask for something to heal a particular part of the body, for example:

J'ai besoin de quelque chose **pour la gorge (pour le nez, pour les yeux, pour l'estomac).**

Or you may ask for a remedy for a particular problem:

J'ai besoin de quelque chose **contre** *(against)* **la toux (contre le rhume des foins, contre la migraine, contre la grippe, contre le mal de mer ou le mal de l'air).**

Or you may ask for a certain type of medicine:

J'ai besoin d'**un tube d'aspirines (de gouttes** [*drops*] **pour le nez ou pour les yeux, de pastilles** [*lozenges*] **pour la gorge, d'antihistaminiques).**

**Question:** In what ways (if any) do French pharmacies differ from the pharmacies you know?

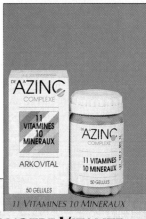

VENDU EN PHARMACIE

**AZINC**

*POUR VOTRE EQUILIBRE ET VOTRE VITALITE*

Arkopharma Laboratoires pharmaceutiques 06511 CARROS - Tél 93.29.11.28

**48 . problèmes de vue**

BPGKMILOFJUNHE
EBKCIPAQEZ
HDUAN.

Laboratoire Conseil Oberlin

**46. le mal au ventre**

Laboratoire Conseil Oberlin

Rendez-vous au
**DRUGSTORE**

## À VOUS! (Exercices de vocabulaire)

**A.  Qu'est-ce que vous avez?** Voici des expressions qu'on emploie pour parler des maux *(ailments)* physiques normaux. Choisissez les symptômes qui correspondent à chaque situation.

SYMPTÔMES: **J'ai mal à la tête (à la gorge, aux yeux, au dos, à l'estomac, au cœur). Je tousse. J'éternue. J'ai le nez qui coule. J'ai le nez bouché. Je n'ai pas d'appétit. J'ai le vertige** *(I'm dizzy).* **J'ai pris un coup de soleil** *(I got sunburned).* **J'ai du mal à dormir** *(I can't sleep).*

1.  Vous avez un rhume.
2.  Vous avez trop mangé.
3.  Vous avez la grippe.
4.  Vous êtes en vacances au bord de la mer.
5.  Vous avez un examen très important et vous êtes nerveux(-se).

Ex. B: ⇄ Have students alternate playing client and
druggist.

**B.  À la pharmacie.** Expliquez au (à la) pharmacien(ne) que vous avez les symptômes qui accompagnent normalement les problèmes médicaux suivants. Il (elle) vous recommandera les médicaments donnés entre parenthèses.

*Modèle:*     une indigestion (pastilles pour l'estomac)
—*Bonjour, Monsieur (Madame). Je peux vous aider?*
—*Oui. Je ne me sens pas très bien. J'ai mal à l'estomac et un peu mal au cœur.*
—*Ah. Vous avez peut-être une petite indigestion. Je vais vous donner des pastilles pour l'estomac.*
—*Merci, Monsieur (Madame).*

1.  un rhume (gouttes pour le nez, sirop contre la toux)
2.  une grippe (aspirine, pastilles pour la gorge)
3.  le rhume des foins (antihistaminiques, gouttes pour les yeux)

R·E·P·R·I·S·E

## Première étape

**C.  Il va avoir...** Vos amis ont tendance à exagérer un peu—c'est-à-dire qu'ils ne se limitent pas. Indiquez où ils vont avoir mal à cause de leur manque *(lack)* de prudence.

*Modèle:*     Michel parle sans arrêt *(nonstop).*
*Il va avoir mal à la gorge.*

1.  Éric mange beaucoup de bonbons.
2.  Anne-Marie regarde la télé pendant des heures et des heures.
3.  Sylvie ne porte jamais de chaussures *(shoes).*
4.  Alain et son frère écoutent leur Walkman seize heures par jour.
5.  Je me brosse les dents très rarement.
6.  Jean-Pierre veut soulever *(lift)* trois grosses boîtes.
7.  Mes amis et moi, nous faisons du jogging dans la rue.
8.  Jacqueline joue de la guitare pendant des heures sans arrêt.

▲▲▲  d

**D.  L'enfance de M. Kerguézec.** Le père de Michel Kerguézec se rappelle sa vie quand il était garçon. Reproduisez ses phrases en mettant les verbes à l'imparfait.

*Modèle:*     Nous habitons à Nantes.
*Nous habitions à Nantes.*

1.  Mon père travaille dans la réfrigération.
2.  Ma mère s'occupe de la maison.
3.  Nous sommes trois enfants.

4. Ma sœur a dix-huit ans.
5. Elle fait des études à l'université.
6. Mon frère et moi, nous allons au lycée.
7. Nous passons l'été à Noirmoutier.
8. Mes parents louent *(rent)* une maison tout près de la mer.
9. Ma sœur aime nager.
10. Moi, je joue au volley sur la plage.
11. Mon père et mon frère pêchent des crabes.
12. Nous nous amusons bien l'été à Noirmoutiers et l'hiver à Nantes.

**E.   André ne peut pas...** Chaque fois que votre camarade de classe mentionne Ex. E: ⇄ ce qu'il(elle) espère faire ce week-end, vous expliquez pourquoi c'est impossible. Utilisez le verbe **pouvoir** et inspirez-vous des images.

*Modèle:*
jouer au football avec André
—*Ce week-end j'espère (je vais) jouer au football avec André.*
—*Mais il ne peut pas (jouer au football); il s'est fait mal au genou.*

1. jouer au tennis avec Micheline

2. faire du jogging avec Thierry

3. jouer au golf avec Lucien et sa sœur

4. faire une promenade avec Anne-Marie

5. aller nager avec Henri

# S·T·R·U·C·T·U·R·E

## L'imparfait (suite)

| | |
|---|---|
| Pendant que **nous parlions, elle regardait** le journal. | While *we were talking, she was looking* at the newspaper. |
| **Elle avait** les yeux bleus. | *She had* blue eyes. (Her eyes *were* blue.) |
| **Je** la **trouvais** jolie. | *I found* her (*thought* she was) pretty. |

In addition to expressing habitual past actions, the imperfect tense is used to tell about several other situations in the past:

1. To indicate that actions *were going on:*

   | | |
   |---|---|
   | Pendant que **nous parlions, elle regardait** la télé. | While *we were talking, she was watching* TV. |

2. To describe physical attributes:

   | | |
   |---|---|
   | **Il avait** les cheveux blonds. | *He had* blond hair. |

3. To express attitudes and beliefs:

   | | |
   |---|---|
   | **Je** les **trouvais** très gentils. | *I found* them very nice. |

4. To express age:

   | | |
   |---|---|
   | **Elle avait** cinquante ans. | *She was* fifty years old. |

5. To describe states of health:

   | | |
   |---|---|
   | **Je ne me sentais pas** très bien. | *I didn't feel* very well. |

6. To set the background or context for a story:

   | | |
   |---|---|
   | **Il était** neuf heures. **J'étais** en visite à Berlin. **C'était** la fin de l'hiver et **il faisait** toujours très froid. **Nous étions** trois dans un petit restaurant. | *It was* 9 o'clock. *I was* visiting Berlin. *It was* the end of winter and *it was* still very cold. *There were* three of us in a small restaurant. |

▲　▲　▲

## APPLICATION

**F.   La soirée de Claire.** Claire Maurant et ses amies ont organisé une soirée. Tous les invités, à l'exception d'André, sont arrivés chez Claire vers 9h. Utilisez l'imparfait et les expressions suggérées pour décrire ce que faisaient les invités quand Alain est finalement arrivé.

> *Modèle:*   Cécile / chanter   *Cécile chantait.*

1. Sacha / écouter la stéréo
2. Michèle / parler avec Yvette
3. Georges et Véronique / danser
4. Claire / chercher des boissons
5. Jacques et Henri / manger
6. Jérôme / regarder la télé
7. M. Matignon / prendre des photos
8. tout le monde / s'amuser bien

**G.   Quand ils étaient jeunes...** Pensez à des photos qui montrent quelques       Ex. G: ⇄
membres de votre famille quand ils (elles) étaient jeunes, puis décrivez-les
à un(e) camarade de classe.

> *Modèle:*   votre père
> *Quand mon père était jeune, il avait les cheveux blonds et il ne portait pas de lunettes. Il était très beau. Il aimait jouer au base-ball et au football américain.*

1. votre père (votre oncle)
2. votre mère (votre tante)
3. votre grand-père (votre grand-mère)

**H.   Hier soir à 8h...** Vous vous préparez à raconter une histoire au sujet de quelque chose qui vous est arrivé *(that happened to you)* ou que vous avez fait. Établissez le contexte en expliquant où vous étiez et ce que vous faisiez au moment où l'incident s'est produit *(occurred)*. Pour la première situation, on vous propose quelques questions pour vous guider. Pour les autres situations, c'est à vous d'imaginer les détails.

1. Hier soir à 8h—Où étiez-vous? Que faisiez-vous? Quel temps faisait-il? Vous vous sentiez bien? Est-ce que vous étiez seul(e) *(alone)* ou avec d'autres personnes? Que faisaient-elles?
2. Ce matin à ___
3. Samedi dernier à 10h (du matin ou du soir)
4. Le jour où la fusée Challenger a explosé
5. Choisissez un moment important de votre vie.

**Student Tape:**
Chapitre 8
Segment 1

# PRONONCIATION *La combinaison ll*

When preceded by a vowel other than **i,** the combination **ll** is pronounced [l]: **elle, football, folle.** When the combination **ill** is at the beginning of a word, the **ll** is also pronounced [l]: **illusion.** However, when the combination **ill** follows a consonant, it may be pronounced either [l] or [j]. In the words **mille, ville, tranquille,** and their derivatives, the **ll** is pronounced [l]. In all other words, the **ll** of **ill** following a consonant is pronounced [j]: **fille, famille.**

**I.** Read each word aloud, being careful to distinguish between the [l] sound and the [j] sound.

elle / mille / fille / ville / famille / Deauville / tranquille / Bastille / intellectuelle / village / illustration / grille / Chantilly / vallée / million / illégitime / tranquillité / guillotine / millionnaire / folle / tranquillement / cédille

# S·T·R·U·C·T·U·R·E

**Suggestion, Devoir** (additional tenses): (1) Quickly review the present of **devoir.** (2) Have students generate the imperfect. (3) Present the past participle. (4) Make a chart showing meanings: owing, necessity, obligation, probability. Have students give a present-tense example for each category; then show the transformation to past.

## *Le verbe irrégulier* **devoir** *(suite)*

**Ils devaient** beaucoup d'argent à leurs parents.

**Elle devait** me retrouver à 7h. J'ai attendu jusqu'à 7h30, mais elle n'est pas venue.

*They owed* their parents a lot of money.

*She was supposed to* meet me at 7 o'clock. I waited until 7:30, but she didn't come.

You have already learned that the verb **devoir** has several meanings, depending on the context of the sentence. In the *present,* it may express:

1. the idea of owing something (money or objects);
2. the notion of obligation *(supposed to . . .);*
3. the idea of probability *(must be . . .).*

In the **passé composé,** it may indicate:

1. the notion of necessity *(had to . . .);*
2. the idea of probability *(must have . . .).*

The *imperfect* expresses meanings similar to two of those of the present:

1. the idea of owing (money or something);
2. the notion of obligation *(was supposed to . . .).*

The exercises that follow will include all three tenses of **devoir.**

▲  ▲  ▲

## APPLICATION

**J.** Remplacez les sujets en italique et faites les changements nécessaires.

1. *Il* a dû aller en ville pour voir quelqu'un. (tu / les autres / Jacqueline / je / nous / vous)
2. *Chantal* n'est pas là? *Elle* a dû oublier. (Henri / vos parents / Marcelle / les Raymond)
3. *Ils* devaient partir lundi. (je / vous / les autres / on / tu / nous)
4. *Elle* doit être malade. (tu / les autres / Jacques / je / vous / nous)

**K.** **Une soirée au théâtre.** Faites des phrases en utilisant le passé composé ou l'imparfait de **devoir** et les expressions données.

1. Vos amis ont organisé une soirée au théâtre, mais plusieurs personnes n'y sont pas allées parce qu'elles avaient d'autres *obligations*. Les personnes suivantes n'ont pas pu participer à la soirée.

*Modèle:*      Paul / travailler      *Paul a dû travailler.*

a. Anne-Marie / aider sa mère
b. Hervé et sa sœur / aller à Bordeaux
c. je / soigner mon rhume
d. Michel / s'occuper de ses petits frères

2. D'autres personnes n'ont pas donné d'explications. Par conséquent, les organisateurs ont proposé des explications *probables*.

*Modèle:*      Catherine / oublier      *Catherine a dû oublier.*

a. Jean / être occupé
b. la cousine de Victor / manquer *(to miss)* son train
c. Édouard et son frère / avoir un accident

3. Enfin, l'absence de certaines personnes était très gênante *(bothersome)* parce qu'elles avaient accepté certaines *responsabilités*.

*Modèle:*      Édouard / organiser une réception après le spectacle
              *Édouard devait organiser une réception après le spectacle.*

a. Marie-Claude / apporter des boissons pour la réception
b. Jean et Claire / amener *(to bring)* les gens qui n'avaient pas de voiture
c. et toi, tu / remercier *(to thank)* les acteurs

**L. Traduisons!** Donnez l'équivalent en français.

1. She has to go home. She is supposed to go home. She was supposed to go home.
2. They have to go to the library. They are probably going to the library. They probably went to the library.
3. He had to leave. He must have left. He was supposed to leave.
4. We have to stay here. We are supposed to stay here. We had to stay here.

▲▲▲▲▲▲▲▲▲▲ **Débrouillons-nous!** ▲▲▲▲▲▲▲▲▲

*Petite révision de l'étape*

Ex. M: ⇄

**M. Échange.** Posez les questions à un(e) autre étudiant(e), qui va vous répondre.

1. À quelle heure est-ce que tu t'es levé(e) ce matin pour aller à ton premier cours? Est-ce que tu dois te lever à ___ heures tous les matins?
2. Qu'est-ce que nous devions faire pour le cours de français aujourd'hui?
3. Combien de temps as-tu dû étudier pour faire ces devoirs?
4. Pourquoi ___ n'est-il (elle) pas en classe aujourd'hui? Pourquoi est-ce que ___ n'était pas en classe la dernière fois?
5. Comment est-ce que tu devais aider tes parents quand tu étais petit(e)? Est-ce que tu devais faire ton lit? Ranger ta chambre? Aider ta mère à préparer les repas? Faire la vaisselle *(do the dishes)?* Est-ce que tu le faisais toujours?

Ex. N: ⇄

**N. À la pharmacie.** What would you say to a pharmacist in the following situations? A classmate will take the role of the pharmacist.

1. You spent six hours on the beach yesterday and can hardly move today.
2. You've been invited to go out on a sailboat, but you think you're going to be seasick.
3. You feel like you're getting sick; your throat is sore and your head hurts.
4. You were out partying very late last night and your stomach feels terrible.
5. You walked all over Paris last night and now your feet hurt.
6. You think that your traveling companion has got the flu.

**À faire chez vous:** CAHIER, Chapitre 8 / 2ᵉ étape

# T R O I S I È M E   É T A P E

## Point de départ

▼▼▼▼▼▼▼▼▼▼▼▼

**Instructor's Tape:**
Santé passe richesse

**Suggestion, Point de départ:**
Have students listen to the dialogue on the Instructor's Tape.

*Santé passe richesse*

Michel Kerguézec regarde, avec ses parents, des photos de ses cousins.

| | | |
|---|---|---|
| M. KERGUÉZEC: | Qui est-ce? Je ne le **reconnais** pas. | recognize |
| MICHEL: | C'est Jean-François. **Qu'est-ce qu'il est fort et musclé!** Il doit **faire de la musculation.** | Boy, is he strong and muscular! to work out with weights |
| M. KERGUÉZEC: | Et ça, c'est bien Mathilde? Elle a **tellement** grossi! Elle doit être **enceinte.** | so much pregnant |
| MME KERGUÉZEC: | Ah, oui. **Par contre,** voilà son mari qui a beaucoup maigri. | On the other hand |
| M. KERGUÉZEC: | Oui, **il est au régime depuis quelques mois.** Michel, regarde ta cousine Annette. Elle a vraiment grandi. | he has been on a diet for several months |
| MICHEL: | Oui, elle doit **faire un mètre soixante-dix.** C'est parce qu'elle mange bien et qu'elle **fait de la gym.** | to be 1m70 tall (about 5′8″) does (gymnastic-type) exercises (not competitive) |
| MME KERGUÉZEC: | Oui. Mais ton oncle Michel et ta tante Élise, ils n'ont pas changé. | |
| M. KERGUÉZEC: | C'est vrai. Ils ne sont pas riches, mon amour, mais ils **gardent leur ligne.** | keep their figures |

L'

ENTRAI-
NEMENT
COMMENCE A
TABLE

CESSPF

VOTRE PHARMACIEN
VOUS CONSEILLE

## Note culturelle

The French express height and weight in terms of meters and kilograms. **Un mètre** is the equivalent of 3.281 feet. Conversely, one foot equals 0.305 meters, and one inch equals 2.539 centimeters. **Un kilo** equals 2.2 pounds. Thus, to describe a person who is 5′10″ and weighs 160 pounds, a French person would say, **Il (elle) fait un mètre soixante-quinze et pèse** *(weighs)* **soixante-treize kilos.** The following chart shows some approximate equivalents:

| *Heights* | | *Weights* | |
|---|---|---|---|
| 5′0″ | 1,50 m | 100 lbs. | 45 kilos |
| 5′5″ | 1,63 m | 120 lbs. | 55 kilos |
| 5′10″ | 1,75 m | 140 lbs. | 64 kilos |
| 6′0″ | 1,80 m | 160 lbs. | 73 kilos |
| 6′2″ | 1,83 m | 180 lbs. | 82 kilos |
| 6′6″ | 1,95 m | 200 lbs. | 93 kilos |

Americans often think of French people as being quite small. It is true that, on the average, French men and women are shorter and weigh less than American men and women, with the average French male measuring 1,72 meters and 75 kilos and the average French female measuring 1,60 meters and 60 kilos. Nevertheless, do not be surprised to find people of all sizes in France.

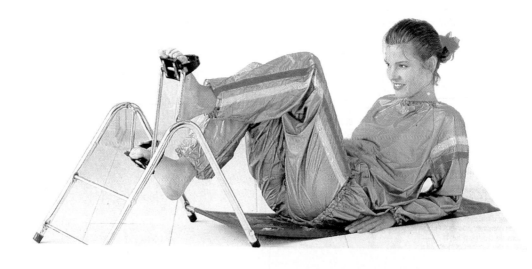

# À VOUS! (Exercices de vocabulaire)

**A. Pourquoi?** L'apparence et la taille *(size)* physique peuvent changer pour plusieurs raisons. En utilisant les expressions suggérées et en vous inspirant des dessins, indiquez pourquoi les personnes indiquées sont comme elles sont.

EXPRESSIONS: **grandir, grossir, rester petit, garder sa ligne, maigrir, manger trop, ne pas manger assez, faire de la gym, être malade, faire de la musculation, faire de l'aérobic, être enceinte**

Françoise

*Modèle:* *Françoise maigrit parce qu'elle est malade. Peut-être qu'elle ne mange pas assez.*

1. Nicolas

2. Suzanne

3. Mme Rinaldi

4. M. Lécuyer

5. Jeanne

6. Nicole

**B. Vous et votre famille.** Faites une description des membres de votre famille. Insistez sur leur taille physique, leurs activités et les changements qui se sont produits.

*Modèle:*   *Mon frère Michel est très grand et très fort. Il mange bien et il fait du sport. Il a beaucoup grandi récemment. Maintenant il fait un mètre quatre-vingt-dix et il pèse quatre-vingt-huit kilos.*

**C. Vous mangez bien?** Ce qu'on mange a beaucoup d'importance pour la santé et pour l'état physique. En suivant le tableau d'aliments, analysez ce que vous avez mangé hier. Vos camarades de classe indiqueront ensuite si vous avez bien mangé ou pas.

*Modèle:*   *Dans le premier groupe, j'ai mangé du fromage pour le petit déjeuner et j'ai pris du lait avec le dîner. Dans le deuxième groupe,...*

▲▲▲  b

Transparency:
8-3 (food chart)

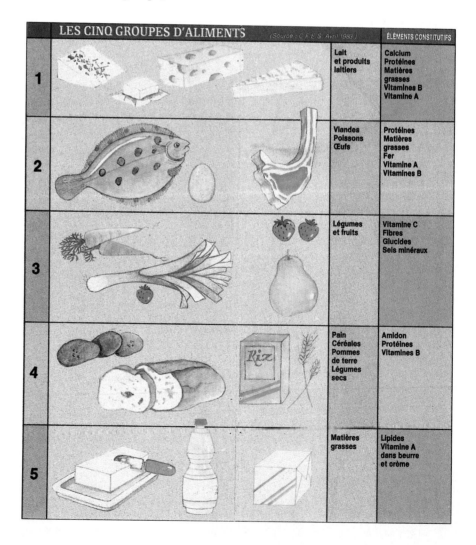

| LES CINQ GROUPES D'ALIMENTS | | ÉLÉMENTS CONSTITUTIFS |
| --- | --- | --- |
| 1 | Lait et produits laitiers | Calcium, Protéines, Matières grasses, Vitamines B, Vitamine A |
| 2 | Viandes, Poissons, Œufs | Protéines, Matières grasses, Fer, Vitamine A, Vitamines B |
| 3 | Légumes et fruits | Vitamine C, Fibres, Glucides, Sels minéraux |
| 4 | Pain, Céréales, Pommes de terre, Légumes secs | Amidon, Protéines, Vitamines B |
| 5 | Matières grasses | Lipides, Vitamine A dans beurre et crème |

(Source : C.F.E.S. Avril 1983)

## R·E·P·R·I·S·E

*Deuxième étape*

**D.  Des plaintes.** *(Complaints.)* Vous jouez le rôle du (de la) pharmacien(ne). En utilisant **prendre, aller** ou le verbe donné ainsi que les expressions entre parenthèses, faites des recommandations à vos clients.

*Modèle:*    J'ai mal à la tête. (cachets d'aspirine)
              *Prenez deux cachets d'aspirine.*

1.  J'ai le nez bouché. (antihistaminiques)
2.  J'ai une grippe. (cachets d'aspirine)
3.  Je tousse. (sirop)
4.  J'ai mal à la gorge. (pastilles)
5.  Je suis toujours fatigué. (se reposer)
6.  J'ai de la fièvre. (cachets d'aspirine)
7.  J'ai mal au ventre. (thé)
8.  J'ai mal partout. (chez le médecin)

**E.  Des reproches... des excuses...** Quand on vous fait un reproche, vous pouvez vous défendre en expliquant que vous étiez obligé(e) de faire autre chose. Imitez le modèle en utilisant le temps convenable de **devoir** et les expressions données.

Ex. E: ⇄

*Modèle:*    écrire à tes grands-parents / faire mes devoirs
              —*Tu devais écrire à tes grands-parents.*
              —*Oui, je sais* (I know), *mais j'ai dû faire mes devoirs.*

1.  préparer le dîner  /  parler avec mon professeur
2.  faire ton lit  /  partir de bonne heure ce matin
3.  téléphoner à ton ami(e)  /  aider ma sœur
4.  te coucher de bonne heure hier soir  /  préparer un examen

Quand on fait un reproche à une autre personne, vous pouvez défendre cette personne en donnant une explication probable de ses actions.

*Modèle:*    Jacqueline / être là avant 7h / avoir un accident
              —*Jacqueline devait être là avant 7h.*
              —*Oui, je le sais, elle a dû avoir un accident.*

5.  Marc  /  arriver avant nous  /  prendre l'autobus
6.  ton père  /  retrouver ta mère au restaurant  /  travailler tard
7.  les autres  /  aller au cinéma avec nous  /  changer de projets
8.  Françoise  /  se lever avant 6h  /  se coucher très tard

# S·T·R·U·C·T·U·R·E

**Grammar:** In the **passé composé, savoir** has a special meaning, *to find out:* **J'ai su les résultats de l'examen hier.** *I found out the exam results yesterday.*

## Le verbe irrégulier *savoir*

—**Savez-vous** où habite Isabelle?
—Non, **je ne sais pas.**
—**Henri sait** son adresse, mais il n'est pas là ce matin.

—*Do you know* where Isabelle lives?
—No, *I don't know.*
—*Henri knows* her address, but he's not here this morning.

---

| **savoir** *(to know)* | |
|---|---|
| je **sais** | nous **savons** |
| tu **sais** | vous **savez** |
| il, elle, on **sait** | ils, elles **savent** |
| PAST PARTICIPLE: **su** (avoir) | IMPERFECT STEM: **sav-** |

---

The verb **savoir** is used to express the following ideas:

1. **Savoir** + infinitive = *to know how (to do something):*

   **Il sait jouer** du piano.    *He knows how to play* the piano.

2. **Savoir que** + clause (subject and verb) = *to know that . . . :*

   **Nous savons qu'ils habitent** à Lyon.    *We know that they live* in Lyon.

3. **Savoir** + language = *to know (how to speak) a language:*

   **Ils savent l'espagnol.**    *They know Spanish.*

4. **Savoir** + factual information = *to know (something):*

   **Vous savez la réponse à la première question?**    *Do you know the answer to the first question?*

Note that **savoir** is also used as a filler in conversation:

Oh, **vous savez (tu sais),** ce n'est pas grave.    Oh, *you know,* it isn't very serious.

▲   ▲   ▲

# APPLICATION

**F.**   Remplacez les sujets en italique et faites les changements nécessaires.

1. *Nous* savons bien jouer au tennis. (je / vous / elles / il / tu)
2. *Vous* savez leur numéro de téléphone? (tu / elle / ils / il / nous)
3. *On* ne sait pas pourquoi il est en retard. (nous / je / elle / elles / tu)
4. *Elle* ne savait pas que le musée était fermé. (il / nous / on / je / ils)

**G.   Qui sait?** Demandez à plusieurs camarades de classe s'ils savent les renseignements suivants.

Ex. G: ○

*Modèle:*       où le professeur habite
            —*Peter, tu sais où le professeur habite?*
            —*Oui, je sais où elle habite. Elle a un appartement près du*
                *campus. ou Non, je ne sais pas.*
            (—*Tu ne sais pas. Je vais demander à Jack.*)

1. où le président de l'université habite
2. pourquoi _____ n'est pas là aujourd'hui
3. le titre du nouveau disque compact de _____
4. la date de l'anniversaire de _____
5. le film qui passe au cinéma _____ ce week-end
6. le numéro de téléphone de _____

**H.   On ne peut pas parce qu'on ne sait pas...** En utilisant les verbes **pouvoir** et **savoir** et les suggestions entre parenthèses, expliquez pourquoi il est impossible de faire ce que proposent vos amis. D'abord, ils veulent parler à une amie qui a déménagé *(moved)*.

Ex. H: ○

*Modèle:*       Téléphonons à Christina. (son nouveau numéro de téléphone)
            *Nous ne pouvons pas téléphoner à Christina. Nous ne savons*
                *pas son nouveau numéro de téléphone.*

1. Eh bien, demande à son père. Il habite ici. (son prénom)
2. Mais c'est facile. Demandons à sa cousine, Marisela. (son nom de famille)
3. Alors, tu dois téléphoner à ses grands-parents à Madrid. J'ai leur numéro. Le voici. (l'espagnol)

Vos amis et vous renoncez donc à l'idée de parler à Christina. Maintenant vous voulez avoir des billets pour une pièce de théâtre qui a beaucoup de succès.

4. Réservons des billets. (les dates)
5. Pas de problème. Tu téléphones pour demander. (le nom du théâtre)
6. Regardons dans le journal. (le titre de la pièce)
7. Michèle doit le savoir. Demande-lui de nous réserver des places. (le prix des billets)

**I.** **Tu sais jouer au golf?** Demandez à un(e) camarade de classe s'il (si elle) sait faire les choses suivantes. Posez-lui la même question au sujet des membres de sa famille.

*Modèle:*     jouer au golf
—*Hélène, tu sais jouer au golf?*
—*Non, je ne sais pas jouer au golf.*
—*Et ta sœur?* Etc.

1. jouer au tennis   2. nager   3. faire de la planche à voile   4. faire du patinage   5. jouer au bridge   6. parler une langue étrangère

**Student Tape:**
Chapitre 8
Segment 1

# PRONONCIATION   *La combinaison **ill** après une voyelle*

When the combination **ill** follows a vowel sound, it is always pronounced [j]. The **i** does *not* represent a separate sound. To pronounce the combination **aille,** produce only two sounds, [a] + [j]. The same is true for **ouille** [uj] and **eille** [ej].

**J.** Read each word aloud. Limit the vowel + **ill** combination to two sounds.

travailler / bataille / Versailles / braille / Marseille / bouteille / vieille / mouiller / fouiller / brouillard

*le palais de Versailles*

# S·T·R·U·C·T·U·R·E

## Les expressions *depuis quand, depuis combien de temps* et *depuis*

—**Depuis quand** est-ce que tu fais du jogging?

—Je fais du jogging **depuis** l'âge de 25 ans.
—**Depuis combien de temps** est-ce que tu fais du yoga?
—Je fais du yoga **depuis** deux ans.

—*How long (since when, since what point in time)* have you been going jogging?
—*I've been jogging since* I was 25 years old.
—*How long (for how much time)* have you been doing yoga?
—*I've been doing yoga for* two years.

**Depuis quand** and **depuis combien de temps** are used to ask questions about something that started in the past and *is continuing in the present:*

| Question | Answer |
| --- | --- |
| **depuis quand?** | **depuis** *(since)* + a specific point in time |
| **depuis combien de temps?** | **depuis** *(for)* + a length of time |

Note that any form of **depuis** is usually accompanied by the *present tense,* since the activity is still going on. The verb is the equivalent of the English *has (have) been (do)ing.* However, in the negative, since the activity stopped some time ago, you may use the **passé composé** to explain that you have *not* done something *since* a specific time or *for* a certain amount of time:

**Je n'ai pas parlé** à Jacques **depuis** le début de mars.
**Je n'ai pas fait de** jogging **depuis** trois jours.

*I haven't spoken* to Jacques *since* the beginning of March.
*I haven't been jogging for* three days.

▲  ▲  ▲

Suggestion, Depuis: (1) To accustom students to this structure, make personal statements: **Je suis professeur de français depuis ____ ans. J'habite à ____ depuis ____ ans. Nous sommes en classe depuis ____ minutes.** Then lead students to answer: **Vous étudiez le français depuis combien de mois? Vous habitez à ____ depuis quand? Vous savez ____ depuis combien de temps?** (2) Write some answers on the board. Use a time line with questions such as: **Vous avez commencé à étudier le français en septembre 19XX. Votre famille a acheté votre maison en 19XX. Le cours de français a commencé à ____ h.** Then show two different ways to express these ideas: **depuis quand** and **depuis combien de temps.** You will probably want to insist on the English equivalents. (3) Save discussion of the **passé composé** after **depuis** until it occurs in exercise examples.

## APPLICATION

**K.  Mme Beaune chez le médecin.** La tante de Mireille Loiseau, Mme Beaune, est malade depuis quelques jours. Elle va donc chez le docteur Lahbabi. Son infirmière *(nurse)* pose quelques questions à Mme Beaune. Utilisez les suggestions entre parenthèses pour reproduire ses réponses.

*Modèle:*      Depuis quand habitez-vous à Paris? (1982)
*J'habite à Paris depuis 1982.*

1.  Ah, bon. Vous habitez donc à Paris depuis neuf ans? (non / ___ ans)
2.  Depuis combien de temps travaillez-vous chez Peugeot? (dix ans)
3.  Depuis quand consultez-vous le docteur Lahbabi? (1989)
4.  Depuis combien de temps est-ce que vous n'êtes pas allée chez le médecin? (six mois)
5.  Depuis combien de temps êtes-vous enrhumée? (trois ou quatre jours)
6.  Et vous avez de la fièvre? Oui? Depuis quand? (hier)
7.  Qu'est-ce que vous prenez? Des antihistaminiques? Depuis combien de temps? (deux jours)
8.  Vous dormez bien? Non? Depuis combien de temps est-ce que vous avez du mal à vous endormir? (deux jours)
9.  Vous avez de l'appétit? Non? Depuis quand est-ce que vous n'avez pas mangé? (avant-hier [*the day before yesterday*])

Ex. L: ⇄

**L.  Un(e) camarade malade.** Quand votre camarade de classe indique qu'il(elle) ne se sent pas très bien, vous essayez de vous renseigner sur son état physique. Utilisez les suggestions entre parenthèses pour lui poser des questions.

*Modèle:*      Oh là là. Ça ne va pas du tout. (depuis combien de temps / se sentir mal)
*Depuis combien de temps est-ce que tu te sens mal?*

1.  Depuis plusieurs jours. Oh, la tête! (depuis quand / avoir mal à la tête)
2.  Depuis lundi. Et la gorge! (depuis combien de temps / avoir mal à la gorge)
3.  Depuis deux jours. C'est peut-être que je suis fatigué(e). (depuis combien de temps / dormir mal)
4.  Depuis trois semaines. Mais j'ai commencé à me coucher de bonne heure. (depuis quand / se coucher avant minuit)
5.  Depuis hier soir. Oh! J'ai envie de vomir. (depuis combien de temps / avoir mal au cœur)
6.  Depuis quelques heures. J'ai faim, mais je ne peux pas manger. (depuis quand / ne pas manger)
7.  Depuis hier. Je vais peut-être aller chez le médecin. (Bonne idée!)

**M.  Traduisons!** Donnez l'équivalent français des phrases suivantes.

1.  I have been feeling poorly for several weeks. I've had a temperature since last Monday.

**Answers,** Ex. M: 1. Je me sens mal depuis plusieurs semaines. J'ai de la fièvre depuis lundi dernier. 2. Mon amie est enrhumée depuis un mois. Elle tousse depuis des jours. 3. Mes parents ont mal à la gorge depuis le début de la semaine. 4. Depuis combien de temps est-ce que tu as (vous avez) mal à l'estomac? 5. Depuis quand est-ce que tu as mal au cœur? 6. Je n'ai pas bien mangé depuis un mois.

2. My friend has had a cold for a month. She has been coughing for days.
3. My parents have had sore throats since the beginning **(le début)** of the week.
4. How long has your stomach been hurting?
5. Since when have you been feeling nauseous?
6. I haven't eaten well for a month.

## ▲ ▲ ▲ ▲ ▲ ▲ ▲ ▲ ▲ ▲ **Débrouillons-nous!** ▲ ▲ ▲ ▲ ▲ ▲ ▲ ▲ ▲ ▲

*Petite révision de l'étape*

**N.  Échange.** Posez les questions à un(e) autre étudiant(e), qui va vous répondre.

Ex. N: ⇄

1. Où est-ce que ta famille habite? Depuis combien de temps?
2. Où est-ce que ton père (ta mère) travaille? Depuis quand?
3. Depuis quand est-ce que tu étudies le français? Depuis combien de temps es-tu à l'université?
4. As-tu un rhume? Depuis combien de temps es-tu enrhumé(e) (n'as-tu pas eu de rhume)?
5. Sais-tu nager? Quel âge avais-tu quand tu as appris à nager?
6. Sais-tu jouer du piano? D'un autre instrument de musique?
7. Sais-tu une langue étrangère autre que le français?
8. Est-ce que tu sais la date du prochain examen dans ce cours?

**O.  Est-ce qu'on est en bonne santé?** Survey some of your classmates about the eating habits and physical condition of their friends and/or family members. Then, without naming names, report to the class your general conclusions about the health of the people you know.

Ex. O: ◯

**À faire chez vous:**
**CAHIER, Chapitre 8 / 3ᵉ étape**

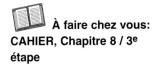

**À faire chez vous:**
**Student Tape**

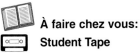

Now that you've completed the first three **étapes** of **Chapitre 8,** do Segment 2 of the STUDENT TAPE. See **CAHIER, Chapitre 8, *Écoutons!,*** for exercises that accompany this segment.

# QUATRIÈME ÉTAPE

## L·E·C·T·U·R·E

### Une consultation gratuite

*This text, from the play* **Knock** *by Jules Romain, is longer than the other readings you have done. Don't try to translate every word; work on capturing the general tone and movement of this scene from a famous French comedy of the early twentieth century.*

*Le docteur Knock est nouvellement arrivé à la commune (le petit village) de Saint-Maurice. Son prédécesseur était vieux et n'avait pas beaucoup de travail. Le docteur Knock est beaucoup plus ambitieux. Il commence par annoncer des consultations gratuites.[1]*

| | |
|---|---|
| KNOCK: | C'est vous qui êtes la première, Madame? *(Il fait entrer la dame en noir et referme la porte.)* Vous êtes bien du canton?[2] |
| LA DAME EN NOIR: | Je suis de la commune. |
| KNOCK: | De Saint-Maurice même? |
| LA DAME: | J'habite la grande ferme[3] qui est sur la route de Luchère. |
| KNOCK: | Elle vous appartient?[4] |
| LA DAME: | Oui, à mon mari et à moi. |

| | |
|---|---|
| KNOCK: | Si vous l'exploitez vous-même, vous devez avoir beaucoup de travail? |
| LA DAME: | Pensez, Monsieur! Dix-huit vaches,[5] deux bœufs, deux taureaux,[6] six chèvres,[7] une bonne douzaine de cochons,[8] sans compter la basse-cour.[9] |
| KNOCK: | Je vous plains.[10] Il ne doit guère vous rester de temps pour vous soigner. |
| LA DAME: | Oh! non. |
| KNOCK: | Et pourtant vous souffrez. |
| LA DAME: | Ce n'est pas le mot. J'ai plutôt de la fatigue. |
| KNOCK: | Oui, vous appelez ça de la fatigue. *(Il s'approche d'elle.)* Tirez la langue.[11] Vous ne devez pas avoir beaucoup d'appétit. |
| LA DAME: | Non. |
| KNOCK: | Vous êtes constipée. |
| LA DAME: | Oui, assez. |
| KNOCK: | *(Il l'ausculte.[12])* Baissez la tête. Respirez.[13] Toussez. Vous n'êtes jamais tombée d'une échelle,[14] étant petite? |
| LA DAME: | Je ne me souviens pas.[15] |
| KNOCK: | *(Il lui palpe[16] le dos, lui presse brusquement les reins.[17])* Vous n'avez jamais mal ici le soir en vous couchant? |
| LA DAME: | Oui, des fois. |
| KNOCK: | Essayez de vous rappeler. Ça devait être une grande échelle. |
| LA DAME: | Ça se peut bien.[18] |
| KNOCK: | C'était une échelle d'environ trois mètres cinquante, posée contre un mur. Vous êtes tombée à la renverse. C'est la fesse[19] gauche, heureusement. Vous vous rendez compte de votre état?[20] |
| LA DAME: | Non. |
| KNOCK: | Tant mieux.[21] Vous avez envie de guérir,[22] ou vous n'avez pas envie? |
| LA DAME: | J'ai envie. |
| KNOCK: | Ce sera long et très coûteux. On ne guérit pas en cinq minutes un mal qui traîne[23] depuis quarante ans. |
| LA DAME: | Depuis quarante ans? |
| KNOCK: | Oui, depuis que vous êtes tombée de votre échelle. |
| LA DAME: | Et combien que ça me coûterait? |
| KNOCK: | Qu'est-ce que valent les veaux actuellement?[24] |
| LA DAME: | Ça dépend... quatre ou cinq cents francs. |
| KNOCK: | Et les cochons gras?[25] |
| LA DAME: | Plus de mille francs. |
| KNOCK: | Ça vous coûtera à peu près deux cochons et deux veaux... Mais ce que je puis vous proposer, c'est de vous mettre en observation. Ça ne vous coûtera presque rien. Au bout de quelques jours vous vous rendrez compte[26] par vous-même de votre état, et vous vous déciderez... Bien. Vous allez rentrer chez vous. Vous êtes venue en voiture?[27] |
| LA DAME: | Non, à pied. |

KNOCK:        Il faut trouver une voiture. Vous vous coucherez en arrivant. Une chambre où vous serez[28] seule, autant que[29] possible. Faites fermer les volets et les rideaux.[30] Aucune[31] alimentation solide pendant une semaine. Un verre d'eau de Vichy toutes les deux heures et, à la rigueur,[32] une moitié de biscuit. À la fin de la semaine, si vos forces et votre gaieté sont revenues,[33] c'est que le mal est moins sérieux qu'on ne pouvait croire. Si, au contraire, vous éprouvez une faiblesse[34] générale, nous commencerons le traitement. C'est convenu?[35]

LA DAME:      *(soupirant[36])* Comme vous voudrez.[37]

Jules Romains, *Knock*

1. free   2. district   3. farm   4. belongs   5. cows   6. bulls   7. goats   8. pigs   9. not counting the poultry yard   10. I feel sorry for you.   11. Stick out your tongue.   12. listens to her heart and lungs   13. Breathe.   14. ladder   15. I don't remember.   16. feels   17. kidneys   18. That's possible.   19. buttock   20. Are you aware of your condition?   21. So much the better.   22. Do you really want to be cured?   23. has been dragging on   24. How much are calves worth these days?   25. fat   26. will realize   27. Did you come by car?   28. will be   29. as much as   30. Have the shutters and blinds closed.   31. no   32. if worst comes to worst   33. have come back   34. feel a weakness   35. Agreed?   36. sighing   37. As you wish.

**Postreading:** Have students compare their impression of doctors with their reactions to Knock. Could this satire extend to other professions? Which ones?

## APPRÉCIATION

**A.** Discuss the following questions with your classmates.

1. What is Knock's objective in this consultation? What is his strategy for attaining his goal?
2. How does the woman react to the doctor? In your opinion, which of her symptoms are real and which are imagined?
3. What do you think of Knock's "prescription" for the woman? What do you imagine the result will be?

R·E·P·R·I·S·E

*Troisième étape*

**B.   Est-ce qu'ils ont beaucoup changé?** En regardant les photos, indiquez si les personnes ont changé au cours des ans *(over the years),* puis suggérez une explication pour les changements ou pour l'absence de changement.

EXPRESSIONS: **grandir, maigrir, grossir, vieillir, ne pas changer, garder sa ligne, manger beaucoup (très peu, trop, moins), se nourrir bien (mal), être au régime, être malade, être enceinte, faire du sport, s'entraîner à**

Mme Brieuc

*Modèle:*   Mme Brieuc

*Mme Brieuc n'a pas changé, elle n'a pas vieilli. Elle se nourrit bien et elle fait de l'aérobic (de la gym, du jogging, etc.).*

1.   Roger Gaillard

2.   Chantal Ferréol

3.   M. Audouard

4.   Mme Durand

5.   M. Coulon

Ex. C: ⇄

**C.   On se retrouve.** Vince Cosimini n'a pas vu sa famille française depuis quelques années. Quand sa sœur française lui rend visite aux États-Unis, ils parlent de ce qu'il y a de neuf dans sa vie. Vous allez jouer avec un(e) camarade de classe les rôles de Vince et de sa sœur française. Utilisez les expressions **depuis combien de temps, depuis quand** et **depuis.**

*Modèle:*     Nous habitons maintenant à Nogent. / Nous nous sommes installés à Nogent en 1989.
—*Nous habitons maintenant à Nogent.*
—*Depuis combien de temps est-ce que vous habitez à Nogent?*
—*Nous nous sommes installés à Nogent en 1989.*
—*Ah, vous habitez à Nogent depuis (trois) ans.*

1. Je suis à l'université. / J'ai commencé mes études en 1991.
2. Je fais de l'aérobic. / J'ai commencé il y a quatre ans.
3. Je parle espagnol. / J'ai commencé à étudier l'espagnol en 1988.
4. Nous avons un chien. / Nous l'avons acheté l'année dernière.
5. Mon père travaille pour Peugeot maintenant. / Il a commencé en 1989.
6. J'ai un petit ami. / J'ai fait sa connaissance en septembre.

▲ ▲ ▲ ▲ ▲ ▲ ▲ ▲ ▲ ▲ ▲ ▲ ▲ ▲ ▲ ▲ ▲ ▲ ▲ ▲ ▲ ▲ ▲ ▲ ▲ ▲ ▲ ▲ ▲

# Point d'arrivée

**À faire chez vous:**
**Student Tape**

**CAHIER, Chapitre 8:**
*Rédigeons! / Travail de fin de chapitre* (including STUDENT TAPE, Chapitre 8, Segment 3)

*Activités orales*

## Exprimons-nous!

To inquire about someone's health in French (in addition to using expressions with **aller**), you may ask:

| | |
|---|---|
| **Comment vous sentez-vous? (Comment est-ce que tu te sens)?** | How do you feel? |

To say that you are well, use expressions such as:

| | |
|---|---|
| **Je me sens (très) bien.** | I feel (very) well. |
| **Je suis en forme.** | I'm feeling great. |

To say that you are not well, use expressions such as:

| | |
|---|---|
| **Je ne me sens pas bien.** | I'm not feeling well. |
| **Je suis souffrant.** | I'm feeling poorly. |

When someone says that he or she is not feeling well, you may seek clarification by asking:

| | |
|---|---|
| **Qu'est-ce qui ne va pas?** | What's wrong? |
| **Qu'est-ce qu'il y a?** | What's the matter? |
| **Qu'est-ce que vous avez (tu as)?** | What's the matter with you? |

**D.  J'ai eu un accident.** Think of a time when you accidentally got hurt. Imagine that it occurred just recently. When a classmate calls you on the phone, tell him/her about your injury and

Ex. D: ⇄ Have students practice in pairs. Then have them "phone" members of other groups to hear about their accidents.

explain, as well as you can, the circumstances of the accident. (When did it happen? Where? What were you doing? With whom? What happened to you?)

Ex. E: △
**Variation,** Ex. E: To review numbers, use the price list card from the KIT. Distribute a copy to each "pharmacist."

Ex. F: ○
**Implementation,** Ex. F: Divide the class into groups of 6 or 8. After pairs have rotated within the groups, each group will choose the person in the "worst shape" to make a presentation to the class.

Ex. G: ○
**Implementation,** Ex. G: Model the hypochondriac conversation before breaking the class into groups.

**E.   Un(e) ami(e) vous aide.** Feeling sick, you call a friend, describe your symptoms, and ask him or her to go to the pharmacy. Your friend does so and describes your symptoms to the pharmacist, who makes a recommendation. Your friend returns and explains the medicine and the pharmacist's recommendation(s).

**F.   Je ne suis pas en forme.** All the members of your group compete to see who is in the worst physical condition. Group members gather their information in a series of one-on-one discussions—that is, two students meet and talk about their health. When they have finished their conversation, each chats with another student, and so on.

**G.   Ça va? Ça ne va pas?** Your class is divided into two types of people—those who are never sick and those who always think they are sick. If you meet a person from the first group, try to persuade him/her that something is really wrong (that is, that he/she doesn't look well, etc.). If you meet a member of the second group, try to persuade him/her that nothing is wrong (that is, that he/she looks great. etc.).

 **Instructor's Tape:**
**M. Ahmed Abdiba,**
**Fès, Maroc**

**Portrait:** Have students listen to recording on Instructor's Tape.

# PORTRAIT
*M. Ahmed Abdiba, Fès, Maroc*

Je suis né au Maroc, à Fès qui est un centre touristique et religieux à l'ouest de Rabat (la capitale). Nous parlions arabe à la maison, mais j'ai appris le français au lycée. À l'âge de 19 ans, je suis venu en France pour faire des études à la Faculté de Pharmacie de Châtenay-Malabry. Depuis plus de 10 ans, je travaille dans une pharmacie à Nantes. Je suis assez heureux, mais j'ai envie de retourner un jour au Maroc pour y établir ma propre pharmacie.

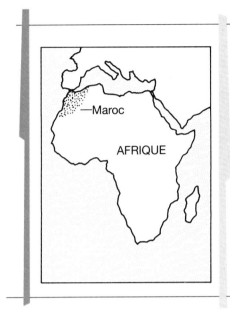

# Profil
## *Le Maroc*

**SITUATION:** à l'extrémité nord-ouest de l'Afrique sur l'Atlantique et la Méditerranée

**SUPERFICIE:** 710 850 km$^2$

**POPULATION:** 24 600 000 habitants

**NOM DES HABITANTS:** Marocains

**CAPITALE:** Rabat

**VILLES IMPORTANTES:** Casablanca, Marrakech, Safi, Agadir, Tanger, Fès

**LANGUE OFFICIELLE:** arabe

**AUTRES LANGUES:** berbère, français, hassania, espagnol

**RELIGION:** musulmans (95,95%)

**CLIMAT:** sec du côté méditerranéen, étés tempérés et hivers doux du côté atlantique, très sec dans les régions présaharienne et saharienne

**ÉCONOMIE:** agriculture, tourisme, artisanat

**HISTOIRE:** d'abord sous l'influence des Espagnols et des Portugais, ensuite colonie française; proclame son indépendance en 1956

**GOUVERNEMENT:** monarchie constitutionnelle

**À discuter:** Quelles images avez-vous du Maroc? Des Marocains? Sur quoi ces images sont-elles fondées?

# L · E · X · I · Q · U · E

## Pour se débrouiller

*Pour parler de sa santé*

Tu (n')as (pas) bonne mine aujourd'hui!
Qu'est-ce que tu as (vous avez)?
Qu'est-ce qu'il y a?
avoir mal à
avoir un accident
se blesser à
se casser

être blessé(e) à
être en bonne santé
être enceinte
être en forme
être malade
se faire mal à
se fouler
se sentir bien (mal)

*Pour décrire ses symptômes* (m.pl.)
  avoir des allergies *(f.pl.)*
  avoir du mal à dormir
  avoir le mal de l'air – airsick
     le mal de mer – seasick
  avoir le rhume des foins – hay fever
  avoir le vertige
  avoir une grippe
    avoir des courbatures *(f.pl.)* – aching
    avoir de la fièvre
    avoir mal à
  avoir un rhume, être enrhumé(e)
    avoir le nez qui coule – runny nose
    avoir le nez bouché – stuffed up
    éternuer – sneeze
    tousser – to cough
  digérer mal
  ne pas avoir d'appétit
  prendre un coup de soleil

*Pour se procurer des médicaments*
  J'ai besoin de...
  J'ai besoin de quelque chose pour *(partie du corps)*.
  J'ai besoin de quelque chose contre *(maladie, symptôme)*.

*Pour faire des excuses*
  devoir
  ne pas pouvoir

*Pour parler de sa taille*
  être au régime
  faire un mètre ___
  garder sa ligne
  grandir
  grossir
  maigrir
  peser ___ kilos

*Pour parler de la durée*
  depuis
  depuis combien de temps?
  depuis quand?

## Thèmes et contextes

*Les activités* (f.pl.) *physiques*
  faire de la gym
  faire de la musculation

*Le corps*
  la bouche
  le bras
  les cheveux *(m.pl.)*
  la cheville – ankle
  le cœur
  le cou – neck
  le coude – elbow
  les dents *(f.pl.)*
  les doigts *(m.pl.)*
  les doigts de pied
  le dos
  les épaules *(f.pl.)*
  l'estomac *(m.)*

  le genou
  la gorge
  la jambe
  la main
  le nez
  l'oreille *(f.)*
  le pied
  le poignet – wrist
  la poitrine – chest
  la tête
  le ventre – stomach
  le visage – face
  les yeux *(m.pl.)*, l'œil *(m.)*

*Les médicaments* (m.pl.)
  les antihistaminiques *(f.pl.)*
  l'aspirine *(f.)*
  un cachet
  un comprimé
  une gélule
  des gouttes *(f.pl.)* pour le nez
                pour les yeux
  des pastilles *(f.pl.)* pour la gorge
  un suppositoire

*Les aliments* (m.pl.)
  les céréales *(f.pl.)*
  les matières grasses *(f.pl.)*
  les poissons *(m.pl.)*
  les produits laitiers *(m.pl.)*
  les protéines *(f.pl.)*
  les vitamines *(f.pl.)*

## Vocabulaire général

do the dishes

*Verbes*
  améliorer
  amener
  faire la vaisselle
  jouer un tour à

  manquer
  s'occuper de
  pouvoir
  ranger

  reconnaître
  remercier
  savoir

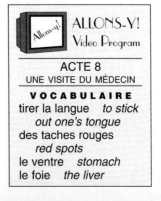

ALLONS-Y!
Video Program

ACTE 8
UNE VISITE DU MÉDECIN

**VOCABULAIRE**
tirer la langue   *to stick out one's tongue*
des taches rouges   *red spots*
le ventre   *stomach*
le foie   *the liver*

# APPENDICE

## Conjugaison des verbes réguliers et irréguliers

| | | INDICATIF | | |
|---|---|---|---|---|
| PRÉSENT | PASSÉ COMPOSÉ | IMPARFAIT | PLUS-QUE-PARFAIT | FUTUR |

## REGULAR VERBS in -er, -ir, -re

### donner

| | | | | |
|---|---|---|---|---|
| je donne | j´ai donné | je donnais | j'avais donné | je donnerai |
| tu donnes | tu as donné | tu donnais | tu avais donné | tu donneras |
| il donne | il a donné | il donnait | il avait donné | il donnera |
| nous donnons | nous avons donné | nous donnions | nous avions donné | nous donnerons |
| vous donnez | vous avez donné | vous donniez | vous aviez donné | vous donnerez |
| ils donnent | ils ont donné | ils donnaient | ils avaient donné | ils donneront |

### finir

| | | | | |
|---|---|---|---|---|
| je finis | j'ai fini | je finissais | j'avais fini | je finirai |
| tu finis | tu as fini | tu finissais | tu avais fini | tu finiras |
| il finit | il a fini | il finissait | il avait fini | il finira |
| nous finissons | nous avons fini | nous finissions | nous avions fini | nous finirons |
| vous finissez | vous avez fini | vous finissiez | vous aviez fini | vous finirez |
| ils finissent | ils ont fini | ils finissaient | ils avaient fini | ils finiront |

### attendre

| | | | | |
|---|---|---|---|---|
| j'attends | j'ai attendu | j'attendais | j'avais attendu | j'attendrai |
| tu attends | tu as attendu | tu attendais | tu avais attendu | tu attendras |
| il attend | il a attendu | il attendait | il avait attendu | il attendra |
| nous attendons | nous avons attendu | nous attendions | nous avions attendu | nous attendrons |
| vous attendez | vous avez attendu | vous attendiez | vous aviez attendu | vous attendrez |
| ils attendent | ils ont attendu | ils attendaient | ils avaient attendu | ils attendront |

## IRREGULAR VERBS avoir and être (helping verbs)

### avoir

| | | | | |
|---|---|---|---|---|
| j'ai | j'ai eu | j'avais | j'avais eu | j'aurai |
| tu as | tu as eu | tu avais | tu avais eu | tu auras |
| il a | il a eu | il avait | il avait eu | il aura |
| nous avons | nous avons eu | nous avions | nous avions eu | nous aurons |
| vous avez | vous avez eu | vous aviez | vous aviez eu | vous aurez |
| ils ont | ils ont eu | ils avaient | ils avaient eu | ils auront |

### être

| | | | | |
|---|---|---|---|---|
| je suis | j'ai été | j'étais | j'avais été | je serai |
| tu es | tu as été | tu étais | tu avais été | tu seras |
| il est | il a été | il était | il avait été | il sera |
| nous sommes | nous avons été | nous étions | nous avions été | nous serons |
| vous êtes | vous avez été | vous étiez | vous aviez été | vous serez |
| ils sont | ils ont été | ils étaient | ils avaient été | ils seront |

## IRREGULAR VERBS in -er

### aller

| | | | | |
|---|---|---|---|---|
| je vais | je suis allé(e) | j'allais | J'étais allé(e) | j'irai |
| tu vas | tu es allé(e) | tu allais | tu étais allé(e) | tu iras |
| il va | il est allé | il allait | il était allé | il ira |
| nous allons | nous sommes allé(e)s | nous allions | nous étions allé(e)s | nous irons |
| vous allez | vous êtes allé(e)(s) | vous alliez | vous étiez allés(e)(s) | vous irez |
| ils vont | ils sont allés | ils allaient | ils étaient allés | ils iront |

| CONDITIONNEL | | IMPÉRATIF | PARTICIPE | SUBJONCTIF | |
| PRÉSENT | PASSÉ | | PRÉSENT | PRÉSENT | PASSÉ |
| --- | --- | --- | --- | --- | --- |
| je donnerais | j'aurais donné | | donnant | que je donne | que j'aie donné |
| tu donnerais | tu aurais donné | donne | | que tu donnes | que tu aies donné |
| il donnerait | il aurait donné | | | qu'il donne | qu'il ait donné |
| nous donnerions | nous aurions donné | donnons | | que nous donnions | que nous ayons donné |
| vous donneriez | vous auriez donné | donnez | | que vous donniez | que vous ayez donné |
| ils donneraient | ils auraient donné | | | qu'ils donnent | qu'ils aient donné |
| je finirais | j'aurais fini | | finissant | que je finisse | que j'aie fini |
| tu finirais | tu aurais fini | finis | | que tu finisses | que tu aies fini |
| il finirait | il aurait fini | | | qu'il finisse | qu'il ait fini |
| nous finirions | nous aurions fini | finissons | | que nous finissions | que nous ayons fini |
| vous finiriez | vous auriez fini | finissez | | que vous finissiez | que vous ayez fini |
| ils finiraient | ils auraient fini | | | qu'ils finissent | qu'ils aient fini |
| j'attendrais | j'aurais attendu | | attendant | que j'attende | que j'aie attendu |
| tu attendrais | tu aurais attendu | attends | | que tu attendes | que tu aies attendu |
| il attendrait | il aurait attendu | | | qu'il attende | qu'il ait attendu |
| nous attendrions | nous aurions attendu | attendons | | que nous attendions | que nous ayons attendu |
| vous attendriez | vous auriez attendu | attendez | | que vous attendiez | que vous ayez attendu |
| ils attendraient | ils auraient attendu | | | qu'ils attendent | qu'ils aient attendu |
| j'aurais | j'aurais eu | | ayant | que j'aie | que j'aie eu |
| tu aurais | tu aurais eu | aie | | que tu aies | que tu aies eu |
| il aurait | il aurait eu | | | qu'il ait | qu'il ait eu |
| nous aurions | nous aurions eu | ayons | | que nous ayons | que nous ayons eu |
| vous auriez | vous auriez eu | ayez | | que vous ayez | que vous ayez eu |
| ils auraient | ils auraient eu | | | qu'ils aient | qu'ils aient eu |
| je serais | j'aurais été | | étant | que je sois | que j'aie été |
| tu serais | tu aurais été | sois | | que tu sois | que tu aies été |
| il serait | il aurait été | | | qu'il soit | qu'il ait été |
| nous serions | nous aurions été | soyons | | que nous soyons | que nous ayons été |
| vous seriez | vous auriez été | soyez | | que vous soyez | que vous ayez été |
| ils seraient | ils auraient été | | | qu'ils soient | qu'ils aient été |
| j'irais | je serais allé(e) | | allant | que j'aille | que je sois allé(e) |
| tu irais | tu serais allé(e) | va | | que tu ailles | que tu sois allé(e) |
| il irait | il serait allé | | | qu'il aille | qu'il soit allé |
| nous irions | nous serions allé(e)s | allons | | que nous allions | que nous soyons allé(e)s |
| vous iriez | vous seriez allé(e)(s) | allez | | que vous alliez | que vous soyez allé(e)(s) |
| ils iraient | ils seraient allés | | | qu'ils aillent | qu'ils soient allés |

| | | INDICATIF | | |
|---|---|---|---|---|
| PRÉSENT | PASSÉ COMPOSÉ | IMPARFAIT | PLUS-QUE-PARFAIT | FUTUR |

**envoyer**

| | | | | |
|---|---|---|---|---|
| j'envoie | j'ai envoyé | j'envoyais | j'avais envoyé | j'enverrai |
| tu envoies | tu as envoyé | tu envoyais | tu avais envoyé | tu enverras |
| il envoie | il a envoyé | il envoyait | il avait envoyé | il enverra |
| nous envoyons | nous avons envoyé | nous envoyions | nous avions envoyé | nous enverrons |
| vous envoyez | vous avez envoyé | vous envoyiez | vous aviez envoyé | vous enverrez |
| ils envoient | ils ont envoyé | ils envoyaient | ils avaient envoyé | ils enverront |

## IRREGULAR VERBS in -ir

**dormir**

| | | | | |
|---|---|---|---|---|
| je dors | j'ai dormi | je dormais | j'avais dormi | je dormirai |
| tu dors | tu as dormi | tu dormais | tu avais dormi | tu dormiras |
| il dort | il a dormi | il dormait | il avait dormi | il dormira |
| nous dormons | nous avons dormi | nous dormions | nous avions dormi | nous dormirons |
| vous dormez | vous avez dormi | vous dormiez | vous aviez dormi | vous dormirez |
| ils dorment | ils ont dormi | ils dormaient | ils avaient dormi | ils dormiront |

*Also:* **endormir, s'endormir, partir, servir, sentir, sortir**

**ouvrir**

| | | | | |
|---|---|---|---|---|
| j'ouvre | j'ai ouvert | j'ouvrais | j'avais ouvert | j'ouvrirai |
| tu ouvres | tu as ouvert | tu ouvrais | tu avais ouvert | tu ouvriras |
| il ouvre | il a ouvert | il ouvrait | il avait ouvert | il ouvrira |
| nous ouvrons | nous avons ouvert | nous ouvrions | nous avions ouvert | nous ouvrirons |
| vous ouvrez | vous avez ouvert | vous ouvriez | vous aviez ouvert | vous ouvrirez |
| ils ouvrent | ils ont ouvert | ils ouvraient | ils avaient ouvert | ils ouvriront |

*Also:* **couvrir, offrir, souffrir**

**venir**

| | | | | |
|---|---|---|---|---|
| je viens | je suis venu(e) | je venais | j'étais venu(e) | je viendrai |
| tu viens | tu es venu(e) | tu venais | tu étais venu(e) | tu viendras |
| il vient | il est venu | il venait | il était venu | il viendra |
| nous venons | nous sommes venu(e)s | nous venions | nous étions venu(e)s | nous viendrons |
| vous venez | vous êtes venu(e)(s) | vous veniez | vous étiez venu(e)(s) | vous viendrez |
| ils viennent | ils sont venus | ils venaient | ils étaient venus | ils viendront |

*Also:* **devenir, revenir, tenir, obtenir, retenir**

## IRREGULAR VERBS in -re

**boire**

| | | | | |
|---|---|---|---|---|
| je bois | j'ai bu | je buvais | j'avais bu | je boirai |
| tu bois | tu as bu | tu buvais | tu avais bu | tu boiras |
| il boit | il a bu | il buvait | il avait bu | il boira |
| nous buvons | nous avons bu | nous buvions | nous avions bu | nous boirons |
| vous buvez | vous avez bu | vous buviez | vous aviez bu | vous boirez |
| ils boivent | ils ont bu | ils buvaient | ils avaient bu | ils boiront |

**connaître**

| | | | | |
|---|---|---|---|---|
| je connais | j'ai connu | je connaissais | j'avais connu | je connaîtrai |
| tu connais | tu as connu | tu connaissais | tu avais connu | tu connaîtras |
| il connaît | il a connu | il connaissait | il avait connu | il connaîtra |
| nous connaissons | nous avons connu | nous connaissions | nous avions connu | nous connaîtrons |
| vous connaissez | vous avez connu | vous connaissiez | vous aviez connu | vous connaîtrez |
| ils connaissent | ils ont connu | ils connaissaient | ils avaient connu | ils connaîtront |

| CONDITIONNEL | | IMPÉRATIF | PARTICIPE | SUBJONCTIF | |
| PRÉSENT | PASSÉ | | PRÉSENT | PRÉSENT | PASSÉ |
|---|---|---|---|---|---|
| j'enverrais | j'aurais envoyé | | envoyant | que j'envoie | que j'aie envoyé |
| tu enverrais | tu aurais envoyé | envoie | | que tu envoies | que tu aies envoyé |
| il enverrait | il aurait envoyé | | | qu'il envoie | qu'il ait envoyé |
| nous enverrions | nous aurions envoyé | envoyons | | que nous envoyions | que nous ayons envoyé |
| vous enverriez | vous auriez envoyé | envoyez | | que vous envoyiez | que vous ayez envoyé |
| ils enverraient | ils auraient envoyé | | | qu'ils envoient | qu'ils aient envoyé |
| je dormirais | j'aurais dormi | dors | dormant | que je dorme | que j'aie dormi |
| tu dormirais | tu aurais dormi | | | que tu dormes | que tu aies dormi |
| il dormirait | il aurait dormi | dormons | | qu'il dorme | qu'il ait dormi |
| nous dormirions | nous aurions dormi | dormez | | que nous dormions | que nous ayons dormi |
| vous dormiriez | vous auriez dormi | | | que vous dormiez | que vous ayez dormi |
| ils dormiraient | ils auraient dormi | | | qu'ils dorment | qu'ils aient dormi |
| j'ouvrirais | j'aurais ouvert | ouvre | ouvrant | que j'ouvre | que j'aie ouvert |
| tu ouvrirais | tu aurais ouvert | | | que tu ouvres | que tu aies ouvert |
| il ouvrirait | il aurait ouvert | ouvrons | | qu'il ouvre | qu'il ait ouvert |
| nous ouvririons | nous aurions ouvert | ouvrez | | que nous ouvrions | que nous ayons ouvert |
| vous ouvririez | vous auriez ouvert | | | que vous ouvriez | que vous ayez ouvert |
| ils ouvriraient | ils auraient ouvert | | | qu'ils ouvrent | qu'ils aient ouvert |
| je viendrais | je serais venu(e) | viens | venant | que je vienne | que je sois venu(e) |
| tu viendrais | tu serais venu(e) | | | que tu viennes | que tu sois venu(e) |
| il viendrait | il serait venu | venons | | qu'il vienne | qu'il soit venu |
| nous viendrions | nous serions venu(e)s | venez | | que nous venions | que nous soyons venu(e)s |
| vous viendriez | vous seriez venu(e)(s) | | | que vous veniez | que vous soyez venu(e)(s) |
| ils viendraient | ils seraient venus | | | qu'ils viennent | qu'ils soient venus |
| je boirais | j'aurais bu | bois | buvant | que je boive | que j'aie bu |
| tu boirais | tu aurais bu | | | que tu boives | que tu aies bu |
| il boirait | il aurait bu | buvons | | qu'il boive | qu'il ait bu |
| nous boirions | nous aurions bu | buvez | | que nous buvions | que nous ayons bu |
| vous boiriez | vous auriez bu | | | que vous buviez | que vous ayez bu |
| ils boiraient | ils auraient bu | | | qu'ils boivent | qu'ils aient bu |
| je connaîtrais | j'aurais connu | connais | connaissant | que je connaisse | que j'aie connu |
| tu connaîtrais | tu aurais connu | | | que tu connaisses | que tu aies connu |
| il connaîtrait | il aurait connu | connaissons | | qu'il connaisse | qu'il ait connu |
| nous connaîtrions | nous aurions connu | connaissez | | que nous connaissions | que nous ayons connu |
| vous connaîtriez | vous auriez connu | | | que vous connaissiez | que vous ayez connu |
| ils connaîtraient | ils auraient connu | | | qu'ils connaissent | qu'ils aient connu |

| PRÉSENT | PASSÉ COMPOSÉ | INDICATIF IMPARFAIT | PLUS-QUE-PARFAIT | FUTUR |
|---------|---------------|---------------------|------------------|-------|
| **croire** | | | | |
| je crois | j'ai cru | je croyais | j'avais cru | je croirai |
| tu crois | tu as cru | tu croyais | tu avais cru | tu croiras |
| il croit | il a cru | il croyait | il avait cru | il croira |
| nous croyons | nous avons cru | nous croyions | nous avions cru | nous croirons |
| vous croyez | vous avez cru | vous croyiez | vous aviez cru | vous croirez |
| ils croient | ils ont cru | ils croyaient | ils avaient cru | ils croiront |
| **dire** | | | | |
| je dis | j'ai dit | je disais | j'avais dit | je dirai |
| tu dis | tu as dit | tu disais | tu avais dit | tu diras |
| il dit | il a dit | il disait | il avait dit | il dira |
| nous disons | nous avons dit | nous disions | nous avions dit | nous dirons |
| vous dites | vous avez dit | vous disiez | vous aviez dit | vous direz |
| ils disent | ils ont dit | ils disaient | ils avaient dit | ils diront |
| **écrire** | | | | |
| j'écris | j'ai écrit | j'écrivais | j'avais écrit | j'écrirai |
| tu écris | tu as écrit | tu écrivais | tu avais écrit | tu écriras |
| il écrit | il a écrit | il écrivait | il avait écrit | il écrira |
| nous écrivons | nous avons écrit | nous écrivions | nous avions écrit | nous écrirons |
| vous écrivez | vous avez écrit | vous écriviez | vous aviez écrit | vous écrirez |
| ils écrivent | ils ont écrit | ils écrivaient | ils avaient écrit | ils écriront |
| *Also:* **décrire** | | | | |
| **faire** | | | | |
| je fais | j'ai fait | je faisais | j'avais fait | je ferai |
| tu fais | tu as fait | tu faisais | tu avais fait | tu feras |
| il fait | il a fait | il faisait | il avait fait | il fera |
| nous faisons | nous avons fait | nous faisions | nous avions fait | nous ferons |
| vous faites | vous avez fait | vous faisiez | vous aviez fait | vous ferez |
| ils font | ils ont fait | ils faisaient | ils avaient fait | ils feront |
| **lire** | | | | |
| je lis | j'ai lu | je lisais | j'avais lu | je lirai |
| tu lis | tu as lu | tu lisais | tu avais lu | tu liras |
| il lit | il a lu | il lisait | il avait lu | il lira |
| nous lisons | nous avons lu | nous lisions | nous avions lu | nous lirons |
| vous lisez | vous avez lu | vous lisiez | vous aviez lu | vous lirez |
| ils lisent | ils ont lu | ils lisaient | ils avaient lu | ils liront |
| **mettre** | | | | |
| je mets | j'ai mis | je mettais | j'avais mis | je mettrai |
| tu mets | tu as mis | tu mettais | tu avais mis | tu mettras |
| il met | il a mis | il mettait | il avait mis | il mettra |
| nous mettons | nous avons mis | nous mettions | nous avions mis | nous mettrons |
| vous mettez | vous avez mis | vous mettiez | vous aviez mis | vous mettrez |
| ils mettent | ils ont mis | ils mettaient | ils avaient mis | ils mettront |
| *Also:* **permettre, promettre** | | | | |

| CONDITIONNEL | | IMPÉRATIF | PARTICIPE | SUBJONCTIF | |
| PRÉSENT | PASSÉ | | PRÉSENT | PRÉSENT | PASSÉ |
|---|---|---|---|---|---|
| je croirais | j'aurais cru | | croyant | que je croie | que j'aie cru |
| tu croirais | tu aurais cru | crois | | que tu croies | que tu aies cru |
| il croirait | il aurait cru | | | qu'il croie | qu'il ait cru |
| nous croirions | nous aurions cru | croyons | | que nous croyions | que nous ayons cru |
| vous croiriez | vous auriez cru | croyez | | que vous croyiez | que vous ayez cru |
| ils croiraient | ils auraient cru | | | qu'ils croient | qu'ils aient cru |
| je dirais | j'aurais dit | | disant | que je dise | que j'aie dit |
| tu dirais | tu aurais dit | dis | | que tu dises | que tu aies dit |
| il dirait | il aurait dit | | | qu'il dise | qu'il ait dit |
| nous dirions | nous aurions dit | disons | | que nous disions | que nous ayons dit |
| vous diriez | vous auriez dit | dites | | que vous disiez | que vous ayez dit |
| ils diraient | ils auraient dit | | | qu'ils disent | qu'ils aient dit |
| j'écrirais | j'aurais écrit | | écrivant | que j'écrive | que j'aie écrit |
| tu écrirais | tu aurais écrit | écris | | que tu écrives | que tu aies écrit |
| il écrirait | il aurait écrit | | | qu'il écrive | qu'il ait écrit |
| nous écririons | nous aurions écrit | écrivons | | que nous écrivions | que nous ayons écrit |
| vous écririez | vous auriez écrit | écrivez | | que vous écriviez | que vous ayez écrit |
| ils écriraient | ils auraient écrit | | | qu'ils écrivent | qu'ils aient écrit |
| je ferais | j'aurais fait | | faisant | que je fasse | que j'aie fait |
| tu ferais | tu aurais fait | fais | | que tu fasses | que tu aies fait |
| il ferait | il aurait fait | | | qu'il fasse | qu'il ait fait |
| nous ferions | nous aurions fait | faisons | | que nous fassions | que nous ayons fait |
| vous feriez | vous auriez fait | faites | | que vous fassiez | que vous ayez fait |
| ils feraient | ils auraient fait | | | qu'ils fassent | qu'ils aient fait |
| je lirais | j'aurais lu | | lisant | que je lise | que j'aie lu |
| tu lirais | tu aurais lu | lis | | que tu lises | que tu aies lu |
| il lirait | il aurait lu | | | qu'il lise | qu'il ait lu |
| nous lirions | nous aurions lu | lisons | | que nous lisions | que nous ayons lu |
| vous liriez | vous auriez lu | lisez | | que vous lisiez | que vous ayez lu |
| ils liraient | ils auraient lu | | | qu'ils lisent | qu'ils aient lu |
| je mettrais | j'aurais mis | | mettant | que je mette | que j'aie mis |
| tu mettrais | tu aurais mis | mets | | que tu mettes | que tu aies mis |
| il mettrait | il aurait mis | | | qu'il mette | qu'il ait mis |
| nous mettrions | nous aurions mis | mettons | | que nous mettions | que nous ayons mis |
| vous mettriez | vous auriez mis | mettez | | que vous mettiez | que vous ayez mis |
| ils mettraient | ils auraient mis | | | qu'ils mettent | qu'ils aient mis |

| | | INDICATIF | | |
| PRÉSENT | PASSÉ COMPOSÉ | IMPARFAIT | PLUS-QUE-PARFAIT | FUTUR |
|---|---|---|---|---|
| **prendre** | | | | |
| je prends | j'ai pris | je prenais | j'avais pris | je prendrai |
| tu prends | tu as pris | tu prenais | tu avais pris | tu prendras |
| il prend | il a pris | il prenait | il avait pris | il prendra |
| nous prenons | nous avons pris | nous prenions | nous avions pris | nous prendrons |
| vous prenez | vous avez pris | vous preniez | vous aviez pris | vous prendrez |
| ils prennent | ils ont pris | ils prenaient | ils avaient pris | ils prendront |
| *Also:* **apprendre, comprendre** | | | | |
| **rire** | | | | |
| je ris | j'ai ri | je riais | j'avais ri | je rirai |
| tu ris | tu as ri | tu riais | tu avais ri | tu riras |
| il rit | il a ri | il riait | il avait ri | il rira |
| nous rions | nous avons ri | nous riions | nous avions ri | nous rirons |
| vous riez | vous avez ri | vous riiez | vous aviez ri | vous rirez |
| ils rient | ils ont ri | ils riaient | ils avaient ri | ils riront |
| **suivre** | | | | |
| je suis | j'ai suivi | je suivais | j'avais suivi | je suivrai |
| tu suis | tu as suivi | tu suivais | tu avais suivi | tu suivras |
| il suit | il a suivi | il suivait | il avait suivi | il suivra |
| nous suivons | nous avons suivi | nous suivions | nous avions suivi | nous suivrons |
| vous suivez | vous avez suivi | vous suiviez | vous aviez suivi | vous suivrez |
| ils suivent | ils ont suivi | ils suivaient | ils avaient suivi | ils suivront |

### IRREGULAR VERBS in -oir

| PRÉSENT | PASSÉ COMPOSÉ | IMPARFAIT | PLUS-QUE-PARFAIT | FUTUR |
|---|---|---|---|---|
| **devoir** | | | | |
| je dois | j'ai dû | je devais | j'avais dû | je devrai |
| tu dois | tu as dû | tu devais | tu avais dû | tu devras |
| il doit | il a dû | il devait | il avait dû | il devra |
| nous devons | nous avons dû | nous devions | nous avions dû | nous devrons |
| vous devez | vous avez dû | vous deviez | vous aviez dû | vous devrez |
| ils doivent | ils ont dû | ils devaient | ils avaient dû | ils devront |
| **pleuvoir** | | | | |
| il pleut | il a plu | il pleuvait | il avait plu | il pleuvra |
| **pouvoir** | | | | |
| je peux | j'ai pu | je pouvais | j'avais pu | je pourrai |
| tu peux | tu as pu | tu pouvais | tu avais pu | tu pourras |
| il peut | il a pu | il pouvait | il avait pu | il pourra |
| nous pouvons | nous avons pu | nous pouvions | nous avions pu | nous pourrons |
| vous pouvez | vous avez pu | vous pouviez | vous aviez pu | vous pourrez |
| ils peuvent | ils ont pu | ils pouvaient | ils avaient pu | ils pourront |

| CONDITIONNEL | | IMPÉRATIF | PARTICIPE | SUBJONCTIF | |
| PRÉSENT | PASSÉ | | PRÉSENT | PRÉSENT | PASSÉ |
|---|---|---|---|---|---|
| je prendrais | j'aurais pris | | prenant | que je prenne | que j'aie pris |
| tu prendrais | tu aurais pris | prends | | que tu prennes | que tu aies pris |
| il prendrait | il aurait pris | | | qu'il prenne | qu'il ait pris |
| nous prendrions | nous aurions pris | prenons | | que nous prenions | que nous ayons pris |
| vous prendriez | vous auriez pris | prenez | | que vous preniez | que vous ayez pris |
| ils prendraient | ils auraient pris | | | qu'ils prennent | qu'ils aient pris |
| je rirais | j'aurais ri | | riant | que je rie | que j'aie ri |
| tu rirais | tu aurais ri | ris | | que tu ries | que tu aies ri |
| il rirait | il aurait ri | | | qu'il rie | qu'il ait ri |
| nous ririons | nous aurions ri | rions | | que nous riions | que nous ayons ri |
| vous ririez | vous auriez ri | riez | | que vous riiez | que vous ayez ri |
| ils riraient | ils auraient ri | | | qu'ils rient | qu'ils aient ri |
| je suivrais | j'aurais suivi | | suivant | que je suive | que j'aie suivi |
| tu suivrais | tu aurais suivi | suis | | que tu suives | que tu aies suivi |
| il suivrait | il aurait suivi | | | qu'il suive | qu'il ait suivi |
| nous suivrions | nous aurions suivi | suivons | | que nous suivions | que nous ayons suivi |
| vous suivriez | vous auriez suivi | suivez | | que vous suiviez | que vous ayez suivi |
| ils suivraient | ils auraient suivi | | | qu'ils suivent | qu'ils aient suivi |
| je devrais | j'aurais dû | | devant | que je doive | que j'aie dû |
| tu devrais | tu aurais dû | dois | | que tu doives | que tu aies dû |
| il devrait | il aurait dû | | | qu'il doive | qu'il ait dû |
| nous devrions | nous aurions dû | devons | | que nous devions | que nous ayons dû |
| vous devriez | vous auriez dû | devez | | que vous deviez | que vous ayez dû |
| ils devraient | ils auraient dû | | | qu'ils doivent | qu'ils aient dû |
| il pleuvrait | il aurait plu | | pleuvant | qu'il pleuve | qu'il ait plu |
| je pourrais | j'aurais pu | | pouvant | que je puisse | que j'aie pu |
| tu pourrais | tu aurais pu | | | que tu puisses | que tu aies pu |
| il pourrait | il aurait pu | | | qu'il puisse | qu'il ait pu |
| nous pourrions | nous aurions pu | | | que nous puissions | que nous ayons pu |
| vous pourriez | vous auriez pu | | | que vous puissiez | que vous ayez pu |
| ils pourraient | ils auraient pu | | | qu'ils puissent | qu'ils aient pu |

| PRÉSENT | PASSÉ COMPOSÉ | INDICATIF IMPARFAIT | PLUS-QUE-PARFAIT | FUTUR |
|---|---|---|---|---|
| **vouloir** | | | | |
| je veux | j'ai voulu | je voulais | j'avais voulu | je voudrai |
| tu veux | tu as voulu | tu voulais | tu avais voulu | tu voudras |
| il veut | il a voulu | il voulait | il avait voulu | il voudra |
| nous voulons | nous avons voulu | nous voulions | nous avions voulu | nous voudrons |
| vous voulez | vous avez voulu | vous vouliez | vous aviez voulu | vous voudrez |
| ils veulent | ils ont voulu | ils voulaient | ils avaient voulu | ils voudront |
| **recevoir** | | | | |
| je reçois | j'ai reçu | je recevais | j'avais reçu | je recevrai |
| tu reçois | tu as reçu | tu recevais | tu avais reçu | tu recevras |
| il reçoit | il a reçu | il recevait | il avait reçu | il recevra |
| nous recevons | nous avons reçu | nous recevions | nous avions reçu | nous recevrons |
| vous recevez | vous avez reçu | vous receviez | vous aviez reçu | vous recevrez |
| ils reçoivent | ils ont reçu | ils recevaient | ils avaient reçu | ils recevront |
| **savoir** | | | | |
| je sais | j'ai su | je savais | j'avais su | je saurai |
| tu sais | tu as su | tu savais | tu avais su | tu sauras |
| il sait | il a su | il savait | il avait su | il saura |
| nous savons | nous avons su | nous savions | nous avions su | nous saurons |
| vous savez | vous avez su | vous saviez | vous aviez su | vous saurez |
| ils savent | ils ont su | ils savaient | ils avaient su | ils sauront |
| **voir** | | | | |
| je vois | j'ai vu | je voyais | j'avais vu | je verrai |
| tu vois | tu as vu | tu voyais | tu avais vu | tu verras |
| il voit | il a vu | il voyait | il avait vu | il verra |
| nous voyons | nous avons vu | nous voyions | nous avions vu | nous verrons |
| vous voyez | vous avez vu | vous voyiez | vous aviez vu | vous verrez |
| ils voient | ils ont vu | ils voyaient | ils avaient vu | ils verront |

## STEM-CHANGING VERBS

| | | | | |
|---|---|---|---|---|
| **acheter** | | | | |
| j'achète | j'ai acheté | j'achetais | j'avais acheté | j'achèterai |
| tu achètes | tu as acheté | tu achetais | tu avais acheté | tu achèteras |
| il achète | il a acheté | il achetait | il avait acheté | il achètera |
| nous achetons | nous avons acheté | nous achetions | nous avions acheté | nous achèterons |
| vous achetez | vous avez acheté | vous achetiez | vous aviez acheté | vous achèterez |
| ils achètent | ils ont acheté | ils achetaient | ils avaient acheté | ils achèteront |
| **appeler** | | | | |
| j'appelle | j' ai appelé | j'appelais | j'avais appelé | j'appellerai |
| tu appelles | tu as appelé | tu appelais | tu avais appelé | tu appelleras |
| il appelle | il a appelé | il appelait | il avait appelé | il appellera |
| nous appelons | nous avons appelé | nous appelions | nous avions appelé | nous appellerons |
| vous appelez | vous avez appelé | vous appeliez | vous aviez appelé | vous appellerez |
| ils appellent | ils ont appelé | ils appelaient | ils avaient appelé | ils appelleront |

| CONDITIONNEL | | IMPÉRATIF | PARTICIPE | SUBJONCTIF | |
| PRÉSENT | PASSÉ | | PRÉSENT | PRÉSENT | PASSÉ |
|---|---|---|---|---|---|
| je voudrais | j'aurais voulu | | voulant | que je veuille | que j'aie voulu |
| tu voudrais | tu aurais voulu | veuille | | que tu veuilles | que tu aies voulu |
| il voudrait | il aurait voulu | | | qu'il veuille | qu'il ait voulu |
| nous voudrions | nous aurions voulu | voulons | | que nous voulions | que nous ayons voulu |
| vous voudriez | vous auriez voulu | veuillez | | que vous vouliez | que vous ayez voulu |
| ils voudraient | ils auraient voulu | | | qu'ils veuillent | qu'ils aient voulu |
| je recevrais | j'aurais reçu | | recevant | que je reçoive | que j'aie reçu |
| tu recevrais | tu aurais reçu | reçois | | que tu reçoives | que tu aies reçu |
| il recevrait | il aurait reçu | | | qu'il reçoive | qu'il ait reçu |
| nous recevrions | nous aurions reçu | recevons | | que nous recevions | que nous ayons reçu |
| vous recevriez | vous auriez reçu | recevez | | que vous receviez | que vous ayez reçu |
| ils recevraient | ils auraient reçu | | | qu'ils reçoivent | qu'ils aient reçu |
| je saurais | j'aurais su | | sachant | que je sache | que j'aie su |
| tu saurais | tu aurais su | sache | | que tu saches | que tu aies su |
| il saurait | il aurait su | | | qu'il sache | qu'il ait su |
| nous saurions | nous aurions su | sachons | | que nous sachions | que nous ayons su |
| vous sauriez | vous auriez su | sachez | | que vous sachiez | que vous ayez su |
| ils sauraient | ils auraient su | | | qu'ils sachent | qu'ils aient su |
| je verrais | j'aurais vu | | voyant | que je voie | que j'aie vu |
| tu verrais | tu aurais vu | vois | | que tu voies | que tu aies vu |
| il verrait | il aurait vu | | | qu'il voie | qu'il ait vu |
| nous verrions | nous aurions vu | voyons | | que nous voyions | que nous ayons vu |
| vous verriez | vous auriez vu | voyez | | que vous voyiez | que vous ayez vu |
| ils verraient | ils auraient vu | | | qu'ils voient | qu'ils aient vu |
| j'achèterais | j'aurais acheté | | achetant | que j'achète | que j'ai acheté |
| tu achèterais | tu aurais acheté | achète | | que tu achètes | que tu aies acheté |
| il achèterait | il aurait acheté | | | qu'il achète | qu'il ait acheté |
| nous achèterions | nous aurions acheté | achetons | | que nous achetions | que nous ayons acheté |
| vous achèteriez | vous auriez acheté | achetez | | que vous achetiez | que vous ayez acheté |
| ils achèteraient | ils auraient acheté | | | qu'ils achètent | qu'ils aient acheté |
| j'appellerais | j'avais appelé | | appelant | que j'appelle | que j'aie appelé |
| tu appellerais | tu avais appelé | appelle | | que tu appelles | que tu aies appelé |
| il appellerait | il avait appelé | | | qu'il appelle | qu'il ait appelé |
| nous appellerions | nous avions appelé | appelons | | que nous appelions | que nous ayons appelé |
| vous appelleriez | vous aviez appelé | appelez | | que vous appeliez | que vous ayez appelé |
| ils appelleraient | ils avaient appelé | | | qu'ils appellent | qu'ils aient appelé |

| | | INDICATIF | | |
|---|---|---|---|---|
| PRÉSENT | PASSÉ COMPOSÉ | IMPARFAIT | PLUS-QUE-PARFAIT | FUTUR |
| **commencer** | | | | |
| je commence | j'ai commencé | je commençais | j'avais commencé | je commencerai |
| tu commences | tu as commencé | tu commençais | tu avais commencé | tu commenceras |
| il commence | il a commencé | il commençait | il avait commencé | il commencera |
| nous commençons | nous avons commencé | nous commencions | nous avions commencé | nous commencerons |
| vous commencez | vous avez commencé | vous commenciez | vous aviez commencé | vous commencerez |
| ils commencent | ils ont commencé | ils commençaient | ils avaient commencé | ils commenceront |
| **espérer** | | | | |
| j'espère | j'ai espéré | j'espérais | j'avais espéré | j'espérerai |
| tu espères | tu as espéré | tu espérais | tu avais espéré | tu espéreras |
| il espère | il a espéré | il espérait | il avait espéré | il espérera |
| nous espérons | nous avons espéré | nous espérions | nous avions espéré | nous espérerons |
| vous espérez | vous avez espéré | vous espériez | vous aviez espéré | vous espérerez |
| ils espèrent | ils ont espéré | ils espéraient | ils avaient espéré | ils espéreront |
| **essayer** | | | | |
| j'essaie | j'ai essayé | j'essayais | j'avais essayé | j'essaierai |
| tu essaies | tu as essayé | tu essayais | tu avais essayé | tu essaieras |
| il essaie | il a essayé | il essayait | il avait essayé | il essaiera |
| nous essayons | nous avons essayé | nous essayions | nous avions essayé | nous essaierons |
| vous essayez | vous avez essayé | vous essayiez | vous aviez essayé | vous essaierez |
| ils essaient | ils ont essayé | ils essayaient | ils avaient essayé | ils essaieront |
| **jeter** | | | | |
| je jette | j'ai jeté | je jetais | j'avais jeté | je jetterai |
| tu jettes | tu as jeté | tu jetais | tu avais jeté | tu jetteras |
| il jette | il a jeté | il jetait | il avait jeté | il jettera |
| nous jetons | nous avons jeté | nous jetions | nous avions jeté | nous jetterons |
| vous jetez | vous avez jeté | vous jetiez | vous aviez jeté | vous jetterez |
| ils jettent | ils ont jeté | ils jetaient | ils avaient jeté | ils jetteront |
| **lever** | | | | |
| je lève | j'ai levé | je levais | j'avais levé | je lèverai |
| tu lèves | tu as levé | tu levais | tu avais levé | tu lèveras |
| il lève | il a levé | il levait | il avait levé | il lèvera |
| nous levons | nous avons levé | nous levions | nous avions levé | nous lèverons |
| vous levez | vous avez levé | vous leviez | vous aviez levé | vous lèverez |
| ils lèvent | ils ont levé | ils levaient | ils avaient levé | ils lèveront |
| **manger** | | | | |
| je mange | j'ai mangé | je mangeais | j'avais mangé | je mangerai |
| tu manges | tu as mangé | tu mangeais | tu avais mangé | tu mangeras |
| il mange | il a mangé | il mangeait | il avait mangé | il mangera |
| nous mangeons | nous avons mangé | nous mangions | nous avions mangé | nous mangerons |
| vous mangez | vous avez mangé | vous mangiez | vous aviez mangé | vous mangerez |
| ils mangent | ils ont mangé | ils mangeaient | ils avaient mangé | ils mangeront |

| CONDITIONNEL | | IMPÉRATIF | PARTICIPE | SUBJONCTIF | |
| PRÉSENT | PASSÉ | | PRÉSENT | PRÉSENT | PASSÉ |
|---|---|---|---|---|---|
| je commencerais | j'aurais commencé | | commençant | que je commence | que j'aie commencé |
| tu commencerais | tu aurais commencé | commence | | que tu commences | que tu aies commencé |
| il commencerait | il aurait commencé | | | qu'il commence | qu'il ait commencé |
| ns commencerions | ns aurions commencé | commençons | | que ns commencions | que ns ayons commencé |
| vs commenceriez | vs auriez commencé | commencez | | que vs commenciez | que vs ayez commencé |
| ils commenceraient | ils auraient commencé | | | qu'ils commencent | qu'ils aient commencé |
| j'espérerais | j'aurais espéré | | espérant | que j'espère | que j'aie espéré |
| tu espérerais | tu aurais espéré | espère | | que tu espères | que tu aies espéré |
| il espérerait | il aurait espéré | | | qu'il espère | qu'il ait espéré |
| nous espérerions | nous aurions espéré | espérons | | que nous espérions | que nous ayons espéré |
| vous espéreriez | vous auriez espéré | espérez | | que vous espériez | que vous ayez espéré |
| ils espéreraient | ils auraient espéré | | | qu'ils espèrent | qu'ils aient espéré |
| j'essaierais | j'aurais essayé | | essayant | que j'essaie | que j'aie essayé |
| tu essaierais | tu aurais essayé | essaie | | que tu essaies | que tu aies essayé |
| il essaierait | il aurait essayé | | | qu'il essaie | qu'il ait essayé |
| nous essaierions | nous aurions essayé | essayons | | que nous essayions | que nous ayons essayé |
| vous essaieriez | vous auriez essayé | essayez | | que vous essayiez | que vous ayez essayé |
| ils essaieraient | ils auraient essayé | | | qu'ils essaient | qu'ils aient essayé |
| je jetterais | j'aurais jeté | | jetant | que je jette | que j'aie jeté |
| tu jetterais | tu aurais jeté | jette | | que tu jettes | que tu aies jeté |
| il jetterait | il aurait jeté | | | qu'il jette | qu'il ait jeté |
| nous jetterions | nous aurions jeté | jetons | | que nous jetions | que nous ayons jeté |
| vous jetteriez | vous auriez jeté | jetez | | que vous jetiez | que vous ayez jeté |
| ils jetteraient | ils auraient jeté | | | qu'ils jettent | qu'ils aient jeté |
| je lèverais | j'aurais levé | | levant | que je lève | que j'aie levé |
| tu lèverais | tu aurais levé | lève | | que tu lèves | que tu aies levé |
| il lèverait | il aurait levé | | | qu'il lève | qu'il ait levé |
| nous lèverions | nous aurions levé | levons | | que nous levions | que nous ayons levé |
| vous lèveriez | vous auriez levé | levez | | que vous leviez | que vous ayez levé |
| ils lèveraient | ils auraient levé | | | qu'ils lèvent | qu'ils aient levé |
| je mangerais | j'aurais mangé | | mangeant | que je mange | que j'aie mangé |
| tu mangerais | tu aurais mangé | mange | | que tu manges | que tu aies mangé |
| il mangerait | il aurait mangé | | | qu'il mange | qu'il ait mangé |
| nous mangerions | nous aurions mangé | mangeons | | que nous mangions | que nous ayons mangé |
| vous mangeriez | vous auriez mangé | mangez | | que vous mangiez | que vous ayez mangé |
| ils mangeraient | ils auraient mangé | | | qu'ils mangent | qu'ils aient mangé |

# LEXIQUES

# LEXIQUE

## Français-anglais

▼▼▼▼▼▼▼▼▼▼▼▼▼▼▼

## A

**à** in; at; to; **— toi** yours; **— qui** to whom; **— la télévision** on television

**abandonner** to abandon

**abbaye** *(f)* abbey

**abondant(e)** abundant

**abonnement** *(m)* subscription; season ticket

**aborder** to approach (a person)

**abréviation** *(f)* abbreviation

**abricot** *(m)* apricot

**abriter** to shelter

**absent(e)** absent

**absolument** absolutely

**abstrait(e)** abstract

**accent** *(m)* accent; stress

**accepter** to accept

**accès** *(m)* access

**accident** *(m)* accident

**accompagner** to accompany

**accomplir** to accomplish

**accomplissement** *(m)* accomplishment

**accord** *(m)* agreement; **d'—** okay; **être d'—** to agree

**accueillir** to greet; to welcome

**achat** *(m)* purchase; **les —s** purchasing (department); **faire des —s** to shop; to go shopping

**acheter** to buy

**acier** *(m)* steel

**acquérir** *(acquis)* to acquire

**acrylique** *(f)* acrylic

**acteur(-trice)** *(m, f)* actor

**actif(-ve)** active; employed

**actifs** *(m pl)* workers

**activité** *(f)* activity

**actuel(le)** current

**actuellement** currently

**addition** *(f)* check (restaurant)

**adieux: faire ses —** to say goodbye

**administrer:** to manage; to run

**adorer** to adore; to love

**adresse** *(f)* address

**adresser: s'— à** to speak to

**aéroport** *(m)* airport

**affaires** *(f pl)* belongings; business; **homme (femme) d'—** businessman (-woman)

**affiche** *(f)* poster

**afficher** to post

**affreux(-euse)** horrible

**afin de** in order to

**Afrique** *(f)* Africa; **— du Sud** South Africa

**âge** *(m)* age; **Quel — as-tu?** How old are you?; **d'un certain —** middle-aged

**âgé(e)** old

**agence** *(f)* agency; **— de location** rental agency; **— immobilière** real estate agency

**agent(e)** *(m, f)* agent; employee

**agir** to act; **Dans cet article il s'agit de...** This article is about. . .

**agréable** pleasant

**agricole** agricultural

**agriculteur(-trice)** *(m, f)* farmer

**aide** *(f)* help

**aider** to help

**ail** *(m)* garlic

**aile** *(f)* wing

**aimer** to like; to love; **— le mieux** to like the best; **— mieux** to like better; to prefer

**ainsi** thus; **— que** as well as

**air: avoir l'—** to seem; to look

**aire** *(f)* **de repos** rest area

**aise: se mettre à l'—** to get comfortable

**aîné(e)** eldest

**aisé(e)** easy

**ajouter** to add

**album** *(m)* album

**alcoolisé(e)** alcoholic (beverages)

**Algérie** *(f)* Algeria

**algérien(ne)** Algerian

**alimentaire** pertaining to food

**alimentation** *(f)* food; **l'— générale** grocery store

**aliments** *(m pl)* foods

**Allemagne** *(f)* Germany

**allemand(e)** German

**aller** to go; **Allez, au revoir.** So long.; **Je vais bien.** I'm fine.; **Ça te va bien.** That looks good on you.; **Qu'est-ce qui ne va pas?** What's wrong?

**aller: — -simple (-retour)** *(m)* one-way (round-trip) ticket

**allergie** *(f)* allergy

**allée** *(f)* path

**alliés** *(m pl)* allies

**allô** hello (on the telephone)

**allumer** to light

**alors** so; then

**amande** *(f)* almond

**amateur(-trice) de** *(m, f)* lover of

**ambassade** *(f)* embassy

**ambigu(-üe)** ambiguous

**ambitieux(-euse)** ambitious

**améliorer** to improve

**aménageable: sous-sol —** basement that can be finished

**aménager: — une maison** to set up a house

**aménagé(e)** set-up; designed

**amener** to bring; to take

**américain(e)** American

**Amérique** *(f)* America

**ameublement** *(m)* furnishings; furniture

**ami(e)** *(m, f)* friend; **petit(e) —(e)** boy(girl)friend

**amidon** *(m)* starch

**amour** *(m)* love; **"mon —"** "my pet"

**amoureux** *(m pl)* lovers

**amoureux(-euse) de** in love with

**amphi = amphithéâtre**

**amphithéâtre** *(m)* amphitheater

**amusant(e)** fun; amusing

**amuse-gueule** *(m)* snack

**amuser: s'—** to have fun

**an** *(m)* year; **depuis 6 —s** for 6 years; **J'ai 19 —s.** I'm 19 (years old).; **le Nouvel —** New Year's

**analyser** to analyze

**ancêtres** *(m pl)* ancestors

**ancien(ne)** old; ancient; former

**anglais(e)** English

**Angleterre** *(f)* England

**animateur(-trice)** *(m, f)* **de radio** radio talk show host

**année** *(f)* year; **d'— en —** from year to year; **les —s 70** the 70s

**anniversaire** *(m)* birthday

**annonce: les petites —s** classified ads

**annoncer** to announce

**annuaire** *(m)* phone book

**annuler** to cancel

**anonyme** anonymous

**anorak** *(m)* ski jacket

**anthropologie** *(f)* anthropology

**antihistaminique** *(m)* antihistamine

**apéritif** *(m)* before-dinner drink

**appareil** *(m)* apparatus; **— de gymnastique** workout machine; **—-photo** camera; **C'est qui à l'—?** Who's calling? (on the telephone)

**apparence** *(f)* appearance

**appartement** *(m)* apartment

**appartenir à** to belong to

**appel** *(m)* call; roll call

**appeler** to call; **Je m'appelle...** My name is. . .

**appétit** *(m)* appetite; **Bon —!** Enjoy your meal!

**apporter** to bring

**apprécier** to appreciate; to like

**apprendre** *(appris)* to learn

**approcher: s' — de** to approach

**approprié(e)** appropriate

**après** after; afterwards; **— avoir fini** after having finished

**après-midi** *(m)* afternoon

**arabe** *(m)* Arabic

**arbre** *(m)* tree

**architecte** *(m, f)* architect

**architecture** *(f)* architecture

**arène** *(f)* arena

**argent** *(m)* money

**argentin(e)** Argentinian

**Argentine** *(f)* Argentina

**armoire** *(f)* dresser

**aromatisé(e)** flavored

**arranger** to arrange; **s'—** to work itself out

**arrêt** *(m)* stop; **sans —** non-stop; **— de bus** bus stop; **— de travail** medical excuse for not being able to work

**arrêter: s'—** to stop

**arrière: à l'—** in back

**arriver** to arrive; to happen

**arrivée** *(f)* arrival

**arrondissement** *(m)* administrative division of Paris

**arroser** to baste

**art** *(m)* art; **beaux —s** fine arts

**artichaut** *(m)* artichoke

**artisanat** *(m)* arts and crafts

**ascenseur** *(m)* elevator

**Asie** *(f)* Asia

**asperges** *(f pl)* asparagus

**aspirine** *(f)* aspirin

**asseoir: s'—** to sit; **Assieds-toi! (Asseyez-vous!)** Sit down!

**assez** rather; **— de** enough

**assiette** *(f)* plate

**assis(e)** seated

**assistant(e)** *(m, f)* teaching assistant

**assister à** to attend

**associer: s'— à** to be associated with

**astronaute** *(m, f)* astronaut

**astronomie** *(f)* astronomy

**atelier** *(m)* studio; workshop; **l'— Michelin** the Michelin plant (factory)

**atteindre** *(atteint)* to reach

**attendre** to wait (for)

**attention: faire — à** to be careful of; to pay attention to

**attirer** to attract

**aube** *(f)* dawn

**auberge** *(f)* inn

**aucun(e)** not a one; **ne... —** none whatsoever

**augmenter** to increase

**aujourd'hui** today

**auquel** to which

**aussi** also; **—...que** as. . .as

**Australie** *(f)* Australia

**australien(ne)** Australian

**autant que** as much as; **— de...que** as much. . .as; **pour —** in as much as

**auto** *(f)* car

**autobus** *(m)* bus

**automatiquement** automatically

**automne** *(f)* autumn

**autonome** autonomous

**autoroute** *(f)* highway

**autre** other

**autrefois** in the past

**autrichien(ne)** Austrian

**avaler** to swallow

**avance: à l'—** in advance; **en —** early

**avancé(e)** advanced

**avancement** *(m)* promotion

**avant** before; **— d'entrer** before entering; **— Jésus-Christ** B.C.

**avant-hier** the day before yesterday

**avantage** *(m)* advantage

**avare** *(m)* miser

**avare** miserly

**avec** with; **l'un — l'autre** with each other

**avenir** *(m)* future; **à l'—** in the future

**aventure** *(f)* adventure

**averse** *(f)* shower (rain)

**avion** *(m)* airplane

**avis** *(m)* opinion; **à mon —** in my opinion; **changer d'—** to change one's mind

**avisé(e)** informed

**avocat(e)** *(m, f)* lawyer

**avoir** *(eu)* to have; **Qu'est-ce que tu as?** What's the matter (with you)?

**ayant: — décidé de** having decided to

## B

**bac = baccalauréat**

**baccalauréat** *(m)* exam taken at the end of secondary school studies

**badge** *(m)* badge

**baguette** *(f)* long loaf of French bread

**baie** *(f)* bay

**baigner: se —** to go swimming

**baignoire** *(f)* bathtub

**baisser** to lower

**bal** *(m)* danse

**balader: se —** to take a stroll

**baladeur** *(m)* portable stereo (Walkman)

**balcon** *(m)* balcony

**balle** *(f)* ball

**ballon** *(m)* ball; balloon

**banane** *(f)* banana

**banc** *(m)* bench

**banlieue** *(f)* suburbs

**banque** *(f)* bank

**barbant: C'est —.** It's boring.

**barbe** *(f)* beard

**barrage** *(m)* dam

**bas** *(m)* bottom

**base** *(f)* **de données** data bank

**bas(se)** low

**base-ball** *(m)* baseball

**baser: en vous basant sur** based on

**basket** *(m)* basketball; **—s** sneakers

**basse-cour** *(f)* barnyard animals

**bataille** *(f)* battle

**bateau** *(m)* boat; **— à voile** sailboat
**bâtiment** *(m)* building
**batterie** *(f)* drums
**beau/bel (belle)** beautiful; **Il fait beau.** It's beautiful weather.
**beaucoup** a lot
**beau-frère** *(m)* brother-in-law
**beau-père** *(m)* stepfather; father-in-law
**bébé** *(m)* baby
**belge** Belgian
**Belgique** *(f)* Belgium
**belle-mère** *(f)* stepmother; mother-in-law
**belle-sœur** *(f)* sister-in-law
**ben = bien**
**béret** *(m)* beret
**bermuda** *(m)* (pair of) shorts
**besoin** *(m)* need; **avoir — de** to need
**beurre** *(m)* butter
**bibliothèque** *(f)* library
**bicyclette** *(f)* bicycle
**bidet** *(m)* low sink used for personal hygiene
**bien** well; **— entendu** of course; **Ça a l'air —.** That seems nice (okay).
**bientôt** soon; **À —.** See you soon.
**bienvenue à** welcome to
**bière** *(f)* beer
**bifteck** *(m)* steak
**bijou** *(m)* (piece of) jewelry
**bikini** *(m)* bikini
**billet** *(m)* ticket; bill (money)
**biographie** *(f)* biography
**biologie** *(f)* biology
**biscuit** *(m)* cookie
**bisque** *(m)* **de homard** creamy lobster soup
**blanc(he)** white
**blessé(e): être — à** to be injured in
**blessure** *(f)* injury; wound
**blé** *(m)* wheat
**bleu(e)** blue
**blond(e)** blond
**blouson** *(m)* jacket
**blue-jean** *(m)* (a pair of) blue jeans
**bœuf** *(m)* beef; steer
**bohème** bohemian
**boire** *(bu)* to drink
**boisson** *(f)* drink; **— gazeuse** carbonated beverage
**boîte** *(f)* box; can
**boîte: — de nuit** nightclub
**bol** *(m)* bowl

**bon** *(m)* coupon
**bon(ne)** good; **Il fait bon.** The weather's nice.
**bonbon** *(m)* (piece of) candy
**bonheur** *(m)* happiness
**bonjour** hi
**bonnet** *(m)* cap, hat
**bord** *(m)* edge; **au — de** along; **— de la mer** seashore
**bordeaux** burgundy (color)
**botanique** *(f)* botany
**bottes** *(f pl)* boots
**bouche** *(f)* mouth; **— de métro** entrance to subway station
**boucher(-ère)** *(m, f)* butcher
**boucles** *(f pl)* **d'oreille** earrings
**bouillabaisse** *(f)* fish soup
**bouillir** to boil
**boulanger(-ère)** *(m, f)* baker
**boulangerie** *(f)* bakery
**boum** *(f)* young people's party
**bourgeois(e)** *(m, f)* middle-class person
**bourse** *(f)* scholarship
**bout** *(m)* end; piece
**bouteille** *(f)* bottle
**boutique** *(f)* shop (small)
**branché(e)** connected; "in"; "with it"
**bras** *(m)* arm
**bref (brève)** brief
**Brésil** *(m)* Brazil
**brésilien(ne)** Brazilian
**Bretagne** *(f)* Brittany
**brie** *(m)* type of French cheese
**brique** *(f)* brick
**brochure** *(f)* brochure
**brodé(e)** embroidered
**bronzer: se faire —** to get a suntan
**brosse** *(f)* brush; **— à dents** toothbrush
**brosser: se — les dents** to brush one's teeth
**brouillard** *(m)* fog; **Il fait du —.** It's foggy.
**bruit** *(m)* noise
**brûler** to burn
**brûlure** *(f)* burn
**brume** *(f)* mist
**brun(e)** brown; brunette
**buanderie** *(f)* laundry room
**bulletin** *(m)* **d'inscription** registration form
**bureau** *(m)* desk; office; **— de poste** post office; **— de tabac** tobacconist's shop
**bustier** *(m)* halter-type top
**but** *(m)* goal

## C

**ça** that; **— va?** How's it going?; **— ira.** It will be okay.; **— va.** That's okay.; **— vous va?** Is that okay with you?; **C'est pour — que...** That's why...; **C'est —.** That's it.; **— fait un an que...** It has been a year since. . .
**cabine** *(f)* **téléphonique** phone booth
**cabinet** *(m)* **de toilette** half-bath
**cachet** *(m)* tablet; pill
**cadeau** *(m)* gift
**cadran** *(m)* dial
**cadre** *(m)* setting; executive; **— supérieur** high-level executive
**cafard: avoir le —** to be depressed
**café** *(m)* cafe; coffee; **— crème** coffee with cream; **— au lait** coffee with hot milk
**cafétéria** *(f)* cafeteria
**cahier** *(m)* notebook
**Caire** *(m)* Cairo
**caisse** *(f)* cash register
**calculatrice** *(f)* calculator
**calculer** to calculate
**calendrier** *(m)* calendar
**calme** calm
**calmer: se —** to calm down
**calvados** *(m)* brandy made from apples
**camarade** *(m, f)* **de classe** classmate; **— de chambre** roommate
**cambrioler** to rob
**cambrioleur** *(m)* robber
**camembert** *(m)* type of French cheese
**caméra** *(f)* movie camera; camcorder
**Cameroun** *(m)* Cameroon
**camion** *(m)* truck
**campagne** *(f)* country; **à la —** in the country
**camping** *(m)* camping
**campus** *(m)* campus
**Canada** *(m)* Canada
**canadien(ne)** Canadian
**canapé** *(m)* couch
**canard** *(m)* duck
**candidat(e)** *(m, f)* candidate
**candidature: lettre de —** application letter; **poser sa —** to apply for a job
**canoë: faire du —** to go canoeing
**canton** *(m)* canton; district
**caoutchouc** *(m)* rubber
**capitale** *(f)* capital

**capteur** *(m)* **solaire**   solar panel
**capuche** *(f)*   hood
**capuchon** *(m)*   hood on a coat
**car** *(m)*   bus
**car**   because
**caractérisé(e)**   characterized
**carafe** *(f)*   carafe
**carnet** *(m)*   note pad; book of tickets
**carotte** *(f)*   carrot
**carrefour** *(m)*   intersection; crossroads
**carrière** *(f)*   career
**carte** *(f)*   card; map; menu; **— de crédit**   credit card; **— de visite** business card; **— postale** postcard
**carton** *(m)*   box
**cas** *(m)*   case; **dans ce — -là**   in that case
**casque** *(m)*   hat
**casquette** *(f)*   cap
**casser**   to break; **Je me suis cassé le bras.**   I broke my arm.
**casserole** *(f)*   cooking pan
**cassette** *(f)*   cassette tape; **— vierge**   blank tape
**catégorie** *(f)*   category
**cathédrale** *(f)*   cathedral
**caution** *(f)*   deposit
**cave** *(m)*   wine cellar
**ce/cet (cette)**   this; that
**ce que**   what; that which
**ceinture** *(f)*   belt; **— de sécurité** seatbelt
**cela**   that
**célébrer**   to celebrate
**célèbre**   famous
**célibataire**   single (not married)
**celui (celle)-là**   that one
**cendres** *(f pl)*   ashes
**cendrier** *(m)*   ashtray
**cent**   hundred; **trente pour —** thirty percent
**centaine: une — de**   about a hundred
**centime** *(m)*   centime
**centimètre** *(m)*   centimeter
**centre** *(m)*   center; **— commercial** shopping mall; **le — -ville** downtown
**céréales** *(f pl)*   cereal
**cerfeuil** *(m)*   chervil
**cerise** *(f)*   cherry
**certain(e)**   certain
**certainement**   certainly
**certitude** *(f)*   certainty
**ces**   these; those
**cesser**   to stop doing
**chacun(e)**   each one

**chaîne** *(f)*   chain; assembly line; **— stéréo**   stereo
**chaise** *(f)*   chair
**chaleur** *(f)*   heat
**chambre** *(f)*   room; **— à coucher** bedroom
**champ** *(m)*   field
**champagne** *(m)*   champagne
**champignon** *(m)*   mushroom
**chance: avoir de la —**   to be lucky
**chandail** *(m)*   sweater
**change: bureau de —**   foreign currency exchange
**changement** *(m)*   change
**changer (de)**   to change
**chanson** *(f)*   song
**chanter**   to sing
**chanteur(-euse)** *(m, f)*   singer
**chapeau** *(m)*   hat
**chapelure** *(f)*   bread crumbs
**chapitre** *(m)*   chapter
**chaque**   each
**charcuterie** *(f)*   pork butcher's shop, delicatessen; cooked meat products that can be bought there
**charcutier(-ère)** *(m, f)*   pork butcher
**charge: —s comprises**   utilities included
**chargé(e)**   full; **— de**   in charge of
**chariot** *(m)*   shopping cart
**charme** *(m)*   charm
**chat** *(m)*   cat
**château** *(m)*   castle; **— -fort**   fortified castle
**chaud(e)**   hot; warm; **Il fait —.** It is warm (hot).
**chauffage** *(m)*   heat; heating
**chauffer**   to heat
**chauffeur** *(m)*   driver
**chausser: Je chausse du 42.**   I take a size 42 (shoe).
**chaussette** *(f)*   sock
**chaussure** *(f)*   shoe
**chauve**   bald
**chef** *(m)*   leader; **— d'entreprise** company president (CEO); **— d'œuvre**   masterpiece
**chemin** *(m)*   road
**cheminée** *(f)*   chimney
**chemise** *(f)*   shirt
**chemisette** *(f)*   short-sleeved shirt
**chemisier** *(m)*   blouse
**chèque** *(m)*   check
**cher (chère)**   dear; expensive
**chercher**   to look for; **— à**   to try to; **aller —**   to go and get
**cheveux** *(m pl)*   hair
**cheville** *(f)*   ankle
**chèvre** *(m)*   goat

**chez**   at the home (place) of; **— le dentiste**   (at, to) the dentist's office; **— vous**   at your house; in your area; **travailler — Kodak** to work for Kodak
**chic**   stylish
**chien** *(m)*   dog
**chiffre** *(m)*   number; digit
**chimie** *(f)*   chemistry
**chimique**   pertaining to chemicals
**Chine** *(f)*   China
**chinois(e)**   Chinese
**chocolat** *(m)*   chocolat; **un —**   hot chocolate
**choisir**   to choose
**choix** *(m)*   choice
**chômage** *(m)*   unemployment; **être au —**   to be unemployed
**chose** *(f)*   thing; **quelque —** something; **autre —**   something else; **quelque — à boire**   something to drink; **quelque — de petit**   something small
**chou** *(m)*   cabbage
**choucroute** *(f)*   sauerkraut
**chouette**   great; neat
**choux-fleur** *(m)*   cauliflower
**chrétien(ne)**   Christian
**-ci: ce jambon —**   this ham
**cidre** *(m)*   cider
**ciel** *(m)*   sky
**cinéaste** *(m, f)*   filmmaker
**cinéma** *(m)*   cinema; movie theater
**ciné-club** *(m)*   film club
**circonstance** *(f)*   circumstance
**circuler**   to circulate
**cité** *(f)* **universitaire**   dormitory complex
**citron** *(m)*   lemon; **un — pressé** lemonade; **un diabolo —**   lemonade mixed with lemon-flavored syrup
**clarinette** *(f)*   clarinet
**clair(e)**   clear; **bleu —**   light blue
**classe** *(f)*   class; **première (deuxième) —**   first (second) class
**classé: site —**   historical site
**classement** *(m)*   ranking
**classer**   to rank
**classique**   classic; classical
**clé** *(f)*   key
**client(e)** *(m, f)*   customer
**climat** *(m)*   climate
**clinique** *(f)*   hospital
**clip** *(m)*   music video
**Coca** *(m)*   Coca-Cola
**cocher** *(m)*   coachman
**cochon** *(m)*   pig
**cœur** *(m)*   heart; **avoir mal au —** to feel nauseated

**coiffer: se —**   to fix one's hair
**coiffeur(-euse)** *(m, f)*   hairdresser
**coiffure** *(f)*   hairstyle
**coin** *(m)*   corner; **— cuisine** kitchenette
**col** *(m)*   collar
**colère** *(f)*   anger
**collège** *(m)*   intermediate or middle school
**collègue** *(m, f)*   colleague
**Colombie** *(f)*   Colombia
**colonie** *(f)*   colony; **— de vacances** children's camp
**coloré(e)**   colored
**combien (de)**   how much; how many
**combinaison** *(f)*   combination
**comédie** *(f)*   comedy
**commande** *(f)*   order
**commander**   to order
**comme**   as
**commencer**   to begin
**comment**   how; **— allez-vous?** How are you?; **— ça va?** How're you doing?; **Comment?** What did you say?; **— est ton frère?** What does your brother look like?
**commentaire** *(m)*   comment
**commerçant(e)** *(m, f)*   small business owner
**commerce** *(m)*   business
**commercial** *(m)*   traveling salesperson
**commercial(e)**   commercial
**commissariat** *(m)* **de police**   police station
**commode** *(f)*   dresser
**commodité** *(f)*   convenience
**commune** *(f)*   municipality
**compagnon** *(m)*   companion
**comparer**   to compare
**complet** *(m)*   suit
**compléter**   to complete
**complètement**   completely; entirely
**compliqué(e)**   complicated
**comportement** *(m)*   behavior
**composé(e) de**   made of
**composer**   to dial
**composter**   to validate (ticket)
**comprendre** *(compris)*   to understand; to be comprised of
**comprimé** *(m)*   capsule
**compris(e)**   included
**comptabilité** *(f)*   accounting
**comptable** *(m, f)*   accountant
**compte: se rendre — de**   to realize; **tenir — de**   to take into account
**compter**   to count
**concentrer**   to concentrate; **se — sur**   to concentrate on

**concerner: en ce qui concerne**   regarding; concerning
**concert** *(m)*   concert
**concombre** *(m)*   cucumber
**concours** *(m)*   competitive exam
**concurrent(e)** *(m, f)*   competitor
**condition** *(f)*   condition
**conduire** *(conduit)*   to drive
**conduite** *(f)*   driving
**conférence** *(f)*   conference; lecture
**confiture** *(f)*   jam
**confluent** *(m)*   confluence
**confort** *(m)*   comfort
**confortable**   comfortable
**congé** *(m)*   time off; **— payé**   paid vacation; **prendre —**   to say good-bye
**congrès** *(m)*   convention
**connaissance** *(f)*   acquaintance; **faire la — de**   to meet
**connaître** *(connu)*   to know; **Je l'ai connu à Paris.**   I met him in Paris.; **Je m'y connais.**   I know what I'm doing.
**connu(e)**   known
**conquis(e)**   conquered
**conseil** *(m)*   (piece of) advice
**conseiller**   to advise; to suggest
**conserves** *(f pl)*   canned foods
**conséquent: par —**   consequently
**consister en**   to consist of
**consommateur(-trice)** *(m, f)*   consumer
**consommé** *(m)*   consommé
**consonne** *(f)*   consonant
**constamment**   constantly
**constipé(e)**   constipated
**construire** *(construit)*   to build
**consulter**   to consult
**contenir** *(contenu)*   to contain
**content(e)**   happy; pleased
**continuer**   to continue
**contradictoire**   contradictory
**contrainte** *(f)*   constraint
**contraire** *(m)*   opposite
**contre**   against; **par —**   on the other hand
**contribuer**   to contribute
**contrôle** *(m)* **des passeports**   passport control desk
**contrôleur** *(m)*   conductor
**convenable**   appropriate
**convenir à**   to suit; to be appropriate for
**convenu: C'est — ?**   Agreed?
**copain (copine)** *(m, f)*   friend
**copieur** *(m)*   photocopier
**coquilles** *(f)* **St. Jacques**   scallops
**corps** *(m)*   body
**correspondant(e)** *(m, f)*   person to whom one is speaking (writing)

**correspondre à**   to correspond to
**corriger**   to correct
**costaud(e)**   strong; heavy-set
**Côte d'Ivoire** *(f)*   Ivory Coast
**côte** *(f)*   coast; rib
**côté** *(m)*   side; **d'un —...d'un autre**   on the one hand... on the other hand; **à — de**   next to; **le café à —**   the cafe next door
**coton** *(m)*   cotton
**cou** *(m)*   neck
**coude** *(m)*   elbow
**coucher**   to sleep; **se —**   to go to bed
**couchette** *(f)*   sleeping berth
**coudre** *(cousu)*   to sew
**couleur** *(f)*   color; **De quelle — est (sont)...**   What color is (are)...; **téléviseur —**   color television
**couloir** *(m)*   hallway
**coup: prendre un — de soleil**   to get sunburned; **— de téléphone (de fil)**   phone call; **donner un — de main à quelqu'un**   to give somebody a hand
**coupe** *(f)*   haircut
**couper**   to cut; **se faire — les cheveux**   to get a haircut
**courageux(-euse)**   courageous
**couramment: parler — le français**   to speak French fluently
**courbature: avoir des —s**   to be aching
**courgette** *(f)*   zucchini
**couronné(e)**   crowned
**cours** *(m)*   course; class; **J'ai — dans 5 minutes.**   I have class in 5 minutes.; **au — de**   during
**course** *(f)*   errand; **faire les —s**   to do the shopping; to run errands
**court(e)**   short
**courtoisie** *(f)*   courtesy
**cousin(e)** *(m, f)*   cousin
**coussin** *(m)*   cushion
**coût** *(m)*   cost
**couteau** *(m)*   knife
**coûter**   to cost; **— cher**   to be expensive
**coûteux(-euse)**   costly
**coutume** *(f)*   custom; **les us et —s**   habits and customs
**couture: la haute —**   high fashion
**couturière** *(f)*   seamstress
**couvent** *(m)*   convent
**couvercle** *(m)*   lid
**couvert(e)**   covered; **Le ciel est —.**   It's cloudy.
**cravate** *(f)*   tie
**crayon** *(m)*   pencil
**créer**   to create

**crème** *(f)* cream
**crêpe** *(f)* crepe
**crevé: pneu —** flat tire
**crever** to die
**crevette** *(f)* shrimp
**crime** *(m)* crime
**crise** *(f)* crisis
**critiquer** to criticize
**croire** *(cru)* to believe; to think
**croiser** to cross; to pass
**croissance** *(f)* growth
**croque-monsieur (madame)** *(m)* open-faced grilled ham and cheese (with poached egg on top)
**crudités** *(f pl)* raw vegetables
**cruel(le)** cruel
**cuillère** *(f)* spoon
**cuillerée** *(f)* **à café** teaspoonful; **— à soupe** tablespoonful
**cuire: faire —** to cook
**cuisine** *(f)* kitchen; cuisine; **faire la —** to cook
**cuisiner** to cook
**cuisiné: un plat —** a prepared dish
**cuisinier(-ère)** *(m, f)* cook; chef
**cuisson** *(f)* cooking time
**cuit(e)** cooked
**curriculum vitae (CV)** *(m)* résumé
**cycliste** *(m, f)* cyclist
**cyclone** *(m)* hurricane

# D

**d'abord** first
**d'accord** okay; **être — avec** to agree with
**dame** *(f)* woman
**Danemark** *(m)* Denmark
**dangereux(-euse)** dangerous
**danois(e)** Danish
**dans** in; **— la rue Balzac** on Balzac Street
**danse** *(f)* dance
**danseur(-euse)** *(m, f)* dancer
**dater de** to date from
**daurade** *(f)* gilt-head (fish)
**davantage** more
**de** from; of
**déballer** to unwrap; to unpack
**débardeur** *(m)* tank top
**débarquement** *(m)* landing
**débarrasser: — la table** to clear the table
**débrouiller: se —** to manage (to do something)
**début** *(m)* beginning; **le — de juin (— juin)** the beginning of June

**débutant(e)** beginner
**décevant(e)** disappointing
**décider (de)** to decide; **se —** to make up one's mind; **C'est décidé!** That's settled!
**décision** *(f)* decision; **prendre une —** to make a decision
**déclarer** to declare; to say
**décontracté(e)** relaxed
**découper** to cut
**décourager** to discourage; **se laisser —** to become discouraged
**découvrir** *(découvert)* to discover
**décrire** *(décrit)* to describe
**décrocher** to unhook; to pick up (phone)
**déçu(e)** disappointed
**défendre** to defend
**défi** *(m)* challenge
**défilé** *(m)* parade
**degré** *(m)* degree
**dégustation** *(f)* tasting
**déguster** to taste; to eat
**dehors** outside; **en — de** outside of
**déjà** already
**déjeuner** *(m)* lunch; **le petit —** breakfast
**déjeuner** to have lunch
**délai** *(m)* delay
**délégué(e)** *(m, f)* delegate
**délicieux(-euse)** delicious
**délier: se —** to become untied
**délimité: une région —e** a defined area
**demain** tomorrow
**demander** to ask (for)
**déménager** to move
**demeurer** to remain; to stay
**demi** *(m)* (a glass of) draft beer
**demi(e)** half; **onze heures et —e** 11:30; **un —-kilo** half a kilogram; **une —e-heure** a half hour
**démission** *(f)* resignation
**demi-frère (sœur)** stepbrother (sister)
**démissionner** to resign
**dense** dense
**dent** *(f)* tooth
**dentifrice** *(m)* toothpaste
**dentiste** *(m, f)* dentist
**dépannage: service de —** towing service
**départ** *(m)* departure
**dépasser** to pass
**dépendre: Ça dépend de...** That depends on...
**dépenser** to spend (money)
**dépêcher: se —** to hurry; **Dépêchez-vous!** Hurry up!

**déplacement** *(m)* movement; trip
**déposer** to drop off
**déprimant(e)** depressing
**depuis** since; for; **— quand** since when; **— combien de temps** for how long; **— des heures** for hours
**dernier(-ère)** last; latest; **le mois —** last month
**dérouler: se —** to take place
**derrière** behind
**des** some
**dès** from; **— que** as soon as
**désastreux(-euse)** disastrous
**descendre** to go down; to get off (train, bus, etc.); **— à un hôtel** to stay at a hotel
**désert(e)** deserted
**désigner** to designate
**désir** *(m)* desire; wish
**désirer** to want
**désolé(e)** sorry
**dessert** *(m)* dessert
**desservir** to serve (an area)
**dessin** *(m)* drawing; **— animé** cartoon
**dessiner** to draw
**dessous: ci- —** below
**dessus: ci- —** above
**détail** *(m)* detail
**détaillé(e)** detailed
**détester** to dislike
**devant** in front of
**développement** *(m)* development
**devenir** *(devenu)* to become
**deviner** to guess
**devoir** *(dû)* to have to; to owe; **Elle devait...** She was supposed to...; **Tu devrais acheter...** You should buy...
**d'habitude** normally; usually
**diable** *(m)* devil
**dialogue** *(m)* dialogue
**différend** *(m)* disagreement
**différer de** to differ from
**difficile** difficult
**difficulté** difficulty; **avoir des —s à faire** to have trouble doing; **en —** in trouble
**diminuer** to diminish
**dinde** *(f)* turkey
**dîner** *(m)* dinner
**dîner** to have dinner
**diplôme** *(m)* diploma; degree
**diplomatie** *(f)* diplomacy
**dire** *(dit)* to say; **C'est-à- —...** That is... (That is to say...); **Ça veut —...** That means...; **Dis...** Say...

**direct(e)** direct
**directement** directly
**directeur(-trice)** *(m, f)* director
**direction** *(f)* direction; management
**discipliné(e)** disciplined
**discothèque** *(f)* discotheque
**discret(-ète)** discreet
**discuter (de)** to discuss
**disponible** available
**disposer de** to have at one's disposal
**disputer: se —** to have a fight (an argument)
**disque** *(m)* record;
**distinctif(-ive)** distinctive
**distinguer** to distinguish
**distribuer** to distribute
**distributeur** *(m)* **automatique de billets** automatic teller machine
**divers** miscellaneous
**diviser** to divide
**divorcer** to (get a) divorce
**doctorat** *(m)* doctoral degree
**doigt** *(m)* finger; **— de pied** toe
**dommage: C'est —.** It's a shame.; **Il est — que...** It is unfortunate that. . .
**donc** therefore; **Mais dis donc...** Look. . .
**donner** to give
**dont** about whom; of which; whose
**dorer** to brown
**dormir** to sleep
**dos** *(m)* back
**dose** *(f)* dose
**douane** *(f)* customs
**double** double
**doublé(e)** lined
**douche** *(f)* shower
**doué(e) pour** talented in
**doute** *(m)* doubt; **sans —** probably
**douter** to doubt
**doux (douce)** soft; mild (climate)
**douzaine** *(f)* dozen
**dramatique** dramatic
**drame** *(m)* drama; **— psychologique** psychological drama
**droit** *(m)* law
**droit: tout —** straight ahead
**droite** *(f)* right
**drôle** funny
**dû (due) à** due to
**dur(e)** hard
**durant** during
**durée** *(f)* length
**durer** to last
**dynamique** dynamic

# E

**eau** *(f)* water; **— minérale** mineral water
**échalote** *(f)* shallot
**échange** *(f)* exchange
**échanger** to exchange
**échappée** *(f)* escape
**écharpe** *(f)* scarf
**échecs** *(m pl)* chess
**échelle** *(f)* ladder
**échouer à** to fail (a test)
**éclair** *(m)* eclair
**école** *(f)* school; **— maternelle** nursery school
**économie** *(f)* economy; **faire des —s** to save money
**écossais(e)** Scottish
**écouter** to listen (to)
**écran** *(m)* screen
**écrire** *(écrit)* to write
**écrivain** *(m)* writer
**effectifs** *(m pl)* personnel
**effectivement** actually
**effectué(e)** completed
**effet** *(m)* effect; **En —** True. . . (That's true. . .)
**efficace** efficient
**égal: Ça m'est —.** It doesn't matter to me.
**également** equally
**église** *(f)* church
**égoïste** selfish
**Égypte** *(f)* Egypt
**égyptien(ne)** Egyptian
**électrique** electric
**élevé(e)** high
**élégant(e)** elegant
**élément** *(m)* element
**élève** *(m, f)* high school student
**éloigner** to move away
**embauche** *(f)* hiring
**embrasser** to kiss
**émincer** to slice
**émission** *(f)* broadcast
**émouvant(e)** moving; touching
**emploi** *(m)* employment; job; use; **— du temps** schedule
**employer** to use
**employé(e)** *(m, f)* employee
**emporter** to take; to bring
**emprunter** to borrow
**en** in; at; to; **— écoutant** while (by) listening to; **si vous — avez besoin** if you need it (some); **voyager — groupe** to travel in a group; **— avion** by plane
**enceinte** pregnant
**enchanté(e)** delighted
**enchères: vente aux —** auction

**encore** still; **— de** more; **pas —** not yet; **— plus** to work even more; **— un an** another year; **— une fois** once again
**encourager** to encourage
**endommagé(e)** damaged
**endroit** *(m)* place
**enduire** to coat
**énergique** energetic
**énerver: s'—** to get upset
**énervé(e)** upset
**enfance** *(f)* childhood
**enfant** *(m)* child
**enfin** finally
**engagement** *(m)* hiring
**engager: s'— à** to take upon oneself (to do something)
**enlever** to take off; to remove
**ennui** *(m)* problem
**ennuyer: s'—** to be bored
**ennuyeux(-euse)** boring
**énormément de** a lot of
**enquête** *(f)* survey
**enregistrer** to register; to record
**enrhumé(e): être —** to have a cold
**enrobé(e)** coated
**enseignement** *(m)* teaching
**enseigner** to teach
**ensemble** together
**ensoleillé(e)** sunny
**ensuite** then; next
**entendre** *(entendu)* to hear; **J'ai entendu dire que...** I heard that. . .; **— parler de** to hear about; **s'— avec** to get along with; **Ça s'entend.** That's understood.
**enthousiasme** *(m)* enthusiasm
**enthousiaste** enthusiastic
**entier(-ère)** entire; whole
**entourer** to surround
**entraînement** *(m)* training
**entraîner: s'— à la musculation** to work out with weights
**entre** between
**entrecôte** *(f)* rib steak
**entrée** *(f)* entrance; first course (of a meal)
**entre-jambes** *(m)* inseam
**entreprise** *(f)* company; business
**entrer (dans)** to enter
**entretemps** in the meantime
**entretien** *(m)* interview
**envie: avoir — de** to want
**environ** about; around
**environnement** *(m)* environment
**environs** *(m pl)* surrounding area
**envoyer** to send
**épater** to impress
**épatant(e)** great

**épaule** *(f)*  shoulder
**épée** *(f)*  sword
**épicerie** *(f)*  grocery store
**épicier(-ère)** *(m, f)*  grocer
**épinards** *(m pl)*  spinach
**éplucher**  to peel
**époque: à cette — -là**  at that time; **à l' — de**  at the time of
**épouser**  to marry
**épouvante: un film d'—**  horror movie
**éprouver**  to feel
**équilibré(e)**  balanced
**équipe** *(f)*  team
**équipé(e)**  equipped
**équitation** *(f)*  horseback riding
**érotisme** *(m)*  eroticism
**escalier** *(m)*  stairs; **— roulant**  escalator
**escalope** *(f)*  cutlet
**escargot** *(m)*  snail
**escarpins** *(m pl)*  pumps
**espace** *(m)*  space; **— vert**  green area
**espadrilles** *(f pl)*  espadrilles
**Espagne** *(f)*  Spain
**espagnol(e)**  Spanish
**espèce** *(f)*  kind; sort
**espèces: payer en —**  to pay cash
**espérer**  to hope
**espionnage** *(m)*  espionnage
**essayer**  to try; to try on (clothing)
**essence** *(f)*  gasoline
**essentiel: Il est — que...**  It is essential that. . .
**essentiellement**  essentially
**est** *(m)*  east
**estomac** *(m)*  stomach
**estrade** *(f)*  platform
**et**  and
**établir**  to establish
**étage** *(m)*  floor; **habiter à l'—**  to live upstairs; **le premier —**  the second floor
**étagères** *(f pl)*  shelves
**étalage** *(m)*  display
**étape** *(f)*  stage or leg of a journey
**état** *(m)*  state; **les États-Unis**  the United States
**été** *(m)*  summer
**éternuer**  to sneeze
**étiquette** *(f)*  label; tag
**étoffe** *(f)*  fabric
**étoile** *(f)*  star
**étonné(e)**  surprised
**étranger: à l'—**  abroad
**étranger(-ère)** *(m, f)*  foreigner
**étranger(-ère)**  foreign

**être** *(été)*  to be; **Comment sont-ils?**  What are they like?; **Nous étions trois.**  There were three of us.
**étroit(e)**  narrow; tight (clothing)
**étude** *(f)*  study
**étudiant(e)** *(m, f)*  college student
**étudier**  to study
**étui** *(m)*  case; holder
**euh...**  uh. . .
**européen(ne)**  European
**eux**  them
**évasé(e)**  flared
**événement** *(m)*  event
**évident(e)**  obvious
**évier** *(m)*  sink
**éviter**  to avoid
**évoluer**  to evolve
**exact(e)**  right; true
**exactement**  exactly
**exagération** *(f)*  exaggeration
**exagérer**  to exaggerate
**examen** *(m)*  exam; **— de fin de semestre**  final exam
**exception: à l'— de**  with the exception of
**exceptionnel(le)**  exceptional
**exclusivement**  exclusively
**excursion: faire une —**  to take a trip
**excuse** *(f)*  excuse
**excuser: Je m'excuse.**  I'm sorry.; Pardon me.; Excuse me.
**exemple** *(m)*  example; **par —**  for example
**exercice** *(m)*  exercise
**exigeant(e)**  demanding
**exiger**  to demand
**explication** *(f)*  explanation
**expliquer**  to explain
**exploiter**  to operate (a business)
**exploser**  to explode
**express** *(m)*  espresso
**exprimer**  to express
**extérieur** *(m)*  exterior; outside
**extra: C'est —!**  That's great!
**extrait** *(m)*  excerpt
**extraordinaire**  extraordinary
**extrême** *(m)*  extreme
**extrémité** *(f)*  extremity

**F**

**fabrication** *(f)*  manufacture
**fabriquer**  to make; to manufacture
**fac = faculté**
**face: en — de**  across from

**fâché(e)**  angry
**facile**  easy
**facilement**  easily
**faciliter**  to facilitate
**façon: de toute —**  in any event; **de — différente**  in a different way
**facturation** *(f)*  billing
**faculté** *(f)*  division of a French university
**faible**  weak
**faiblesse** *(f)*  weakness
**faïence** *(f)*  earthenware
**faillite** *(f)*  bankruptcy
**faim** *(f)*  hunger; **avoir (grand-)—**  to be (very) hungry
**faire** *(fait)*  to do; to make; **— un mètre 70**  to be 1m70 tall; **— construire**  to have built
**fait: en —**  in fact
**familial(e)**  pertaining to the family
**famille** *(f)*  family
**fantastique**  fantastic; **film —**  fantasy film
**farine** *(f)*  flour
**fascinant(e)**  fascinating
**fast-food** *(m)*  fast food; **un —**  a fast-food restaurant
**fatigué(e)**  tired
**faut: il me —**  I need; **Il — combien de temps pour aller...**  How long will it take to go. . .; **Il — ...**  It is necessary. . .
**fauteuil** *(m)*  armchair
**faux (fausse)**  false
**faux-pas** *(m)*  foolish mistake
**faux: chanter —**  to sing off-key
**femme** *(f)*  woman; wife
**fente** *(f)*  slot
**fer** *(m)*  iron
**ferme** *(f)*  farm
**fermé(e): — à clé**  locked
**fermer**  to close
**ferroviaire**  pertaining to railroads
**fesse** *(f)*  buttock
**festival** *(m)*  festival
**fête: jour de —**  holiday
**fêter**  to celebrate
**feux** *(m pl)* **d'artifice**  fireworks
**fiancé(e)** *(m, f)*  fiancé
**fiancer: se — (avec)**  to get engaged (to)
**ficelle** *(f)*  string
**fier (fière)**  proud
**fièvre** *(f)*  fever
**figé(e)**  fixed
**figure** *(f)*  face

**fil** *(m)* thread
**file** *(f)* line
**filet** *(m)* mesh bag for carrying groceries
**filiale** *(f)* subsidiary
**fille** *(f)* girl; daughter; **petite —** granddaughter
**film** *(m)* movie
**fils** *(m)* son; **petit —**
**fin** *(f)* end
**fin(e)** thin; fine
**finalement** finally
**financier(-ère)** financial
**finir** to finish; **Elle a fini par avoir sa voiture.** She finally got her car.
**firme** *(f)* firm; company
**fixer** to set (a date)
**fleur** *(f)* flower
**fleuve** *(m)* river
**flipper** *(m)* pinball
**flûte** *(f)* flute
**foi** *(f)* faith
**fois** *(f)* time; **une — par an** once a year; **des —** at times
**foisonner** to abound
**follement** madly, wildly
**foncé: bleu —** dark blue
**fonctionnaire** *(m, f)* civil servant
**fond** *(m)* background
**fondé(e)** founded
**fondre: faire —** to melt
**foot = football**
**football** *(m)* soccer; **— américain** football
**force** *(f)* strength
**forcé(e)** forced
**forêt** *(f)* forest
**formation** *(f)* education; **— permanente** continuing education
**forme: être en —** to be in shape; **sous — de** in the form of
**former** to form
**formidable** great; tremendous
**fort(e)** strong
**fort: parler —** to talk loudly
**fou/fol (folle)** crazy; **un argent —** a ridiculous amount of money
**foulard** *(m)* scarf
**fouler: se —** to sprain
**four** *(m)* oven; **— à micro-ondes** microwave oven
**fourchette** *(f)* fork
**fournir** to furnish
**foyer** *(m)* hearth; home
**frais (fraîche)** fresh; **Il fait —.** It's cool.
**fraise** *(f)* strawberry; **— à l'eau** water with strawberry-flavored syrup; **un diabolo —** limonade

mixed with strawberry-flavored syrup; **un lait —** milk with strawberry syrup
**framboise** *(f)* raspberry
**franc** *(m)* franc
**français(e)** French
**francophone** French-speaking
**frapper** to knock
**fréquemment** frequently
**frère** *(m)* brother
**frigo** *(m)* refrigerator
**frisé(e)** curly
**frissons** *(m pl)* chills
**frites** *(f pl)* French fries
**frivole** frivolous
**froid** *(m)* cold
**froid(e)** cold; **Il fait —.** It is cold.
**fromage** *(m)* cheese
**fruit** *(m)* fruit; **—s de mer** seafood
**fumée** *(f)* smoke
**fumer** to smoke
**fumeur (non-fumeur)** smoking (non-smoking)
**funk** *(m)* funk music
**furieux(-euse)** furious
**fusée** *(f)* rocket
**futur** *(m)* future

## G

**gagner** to win; to earn
**gamme** *(f)* line (of products); **haut de —** top of the line
**gant** *(m)* glove; **— de toilette** wash cloth
**garage** *(m)* garage
**garçon** *(m)* boy; waiter
**garder** to keep; **— sa ligne** to keep one's figure
**gare** *(f)* train station
**garni(e)** garnished
**gastronomique** gastronomical
**gâte-sauce** *(m)* kitchen boy
**gâté(e)** spoiled
**gâteau** *(m)* cake
**gauche** *(f)* left
**Gaule** *(f)* Gaul
**géant(e)** giant
**gélule** *(f)* capsule
**gênant(e)** bothersome
**général(e)** general; **en —** in general
**généralement** generally
**généreux(-euse)** generous
**génie** *(m)* genius
**genou** *(m)* knee

**genre** *(m)* kind; type; gender
**gens** *(m, f pl)* people
**gentil(le)** kind; nice
**géologie** *(f)* geology
**gérant(e)** *(m, f)* manager
**gérer** to manage
**geste** *(m)* gesture
**gestion** *(f)* management
**gigot** *(m)* **d'agneau** leg of lamb
**gilet** *(m)* vest; sweater
**glace** *(f)* ice cream; ice
**golf** *(m)* golf
**golfe** *(m)* gulf
**gorge** *(f)* throat
**gothique** Gothic
**goût** *(m)* taste
**goutte** *(f)* drop
**gouvernement** *(m)* government
**gradins** *(m pl)* tiered seats; bleachers
**grammaire** *(f)* grammar
**gramme** *(m)* gram
**grand(e)** big; large; tall; great
**grand'chose: pas —** not much
**grand-mère** *(f)* grandmother
**grand-père** *(m)* grandfather
**Grande-Bretagne** *(f)* Great Britain
**grandir** to grow
**gras(se)** fat
**gratiné(e)** with melted cheese
**gratuit(e)** free
**grave** serious
**graver** to engrave
**grec(que)** Greek
**Grèce** *(f)* Greece
**griffe** *(f)* label (clothes)
**grillé(e)** grilled
**grille-pain** *(m)* toaster
**grippe** *(f)* flu
**gris(e)** gray
**gros(se)** big; fat
**grossir** to gain weight
**groupe** *(m)* group
**groupement** *(m)* grouping
**gruyère** *(m)* type of French cheese
**guère: ne... —** hardly
**guérir** to cure; to heal
**guerre** *(f)* war; **la Seconde — mondiale** World War II
**guichet** *(m)* window (bank; train station; etc.)
**guide** *(m)* guide
**guitare** *(f)* guitar
**gym: faire de la —** to work out; to exercise
**gymnase** *(m)* gymnasium

# H

**habile** clever
**habillement** *(m)* clothing
**habiller: s'—** to dress; to get dressed
**habitant(e)** *(m, f)* inhabitant
**habiter** to live
**habité(e)** inhabited
**habituer: s'— à** to get used to
**haricot** *(m)* bean
**hausse: en —** increasing
**hébergement** *(m)* lodging
**héberger** to lodge
**hein?** huh?
**hélas** alas
**henné** *(m)* henna
**hésiter à** to hesitate
**heure** *(f)* hour; **à 10 —s** at ten o'clock; **Quelle — est-il?** What time is it?; **À tout à l'—.** See you in a while.; **l'— du déjeuner** lunch time; **à quelle —...** (at) what time...; **de (très) bonne —** (very) early; **les —s de pointe** rush hour; **24 —s sur 24** 24 hours a day; **130 km à l'—** 130 km per hour; **à l'—** on time
**heureusement** fortunately
**heureux(-euse)** happy
**hier** yesterday
**hiérarchie** *(f)* hierarchy
**histoire** *(f)* history; story
**historique** historic
**hiver** *(m)* winter
**homard** *(m)* lobster
**homme** *(m)* man
**honnête** honest
**honneur: invité d'—** guest of honor
**hôpital** *(m)* hospital
**horaire** *(m)* timetable; schedule
**horreur: avoir — de** to hate; **film d'—** horror movie
**hors-d'œuvre** *(m)* appetizer
**hors: — campus** off-campus
**hôtel** *(m)* hotel; **— de ville** city hall
**hôtelier(-ère)** *(m, f)* hotel owner
**hôtesse** *(f)* hostess
**huile** *(f)* oil
**humain(e)** human
**humeur: de bonne (mauvaise) —** in a good (bad) mood
**humoriste** *(m, f)* humorist

# I

**ici** here
**idéaliste** idealistic

**idée** *(f)* idea
**identifier** to identify
**île** *(f)* island
**illustré(e)** illustrated
**image** *(f)* image; picture
**imaginaire** imaginary
**imaginer** to imagine
**imiter** to imitate
**immangeable** inedible
**immeuble** *(m)* apartment building
**impatient(e)** impatient
**importance** *(f)* importance
**important(e)** important; **L'—, c'est que...** The important thing is that. . .
**imposé(e)** imposed
**impôts** *(m pl)* taxes
**impression: avoir l'—** to have the impression
**impressionnant(e)** impressive
**impressionner** to impress
**imprimé(e)** print (material)
**inaugurer** to inaugurate
**incendie** *(m)* fire
**incertitude** *(f)* uncertainty
**inclure** *(inclus)* to include
**Inde** *(f)* India
**indépendance** *(f)* independence
**indépendant(e)** independent
**indicatif** *(m)* area code; indicative
**indien(ne)** Indian
**indigestion** *(f)* indigestion
**indiquer** to indicate; to show; to point out
**indiscret(-ète)** indiscreet
**indispensable** essential
**industrie** *(f)* industry
**inévitable** inevitable
**infiniment** infinitely
**infirmier(-ère)** *(m, f)* nurse
**influencer** to influence
**informatique** *(f)* computer science
**ingénieur** *(m)* engineer
**inondé(e)** flooded
**inoubliable** unforgettable
**inquiéter: s'—** to worry
**inscrire: s'—** to enroll
**insister (pour que)** to insist (that)
**inspirer: s'— de** to get inspiration from
**installer: s'—** to move; to get settled
**instant** *(m)* moment
**institut** *(m)* institute
**instituteur(-trice)** *(m, f)* grade school teacher
**intellectuel(le)** intellectual
**intelligent(e)** bright

**intention: avoir l'— de** to intend
**interdit(e)** forbidden
**intéressant(e)** interesting
**intéresser: s'— à** to be interested in
**intérêt** *(m)* interest
**intérieur: à l'— de** inside
**interphone** *(m)* intercom
**interroger** to question
**interrompu(e)** interrupted
**interview** *(f)* interview
**interviewer** to interview
**introduire: s'— dans** to enter
**introverti(e)** introverted
**inventer** to invent
**investissement** *(m)* investment
**invité(e)** *(m, f)* guest
**Irak** *(m)* Iraq
**Iran** *(m)* Iran
**iranien(ne)** Iranian
**Israël** *(m)* Israel
**israélien(ne)** Israeli
**italien(ne)** Italian
**itinéraire** *(m)* itinerary

# J

**jamais** ever; **ne... —** never
**jambe** *(f)* leg
**jambon** *(m)* ham
**Japon** *(m)* Japan
**japonais(e)** Japanese
**jardin** *(m)* garden
**jaune** yellow
**jazz** *(m)* jazz
**jean = blue-jean**
**jeu** *(m)* game; **— vidéo** video game
**jeune** young
**jeunesse** *(f)* youth; childhood
**job** *(m)* job
**jogging** *(m)* sweatsuit; jogging; **faire du —** to go jogging
**joie** *(f)* joy
**joli(e)** pretty
**jouer** to play; **— à** to play (a sport); **— de** to play (a musical instrument); **— un tour à** to play a trick on
**jouet** *(m)* toy
**jour** *(m)* day; **de nos —** nowadays; **Quel — sommes-nous?** What day is it?; **un —** some day; **huit —s** a week; **quinze —s** two weeks
**journal** *(m)* newspaper
**journalisme** *(m)* journalism
**journaliste** *(m, f)* journalist
**journée** *(f)* day

**jovial(e)** jovial; jolly
**juger** to judge
**jupe** *(f)* skirt
**jus** *(m)* juice; **— d'orange** orange juice
**jusqu'à** to; until
**justement** exactly; precisely

# K

**karaté** *(m)* karate
**ketchup** *(m)* ketchup
**kilo** *(m)* kilo
**kir** *(m)* white wine with black currant liqueur

# L

**laboratoire** *(m)* laboratory
**lacer** to tie (shoes)
**laid(e)** ugly
**laine** *(f)* wool
**laisser** to leave; **— un mot** to leave a message
**lait** *(m)* milk
**laitier: produits —s** dairy products
**lampe** *(f)* lamp
**là** there; **ce jour - —** that day; **— -bas** over there
**langoustine** *(f)* prawn
**langue** *(f)* language; tongue; **tirer la —** to stick out one's tongue
**lapin** *(m)* rabbit
**large** wide; **pantalon —** baggy pants
**lavabo** *(m)* sink (bathroom)
**laver** to wash
**lèche-vitrines: faire du —** to window-shop
**leçon** *(f)* lesson
**lecture** *(f)* reading
**légende** *(f)* legend
**léger(-ère)** light
**légèrement** lightly; slightly
**légume** *(m)* vegetable
**lendemain** *(m)* the following day; **le — matin** the next morning
**lequel (laquelle)** which one
**lesquel(le)s** which ones
**lessive: faire la —** to do the laundry
**lettre** *(f)* letter; **les —s** liberal arts
**lever: se —** to get up
**lèvre** *(f)* lip
**libanais(e)** Lebanese
**liberté** *(f)* freedom

**librairie** *(f)* bookstore
**libre** free
**libre-service** *(m)* self-service store
**Libye** *(f)* Libya
**lien** *(m)* bond; link
**lieu** *(m)* place; **— de rencontre** meeting place; **avoir —** to take place
**ligne** *(f)* line
**limité(e)** limited
**limonade** *(f)* lemon-flavored soft drink
**linge** *(m)* laundry
**linguistique** *(f)* linguistics
**lire** *(lu)* to read
**liste** *(f)* list
**lit** *(m)* bed; **au —** in bed
**litre** *(m)* liter
**littérature** *(f)* literature
**livraison** *(f)* **des bagages** baggage claim area
**livre** *(f)* pound
**livre** *(m)* book
**location** *(f)* rental
**loden** *(m)* a kind of coat fabric
**logement** *(m)* dwelling; housing
**logiciel** *(m)* software
**loin de** far from
**lointain(e)** faraway
**long(ue)** long; **le — de** along
**longtemps** a long time
**lorsque** when
**louer** to rent
**lourd(e)** heavy
**loyer** *(m)* rent
**lucarne** *(f)* dormer window; skylight
**luge: faire de la —** to go bobsledding
**lunettes** *(f pl)* eyeglasses; **— de soleil** sunglasses
**luxe** *(m)* luxury; **hôtel de —** luxury hotel
**luxueux(-euse)** luxurious
**lycée** *(m)* high school
**lycéen(ne)** *(m, f)* high school student

# M

**machine** *(f)* machine; **— à laver** washing machine; **— à écrire** typewriter
**Madame** Ma'am; Mrs.
**Mademoiselle** Miss; young lady
**magasin** *(m)* store; **grand —** department store; **— de sport** sporting goods store

**magazine** *(m)* magazine
**magnétoscope** *(m)* videocassette recorder (VCR)
**maigrir** to lose weight
**maille jersey** *(f)* knitted fabric
**maillot** *(m):* **— de bain (de surf)** bathing suit; **— de corps** body suit; undershirt
**main** *(f)* hand
**maintenant** now
**mais** but
**maïs** *(m)* corn
**maison** *(f)* house; **à la —** at home
**maître** *(m)* master
**maîtrise** *(f)* master's degree
**majestueux(-euse)** majestic
**majorité** *(f)* majority
**mal** *(m)* illness; pain; **— de mer** seasickness; **— de l'air** airsickness; **avoir —** to hurt; to ache; **avoir — à la tête** to have a headache; **Elle s'est fait — à la jambe.** She hurt her leg.; **avoir du — à** to have trouble
**mal** poorly; **Pas —.** Not bad.; **pas — de** quite a bit (lot) of
**malade** sick; ill
**malgré** in spite of; despite
**malheureux: C'est —.** It's unfortunate.
**malhonnête** dishonest
**manche** *(f)* sleeve; **la Manche** the English Channel
**manger** to eat
**manières** *(f pl)* manners
**manifestation** *(f)* demonstration
**mannequin** *(m)* fashion model
**manque** *(m)* lack
**manquer** to miss; to be lacking; **Elle me manque.** I miss her; **Je n'y manquerai pas.** I won't forget.
**manteau** *(m)* coat
**manuel** *(m)* textbook
**manuscrit(e)** handwritten
**marché** *(m)* market; **— en plein air** open-air market; **— aux puces** flea market; **Marché Commun** Common Market
**marché: bon —** inexpensive
**marcher** to walk; to work
**mari** *(m)* husband
**marié(e)** married
**marine: bleu —** navy blue
**marinière** *(f)* striped top
**marketing** *(m)* marketing
**Maroc** *(m)* Morocco
**marocain(e)** Moroccan

**marque** *(f)* brand
**marquer** to show (one's reaction)
**marqué(e)** marked; **un nom —
dessus** a name marked on it
**marrant: C'est pas —.** It's not
funny.
**marre: en avoir — de** to be fed up
with
**marron** brown
**marron** *(m)* chestnut
**massé(e)s** amassed
**match** *(m)* game
**mathématiques** *(f pl)* math
**maths = mathématiques**
**matière** *(f)* material; **—s** school
subjects; **— première** main in-
gredient; **— grasse** fat
**matin** *(m)* morning
**mauvais(e)** bad; **Il fait —.** The
weather is bad.
**mayonnaise** *(f)* mayonnaise
**mécanicien(ne)** *(m, f)* mechanic
**médecin** *(m)* doctor
**médecine** *(f)* medicine; **faire sa
—** to study medicine
**médical(e)** medical
**médicament** *(m)* medicine;
medication
**Méditerranée: Mer —** Mediterranean Sea
**meilleur(e)** best; **— que** better
than
**mélange** *(m)* mix
**mélanger** to mix
**melon** *(m)* melon
**membre** *(m)* member
**même** even; same; **lui- —** himself; **quand —** anyway
**mémé** *(f)* grandmother
**mener** to lead
**menthe** *(f)* mint; **— à l'eau**
water with mint-flavored syrup;
**un diabolo — limonade** mixed
with mint-flavored syrup
**mentionner** to mention
**menu** *(m)* menu; **— à prix fixe**
set menu
**mer** *(f)* sea; **la — des Caraïbes**
the Caribbean Sea
**mère** *(f)* mother
**merci** thank you
**merveille** *(f)* marvel
**merveille: à —** beautifully
**message** *(m)* message
**mesure: dans quelle —** in what
way; to what extent
**mesurer** to measure
**météo** *(f)* weather forecast
**métier** *(m)* profession

**mètre** *(m)* meter
**métrique** metric
**métro** *(m)* subway
**mettre** *(mis)* to put; **— une heure
pour aller** to take an hour to
go; **— en service** to place into
service; **— la table (le couvert)**
to set the table
**meublé(e)** furnished
**meubles** *(m pl)* furniture
**mexicain(e)** Mexican
**Mexique** *(m)* Mexico
**mi-: cheveux — -longs** mid-
length hair
**midi** *(m)* noon; **le Midi** the
southern part of France
**miel** *(m)* honey
**mieux** better; **— que** better
than; **faire de son — pour** to
do one's best to; **Je vais —.** I'm
feeling better.; **Tant —.** So
much the better.
**migraine** *(f)* migraine headache
**mijoter** to simmer
**milieu** *(m)* middle; **au — de** in
the middle of
**milk-shake** *(m)* milkshake
**mille** thousand
**mille-feuille** *(m)* napoleon
(pastry)
**milliard** *(m)* billion
**milliardaire** *(m)* billionaire
**millier: des —s de** thousands of
**million** *(m)* million
**minable** pathetic
**mince** thin
**mine: avoir bonne (mauvaise) —**
to look good (bad)
**minuit** *(m)* midnight
**minute** *(f)* minute
**miroir** *(m)* mirror
**mis(e) à jour** updated
**mise** *(f)* **en scène** staging; production (play or movie)
**mocassins** *(m pl)* loafers
**moche** ugly
**mode** *(f)* fashion; **à la —** in
fashion
**mode** *(m)* method
**modèle** *(m)* model
**moderne** modern
**moderniser** to modernize
**moindre** least
**moins (de)** less; **— que** less
than; **— de…que** less. . .than;
**neuf heures — le quart** 8:45;
**au —** at least; **le (la) —** the
least

**mois** *(m)* month; **au — de juin**
in June
**moitié** *(f)* half
**moment** *(m)* moment; **au — où**
when; at the time when; **à tout —**
at any time; **en ce —** now
**monarchie** *(f)* monarchy
**monde** *(m)* world; people; **tout le
—** everybody
**mondial(e)** international
**monnaie** *(f)* change (money);
**pièce de —** coin
**monsieur** *(m)* gentleman; Mr.;
**Merci, —.** Thank you, Sir.
**monstre** *(m)* monster
**montagne** *(f)* mountain
**montagneux(-euse)** mountainous
**montant: baskets —s** high-top
sneakers
**monter** to go up; **— dans le train**
to get on the train
**montrer** to show
**moquer: se — de** to make fun of
**morceau** *(m)* piece
**mort** *(f)* death
**mot** *(m)* word
**motiver** to motivate
**moto = motocyclette**
**motocyclette** *(f)* motorcycle
**moule** *(f)* mussel
**mourir** *(mort)* to die
**moustache** *(f)* moustache
**mousse** *(f)* mousse
**moutarde** *(f)* mustard
**mouton** *(m)* sheep; mutton
**moyen** *(m)* means
**moyen(ne)** average
**mur** *(m)* wall
**musclé(e)** muscular
**musculation** *(f)* weightlifting
**musée** *(m)* museum
**musical(e)** musical
**musicien(ne)** *(m, f)* musician
**musique** *(f)* music; **— classique**
classical music; **— populaire**
popular music
**musulman(e)** Moslem
**mystérieux(-euse)** mysterious

# N

**nager** to swim
**naïf (naïve)** naive
**naissance** *(f)* birth
**naître** *(né)* to be born
**natal(e)** of birth
**nationalité** *(f)* nationality
**nature** *(f)* nature

**naturel(le)**   natural
**navré(e)**   very sorry
**né(e): Je suis —**   I was born
**néanmoins**   nevertheless
**nécessaire**   necessary
**négliger**   to neglect
**neige** *(f)*   snow
**neiger: Il neige.**   It is snowing.
**nerveux(-euse)**   nervous
**nettoyer**   to clean
**neuf (neuve)**   new
**neutralité** *(f)*   neutrality
**nez** *(m)*   nose; **avoir le — qui coule**   to have a runny nose; **avoir le — pris (bouché)**   to be stuffed up
**ni: ne...—... —**   neither. . .nor
**niveau** *(m)*   level
**Noël** *(m)*   Christmas
**noir(e)**   black
**noix** *(f)*   nut
**nom** *(m)*   name; noun; **— de famille**   last name
**nombre** *(m)*   number; **le plus grand — (de)**   the most
**nombreux(-euse)**   numerous; **une famille —**   a large family
**nommer**   to name
**nommé(e)**   called; **— d'après**   named after
**non**   no
**nord** *(m)*   north
**normal(e)**   normal
**normalement**   normally; usually
**norvégien(ne)**   Norwegian
**note** *(f)*   grade
**nouer: des liens se nouent**   bonds are formed
**nourrir: se — bien**   to eat well
**nourriture** *(f)*   food
**nouveau/nouvel (nouvelle)**   new
**nouvelle** *(f)*   (piece of) news; **les —s**   news
**nouvellement**   newly
**Nouvelle-Orléans, la** *(f)*   New Orleans
**Nouvelle Zélande** *(f)*   New Zealand
**nôtres: être des —**   to join us
**nuage** *(m)*   cloud
**nuageux(-euse)**   cloudy
**numéro** *(m)*   number; **— de téléphone**   telephone number

## O

**obéir à**   to obey
**obélisque** *(m)*   obelisk

**objet** *(m)*   object
**obligatoire**   mandatory; obligatory
**obligé(e) de**   obliged to
**obliger**   to oblige
**obsédé(e) par**   obsessed with
**obtenir** *(obtenu)*   to get; to obtain
**obtention** *(f)*   obtaining
**occasion** *(f)*   chance; opportunity; **avoir l'— de**   to have the opportunity to; **d'—**   used
**occidental(e)**   western
**occupé(e)**   busy
**occuper**   to occupy; **s'— de**   to take care of
**œil** *(m)* *(pl: yeux)*   eye
**œuf** *(m)*   egg
**officiel(le)**   official
**offre** *(f)*   offer; **les — d'emploi**   want ads
**offrir** *(offert)*   to offer; to give as a gift
**oignon** *(m)*   onion
**omelette** *(f)*   omelet; **— aux fines herbes**   mixed herb omelet
**omnibus** *(m)*   local train
**on**   one; you; we; they; people
**oncle** *(m)*   uncle
**ONU (Organisation des Nations Unies)** *(f)*   United Nations
**opinion** *(f)*   opinion
**optimiste**   optimistic
**or** *(m)*   gold
**orage** *(m)*   storm
**orange**   orange
**Orangina** *(m)*   carbonated orange-flavored soft drink
**ordinateur** *(m)*   computer
**ordre** *(m)*   order
**oreille** *(f)*   ear
**organisateur(-trice)** *(m, f)*   organizer
**organiser**   to organize; **s'—**   to get organized
**organisme** *(m)*   organization
**orgue** *(f)*   organ
**original(e)**   original
**origine** *(f)*   origin
**ou**   or
**où**   where; **le jour —...**   the day when. . .
**oublier**   to forget
**ouest** *(m)*   west
**oui**   yes
**ours** *(m)*   bear
**ouvert(e)**   open
**ouvrage** *(m)*   work
**ouvrier(-ère)** *(m, f)*   factory or manual worker

## P

**P.J. (pièce jointe)**   Enclosure (in a letter)
**page** *(f)*   page; **à la — 3**   on page 3
**pain** *(m)*   bread; **un petit —**   roll; **— de mie**   American type bread; **— grillé**   toast
**paire** *(f)*   pair
**palais** *(m)*   palace; **— de justice**   courthouse
**pâle**   pale
**palper**   to feel
**pamplemousse** *(m)*   grapefruit
**paner**   to bread
**panier** *(m)*   basket
**panne: avoir une — d'essence**   to run out of gas; **tomber en —**   to break down; **— de voiture (de moteur)**   automobile breakdown
**pansement** *(m)*   bandage
**pantalon** *(m)*   (pair of) pants
**Pâques** *(f pl)*   Easter
**papeterie** *(f)*   stationery store
**papier** *(m)*   paper; **—toilette (hygiénique)**   toilet paper
**paquet** *(m)*   package
**par**   by; per; **— ici (là)**   this (that) way
**paragraphe** *(m)*   paragraph
**paraître** *(paru)*   to appear
**parc** *(m)*   park
**parce que**   because
**pardessus** *(m)*   overcoat
**pardon...**   excuse me. . .
**pareil(le)s** *(m, f pl)*   peers; equal
**parenthèses** *(f pl)*   parentheses
**parents** *(m pl)*   parents; relatives
**paresseux(-euse)**   lazy
**parfait(e)**   perfect
**parfaitement**   perfectly
**parfois**   sometimes
**parfum** *(m)*   perfume
**parisien(ne)**   Parisian
**parking** *(m)*   parking lot
**parler**   to speak
**parmi**   among
**parole** *(f)*   word; **adresser la — à quelqu'un**   to speak to someone
**part** *(f)*   piece; **C'est de la — de qui?**   Who's calling? (on the phone); **nulle —**   no where; **quelque —**   somewhere
**partager**   to share
**partenaire** *(m, f)*   partner
**parti** *(m)*   political party
**participer à**   to take part in
**particulier: en —**   in particular

**particulièrement** particularly
**partie** *(f)* part; **en —** in part; **faire une — de tennis** to play a game of tennis; **faire — de** to be a part of
**partir** *(parti)* to leave; to go away; **à — de** beginning (with, in)
**partout** everywhere
**paru(e)** appeared
**pas: ne... —** not; **N'est-ce — ?** Right? Isn't that so?
**passager(-ère)** *(m, f)* passenger
**passant(e)** *(m, f)* passerby
**passé** *(m)* past
**passé(e): le mois —** last month
**passeport** *(m)* passport
**passer** to be playing (movie); to spend (time); to stop by; to go by (time); **se —** to happen; **— par** to go through; **— avant** to be more important than; **— un examen** to take a test
**passionnant(e)** exciting
**pastille** *(f)* lozenge
**pâté** *(m)* pâté (meat spread)
**pâtes** *(f pl)* pasta
**pâtisserie** *(f)* pastry shop; pastry
**pâtissier(-ère)** *(m, f)* pastry chef
**patiemment** patiently
**patience** *(f)* patience
**patient(e)** patient
**patinage: faire du —** to go skating
**patron** *(m)* pattern (sewing)
**patron(ne)** *(m, f)* boss
**pauvre** poor
**pavé** *(m)* rectangular piece of ice cream
**payant(e)** which must be paid for
**payer** to pay (for)
**pays** *(m)* country; **— voisins** neighboring countries
**Pays-Bas** *(m pl)* Netherlands
**péage: autoroute à —** toll road
**peau** *(f)* skin
**pêche** *(f)* peach
**pêche: aller à la —** to go fishing
**pêcher** to fish
**peigne** *(m)* comb
**peine** *(f)* trouble; **Ce n'est pas la —.** Don't bother.
**peinture** *(f)* painting
**pendant** during; **— une heure** for an hour; **— que** while
**pendre** *(pendu)* to hang; **— la crémaillère** to have a house-warming party
**pendulette** *(f)* small clock

**penser** to think; **— à** to think about; **Qu'est-ce que tu en penses?** What do you think about it?
**pension** *(f)* boarding house; inn
**pépé** *(m)* grandfather
**percé(e)** pierced
**perdre** *(perdu)* to lose; **— du temps** to waste time
**père** *(m)* father
**perfectionner** to perfect
**période** *(f)* period
**perle** *(f)* pearl
**permettre** *(permis)* to permit
**Pérou** *(m)* Peru
**Perrier** *(m)* carbonated mineral water
**persil** *(m)* parsley
**personnage** *(m)* character
**personnalité** *(f)* personality
**personne** *(f)* person; **3 —s** 3 people; **ne... —** nobody
**personnel** *(m)* personnel
**personnel(le)** personal
**personnellement** personally
**peser** to weigh
**pessimiste** pessimistic
**petit(e)** small; short
**peu: à — près** nearly; **si — de** so little (few); **un —** a little
**peur: avoir — (de)** to be afraid (of); **faire —** to frighten
**peut-être** perhaps; **— que oui, — que non** maybe, maybe not
**pharmaceutique** pharmaceutical
**pharmacie** *(f)* drug store
**pharmacien(ne)** *(m, f)* pharmacist
**Philippines** *(f pl)* Philippines
**philosophie** *(f)* philosophy
**photo** *(f)* photograph
**photographe** *(m, f)* photographer
**photographier** to photograph
**photo-reportage** *(m)* photo essay
**phrase** *(f)* sentence
**physique** *(f)* physics
**physique** physical
**piano** *(f)* piano
**pièce** *(f)* room; **— de théâtre** play; **— de monnaie** coin
**pied** *(m)* foot; **à —** on (by) foot
**pique-nique** *(m)* picnic
**piqûre** *(f)* shot
**piscine** *(f)* swimming pool
**pistolet** *(m)* gun
**pittoresque** picturesque
**pizza** *(f)* pizza

**placard** *(m)* closet
**place** *(f)* seat; place; central square
**plage** *(f)* beach
**plaie** *(f)* wound
**plaindre: se —** to complain; **Je vous plains.** I feel sorry for you.
**plainte** *(f)* complaint
**plaît: s'il vous (te) —** please
**plaisir** *(m)* pleasure
**plan** *(m)* map; floor plan
**planche: faire de la — à voile** to windsurf
**plancher** *(m)* floor
**plante** *(f)* plant
**plat** *(m)* dish
**plein: faire le —** to get a full tank of gas
**pleurer** to cry
**pleuvoir: Il pleut.** It is raining.
**plongée sous-marine: faire de la —** to go skin-diving
**pluie** *(f)* rain
**plupart: la — de** most; the majority of
**plus** more; **— que** more than; **— de...que** more. . .than; **— tard** later; **non —** neither; **25 francs de —** 25 francs more; **de (en) —** in addition; **ne... —** no longer; not anymore
**plusieurs** several
**plutôt** rather
**pneu** *(m)* tire
**poche** *(f)* pocket
**pochette** *(f)* wallet
**poêle** *(f)* frying pan
**poète** *(m)* poet
**poignet** *(m)* wrist
**pointure** *(f)* shoe size
**poire** *(f)* pear
**poireau** *(m)* leek
**pois** *(m pl)* polka dots; **des petits —** peas
**poisson** *(m)* fish
**poitrine** *(f)* chest
**poivre** *(m)* pepper
**poivrer** to pepper
**poli(e)** polite
**policier: un film —** detective movie
**politique** *(f)* politics
**politique** political
**polo jersey** *(m)* polo shirt
**polonais(e)** Polish
**polyester** *(m)* polyester
**pomme** *(f)* apple; **— de terre** potato; **—s frites** French fries
**pont** *(m)* bridge

**porc** *(m)* pork
**porte** *(f)* door; gate (airport)
**porté(e): être — sur les arts** to be fond of the arts
**porte-clés** *(m)* keychain
**portefeuille** *(m)* wallet
**porter** to wear; **— sur** to be about
**portugais(e)** Portuguese
**Portugal** *(m)* Portugal
**poser** to place; to pose; **— une question** to ask a question
**posséder** to possess
**possession** *(f)* possession
**poste** *(m)* job
**poster** *(m)* poster
**postier(-ère)** *(m, f)* postal worker
**potage** *(m)* soup
**poulet** *(m)* chicken
**poupée** *(f)* doll
**pour** for; in order to
**pourboire** *(m)* tip
**pourcentage** *(m)* percentage
**pourquoi** why
**poursuivre** *(poursuivi)* to pursue; to undertake; **—** to continue
**pourtant** yet; nevertheless
**pouvoir** *(pu)* to be able; **Ça se peut bien.** That's possible.; **Il se peut que...** It is possible that. . .
**pratique** practical
**précaire** precarious
**préciser** to give details
**prédécesseur** *(m)* predecessor
**préférable: Il est — que...** It is preferable that. . .
**préféré(e)** favorite
**préférence: de —** preferably
**préférer** to prefer
**premier(-ère)** first
**premièrement** first of all
**prendre** *(pris)* to take; **— quelque chose** to have something to eat; to buy (a ticket); **— une correspondance** to change trains (subway); **s'y —** to go about (doing something)
**prénom** *(m)* first name
**préoccuper: se — de** to worry about
**préparatifs: faire des —** to make plans
**préparer** to prepare; **se — à** to get ready to; **se — pour** to get ready for; **— un examen** to study for a test
**près de** close to
**prescrire** *(prescrit)* to prescribe

**présentation** *(f)* introduction
**présenter** to present; to introduce
**président(e)** *(m, f)* president
**presque** almost
**pressé(e)** in a hurry
**pression** *(f)* pressure
**prêt(e)** ready
**prêter** to lend; **— à la confusion** to lead to confusion
**prévenir** *(prévenu)* to warn
**prévoir** *(prévu)* to predict
**prier: Je vous (t') en prie.** You're welcome.
**primaire** primary
**principal(e)** main
**printemps** *(m)* spring
**privé(e)** private
**privilégié(e)** privileged
**prix** *(m)* price; prize
**probable: Il est peu — que...** It is unlikely that. . .
**probablement** probably
**problème** *(m)* problem
**prochain(e)** next
**proche** close to; nearby
**procurer: se —** to get
**produire: se —** to occur
**produit** *(m)* product
**prof = professeur**
**professeur** *(m)* teacher
**professionnel(le)** professional
**programme** *(m)* program
**programmeur(-euse)** *(m, f)* computer programmer
**progrès: faire des —** to make progress
**projets** *(m pl)* plans
**promenade: faire une —** to take a walk (ride)
**promener** to walk; **se —** to go for a walk
**promesse** *(f)* promise
**pronom** *(m)* pronoun
**propos: à — de** about
**proposer** to propose
**propre** own
**prospère** prosperous
**protéger** to protect
**protéine** *(f)* protein
**provenance: en — de** coming from
**province** *(f)* province
**prudence** *(f)* prudence; care
**psychiatrie** *(f)* psychiatry
**psychologie** *(f)* psychology
**public (publique)** public
**publicité** *(f)* advertising; advertisement

**publier** to publish
**puis** then; next
**pull-over** *(m)* sweater
**punir** to punish

**Q**

**quai** *(m)* platform (train station)
**qualifié(e)** qualified
**qualité** *(f)* quality
**quand** when
**quart** *(m)* quarter-liter bottle
**quart: midi et —** 12:15; **midi moins le —** 11:45
**quartier** *(m)* neighborhood
**que** what; whom; which; that; **ne... —** only
**quel(le)** what; which; **— que soit le niveau** whatever the level
**quelquefois** sometimes
**quelques** a few
**quelqu'un** someone
**quelques-un(e)s (de)** some (of)
**qu'est-ce que: — c'est?** What is it?; **—'il est fort!** How strong he is!; **—'il y a?** What's the matter?
**question** *(f)* question
**qui** who; which; that; whom; **à —** to whom; **— est-ce?** Who is it?
**quitter** to leave; **Ne quittez pas.** Don't hang up. (telephone)
**quoi** what; **Il n'y a pas de —.** You're welcome.; **Quoi?** What'd you say?; **— d'autre?** What else?

**R**

**raccrocher** to hang up (phone)
**raconter** to tell (a story)
**radio-cassette** *(f)* radio/tape player
**radioréveil** *(m)* clock radio
**radis** *(m)* radish
**raffinement** *(m)* de pétrole oil refining
**raide** straight (hair)
**raison** *(f)* reason; **la — pour laquelle** the reason why; **avoir —** to be right
**raisonnable** reasonable
**ramener** to bring back
**randonnée: faire une —** to go for a hike
**rang** *(m)* rank
**ranger** to put in order; to clean up

**râpé(e)** grated; worn
**rapidement** quickly
**rappeler** to call again; to remind; **se —** to remember
**rapport** *(m)* relationship
**raquette** *(f)* racket
**rarement** rarely
**rasant: C'est —.** It's boring.
**rassasier** to satisfy
**rassurer** to reassure
**rater** to fail (a test)
**ravi(e)** delighted
**ravin** *(m)* ravine
**rayé(e)** striped
**rayon** *(m)* department (of a store)
**rayure: à —s** striped
**réaction** *(f)* reaction
**réagir** to react
**réaliste** realistic
**réalité** *(f)* reality
**rébus** *(m)* puzzle
**récemment** recently
**recenser** to make an inventory of
**réception** *(f)* reception; front desk (hotel)
**recette** *(f)* recipe
**recevoir** *(reçu)* to receive
**réchauffer** to heat
**recherche** *(f)* research; search; **faire des —s** to do research
**recommander** to recommend
**reconnaître** *(reconnu)* to recognize
**reconstruire** *(reconstruit)* to reconstruct
**recruter** to recruit
**récupérer** to recover
**recyclage: cours de —** refresher course
**réduire** *(réduit)* to reduce
**redoubler: — un cours** to take a course again
**refaire** *(refait)* to do (make) again
**réfléchir à** to think over; to reflect (about something)
**refléter** to reflect
**refuser** to refuse; to turn down
**regard** *(m)* look
**regarder** to watch; to look at
**régime: être au —** to be on a diet
**règle** *(f)* rule
**régler** to arrange; to pay
**régner** to reign
**regret** *(m)* regret
**regretter** to be sorry
**régulièrement** regularly
**rein** *(m)* kidney
**rejoindre** *(rejoint)* to join

**réjouir: se — (de)** to be delighted (about)
**relax** relaxed
**relevé** *(m)* **de notes** transcript
**relevé(e)** recorded
**relier** to connect
**religieuse** *(f)* creampuff
**religieux(-euse)** religious
**remarque** *(f)* remark
**remarquer** to notice
**remerciement** *(m)* thanks; acknowledgment
**remercier** to thank
**remonter: — aux source** to go back to the source
**remplacer** to replace
**remplir** to fill out (a form)
**remuer** to stir
**rémunération** *(f)* salary
**rencontrer** to meet
**rendez-vous** *(m)* meeting; appointment
**rendre** *(rendu)* to return (something); **— visite à** to visit (a person); **— facile** to make easy
**renommée** *(f)* renown
**renoncer à** to give up
**renseignements** *(m pl)* information
**renseigner: se — (sur)** to get information (about)
**rentable** profitable
**rentrer** to go home; to go back; to go back to school
**rentrée** *(f)* beginning of the school year
**renverse: tomber à la —** to fall over backwards
**repartir** to leave again
**repas** *(m)* meal
**répéter** to repeat
**répondre à** *(répondu)* to answer
**réponse** *(f)* answer
**repos** *(m)* rest
**reposer: se —** to rest
**reprendre: — le train** to get back on the train
**représenter** to represent
**reproche: faire un — à quelqu'un** to blame someone
**reproduire** *(reproduit)* to reproduce
**réseau** *(m)* network
**réserver** to reserve; to put aside
**résidence** *(f)* **universitaire** dormitory
**respirer** to breathe
**responsabilité** *(f)* responsibility

**responsable** responsible
**ressortissant(e)** *(m, f):* **— d'un pays** national
**ressources** *(f pl)* resources
**restaurant** *(m)* restaurant
**rester** to stay; **Il n'en reste plus.** There aren't anymore (left).; **l'argent qui me reste** the money I have left
**résultats** *(m pl)* results
**résumé** *(m)* summary
**retard: être en —** to be late
**rétablir** to reestablish
**retour** *(m)* return trip; **être de —** to be back; **Te voilà de —!** You're back!
**retourner** to go back
**retrait** *(m)* withdrawal
**retraite** *(f)* retirement; **être à la —** to be retired
**retrouver** to meet
**réunir** to bring together; **se —** to meet; to get together
**réussi(e): Les escalopes étaient — es.** The cutlets turned out well.
**réussir à** to succeed; to pass (a test); **— un voyage** to have a successful trip
**réussite** *(f)* success
**réveil-matin** *(m)* alarm clock
**réveiller: se —** to wake up
**revenir** *(revenu)* to come back; **faire —** to soften up
**rêver** to dream
**revers** *(m)* reverse side; **au — du col** inside the collar
**révision** *(f)* review
**revoir: au —** good-bye
**revue** *(f)* magazine
**rez-de-chaussée** *(m)* ground floor
**rhume** *(m)* cold; **— des foins** hay fever
**riche** rich
**richesse** *(f)* wealth
**rideau** *(m)* curtain
**rien: ne —** nothing: **Ça ne fait —.** It doesn't matter.; **De —.** You're welcome.
**rigueur: à la —** if need be
**rissoler** to brown
**rive** *(f)* bank (of a river)
**riz** *(m)* rice
**robe** *(f)* dress
**robot** *(m)* robot
**rock** *(m)* rock music
**roi** *(m)* king
**rôle** *(m)* role
**roman** *(m)* novel

**roman(e)**  Romanesque
**ronde** *(f)*  round
**rosbif** *(m)*  roast beef
**rose**  pink
**rôti** *(m)*  roast
**roue** *(f)*  wheel
**rouge**  red
**route** *(f)*  road; **en — pour**  on the way to
**routier(-ère)**  pertaining to roads
**roux: avoir les cheveux —**  to have red hair
**Royaume-Uni** *(m)*  United Kingdom
**rude**  harsh
**rue** *(f)*  street
**ruines** *(f pl)*  ruins
**rural(e)**  rural
**russe**  Russian

**S**

**sac** *(m)*  bag; **— à main**  purse, handbag; **— à dos**  backpack; **— de voyage**  travel bag
**sage: Sois —.**  Be good.
**saignant(e)**  rare (meat)
**saison** *(f)*  season
**salade** *(f)*  salad; head of lettuce
**salaire** *(m)*  salary
**salarié(e)** *(m, f)*  salaried worker
**sale**  dirty
**saler**  to salt
**salle** *(f)*  room; **— de bains**  bathroom; **— de classe**  classroom; **— à manger**  dining room; **— de séjour**  living room; **— de remise en forme**  exercise room
**salon** *(m)* **d'essayage**  fitting room; **— du cheval**  horse show
**salopette** *(f)*  overalls
**saluer**  to greet
**salut**  hello; good-bye
**salutation** *(f)*  greeting
**sandales** *(f pl)*  sandals
**sandwich** *(m)*  sandwich
**sang** *(m)*  blood
**sans**  without; **— faire**  without doing
**santé** *(f)*  health; **en bonne —**  in good health
**satisfait(e) (de)**  satisfied (with)
**sauce** *(f)*  sauce
**saucisse** *(f)*  sausage
**saucisson** *(m)*  salami
**sauf**  except
**sauver: se —**  to run away; to escape

**saveur** *(f)*  flavor
**savoir** *(su)*  to know
**savon** *(m)*  soap
**savoureux(-euse)**  savory; flavorful
**saxophone** *(m)*  saxophone
**scène** *(f)*  scene
**science** *(f)*  science; **— politique**  political science; **—s économiques**  economics; **— fiction**  science fiction
**scolaire**  pertaining to school
**sculpture** *(f)*  sculpture
**séance** *(f)*  showing (of a film)
**sec (sèche)**  dry
**sécher: — un cours**  to skip a class
**séchoir** *(m)*  dryer
**second(e)**  second; **un billet de seconde**  a second-class ticket
**secondaire**  secondary
**secours** *(m)*  help
**secret(-ète)**  secret
**secrétaire** *(m, f)*  secretary
**séjour** *(m)*  stay
**sel** *(m)*  salt
**sélectionner**  to select
**selon**  according to
**semaine** *(f)*  week; **en —**  during the week
**sembler**  to seem
**semelle** *(f)*  sole
**Sénégal** *(m)*  Senegal
**sénégalais(e)**  Senegalese
**sens** *(m)*  direction; sense; **bon —**  common sense
**sensass = sensationnel**
**sensationnel(le)**  sensational
**sensible**  noticeable
**sentir: se —**  to feel; **se — bien (mal)**  to feel well (poorly)
**séparément**  separately
**série** *(f)*  series
**sérieusement**  seriously
**sérieux(-euse)**  serious
**serveur(-euse)** *(m, f)*  waiter (waitress)
**service** *(m)*  service; **— compris**  tip included; **— de table**  dinner service; **demander un —**  to ask for a favor; **les —s**  service industry
**serviette** *(f)*  towel; briefcase
**servir** *(servi)*  to serve
**serviteur** *(m)*  servant
**seul(e)**  alone; **un — ticket**  a single ticket
**seulement**  only

**shampooing** *(m)*  shampoo
**shopping: faire du —**  to shop
**short** *(m)*  (pair of) shorts
**si**  if; **— grand**  so big; **— longtemps**  such a long time
**siècle** *(m)*  century
**siège** *(m)*  seat; **— avant (arrière)**  front (back) seat
**signaler**  to point out
**signalisation** *(f)* **routière**  road signs
**signe** *(m)*  sign; symbol
**signer**  to sign
**signifier**  to signify; to mean
**silencieux(-euse)**  silent
**simple: hamburger —**  single hamburger
**simplement**  simply
**sincère**  sincere
**sirop** *(m)*  syrup
**situation** *(f)*  situation; location
**situé(e)**  located
**ski: faire du — (de piste/de fond/ nautique)**  to go (downhill/cross-country/water) skiing
**SNCF** *(f)*  French national railroad company
**société** *(f)*  company
**sociologie** *(f)*  sociology
**sœur** *(f)*  sister
**sofa** *(m)*  sofa
**soi-même**  oneself
**soie** *(f)*  silk
**soif** *(f)*  thirst; **avoir —**  to be thirsty
**soigner**  to care for; **se —**  to take care of oneself
**soigneusement**  carefully
**soir** *(m)*  evening
**soirée** *(f)*  party
**soit...soit**  either. . .or
**solde: en —**  on sale
**soldes** *(f pl)*  sale items
**sole** *(f)*  sole (fish)
**soleil** *(m)*  sun; **Il fait du —.**  It is sunny.
**solliciter**  to solicit; **Je me permets de — le poste.**  I would like to apply for the job.
**solution** *(f)*  solution
**somptueux(-euse)**  sumptuous
**sondage** *(m)*  survey
**sonner**  to ring
**sorbet** *(m)*  Italian ice
**sorte** *(f)*  kind; type
**sortie** *(f)*  exit; outing
**sortir** *(sorti)*  to leave; to go out
**soudain**  suddenly

**souffrant(e): être —** to be feeling poorly

**souffrir** *(souffert)* to suffer

**souhaiter** to wish; **— la bien-venue** to welcome

**souhaité(e)** desired

**soulagement** *(m)* relief

**soulagé(e)** relieved

**soulever** to lift

**soulier** *(m)* shoe

**soupçonner** to suspect

**soupe** *(f)* soup

**souper** *(m)* dinner; supper (evening meal)

**souper** to have supper (dinner)

**soupirer** to sigh

**sous-sol** *(m)* basement

**sous** under; **— la pluie** in the rain

**soutenir** to support

**souvenir** *(m)* souvenir; memory

**souvenir: se — de** to remember

**souvent** often

**spacieux(-euse)** spacious

**spectacle** *(m)* show; **— son et lu-mière** light and sound show

**spécial(e)** special

**spécialisation** *(f)* major (in college)

**spécialiser: se — en français** to major in French

**spécialité** *(f)* specialty

**spiritueux** *(m pl)* spirits

**sport** *(m)* sport; **faire du —** to participate in sports

**sportif(-ive)** sports-minded

**stade** *(m)* stadium

**stage** *(m)* practicum; internship

**standard** *(m)* switchboard

**station** *(f)* station; **— -service** service station; **— balnéaire** seaside resort; **— de métro** subway station; **— de ski** ski resort

**stationnement** *(m)* parking

**stationner** to park

**statue** *(f)* statue

**statut** *(m)* status

**stress** *(m)* stress

**studieux(-euse)** studious

**style** *(m)* style

**stylo** *(m)* pen

**substituer** to substitute

**succès** *(m)* success

**succursale** *(f)* branch office

**sucre** *(m)* sugar

**sucreries** *(f pl)* sweets

**sud** *(m)* south; **au — (de)** to the south (of)

**suédois(e)** Swedish

**suffire** to be enough

**suggérer** to suggest

**Suisse** *(f)* Switzerland

**suisse** Swiss

**suite** *(f)* continuation; **par la —** in the end

**suivant(e)** following

**suivi(e) de** followed by

**suivre** *(suivi)* to follow; **— un cours** to take a class

**sujet** *(m)* subject; **au — de** about

**super: C'est —!** That's great!

**superficie** *(f)* area

**supérieur(e)** superior; **l'en-seignement —** higher education

**supermarché** *(m)* supermarket

**supplément: payer un —** to pay extra

**supplémentaire** extra

**supporter** to bear; to stand; to put up with

**sur** on; about; **un — trois** one out of three

**sûr(e)** sure; **bien —** of course

**surgelé(e)** frozen

**surprenant(e)** surprising

**surpris(e)** surprised

**surprise-partie** *(f)* party

**surtout** especially

**svelte** thin

**sweat = sweatshirt**

**sweatshirt** *(m)* sweatshirt

**syllabe** *(f)* syllable

**sympa = sympathique**

**sympathique** nice

**symptôme** *(m)* symptom

**synagogue** *(f)* synagogue

**syndicat** *(m)* **d'initiative** tourist bureau

**Syrie** *(f)* Syria

**système** *(m)* system

## T

**t'as = tu as**

**t'es = tu es**

**T-shirt** *(m)* t-shirt

**tabac** *(m)* tobacco

**tableau** *(m)* chart; table; chalkboard; painting

**taille** *(f)* size

**tailleur** *(m)* suit

**taire: se —** *(tu)* to be quiet

**talon** *(m)* heel

**tante** *(f)* aunt

**tant...que** as much. . .as

**taper** to type

**tapis** *(m)* rug

**tard** late

**tardif(-ve)** late

**tarte** *(f)* pie

**tartelette** *(f)* tart

**tasse** *(f)* cup

**taureau** *(m)* bull

**taux** *(m)* rate

**taxi** *(m)* taxi

**technologie** *(f)* technology

**tel(le) que** such as

**télécarte** *(f)* debit card for making phone calls

**télécopieur** *(m)* fax machine

**téléphone** *(m)* telephone

**téléphoner à** to call

**téléviseur** *(m)* television; **— couleur** color television

**télévisé(e)** televised

**télévision** *(f)* television

**tellement** so; really; **— de** so much (so many)

**témoin** *(m)* witness

**tempéré(e)** temperate

**temps** *(m)* time; weather; tense (verb); **Quel — fait-il?** What's the weather like?; **avoir le — de** to have the time to; **de — en —** from time to time; **en même —** at the same time; **les — à venir** the future

**tendance: avoir — à** to tend to

**tendre à** to tend to

**tendu(e)** tense

**tenir: — une promesse** to keep a promise; **Tiens!** Hey!

**tennis** *(m)* tennis; **faire du —** to play tennis

**tenter: — sa chance** to try one's luck

**tenu(e) par** owned by

**tenue** *(f)* outfit

**terminer** to finish; **se —** to end

**terrasse** *(f)* terrace; sidewalk in front of a café

**terrine** *(f)* pâté

**tête** *(f)* head

**TGV (Train à Grande Vitesse)** *(m)* French high-speed train

**thé** *(m)* tea; **— -nature** plain tea; **— -citron** tea with lemon; **— au lait** tea with milk

**théâtre** *(m)* theater

**thon** *(m)* tuna

**timbre** *(m)* postage stamp

**timide** shy

**tiroir** *(m)*   drawer
**tissu** *(m)*   material; fabric
**toast** *(m)*   toast
**toile** *(f)*   linen; canvas; sailcloth
**toilettes** *(f pl)*   bathroom; restrooms
**toit** *(m)*   roof
**tomate** *(f)*   tomato
**tomber: — malade**   to become sick
**ton** *(m)*   tone
**tonalité** *(f)*   dial tone
**totalité** *(f)*   entirety
**toucher: tout ce qui touche à la vente**   all that concerns selling
**toujours**   always; still
**tour** *(f)*   tower
**tour: faire un — (à vélo/en voiture/à moto)**   to take a ride (on a bike/in a car/on a motorcycle); **faire un — à pied**   to go for a walk; **à son —**   in turn; **à — de rôle**   in turn; **le — de taille**   waist size; **le — de poitrine**   chest size; **le — de hanches (bassin)**   hip size
**tourisme: faire du —**   to go sightseeing
**touriste** *(m, f)*   tourist
**tourner**   to turn; **— à droite**   to turn right
**tousser**   to cough
**tout(e)**   all; **toute une boîte**   a whole box
**tout: pas du —**   not at all; **tous les ans**   every year; **tous les deux**   both; **— à fait**   exactly; **— de suite**   right away; immediately; **— naturellement**   quite naturally; **— près**   very close
**toux** *(f)*   cough
**traditionnel(le)**   traditional; conservative
**traduction** *(f)*   translation
**traduire** *(traduit)*   to translate
**trafic** *(m)*   traffic
**train** *(m)*   train
**train: en — de**   in the process of
**traîner**   to lie around; to drag
**trait** *(m)* **de caractère**   character trait
**traitement** *(m)*   treatment
**traître** *(m)*   traitor
**tranche** *(f)*   slice
**transistor** *(m)*   transistor radio
**transport** *(m)*   transportation
**travail** *(m)*   work; job; **— (à mi-temps/à plein temps)**   (part-time/full-time) work; **des travaux pratiques**   lab work

**travailler**   to work
**travailleur(-euse)** *(m, f)*   worker
**travailleur(-euse)**   hard-working
**travers: à —**   across; over
**traverser**   to cross
**trembler**   to tremble
**très**   very
**tricoter**   to knit
**trimestre** *(m)*   trimester
**triomphe** *(m)*   triumph
**triste**   sad
**trombone** *(m)*   trombone
**tromper: se —**   to be mistaken; **se — de route**   to take the wrong road
**trompette** *(f)*   trumpet
**trop (de)**   too much; too many
**troquer**   to trade
**trouver**   to find; to think; **se —**   to be located
**truite** *(f)*   trout
**tube** *(m)*   tube
**Tunisie** *(f)*   Tunisia
**tunisien(ne)**   Tunisian
**turc (turque)**   Turkish
**typiquement**   typically

## U

**URSS** (former) *(f)*   USSR (former)
**uni(e)**   one color
**Union Soviétique** *(f)*   Soviet Union
**université** *(f)*   university
**urgence: en cas d'—**   in case of emergency
**usagé(e)**   used; worn
**utile**   useful
**utiliser**   to use

## V

**vacances** *(f pl)*   vacation
**vacanciers** *(m pl)*   vacationers
**vache** *(f)*   cow
**vachement = très**
**vague** *(f)*   wave
**vaisselle: faire la —**   to do the dishes
**val: le — de Loire**   the Loire Valley
**vallée** *(f)*   valley
**valise** *(f)*   suitcase; **faire les —s**   to pack
**valoir**   to be worth; **Il vaut mieux (que)...**   It is better to (that). . .

**vanille** *(f)*   vanilla
**varier**   to vary
**varié(e)s**   various
**variété** *(f)*   variety
**veau** *(m)*   calf; veal
**vélo** *(m)*   bicycle
**vélomoteur** *(m)*   moped
**vendeur(-euse)** *(m, f)*   salesperson
**vendre** *(vendu)*   to sell; **à —**   for sale
**Venezuela** *(m)*   Venezuela
**vénézuélien(ne)**   Venezuelan
**venir** *(venu)*   to come; **— de**   to have just
**ventes** *(f pl)*   sales
**ventre** *(m)*   stomach
**verglas** *(m)*   ice on the road
**véritable**   real
**vérité** *(f)*   truth
**verre** *(m)*   glass
**vers**   toward; **— 10h**   around 10:00
**verser**   to pour
**vert(e)**   green
**vertige: avoir le —**   to be dizzy
**veste** *(f)*   sport jacket
**vêtement** *(m)*   article of clothing; **—s**   clothes
**vêtu(e)**   dressed
**viande** *(f)*   meat
**vidéo** *(f)*   videotape
**vidéo-clip** *(m)*   music video
**vie** *(f)*   life
**vieillir**   to grow old
**Viêt-Nam** *(m)*   Viet Nam
**vietnamien(ne)**   Vietnamese
**vieux/vieil (vieille)**   old
**vigne** *(f)*   vine
**vignoble** *(m)*   vineyard
**village** *(m)*   village
**ville** *(f)*   city; **en —**   to (in) town
**vin** *(m)*   wine
**vinaigre** *(m)*   vinegar
**violet(te)**   purple
**violon** *(m)*   violin
**visa** *(m)*   visa
**visage** *(m)*   face
**visite: être en —**   to be visiting; **rendre — à**   to visit (a person)
**visiter**   to visit (a place)
**vitamines** *(f pl)*   vitamins
**vite**   quickly
**vitesse** *(f)*   speed; **— maximale**   maximum speed
**vitrine** *(f)*   window
**Vittel** *(m)*   non-carbonated mineral water
**vivant(e)**   alive; living; **couleurs —es**   bright colors

**vivre** *(vécu)* to live
**vocabulaire** *(m)* vocabulary
**voici** here's; **Le —.** Here it (he) is.
**voie** *(f)* track; lane
**voilà** there's
**voile: faire de la —** to go sailing
**voir** *(vu)* to see; **faire —** to show; **Voyons...** Let's see...; **On verra.** We'll see.
**voire** or even
**voisin(e)** *(m, f)* neighbor
**voiture** *(f)* car; **— de fonction** company car
**voix** *(f)* voice; **à haute —** aloud
**vol** *(m)* flight
**voler** to steal
**volet** *(m)* shutter

**volley** *(m)* volleyball
**volonté** *(f)* will; **bonne —** willingness
**volontiers** gladly; willingly
**vomir** to vomit
**vouloir** *(voulu)* to want; to wish; **Je voudrais...** I would like...; **Je veux bien.** Gladly. (With pleasure.)
**voyage: faire un —** to take a trip
**voyager** to travel
**voyageur(-euse)** *(m, f)* traveler
**voyelle** *(f)* vowel
**vrai(e)** true; **à — dire** to tell the truth; **C'est vrai.** That's right
**vraiment** really
**vu(e)** seen; **bien —** highly regarded

**vue** *(f)* sight; **à première —** at first sight

## W — Z

**Walkman** *(m)* Walkman
**W.C.** *(m pl)* toilet
**wagon** *(m)* car (of a train)
**week-end** *(m)* weekend
**western** *(m)* western (film)
**y** there; **il — a** there is; there are; **Allons- —!** Let's go!; **il — a 3 jours** 3 days ago
**yaourt** *(m)* yogurt
**Zaïre** *(m)* Zaire
**Zut!** Darn!

## A

**a** un (une)
**to abandon** abandonner
**abbey** abbaye *(f)*
**abbreviation** abréviation *(f)*
**able: to be —** pouvoir *(pu)*
**about** à propos de; environ; sur; au sujet de; **— whom (which)** dont; **— a hundred** une centaine de; **to be —** porter sur
**above** ci-dessus
**abroad** à l'étranger
**absent** absent(e)
**absolutely** absolument
**abstract** abstrait(e)
**abundant** abondant(e)
**accent** accent *(m)*
**to accept** accepter
**access** accès *(m)*
**accident** accident *(m)*
**to accompany** accompagner
**to accomplish** accomplir
**accomplishment** accomplissement *(m)*
**according to** selon
**accountant** comptable *(m, f)*
**accounting** comptabilité *(f)*
**accusation** reproche *(m)*
**ache: to be aching** avoir des courbatures
**acquaintance** connaissance *(f)*
**to acquire** acquérir *(acquis)*
**across** à travers; **— from** en face de
**acrylic** acrylique *(f)*
**to act** agir
**active** actif(-ve)
**activity** activité *(f)*
**actor** acteur(-trice) *(m, f)*
**actually** effectivement
**to add** ajouter
**addition: in —** de plus
**address** adresse *(f)*
**advance: in —** à l'avance
**advanced** avancé(e)
**advantage** avantage *(m)*

**adventure** aventure *(f)*
**advertisement** publicité *(f)*
**advertising** publicité *(f)*
**advice** conseil *(m)*
**to advise** conseiller
**aerobics: to do —** faire de l'aérobic
**afraid: to be — (of)** avoir peur (de)
**Africa** Afrique *(f)*; **South —** Afrique du Sud
**after** après; **— having finished** après avoir fini
**afternoon** après-midi *(m)*
**afterwards** après
**again: once —** encore une fois
**against** contre
**age** âge *(m)*
**agent** agent(e) *(m, f)*
**to agree** être d'accord; **Agreed?** C'est convenu?
**agricultural** agricole
**ailment** mal *(m)*
**airplane** avion *(m)*
**airport** aéroport *(m)*
**airsickness** mal *(m)* de l'air
**alarm clock** réveil-matin *(m)*
**alas** hélas
**album** album *(m)*
**alcoholic (beverages)** alcoolisé(e)
**Algeria** Algérie *(f)*
**Algerian** algérien(ne)
**alive** vivant(e)
**all** tout(e); **— the better.** Tant mieux.; **— day** toute la journée; **— red** tout(e) rouge; **at —** du tout
**allergy** allergie *(f)*
**allies** alliés *(m pl)*
**almond** amande *(f)*
**almost** presque
**alone** seul(e)
**along** le long de; au bord de; **to get — with** s'entendre avec
**aloud** à haute voix
**already** déjà
**also** aussi

**always** toujours
**ambiguous** ambigu(-üe)
**ambitious** ambitieux(-euse)
**America** Amérique *(f)*
**American** américain(e)
**among** parmi
**amphitheater** amphithéâtre *(m)*
**ancestors** ancêtres *(m pl)*
**and** et
**anger** colère *(f)*
**angry** fâché(e)
**ankle** cheville *(f)*
**to announce** annoncer
**anonymous** anonyme
**another** un(una) autre; **— year** encore un an
**to answer** répondre (à)
**answer** réponse *(f)*
**anthropology** anthropologie *(f)*
**antihistamine** anti-histaminique *(m)*
**anymore: not —** ne...plus
**anyway** quand même
**apartment** appartement *(m)*; **— building** immeuble *(m)*
**to appear** paraître *(paru)*
**appearance** apparence *(f)*
**appetite** appétit *(m)*
**appetizer** hors-d'œuvre *(m)*
**apple** pomme *(f)*
**apply: to — for a job** poser sa candidature
**appointment** rendez-vous *(m)*
**to appreciate** apprécier
**to approach (a person)** aborder
**appropriate** approprié(e); convenable
**apricot** abricot *(m)*
**Arabic** arabe *(m)*
**architect** architecte *(m, f)*
**architecture** architecture *(f)*
**area** superficie *(f)*
**area code** indicatif *(m)*
**arena** arène *(f)*
**Argentina** Argentine *(f)*
**Argentinian** argentin(e)
**to argue** se disputer

**arm** bras *(m)*
**armchair** fauteuil *(m)*
**to arrange** arranger; régler
**arrival** arrivée *(f)*
**to arrive** arriver
**around: — 10:00** vers 10h
**art** art *(m)*
**artichoke** artichaut *(m)*
**as** comme; **— old —** aussi vieux que
**ashes** cendres *(f pl)*
**ashtray** cendrier *(m)*
**Asia** Asie *(f)*
**to ask (for)** demander; **to — a question** poser une question; **to — for a favor** demander un service
**asparagus** asperges *(f pl)*
**aspirin** aspirine *(f)*
**assembly line** chaîne *(f)*
**associated: to be — with** s'associer à
**astronaut** astronaute *(m, f)*
**astronomy** astronomie *(f)*
**at** à; en; **to work — Kodak** travailler chez Kodak
**to attend** assister à
**to attract** attirer
**auction** vente *(f)* aux enchères
**aunt** tante *(f)*
**Australia** Australie *(f)*
**Australian** australien(ne)
**Austrian** autrichien(ne)
**automatic teller machine** distributeur *(m)* automatique de billets
**automatically** automatiquement
**autonomous** autonome
**autumn** automne *(f)*
**available** disponible
**average** moyen(ne)
**to avoid** éviter

# B

**B.C.** avant Jésus-Christ
**baby** bébé *(m)*
**back** dos *(m)*; **in —** à l'arrière; **to get — on the train** reprendre le train; **to be —** être de retour; **You're back!** Te voilà de retour!
**background** fond *(m)*
**backpack** sac *(m)* à dos
**backwards** à la renverse
**bacon** bacon *(m)*
**bad** mauvais(e); **The weather is —.** Il fait mauvais.
**badge** badge *(m)*
**bag** sac *(m)*

**baggage claim** livraison *(f)* des bagages
**baker** boulanger(-ère) *(m, f)*
**bakery** boulangerie *(f)*
**balanced** équilibré(e)
**balcony** balcon *(m)*
**bald** chauve
**ball** balle *(f)*; ballon *(m)*
**banana** banane *(f)*
**bandage** pansement *(m)*
**bank** banque (f); **(of a river)** rive *(f)*; **data —** base *(f)* de données
**bankruptcy** faillite *(f)*
**baseball** base-ball *(m)*
**basement** sous-sol *(m)*
**basket** panier *(m)*
**basketball** basket *(m)*
**bathing suit** maillot *(m)* de bain (de surf)
**bathroom** salle *(f)* de bains; cabinet *(m)* de toilette; toilettes *(f pl)*
**bathtub** baignoire *(f)*
**battle** bataille *(f)*
**bay** baie *(f)*
**to be** être *(été)*
**beach** plage *(f)*
**bean** haricot *(m)*
**bear** ours *(m)*
**to bear** supporter
**beard** barbe *(f)*
**beautiful** beau/bel (belle); **It's — weather.** Il fait beau.
**beautifully** à merveille
**because** parce que; car
**to become** devenir *(devenu)*; **to — sick** tomber malade
**bed** lit *(m)*; **in —** au lit; **to go to —** se coucher
**bedroom** chambre *(f)* à coucher
**beef** bœuf *(m)*
**beer** bière *(f)*; **glass of draft —** demi *(m)*
**before** avant; **— entering** avant d'entrer
**before-dinner drink** apéritif *(m)*
**to begin** commencer
**beginner** débutant(e)
**beginning** début *(m)*; **— with (in)** à partir de; **— of the school year** rentrée *(f)*
**behavior** comportement *(m)*
**behind** derrière
**Belgian** belge
**Belgium** Belgique *(f)*
**to believe** croire *(cru)*
**belongings** affaires *(f pl)*
**below** ci-dessous
**belt** ceinture *(f)*
**bench** banc *(m)*

**beret** béret *(m)*
**berth** couchette *(f)*
**best** meilleur(e); mieux; **to do one's — to** faire de son mieux pour
**better: — than** meilleur(e) que; mieux que; **It is — to. . .** Il vaut mieux...; **It would be — that. . .** Il vaut mieux que...; **All the —.** Tant mieux.
**between** entre
**bicycle** bicyclette *(f)*; vélo *(m)*
**big** grand(e); gros(se)
**bikini** bikini *(m)*
**bill (money)** billet *(m)*
**billing** facturation *(f)*
**billion** milliard *(m)*
**billionaire** milliardaire *(m)*
**biography** biographie *(f)*
**biology** biologie *(f)*
**birth** naissance *(f)*; **of —** natal(e)
**birthday** anniversaire *(m)*
**black** noir(e)
**blank: — tape** cassette vierge
**blond** blond(e)
**blood** sang *(m)*
**blouse** chemisier *(m)*
**blue** bleu(e); **— jeans** blue-jean *(m)*; jean *(m)*
**boarding house** pension *(f)*
**boat** bateau *(m)*
**bobsled** luge *(f)*; **to go bobsledding** faire de la luge
**body** corps *(m)*; **— suit** maillot *(m)* de corps
**bohemian** bohème
**bond** lien *(m)*
**book** livre *(m)*; **— of tickets** carnet *(m)*
**bookstore** librairie *(f)*
**boots** bottes *(f pl)*
**bored: to be —** s'ennuyer
**boring** ennuyeux(-euse); barbant(e); rasant(e)
**born: I was —** Je suis né(e)
**to borrow** emprunter
**boss** patron(ne) *(m, f)*
**botany** botanique *(f)*
**both** tous (toutes) les deux
**bother: Don't —.** Ce n'est pas la peine.
**bothersome** gênant(e)
**bottle** bouteille *(f)*
**bowl** bol *(m)*
**box** boîte *(f)*; carton *(m)*
**boy** garçon *(m)*; **— friend** petit ami
**branch office** succursale *(f)*

**brand**   marque *(f)*
**Brazil**   Brésil *(m)*
**Brazilian**   brésilien(ne)
**bread**   pain *(m)*
**to break down (car)**   avoir une panne (de moteur)
**breakdown**   panne *(f)* de voiture (de moteur)
**breakfast**   petit déjeuner *(m)*
**brick**   brique *(f)*
**bridge**   pont *(m)*
**brief**   bref (brève)
**briefcase**   serviette *(f)*
**bright: — colors**   couleurs vives
**to bring**   amener; apporter; **to — back**   ramener; **to — together** réunir
**Brittany**   Bretagne *(f)*
**broadcast**   émission *(f)*
**brochure**   brochure *(f)*
**brother**   frère *(m)*; **— -in-law** beau-frère
**brown**   marron; brun(e)
**brunette**   brun(e)
**brush**   brosse *(f)*
**to build**   construire *(construit)*
**building**   bâtiment *(m)*
**bull**   taureau *(m)*
**bunch (radishes, etc.)**   botte *(f)*
**burgundy (color)**   bordeaux
**burn**   brûlure *(f)*
**to burn**   brûler
**bus**   autobus *(m)*; car *(m)*
**business**   affaires *(f pl)*; commerce *(m)*; **— card**   carte *(f)* de visite
**businessman (-woman)**   homme (femme) d'affaires
**but**   mais
**butcher**   boucher(-ère) *(m, f)*
**butter**   beurre *(m)*
**buttock**   fesse *(f)*
**to buy**   acheter; un billet **— a ticket**   prendre
**by**   par; **— plane**   en avion; **— using**   en utilisant

**C**

**cabbage**   chou *(m)*
**cafeteria**   cafétéria *(f)*
**café**   café *(m)*
**Cairo**   Le Caire *(m)*
**cake**   gâteau *(m)*
**to calculate**   calculer
**calculator**   calculatrice *(f)*
**calendar**   calendrier *(m)*
**calf**   veau *(m)*
**call**   appel *(m)*

**to call**   téléphoner à; appeler; **to — again**   rappeler
**called**   nommé(e)
**calm**   calme
**camcorder**   caméra *(f)*
**camera**   appareil-photo *(m)*
**Cameroon**   Cameroun *(m)*
**camp**   colonie *(f)* de vacances
**camping**   camping *(m)*
**campus**   campus *(m)*
**can**   boîte *(f)*
**Canada**   Canada *(m)*
**Canadian**   canadien(ne)
**to cancel**   annuler
**candy**   bonbon *(m)*
**canned foods**   conserves *(f pl)*
**canoe: to go canoeing**   faire du canoë
**canvas**   toile *(f)*
**capital**   capitale *(f)*
**cap**   bonnet *(m)*; casquette *(f)*
**capsule**   gélule *(f)*
**car**   auto *(f)*; voiture *(f)*; **— of a train**   wagon *(m)*
**carbonated**   gazeux(-euse)
**card**   carte *(f)*; **credit —**   carte de crédit
**care: to take — of**   s'occuper de; **to take — of oneself**   se soigner
**career**   carrière *(f)*
**careful: to be — (of)**   faire attention (à)
**carefully**   soigneusement
**carrot**   carotte *(f)*
**cartoon**   dessin *(m)* animé
**case**   cas *(m)*
**cash register**   caisse *(f)*
**cassette tape**   cassette *(f)*
**castle**   château *(m)*
**cat**   chat *(m)*
**category**   catégorie *(f)*
**cathedral**   cathédrale *(f)*
**cauliflower**   choux-fleur *(m)*
**CD**   compact disque *(m)*
**to celebrate**   célébrer; fêter
**center**   centre *(m)*
**centimeter**   centimètre *(m)*
**century**   siècle *(m)*
**cereal**   céréales *(f pl)*
**certain**   certain(e)
**certainly**   certainement
**certainty**   certitude *(f)*
**chain**   chaîne *(f)*
**chair**   chaise *(f)*
**chalkboard**   tableau *(m)*
**challenge**   défi *(m)*
**champagne**   champagne *(m)*
**chance (opportunity)**   occasion *(f)*; **to have the — to**   avoir l'occasion de

**change**   changement *(m)*
**change (money)**   monnaie *(f)*
**to change**   changer; **to — one's mind**   changer d'avis; **to — trains (subway)**   prendre une correspondance
**chapter**   chapitre *(m)*
**character**   personnage *(m)*; **— trait**   trait *(m)* de caractère
**characterized**   caractérisé(e)
**charge: in — of**   chargé(e) de
**charm**   charme *(m)*
**chart**   tableau *(m)*, diagramme *(m)*
**cheap**   bon marché
**check**   chèque *(m)*; **(in a restaurant)**   addition *(f)*
**cheese**   fromage *(m)*
**chef**   cuisinier(-ère) *(m, f)*
**chemistry**   chimie *(f)*
**cherry**   cerise *(f)*
**chess**   échecs *(m pl)*
**chest**   poitrine *(f)*
**chestnut**   marron *(m)*
**chicken**   poulet *(m)*
**child**   enfant *(m)*
**childhood**   enfance *(f)*; jeunesse *(f)*
**chills**   frissons *(m pl)*
**chimney**   cheminée *(f)*
**China**   Chine *(f)*
**Chinese**   chinois(e)
**chocolat**   chocolat *(m)*
**choice**   choix *(m)*
**to choose**   choisir
**Christian**   chrétien(ne)
**Christmas**   Noël *(m)*
**church**   église *(f)*
**cider**   cidre *(m)*
**to circulate**   circuler
**circumstance**   circonstance *(f)*
**city**   ville *(f)*; **— hall**   hôtel *(f)* de ville
**civil servant**   fonctionnaire *(m, f)*
**clarinet**   clarinette *(f)*
**class**   classe *(f)*; cours *(m)*; **first (second) —**   première (deux-ième) classe; **in —**   en classe; **I have — in 5 minutes.**   J'ai cours dans 5 minutes.
**classic, classical**   classique
**classified ads**   petites annonces
**classmate**   camarade *(m, f)* de classe
**to clean**   nettoyer
**clear**   clair(e)
**to clear the table**   débarrasser la table
**clever**   habile; intelligent
**climate**   climat *(m)*
**clock radio**   radioréveil *(m)*

**to close**  fermer
**close to**  près de; proche
**closet**  placard *(m)*
**clothes**  vêtements *(m pl)*
**clothing**  habillement *(m)*
**cloud**  nuage *(m)*; **It's cloudy.**  Le ciel est nuageux (couvert).
**coast**  côte *(f)*
**coat**  manteau *(m)*
**coated**  enrobé(e)
**Coca-Cola**  Coca *(m)*
**coffee**  café *(m)*
**coin**  pièce *(f)* de monnaie
**cold**  froid(e); froid *(m)*; **to have a — **  avoir un rhume; **It is —.**  Il fait froid
**collar**  col *(m)*
**colleague**  collègue *(m, f)*
**Colombia**  Colombie *(f)*
**colony**  colonie *(f)*
**color**  couleur *(f)*
**colored**  coloré(e)
**comb**  peigne *(m)*
**combination**  combinaison *(f)*
**to come**  venir *(venu)*; **to — back** revenir; **to — across**  rencontrer
**comedy**  comédie *(f)*
**comfort**  confort *(m)*
**comfortable**  confortable; **to get —**  se mettre à l'aise
**coming from**  en provenance de
**comment**  commentaire *(m)*
**commercial**  commercial(e)
**companion**  compagnon *(m)*
**company**  entreprise *(f)*; société *(f)*; firme *(f)*
**to compare**  comparer
**competitor**  concurrent(e) *(m, f)*
**to complain**  se plaindre
**complaint**  plainte *(f)*
**completely**  tout(e); complètement
**complicated**  compliqué(e)
**comprised: to be — of** comprendre
**computer**  ordinateur *(m)*; **— programmer**  programmeur(-euse) *(m, f)*; **— science**  informatique *(f)*
**to concentrate**  concentrer; **to — on**  se concentrer sur
**concerning**  en ce qui concerne
**concert**  concert *(m)*
**conference**  conférence *(f)*
**confluence**  confluent *(m)*
**to connect**  relier
**conquered**  conquis(e)
**consequently**  par conséquent
**conservative**  traditionnel(le)
**to consist of**  consister en

**consonant**  consonne *(f)*
**constantly**  constamment
**constipated**  constipé(e)
**constraint**  contrainte *(f)*
**to consult**  consulter
**consumer**  consommateur(-trice) *(m, f)*
**to contain**  contenir
**continuation**  suite *(f)*
**to continue**  continuer; poursuivre; **to be continued**  à suivre
**contradictory**  contradictoire
**to contribute**  contribuer
**convent**  couvent *(m)*
**convention**  congrès *(m)*
**cook**  cuisinier(-ère) *(m, f)*
**cooked**  cuit(e)
**cookie**  biscuit *(m)*
**cool: It's —**  Il fait frais.
**corn**  maïs *(m)*
**corner**  coin *(m)*
**to correct**  corriger
**cost**  coût *(m)*
**to cost**  coûter
**costly**  coûteux(-euse)
**cotton**  coton *(m)*
**couch**  canapé *(m)*
**cough**  toux *(f)*; **to —**  tousser
**to count**  compter
**country**  pays *(m)*; campagne *(f)*; **in the —**  à la campagne
**courageous**  courageux(-euse)
**course**  cours *(m)*; **first — (of a meal)**  entrée *(f)*
**course: of —**  bien sûr; bien entendu
**courtesy**  courtoisie *(f)*
**cousin**  cousin(e) *(m, f)*
**covered**  couvert(e)
**cow**  vache *(f)*
**crazy**  fou/fol (folle)
**cream**  crème *(f)*; **— fouettée** whipped cream
**to create**  créer
**crepe**  crêpe *(f)*
**crime**  crime *(m)*
**crisis**  crise *(f)*
**to criticize**  critiquer
**to cross**  traverser
**to cry**  pleurer
**cucumber**  concombre *(f)*
**cuisine**  cuisine *(f)*
**cup**  tasse *(f)*
**current**  actuel(le)
**currently**  actuellement
**curtain**  rideau *(m)*
**cushion**  coussin *(m)*

**custom**  coutume *(m)*
**customer**  client(e) *(m, f)*
**customs**  douane *(f)*
**to cut**  couper
**cutlet**  escalope *(f)*
**cyclist**  cycliste *(m, f)*

# D

**dairy products**  produits laitiers
**damaged**  endommagé(e)
**dance**  danse *(f)*
**dancer**  danseur(-euse) *(m, f)*
**dangerous**  dangereux(-euse)
**Danish**  danois(e)
**danse**  bal *(m)*
**dark: — blue**  bleu foncé
**Darn!**  Zut!
**to date from**  dater de
**daughter**  fille *(f)*
**dawn**  aube *(f)*
**day**  jour *(m)*; journée *(f)*; **What — is it?**  Quel jour sommes-nous?; **the following —**  lendemain *(m)*
**dear**  cher (chère)
**death**  mort *(f)*
**to decide**  décider (de)
**decision**  décision *(f)*; **to make a —**  prendre une décision
**to declare**  déclarer
**degree**  diplôme *(m)*
**delay**  délai *(m)*
**delegate**  délégué(e) *(m, f)*
**delicious**  délicieux(-euse)
**delighted**  ravi(e); enchanté(e); **to be —**  se réjouir
**to demand**  exiger
**demanding**  exigeant(e)
**demonstration**  manifestation *(f)*
**Denmark**  Danemark *(m)*
**dense**  dense
**dentist**  dentiste *(m, f)*
**department (of a store)**  rayon *(m)*
**departure**  départ *(m)*
**to depend: That —s on...**  Ça dépend de...
**depressed: to be —**  avoir le cafard *(fam)*
**depressing**  déprimant(e)
**to describe**  décrire *(décrit)*
**deserted**  désert(e)
**to designate**  désigner
**desire**  désir *(m)*
**desired**  souhaité(e)
**desk**  bureau *(m)*; **front — (hotel)**  réception *(f)*
**despite**  malgré

**dessert** dessert *(m)*
**detail** détail *(m)*; **to give —s** préciser
**detailed** détaillé(e)
**detective movie** film *(m)* policier
**development** développement *(m)*
**devil** diable *(m)*
**dial** cadran *(m)*; **to —** composer; **— tone** tonalité *(f)*
**dialogue** dialogue *(m)*
**to die** mourir *(mort)*; crever
**diet: to be on a —** être au régime
**to differ from** différer de
**difficult** difficile
**digit** chiffre *(m)*
**to diminish** diminuer
**dining room** salle *(f)* à manger
**dinner** dîner *(m)*; **to have —** dîner
**diploma** diplôme *(m)*
**diplomacy** diplomatie *(f)*
**direct** direct(e)
**direction** direction *(f)*; sens *(m)*; **(of a movie, play)** mise en scène *(f)*
**directly** directement
**director** directeur(-trice) *(m, f)*
**dirty** sale
**disagreement** différend *(m)*
**disappointed** déçu(e)
**disappointing** décevant(e)
**disastrous** désastreux(-euse)
**disciplined** discipliné(e)
**discotheque** discothèque *(f)*
**to discourage** décourager
**to discover** découvrir *(découvert)*
**discreet** discret(-ète)
**to discuss** discuter (de)
**dish** plat *(m)*
**dishonest** malhonnête
**to dislike** détester
**display** étalage *(m)*
**distinctive** distinctif(-ive)
**to distinguish** distinguer
**to distribute** distribuer
**to divide** diviser
**divorce: to (get a) —** divorcer
**to do** faire *(fait)*
**doctor** médecin *(m)*
**doctoral degree** doctorat *(m)*
**dog** chien *(m)*
**doll** poupée *(f)*
**door** porte *(f)*
**dormitory** résidence *(f)* universitaire; **— complex** cité *(f)* universitaire
**dose** dose *(f)*
**doubt** doute *(m)*
**to doubt** douter

**down: to go —** descendre
**downtown** centre-ville *(m)*
**dozen** douzaine *(f)*
**drama** drame *(m)*
**dramatic** dramatique
**to draw** dessiner
**drawer** tiroir *(m)*
**drawing** dessin *(m)*
**to dream** rêver
**dress** robe *(f)*
**dressed** habillé(e); vêtu(e); **to get —** s'habiller
**dresser** commode *(f)*
**drink** boisson *(f)*; **to —** boire *(bu)*
**to drive** conduire
**driver** chauffeur *(m)*
**driving** conduite *(f)*
**drop** goutte *(f)*
**to drop off** déposer
**drug store** pharmacie *(f)*
**drums** batterie *(f)*
**dry** sec (sèche)
**dryer** séchoir *(m)*
**duck** canard *(m)*
**due to** dû (due) à
**during** durant, au cours de; **— the week** en semaine
**duty-free** hors taxes; exempt de droit
**dwelling** logement *(m)*
**dynamic** dynamique

**E**

**each** chaque; **— one** chacun(e); **with — other** l'un(e) avec l'autre
**ear** oreille *(f)*
**early** de bonne heure; en avance
**to earn** gagner
**earrings** boucles *(m pl)* d'oreille
**easily** facilement
**east** est *(m)*
**Easter** Pâques *(f pl)*
**easy** facile; aisé(e)
**to eat** manger
**eclair** éclair *(m)*
**economics** sciences économiques
**economy** économie *(f)*
**edge** bord *(m)*
**education** formation *(f)*; **continuing —** formation permanente; **higher —** enseignement supérieur
**effect** effet *(m)*
**efficient** efficace
**egg** œuf *(m)*

**Egypt** Égypte *(f)*
**Egyptian** égyptien(ne)
**either. . .or** soit...soit
**elbow** coude *(m)*
**eldest** aîné(e)
**electric** électrique
**elegant** élégant(e)
**element** élément *(m)*
**elevator** ascenseur *(m)*
**embassy** ambassade *(m)*
**embroidered** brodé(e)
**emergency: in case of —** en cas d'urgence
**employee** employé(e) *(m, f)*; agent(e) *(m, f)*
**employment** emploi *(m)*
**enclosure (in a letter)** P.J. (pièce jointe)
**to encourage** encourager
**end** fin *(f)*; bout *(m)*; **in the —** pour finir; par la suite
**to end** (se) terminer
**energetic** énergique
**engaged: to get — (to)** se fiancer (avec)
**engineer** ingénieur *(m)*
**England** Angleterre *(f)*
**English** anglais(e)
**English Channel** Manche *(f)*
**to engrave** graver
**enjoy: — your meal!** Bon appétit!
**enough** assez (de); **to be —** suffire
**to enroll** s'inscrire
**to enter** entrer dans; s'introduire dans
**enthusiasm** enthousiasme *(m)*
**enthusiastic** enthousiaste
**entire** entier(-ère)
**entirely** complètement
**entirety** totalité *(f)*
**entrance** entrée *(f)*
**environment** environnement *(m)*
**equally** également
**equipped** équipé(e)
**errand** course *(f)*; **to run —s** faire les courses
**escalator** escalier *(m)* roulant
**to escape** se sauver
**espadrilles** espadrilles *(f pl)*
**especially** surtout
**espionage** espionnage *(m)*
**espresso** express *(m)*
**essential** indispensable; **It is — that. . .** Il est essentiel que...
**essentially** essentiellement
**to establish** établir
**European** européen(ne)
**even** même; **or —** voire

**evening** soir *(m)*

**event** événement *(m)*; **in any —** de toute façon

**ever** jamais

**every: — week** toutes les semaines; **— year** tous les ans; **— body** tout le monde; **—where** partout

**to evolve** évoluer

**exact** exact(e)

**exactly** exactement; justement; tout à fait

**exaggeration** exagération *(f)*

**exam** examen *(m)*; **competitive —** concours *(m)*; **final —** examen de fin de semestre

**example** exemple *(m)*; **for —** par exemple

**except** sauf

**exception: with the — of** à l'exception de

**exceptional** exceptionnel(le)

**excerpt** extrait *(m)*

**exchange** échange *(f)*; **foreign currency —** bureau *(m)* de change; **to —** échanger

**exciting** passionnant(e)

**exclusively** exclusivement

**excuse** excuse *(f)*; **— me. . .** Pardon...

**executive** cadre *(m)*; **high-level —** cadre supérieur

**exercise** exercice *(m)*

**exit** sortie *(f)*

**expensive** cher (chère); **to be —** coûter cher

**to explain** expliquer

**explanation** explication *(f)*

**to express** exprimer

**exterior** extérieur *(m)*

**extra** supplémentaire

**extraordinary** extraordinaire

**extreme** extrême *(m)*

**extremity** extrémité *(f)*

**eye** œil (pl yeux) *(m)*

**eyeglasses** lunettes *(f pl)*

**F**

**fabric** tissu *(m)*

**face** figure *(f)*; visage *(m)*

**to facilitate** faciliter

**fact: in —** en fait

**to fail (a test)** rater; échouer à

**faith** foi *(f)*

**false** faux (fausse)

**family** famille *(f)*; **pertaining to the —** familial(e)

**famous** célèbre

**fantastic** fantastique

**fantasy: — movie** film *(m)* fantastique

**far (from)** loin (de)

**faraway** lointain(e)

**farm** ferme *(f)*

**farmer** agriculteur(-trice) *(m, f)*

**fascinating** fascinant(e)

**fashion** mode *(f)*; **high —** haute couture; **in —** à la mode

**fast food** fast-food *(m)*; **a — restaurant** un fast-food

**fat** gros(se); gras(se)

**fatality** fatalité *(f)*

**father** père *(m)*; **— -in-law, stepfather** beau-père

**favorite** préféré(e)

**fax machine** télécopieur *(m)*

**fed: to be — up with** en avoir marre de

**to feel** se sentir; **I'm feeling better.** Je vais mieux.

**festival** festival *(m)*

**fever** fièvre *(f)*; **hay—** rhume *(m)* des foins

**few: a —** quelques; **so —** si peu de

**fiance** fiancé(e) *(m, f)*

**field** champ *(m)*

**to fill out (a form)** remplir

**filled** chargé(e); rempli(e)

**filmmaker** cinéaste *(m f)*

**finally** finalement; enfin; **She — got her car.** Elle a fini par avoir sa voiture.

**financial** financier(-ère)

**to find** trouver

**fine: I am —.** Je vais bien.

**finger** doigt *(m)*

**to finish** finir; terminer

**fire** incendie *(m)*

**fireworks** feux *(m pl)* d'artifice

**first** premier(-ère); **— of all** d'abord; premièrement

**fish** poisson *(m)*; **— soup** bouillabaisse *(f)*

**fishing** pêche *(f)*; **to go —** aller à la pêche

**fitting room** salon *(m)* d'essayage

**to fix one's hair** se coiffer

**fixed** figé(e); décidé(e)

**flavor** saveur *(f)*

**flight** vol *(m)*

**flooded** inondé(e)

**floor** plancher *(m)*; étage *(m)*; **—plan** plan *(m)*; **ground —** rez-de-chaussée *(m)*

**flour** farine *(f)*

**flower** fleur *(f)*

**flu** grippe *(f)*

**fluently: to speak French —** parler couramment le français

**flute** flûte *(f)*

**fog** brouillard *(m)*

**foggy: It's —.** Il fait du brouillard.

**to follow** suivre *(suivi)*; **followed by** suivi(e) de; **following** suivant(e)

**food** alimentation *(f)*; nourriture *(f)*; aliments *(m pl)*

**foot** pied *(m)*

**football** football *(m)* américain

**for** pour; **— an hour** pendant une heure; **— hours** depuis des heures

**forbidden** interdit(e)

**forced** forcé(e)

**foreign** étranger(-ère)

**foreigner** étranger(-ère) *(m, f)*

**forest** forêt *(f)*

**to forget** oublier

**fork** fourchette *(f)*

**form: in the — of** sous forme de; **to —** former

**former** ancien(ne)

**fortunately** heureusement

**founded** fondé(e)

**free** gratuit(e); libre

**freedom** liberté *(f)*

**French** français(e)

**French fries** (pommes) frites *(f pl)*

**French-speaking** francophone

**frequently** fréquemment

**fresh** frais (fraîche)

**friend** ami(e) *(m, f)*; copain (copine) *(m, f)*

**to frighten** faire peur (à)

**frivolous** frivole

**from** de; **— the beginning** dès le début

**front: in — of** devant

**frozen** surgelé(e)

**fruit** fruit *(m)*

**frying pan** poêle *(f)*

**fun: to have —** s'amuser; **to make — of** se moquer de

**funny** drôle; amusant(e); **It's not —.** C'est pas marrant.

**furious** furieux(-euse)

**to furnish** fournir; **to — a house** aménager une maison

**furnished** meublé(e)

**furnishings** ameublement *(m)*

**furniture** meubles *(m pl)*

**future** futur *(m)*; avenir *(m)*

**G**

**to gain weight** grossir

**game** jeu *(m)*; match *(m)*; **to play a — of tennis** faire une partie de tennis

**garage**  garage *(m)*
**garden**  jardin *(m)*
**garlic**  ail *(m)*
**garnished**  garni(e)
**gasoline**  essence *(f)*; **to get a full tank of —**  faire le plein
**gastronomical**  gastronomique
**gate (airport)**  porte *(f)*
**gender**  genre *(m)*
**general**  général(e); **in —**  en général
**generally**  généralement
**generous**  généreux(-euse)
**genius**  génie *(m)*
**gentleman**  monsieur *(m)*
**geology**  géologie *(f)*
**German**  allemand(e)
**Germany**  Allemagne *(f)*
**gesture**  geste *(m)*
**to get**  obtenir *(obtenu)*; **to — in (car, bus, etc.)**  monter dans; **to — off**  descendre de; **to — back**  récupérer; **to — settled**  s'installer; **to — up**  se lever; **to — upset**  s'énerver; **to — used to**  s'habituer à
**giant**  géant(e)
**gift**  cadeau *(m)*
**girl**  fille *(f)*; **—friend**  petite amie
**to give**  donner
**gladly**  volontiers; Je veux bien.
**glass**  verre *(m)*
**glove**  gant *(m)*
**to go**  aller; **Let's — !**  Allons-y!; **to — and get**  aller chercher; **to — back**  rentrer, retourner; **to — by (time)**  passer; **to — about (doing something)**  s'y prendre
**goal**  but *(m)*
**goat**  chèvre *(f)*
**gold**  or *(m)*
**golf**  golf *(m)*
**good**  bon(ne); **Be —.**  Sois sage.
**good-bye**  au revoir; salut; **to say —**  prendre congé
**government**  gouvernement *(m)*
**grade**  note *(f)*
**gram**  gramme *(m)*
**grammar**  grammaire *(f)*
**grand: — daughter**  petite fille; **— son**  petit fils; **— father**  grand-père; **— mother**  grand-mère
**grapefruit**  pamplemousse *(m)*
**grated**  râpé(e)
**gray**  gris(e)
**Great Britain**  Grande-Bretagne *(f)*

**great**  grand(e); **That's — !**  C'est extra (épatant, chouette)!
**Greece**  Grèce *(f)*
**Greek**  grec(que)
**green**  vert(e)
**to greet**  saluer; accueillir
**greeting**  salutation *(f)*
**grilled**  grillé(e)
**grocer**  épicier(-ère) *(m, f)*
**grocery store**  alimentation *(f)* générale; épicerie *(f)*
**ground floor**  rez-de-chaussée *(m)*
**group**  groupe *(m)*
**growth**  croissance *(f)*
**to guess**  deviner
**guest**  invité(e) *(m, f)*
**guide**  guide *(m)*
**guitar**  guitare *(f)*
**gulf**  golfe *(m)*
**gun**  pistolet *(m)*
**gymnasium**  gymnase *(f)*

## H

**hair**  cheveux *(m pl)*; **—cut**  coupe *(f)*; **—dresser**  coiffeur(-euse) *(m, f)*; **—style**  coiffure *(f)*
**half**  moitié *(f)*; demi(e)
**hallway**  couloir *(m)*
**ham**  jambon *(m)*
**hand**  main *(f)*; **on one — . . . on the other**  d'un côté...de l'autre; **to give somebody a —**  donner un coup de main à quelqu'un
**handwritten**  manuscrit(e)
**to hang**  pendre *(pendu)*; **to — up (phone)**  raccrocher
**to happen**  se passer
**happiness**  bonheur *(m)*
**happy**  heureux(-euse); content(e)
**hard**  dur(e); **— working**  travailleur(-euse)
**hardly**  ne...guère
**harsh**  rude
**hat**  chapeau *(m)*
**to hate**  avoir horreur de
**to have**  avoir *(eu)*; **(something to eat)**  prendre *(pris)*; **to — to**  devoir *(dû)*; **to — one's hair cut**  se faire couper les cheveux; **having decided to**  ayant décidé de
**head**  tête *(f)*
**health**  santé *(f)*; **in good —**  en bonne santé; **your good health!**  Santé!
**to hear**  entendre *(entendu)*; **to — about**  entendre parler de; **to — that**  entendre dire que

**heart**  cœur *(m)*
**heat**  chaleur *(f)*
**heating**  chauffage *(m)*
**heavy**  lourd(e); **— -set**  costaud(e)
**heel**  talon *(m)*
**hello**  salut; bonjour; allô
**help**  aide *(f)*; secours *(m)*
**to help**  aider
**henna**  henné *(m)*
**here**  ici; **Here's. . .** Voici...
**to hesitate**  hésiter
**Hey!**  Tiens!
**hierarchy**  hiérarchie *(f)*
**high**  élevé(e)
**highway**  autoroute *(f)*
**hike: to go for a —**  faire une randonnée
**to hire**  embaucher
**historic**  historique
**history**  histoire *(f)*
**holiday**  jour de fête
**home: at the — of**  chez; **at —**  à la maison; **to go —**  rentrer
**honest**  honnête
**honey**  miel *(m)*
**hood**  capuche *(f)*; capuchon *(m)*
**to hope**  espérer
**horrible**  affreux(-euse)
**horror movie**  film *(m)* d'épouvante
**horseback riding**  équitation *(f)*
**hospital**  hôpital *(m); clinique (f)*
**hostel:  youth —**  auberge *(f)* de jèunesse
**hostess**  hôtesse *(f)*
**hot**  chaud(e)
**hotel**  hôtel *(m)*; **— owner**  hôtelier(-ère) *(m, f)*
**hour**  heure *(f); 24 —s a day*  24 heures sur 24; **130 km per —**  130 km à l'heure; **rush —**  heures de pointe
**house**  maison *(f)*
**housing**  logement *(m)*
**how**  comment; **— much ( — many)**  combien (de); **— are you?**  Comment allez-vous? (Comment ça va?); **— strong he is!**  Qu'est-ce qu'il est fort!; **— long will it take to go. . .**  Il faut combien de temps pour aller...
**huh?**  hein?
**human**  humain(e)
**hunger**  faim *(f)*
**hungry: to be (very) —**  avoir (grand) faim
**to hurry**  se dépêcher; **in a —**  pressé(e)
**husband**  mari *(m)*

# I

**ice cream** glace *(f)*
**idea** idée *(f)*
**idealistic** idéaliste
**to identify** identifier
**if** si
**illness** mal *(m)*
**illustrated** illustré(e)
**image** image *(f)*
**imaginary** imaginaire
**to imagine** imaginer
**immediately** tout de suite
**impatient** impatient(e)
**importance** importance *(f)*
**important** important(e)
**imposed** imposé(e)
**to impress** impressionner; épater
**impression: to have the — (of, that)** avoir l'impression (de, que)
**impressive** impressionnant(e)
**to improve** améliorer
**in** à; en; dans
**to inaugurate** inaugurer
**to include** inclure *(inclus)*
**included** compris(e)
**to increase** augmenter
**increasing** en hausse
**independence** indépendance *(f)*
**independent** indépendant(e)
**India** Inde *(f)*
**Indian** indien(ne)
**to indicate** indiquer
**indigestion** indigestion *(f)*
**indiscreet** indiscret(-ète)
**industry** industrie *(f)*
**inedible** immangeable
**inevitable** inévitable
**to influence** influencer
**information** renseignements *(m pl)*; **to get — (about)** se renseigner (sur)
**informed** avisé(e)
**inhabitant** habitant(e) *(m, f)*
**inhabited** habité(e)
**injury** blessure *(f)*
**inn** pension *(f)*; auberge *(f)*
**inseam** entre-jambes *(m)*
**inside** à l'intérieur de
**to insist (that)** insister (pour que)
**institute** institut *(m)*
**intellectual** intellectuel(le)
**to intend to** avoir l'intention (de)
**intercom** interphone *(m)*
**interest** intérêt *(m)*
**interested: to be — in** s'intéresser à
**interesting** intéressant(e)

**international** international(e); mondial(e)
**to interrogate** interroger
**interrupted** interrompu(e)
**intersection** carrefour *(m)*
**interview** interview *(f)*; entretien *(m)*; **to —** interviewer
**to introduce** présenter
**introduction** présentation *(f)*
**introverted** introverti(e)
**to invent** inventer
**investment** investissement *(m)*
**Iran** Iran *(m)*
**Iranian** iranien(ne)
**Iraq** Irak *(m)*
**iron** fer *(m)*
**island** île *(f)*
**Israel** Israël *(m)*
**Israeli** israélien(ne)
**Italian** italien(ne)
**itinerary** itinéraire *(m)*
**Ivory Coast** Côte d'Ivoire *(f)*

# J

**jacket** blouson *(m)*; **sports —** veste *(f)*
**jam** confiture *(f)*
**Japan** Japon *(m)*
**Japanese** japonais(e)
**jazz** jazz *(m)*
**jewelry** bijoux *(m pl)*
**job** job *(m)*; poste *(m)*; travail *(m)*; emploi *(m)*
**to jog** faire du jogging
**to join** rejoindre *(rejoint)*; **to — us** être des nôtres
**jolly** jovial(e)
**journalism** journalisme *(m)*
**journalist** journaliste *(m, f)*
**joy** joie *(f)*
**to judge** juger
**juice** jus *(m)*; **fruit —** jus *(m)* de fruit
**just: I have — arrived.** Je viens d'arriver

# K

**karate** karaté *(m)*
**to keep** garder; **to — a promise** tenir une promesse
**ketchup** ketchup *(m)*
**key** clé *(f)*
**keychain** porte-clés *(m)*
**kidney** rein *(m)*

**kilogram** kilo *(m)*
**kind (nice)** gentil(le)
**kind (type)** genre *(m)*; sorte *(f)*
**king** roi *(m)*
**to kiss** embrasser
**kitchen** cuisine *(f)*
**knee** genou *(m)*
**knife** couteau *(m)*
**to knit** tricoter
**to knock** frapper
**to know** connaître *(connu)*; savoir *(su)*; **I — what I'm doing.** Je m'y connais.
**known** connu(e)

# L

**label** étiquette *(f)*; griffe *(f)*
**laboratory** laboratoire *(m)*
**lack** manque *(m)*
**ladder** échelle *(f)*
**lamp** lampe *(f)*
**landing** débarquement *(m)*
**lane** voie *(f)*
**language** langue *(f)*
**large** grand(e); **— family** famille nombreuse
**last** dernier(-ère); passé(e)
**to last** durer
**late** tard; en retard; tardif(-ve)
**later** plus tard
**latest** dernier(ère)
**laundry** linge *(m)*; **to do the —** faire la lessive; **— room** buanderie *(f)*
**law** droit *(m)*
**lawyer** avocat(e) *(m, f)*
**lazy** paresseux(-euse)
**to lead** mener
**leader** chef *(m)*
**to learn** apprendre *(appris)*
**least** moindre; **the —** le (la) moins; **at —** au moins
**to leave** quitter; sortir *(sorti)*; partir *(parti)*; **to — again** repartir; **to take —** prendre congé
**Lebanese** libanais(e)
**lecture** conférence *(f)*
**leek** poireau *(m)*
**left** gauche *(f)*
**left: the money I have —** l'argent qui me reste
**leg** jambe *(f)*
**legend** légende *(f)*
**lemon** citron *(m)*
**lemonade** citron *(m)* pressé
**to lend** prêter
**length** durée *(f)*

**less** moins; — ...**than** moins
de...que
**lesson** leçon *(f)*
**letter** lettre *(f)*; **application —**
lettre de candidature
**lettuce** salade *(f)*
**level** niveau *(m)*
**liberal arts** lettres *(f pl)*
**library** bibliothèque *(f)*
**Libya** Libye *(f)*
**life** vie *(f)*
**to light** allumer
**light: — blue** bleu clair
**light** léger(-ère)
**lightly** légèrement
**to like** aimer; aimer bien; **to —**
**better** aimer mieux; **to — the**
**best** aimer le mieux; **I would**
**like...** Je voudrais...
**limited** limité(e)
**line** ligne *(f)*; file *(f)*
**lined** doublé(e)
**linguistics** linguistique *(f)*
**lip** lèvre *(f)*
**list** liste *(f)*
**to listen (to)** écouter
**liter** litre *(m)*
**literature** littérature *(f)*
**little** un peu; **so —** si peu (de)
**to live** vivre *(vécu);* habiter
**living room** salle *(f)* de séjour
**loafers** mocassins *(m pl)*
**lobster** homard *(m)*
**located** situé(e); **to be —** se
trouver
**location** situation *(f)*
**locked** fermé(e) à clé
**to lodge** héberger
**lodging** hébergement
**long** long(ue)
**look** regard *(m);* **to — (seem)**
avoir l'air; **to — at** regarder; **to**
**— for** chercher; **That looks**
**good on you.** Ça te va très bien.
**to lose** perdre; **to — weight**
maigrir
**lot: a — (of)** beaucoup (de); énormément (de)
**loudly: to talk —** parler fort
**love** amour *(m);* **to —** aimer;
adorer; **to be in — with** être
amoureux(-euse) de
**lover: — of** amateur(-trice) de *(m,*
*f);* **—s** amoureux *(m pl)*
**low** bas(se)
**lozenge** pastille *(f)*
**lucky: to be —** avoir de la chance
**lunch** déjeuner *(m);* **to have —**
déjeuner; **— time** l'heure du
déjeuner

**luxurious** luxueux(-euse)
**luxury** luxe *(m)*

## M

**made of** composé(e) de
**magazine** magazine *(m)*; revue *(f)*
**main** principal(e)
**major (in college)** spécialisation
*(f)*; **to — in French** se spécialiser en français
**majority** majorité *(f)*
**to make** faire *(fait);* fabriquer; **to**
**— beautiful** rendre beau
**man** homme *(m)*
**to manage** gérer; **to — to do**
**something** se débrouiller
**management** gestion *(f)*
**manager** gérant(e) *(m, f)*
**mandatory** obligatoire
**manners** manières *(f pl)*
**manufacture** fabrication *(f)*
**to manufacture** fabriquer
**many** beaucoup; **so —** tellement
(de); **as — as** tant que; autant
que; **as — ...as** autant de...que
**map** carte *(f)*; plan *(m)*
**marked** marqué(e)
**market** marché *(m)*; **flea —**
marché aux puces; **Common —**
Marché Commun
**marketing** marketing *(m)*
**married** marié(e) **to get —** se
marier
**to marry** épouser
**marvel** merveille *(f)*
**master** maître *(m)*; **—'s degree**
maîtrise *(f)*
**masterpiece** chef d'œuvre
**material** matière *(f)*
**math** mathématiques *(f pl)*
**matter: It doesn't —.** Ça m'est
égal.; Ça ne fait rien.; **What's the**
**— ?** Qu'est-ce que tu as?; Qu'est-
ce qu'il y a?
**maybe** peut-être
**mayonnaise** mayonnaise *(f)*
**meal** repas *(m)*
**to mean** signifier; **That means...**
Ça veut dire...
**means** moyen *(m)*
**meantime: in the —** entretemps;
en attendant
**to measure** mesurer
**meat** viande *(f)*
**mechanic** mécanicien(ne) *(m, f)*
**medical** médical(e)
**medicine** médecine *(f);* **to study**
**—** faire sa médecine

**medication** médicament *(m)*
**Mediterranean Sea** Mer
Méditerranée
**to meet** faire la connaissance de;
rencontrer; retrouver; se retrouver; se réunir; **I met him in**
**Paris.** Je l'ai connu à Paris.
**meeting** rendez-vous *(m)*; congrès
*(m);* réunion *(f)*
**melon** melon *(m)*
**member** membre *(m)*
**memory** souvenir *(m)*
**menu** carte *(f)*; menu *(m)*
**message** message *(m)*; **to leave a**
**—** laisser un mot
**meter** mètre *(m)*
**method** mode *(f)*
**metric** métrique
**Mexican** mexicain(e)
**Mexico** Mexique *(m)*
**middle** milieu *(m)*; **— -aged**
d'un certain âge; **— -class**
bourgeois(e)
**midnight** minuit *(m)*
**migraine headache** migraine *(f)*
**mild (climate)** doux (douce)
**milk** lait *(m)*; **—shake** milk-
shake *(m)*
**million** million *(m)*
**mint** menthe *(f)*
**minute** minute *(f)*
**mirror** miroir *(m)*
**miser** avare *(m)*
**miserly** avare
**to miss: I — her** Elle me manque.
**mistake: to make a —** se tromper
**mix** mélange *(m)*
**to mix** mélanger
**model** modèle *(m)*; **fashion —**
mannequin *(m)*
**modern** moderne
**to modernize** moderniser
**moment** instant *(m);* moment *(m)*
**monarchy** monarchie *(f)*
**money** argent *(m)*
**monster** monstre *(m)*
**month** mois *(m)*
**mood: in a good (bad) —** de
bonne (mauvaise) humeur
**moped** vélomoteur *(m)*
**more** davantage; encore de; **—**
**than** plus que; **— ...than**
plus de...que; **25 francs —** 25
francs de plus; **no —** ne...plus
**morning** matin *(m)*
**Moroccan** marocain(e)
**Morocco** Maroc *(m)*
**Moslem** musulman(e)
**most** la plupart de; **the —** le
plus (de)

**mother** mère *(f)*; **— -in-law, step-mother** belle-mère
**to motivate** motiver
**motorcycle** moto *(f)*; motocyclette *(f)*
**mountain** montagne *(f)*
**mountainous** montagneux(-euse)
**mousse** mousse *(f)*
**moustache** moustache *(f)*
**mouth** bouche *(f)*
**movement** mouvement *(m)*; déplacement *(m)*
**movie** film *(m)*; **—s, — theater** cinéma *(m)*; **— camera** caméra *(f)*
**moving** émouvant(e)
**much: so —** tellement (de); **as — as** tant que; autant que; **as — ...as** autant de...que
**muscular** musclé(e)
**museum** musée *(m)*
**mushroom** champignon *(m)*
**music** musique *(f)*; **classical —** la musique classique; **popular —** la musique populaire; **— video** (vidéo-)clip *(m)*
**musical** musical(e)
**musician** musicien(ne) *(m, f)*
**mussel** moule *(f)*
**mustard** moutarde *(f)*
**mutton** mouton *(m)*
**my** mon; ma; mes
**mysterious** mystérieux(-euse)

## N

**naive** naïf (naïve)
**to name** nommer
**name** nom *(m)*; **first —** prénom *(m)*; **last —** nom de famille; **My — is. . .** Je m'appelle...
**nationality** nationalité *(f)*
**natural** naturel(le)
**nature** nature *(f)*
**nauseated: to feel —** avoir mal au cœur
**navy: — blue** bleu marine
**near** proche; près (de)
**nearly** à peu près; presque
**neat** chouette
**necessary** nécessaire; **It is — (that). . .** Il faut (que)...
**neck** cou *(m)*
**need** besoin *(m)*; **to —** avoir besoin de; **I — . . .** Il me faut...; **if — be** à la rigueur
**to neglect** négliger
**neighbor** voisin(e) *(m, f)*
**neighborhood** quartier *(m)*

**neither** non plus; **— . . .nor** ne...ni...ni
**nervous** nerveux(-euse)
**Netherlands** Pays-Bas *(m pl)*
**network** réseau *(m)*
**neutrality** neutralité *(f)*
**never** ne...jamais
**nevertheless** néanmoins
**new** nouveau/nouvel (nouvelle); neuf (neuve)
**New Orleans** Nouvelle-Orléans *(f)*
**newly** nouvellement
**news** nouvelles *(f pl)*
**newspaper** journal *(m)*
**New Year's** le Nouvel An
**New Zealand** Nouvelle Zélande *(f)*
**next** prochain(e); **— to** à côté de; **the cafe — door** le café à côté; **the — morning** le lendemain matin
**nice** sympathique; **It's — (weather).** Il fait bon.
**nightclub** boîte *(f)* de nuit
**no** non
**nobody** ne...personne
**noise** bruit *(m)*
**none whatsoever** ne...aucun(e)
**noon** midi *(m)*
**normal** normal(e)
**normally** normalement; d'habitude
**north** nord *(m)*
**Norwegian** norvégien(ne)
**nose** nez *(m)*; **to have a runny —** avoir le nez qui coule;
**not: — bad** pas mal; **— at all** pas du tout; **— much** pas grand'chose; **— yet** pas encore
**note pad** carnet *(m)*
**notebook** cahier *(m)*
**to notice** s'apercevoir de; remarquer
**noticeable** sensible; remarquable
**noun** nom *(m)*
**novel** roman *(m)*
**now** maintenant; en ce moment
**nowadays** de nos jours
**nowhere** nulle part
**number** numéro *(m)*; nombre *(m)*
**numerous** nombreux(-euses)
**nurse** infirmier(-ère) *(m, f)*
**nut** noix *(f)*

## O

**obey** obéir à
**object** objet *(m)*
**to oblige** obliger

**obsessed with** obsédé(e) par
**obvious** évident(e)
**occupation** métier *(m)*
**occupied** occupé(e)
**to occupy** occuper
**o'clock: 10 —** 10 heures
**of** de
**off-campus** hors campus
**offer** offre *(f)*
**to offer** offrir *(offert)*
**office** bureau *(m)*
**official** officiel(le)
**often** souvent
**oil** huile *(f)*
**okay** d'accord; **Is that —?** Ça vous va?; **It will be —.** Ça ira.
**old** vieux/vieil (vieille); ancien(ne); âgé(e); **How — are you?** Quel-âge as-tu?; **to grow —** vieillir
**omelet** omelette *(f)*
**on** sur; **— Balzac Street** dans la rue Balzac; **— Mondays** le lundi; **— page 3** à la page 3; **— sale** en solde; **— television** à la télévision; **— the other hand** par contre; **— the phone** au téléphone; **— the way to** en route pour; **— time** à l'heure
**one-way (ticket)** aller-simple *(m)*; **(street)** à sens unique
**oneself** soi-même
**onion** oignon *(m)*
**only** ne...que; seulement
**to open** ouvrir *(ouvert)*
**opinion** opinion *(f)*; **in my —** à mon avis
**opportunity** occasion *(f)*
**opposite** contraire *(m)*
**optimistic** optimiste
**or** ou
**orange** orange *(f)*
**order** commande *(f)*; ordre *(m)*; **in — to** afin de; pour
**to order** commander
**organ** orgue *(f)*
**organization** organisme *(m)*; organisation *(f)*
**to organize** organiser
**organized: to get —** s'organiser
**organizer** organisateur(-trice) *(m, f)*
**origin** origine *(f)*
**original** original(e)
**other** autre
**out: to go —** sortir *(sorti)*; **one — of three** un sur trois
**outfit** tenue *(f)*
**outing** sortie *(f)*
**outside (of)** à l'extérieur (de); en dehors (de)

**oven** four (m); **microwave —** four à micro-ondes
**over** sur; dessus; par-dessus
**overalls** salopette (f)
**overcoat** manteau (m); pardessus (m)
**to owe** devoir (dû)
**own** propre

## P

**to pack** faire les valises
**package** paquet (m)
**painting** peinture (f); tableau (m)
**pair** paire (f)
**palace** palais (m)
**pale** pâle
**pan** casserole (f)
**pants** pantalon (m)
**parade** défilé (m)
**paragraph** paragraphe (m)
**parentheses** parenthèses (f pl)
**parents** parents (m pl)
**Parisian** parisien(ne)
**park** parc (m)
**to park** stationner
**parking** stationnement (m); **— lot** parking (m)
**part** partie (f); **in —** en partie; **to be a — of** faire partie de
**particular: in —** en particulier
**particularly** particulièrement
**partner** partenaire (m, f)
**party** boum (f); soirée (f); surprise-partie (f)
**to pass** dépasser; **to — a test** réussir à un examen
**passenger** passager(-ere) (m, f)
**passerby** passant(e) (m, f)
**passport** passeport (m)
**past** passé (m); **in the —** autrefois
**pasta** pâtes (f pl)
**pastry, pastry shop** pâtisserie (f); **— chef** pâtissier(-ère) (m, f)
**path** allée (f); chemin (m)
**patience** patience (f)
**patient** patient(e)
**patiently** patiemment
**pattern (sewing)** patron (m)
**to pay (for)** payer, régler; **to — attention** faire attention; **to — cash** payer en espèces; **to — extra** payer un supplément
**peach** pêche (f)
**pear** poire (f)
**pearl** perle (f)
**peas** petits pois (m pl)
**to peel** éplucher

**pen** stylo (m)
**pencil** crayon (m)
**people** gens (m f pl); peuple (m)
**pepper** poivre (m)
**per** par
**percent: thirty —** trente pour cent
**percentage** pourcentage (m)
**perfect** parfait(e)
**to perfect** perfectionner
**perfectly** parfaitement
**perfume** parfum (m)
**perhaps** peut-être
**period** période (f)
**to permit** permettre (permis)
**person** personne (f)
**personal** personnel(le)
**personality** personnalité (f)
**personally** personnellement
**personnel** personnel (m); effectifs (m pl)
**to persuade** décider
**Peru** Pérou (m)
**pessimistic** pessimiste
**pharmaceutical** pharmaceutique
**pharmacist** pharmacien(ne) (m, f)
**Philippines** Philippines (f pl)
**philosophy** philosophie (f)
**photocopier** copieur (m)
**photograph** photo (f)
**to photograph** photographier
**photographer** photographe (m, f)
**physics** physique (f)
**physical** physique
**piano** piano (m)
**pick: to — up (phone)** décrocher
**picnic** pique-nique (m)
**picturesque** pittoresque
**pie** tarte (f)
**piece** bout (m); morceau (m); part (f)
**pierced** percé(e)
**pig** cochon (m)
**pinball** flipper (m)
**pink** rose
**pity: It's a —.** C'est dommage.
**pizza** pizza (f)
**place** endroit (m); lieu (m); **meeting —** lieu de rencontre
**plans** préparatifs (m pl); projets (m pl)
**plant** plante (f)
**plate** assiette (f)
**platform (train station)** quai (m)
**play** pièce (f) de théatre
**to play** jouer; **(sport)** jouer à; **(musical instrument)** jouer de; **to — tennis** faire du tennis
**playing: to be — (movie)** passer
**pleasant** agréable
**pleased** content(e)

**please** s'il vous (te) plaît
**pleasure** plaisir (m)
**pocket** poche (f)
**poet** poète (m)
**to point out** signaler
**police station** commissariat (m) de police
**Polish** polonais(e)
**polite** poli(e)
**political** politique; **— party** parti (m); **— science** science (f) politique
**politics** politique (f)
**polka dots** pois (m pl)
**polo shirt** polo jersey (m)
**polyester** polyester (m)
**poor** pauvre
**poorly** mal
**pork** porc (m)
**Portugal** Portugal (m)
**Portuguese** portugais(e)
**position** situation (f); poste (m)
**to possess** posséder
**possession** possession (f)
**possible: It is — that. . .** Il se peut que...; **That's —.** Ça se peut bien.
**to post** afficher
**post office** bureau (m) de poste
**postage stamp** timbre (m)
**postal worker** postier(-ère) (m, f)
**postcard** carte (f) postale
**poster** affiche (f); poster (m)
**pound** livre (f)
**to pour** verser
**practical** pratique
**practicum** stage (m)
**prawn** langoustine (f)
**precarious** précaire
**predecessor** prédécesseur (m)
**to predict** prévoir (prévu)
**to prefer** préférer; aimer mieux
**preferable: It is — that. . .** Il est préférable que...
**preferably** de préférence
**pregnant** enceinte
**preparations** préparatifs (m pl)
**to prepare** préparer
**to prescribe** prescrire (prescrit)
**to present** présenter
**president** président(e) (m, f)
**pressure** pression (f)
**pretty** joli(e)
**price** prix (m)
**primary** primaire
**private** privé(e)
**privileged** privilégié(e)
**prize** prix (m)
**probably** probablement; sans doute
**problem** problème (m); ennui (m)

**process: in the — of** en train de
**product** produit *(m)*
**profession** métier *(m)*; profession *(f)*
**professional** professionnel(le)
**profitable** rentable
**program** programme *(m)*
**progress: to make —** faire des progrès
**promise** promesse *(f)*
**promotion** avancement *(m)*
**pronoun** pronom *(m)*
**to propose** proposer
**prosperous** prospère
**to protect** protéger
**protein** protéine *(f)*
**proud** fier (fière)
**province** province *(f)*
**psychiatry** psychiatrie *(f)*
**psychology** psychologie *(f)*
**public** public (publique)
**to publish** publier .
**pumps** escarpins *(m pl)*
**to punish** punir
**purchase** achat *(m)*; **to —** acheter
**purchasing (department)** achats *(m pl)*
**purple** violet(te)
**purse** sac *(m)* à main
**to pursue** poursuivre *(poursuivi)*
**to put** mettre *(mis)*; **to — up with** supporter
**puzzle** rébus *(m)*; énigme *(f)*

# Q

**qualified** qualifié(e)
**quality** qualité *(f)*
**question** question *(f)*
**quickly** rapidement; vite
**quiet: to be —** se taire
**quite: — a bit of** pas mal de; **— naturally** tout naturellement

# R

**R&B music** funk *(m)*
**rabbit** lapin *(m)*
**racket** raquette *(f)*
**rain** pluie *(f)*; **in the —** sous la pluie
**to rain** pleuvoir *(plu)*; **It's raining.** Il pleut.
**to rank** classer
**ranking** classement *(m)*
**rare** rare; **— (meat)** saignant(e)
**rarely** rarement

**rate** taux *(m)*
**rather** plutôt; assez
**ravine** ravin *(m)*
**to reach** atteindre *(atteint)*
**to react** réagir
**reaction** réaction *(f)*
**to read** lire *(lu)*
**reading** lecture *(f)*
**ready** prêt(e); **to get — (to)** se préparer (pour)
**real** véritable
**real estate agency** agence *(f)* immobilière
**realistic** réaliste
**reality** réalité *(f)*
**to realize** se rendre compte de
**really** vraiment
**reason** raison *(f)*; **the — why** la raison pour laquelle
**reasonable** raisonnable
**to reassure** rassurer
**to receive** recevoir *(reçu)*
**recently** récemment
**reception** réception *(f)*
**recipe** recette *(f)*
**to recognize** reconnaître *(reconnu)*
**to recommend** recommander
**to reconstruct** reconstruire *(reconstruit)*
**record** disque *(m)*
**to recruit** recruter
**red** rouge; **to have — hair** avoir les cheveux roux
**to reduce** réduire *(réduit)*
**to reestablish** rétablir
**to reflect** refléter
**refresher course** cours *(m)* de recyclage
**refrigerator** frigo *(m)*
**to refuse** refuser
**regarding** en ce qui concerne
**to register** enregistrer
**registration form** bulletin *(m)* d'inscription
**regularly** régulièrement
**to reign** régner
**relationship** rapport *(m)*
**relatives** parents *(m pl)*
**relaxed** décontracté(e); relax
**relief** soulagement *(m)*
**relieved** soulagé(e)
**religious** religieux(-euse)
**to remain** demeurer
**remark** remarque *(f)*
**to remember** se rappeler; se souvenir (de)
**to remind** rappeler
**renowned** renommé(e)

**rent** loyer *(m)*
**to rent** louer
**rental** location *(f)*; **— agency** agence *(f)* de location
**to repeat** répéter
**to replace** remplacer
**to represent** représenter
**to reproduce** reproduire *(reproduit)*
**research** recherche *(f)*; **to do —** faire des recherches
**to reserve** réserver
**to resign** démissionner
**resignation** démission *(f)*
**resources** ressources *(f pl)*
**responsibility** responsabilité *(f)*
**responsible** responsable
**rest** repos *(m)*; **to —** se reposer; **— area** aire *(f)* de repos
**restaurant** restaurant *(m)*
**results** résultats *(m pl)*
**retired: to be —** être à la retraite
**to return (give back)** rendre *(rendu)*
**return trip** retour *(m)*
**review** révision *(f)*
**résumé** curriculum vitae (CV) *(m)*
**rib** côte *(f)*
**rice** riz *(m)*
**rich** riche
**right** droite *(f)*
**right (correct)** vrai; exact; **to be —** avoir raison
**to ring** sonner
**river** fleuve *(m)*
**road** chemin *(m)*; route *(f)*; **— signs** signalisation *(f)* routière; **pertaining to —s** routier(-ière)
**to rob** cambrioler
**robber** cambrioleur *(m)*
**rock music** rock *(m)*
**rocket** fusée *(f)*
**role** rôle *(m)*
**roof** toit *(m)*
**room** chambre *(f)*; pièce *(f)*; salle *(f)*; **—mate** camarade *(m, f)* de chambre; **bath—** salle de bains; **class—** salle de classe (cours)
**round-trip (ticket)** aller-retour *(m)*
**rubber** caoutchouc *(m)*
**rug** tapis *(m)*
**ruins** ruines *(f pl)*
**rule** règle *(f)*
**to run (business)** exploiter; **manage** gérer; **to — away** se sauver; **to — out of gas** avoir une panne d'essence
**rural** rural(e)
**Russian** russe

# S

**sad**  triste

**sail: — boat**  bateau *(m)* à voile; **to go sailing**  faire de la voile

**salad**  salade *(f)*

**salary**  salaire *(m)*

**sale: for —**  à vendre

**sales**  ventes *(f pl)*; soldes *(f pl)*

**salesperson**  vendeur(-euse) *(m, f)*

**same**  même

**sandals**  sandales *(f pl)*

**sandwich**  sandwich *(m)*

**satisfied (with)**  satisfait(e) (de)

**to satisfy**  rassasier

**to save (money)**  faire des économies

**savory**  savoureux(-euse)

**saxophone**  saxophone *(m)*

**to say**  dire *(dit)*; déclarer; **to — goodbye**  faire ses adieux; **Say. . .**  Dis... (Dites...)

**scallops**  coquilles Saint-Jacques *(f)*

**scarf**  écharpe *(f)*; foulard *(m)*

**scene**  scène *(f)*

**schedule**  emploi *(m)* du temps; horaire *(m)*

**scholarship**  bourse *(f)*

**school**  école *(f)*; **high —**  lycée *(m)*; **intermediate (middle) —**  collège *(m)*; **nursery —**  école maternelle; **pertaining to —**  scolaire

**science**  science *(f)*; **— fiction**  science fiction *(f)*

**Scottish**  écossais(e)

**screen**  écran *(m)*

**sculpture**  sculpture *(f)*

**sea**  mer *(f)*; **—food**  fruits *(m pl)* de mer

**seamstress**  couturière *(f)*

**search**  recherche *(f)*

**seashore**  bord *(m)* de la mer

**seasickness**  mal *(m)* de mer

**seaside resort**  station *(f)* balnéaire

**season**  saison *(f)*

**seat**  place *(f)*; **front (back) —**  siège *(m)* avant (arrière)

**seatbelt**  ceinture *(f)* de sécurité

**seated**  assis(e)

**second**  deuxième; second(e); **--class ticket**  billet *(m)* de seconde; **— floor**  premier étage

**secondary**  secondaire

**secret**  secret(-ète)

**secretary**  secrétaire *(m, f)*

**to see**  voir *(vu)*; **— you in a while.**  À tout à l'heure.; **— you soon.**  À bientôt.; **Let's see. . .**  Voyons...; **We'll see. . .**  On verra...

**to seem**  sembler; avoir l'air

**to select**  sélectionner

**selfish**  égoïste

**to sell**  vendre *(vendu)*

**to send**  envoyer

**Senegal**  Sénégal *(m)*

**Senegalese**  sénégalais(e)

**sensational**  sensationnel(le)

**sense**  sens *(m)*; **common —**  bon sens

**sentence**  phrase *(f)*

**separately**  séparément

**series**  série *(f)*

**serious**  grave; sérieux(-euse)

**seriously**  sérieusement

**servant**  serviteur *(m)*

**to serve**  servir; desservir

**service**  service *(m)*; **— station**  station-service *(f)*

**to set (a date)**  fixer; **to — the table**  mettre la table (le couvert)

**setting**  cadre *(m)*

**several**  plusieurs

**to sew**  coudre *(cousu)*

**shame: It's a — .**  C'est dommage.

**shampoo**  shampooing *(m)*

**to share**  partager

**to shelter**  abriter

**shelves**  étagères *(f pl)*

**shirt**  chemise *(f)*; **short-sleeved —**  chemisette *(f)*

**shoe**  chaussure *(f)*; soulier *(m)*; **— size**  pointure *(f)*

**to shop (go shopping)**  faire des achats; faire du shopping; faire les courses

**shopping mall**  centre *(m)* commercial

**short**  court(e); petit(e)

**shorts**  short *(m)*; bermuda *(m)*

**shot**  piqûre *(f)*

**should: you — buy**  tu devrais acheter

**shoulder**  épaule *(f)*

**show**  spectacle *(m)*

**to show**  montrer; faire voir; indiquer; **to — one's reaction**  marquer sa réaction

**shower**  douche *(f)*

**showing (of a film)**  séance *(f)*

**shrimp**  crevette *(f)*

**shutter**  volet *(m)*

**shy**  timide

**sick**  malade

**side**  côté *(m)*

**sidewalk (of a café)**  terrasse *(f)*

**to sigh**  soupirer

**sight**  vue *(f)*; **at first —**  à première vue

**sightseeing: to go —**  faire du tourisme

**sign**  signe *(m)*

**to sign**  signer

**to signify**  signifier

**silent**  silencieux(-euse)

**silk**  soie *(f)*

**simply**  simplement

**since**  depuis; **— when**  depuis quand; **It has been a year —...**  Ça fait un an que...

**sincere**  sincère

**to sing**  chanter; **to — off-key**  chanter faux

**singer**  chanteur(-euse) *(m, f)*

**single (not married)**  célibataire

**sink**  évier *(m)*; lavabo *(m)*

**sister**  sœur *(f)*; **—-in-law,**  belle-sœur; **step —**  demi-sœur

**to sit**  s'asseoir; **— down!**  Assieds-toi! (Asseyez-vous!)

**situation**  situation *(f)*

**size**  taille *(f)*; **I take a — 42 (shoe).**  Je chausse du 42.

**skating: to go —**  faire du patinage

**ski: to go (downhill/cross-country/water) skiing**  faire du ski (de piste/de fond/nautique); **— jacket**  anorak *(m)*; **— resort**  station *(f)* de ski

**skin**  peau *(f)*

**skindiving: to go —**  faire de la plongée sous-marine

**to skip a class**  sécher un cours

**skirt**  jupe *(f)*

**sky**  ciel *(m)*

**to sleep**  dormir; coucher

**sleeve**  manche *(f)*

**slightly**  légèrement

**slot**  fente *(f)*

**small**  petit(e)

**smoke**  fumée *(f)*

**to smoke**  fumer

**smoking (non-smoking)**  fumeur (non-fumeur)

**snack**  amuse-gueule *(m)*

**snail**  escargot *(m)*

**sneakers**  baskets *(m pl)*; **high-top —**  baskets montants

**to sneeze**  éternuer

**so**  alors; **— big**  si grand

**soap**  savon *(m)*

**soccer**  football *(m)*

**sociology**  sociologie *(f)*

**sock**  chaussette *(f)*

**sofa**  sofa *(m)*

**soft**  doux (douce)

**software**  logiciel *(m)*

**sole**  semelle *(f)*

**to solicit**  solliciter
**solution**  solution *(f)*
**some**  des; **— day**  un jour; **— (of)**
  quelques-un(e)s (de)
**someone**  quelqu'un
**something**  quelque chose; **— else**
  autre chose; **— small**  quelque
  chose de petit; **— to drink**  quelque chose à boire
**sometimes**  parfois; quelquefois
**somewhere**  quelque part
**son**  fils *(m)*
**soon**  bientôt
**sorrow**  chagrin *(m)*; tristesse *(f)*
  **to my —**  à mon (grand) regret
**sorry**  désolé(e); navré(e); **to be —**
  regretter; **I feel — for you.**  Je
  vous plains.; **I'm —.**  Je
  m'excuse.
**soup**  soupe *(f)*; potage *(m)*
**south**  sud *(m)*
**souvenir**  souvenir *(m)*
**Soviet Union**  (former) Union Soviétique *(f)*
**space**  espace *(m)*
**spacious**  spacieux(-euse)
**Spain**  Espagne *(f)*
**Spanish**  espagnol(e)
**to speak**  parler; **to — to someone**
  s'adresser à quelqu'un, adresser la
  parole à quelqu'un
**special**  spécial(e)
**specialty**  spécialité *(f)*
**speed**  vitesse *(f)*
**to spend (money)**  dépenser;
  **(time)**  passer le temps
**spinach**  épinards *(m pl)*
**spite: in — of**  malgré
**spoiled**  gâté(e)
**spoon**  cuiller (cuillère) *(f)*
**sport: to participate in —s**  faire
  du sport; **—jacket**  veste *(f)*; **—s
  -minded**  sportif(-ive); **—ing
  goods store**  magasin *(m)* de
  sport
**to sprain**  se fouler
**spring**  printemps *(m)*
**square: (in a town)**  place *(f)*
**stadium**  stade *(m)*
**stairs**  escalier *(m)*
**to stand (put up with)**  supporter
**star**  étoile *(f)*
**state**  état *(m)*
**statue**  statue *(f)*
**status**  statut *(m)*
**stay**  séjour *(m)*
**to stay**  rester; **to — at a hotel**
  descendre à un hôtel
**to steal**  voler
**steel**  acier *(m)*
**steer**  bœuf *(m)*

**step: — -brother**  demi-frère; **—
  -father**  beau-père; **— -mother**
  belle-mère; **— -sister**  demi-sœur
**stereo**  chaîne *(f)* stéréo
**still**  encore; toujours
**stomach**  ventre *(m)*; estomac *(m)*
**stop**  arrêt *(m)*; **bus —**  arrêt d'autobus; **non— -**  sans arrêt; **to —**
  s'arrêter; cesser; **to — by**  passer
**store**  magasin *(m)*
**storm**  orage *(m)*
**story**  histoire *(f)*
**straight: — hair**  cheveux raides;
  **— ahead**  tout droit
**strawberry**  fraise *(f)*
**street**  rue *(f)*
**strength**  force *(f)*; **regain one's
  strength**  regagner ses forces
**stress**  stress *(m)*
**string**  ficelle *(f)*
**striped**  rayé(e); à rayures
**strong**  fort(e)
**student**  (high school)  élève *(m,
  f)*; lycéen(ne) *(m, f)*; **(college)**
  étudiant(e) *(m, f)*
**studious**  studieux(-euse)
**study**  étude *(f)*; **to —**  étudier; **to
  — for a test**  préparer un
  examen
**stuffed: to be — up**  avoir le nez
  pris (bouché)
**style**  style *(m)*
**stylish**  chic
**subject**  sujet *(m)*; **school —s**
  matières *(f pl)*
**subscription**  abonnement *(m)*
**subsidiary**  filiale *(f)*
**to substitute**  substituer
**suburbs**  banlieue *(f)*
**subway**  métro *(m)*; **— station**
  station *(f)* de métro
**to succeed**  réussir
**success**  succès *(m)*; réussite *(f)*
**such: — as**  tel(le) que; **— a long
  time**  si longtemps
**suddenly**  soudain
**to suffer**  souffrir *(souffert)*
**sugar**  sucre *(m)*
**to suggest**  suggérer; conseiller
**suit**  complet *(m)*; tailleur *(m)*
**to suit (be appropriate for)**  convenir à
**suitcase**  valise *(f)*
**summary**  résumé *(m)*
**summer**  été *(m)*
**sumptuous**  somptueux(-euse)
**sun**  soleil *(m)*; **—burn**  coup *(m)*
  de soleil; **—glasses**  lunettes *(f)*
  de soleil; **to get a —tan**  se faire
  bronzer

**sunny**  ensoleillé(e); **It's —.**  Il
  fait du soleil.
**superior**  supérieur(e)
**to support**  soutenir *(soutenu)*
**suppose: She was supposed to. . .**
  Elle devait...
**sure**  sûr(e)
**surprised**  étonné(e); surpris(e)
**surprising**  surprenant(e)
**to surround**  entourer
**surrounding area**  environs *(m
  pl)*
**survey**  enquête *(f)*; sondage *(m)*
**to suspect**  soupçonner
**to swallow**  avaler
**to sweat**  transpirer
**sweater**  pull-over *(m)*; chandail
  *(m)*; gilet *(m)*
**sweatsuit**  jogging *(m)*
**sweatshirt**  sweat(shirt) *(m)*
**Swedish**  suédois(e)
**sweets**  sucreries *(f pl)*
**to swim**  nager; se baigner
**swimming pool**  piscine *(f)*
**Swiss**  suisse
**switchboard**  standard *(m)*
**Switzerland**  Suisse *(f)*
**sword**  épée *(f)*
**syllable**  syllabe *(f)*
**symptom**  symptôme *(m)*
**synagogue**  synagogue *(f)*
**Syria**  Syrie *(f)*
**syrup**  sirop *(m)*
**system**  système *(m)*

**T**

**t-shirt**  T-shirt *(m)*
**table**  table *(f)*
**tablet (pill)**  cachet *(m)*; comprimé
  *(m)*
**to take**  prendre *(pris)*; **to — (a
  person)**  amener; **to — a class**
  suivre un cours; **to — a class
  over**  redoubler un cours; **to — a
  ride (on a bike/in a car/on a
  motorcycle)**  faire un tour (à
  vélo/en voiture/à moto); **to — a
  stroll**  se balader; **to — a test**
  passer un examen; **to — a trip**
  faire un voyage; **to — a walk
  (ride) in town**  faire un tour en
  ville; **to — a walk**  faire une
  promenade; **to — an hour to go**
  mettre une heure pour aller; **to —
  care of**  s'occuper de; **to — it
  easy**  se calmer; **to — leave**
  prendre congé; **to — off**  enlever;

**to — part in**  participer à; **to — place**  se dérouler; avoir lieu; **to — the wrong road**  se tromper de route
**talented in**  doué(e) pour
**tall**  grand(e)
**to tan**  se faire bronzer; **tanned**  bronzé(e)
**tank top**  débardeur (m)
**tart**  tartelette (f)
**taste**  goût (m); **to —**  déguster
**taxes**  impôts (m pl)
**taxi**  taxi (m)
**tea**  thé (m)
**to teach**  enseigner
**teacher**  professeur (m); **grade school —**  instituteur(-trice) (m, f)
**teaching**  enseignement (m); **— assistant**  assistant(e) (m, f)
**team**  équipe (f)
**technology**  technologie (f)
**telephone**  téléphone (m); **— number**  numéro (m) de téléphone; **— booth**  cabine (f) téléphonique; **— call**  coup (m) de téléphone (fil); **— book**  annuaire (m)
**televised**  télévisé(e)
**television**  téléviseur (m); télévision (f)
**to tell**  raconter
**temperate**  tempéré(e)
**to tend**  avoir tendance à; tendre à
**tennis**  tennis (m); **— shoes**  souliers (m pl) de tennis
**tense**  tendu(e)
**terrace**  terrasse (f)
**terrible**  affreux(-euse)
**textbook**  manuel (m)
**to thank**  remercier; **— you**  merci; **—s**  remerciements (m pl)
**that**  cela; ça; **— day**  ce jour-là; **— is ( — is to say)**  c'est-à-dire; **— one**  celui (celle)-là; **— way**  par là; **—'s it.**  C'est ça.; **—'s okay.**  Ça va.
**theater**  théâtre (m)
**then**  puis; ensuite; alors
**there**  y; là; là-bas; **— is (are)**  il y a; **—'s...**  voilà...
**therefore**  donc
**these (those)**  ces
**thin**  mince; svelte; fin(e)
**thing**  chose (f)
**to think**  penser; croire (cru); **to — about**  penser à, réfléchir à
**thirst**  soif (f); **to be thirsty**  avoir soif
**this (that)**  ce/cet (cette)

**thousand**  mille; **—s of**  des milliers de
**thread**  fil (m)
**throat**  gorge (f)
**through: to go —**  passer par
**thus**  ainsi
**ticket**  billet (m)
**to tie (shoes)**  lacer
**tie**  cravatte (f)
**tight (clothing)**  étroit(e)
**time**  temps (m); **a long —**  longtemps; **at that —**  à cette époque-là; **three —s**  trois fois; **at the same —**  en même temps; **at the — of**  à l'époque de; **at any —**  à tout moment; **at what —**  à quelle heure; **from — to —**  de temps en temps; **to have the — to**  avoir le temps de; **How many —s?**  Combien de fois; **What — is it?**  Quelle heure est-il?
**timetable**  horaire (m)
**tip**  pourboire (m)
**tire**  pneu (m); **flat —**  pneu crevé
**tired**  fatigué(e)
**to**  à; en; jusqu'à
**toast**  toast (m); pain (m) grillé
**toaster**  grille-pain (m)
**tobacco**  tabac (m); **— store**  bureau (m) de tabac
**today**  aujourd'hui
**toe**  doigt (m) de pied
**together**  ensemble
**toilet**  toilette (f); W.C. (m); **— paper**  papier (m) toilette (hygiénique)
**toll road**  autoroute à péage
**tomato**  tomate (f)
**tomorrow**  demain
**tone**  ton (m)
**tongue**  langue (f)
**too**  trop; **— much (many)**  trop de
**tooth**  dent (f); **—brush**  brosse (f) à dents; **—paste**  dentifrice (m)
**tourist**  touriste (m, f); **— bureau**  syndicat (m) d'initiative; office (m) de tourisme
**toward**  vers
**towel**  serviette (f)
**tower**  tour (f)
**towing service**  service (m) de dépannage
**town**  ville (f); **in (to) —**  en ville
**toy**  jouet (m)
**track**  voie (f)
**trade (profession)**  métier (m); **(business)**  commerce (m)

**traditional**  traditionnel(le)
**traffic**  trafic (m)
**train**  train (m); **— station**  gare (f)
**training**  entraînement (m)
**traitor**  traître (m)
**transistor radio**  transistor (m)
**to translate**  traduire (traduit)
**translation**  traduction (f)
**transportation**  transport (m)
**to travel**  voyager; **— bag**  sac (m) de voyage
**traveler**  voyageur(-euse) (m, f)
**treatment**  traitement (m)
**tree**  arbre (m)
**to tremble**  trembler
**trimester**  trimestre (m)
**trip: to take a —**  faire une excursion (un voyage)
**triumph**  triomphe (m)
**trombone**  trombone (m)
**trouble**  peine (f); **in —**  en difficulté; **to have — doing**  avoir des difficultés à faire
**trout**  truite (f)
**truck**  camion (m)
**true**  vrai(e); **That's —.**  C'est vrai.; En effet.
**trumpet**  trompette (f)
**truth**  vérité (f)
**to try, to try on (clothing)**  essayer; **to — to**  chercher à; **to — one's luck**  tenter sa chance
**tube**  tube (m)
**tuna**  thon (m)
**Tunisia**  Tunisie (f)
**Tunisian**  tunisien(ne)
**turkey**  dinde (f)
**Turkish**  turc(que)
**turn: in —**  à tour de rôle; à son tour; tour à tour
**to turn**  tourner
**to type**  taper
**typewriter**  machine (f) à écrire
**typically**  typiquement

**U**

**U.S.S.R.**  (former) U.R.S.S. (f)
**ugly**  laid(e); moche
**\*uh...**  euh...
**uncertainty**  incertitude (f)
**uncle**  oncle (m)
**to understand**  comprendre (compris)
**understood: That's —.**  Ça s'entend.
**unemployed: to be —**  être au chômage

**unemployment**  chômage *(m)*;
**unforgettable**  inoubliable
**unfortunate: That's —.**  C'est
malheureux.; **It is — that. . .**
C'est dommage que...
**United Kingdom**  Royaume-Uni
*(m)*
**United Nations**  ONU *(f)* (Organisation des Nations Unies)
**university**  université *(f)*
**unlikely: It is — that. . .**  Il est
peu probable que...
**until**  jusqu'à
**up: to go —**  monter
**updated**  mis(e) à jour
**upset**  énervé(e)
**upstairs**  à l'étage
**use**  emploi *(m)*; **to —**  employer;
utiliser
**used**  d'occasion; usagé(e)
**used to**  habitué(e) à
**useful**  utile
**usually**  d'habitude; normalement
**utilities**  charges *(f pl)*

## V

**vacation**  vacances *(f pl)*; **paid —**
congé *(m)* payé
**vacationers**  vacanciers *(m pl)*
**to validate (ticket)**  composter
**vanilla**  vanille *(f)*
**variety**  variété *(f)*
**various**  varié(e)s
**to vary**  varier
**veal**  veau *(m)*
**vegetable**  légume *(m)*; **raw —s**
crudités *(f pl)*
**Venezuela**  Venezuela *(m)*
**Venezuelan**  vénézuélien(ne)
**verb**  verbe *(m)*
**very**  très; **— close**  tout près
**vest**  gilet *(m)*
**video game**  jeu *(m)* vidéo
**videocassette**  vidéo *(f)*; **— recorder (VCR)**  magnétoscope
*(m)*
**Viet Nam**  Viêt-Nam *(m)*
**Vietnamese**  vietnamien(ne)
**village**  village *(m)*
**vine**  vigne *(f)*
**vinegar**  vinaigre *(m)*
**vineyard**  vignoble *(m)*
**violin**  violon *(m)*
**visa**  visa *(m)*
**to visit (a place)**  visiter; **(a person)**  rendre visite à
**vitamins**  vitamines *(f pl)*

**vocabulary**  vocabulaire *(m)*
**voice**  voix *(f)*
**volleyball**  volley *(m)*
**to vomit**  vomir
**vowel**  voyelle *(f)*

## W

**to wait (for)**  attendre *(attendu)*
**waiter**  garçon *(m)* de café; serveur
*(m)*
**waitress**  serveuse *(f)*
**to wake up**  se réveiller
**to walk**  marcher; promener; **to go
for a —**  se promener
**Walkman**  Walkman *(m)*; baladeur
*(m)*
**wall**  mur *(m)*
**wallet**  portefeuille *(m)*
**to want**  vouloir *(voulu)*; désirer;
avoir envie de; **— ads**  offres *(f
pl)* d'emploi
**war**  guerre *(f)*; **World — II**  la
Seconde guerre mondiale
**warm**  chaud(e); **It is — (hot).**  Il
fait chaud.
**to warn**  prévenir *(prévenu)*
**to wash**  laver
**washing machine**  machine *(f)* à
laver
**waste: to — time**  perdre du temps
**to watch**  regarder
**water**  eau *(f)*; **mineral —**  eau
minérale
**wave**  vague *(f)*
**way: in a different —**  de façon
différente; **in what —**  de quelle
façon
**weak**  faible
**weakness**  faiblesse *(f)*
**wealth**  richesse *(f)*
**to wear**  porter
**weather**  temps *(m)*; **What's the
— like?;** Quel temps fait-il?; **— report**  météo *(f)*
**week**  semaine *(f)*; **—end**  week-
end *(m)*
**to weigh**  peser
**weightlifting**  musculation *(f)*
**welcome: — to**  bienvenue à; **to —**
accueillir; souhaiter la bienvenue;
**You're —.**  Je vous (t')en prie./
De rien./Il n'y a pas de quoi.
**well**  bien; **as — as**  ainsi que;
aussi bien que
**west**  ouest *(m)*
**western (film)**  western *(m)*

**western**  occidental(e)
**what**  que; quel(le); ce qui; ce que;
**— is it?**  Qu'est-ce que c'est?; **—
did you say?**  Comment? Quoi?
Vous dîtes?; **— else?**  Quoi
d'autre?; **— are they like?**
Comment sont-ils?; **— do you
think about it?**  Qu'est-ce que
tu en penses?; **— does your
brother look like?**  Comment
est ton frère?
**whatever: — the level**  quel que
soit le niveau
**wheat**  blé *(m)*
**wheel**  roue *(f)*
**when**  quand; lorsque; **the day —
. . .**  le jour où...; **at the time —**
au moment où
**where**  où
**which**  quel(le); **— one**  lequel
(laquelle); **— ones**  lesquel(le)s;
**that —**  ce que; **to —**  auquel (à
laquelle); **of —**  dont
**while**  pendant que; **— waiting**
en attendant
**white**  blanc(he)
**who**  qui; **—'s calling?**  C'est de
la part de qui?; C'est qui à l'appareil?; **— is it?**  Qui est-ce?
**whole**  entier(-ère)
**whom: to —**  à qui
**whose**  dont
**why**  pourquoi; **That's why. . .**
C'est pour ça que...
**wide**  large
**wife**  femme *(f)*
**willingly**  volontiers
**willingness**  volonté *(f)*
**to win**  gagner
**wind**  vent *(m)*; **It's windy.**  Il
fait du vent.
**window (of a house)**  fenêtre *(f)*;
**(of a shop)**  vitrine *(f)*; **(of a
bank, etc.)**  guichet *(m)*; **to —
-shop**  faire du lèche-vitrines
**to windsurf**  faire de la planche à
voile
**wine**  vin *(m)*; **— cellar**  cave *(m)*
**wing**  aile *(f)*
**winter**  hiver *(m)*
**to wish**  souhaiter
**with**  avec
**withdrawal**  retrait *(m)*
**without**  sans; **— doing anything**
sans rien faire
**witness**  témoin *(m)*
**woman**  femme *(f)*; dame *(f)*
**wool**  laine *(f)*
**word**  mot *(m)*; parole *(f)*

**work**   travail *(m);* **(part-time/full-time)** **—**   travail (à mi-temps/à plein temps); **to —**   travailler; **(of a machine)**   marcher; **to — hard**   travailler dur; **to — itself out**   s'arranger; **to — out (exercise)**   s'entraîner

**worker**   travailleur(-euse) *(m, f);* **factory —**   ouvrier(-ère) *(m, f)*

**workout machine**   appareil *(m)* de gymnastique

**world**   monde *(m)*

**worn**   râpé(e); usagé(e)

**to worry (about)**   s'inquiéter (de); s'en faire au sujet de

**wound**   plaie *(f);* blessure *(f)*

**wrist**   poignet *(m)*

**to write**   écrire *(écrit)*

**writer**   écrivain *(m)*

**wrong: to take the — train**   se tromper de train; **What's —?**   Qu'est-ce qui ne va pas?

## XYZ

**year**   an *(m);* année *(f);* **from — to —**   d'année en année

**yellow**   jaune

**yes**   oui

**yesterday**   hier; **the day before —**   avant-hier

**yet**   pourtant

**yogurt**   yaourt *(m)*

**young**   jeune; **— people**   les jeunes

**yourself**   vous-même

**youth**   jeunesse *(f)*

**Zaire**   Zaïre *(m)*

**zucchini**   courgette *(f)*

# INDEX

# Photo Credits

Photos on the following pages were taken by **Jonathan Stark,** Heinle & Heinle Photo/Video Specialist.

15, 17, 27, 30, 36, 39, 49, 89, 127, 137, 149, 173, 211, 224, 241, 253, 271 *bottom left and right,* 272 *top left and bottom right,* 273, 289, 299, 309, 345, 366, 389, 393, 395, 423, 443, 444, 445, 453, 456, 463, 485, 487, 533, 534 *top,* 583

All other photos except those on the following pages were taken by **Stuart Cohen.**

2, **Stuart Cohen/COMSTOCK;** 11, **Bernard Jaubert/SIPA IMAGE;** 71, **Peter Menzel/STOCK BOSTON;** 145, **Nicholas Raducanu;** 163, **SUPERSTOCK;** 168, *bottom right* **P. Amranand/SUPERSTOCK,** *others* **SUPERSTOCK;** 169, *top left* **S. Vidler/SUPERSTOCK;** *upper right* **P. Amranand/SUPERSTOCK,** *upper and lower center* **O. Troisfontaines/SUPERSTOCK,** *bottom left* **Tabuteau/The Image Works,** *bottom right* **SUPERSTOCK;** 170, *top and bottom left* **P. J. Sharpe/SUPER-STOCK,** *center right* **S. Vidler/SUPERSTOCK,** *center left* **SUPERSTOCK,** *bottom right* **K. Kitagawa/SUPERSTOCK;** 171, *top left and right* **SUPERSTOCK,** *center and bottom right* **S. Vidler/SUPERSTOCK,** *bottom left* **P. Amranand/SUPER-STOCK;** 195, **Nicholas Raducanu;** 207, **SUPERSTOCK;** 242, **SUPERSTOCK;** 249, **S. Vidler/SUPERSTOCK;** 255, **SUPERSTOCK;** 265, **Nicholas Raducanu;** 271, *top* **Nicholas Raducanu;** 272, *bottom left* **Nicholas Raducanu;** 280, **Stuart Cohen/COMSTOCK;**326, **S. Vidler/SUPERSTOCK;** 330, *left* **C. Lipnitzki-Viollet,** *right* **Collection Viollet;** 340, *top left and right, and bottom right* **S. Vidler/SUPER-STOCK,** *top center and second right* **R. Llewellyn/SUPERSTOCK,** *top and center right* **SUPERSTOCK;** 341, *top left* **K. Kitagawa/SUPERSTOCK,** *top and bottom right* **S. Vidler/SUPERSTOCK,** *center and bottom left* **H. Kanus/SUPERSTOCK,** *center right* **R. Chen/SUPERSTOCK;** 342, *top right and left* **S. Vidler/SUPER-STOCK,** *center and bottom* **SUPERSTOCK;** 343, *top left* **E. Streichan/SUPER-STOCK,** *top right and bottom left* **S. Vidler/SUPERSTOCK,** *bottom right* **Mia + Klaus/SUPERSTOCK;** 404 **Topham/The Image Works;** 420, **Nicholas Raducanu;** 425, **Pierre Valette;** 426, *top* **P. Amranand SUPERSTOCK,** *bottom left* **P.J. Sharpe/SUPERSTOCK,** *bottom center* **E. Faure/SUPERSTOCK;** 427, *top left and right* **M. Antman/The Image Works,** *center right* **B. Bausse/SUPERSTOCK,** *center* **Russel Dian/MONKMEYER,** *bottom left* **Hugh Rogers/Monkmeyer,** *bottom right* **Mike Mazzachi/STOCK BOSTON;** 436 **M. Antman/The Image Works;** 480, *top left* **SUPERSTOCK,** *top right and center left* **G. Ricatto/SUPERSTOCK,** *center right* **O. Warren/SUPERSTOCK,** *bottom right and left* **H. Kanus/SUPERSTOCK;** 481, *top left* **M. Burgess/SUPERSTOCK,** *top right* **G. Ricatto/SUPERSTOCK,** *second left* **D. Nunclo/SUPERSTOCK,** *third left* **Holton Collection/SUPERSTOCK,** *center and bottom right* **SUPERSTOCK;** 482, *three left* **Mia + Klaus/SUPERSTOCK,** *two top right and bottom right* **S. Vidler/SUPERSTOCK,** *center right* **Malak/SUPERSTOCK;** 483, *two top left and bottom right* **M. Burgess/SUPER-STOCK,** *third left* **C. May/SUPERSTOCK,** *fourth left* **C. Harris/SUPERSTOCK,** *bottom left* **G. Jacobs/SUPERSTOCK,** *top right* **H. Linker/SUPERSTOCK,** *second right* **S. Vidler/SUPERSTOCK,** *third right* **K. Scholz/SUPERSTOCK;** 534, *bottom* **Peter Menzel/STOCK BOSTON;** 548, *left* **Ray Stott/The Image Works,** *top right* **J.J. Gonzalez/The Image Works,** *bottom right* **Mark Antman/The Image Works;** 554, **C. Parry/The Image Works;** 559, **FourByFive;** 599, **SUPERSTOCK**

## Text Credits

**158,** from SNCF brochure "Histoire des billets"; **203,** "Déjeuner du matin" Editions Gallimard, 1949; **289-291,** "Demain la faculté", *Phosphore* magazine; **424,** "La mode et vous", *Ça va* magazine, vol. 22, no. 3, dec. 1986/jan. 1987; **469-470,** "Les mouvements de la mode expliqués", Editions Robert Laffont, 1984; **486-489,** text and charts from Gérard Mermet, *Francoscopie 1995,* © Larousse, 1994; **523;** "Bonnes manières: le guide du parfait Européen", *Journal français d'Amérique,* Vol. 12, no. 9, mai 1990; **584,** "Etes-vous gourmand?" *Ça va* magazine: **609,** recipe from *Elle* magazine; **620,** recipes from *Cuisine de Mapie,* pp. 346, 329, 399; **621,** *L'Avare,* by Molière

## Realia Credits

**111,** brochure: Office de tourisme, Arles; **119,** brochure: Office de tourisme, Fougères, **138,** map: Régie autonome des transports parisiens; **168,** map from Michelin, Paris Atlas n° 11; **169,** brochure: Département Communications, Etablissement public de la Villette; **190,** brochure: Office de tourisme, Paris; **218, 234,** Fnac; **309,** medicine boxes: Végétoserum, Laboratoire Phosma, S.A.; Aspirine du Rhône, Rhinofluimicil, Laboratoire Zambon France, S.A.; **310,** Vitamines Azinc; **322,** chart by Ricq Etienne reproduced from *Le Chasseur français,* février 1986; **346-347,** brochure: Courtesy of the Institut de Touraine; **357, 358, 359, 370,** © MICHELIN from the *Michelin Guide Rouge, France* (1995), Permission No. 95-433; **381, 382,** brochures: Association Québecoise des écoles des français, Délégation du Québec; **408,** brochure: Passy-Kennedy; **424, 438, 450, 457, 459,** selections: catalogue, *La Redoute;* **424,** ad: Le Printemps; **426,** logo courtesy of Jacques Esterel, logo courtesy of Lacoste; **437,** floor plan: Galeries Lafayette; "Aux Trois Quartiers", Office de tourisme, Paris; **490,** Cadillac Plastic; *bottom right* Advertisement image reprinted with permission from Microsoft Corporation; **491,** William Saurin; **492,** Schweppes, Peudouce, BASF; **493,** *L'Express* magazine; **501,** Toshiba; **504,** Moulinex Perrier-Jouët; **505,** Pelikan, Mammouth, **515,** Courtesy of Kodak-Pathé; **535, 537, 538, 539, 549, 550, 558,** Société National des Chemins de Fer; **560,** from the Michelin Map no. 254 Provence-Côte d'Azur édition 1995, © MICHELIN, Permission No. 95-433; **587,** brochure: Comité départemental du tourisme de l'Ain; **608,** Revue française des télécommunications (Ministère des Postes); **609,** recipe from *Elle* magazine; **620,** recipes from *cuisine de Mapie*